SHIP

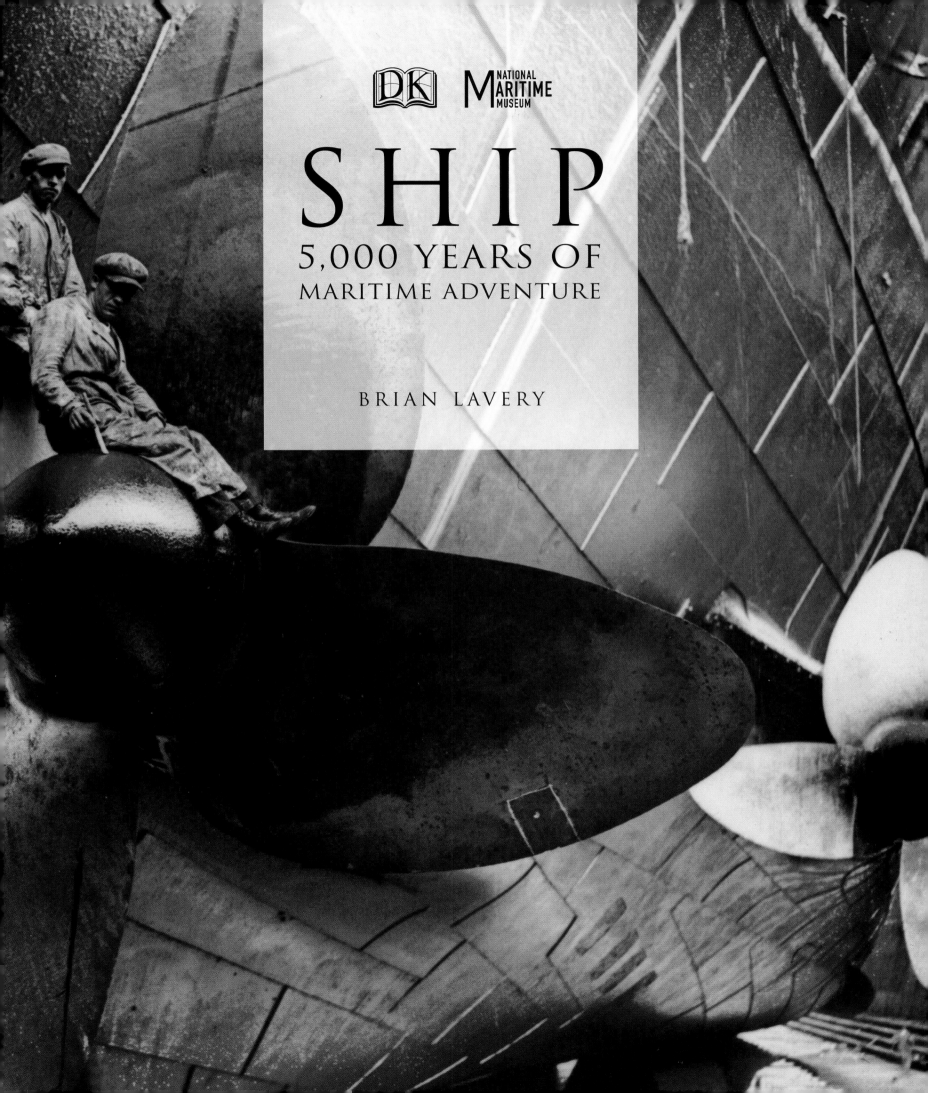

SHIP

5,000 YEARS OF MARITIME ADVENTURE

BRIAN LAVERY

LONDON, NEW YORK, MUNICH,
MELBOURNE, and DELHI

Senior Editor Peter Frances
Project Editors Sarah Larter, Gill Pitts
Editors Georgina Garner, Ben Hoare, Giles Sparrow,
David and Sylvia Tombesi-Walton, Nikky Twyman
Indexer Jane Parker

Senior Art Editor Sunita Gahir
Project Art Editors David Ball,
Vanessa Marr, Lee Riches
Designers Paul Drislane, Simon Murrell
Picture Researcher Louise Thomas
Illustrators Tim Loughead, John Plumer
DTP Designers John Goldsmid, Paul Maguire,
Rajen Shah, Adam Shepherd
Production Controller Melanie Dowland

Managing Editor Liz Wheeler
Managing Art Editor Philip Ormerod
Category Publisher Jonathan Metcalf
Art Director Bryn Walls

Special Photography Gary Ombler

NMM Project Co-ordinator Rachel Giles
Consultant Simon Stephens
Picture Co-ordinator Eleanor Driscoll
Photographer Enzo di Cosmo

Smithsonian Consultant Paul F. Johnston
Project Co-ordinators Katie Mann, Ellen Nanney

First published in Great Britain in 2004 by
Dorling Kindersley Limited
80 Strand, London WC2R 0RL
A Penguin Company
Copyright © 2004 Dorling Kindersley Limited
Reprinted with corrections in 2005.

Text © 2004 the National Maritime Museum

2 4 6 8 10 9 7 5 3
023-SD075-Oct/04

A CIP catalogue record for this book
is available from the British Library

ISBN 978-1-4053-0589-1

Colour reproduction by GRB, Italy
Printed and bound in China

see our complete catalogue at
www.dk.com

CONTENTS

FOREWORD

As a child, I sailed onboard Union Castle ships that carried Royal Mail to South Africa. The smell of tarred rope, the cries of stevedores, the creaking of riveted hulls, and the changing moods of the sea were among the earliest influences on a maritime career that already spans five decades.

It was perhaps inevitable that I would run away to sea, joining the Royal Navy at the age of 15. Serving "before the mast" in a destroyer, I learned at first hand the ways of the sea and the hierarchies of those who sail it. Joseph Conrad seemed to be expressing my

experiences, and in those youthful days I read every one of his engagingly evocative books.

Later, after becoming an officer and training at the renowned Britannia Royal Naval College in Dartmouth, I bought my first boat – a humble affair that leaked – and was bitten by the often uncomfortable and sometimes terrifying sport of ocean racing. Qualifying as a skipper, I was fortunate to compete as Chief Mate in the Navy's yacht *Adventure* in the first Whitbread Round the World Race, where I sampled great oceans from a yacht and our team won three out of four legs of the race.

Subsequently, with growing professional experience, I commanded a minehunter, two destroyers, a destroyer squadron, and the aircraft carrier *Invincible*, travelling the globe in the process. These days, when I am not indulging my passion for maritime heritage here in this superb museum in Greenwich, London, I cruise the family sloop around the magical swathways and inlets of England's east coast, where time slows down and a few craftsmen still build boats using traditional skills. A common theme in these experiences is the fellowship of the sea: the bond between those who know the

sea, whether from a vantage point ashore or through plying it for trade, diplomacy, migration, or recreation, and who respect its power and cherish its resources. The sea knows no international boundaries; it shapes professional relationships and recognizes skills and competencies that transcend nationalism. The sea is one of life's greatest levellers, uniting people and demanding teamwork, know-how and good humour.

This wonderful book, beautifully written and presented, sums up the international human relationship with the sea by tracing and radiating enthusiasm for ships and people and for today's seafaring across the world. The book also tackles future directions and influences and rightly considers the impact of mankind on the sustainability of the medium that underpins the Earth's life-support system.

It is a truly comprehensive work by an author who, over many years, has contributed very substantially to our knowledge and understanding of maritime affairs. I congratulate him, those who have contributed specialist details, the publishers, and everyone involved in producing it, and I commend it to readers with an interest in the sea. It will be enjoyed not least by those who have made the sea their life's work or their pleasure, or who – like me – have had the fortune to earn a living by combining the two.

ROY CLARE
REAR ADMIRAL

FORMER DIRECTOR
NATIONAL MARITIME MUSEUM, UK

1

NAVAL DOMINATION
The Roman emperor Trajan presides at the stern of a trireme on this carved column commemorating victory against the Dacians in AD 105–106. The Romans' naval superiority was the culmination of thousands of years of maritime achievement in the Mediterranean.

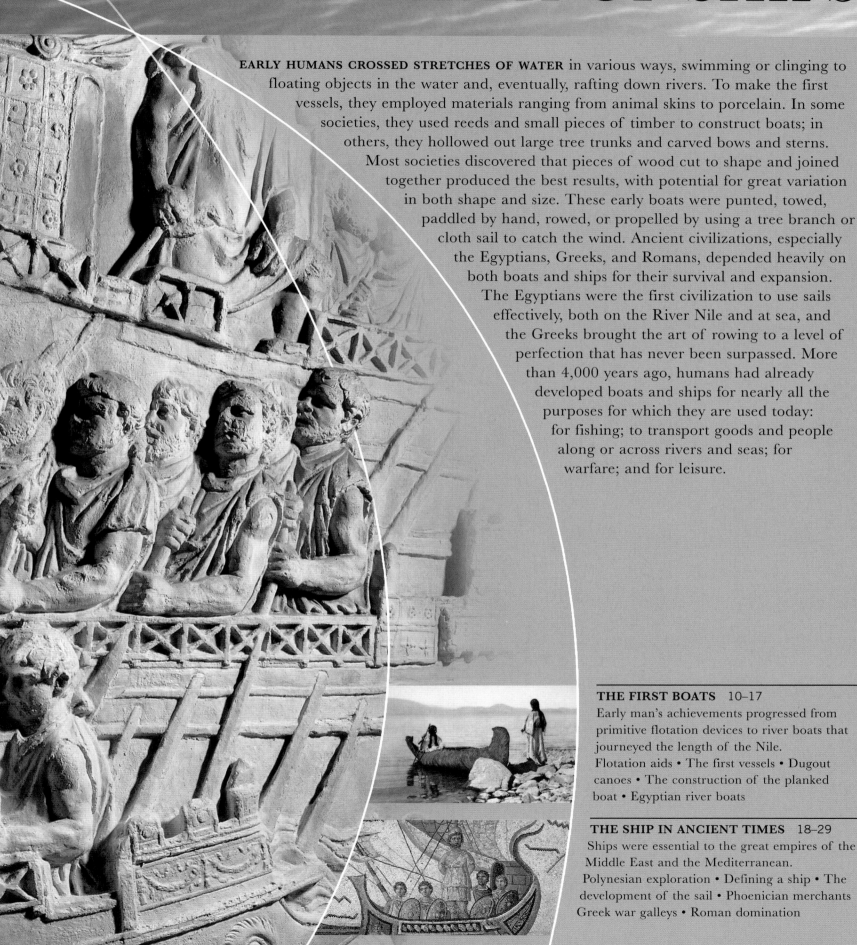

THE BIRTH OF SHIPS

EARLY HUMANS CROSSED STRETCHES OF WATER in various ways, swimming or clinging to floating objects in the water and, eventually, rafting down rivers. To make the first vessels, they employed materials ranging from animal skins to porcelain. In some societies, they used reeds and small pieces of timber to construct boats; in others, they hollowed out large tree trunks and carved bows and sterns. Most societies discovered that pieces of wood cut to shape and joined together produced the best results, with potential for great variation in both shape and size. These early boats were punted, towed, paddled by hand, rowed, or propelled by using a tree branch or cloth sail to catch the wind. Ancient civilizations, especially the Egyptians, Greeks, and Romans, depended heavily on both boats and ships for their survival and expansion. The Egyptians were the first civilization to use sails effectively, both on the River Nile and at sea, and the Greeks brought the art of rowing to a level of perfection that has never been surpassed. More than 4,000 years ago, humans had already developed boats and ships for nearly all the purposes for which they are used today: for fishing; to transport goods and people along or across rivers and seas; for warfare; and for leisure.

SKIN BOAT (*QUFFA*) USED ON THE TIGRIS AND EUPHRATES RIVERS, MESOPOTAMIA

> " My changeling mother conceived me, in secret she bore me. She set me in a basket of rushes, with bitumen she sealed my lid. She cast me into the river which rose not over me "

KING SARGON OF AKKAD, Sumerian king, Mesopotamia, *c.*2334–2279 BC

THE FIRST BOATS

HUNDREDS OF MILLIONS OF YEARS AFTER LIFE CRAWLED OUT OF THE OCEANS, MAN RETURNED TO THE WATER – IN POTS, IN BASKETS, ON RAFTS AND, EVENTUALLY, IN THE FIRST BOATS.

There is no single line of evolution for the development of the boat. Early vessels emerged gradually and were often unique to the societies that originated them, and the traditional maritime practices of some early peoples remained relatively unchanged for thousands of years. Local needs, resources, and geographical circumstances dictated the maritime developments of early communities, but in some societies, such as ancient Egypt, one improvement led to another, and as small craft travelled to nearby lands their advances spread, along with the goods the boats carried.

According to the Book of Genesis, God ordered Noah to build "an Ark of gopher wood", sealed with pitch inside and outside, 300 cubits long, 50 broad, and 30 deep, three storeys high, with a door in the side. Apart from this example of divine instruction, the birth of ships was a long process. Humans learned to use the water slowly, to cross streams and rivers, lakes and estuaries, and, eventually,

seas and oceans. Early vessels progressed from flotation aids to small boats and finally, after thousands of years, to ships capable of making long voyages across the sea. The sea is a dangerous, unstable, and hostile place and, with anything less than God's authority, humans ventured on to it with caution.

Flotation aids

Early human settlements were always close to a water supply, for drinking and irrigation, and perhaps for food from fishing. As primitive humans evolved and began to venture farther afield to hunt and trade, they encountered streams too big to step over, as well as vast expanses of water – rivers, seas, and oceans. They could wade through a stream if it was not too deep, too cold, too fast-flowing, nor inhabited by predators such as crocodiles. Or they could learn to swim, but this was a much less common skill than it is today, and it would not solve all their problems. Early humans

KEY EVENTS

*c.*50,0000 BC **FIRST AUSTRALIANS**
Migrants from Southeast Asia reach northern Australia using rafts, becoming the region's first human inhabitants.

*c.*4000 BC **RAFT MIGRATION** A second wave of migrants from Southeast Asia, the Austronesians, voyage beyond Australia to settle on islands in the western Pacific.

*c.*3500 BC **BETWEEN TWO RIVERS** Ancient Mesopotamian civilization begins to thrive on the Tigris and Euphrates rivers. Trade goods are transported along the rivers on rafts.

*c.*3100 BC **THE FIRST SAIL** Ancient Egyptians use sailing craft on the River Nile. The craft are depicted in a vase painting, the first recorded use of a true sail.

*c.*2700 BC **THE FIRST PLANK BOATS** The Egyptians begin to sew pieces of timber together to build stronger hulls and even larger boats.

STILL WATERS
An American Indian Kootenai child waits on the banks of Flathead Lake, Montana, USA, in 1910. Traditionally, the Kootenai made their canoes from bark or by stretching elk hides over a frame of fir strips or saplings but, since Western colonization, most canoes have been made of wood or canvas.

observed their environment, and they began to use materials such as reeds, logs, and inflated animal skins to help them float across water. Using these simple aids exacted some skill – the expression "as easy as falling off a log" stresses the difficulty – but this acquired skill of floating on and moving in the water allowed early humans to carry goods up and, especially, down river and to extend their fishing and hunting ranges. Across the world, each civilization adopted its local resources to the water, but, with such primitive craft, skill and luck were still required to avoid danger.

The first vessels

The true beginning of maritime history was the development of the raft and the boat, watertight structures in which sailors, passengers, and their goods were kept dry. A simple adaptation involved taking vessels that were used on land for cooking and storage and utilizing them on

FLOATING ON AIR
Supported by an inflated animal bladder, an ancient Assyrian fishes on the Tigris river in Mesopotamia, in about 2,600 BC.

water. An earthenware pot is clearly vulnerable in rough, deep, or rocky waters, but they were used on the marshy waters of the Nile Delta, on the Mediterranean by the Greeks around 600 BC, and on Bangladeshi rivers until recently.

By 4000 BC, Austronesian migrants had reached the islands of the western Pacific using crude rafts, and in the northern hemisphere communities had begun to flourish around river deltas and irrigated waterways in Egypt and Mesopotamia (modern Iraq). From reliefs of this time, we know that on the Nile Delta the ancient Egyptians bound papyrus reeds together to make rafts, and on the Tigris and Euphrates rivers in Mesopotamia even larger craft were in use.

Again, the development of these first vessels was dictated by local water conditions, local needs, and local skills. For more than 2,500 years, the Mesopotamians used wooden rafts called *keleks*, supported by inflated skins, to transport goods along the lower Euphrates river. The inflated or stuffed animal hides protected the raft in the swift and rocky river. Once the sailors had made it downstream to lower Mesopotamia, where

FOWLING IN THE MARSHES
This 18th-Dynasty (c.1400 BC) tomb relief from Thebes, Egypt, depicts the deceased and his family hunting or "fowling" on a papyrus-reed raft on the Nile Delta.

SEALSKIN BOAT

This Inuit kayak holds one person; when paddled by a woman, it is called an umiak. Here, it sits on a sledge for transport across the ice.

whalebone arch

TAUT AND DRY

Sealskins are pinned taut and laid in the sun to dry. From Alaska to Greenland, the Inuits stretched animal hides over frameworks to build skin boats.

tribe, knew how to make a canoe from the bark of a tree, although it is not known how long ago they began to practise this.

The log canoe or dugout is a simple boat to make, produced by burning and cutting out the interior of a single tree trunk. The log boat floats easily, in some circumstances even when waterlogged; it does not leak (although extended log boats may let in water); there is no need to join pieces of wood together with watertight joints; and it can be made into many different shapes. Early societies probably discovered many of the basic techniques of naval architecture through the development of the log canoe. For example, it was discovered that a pointed bow and stern was relatively efficient and that a rounded hull tended to perform better than a square

wood was scarce, the logs could be sold along with the goods, and the skins could be deflated and carried back upstream. The people of west Africa bound together lightweight wood to make their offshore fishing rafts (see below); in the warmer coastal waters where these craft were used, it was not important to be sitting above the water. On Lake Titicaca in South America, however, the Incas built boat-like rafts that kept their occupants high and dry, above the cold water (see p.14).

The skin or hide vessel, made from animal hides stretched over a wooden frame, was one of the earliest types of boat. It was lightweight and could often be carried across land, but it was easily holed in areas with rapids or rocks. According to Assyrian reliefs, by 900 BC the *quffa* – a round skin boat – was a common sight on the Tigris and Euphrates rivers. The hide boat was common to many locations: the Irish currach, the British coracle, and the Indian *paracil* were all rounded hide boats. Further north, Inuit fishermen and women kept themselves dry with their tightly laced sealskin kayaks and umiaks.

Boats could be also made out of basketwork and waterproofed with vegetable oil, as in Vietnam up to the 20th century AD, and American Indians, such as the Kootenai

FISHING RAFT

This ocean-going west African fishing craft is lashed together. It lets in water, but its boat-like shape ensures that neither the occupants nor their catch are swept overboard as they work against the surf.

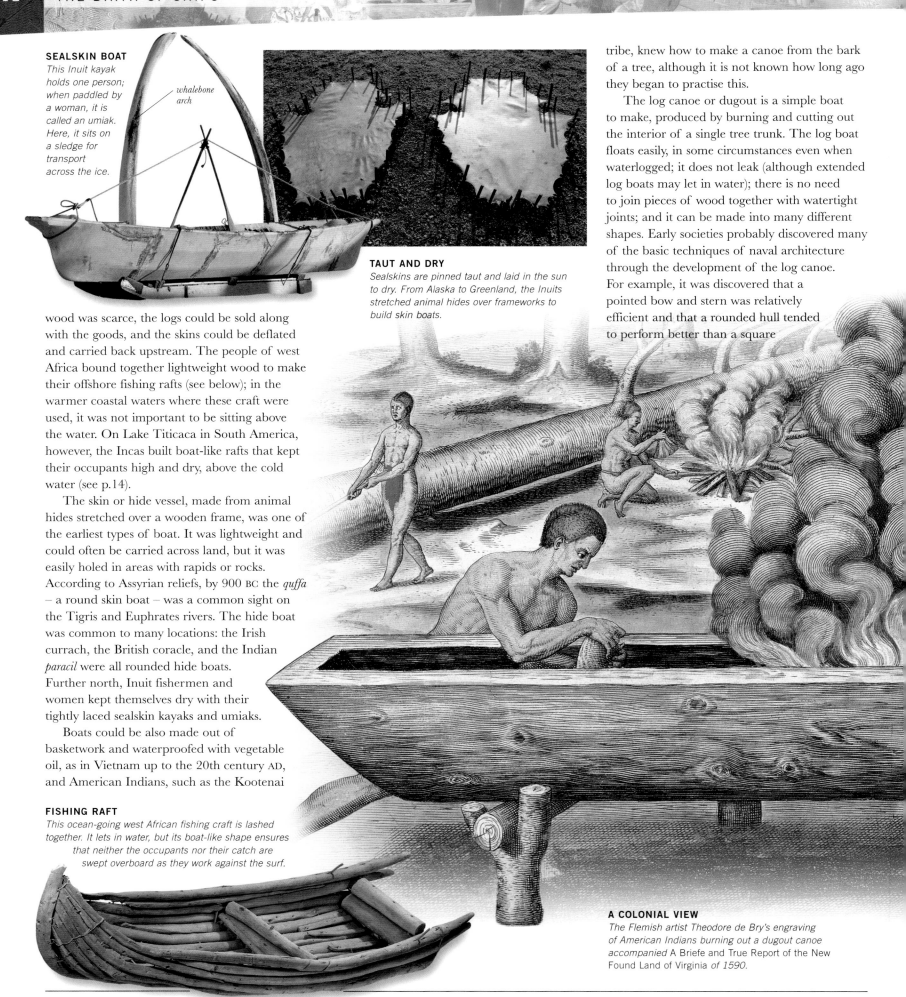

A COLONIAL VIEW

The Flemish artist Theodore de Bry's engraving of American Indians burning out a dugout canoe accompanied A Briefe and True Report of the New Found Land of Virginia *of 1590.*

one. But great variety was possible in the shape of the bow and stern: the offshore Salish boat of northwest America had a spoon-like bow and an overhanging stern; and the Nootka tribe from the same region created boats with a straight bow and an angled stern.

Extending the log boat

The log canoe had a major limitation: it could not be bigger than the tree from which it was made. Tree trunks in most parts of the world are long and rather thin, and on their own they tend to make a rather unstable craft, liable to capsize unless handled very carefully. Early boatbuilders tackled this problem in various ways. The natives of the Danish island of Bornholm, in the Baltic, were expanding their dugouts

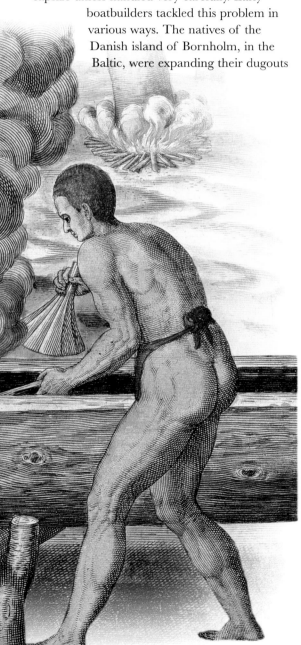

in the 1st century AD. They hewed the sides of the dugout as thinly as possible, before applying heat and gradually inserting longer and longer stretchers. The sides expanded slowly, forcing the ends of the boat to curve up. This allowed the beam to be expanded up to twice its original size. Great skill was required to expand a log boat without bursting it, but this was a common practice in many parts of the world until recently. Like the log canoe, the expanded log boat was probably very precious to its owner, as it took both time and effort to make.

Another method of expansion was to join two trees together, side by side. A rare form of paired log boat consisted of two trees shaped to form a single hull when put together, but the most common method was to make two complete hulls and set them about a metre apart, joined by planks. This was very common

MAORI BAILER
This bailer, which was held by its handle (or spine), dates from Cook's voyage of 1772–75. It was used to scoop the water rapidly from a log canoe.

in the islands of the Pacific and was observed by many 18th-century explorers, including the British mariner James Cook. The hulls might be the same size, as in New Zealand, Hawaii, and Tasmania, or one might be smaller, as in Fiji.

The paired log boat was just a short step from the outrigger canoe, which consisted of a single hull for carrying goods and people, and an outrigger, which provided stability and was often only a simple wooden cylinder, located about a metre from the hull. Some were double-ended so that they could reverse direction when the wind changed, keeping the wind on the same side as the sail; others had a discernible bow and stern, and usually had the outrigger to port. Craft observed in Indonesia from AD 800 onwards had an outrigger on each side.

The addition of timber pieces to the log boat eventually provided an evolutionary path to the plank boat (see panel, below). Boatbuilders began to

SHIP CONSTRUCTION

The advent of the plank boat allowed larger ships and a much greater variety of hull form. Most ancient civilizations constructed the shell of the hull first, later inserting the frame for extra strength. The first plank boats, built by the Egyptians, were probably sewn together. Later, in classical times, the standard method was to cut each plank to shape, then bore its edges to fit

tenons that would join it to the next plank. The best-known example of this is a merchant ship of about 300 BC, discovered off northern Cyprus. The third method of frame-first construction was clinker-building (see p.34), in which the planks were overlapped. This was less labour-intensive and also produced a very strong hull, but the overlaps led to a less smooth shape.

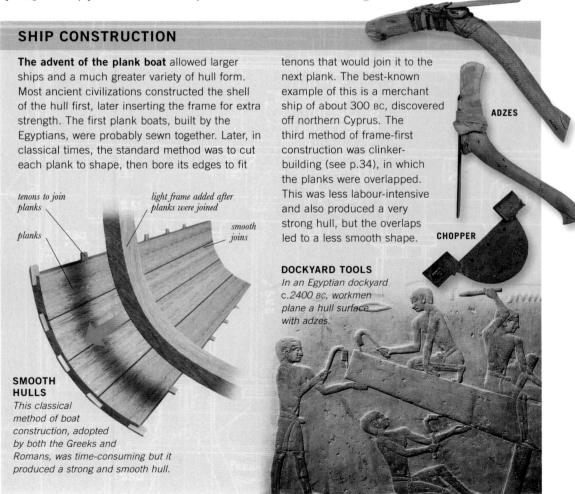

ADZES

CHOPPER

tenons to join planks

planks

light frame added after planks were joined

smooth joins

SMOOTH HULLS
This classical method of boat construction, adopted by both the Greeks and Romans, was time-consuming but it produced a strong and smooth hull.

DOCKYARD TOOLS
In an Egyptian dockyard c.2400 BC, workmen plane a hull surface with adzes.

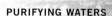

smooth
hull of
beaten gold

oars passed
through holes in
hull (grommets)

yard

mast

CURRACH
*Dating from about
100 BC, this tiny boat was unearthed in AD 1891 as part of
a Celtic gold cache at Broighter, Northern Ireland. Thought
to be a model of an early Irish currach, it is complete with
mast, yard, oars, and seats for 18 oarsmen.*

extend canoes by adding planks to their sides. These are known as washstrakes to modern boatbuilders. Many of the log boats excavated in northern Europe had holes along their sides where such pieces could be fitted, although the actual planks were rarely found and were perhaps only used in bad weather or on long voyages. Boats recorded off the Malabar Coast of India in 1610 showed two planks in place; another report of 1834 spoke of several types of log boats in use at once.

The log that had originally formed the entire hull declined in status to become the keel, and the planks and the frame that supported it became all the more important. The wooden

ABOVE THE TREELINE
*These boats are made from bundles of reeds
and moored to floating reed islands high in
the Andes on Lake Titicaca, South America.*

REED BOAT
*Made from
totora reeds
growing in Lake
Titicaca, this Inca
craft has a high
dome, allowing its
sailor to keep dry
above the water.*

boat had developed beyond the initial limitations of the materials of which it was constructed, and now it could be made ever-larger and in many more different shapes.

This was not the only path to the advent of the plank boat. In Egypt, reed boats evolved into plank boats from around 2700 BC, and in Scandinavia and the British Isles skin and hide boats evolved along the same lines – there is still some debate as to whether the Broighter boat of Northern Ireland (see left) is actually a model of a hide or a plank boat. The development of the plank boat demanded new methods of creating strong and watertight joints. Metalworking was rare in ancient times, and these first plank boats were sewn together. Making these boats was very labour-intensive. The wood close to the join often needed to be shaped in suitable ridges, holes needed to be drilled to take the sewing material, whether leather or twine, and caulking material had to be placed between the planks to keep the water out. Sewn boats have been found in several sites in northern Europe, and they predominated in the islands of the Indian Ocean until the 15th century.

According to different sources, the ancient Greeks used either flax, hemp, or linen to sew their boats, while the ancient tribe of Liburnians from the eastern coast of the Adriatic used leather to hold their boats together. A 15-m (50-ft) long Bronze Age plank boat discovered at Dover, England, in 1992, and dated to about 1300 BC, was stitched with slender yew branches, and its seams were plugged with compressed moss.

Wooden pegs, called trenails or treenails, could also be used to fasten frames and planks together, although this method was rare in early periods. Bronze was too soft to use as nails, but boatbuilders used metal to make their axes and adzes. Unlike iron-fastened boats, sewn boats were immune to corrosion.

THE RIVERS OF THE UNDERWORLD
*The ram-headed god Khnum is depicted here
journeying down a river in the underworld with the
goddess Isis. Both Khnum and Isis were closely
identified with the annual flood.*

PURIFYING WATERS
*This breastplate was worn by Queen Ahhotep (1590–30 BC)
and depicts her son Ahmose I standing on a riverboat as
the gods Re (left, with the head of a falcon) and Amun
anoint him with sacred water. The river was central to all
areas of life on the Nile Delta, including ritual and religion.*

OARS AND PADDLES

A boat needs some means of propulsion. If conditions allow, it can be towed or it can be moved by punting – using a pole to push against the bed of the river – but a more effective and adaptable way is to paddle by hand or by using a pole with a flat surface at one end as a paddle. Facing in the direction of travel, the paddler leans forward or stands up, places his paddle as far forward in the water as he can, and then pulls it back towards himself, propelling the boat forwards.

Rowing is a more complex idea. Usually the rower sits with his back facing the forward course of the vessel, and the oar is pivoted near its centre. In Greek triremes, the oarsman stayed in his seat, directed the oars behind him, and leaned backward with the stroke, his feet braced against a bar. An oarsman uses his whole body in every stroke, not just his arms and back as in paddling, thus propelling the vessel more quickly.

EGYPTIAN FUNERARY BARGE
In ancient Egyptian times, an oarsman would stand up when placing his blade in the water and then sit down on the stroke so that his weight assisted in the process.

BOATS FOR THE AFTERLIFE
In 1895, six wooden boats were found buried near the pyramid of Senusret III, an Egyptian king of the 12th Dynasty (c.1900 BC). Along with other possessions, boats were thought to be needed by pharaohs in the afterlife.

Egypt and the Nile

Derived from the Greek for "between the rivers", Mesopotamia was the world's first acknowledged civilization, flourishing between 3500 and 1600 BC. Its cities were built along the Tigris and Euphrates rivers, and its farmers irrigated the land along the southern banks of the Euphrates, but its rivers were not amenable to the development of navigation. The next great civilization to arise, Egypt, was centred around another river. The Nile flooded annually, producing a rich black soil, and most Egyptians lived in settlements along the edges of the river and in its fertile valleys or wadis. The river was the main artery of the country, and it played an integral role in religion, ritual, and everyday life.

The banks of the Nile grew papyrus reeds, providing the main material for early river and funerary craft. Around 2700 BC, the Egyptians realized that these reed boats could not support enough cargo, especially the stone for their pyramids. They found ways to use the small pieces of timber available to them, joining them together to make a complex structure of ribs and planks. With the development of the plank boat came the need for greater timber resources.

The most important development of this time was the invention of the sail. The Egyptians paddled or rowed their craft down the Nile, assisted by the current that came from the south, but they probably began to sail by holding up a palm frond at the bow of their boats, letting the wind that prevailed from the north carry them back upstream. By about 3100 BC, they had evolved the true sail. With both the plank and the sail boat behind them, they were ready to take an even greater step: to move their craft on to the Mediterranean Sea and, in effect, invent the ship.

EARLY VESSELS

Many different boats have evolved around the world over the centuries. Knowledge of their development is usually sketchy and not always based on hard archaeological evidence. Often a very early boat type has apparently survived the centuries almost into the present day, but it is not certain how much it has changed. A common progression is from a flotation aid to a raft that does not keep the user totally dry. The next stage is a watertight vessel in which passengers and cargo are out of the water.

GONE FISHING
North American Indians used dugout canoes as fishing vessels, as portrayed by the European artist Theodore de Bry in 1590.

Flotation aids

Inflated animal skins can be used to help the traveller stay afloat in a reasonably warm, narrow river that is free of dangerous predators. A carving from around 870 BC (bottom) shows Assyrian soldiers escaping to a fortress. Two are supported by animal skins, inflating them as they go. Pottery vessels were used as river craft when the conditions were not too rough; a picture on a vase in the Vatican (below) shows the Greek hero Heracles in such a vessel.

DETAIL FROM ATHENIAN VASE, c.480 BC

ASSYRIAN CARVING

INFLATED ANIMAL SKIN	
Origin Assyria (Iraq)	Date c.480 BC
Length About 1m (3ft)	
Main material Animal skin	

Hide and bark boats

Animal skins that are sewn together can form the watertight outer part of a boat with a wooden frame. This was used in many parts of the world, including America, China, Arabian Peninsula, and Atlantic Europe. Hide boats are very light – about half the weight of an equivalent plank boat – and can be lifted or beached easily, but there are practical limits to their size. Middle Eastern hide boats are known to date from about 700 BC and are still in use. The origins of the Irish currach are obscure, although it was used in the sixth century AD by St. Columba to spread Christianity around the Scottish islands. There is a crude carving of a currach on a medieval pillar in Bantry, but the first detailed drawing is from the 17th century. This type of boat survived well into the 20th century.

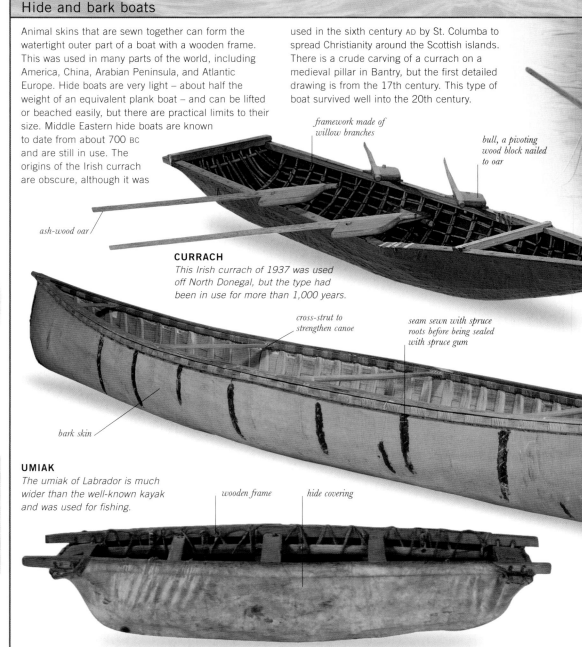

framework made of willow branches

bull, a pivoting wood block nailed to oar

ash-wood oar

CURRACH
This Irish currach of 1937 was used off North Donegal, but the type had been in use for more than 1,000 years.

cross-strut to strengthen canoe

seam sewn with spruce roots before being sealed with spruce gum

bark skin

UMIAK
The umiak of Labrador is much wider than the well-known kayak and was used for fishing.

wooden frame

hide covering

Rafts

The raft is an obvious way of building a boat using relatively small pieces of timber, and it produces a broader, more stable base than that of a log canoe. However, unless the boatbuilder is very skilled, the wood tends to become very wet in rough weather and the boat breaks up easily. The raft has been used in many parts of the world at various times, including ancient Egpyt, east Africa, India, and Bronze Age England in a heavily modified form, and it has found uses in more recent times where conditions are suitable. The sailing log raft from Taiwan (right) has a more sophisticated form than the Polynesian one (left), approaching the shape of a boat, and this may have been one route by which boats evolved.

POLYNESIAN LOG RAFT
This raft from Polynesia is very simple in shape, simply a few planks lashed together to form a platform.

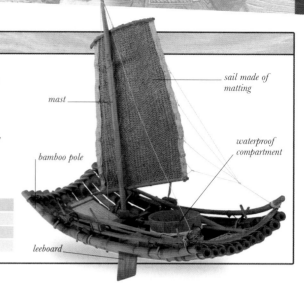

sail made of matting

mast

waterproof compartment

bamboo pole

leeboard

SAILING LOG RAFT
Origin Taiwan	**Date** Prehistory to present day
Length About 5m (16ft 5in)	**Propulsion** Sail and paddle
Main materials Wooden hull, matting sail	

Log boats

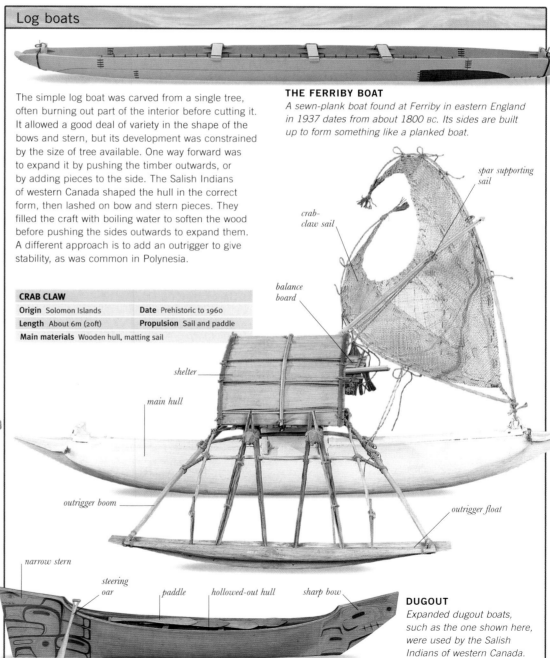

The simple log boat was carved from a single tree, often burning out part of the interior before cutting it. It allowed a good deal of variety in the shape of the bows and stern, but its development was constrained by the size of tree available. One way forward was to expand it by pushing the timber outwards, or by adding pieces to the side. The Salish Indians of western Canada shaped the hull in the correct form, then lashed on bow and stern pieces. They filled the craft with boiling water to soften the wood before pushing the sides outwards to expand them. A different approach is to add an outrigger to give stability, as was common in Polynesia.

THE FERRIBY BOAT
A sewn-plank boat found at Ferriby in eastern England in 1937 dates from about 1800 BC. Its sides are built up to form something like a planked boat.

spar supporting sail

crab-claw sail

balance board

shelter

main hull

outrigger boom

outrigger float

CRAB CLAW
Origin Solomon Islands	**Date** Prehistoric to 1960
Length About 6m (20ft)	**Propulsion** Sail and paddle
Main materials Wooden hull, matting sail	

BASKET BOAT
One building method involves making a boat from basketwork and blocking the holes to make it watertight. This is common in places such as Iraq and Vietnam.

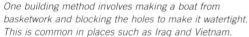

bark is positioned with the grain running longitudinally, allowing sheets to be sewn together more easily

BARK CANOE
Origin North America	**Date** Prehistory to present day
Length About 6m (20ft)	**Propulsion** Paddle
Main material Tree bark	

narrow stern

steering oar

paddle

hollowed-out hull

sharp bow

DUGOUT
Expanded dugout boats, such as the one shown here, were used by the Salish Indians of western Canada.

COIN COMMEMORATING GREEK VICTORY IN THE
BATTLE OF SALAMIS, 480 BC

> ❝The hulls of ships were
> overset; the sea was hid
> from sight, covered with
> wreckage and the death
> of men; the reefs and
> headlands were with
> corpses filled, and in
> disordered flight each
> ship was rowed.❞

AESCHYLUS, Greek poet and participant
in the Battle of Salamis, **480** BC

KEY EVENTS

*c.*1000 BC **POLYNESIAN MIGRATIONS** Using
advanced skills in navigation, the islanders of
Samoa, Tonga, and Fiji begin to explore and
colonize islands farther into the Pacific Ocean.

*c.*1000 BC **THE GREEK WARSHIP** The Greek
city-states customize the war galley, complete
with battering ram to sink enemy ships.

*c.*600 BC **THE TRIREME** The Corinthians
develop the three-levelled galley, fast and
manoeuvrable in battle and on the open sea.

480 BC **THE BATTLE OF SALAMIS** Directed
by the Athenian Themistocles, a combined
Greek fleet reverses the advance of the Persians
with a decisive naval victory at Salamis, Greece.

31 BC **BATTLE OF ACTIUM** The Roman Navy's
victory over the forces of Antony and Cleopatra
establishes its maritime supremacy, under
which peace reigns and trade flourishes in the
Mediterranean.

HOMERIC TALES AND VOYAGES
*Tied to the mast of his ship, the Greek hero
Odysseus listens safely to the deadly song of the
Sirens. Much of our knowledge of Bronze Age
maritime practices comes from Homeric legends.*

THE SHIP IN ANCIENT TIMES

AS NEW CIVILIZATIONS ROSE AND FELL, NAVAL DOMINANCE BECAME CRUCIAL, AND IT WAS IN THE MEDITERRANEAN THAT THE EARLY SHIPS REALLY SET SAIL.

Polynesian voyages

The Polynesians were responsible for the earliest and greatest feats of maritime exploration: the discovery and colonization of thousands of previously uninhabited islands across the vast Pacific Ocean. Around 60,000 BC, early humans crossed the land bridges of southeast Asia (formed by the low sea levels of the last Ice Age), and using floats, rafts, and primitive boats they forded short straits between islands, moving south and eventually settling in Australia and New Guinea. An epoch later, around 2500 BC, Austronesian migrants from southern Asia began to move farther east into the Pacific as well as west into the Indian Ocean. From 1000 BC, their descendants, the Polynesians of Samoa, Tonga, and Fiji, began to make even longer sea voyages, reaching Hawaii in about AD 400, Easter Island in about AD 300, New Zealand in about AD 1200 and Chatham Island in about AD 1500.

It is presumed that the Polynesians travelled by sailing upwind when the predominantly easterly winds flagged – all prudent sailors like to know that they can make their way home again – but it is probable that exploration also resulted from fishing craft being blown off course. The Norwegian explorer and archaeologist Thor Heyerdahl postulated that the Polynesians had originated in South America and migrated westwards, sailing with, and not against, the prevailing winds. In 1947, Heyerdahl successfully sailed 8,000km (5,000 miles) from Peru to Polynesia on an ancient-Peruvian-style balsa raft replica, the *Kon Tiki*.

SPEED AND BALANCE
Hawaiian canoes were traditionally made from local koa wood, and sailed with a single outrigger to aid balance; when the wind was still, they were paddled. Modern replicas of traditional outrigger canoes are raced annually at Oahu, Hawaii.

Both ethnographic and archaeological evidence, however, suggests that Polynesian migration came from the opposite direction.

The rapid acceleration of these first episodes of migration into the Pacific Ocean indicates that the Polynesians had highly developed methods of navigation. The islands of the Pacific are small and difficult to find. Their archipelagos are also widely spaced, although within each island group it is often possible to glimpse one island from another. At sea, these Pacific sailors used a complex system of navigation involving the stars, winds, currents, fish, and bird movements. They could predict the appearance of an island on the horizon by observing the flight patterns of birds, the swell of the ocean, the formation of the clouds, and even by recognizing the smell of the land. Detailed knowledge of the stars helped them to keep their course. In these tropical waters, the stars were rarely obscured by clouds.

Direct evidence of Polynesian craft of this time is rare, but additional information is contained in accounts of the boats that

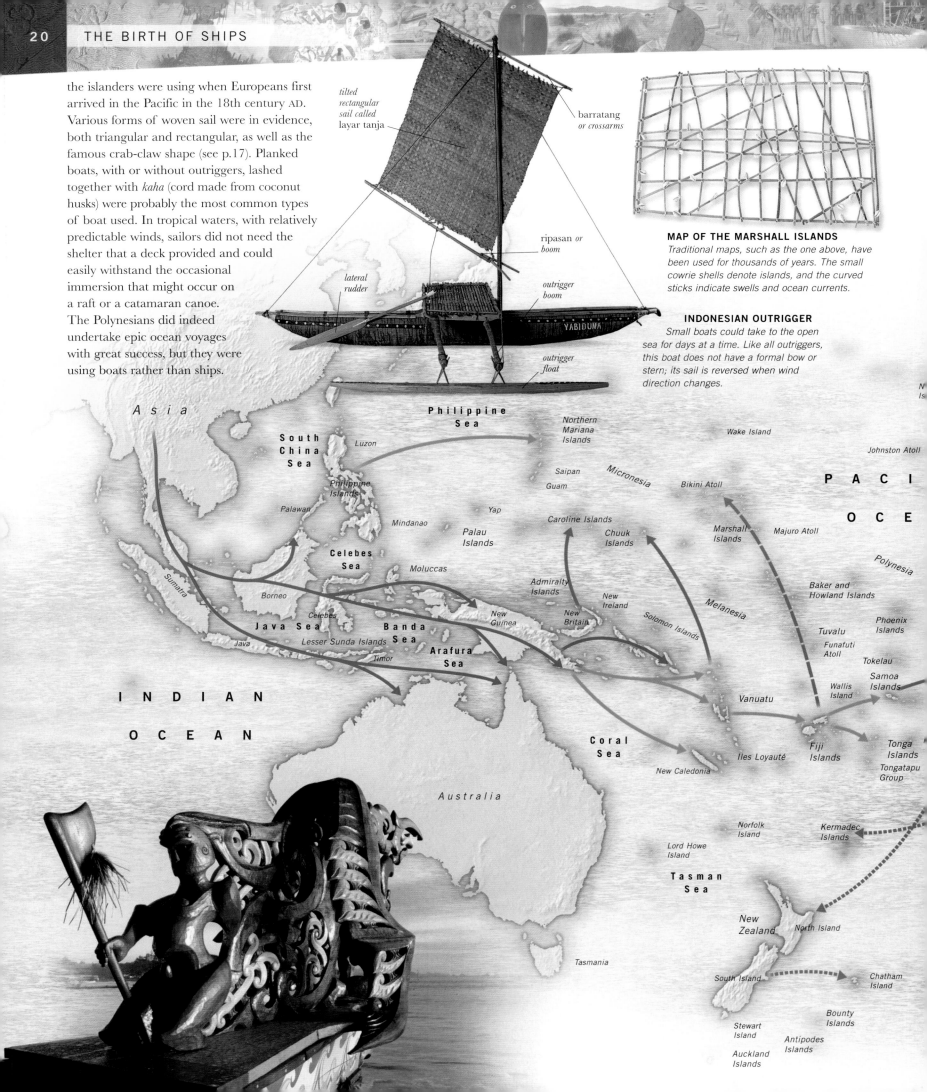

the islanders were using when Europeans first arrived in the Pacific in the 18th century AD. Various forms of woven sail were in evidence, both triangular and rectangular, as well as the famous crab-claw shape (see p.17). Planked boats, with or without outriggers, lashed together with *kaha* (cord made from coconut husks) were probably the most common types of boat used. In tropical waters, with relatively predictable winds, sailors did not need the shelter that a deck provided and could easily withstand the occasional immersion that might occur on a raft or a catamaran canoe. The Polynesians did indeed undertake epic ocean voyages with great success, but they were using boats rather than ships.

tilted rectangular sail called layar tanja

barratang *or crossarms*

ripasan *or boom*

lateral rudder

outrigger boom

outrigger float

YABIDUNA

MAP OF THE MARSHALL ISLANDS
Traditional maps, such as the one above, have been used for thousands of years. The small cowrie shells denote islands, and the curved sticks indicate swells and ocean currents.

INDONESIAN OUTRIGGER
Small boats could take to the open sea for days at a time. Like all outriggers, this boat does not have a formal bow or stern; its sail is reversed when wind direction changes.

Asia

Philippine Sea

South China Sea

Luzon

Northern Mariana Islands

Wake Island

Johnston Atoll

Saipan

Guam

Micronesia

Bikini Atoll

PACI

OCE

Philippine Islands

Palawan

Yap

Caroline Islands

Chuuk Islands

Marshall Islands

Majuro Atoll

Mindanao

Palau Islands

Celebes Sea

Moluccas

Polynesia

Baker and Howland Islands

Sumatra

Borneo

Admiralty Islands

New Ireland

New Britain

Solomon Islands

Melanesia

Phoenix Islands

Tuvalu

Celebes

Java Sea

Banda Sea

New Guinea

Funafuti Atoll

Tokelau

Java

Lesser Sunda Islands

Arafura Sea

Samoa Islands

Timor

Wallis Island

INDIAN

OCEAN

Vanuatu

Fiji Islands

Tonga Islands

Coral Sea

Iles Loyauté

Tongatapu Group

Australia

New Caledonia

Norfolk Island

Kermadec Islands

Lord Howe Island

Tasman Sea

New Zealand

North Island

South Island

Chatham Island

Tasmania

Stewart Island

Antipodes Islands

Bounty Islands

Auckland Islands

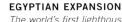

What is a ship?

Around 2500 BC, in the eastern Mediterranean, small boats began to develop into ships, but the difference is not easy to define. Fishing vessels are always boats, regardless of size or function, and in the Royal and United States navies of the present day, submarines are always referred to as boats because of their origins as quite small craft. With some exceptions, it is safe to say that a ship is generally larger than a boat. It is not enough to say, however, that a boat is a small craft for crossing rivers and narrow seas, while a ship is larger and designed to traverse oceans; in ancient times, great distances and areas of water were crossed by small Polynesian canoes and Irish currachs, and now, in modern times, adventurers compete to cross oceans in the smallest craft possible.

To define a ship or a boat, it is helpful to consider the kind of accommodation onboard. Normally, a ship has decks under which crew and passengers can shelter and where cargo can be protected. Again, however, this is not completely inclusive: the famous Viking longships and the classical galley are indisputably ships,

but the longship had no real sheltered decks, and galleys were not designed for long passages but were drawn up on beaches overnight.

Modern ships may be larger and more populous than whole towns of early modern times, but tiny craft are still used for leisure and fishing – some of these we call ships, and others we call boats. Despite the development of the ship, the old continues to exist alongside the new.

The Egyptians at sea

The Egyptians developed the sail by around 3500 BC. They began to build a variety of river and seagoing sailing craft, becoming the world's major naval power for almost the next 2,000 years. Progress in Egyptian shipbuilding was recorded effectively but unsystematically on tomb reliefs and on pottery, and a complete and intact boat from about 2550 BC, found at Cheops in the 20th century AD (see p.27), offers further insight into early ship design.

Pharaoh Sahure's fleet of seagoing ships of around 2475 BC show their origin in river boats, with long, narrow, spoon-like hulls and large overhangs at the bow and stern. They had bipod masts, made from two logs tethered together at the top, and rope trusses from bow to stern, all of which helped to strengthen the hull. Queen Hatshepsut's ships, one thousand

EGYPTIAN EXPANSION
The world's first lighthouse was built in about 29 BC at Alexandria, an important trading port between the Nile and the Mediterranean.

years later, had finer lines. Single pole masts carrying wide, billowing sails gave these ships better sailing qualities. They travelled the length of the Red Sea, from Egypt to Ethiopia or perhaps Somalia, but they still carried a full complement of rowers, essential in areas with such light and unreliable winds. Ramses III's fleet of around 1190 BC is depicted repelling a naval invasion from the eastern Mediterranean. Ramses' ships had much lower bows and sterns than their predecessors, although they still had curved hulls. The craft of the invaders are shown with straight stem and stern posts, decorated with birds' heads.

THE FIRST SHIPS

The earliest known depiction of a boat under sail is on an Egyptian vase, dating from about 3100 BC (see below). Riverboats, which ran up the Nile with the wind at their back, had a tall, narrow sail on a mast placed well forward of the ship. The birth of the seagoing sailing ship was sometime between 3500 BC and 2500 BC. By 2500 BC, the sail had evolved to a broad, shallow shape, more suitable for furling during strong winds on long voyages, when oars could be used. Early seagoing craft had bipod masts, but these soon gave way to a single pole mast, which could carry the sail on either side and, located near the middle of the ship, helped to balance the vessel when the wind came from the side.

Hawaiian Islands
Kauai Oahu
       Maui
Hawaii

C

Palmyra Atoll
Tabuaeran
  Kiritimati
Jarvis
Island   Line Islands
Malden Island
Starbuck Island

orthern Cook
Islands
      Vostok   Caroline
      Island   Island
                    Tuamotu
                    Islands
    Society   Tahiti
    Islands
outhern Cook
Islands
    Iles Australes   Iles Gambier

Marquesas
Islands

POLYNESIAN MIGRATION
From around 10,000 BC, a series of migrations carried the Polynesian peoples out of southeast Asia and across the South Pacific, ultimately leading to the colonization of an area reaching from Hawaii in the north, to New Zealand in the south, and Easter Island in the east.

Pitcairn
Island   Henderson
           Island

Sala y Gomez

Easter
Island

P A C I F I C

O C E A N

N

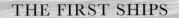

PACIFIC MIGRATIONS	
Earliest migrations	
⟶	Pre-10,000 BC
Austronesian migrations	
⟶	2500 BC–1000 BC
Polynesian migrations	
⟶	1000 BC –1 BC
⟶	AD 1–500
⟶	AD 500–1500

1,000   0 km   1,000
1,000   0 miles   1,000

MERCHANT *HIPPOS*
Decorated with the head of a horse and the tail of a fish, these Phoenician merchant ships of about 700 BC, known as hippos, *are towing cedar wood from Assyria.*

The Nile provided the Egyptians with most but not all of their resources, so they began to venture into the Mediterranean Sea. Their known voyages were short coastal journeys to the Levant (the modern eastern Mediterranean countries). Timber, mainly for shipbuilding, was imported from Lebanon, copper came from Cyprus, and tin from Asia Minor.

The earliest identifiable seagoing merchant ships are depicted on a mural in Thebes, dated around 1400 BC, although merchant ships undoubtedly existed much earlier. They have short, fat hulls with raised palisades, to protect the above-deck cargo, and the wide, shallow sails of seagoing ships; there is no sign of oars. They are transporting jars containing wine and oil from a Levantine port.

The Phoenicians

During the decline of Egyptian power, which culminated in the collapse of New Kingdom in 1085 BC, there were two or three centuries of dark ages, from which little is known about ships and seamanship. From around 900BC, the Phoenicians became the leading sea power. Possibly starting from the Syrian and Palestinian coasts, they established a colony in Carthage (modern Tunisia) around 814 BC. They were natural sailors and began to dominate trade, sailing along the length of the Mediterranean and, in far more difficult waters, along the west

PHOENICIAN SHIP
This late Egyptian clasp depicts a Phoenician ship complete with an above-deck cabin and a ram.

THE GALLEY

Homer's *Odyssey* gives a description of the crew of a Greek galley sailing in a fair wind under the command of Odysseus's son:

Telemachus shouted out commands to his shipmates: 'All lay hands to tackle!' They sprang to orders, hoisting the pinewood mast, they stepped it firm in its blocks amidships, lashed it fast with stays and with braided rawhide halyards hauled the white sail high. Suddenly wind hit full and the canvas bellied out and a dark blue wave, foaming up at the bow, sang out loud and strong as the ship made way, skimming the whitecaps, cutting towards her goal.

HOMER, *The Odyssey*, **c.700** BC

coast of Spain, to the Canary Islands, and the west African coast. Although the Phoenicians invented the alphabet and brought it to Europe, their voyages and vessels are known only from the accounts of their rivals, the Egyptians and the Greeks. The Greeks called the Phoenician trading ships *gauloi* or tubs, implying that the craft were short and fat, and *hippo* or horses because of the figureheads that fronted them.

A relief from about 700 BC shows Phoenician galleys with very pointed, curved rams, single rows of oarsmen, curved sterns, and fighting decks with shields along their sides. These ships probably protected the merchant ships. They appear short and fat by later galley standards, although it is impossible to judge the accuracy of the sculptor's perspective. Less warlike vessels also appear in the relief, without rams but still propelled by oars and with a deck above, carrying distinguished-looking passengers.

The Greek galley

The galley was to become the dominant fighting ship of the eastern Mediterranean, but early galleys were simply ships with single levels of oarsmen. The slower, sturdier ships were used to transport goods, while faster galleys, with slim, lightly built hulls, were used to carry messages or important personages. In the Aegean Sea from 2200 to 1450 BC, the thriving Minoan civilization established the first navy to protect its merchant ships at sea. The Egyptians adapted their galleys for raiding, using warrior-oarsmen who could fight as well as row – any type of ship could transport troops on forays, but these galleys carried marines who could also fight enemy craft hand-to-hand on the water. Around 1000 BC, the Greek peoples of the Aegean added a ram to the lighter form of galley, creating the first true warship, capable of sinking an enemy.

The most detailed information about early galleys comes from stories credited to the Greek poet Homer. It has never been established whether these tales were written by a single person or were the culmination of an oral tradition but, at some stage around 700 BC, the epic poem *The Odyssey* was recorded. This account of the hero Odysseus's long voyage home from the siege of Troy (thought to be based on a battle that occurred around 1200 BC)

THE OARS OF THE TRIREME

It is with a combination of conjecture and practical experimentation that modern scholars attempt to explain how the three levels of oarsmen were organized in a Greek trireme. From documentary sources, we know that each oarsman took up 2 cubits or 96cm (38in) and that each man had his own oar. The oars were 9 or 9.5 cubits long; with the larger oars used near the centre of the ship, rather than on a specific level. It has been established that the thranites were the upper level of oarsmen, the zygites the

TIER STRUCTURES

Two alternative methods of arranging tiers of oarsmen are shown here. The exact positions are still debated but the reconstructed trireme Olympias (see pp.24–25) demonstrated the practicality of the positioning shown on the left.

middle, and the thalamites the lowest. The idea of three men pulling on one oar has been ruled out. Three separate decks of oarsmen directly above one another have also been discounted, for this would place the highest level of oarsmen too far above the water. The English classical scholar John Morrison took a clue from the fifth-century BC comedy *The Frogs*, by the Athenian playwright Aristophanes, which mentions an upper oarsman's habit of "breaking wind in the face of the thalamite", and suggested that the tiers were staggered, with the seat of one level with the shoulders of the oarsman below. No modern trireme replica has been able to reach, under oar, the speeds of up to 8.6 knots claimed by the highly trained Athenians.

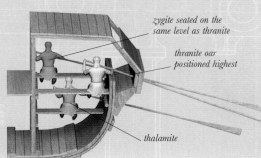

thranite
zygite seated below thranite
thalamite

zygite seated on the same level as thranite
thranite oar positioned highest
thalamite

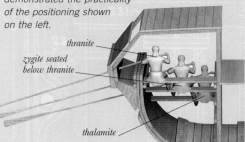

TIED TO THE MAST

This Greek amphora of around 520 BC shows Odysseus bound to the mast of his ship to resist the lure of the Sirens.

describes the construction and sailing of galleys (see panel, opposite). Homer details the building of a galley: "he bored through all his planks and wedged them snugly, knocking them home together, locked with pegs and joints". He also lodges his contempt of those nations who do not use the sea: "they have no shipwrights in their country to build sound vessels to serve their needs, to visit foreign towns and townsfolk as men elsewhere

do in their voyages." According to Homer, other people loved the sea – he describes the Phaeacians as proud to be "oarsmen and seamen of renown". The oarsmen of *The Odyssey* are not slaves but free men who delight in the teamwork and athleticism of their craft.

The Greek galley of Odysseus's journey was probably the penteconter, the single-decked 50-oared ship that became the standard and most powerful vessel in the Mediterranean by the sixth century BC. Following this, the Greeks perfected the addition of a second row of oarsmen, and the bireme was born. This construction could double the power of a galley

MINOAN NAVY

The world's first navy (depicted on this fresco from the 16th century BC) was built by the Minoans of Crete to protect their trading interests.

of the standard length, or produce a shorter and more manoeuvrable ship with greater ramming power. By about 600 BC, the Corinthians reached the next stage and built the famous trireme, with its three levels of oars. The trireme was copied by the various city-states, such as Athens and Sparta, and by 500 BC it was the most successful warship in the eastern Mediterranean. As the Greek city-states increased in power and conflict between them intensified, hundreds of ships were built. The trireme was the most technologically advanced warship of its age, tested and refined in numerous campaigns and battles over several

centuries. Naval power in Greece became increasingly concentrated, as the newly democratic state of Athens formed alliances with other Greek states to defend their territories from Persian invasion. Their greatest naval victory was in 480 BC, when a fleet of Greek triremes and penteconters joined together to defeat the larger but ultimately unwieldy Persian force in the Battle of Salamis (see panel, below).

UNDER SAIL
All oars are out as the Olympias raises its sails. In fact, the two sails of the Greek trireme were probably not used while the ship was under oar, nor while in battle. Except over long periods, rowing was generally faster than sailing.

THE BATTLE OF SALAMIS

In 480 BC, after defeat by the Persians at Thermopylae, the Athenians evacuated their capital and joined their Greek allies off the island of Salamis, with the Persians in pursuit. Drawn up between the island and the mainland, the Greek fleet under the Spartan Eurybiades numbered around 300 triremes. Faced with a Persian fleet of around 1,000 larger ships, the Greek coalition favoured retreat. The Athenian leader Themistocles, however, convinced of

the advantage of their position, leaked these plans to the Persian King Xerxes who, dividing his forces, blocked both mouths of the Bay of Eleusis and, at dawn, attacked. Entering the narrow channel, the Persian fleet was divided by the small island of Psyttaleia. Themistocles attacked the disordered left wing and forced it back on the right wing, which was attacked by the Spartans. A final flank of Corinthian ships moved forward, and a melee developed, in which the manoeuvrability of the smaller Greek ships proved decisive. The Greeks lost 40 ships, the Persians 200. The battle reversed the Persian advance, and confirmed the ram as the main naval weapon of the age.

No wreck of a trireme has ever been located, for they were often dismantled, and being lightweight vessels would have broken up easily in the sea. Pictures on vases and carvings tend to take the ships' detail for granted, and there has been much modern debate regarding the construction of the three levels. In 1986, the Hellenic Navy completed a full-scale replica of a trireme, the *Olympias*, with staggered tiers of oarsmen (see panel, p.23). Rowed by volunteers from around the world, the *Olympias* achieved a cruising speed of 5.8 knots during a series of time trials.

Despite the fact that it was not easy to fit three levels of oarsmen into a hull, surviving written records show that vessels with even larger numbers of oarsmen were built. Around the fourth century BC, Dionysus of Sicily, known as the Tyrant of Syracuse, began to colonize the Adriatic using galleys with four or five levels to the oars. One of the most powerful leaders in history, Alexander the Great, the king of the Greek state of Macedon,

BATTLE OF SALAMIS
- Persian coalition ships
- Greek coalition ships
→ Persian advance
→ Greek advance
⇢ Greek decoy

AEGEAN SEA
site of battle — Athens
Peloponnese — Salamis
Saronic Gulf

Eleusis
Bay of Eleusis
Megara
Corinthians
Megara Gulf
Athenians
Egyptians
Salamis
Spartans
Psyttaleia
Piraeus
Salamis
Ionians   *Phoenicians*
Saronic Gulf
N

1,000   0 km   1,000
1,000   0 miles   1,000

SUBTERFUGE
On the morning of the battle, a small decoy fleet raised sail and retreated north. The Egyptians were fooled and never entered battle.

expanded his empire from Greece to India, taking over the galley fleets of the states he conquered, before his death in 323 BC. There is mention of ships with up to 30 levels of oarsmen in the great fleets of this time. This might be possible if several men pulled at one oar, as was common in later times, or if two hulls were combined in a catamaran arrangement – the "forty" of Ptolemy IV, ruler of Egypt from 222 to 205 BC and the founder and creator of the Pharos lighthouse, probably consisted of two plank hulls linked together.

The Dover Boat

Although most progress in the development of ancient ships took place in the Mediterranean, the peoples of northern Europe took to the seas just as early as the Egyptians. The remains of a large cargo boat discovered at Dover, England, in 1992 have been carbon-dated to approximately 3,550 years ago. Its size and location suggest that it may have been used for trading across the English Channel, and this is supported by other finds of goods that must have originated in continental Europe. The boat fits into the northern European tradition of the time, as established from other archaeological finds such as the late Bronze Age boats found at North Ferriby, in northern England. The Dover Boat was about 9.5m (31ft) long with a crew of perhaps 18 paddlers. It had a flat bottom consisting of two planks held together by wedges, with side planks stitched on.

SWALLOWED BY A WHALE
Discovered asleep during rough weather, Jonah finds out that sailors are always suspicious, especially during a storm.

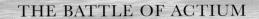

Roman ships

Although not natural seamen themselves, the Romans adopted the galley from the Greeks and used it to good effect in their wars against Carthage in the second and third centuries BC. The Romans' power was rooted in the army, and in naval battle they used marines, who surged across gangways to board enemy ships when they drew alongside, and fought with spear and sword. The ram, although still important, was secondary. The Romans built towers on their ships so their archers could fire from greater height, and they adopted the shipboard catapult from Alexander the Great. They built ever-larger galleys with an emphasis on size rather than manoeuvrability, but they also used smaller, faster, single-level galleys called liburnians for reconnaissance and communication during battle. During the First Punic War with Carthage (264–241 BC), the Romans carried 120 marines in their fighting ships – Athenian galleys had normally carried no more than 14 additional soldiers.

The Battle of Actium in 31 BC (see panel, right) left the new Emperor Augustus with no rivals at sea, and galleys were now confined to anti-piracy patrols and imperial expansion. Roman ships ventured out of the Mediterranean into western and northern Europe, carrying troops as far as Britain during the invasions of 55 and 54 BC. In the Mediterranean, the galleys kept the peace and controlled trade routes. Merchant ships traded fish, olive oil, and wine along the Mediterranean and kept Rome supplied with grain from Egypt. These cargos were carried in amphoras – large jars with narrow necks and a handle on each side, weighing around 23kg (50lb) when empty and twice as much when full. A dock worker could carry one balanced on his shoulder, and they could be stowed

ROMAN REMAINS
This bronze goose figurehead (above) and iron anchor (right) were typical additions to a Roman galley.

THE BATTLE OF ACTIUM

On 2 September 31 BC, the army of the Roman statesman Mark Antony lay under seige and starving at Actium, western Greece, with their opponents waiting at the narrow Gulf of Ambracia. Antony and his lover Cleopatra, Queen of Egypt, had disputed control of the Roman Empire with Octavian, the heir of Julius Caesar. Antony's fleet of large galleys was drawn up in three squadrons across the entrance of the gulf, with Cleopatra's force of 60 ships behind them. Octavian's naval commander, Agrippa, attacked with three squadrons made up of mostly smaller and faster

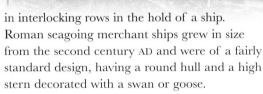

liburnians, and surrounded Antony's larger ships as they emerged, destroying them with fire arrows (below). Cleopatra and her ships fled, followed by Antony and some of his fleet, but the rest were overpowered and the besieged army was forced to surrender. One year later, Anthony and Cleopatra committed suicide, and by 27 BC Octavian had adopted the name Augustus and ruled unchallenged as the first Roman Emperor. The Battle of Actium marked the end of the maritime threat from the east to Roman rule. It also signalled the end for the great galley.

in interlocking rows in the hold of a ship. Roman seagoing merchant ships grew in size from the second century AD and were of a fairly standard design, having a round hull and a high stern decorated with a swan or goose.

St. Paul's journey from Jerusalem to Rome in 60 AD is detailed in the Acts of the Apostles in the Bible, and was typical of the voyages of the time, apart from its conclusion in a shipwreck. He was transported on a ship belonging to the Imperial Regiment, first sailing north and around Cyprus, before changing to an Alexandrian merchant ship carrying grain bound for Rome. In unfavourable winds, they put into the port of Fair Havens, Crete, for shelter. Despite Paul's warning about the approach of winter, it was decided to head for Rome. The ship was driven before a northeast wind and blown off course. Taking shelter off a small

island, the crew undergirded the ship (bracing it with rope) in order to strengthen the hull, but after 14 days they ran aground at what is now St. Paul's Bay, Malta. Three months later, Paul's voyage resumed on another Alexandrian merchant ship, which had wintered on the island. It put into Syracuse on Sicily, then followed a southerly wind to Rome.

Long journeys for trade and exploration could now be made relatively confidently. The Mediterranean peoples had developed two types of vessel, the long ship (or galley) and the round ship (or merchantman), which would dominate the seas well into the modern age, more than one thousand years after the Roman Empire fell.

SMALL MERCHANTS
Many Roman merchantmen for long voyages, such as the one shown here, were two-masted. Some also used topsails.

EGYPTIAN SHIPS

The ancient Egyptian civilization, based around the River Nile, was the first culture to develop sailing ships on a large scale and the first to venture into the open sea with them. Although ancient Egypt was held back by a shortage of shipbuilding materials, such as timber, it produced a variety of craft. There are few written records, but pictures and models have been found in tombs – and even a real boat in one case.

LATE EGYPTIAN SHIP
This contemporary wall painting shows an Egyptian ship of the period 664–332 BC with a crescent-shaped yard.

Seagoing craft

Around 3500 BC, the Egyptians made the historic leap from the Nile into the Mediterranean. A model (below) based on a relief on the tomb of Sahure shows triple rudders, a bipod mast (lowered here), and oars. A rope truss braces the long hull against the stresses of the sea.

taut rope truss to prevent boat from sagging

bipod mast

stern

SAHURE SHIP

Date *c.*2450 BC	Propulsion Sail
Length Not known	Material Wood

Sailing craft

Sails were very useful on the Nile, where the current runs one way and the prevailing wind the other. Early Egyptian sails were far broader than high, with poles at the head and foot to open them (right). Later sails were narrower and taller, with only a yard at the head to spread them. The mast was supported by several backstays, running from its head to the stern of the ship, and a smaller number of forestays. Some ships had bipod masts.

SAILING BOAT

Date *c.*1900 BC	Propulsion Sail
Length Not known	Material Wood

Rowing craft

Rowing was the most obvious means of propulsion on the Nile. The Egyptians tended to use their oars at a very steep angle. A boat (below) in the pyramid of King Cheops (or Khufu), discovered unassembled in 1954, provides the most complete picture of an Egyptian river craft.

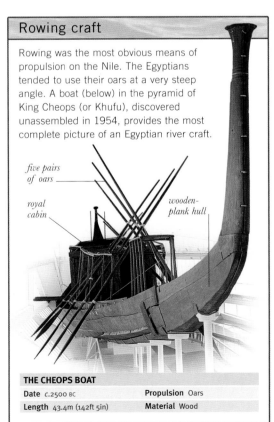

five pairs of oars

royal cabin

wooden-plank hull

THE CHEOPS BOAT

Date *c.*2500 BC	Propulsion Oars
Length 43.4m (142ft 5in)	Material Wood

Funerary craft

Egyptian boats were used for many purposes, including transporting corpses to their tombs, and the Cheops boat (left) may have been used in this way for the king. A very simple model (below) discovered in a tomb at Thebes shows a boat with a very curved stern carrying a rectangular coffin, with a crew of eight, probably rowers. Its colouring and shape suggest that it was made of reed, just as all the earliest boats were. Much larger craft were used to transport stone obelisks and the materials for pyramids.

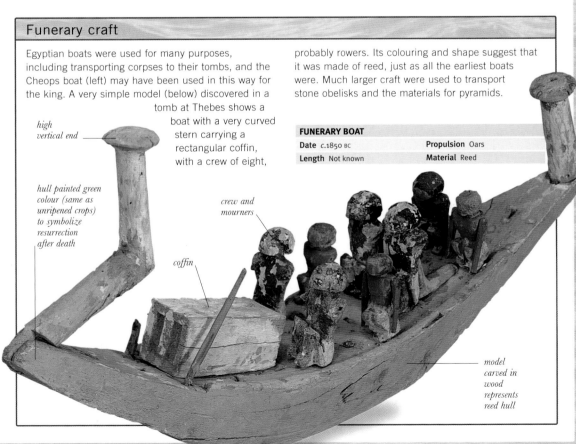

high vertical end

hull painted green colour (same as unripened crops) to symbolize resurrection after death

crew and mourners

coffin

FUNERARY BOAT

Date *c.*1850 BC	Propulsion Oars
Length Not known	Material Reed

model carved in wood represents reed hull

GALLEYS

The Phoenicians, Greeks, and Romans all used the rowing galley as their main means of domination in the Mediterranean over a period of more than a thousand years. The galley developed from a single tier of oars in Phoenician times to great, if impracticable, multi-tiered vessels under the Romans. There were various standard types of galley, most notably the great trireme associated with early Athens.

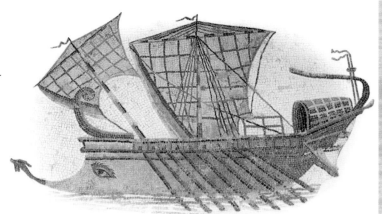

GALLEY MOSAIC
This Roman mosaic shows a galley with a single bank of oars, two sails, and an eye painted on its prow.

Phoenician galleys

The Phoenicians of the eastern Mediterranean were among the first people to carry out an extensive seaborne trade. Besides their merchant ships, they built galleys for warfare. A carving from Nineveh (below) shows a galley with two rows of oars, an upper deck surrounded with shields, and a pointed ram bow.

PHOENICIAN WAR GALLEY	
Origin Lebanon/Syria	**Date** *c.*700 BC
Length Not known	**Crew** At least 32 rowers

ram bow

Greek galleys

Ancient Greece was divided into city states, some on islands and some on mainland coastal areas. Piracy and rivalry between the states, followed by foreign invasion, led to almost constant warfare from about 700 BC. Over many centuries, they developed the galley into the classic trireme, with three levels of oars, then into even larger vessels. An image on a vase (below) shows what might be a pentaconter, so called because it had around 50 oars. The carving (right) shows a trireme.

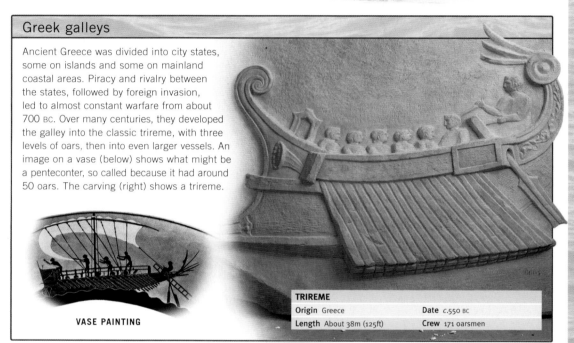

VASE PAINTING

TRIREME	
Origin Greece	**Date** *c.*550 BC
Length About 38m (125ft)	**Crew** 171 oarsmen

Roman galleys

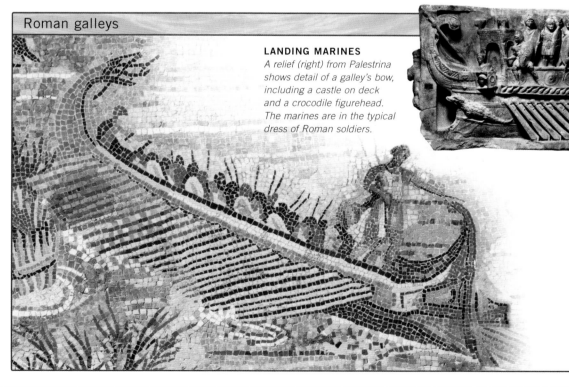

LANDING MARINES
A relief (right) from Palestrina shows detail of a galley's bow, including a castle on deck and a crocodile figurehead. The marines are in the typical dress of Roman soldiers.

Although the Romans were not natural seafarers like the Phoenicians and many of the Greeks, they adopted the galley to fight their wars with Carthage, across the Mediterranean, and used it to expand their empire as far north as Britain, in a much more hostile maritime environment. The pictorial evidence suggests that the Romans relied more on crew than the Greeks and less on the ram, although the ram was kept in service. With no equivalent naval power to fight in the days of their empire, the Romans tended to use their galleys mostly to land marines. The later Roman Empire's navies were principally manned by Greeks. A mosaic (left) in the Palazzo Barbarini at Palestrina in Italy shows a two-level galley of the first century, with the oars operating through an oar box on each side and marines drawn up ready on the deck.

ROMAN GALLEY	
Origin Rome	**Date** *c.*250 BC
Length About 55m (180ft)	**Crew** About 300

ANCIENT MERCHANT VESSELS

Rowing galleys were by far the most famous ships of the ancient Mediterranean world, but the Greeks and Romans also used fleets of sailing merchant ships for carrying goods as well as for pleasure sailing. The Roman merchant ship traditionally had a rounded hull, a feature common to Mediterranean cargo ships for many centuries. These vessels reached quite substantial sizes, and "ten-thousanders", able to carry that number of amphoras or sacks of grain (about 400 tons), seem to have been quite common.

MERCHANT SHIP IN PORT
This view of a ship's stern shows sails, a side rudder, and an overhanging stern. It is taken from a Roman mosaic.

Small craft

A relief from Utica (below) shows a small ship with the foremast raked well forward and the mainmast almost vertical. The boat is steered by one man, but more would have been needed for handling sails.

TWO-MASTED BOAT

Origin Roman	**Date** *C.*AD 200
Length Not known	**Propulsion** Sail

Roman pleasure craft

Several pictures show Roman craft being used for leisure. The Emperor Caligula himself had huge houseboats built for use on Lake Nemi, which were recovered in the 1930s and give much detailed information about Roman shipbuilding techniques. A wall painting (below) from early in the first century AD shows a brightly painted rowing boat with many of the features of a galley. None of these vessels seems suitable for use on the open sea.

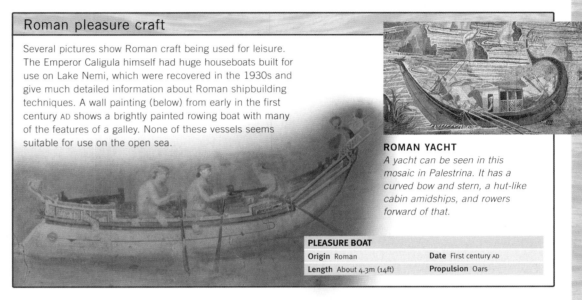

ROMAN YACHT
A yacht can be seen in this mosaic in Palestrina. It has a curved bow and stern, a hut-like cabin amidships, and rowers forward of that.

PLEASURE BOAT

Origin Roman	**Date** First century AD
Length About 4.3m (14ft)	**Propulsion** Oars

Large merchantmen

The Romans developed some very large merchant ships, largely for carrying grain from the Nile Valley, via Alexandria, to feed the city of Rome. The swan-neck motif at the stern was almost a universal feature of merchant ships. Square sails were common, and the two-masted rig was not unusual.

MERCHANT SHIP

Origin Roman	**Date** *C.* AD 200
Length About 26m (85ft)	**Propulsion** Sail

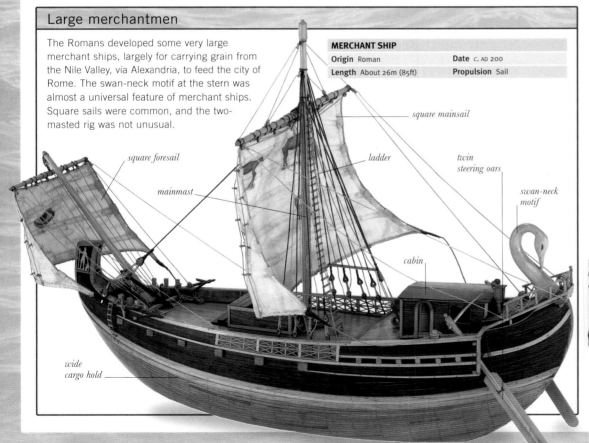

square foresail

mainmast

square mainsail

ladder

twin steering oars

swan-neck motif

cabin

wide cargo hold

River craft

River transport was important to the Roman Empire, and it was undertaken through the native waters of the Tiber and the great French and German rivers, as well as the Nile. Shallow-draft boats were designed for some rivers. A relief from the south of France shows a boat, carrying heavy casks, being towed by two men by means of ropes mounted on a post. More men would probably have been needed in practice, and larger boats could be pulled by teams of oxen. Another relief (below), probably from the port of Ostia at the mouth of the Tiber, shows three boats under sail in the rough waters at the mouth of the harbour of Portus.

RIVER BOAT

Origin Roman	**Date** Third century AD
Length Not known	**Propulsion** Sail

2

NAVAL WARFARE
The Battle of Sluys, as depicted here in Jean Froissart's chronicle of the 100 Years' War, was fought in 1340. Naval warfare was uncommon in medieval times, and warships were often converted from merchant ships.

SAILORS OF THE SEAS

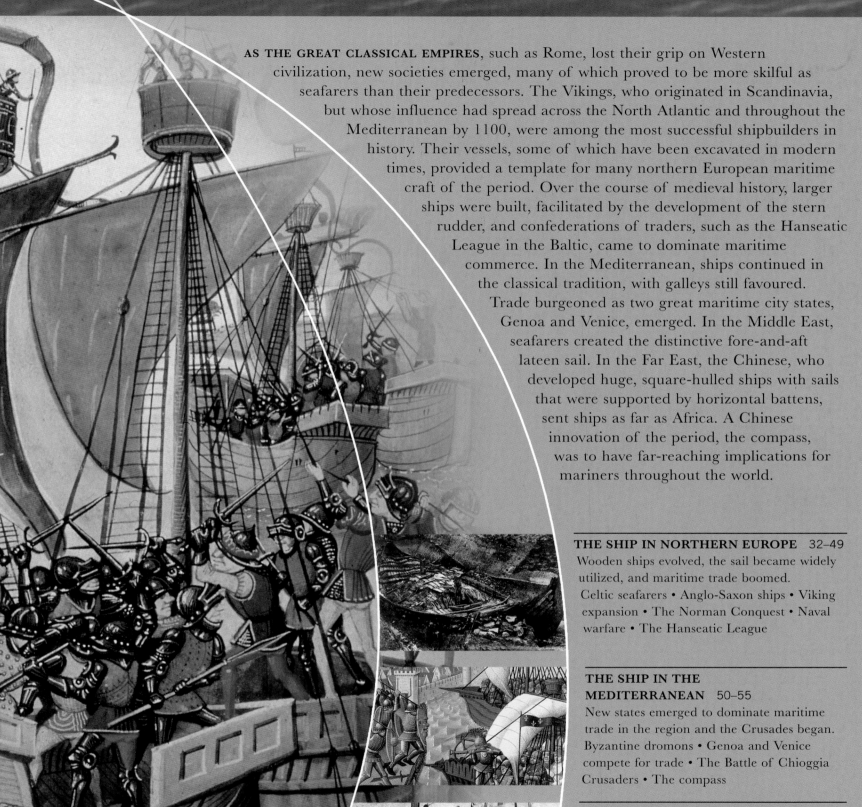

AS THE GREAT CLASSICAL EMPIRES, such as Rome, lost their grip on Western civilization, new societies emerged, many of which proved to be more skilful as seafarers than their predecessors. The Vikings, who originated in Scandinavia, but whose influence had spread across the North Atlantic and throughout the Mediterranean by 1100, were among the most successful shipbuilders in history. Their vessels, some of which have been excavated in modern times, provided a template for many northern European maritime craft of the period. Over the course of medieval history, larger ships were built, facilitated by the development of the stern rudder, and confederations of traders, such as the Hanseatic League in the Baltic, came to dominate maritime commerce. In the Mediterranean, ships continued in the classical tradition, with galleys still favoured. Trade burgeoned as two great maritime city states, Genoa and Venice, emerged. In the Middle East, seafarers created the distinctive fore-and-aft lateen sail. In the Far East, the Chinese, who developed huge, square-hulled ships with sails that were supported by horizontal battens, sent ships as far as Africa. A Chinese innovation of the period, the compass, was to have far-reaching implications for mariners throughout the world.

THE SHIP IN NORTHERN EUROPE

TRADE AND THE URGE TO EXPLORE DROVE THE CELTS, VIKINGS, AND OTHER NORTHERN PEOPLES TO BECOME GREAT SHIPBUILDERS AND SEAFARERS.

WEATHER VANE FOR VIKING SHIP, 12TH CENTURY

> *" ... thus putting to sea with a favourable breeze, we were enabled, without the slightest fatigue, to reach our island that same day. "*
>
> **ST. COLUMBA**, *Life of Columba*, written by Adamnán of Iona, **early 7th century** AD

KEY EVENTS

563 ST. COLUMBA ARRIVES IN IONA The Irish monk crosses the Irish Sea in a curach to found a monastery off Scotland's west coast.

625 SUTTON HOO BURIAL At about this time, King Raedwald of Anglia in southeast England is ceremonially buried in a ship. The wooden craft is later uncovered in 1939.

790 VIKING RAIDS BEGIN Vikings start to cross the North Sea in fleets of longships to launch raids on western Europe.

1001 VIKINGS REACH NORTH AMERICA Having reached Iceland in 870, Viking explorers sail to Greenland in 890 and Canada in 1001.

1066 NORMAN CONQUEST William the Conqueror sails to England in an invasion fleet of 700 ships, defeating King Harold at Hastings.

1143 LÜBECK FOUNDED The German Baltic port of Lübeck is set to become the chief city of the emerging Hansa League of merchants.

1340 BATTLE OF SLUYS Several hundred English and French ships fight one of the largest sea battles of the medieval period.

EXCAVATING A VIKING LONGSHIP
Several exciting discoveries, such as the unearthing of the Oseberg ship on a farm in Norway in 1904, have contributed to our knowledge of early craft in northern Europe. The Oseberg ship shows the Vikings' mastery of the "clinker" method of hull construction.

After the fall of Rome in AD 476, Europe entered the early medieval period, which is sometimes referred to as the Dark Ages, due in part to the scarcity of written historical records. Evidence about ships and shipbuilding in northern Europe mainly comprises brief descriptions by monks and other contemporary chroniclers and rare discoveries of wrecks or ship burials in which the vessels are in varying stages of decay. Most illustrations of ships from the early medieval period are contained in much later manuscripts from the 11th to 14th centuries. However, it seems likely that northern European cultures had been building seagoing vessels for as long as Mediterranean civilizations such as the Greeks and Romans (see pp.23–26).

During the Bronze Age (from about 2000 BC), the peoples of present-day Denmark, Norway, and Sweden are known to have used boats to cross

IRISH CURACH
Two Irish men can be seen paddling a curach in this illustration from an English manuscript of the late 13th century. The craft's light framework is clearly visible.

fjords and lakes and to travel between islands. These vessels were forerunners of Viking boats such as the longship (see pp.35–36), one of the most successful of all medieval ship designs. Shipbuilding and seafaring skills would prove to form the foundation for Viking achievement.

The other great seafarers of northwestern Europe at this time were the Saxons (see p.34) and the Celts. In 49 BC, Julius Caesar mentioned that the Celtic tribes of Ireland, Wales, and western England possessed large boats able to carry several men. These craft were the basis of a tradition of shipbuilding that enabled the Celts to undertake impressive voyages of exploration.

Celtic craft

On Ireland's west coast, the lack of trees led to the development of hide boats at an early stage. The currach, or curragh, was a banana-shaped boat made from animal skins stretched across a light wicker frame. It was powered mainly by paddles but also carried a sail. Although there is little archaeological evidence about what the currach looked like, indirect evidence comes from a vague carving

on a pillar in the Irish town of Bantry and from a small model made out of thin gold sheet (see p.14). Similar canvas boats are also in use in parts of Ireland to this day.

Despite the currach's fragile appearance, it was sturdy enough for sea fishing and transport to islands out of sight of the mainland. In the middle of the sixth century AD, St. Brendan, an abbot who founded a large monastery at Clonfert in Galway, used a currach to make a legendary voyage out into the Atlantic Ocean.

VOYAGE OF ST. BRENDAN
This woodcut published in 1621 depicts St. Brendan's voyage of discovery in the sixth century AD, during which a whale was said to have surfaced to enable the saint to say mass on its back.

He is supposed to have discovered a "land of promise", which featured on sea charts for many centuries afterwards. The extraordinary journey of Brendan the Navigator, as he is often known, has been the subject of much debate among historians. Among the theories put forward are that Brendan reached the Canary Islands, Iceland, or even Newfoundland. However, myth and fact are inextricably linked in accounts from the early Christian period, so perhaps the most valuable thing to emerge from the story of Brendan's voyage is its insight into currach construction. We are told that the monks used iron tools to prepare the boat's frame, tarred the hides to make them waterproof, and fitted a steering oar and sail, although with a side wind the boat was likely to be blown off course.

Another Irish monk of the sixth century AD, St. Columba, used his mastery of the currach to cross the Irish Sea. Born in Donegal to a princely line, Columba was a pupil of the bishop, St. Fillian. He built a monastery at Durrow and several other churches in Ireland, but in AD 563 he left the island, apparently due to a banishment after a political struggle. Sharing his boat with 12 companions, Columba arrived on the tiny Hebridean island of Iona and used it as a base to convert the Picts of western Scotland to Christianity. He founded several monasteries in the area, although not the later medieval ones that can be seen today on Iona and the island of Oronsay.

Anglo-Saxon ships

Brendan and Columba lived in an age of religious and political upheaval typified by big population movements in much of northern Europe. Britain, in particular, was a land of competing kingdoms, especially after the Romans retreated in AD 409. The Romans were succeeded by several Germanic peoples: the Angles, who founded East Anglia; the Saxons of Essex, Wessex, and Sussex; and the Jutes, who settled in Kent. Huge stone Saxon shore forts along the southeast coast of England date from the twilight years of the Roman occupation and were a defence against raids by such peoples. Ships of various kinds played a key role in all these movements of people and culture. In 1939, spectacular evidence of the type of ship used by the Saxons was found at Sutton Hoo in Suffolk, near the East Anglian coast. The ship in question was used to bury a powerful Anglian king, Raedwald, in about AD 625, together with a fabulous treasure of gold and silver jewellery, armour, combs, clasps, buckles, and ornate weapons.

SUTTON HOO HELMET
This seventh-century Anglo-Saxon ceremonial helmet from the ship burial at Sutton Hoo features metalwork of astonishing quality. Ship burials were commonly used for rulers in East Anglia and Sweden at the time.

overlapping planks, or strakes

nail joins planks together

light frame added after planks joined

CLINKER BUILD
The Sutton Hoo and Graveney Saxon ships both used the clinker method of hull construction. Planks, or strakes, were laid one on top of the other and fixed with iron nails. The overlapping timbers were then strengthened with light transverse frames. The Sutton Hoo ship had nine strakes on each side and 26 frames.

Only the shape of the ship remained, for the timbers and iron fastenings had long since rotted away, leaving an impression in the sandy ground. Nevertheless, the "ghosted" outline revealed much about Anglo-Saxon shipbuilding. The ship had long, curved stern and stem posts, and was clinker-built – that is, the hull was formed from overlapping planks. It would have closely resembled Viking longships built 150 to 200 years later, such as the Oseberg ship (see p.36).

Another, much larger vessel from a similar shipbuilding tradition was found in marshes at Graveney in Kent. It dates from about AD 1000 and differs from the Viking longships of its time in that it has a fuller cross section, a smaller keel that makes the boat almost flat-bottomed, and larger frame timbers. It was probably a sea-going trading vessel, and it has been estimated that it would have been able to carry a cargo of seven or more tonnes.

Early Viking craft

The 300 or so years from the mid-8th to the mid-11th century are traditionally known as northern Europe's Viking Age. The Vikings were a group of peoples from Denmark, Sweden, and Norway, many of whom were settled farmers, traders, and craftsmen rather than seaborne raiders, so their traditional reputation as bloodthirsty plunderers is misleading. However, there is no doubt that ships lay at the heart of Viking success, enabling them to explore far-flung lands and expand overseas. In Scandinavia, more than in other areas of Europe, the ship was by far the most effective means of transport. Much of the region was mountainous and marshy, and it was bisected by many fjords and rivers, while roads were scarce. Fortunately for archaeologists, the Scandinavians developed a tradition of burying their high-ranking chieftains and nobles in ships and boats beneath

OARED VIKING SHIP
The arrival of Viking ships in British waters had a huge impact on local people, and the strange craft were documented in several Anglo-Saxon manuscripts, including this somewhat fanciful depiction.

SHIP'S INTERIOR
This view inside a replica Viking ship – the front view is shown below – demonstrates the way in which cross-beams were used to add strength to the hull. The crosswise timbers could support a deck and were secured to the planks at the sides with curved "knees".

MERCHANT SHIP
This is a replica of a trading vessel originally found at Roskilde in Denmark. It had a very high prow to stop the boat tipping forwards in rough water and a pronounced keel to keep it on course in a crosswind. The ship would have been ideal for use in the Baltic Sea.

huge burial mounds. A few of these vessels have been recovered, offering a valuable insight into the Viking seafaring tradition. The earliest is the Hjortspring war canoe from Denmark, dated to the 2nd or 3rd century BC, which already shows signs of a structure based around a strong outer shell with an internal strengthening frame (see p.46). The Nydam boat of AD 350–400, found in a peat bog in northern Germany, was a heavy open rowing boat made of oak. This 24-m (80-ft) vessel incorporated a more sophisticated clinker-built hull, with five planks on each side, and was operated by 30 oarsmen.

Development of the sail

Apart from the development of a multi-planked hull with fine lines for moving through the water, the most significant innovation in Scandinavian waters was the introduction of the sail. This followed another refinement – a strong central keel – which provided a fixture for the mast

and helped to prevent the ship being driven sideways in a crosswind. The change happened relatively late in Scandinavia: whereas the Irish Celts and Anglo-Saxons were using sails by the sixth century AD (long after the Mediterranean civilizations), the Vikings appear not to have experimented with them for at least another 100 years.

SETTING SAIL
This 12th-century English manuscript depicts a sail boat of the type in use in Britain during the seventh century AD.

MEMORIAL STONE
Ships feature prominently on numerous upright stone slabs, or steles, erected by the Vikings on the Baltic island of Gotland. The picture stone shown here includes a carving of a boat with a large rectangular sail, complete with rigging.

The Oseberg ship

Viking ship designs developed rapidly throughout the eighth and ninth centuries AD. The use of sails became more widespread, and as a result hulls became wider and keels deeper in order to keep the vessels stable. In most vessels, masts were removable (though in the later ocean-going *knorrs* they were permanently fixed in place). In either case, the mast called for the addition of a strong supporting framework, with a strong beam called a keelson along the vessel's midline.

One of the most impressive remnants of the period is the Oseberg ship, discovered in a ceremonial burial mound in Norway in 1904. It is an extreme development of a longship, and not particularly seaworthy – it was probably used for ceremonial occasions or inshore trips. Artefacts found with it suggest the ship and its occupants were buried in the late ninth century AD, although the ship itself dates to about AD 800. This makes it the earliest known Viking vessel with a mast, although it probably relied more on oars for propulsion.

The elaborate decoration of the ship, and the high quality of the objects inside it, suggest that the materials recovered at Oseberg are the remains of a royal burial. It contained the skeletons of two

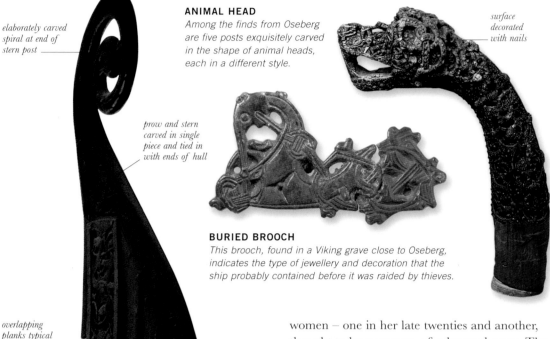

elaborately carved spiral at end of stern post

prow and stern carved in single piece and tied in with ends of hull

overlapping planks typical of clinker build

single mast about 10m (33ft) tall

carved human and animal figures

ANIMAL HEAD
Among the finds from Oseberg are five posts exquisitely carved in the shape of animal heads, each in a different style.

surface decorated with nails

BURIED BROOCH
This brooch, found in a Viking grave close to Oseberg, indicates the type of jewellery and decoration that the ship probably contained before it was raided by thieves.

women – one in her late twenties and another, thought to be a servant, of advanced years. The servant may have been sacrificed as part of the burial ceremony; the Vikings certainly sacrificed animals and people to accompany their high-ranking nobles into the afterlife.

During the excavation, archaeologists found signs that the burial had been raided in earlier centuries by treasure hunters. They would almost certainly have removed any gold and silver objects they could find, but they left the rest intact, and painstaking reconstruction now reveals the highly developed craftsmanship of the Vikings and the many hours they spent on the adornment of their most important ships.

The Viking raids

Initially, the Scandinavians used their ships largely for coastal travel in shallow waters. They were mostly a peaceful farming people, settling the shores of the Baltic. But the favourable climate of the time allowed their population to boom, increasing their need for cultivable land and putting them on a path to colonization and ultimately conflict with western Europe. The first "raids" were in fact aimed at settling unused land in islands such as the Orkneys and Shetlands, where settlers, particularly from Norway, established farming outposts. However, others turned to the Viking way, embarking on "pirate raids" that involved

THE OSEBERG STERN
The reconstructed prow of the Oseberg ship is decorated with stylized carvings of animals and humans. The stern post rises up and curves round to form the tail of a snake – the snake's head decorates the stem.

RAIDERS IN FRANCE
A longship under the power of its oarsmen was the fastest vessel of its era, with an almost flat bottom and shallow draft that allowed it to sail far upriver and beach itself with alarming speed in an early form of amphibious warfare.

typical square sail

flat deck for horses and equipment

steering oar

ROSKILDE WARSHIP
The longship on which this model was based was one of five vessels found at Roskilde Fjord in Denmark in 1959. The Danes took the longship design to a greater extreme than the Norwegians: this vessel was some 18m (59ft) long.

shields line the gunwales

READY FOR WAR
Typical Viking weapons included long-handled axes (left), while armour consisted of chain-mail shirts (below), round shields, and helmets in a variety of styles (although rarely with horns). Chainmail was hand-made in a lengthy process, and a mail shirt was a valuable possession.

raping and looting in the fertile green countries they found as they sailed southwest into the Atlantic. Often these raids were conducted by Scandinavian kings and princes, almost as a diversion from political warfare at home. In other cases, exiles and fugitives from the law turned to the Viking life.

At first, the raiders concentrated on attacking the wealthy Celtic monasteries around the coasts of England and Ireland, but from about AD 800 onwards, mainly due to population pressure at home, the Vikings became conquerors and settlers rather than plunderers. Aided by seafaring technology that no-one else could match or defend themselves against, they conquered most of eastern and northern England during the ninth century AD, creating an independent region known as the Danelaw. Their advance was eventually stemmed by King Alfred the Great, who ruled from AD 871 to 899 and united England for the first time. Alfred relied largely on land warfare and fortifications to repel Viking raiders, but in his last years he founded the first English Navy, with ships based on Norse design, although they were larger and higher than Viking craft.

In Ireland, the Vikings settled Dublin in about AD 840. In AD 859–62, they raided Spain, where they were defeated, and ventured further into the Mediterranean, raiding the coasts of Morocco and Italy and returning with African prisoners.

It would be a mistake to think that all Viking craft were as decorated as the Oseberg ship or as streamlined as the longship. The ship burials

that have been excavated are those of wealthy and powerful people, who presumably had ships to match. Alongside these few awe-inspiring vessels were probably many more robust merchant ships and smaller inshore boats, few of which have been preserved either as burials or in historic records.

SEAMANSHIP AND NAVIGATION

Viking navigation was done with simple equipment but a deep understanding of the sea and the sky. Navigational wisdom was passed on by word of mouth. The Vikings had no compasses, so they had to rely on the Sun and stars to find direction when out of sight of land. With no sextants to accurately measure the positions of celestial bodies, they may have used an oral tradition of "zenith stars", memorizing which stars passed directly overhead when seen from different lines of latitude.

curved line marks path of post shadow through the day at a known latitude

centre post

if the ship stays on its latitude, the shadow falls on the curve

straight line divides north and south

line is accurate only for a few days each year

SUN SHADOW BOARD
This ingenious device enabled Viking navigators to work out the elevation of the Sun at any time of day, in order to sail along a line of latitude.

LEIF ERIKSSON

Leif Eriksson was the second son of Erik the Red, founder of the Viking colony in Greenland, but little is known of his early years. He is thought to have been born in Greenland around AD 975 and sailed as a young man to Norway, where he was converted to Christianity by King Olaf I in AD 1000. He returned to Greenland the following year as a missionary for the new religion, where, according to the *Greenlander's Saga*, he heard talk of a new land to the west, sighted by Icelander Bjarni Herjulfsson some 14 years previously. Eriksson set out in search of this new land, making three landfalls along the North American coast – thought to have been in Labrador, Newfoundland, and (perhaps) northern Newfoundland, where he and his crew overwintered. Other sources say Eriksson found the new continent by accident, having been driven off course on his return to Greenland.

Expansion and trade

While Norse contact with western Europe was largely a story of plunder and blackmail, elsewhere Vikings undertook very different voyages. From around AD 800, they traded their way south from the Baltic, carrying their shallow-hulled inshore boats between rivers when they had to. In this way, they moved deep into Russia along the Volga and Dnieper rivers, eventually reaching the Black Sea and the Caspian Sea, where they traded with Byzantium and the rich civilizations of central Asia.

Meanwhile in western Europe, the Vikings were developing political ambitions. Norse and Danish leaders carved out territories in several countries, and rulers with an eye to protecting themselves invited them into the nobility, and even into their own families through marriage. This was how, in 1016, Cnut became the Viking king of England. In the next decade, he inherited the throne of Denmark and seized Norway and parts of Sweden, establishing his own short-lived empire.

Across the Atlantic

Elsewhere, the Norsemen pushed steadily west. They settled the Faroe Islands, some 200 miles west of Norway, around 870,

NORSE GODS IN ICELAND

Found on a farm at Akureyri in Iceland, this small bronze statue depicts the Norse god Thor holding a lightning bolt. It dates from about AD 1000.

and soon went on to colonize Iceland. According to legend, many of the Atlantic discoveries happened by accident, but even if the discoveries were due to luck, the opportunist Norse people were quick to take advantage of them. They were fortunate to live at a time when the climate was, on average, somewhat warmer than today, and as a result the islands of the north Atlantic were far more hospitable. Iceland soon became a major colony, home to some 60,000 settlers from western Norway at its peak, while the more intrepid explorers pushed on to Greenland. This new island was named by Erik the Red, who explored its coast in the early 980s

VIKING VOYAGERS

The 23-m (76-ft) Gokstad ship (a reconstruction of which is shown here) is probably typical of the vessels the Vikings used on their voyages of discovery (outlined on the map). In 1893, another replica of the Gokstad ship crossed the Atlantic Ocean from Norway to Newfoundland in just four weeks.

Map labels

North America

Greenland

Labrador Sea

Iceland

L'Anse aux Meadows

Newfoundland

Norway

Oslo

Russia

Baltic Sea

Asia

Ireland

Dublin

York

London

Paris

Europe

Caspian Sea

ATLANTIC OCEAN

Black Sea

Marseille

Rome

Spain

Mediterranean Sea

Africa

N

VIKING TRADE

→ maritime exploration routes

--▸ routes of exploration via rivers and overland

500   0 km   500

500   0 miles   500

THE VIKINGS IN NORTH AMERICA

The sites of most Viking landings in North America are still unknown, but there are scraps of archaeological evidence showing a short-lived settlement at L'Anse aux Meadows, on the northern tip of Newfoundland, around AD 1000. This may be the site of Leifsbúdir (Leif's Settlement), where Eriksson and his crew overwintered on their voyage of discovery. After the return of this first

expedition, two more were dispatched to explore further inland – one was led by Leif's brother Torvald, the other by Icelandic merchant Thórfin Thordarson. Both clashed with American Indians, and attempts at exploration were soon abandoned. By 1121, when Erik Gnúpsson travelled from Greenland "in search of Vinland", the continent seems to have receded into folk memory, although several Norse sagas assume its existence to be common knowledge.

LEIF ERIKSSON
This romanticized 19th-century painting shows Eriksson's boat nearing the coast of Vinland.

and settled there in AD 985–86, followed by some 25 shiploads of immigrants. The Greenland colony flourished for several centuries while the climate remained favourable, and it was a base for the Norse discovery and exploration of North America (see panels, above and left), but it was finally abandoned some time in the early 15th century.

Throughout this period, Viking ships were steadily being developed for new roles. The favoured vessel for long voyages in the open ocean was the *knorr*, a relatively short and broad boat with a deep draft and high gunwhales. These features made the *knorr* a stable cargo transport, but limited its number of oars – especially since it could not carry cargo and seat oarsmen at the same time. Instead the vessel had to rely largely on the wind, so it was fitted with a tall fixed mast and a large, square-rigged sail.

For warfare and inshore journeys, however, the longship still ruled. As Norse society coalesced under fewer, wealthier rulers, longship proportions became ever more

DECORATIVE CARVING
Discovered amid Viking ruins in Greenland, this wooden object, carved with animal heads and inscribed with the name "Helge", is thought to have been a boat tiller.

extreme, culminating in the dragon-ship or *drakkar*, which could require up to 60 oarsmen. Such fearsome ships were so expensive that only a king could afford them – and they provided an effective means of enforcing his rule.

NEWFOUNDLAND SETTLEMENT
This model of a small Viking landing boat stands on the site of the Norse settlement at L'Anse Aux Meadows, Newfoundland, alongside a replica of a sod-built house of the kind Leif Eriksson's men would have overwintered in.

RAIDERS ON NORMANDY
This illustration from a late-11th-century French manuscript records a Viking longboat attack on northern France. Although the boat is truncated, it clearly shows distinctive Viking features such as a hull built of long strakes and a steersman holding the tiller at the rear.

BOAT-BUILDING IN THE BAYEUX TAPESTRY
This scene depicts the preparation of the invasion fleet, and is preceded by images of trees being chopped down and shaped into long planks or strakes. Given the speed with which William launched his attack, it is likely that he commandeered most of his fleet – perhaps only building some of his horse transports from scratch.

Norman conquests

Following repeated Viking raids on France, early in the tenth century the French king offered land to a group of Norsemen in return for immunity from their attacks. These settlers became known as the Normans, and the area of northern France in which they settled, Normandy.

From this base, the Norman nobility extended their interests in new directions. In 1060, Norman knights led an invasion of Sicily, wresting it from its previous Arab control. A more famous Norman conquest followed six years later, when the Norman Duke William seized the throne of England from his rival Harold Godwinson.

William was an astute politician, and he ordered the conquest to be commemorated in a unique form – the 70-m (230-ft) Bayeux Tapestry. The tapestry records the story of the invasion and its background in detail, and reveals a great deal about the Norman sailing tradition.

The dispute over the crown arose from medieval laws and customs – William asserted that Harold, during a visit to his court in 1064, had pledged allegiance and support for William's claim to the English throne, promised him by his cousin, King Edward the Confessor, some years before. However, when Edward died, Harold himself was crowned king, and the enraged William prepared for war. The Bayeux tapestry records the building and preparation of a great invasion fleet of about 700 ships.

These ships were essentially similar to those used by the Vikings during the previous two centuries – but the Normans had developed the art of land warfare and had learned to use cavalry instead of infantry as their main attacking force. For this reason, about half of their ships were horse transports, each carrying perhaps six to ten animals, and similar to the cargo ship discovered at Roskilde in Denmark. The rest were more traditional Viking longships. However, the Normans apparently did not hang their shields over the sides of the boat – the move to cavalry meant the shields were no longer round but kite-shaped to suit a horseman, so they were stowed inboard.

WILLIAM OF NORMANDY
After the conquest, William exerted his new authority over England, issuing coins such as this one. He installed a Norman nobility and commissioned a great survey of lands – the Domesday book. But he had to face constant rebellions, and battles with the Welsh and Scots.

In the prelude to the battle, the Bayeux tapestry also reveals some interesting details of English ships of the time. The English rulers themselves were of Danish descent, so English ships show unsurprising similarities to the Norman ones. One significant difference is a gap along the line of oar ports in the centre – this may indicate a platform for hand-to-hand fighting between ships, and its origins can be traced as far back as Alfred the Great's first English Navy.

However, the English Fleet could play no part in repelling the Norman Conquest – they were too far away when William's fleet made its surprise overnight crossing from the mouth of the Somme River to southeast England. The Normans came ashore unopposed at Pevensey

INVASION FLEET
This sequence shows William's ships crossing the English Channel. According to some estimates, the fleet carried 8,000–10,000 men and about 2,000 horses.

on 28 September 1066. Word reached Harold three days later in the north of England, where he had just defeated an invading force led by the Norwegian King Harald Hardrada. Harold turned his army around and marched south, pausing at London for reinforcements. After an epic journey, he confronted William's forces near Hastings on 14 October, but after a long day's battle Harold was killed and the English Army routed. William's followers, many of whom were mercenaries fighting because he had promised them land, became the new ruling class of England.

THE ENGLISH NAVY
This scene from the Bayeux Tapestry depicts Harold Godwinson's fleet on the way to Normandy, where he will meet William and swear his fateful oath of fealty. English ships in the tapestry have little to distinguish them from Norman ones – the most obvious difference is the central gap in the oar ports along the side.

The cog and the hulk

The standard northern European ship during the medieval period was the cog, which was descended from Viking cargo vessels. It was primarily clinker built (see p.34), although the top part of the hull was carvel constructed. Cog hulls were shorter and fatter than their Nordic predecessors, and they were constructed with a straight stern and bow, a development that was contemporary with the adoption of the stern rudder (see panel, opposite). Cogs had a single mast and a square sail. A spar called the bowsprit projected forward at the prow. This was used to pull forward the bowlines, which were attached to the edges of the sail, and help the ship sail closer to the wind. By the middle of the 14th century, the cog was the standard ship of the Hanseatic League (see p.45) and was capable of carrying up to 200 tonnes of cargo.

COG REPLICA
In 1962, the remains of a cog, which was wrecked in about 1380, were found near Bremen, Germany. This replica was constructed in Kiel, using 14th-century shipbuilding techniques. The cog has a single mast, with one square sail.

100 YEARS' WAR
These 15th-century English warships, which were illustrated by Jean Froissart, are packed with archers and knights ready to fight the French during the 100 Years' War. The symbols of England and St. George adorn the ships.

Another traditional ship that was prevalent in northern Europe was the hulk. It was also clinker built and fitted with a single mast. However, in this case the planks of the hull did not sit flush against the stem and stern posts, as was the Viking tradition. Instead, they curved upwards, almost parallel to the posts and ended at a point above. The hulk was possibly of Germanic origin, and it may reflect the survival of a Roman shipbuilding tradition in northwest Europe long after the Romans themselves had departed. Evidence of the hulk has been found on the seals of several English towns, and this type of ship is also carved on the font of Winchester Cathedral, in southern England. However, it left no surviving tradition, perhaps because it was less adaptable than the cog.

SEAL OF MALDON
Much of what we know about the appearance of medieval ships comes from town seals, such as this one from Maldon, England.

Naval warfare

Naval warfare was rare in medieval northern Europe, and when sea battles did take place they were often an extension of land action. Ships were armed with archers, who attacked their opponents with bows and arrows, and soldiers, who boarded enemy ships and favoured hand-to-hand combat. Often warships were merchant cogs that were converted for combat. A fighting platform was added at the top of the mast to give extra height for bowmen and lancers. The vessels also had castellated wooden platforms built in the bow and stern (the after-castle and forecastle). These became larger and more permanent over the years, and were also adopted by merchant craft, as they provided extra shelter for the crew.

In the 13th century, the Cinque Ports were established along the southeast coast of England. The five towns that originally made up the association were Hastings, Romney, Hythe, Dover, and Sandwich, although later additions included Winchelsea and Rye. These towns were given trading privileges in the English Channel in return for supplying ships for the monarch's service when requested. The Cinque Ports' control of the primary crossings along this stretch of water was important at a time when the English king retained possessions on both sides of it. As the Baltic and its entrance came under the control of the Hanseatic League, the narrow waters close to the Straits of Dover became the main focus of maritime conflict. In 1213, as the French Army besieged the Count of Flanders, an English Fleet of 500 ships attacked over 1,000 weakly defended French ships at Damme. Hundreds of the ships were captured and many more destroyed.

Between 1337 and 1453, the Hundred Years' War raged between England and France. The most important sea battle, and the first key action of the long war, was the Battle of Sluys,

dominated all its contemporaries. The 1,300-tonne vessel was launched in 1418 and was one of several ships in Henry's fleet that was built to counter the French. It was unsurpassed in size until Charles I built the *Sovereign of the Seas* in 1637 (see p.105). She was about 60m (200ft) long, and one of her two masts extended a similar distance vertically. The ship pushed the system of clinker building to its limits, as her hull was constructed using three layers of wood. The *Grace Dieu* saw little active service and spent most of her life berthed near Southampton, where she caught fire in 1439. However, her wreck was preserved under a layer of mud, and her remains can still be seen at very low tides, providing a unique archaeological record of a medieval warship.

> ❝ I never saw so large and beautiful a construction. ❞
>
> **LUCA DI MASSI DEGLI ALBIZZI,**
> captain of the Florentine Galleys,
> describing Henry V's ship the *Grace Dieu*, **1430**

which occurred in June 1340. The French planned to invade England, and had assembled a fleet that also included Spanish and Genoese vessels and consisted of 202 sailing ships, 6 galleys, and 22 barges. The vessels were anchored and chained together in three lines, along a narrow channel at Sluys, on the approach to Bruges. The English Fleet, led by King Edward III in his cog *Thomas*, numbered about 260 ships. It approached the stationary fleet unexpectedly and used its superior mobility to render the French a crushing defeat, during which thousands were killed.

During the course of the war, the English used ships many times to attack and invade France. Henry V, one of the most iconic of English kings, was perhaps the first monarch to possess a great ship, the *Grace Dieu*, a vessel that

THE DEVELOPMENT OF THE RUDDER

The simplest way to steer a ship is to hang an oar over the side and turn it to increase or decrease the drag on one side of the vessel. Viking ships used a vertical steering oar, attached to the side and hanging almost vertically. Because the oar pivoted about its centre, the forces pushing on it from each side were almost equal, making it easy to turn. From the 12th century onwards, ships were increasingly built with rudders hung from hinges on the stern. A fixed rudder on the centre line made steering simpler, but had some disadvantages. It usually pivoted along one edge, so it was no longer balanced and needed more force to turn it, For maximum effect, the shape of the stern also had to allow water to reach the rudder, which required major changes to ship design. However, a rudder could be moved by a larger tiller, and later by mechanical devices, such as the whipstaff and steering wheel, allowing bigger ships to be built. Isambard Kingdom Brunel's huge *Great Britain* of 1843 reintroduced a form of balanced rudder, pivoting about its centre.

VIKING STEERING OAR
The stern of a Viking boat had a steering oar attached to its side, manoeuvred by a tiller. The oar could be pulled up when beaching the vessel.

STERN RUDDER
This photograph shows a replica of the rudder of the 14th-century Bremen Cog. These merchant craft were the first to use this type of device.

hinges attach rudder to stern post

rudder sits on centre line of ship

horizontal tiller allows oar to be turned with little effort

oar attaches to gunwales, so it does not require support

flat, broad steering oar

Scottish longships

A variant on the Viking longship emerged in Scotland in the 12th century: the West Highland galley, which was also known as the birlinn. These light, fast vessels, which were common on the lochs and around the islands of western Scotland throughout the medieval period, had a single, centrally positioned mast with a square sail. Unlike Viking ships, West Highland galleys had a straight stern and were manoeuvred using a rudder rather than a steering oar. These ships were probably instrumental in the 1156 sea battle near the isle of Islay, in which Somerled, the clan chief of Argyll, overthrew his Norwegian overlords. From this point, until the Scottish crown took control of the region in 1498, the inhabitants of the West Highlands and the Hebrides maintained an almost independent naval power.

BIRLINN
No remains of a West Highland galley have ever been discovered. However, many carvings of such vessels exist, such as this one from Kilmory Chapel in Argyll.

Northern European trade

The medieval period witnessed a boom in maritime commerce in northern Europe. In the Baltic, trade was dominated by cogs of the Hanseatic League (see panel, opposite). This centred on the German port of Lübeck, which was established in 1143. Other leading members of the trading confederation included the German cities of Bremen, Hamburg, Stralsund, Danzig (modern Gdansk), Kiel, and Dortmund. The league also established four *kontore* (counting houses), which were trading centres further afield in Novgorod, Russia; Bergen, Norway; Bruges, Flanders (part of modern Belgium); and London, England. Hanseatic ships traded along the entire Atlantic coast of Europe and also sent ships to Portugal and the Mediterranean. They shipped a variety of cargoes, including wool and cloth, which was exported from England; timber from Norway; wine and salt from France and Spain; herring from the North Sea and the Baltic; and furs and timber from Russia.

Wine was one of the primary commodities of the age, and its production was dominated by France. Despite constant conflict between England and France in medieval times, Gascony and its chief city, Bordeaux, exported up to 20,000 tuns of wine to England every year, and about three times that amount to other areas. The tun was a type of wooden cask that carried 954 litres (252 gallons) of liquid, according to an English statute of 1423. Wooden casks, which were also known as barrels, were the standard container of the age. Made from staves that were held together by wooden or iron hoops, they were made in varying sizes according to the goods in question. They were used to protect goods in leaky holds, to preserve cargoes such as salted fish in almost airtight conditions, and to transport liquids. They were also easy to manage, as they could be rolled on land, and they stacked neatly in a ship's hold.

Mediterranean ships, such as carracks (see p.80) sometimes made their way into northern waters, where they created a sensation because of their great size and rich, exotic cargoes. A Genoese carrack that put in to Sandwich, southeast England, in 1383 was described by a contemporary

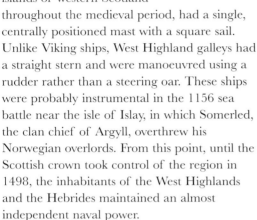

ENGLISH MERCHANTS
This bustling scene shows an un-named English port in the 13th century. A fleet of merchant ships are moored in the harbour.

THE HANSEATIC LEAGUE

The Hanseatic League, an alliance of trading cities in the Baltic region, established itself during the 13th century. Although it had no formal state authority and was run by irregular meetings of its diet (council), it was the most important economic power in northern Europe in the medieval period. The organization had the ability to apply economic sanctions on states and cities that failed to adhere to their terms. The League was also prepared to go to war to protect its trade routes. In May 1370, after a decade-long conflict, King Valdemar IV of Denmark signed a treaty with the confederation. He conceded Denmark's right to trade, gave the merchants a veto on the appointment of the Danish king, and lost control of the four fortresses that guarded the entrance to the sound between the North Sea and the Baltic. This represented the height of Hanseatic power. The Hanseatic League dominated northern European trade until English and Dutch merchants began to overtake it. It was formally disbanded in 1669.

SEALS OF HANSEATIC TOWNS
These wax seals, attached to an official document, represent some of the towns that made up the Hanseatic League. Lübeck's seal, bearing the distinctive image of a single-masted Hanseatic cog, is bottom left.

HANSEATIC HAMBURG
This image, which is taken from the city's charter, shows Hamburg in 1497, when the Hanseatic League dominated maritime trade in northern Europe. Hundreds of cogs, some of which can be seen in this image, were constructed to transport goods all over Europe.

observer as "of astonishing size, full of treasures [such as] fruit, spices of various kinds, oil and so forth." Florentine and Venetian galleys and Genoese carracks are also known to have visited Southampton in 1430.

English maritime commerce began to flourish in the second half of the 15th century, as a result of the expansion of the wool trade. By the end of the century, 80 per cent of the ships transporting wool from England to the Mediterranean were English, the rest were Italian. Dutch and Flemish traders also began to establish themselves in the 15th century. Their main innovation of this period was the *buss*, which was an extremely large fishing boat for the times, and went on to dominate the herring industry in the centuries that followed (see p.248).

The most daring seamen of the 15th century were the Basques, who inhabited the region around the southern end of the Bay of Biscay and the western Pyrenees. They were the first to pursue whales, and travelled from the Bay of Biscay, up through the North Sea, and across the Atlantic to Iceland, and Greenland. They also discovered abundant cod stocks in the North Atlantic, and may have reached North America, like the Vikings before them, although there is no concrete evidence for this.

By the early 16th century, the development of new and more efficient ships set the stage for a remarkable period in history, as European explorers sailed further than ever before.

PORT OF ANTWERP
This image shows the port of Antwerp in 1585, when it was seized by the Duchy of Parma and began to decline. During the 15th century, the Flemish port rose to become one of the most important trading cities in Europe.

VIKING SHIPS

The Norsemen of Sweden, Denmark, and Norway lived among islands, lakes, and fjords and were as close to the sea as any people in history. Using local materials, such as skins and wood, they developed seaworthy boats and ships that influenced European design for many centuries. Their raids and settlements throughout Europe and the North Atlantic are testament to the seaworthiness of their ships and earned them the name of the Vikings, which implies a kind of piracy. Their ships were small by Mediterranean or later North European standards and usually undecked. They had only a single mast and sail and could be rowed when necessary. They had a shallow draft and were light enough to be dragged over land.

MODERN VIKING SHIP
This photograph shows the Saga Sigler, a modern replica of a Viking ship, sailing in Sydney Harbour, Australia, in 1985.

Skin boats

It seems likely that the Norse peoples started their boatbuilding with log boats, then moved on to animal skins stretched on wooden frames, a method that was quite common in many parts of the world, and one that matched the materials and tools available to them. However, there is no direct archaeological evidence to confirm this, as such craft are unlikely to survive. The numerous Bronze Age rock carvings in Scandinavia are the subject of much debate, and it is not clear how far they were meant to be realistic. The ones at Kalnes (right), in southern Norway, like many others, appear to show the frames of such boats, with a long,

protruding keel, vertical supports, and several paddlers, or oarsmen. This might be seen as the origin of the wooden keel, which was an essential feature of Viking ships and allowed them to be dragged over land in circumstances in which a flat bottom might have been damaged more easily. From this it was natural to replace some of the hides with sewn planks, as seems to have happened with the Hjortspring boat (below), which also has long projections in the bows and stern.

SKIN BOAT

Origin Norway		**Date** Not known
Length Not known		**Crew** 6 oarsmen or paddlers

Early planked boats

The step from skin boats to planking was apparently well underway by the fourth century BC. The Nydam boat (below), of which three were discovered in a lake in northern Germany in 1863, is far more advanced than the Hjortspring boat (below, right). It shows clinker construction, with overlapping planks. There is no evidence of sails, but there are thole pins to support oars. The Nydam boat, together with other archaeological finds such as the Sutton

Hoo boat in England (see p.34), demonstrate that the clinker style of construction was used by boatbuilders other than the Vikings. Planked wooden boats allowed much more scope for development in size and produced stronger vessels that could be taken on long voyages in the open sea.

THE NYDAM BOAT

Origin Germany		**Date** AD 350–400
Length 23m (75ft)		**Crew** 30 oarsmen, plus helmsmen

internal frame

thole pin supports oar

oar

clench nail

bow

steering oar

clinker-built hull

HJORTSPRING
The Hjortspring boat (350–300 BC) has room for about 20 paddlers, but there are no signs that it was rowed.

Longships

The Viking longship of the ninth to eleventh centuries is one of the classic ships of all time – the culmination of several centuries of development. It carried the Vikings across the Atlantic, into the Mediterranean, and up the rivers of Russia. We know a good deal about these craft because of the Viking custom of burying their leaders in them, as at Gokstad, Oseberg, and Tune in Norway. These ships, though, are essentially light passenger or cargo vessels rather than fully fledged longships. The nearest we have to the latter are the two warships found at Skuldelev in Denmark. One was more than 27m (90ft) long. Contemporary records say longships could be up to 42.6m (140ft) long.

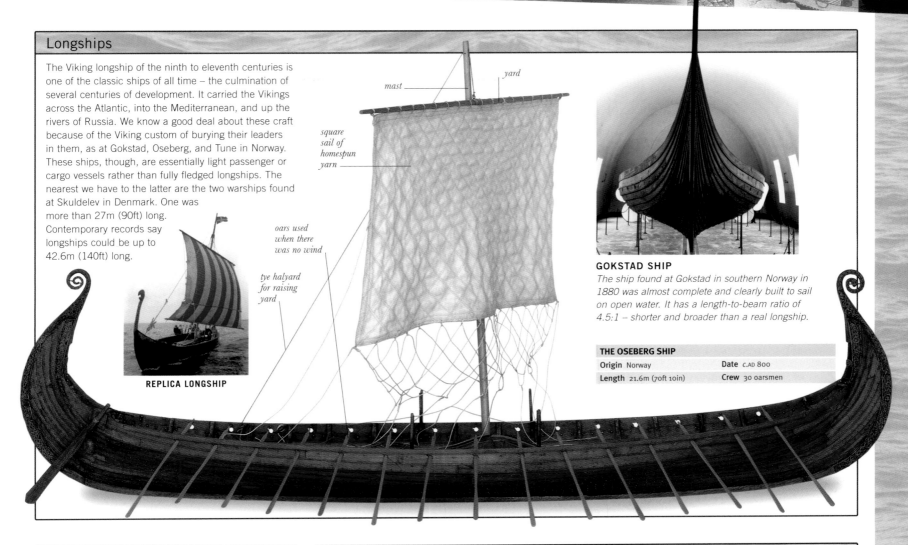

mast

yard

square sail of homespun yarn

oars used when there was no wind

tye halyard for raising yard

REPLICA LONGSHIP

GOKSTAD SHIP
The ship found at Gokstad in southern Norway in 1880 was almost complete and clearly built to sail on open water. It has a length-to-beam ratio of 4.5:1 – shorter and broader than a real longship.

THE OSEBERG SHIP	
Origin Norway	Date c.AD 800
Length 21.6m (70ft 10in)	Crew 30 oarsmen

Sailing boats

The Norsemen seem to have started sailing by holding up a leafy branch in the bows of a boat. A series of stones (below) in Gotland, Sweden, show more sophisticated arrangements, with shrouds supporting the mast and crew members holding the lower edge of the sail. Like all Viking craft, these wooden sailing boats could be rowed.

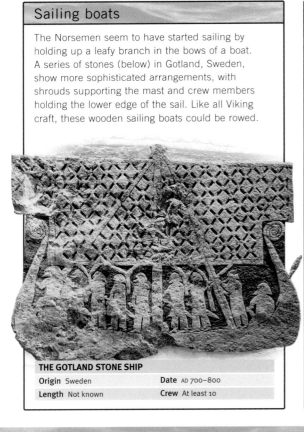

THE GOTLAND STONE SHIP	
Origin Sweden	Date AD 700–800
Length Not known	Crew At least 10

Cargo ships

The Norsemen did not spend all their time raiding and had quite a sophisticated trading community. Of five ships excavated from Roskilde Fjord at Skuldelev in Denmark in 1962, one was a trading ship about 13.8m (45ft 3in) long, capable of carrying about 350 cubic metres (12,360 cubic ft) of cargo. Another is a trading ship of a type called a knorr (right). This ship's timber indicates she was built in Norway. She is bigger than the others, with higher sides, but is clinker-built and single-masted, like almost all Norse seagoing ships.

SKULDELEV KNORR	
Origin Norway	Date 11th century
Length 16–17m (52ft 6in–56ft)	Crew 8

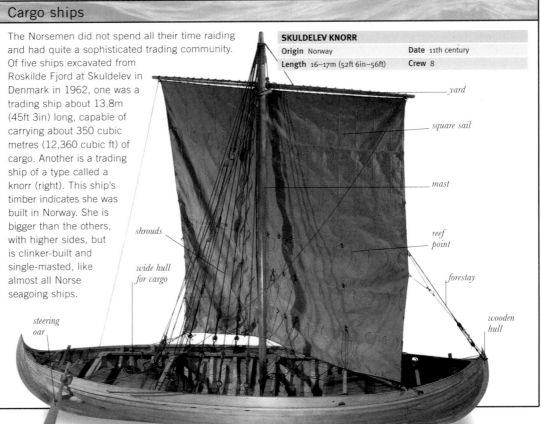

yard

square sail

mast

reef point

forestay

wooden hull

shrouds

wide hull for cargo

steering oar

MEDIEVAL SHIPS

The medieval period saw two shipbuilding traditions in Europe. In the north, the Norsemen were no longer predatory, but their clinker shipbuilding style was still used by the Hanseatic League and the traders of England and northern France and modified by the stern rudder. In the Mediterranean, classical traditions were adapted by Arab mariners, but ships can still be classified into galleys, both merchant and warship, and cargo-carrying round ships.

FRENCH COUNCIL
In this painting, the King of France is holding a council at Sluys in 1340. Warships can be seen on the left.

Medieval galleys

The galley remained the main fighting ship in the Mediterranean, although it rarely ventured into rougher waters. The example illustrated below shows the system of rowing with three oarsmen on each bench, a decorated canopy for the officers in the stern, and a plainer one forward.

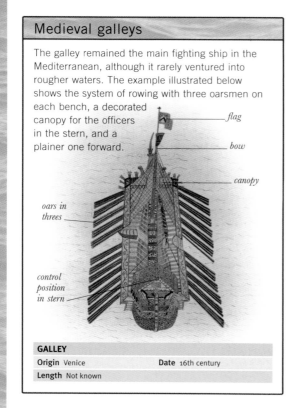

flag
bow
canopy
oars in threes
control position in stern

GALLEY

Origin Venice	Date 16th century
Length Not known	

West Highland galleys

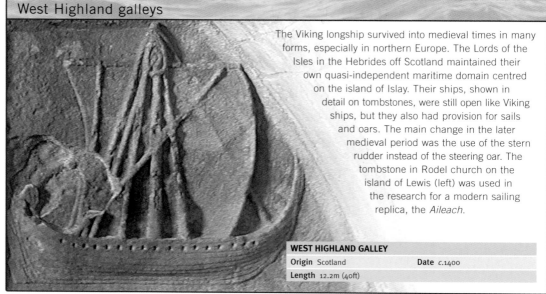

The Viking longship survived into medieval times in many forms, especially in northern Europe. The Lords of the Isles in the Hebrides off Scotland maintained their own quasi-independent maritime domain centred on the island of Islay. Their ships, shown in detail on tombstones, were still open like Viking ships, but they also had provision for sails and oars. The main change in the later medieval period was the use of the stern rudder instead of the steering oar. The tombstone in Rodel church on the island of Lewis (left) was used in the research for a modern sailing replica, the *Aileach*.

WEST HIGHLAND GALLEY

Origin Scotland	Date c.1400
Length 12.2m (40ft)	

Warships

North European merchant ships could be converted into warships by adding wooden castles in the bow and stern, as shown on the seal of the English port of Dunwich (right). Later, the castles became both larger and more solid.

SHIP OF DUNWICH

Origin England	Date Late 12th century
Length Not known	

Hulks

The hulk, or hulc, differed from the ship of Viking descent, which is sometimes known as the "keel", in that it had no keel and the planking of the bows and stern rose up parallel to the bow and stern posts, rather than each plank coming to an end against the posts. It was essentially a Mediterranean type in the Roman tradition, but the hulk was not unknown in the seas of northern Europe, as a picture of Henry I of England (right) shows.

HULK

Origin Probably England or France	Date c.1130
Length Not known	

Coccas

The great Italian ports of Genoa and Venice had their own styles of shipbuilding, as did other Christian ports such as Marseilles and Ragusa (Dubrovnik in modern Croatia) and the Turkish and North African ports, although not much detail is known about them. The cocca was the Mediterranean equivalent of the German and north European cog, with a longer hull than the classical Mediterranean round ship (see below, right). A model (right) in a museum in Venice shows a later example, with four masts rather than two. The projection over the bow was to become a common feature on galleons. The ship has a protruding lower bow that is probably an exaggeration by a sailor model-maker who did not have access to accurate data. The ship also has what appear to be bilge keels, which, if accurate, would have helped prevent rolling.

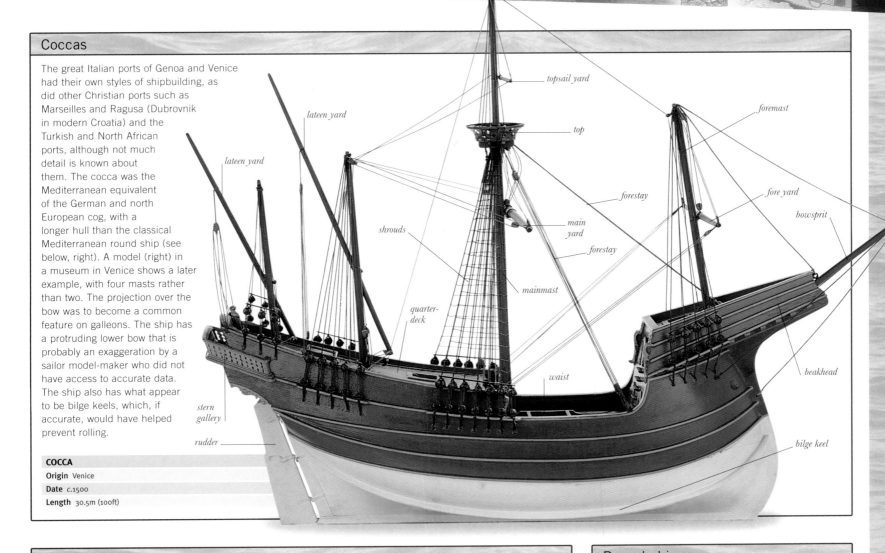

lateen yard

lateen yard

topsail yard

top

foremast

forestay

shrouds

main yard

fore yard

bowsprit

forestay

mainmast

quarter-deck

waist

beakhead

stern gallery

rudder

bilge keel

COCCA	
Origin	Venice
Date	c.1500
Length	30.5m (100ft)

Cogs

The standard vessel of the powerful Hanseatic League was the cog or kogge, which usually had high posts at the bow and stern, but a straight stem and stern posts in later versions. The seal of Lübeck (below), the central port of the League, dates from 1224 and shows a ship with the old-fashioned steering oar, as well as some details of hull construction.

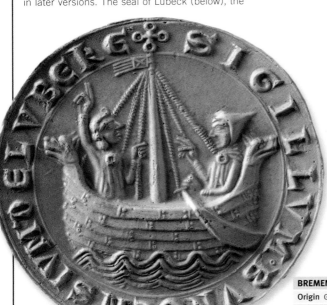

THE SEAL OF KIEL
The 1365 seal of Kiel, another Hanseatic port, shows the main technological change of the last century, the stern rudder.

BREMEN KOGGE			
Origin	Germany	**Date**	c.1380
Length	23.5m (77ft)		

Round ships

The meaning of the term round ship is seen in a 15th-century image (below) of the English King Arthur and his knights by a French artist. The vessel has a two-masted rig with a small foresail.

ROUND SHIP

ROUND SHIP			
Origin	France	**Date**	c.1400
Length	Not known		

15TH-CENTURY RELIEF OF A GALLEY

> " Out of the joy of
> our hearts, we sang
> *Te Deum Laudamus* with
> loud voices, and directed
> our prow towards
> Joppa, commonly
> called Jaffa. "

FELIX FABRI, describing the safe arrival
of pilgrims at the Holy Land after an
arduous sea voyage, **1480–83**

KEY EVENTS

1095 PAPAL BLESSING A sermon by Pope
Urban II leads to the Crusades, in which troop
transports play an important part.

1189 THIRD CRUSADE Richard I of England
and Philip Augustus of France despatch large
fleets to the Holy Land.

1277 TRADE WITH NORTHERN EUROPE
For the first time, a Genoese cargo ship docks
in Bruges, establishing a major new trade route.

1295 TRIUMPHANT RETURN Marco Polo
arrives in Venice after a two-year sea voyage
from China. He had been away for 24 years.

1347 BLACK DEATH REACHES EUROPE A
Genoese ship sailing from the Black Sea port of
Caffa (now Feodosiya) carries plague to Sicily.

1380 BATTLE OF CHIOGGIA Venetian galleys
finally defeat the Genoese, confirming Venice as
the dominant maritime power in Italy.

1453 FALL OF CONSTANTINOPLE The Turks
capture the Byzantine capital, enabling Turkish
fleets to control more Mediterranean trade.

THE SHIP IN THE MEDITERRANEAN

AFTER THE DECLINE OF ROME, MEDITERRANEAN STATES GREW RICH FROM TRADE. THEIR SHIPS ALSO CARRIED CRUSADERS – AND PLAGUE.

For sailors in the early medieval period, the Mediterranean was a less harsh environment than the North Sea or Atlantic coasts. This enclosed sea was too small for the wind to create huge waves, and there was practically no tide, just a few dangerous local currents, such as in the Straits of Messina between Sicily and Italy. Seamen rarely had to go out of sight of land for more than a day or so, and usually followed coastal passages. Apart from along sections of North Africa's coast, there were few underwater obstructions or sandbanks. Above all, the weather was more clement than further north, although squalls were not unusual. The clear skies and horizons made navigation easier.

Shipping in the Mediterranean was in many ways separated from that in other parts of the world in medieval times. Phoenician traders, Roman war fleets, and Italian merchants had ventured outside the sea, but this was far from

PERILOUS VOYAGE OF ULYSSES
In the legend of Ulysses, the turbulent straits between Sicily and mainland Italy turned into a passage between the monstrous rocks Scylla and Charybdis, illustrated here.

easy due to the strong current that ran inwards through the Straits of Gibraltar. Certain types of ship were unique to the Mediterranean or in use there at different times to other parts of the world. For example, galleys remained the supreme naval weapon until well after 1600, whereas the galleon (see p.100) was dominant in western Europe.

The Roman Empire had provided a unified culture and rule throughout the Mediterranean, but it slowly began to fall apart in the fifth century AD and was invaded by the Visigoths, Vandals, and Ostrogoths. However, the former empire's eastern half, known as the Byzantine Empire, continued to flourish. Since AD 324, its capital had been Constantinople (now Istanbul) – a well-positioned port at the crossroads between Europe and Asia. The Byzantine emperors built up a fleet of swift, light galleys called dromons. Dromons were armed with the devastating weapon of Greek fire, probably a compound of sulphur, for burning opposing ships.

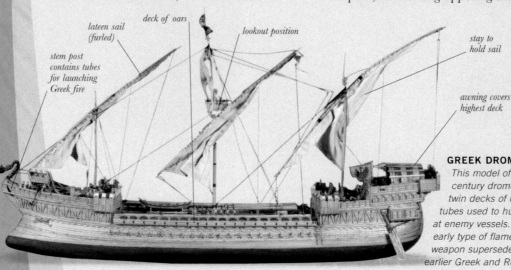

lateen sail (furled)

deck of oars

lookout position

stay to hold sail

stem post contains tubes for launching Greek fire

awning covers highest deck

GREEK DROMON
This model of a tenth-century dromon shows the twin decks of oars and the tubes used to hurl Greek fire at enemy vessels. Similar to an early type of flamethrower, this weapon superseded the ram of earlier Greek and Roman galleys.

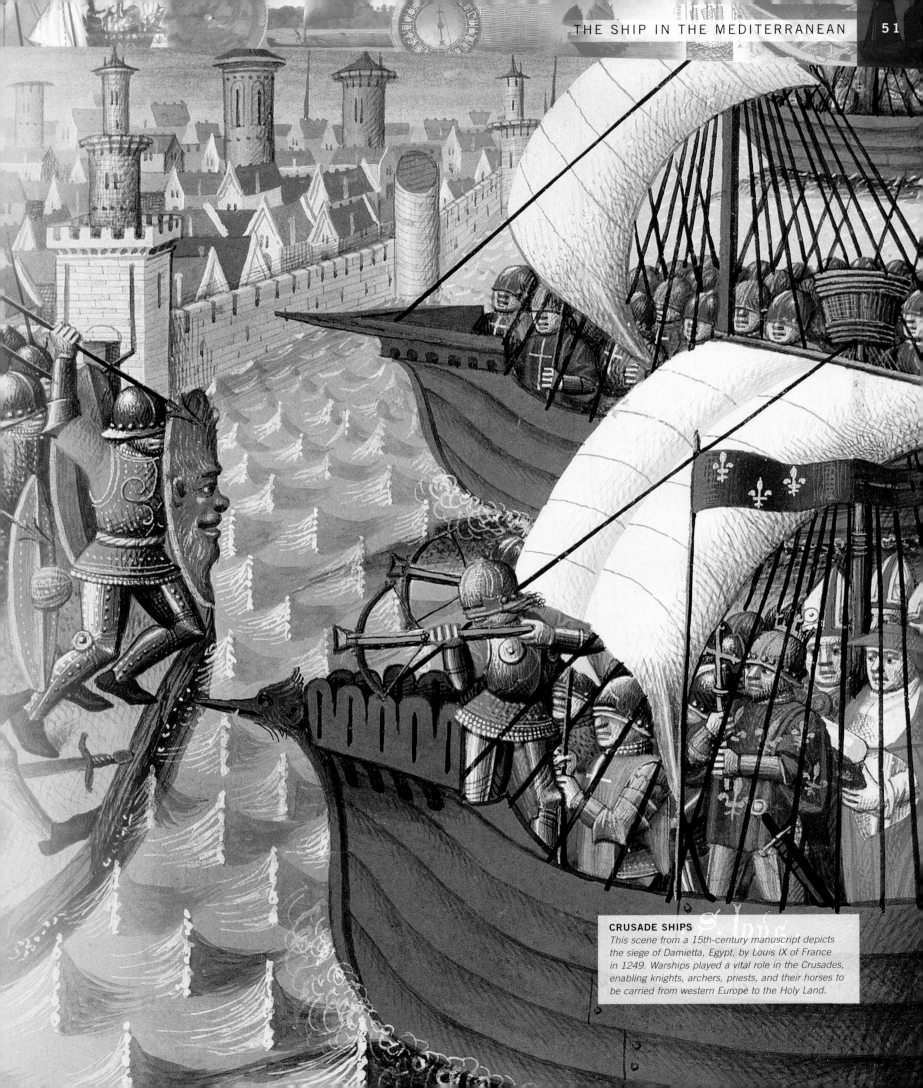

CRUSADE SHIPS
This scene from a 15th-century manuscript depicts the siege of Damietta, Egypt, by Louis IX of France in 1249. Warships played a vital role in the Crusades, enabling knights, archers, priests, and their horses to be carried from western Europe to the Holy Land.

There were also upheavals in other parts of the Mediterranean. In the seventh century AD, Arab tribes moved out from the Arabian Peninsula to take control of much of North Africa. During the following century, they crossed the Straits of Gibraltar and conquered most of Spain. The western Mediterranean was beset by long-term conflict, but trade flourished in the expanding Islamic world, spreading ideas as well as trade.

Even less is known about the Dark Ages of Mediterranean shipping, from the third to the ninth century AD, than the same period in northern waters. Far fewer wrecks and ship burials have been discovered and studied. By the time concrete historical evidence begins to

LEAVING VENICE
Marco Polo was among several great explorers produced by the Venetian mercantile class. This page in a 14th-century edition of the Travels of Marco Polo *depicts his departure from Venice in 1271, bound for Acre (now Akko in Israel).*

reappear, most ships had started to carry a narrow, triangular sail instead of square sails. This was known as the lateen sail (see p.57). It gets its name from *latium*, the ancient name for Rome and the surrounding region. Probably first developed by Arabs, the lateen sail became almost universal in the medieval Mediterranean.

In 1977–79, divers explored a small Byzantine cargo ship wrecked at Serçe Limani, a bay on the coast of Turkey. Its hull was made by nailing planks to frames. Since the vessel has been accurately dated to 1024–25, it is the first known example of the modern, frame-first method of ship construction.

GENOESE COIN
The currencies of the Italian city-states were arguably as important to international trade in medieval Europe as the US dollar is today. The two sides of a 13th-century coin are shown here.

Rival ports

Several important Italian ports grew up after Rome's decline. Originally a backwater of islands and lagoons, Venice became a great trading city between the ninth and eleventh centuries. Its ships visited the eastern Mediterranean, developing a slave trade with Egypt, and Venice also benefited from the land route to China established by Marco Polo. The Venetians used some galleys for carrying cargo and had merchantmen with sturdy hulls derived from Roman cargo ships (see p.26). At its peak in about 1400, Venice claimed to have as many as 3,000 ships with 38,000 sailors.

During the 11th and 12th centuries, the port of Genoa, on the other side of Italy, became a great naval and commercial power to rival Venice, with which it fought four wars in the century after 1282. However, in 1380 its fleet was defeated close to Venice at the Battle of Chioggia, confirming Venetian supremacy.

Mediterranean trading ships of the early medieval period were often much smaller than in Roman times, and huge grain-carriers were

no longer used. The typical ship had a round hull that was carvel-built in the style of the hulk (see p.42); that is, the side planks were laid flush to create a smooth finish. Larger ships had castle-like platforms at each end and two steering oars. The merchants of the region were apparently influenced by the capacious hulls of the north European cogs (see p.42) that appeared in the Mediterranean during the Crusades, and they began to adopt these ships' shape.

The Black Death

Venetian and Genoese merchants carried precious metals, silk, wine, and other luxuries to England and Flanders, but in 1347 they took with them a much deadlier cargo: plague. Bubonic plague originated in the East, perhaps in China, and in Europe it probably reached Sicily first, onboard

VENETIAN NAVAL POWER
In 1379, the Genoese laid siege to Chioggia, near Venice, where they suffered a crushing defeat by the Venetian fleet the following year. The lateen rig of the Venetian galleys can be seen in this 16th-century painting.

a Genoese merchant ship travelling from the port of Caffa (now Feodosiya) on the Black Sea. Many of the ship's crew had caught the plague while in Caffa, and the ship's hold was probably carrying infected black rats. It is thought that the movement of infected rats and seamen onboard merchant ships throughout Europe was a major factor in the plague's rapid spread.

The Crusades

The transfer of new shipbuilding techniques between the Mediterranean and the rest of Europe was made possible not only by trade but also by war – and the Crusades in particular. The Crusades were

SCOURGE OF SALADIN
Richard I (left) and Saladin (right) fight a duel in this interpretation of the Third Crusade, contained in the Luttrell Psalter, an English manuscript of the 1340s.

Christian-inspired military campaigns to counter Muslim advances in the Holy Land. They began with a fiery sermon by Pope Urban II in 1095, inspiring leaders such as Robert of Normandy and Robert II of Flanders to raise armies and take them to the area. In all, there were eight crusades between 1147 and 1270, of which the best known was the Third Crusade, launched after the Saracen leader Saladin captured Jerusalem in 1187. It was led by the ageing Holy Roman Emperor Frederick Barbarossa, Richard I of England (see panel, opposite), and Philip Augustus of France.

The Crusades led to new uses for ships and to the growth of certain Mediterranean ports. Marseilles, Genoa, and Venice were used as bases where troops from western Europe were assembled. They also provided local ships to supplement those brought from

CRUSADER'S ARMOUR
The Christian Cross featured prominently on the helmets and weapons of European knights in the Crusades, as well as on the flags and prows of their ships.

TROOP TRANSPORT
This 14th-century illustration shows a knight and his retinue bound for Palestine. The Third Crusade was the first time that ships from northern Europe had entered the Mediterranean in such large numbers.

The third son of King Henry II and Eleanor of Aquitaine, Richard I (1157–99) outlived his brothers and became king in 1189. Richard the Lion-hearted, as he was known, had already taken the vow of a crusader and was to spend only six months of his ten-year reign in England. In 1190, he set off to join the Third Crusade, travelling by land to Marseilles, where he joined his fleet. The first medieval English king to realize the importance of sea power, Richard conquered Cyprus in 1191 en route to the Holy Land, but failed to take Jerusalem from the Turks. He died of wounds received during a skirmish at Chaluz in France.

the north; for example, in 1268, Louis IX of France ordered a fleet of two-decked ships with lateen rig from Venetian shipbuilders.

In the 12th and 13th centuries, mounted knights were at the centre of military tactics, so ships that could transport horses were vital. The Normans had already used improvised horse transports to invade England in 1066 (see pp.40-–41), and this type of vessel was common in wars involving the Sicilians or the Byzantine Empire. However, the Crusades involved travel on a larger scale, over hundreds of kilometres.

The earliest horse transports were rowed, but sailing transports were the norm in the later Crusades. An English account of 1270 explains how they were used: "… the port of the ship was opened and all the horses we wanted to take overseas were put inside. Then the port was closed and well caulked, just as when a cask is submerged, because, once the ship is on the high seas, the entire port is in the water." Some ships had a ramp, down which a knight could ride straight onto a beach – making them the forerunners of 20th-century landing craft.

The crusaders were innovative in other ways, too. In the Third Crusade, their ships may have incorporated a stern rudder – increasingly used in place of the steering oar in northern Europe by the late 12th century – and its navigators may have used compasses (see panel, right).

Pilgrimages to the Holy Land

Many people in medieval times hoped to go on a pilgrimage to shrines in the Holy Land, creating more demand for space on ships. In the early 1480s, Brother Felix Fabri, a German monk, travelled to Palestine for the second time. His account provides a fascinating insight into life onboard a Mediterranean galley.

Fabri and his companions chartered a galley in Venice. Although it often stopped in harbour to allow the passengers to buy provisions, the captain provided them with "a sufficiency of good bread and biscuit, wine and sweet water, freshly put onboard, with meat, eggs, and other eatables of the same sort". The passengers were protected "from being attacked or ill-used by the galley-slaves [who] were fed most wretchedly … [They] always sleep on the boards of their rowing benches … Both by day and night they are always in the open air ready for work". The ship used favourable winds as much as

TURKS AT GENOA
This miniature from the Book of Suleiman I, *produced by Nasuh al-Matraki in 1545, shows Ottoman dromons blockading Genoa. The Turkish Fleet changed the balance of naval power in the Mediterranean.*

possible. In contrast, rowing was slow and laborious. The galley finally reached Jaffa 43 days after leaving Venice.

Before Fabri's voyage, the Ottoman Turks captured Constantinople in 1453, ending the power of the successor to the Roman Empire. The city's fall dispersed scholars around Europe, spreading new ideas, and severed the main route between Europe and the East, forcing travellers and merchants to look for new routes. Later in the 15th century, the Spanish reconquered their land from the Moors. They continued to expand in Europe, North Africa, and the rest of the world, having developed the skills and the ships that would enable them to do this by sea.

THE DEVELOPMENT OF THE COMPASS

The Crusades created a need for more sophisticated navigation, so it is perhaps no coincidence that in Europe compasses were first described in Italy in 1187, at the time of the Third Crusade. These resembled Chinese devices dating from the 11th century and may have been imported by Arab traders. The essential part of a compass is the iron needle, which is magnetized by rubbing it with a piece of iron called the lodestone. At first, the needle was floated in a bowl of water until it pointed north. The alternative method, which became more common, was for the needle to pivot on a pin inside a bowl. Later, the "compass rose" was fitted above the needle. It was graduated with the other points of the compass, so that a ship's heading or the bearing of an object could be established.

GERMAN COMPASS
This instrument, made in 1550–1600, incorporates a horizontal dial calibrated for latitude 49° north.

NAVIGATIONAL AID
This portable Chinese device combines a magnetic compass with a sundial, both of which were vital aids to navigation.

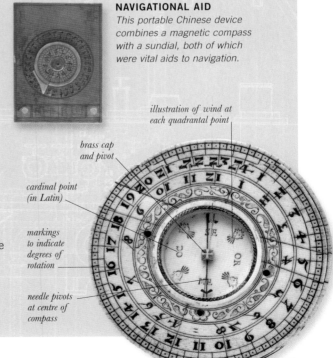

illustration of wind at each quadrantal point

brass cap and pivot

cardinal point (in Latin)

markings to indicate degrees of rotation

needle pivots at centre of compass

19TH-CENTURY CHINESE COMPASS

> The ships which sail the Southern Sea are like houses. When their sails are spread they are like great clouds in the sky.

CHINESE HISTORIAN, describing the treasure ships of the Ming Dynasty, **early 1400s**

KEY EVENTS

485 BC GRAND CANAL, CHINA The canal's first section, joining the Yangtze (Chang Jiang) and Yellow River (Huang He), opens to traffic.

218 BC HSU FU'S SECOND VOYAGE The Chinese sea captain Hsu Fu sets sail into the Pacific in search of the "Eastern Isles" (Japan).

AD 711 INVASION OF SPAIN The Moors send a fleet from North Africa to southern Spain, where their army defeats the Visigoths.

AD 727 ARABS REACH CHINA Merchants sailing in dhows are known to have reached China from the Middle East by this date.

1325 DEPARTURE OF IBN BATTUTA The Moroccan explorer begins his epic travels by sea to Arabia, southern Asia, and east Africa.

1431 ZHENG HE'S FINAL VOYAGE A huge fleet of junks commanded by Zheng He departs on a two-year journey of exploration around the Indian Ocean and western Pacific.

MERCHANT'S DHOW
A dhow's crew is depicted manhandling sails in this painting from a 13th-century Arab manuscript. During the medieval period, dhows were the dominant ships in waters under Arab influence, carrying the bulk of the region's trade and helping to spread Islam and Arab culture. Chinese junks occupied a comparable role in the western Pacific.

THE SHIP IN THE EAST

FOR HUNDREDS OF YEARS BEFORE THE EMERGENCE OF EUROPEAN EMPIRES IN ASIA, THE ARABS AND CHINESE DOMINATED SHIPPING IN THE EAST, PRODUCING SOME OF THE MOST ADVANCED SHIPS OF THE TIME.

As far back as the early medieval period and probably beyond, the shipbuilding culture of the Mediterranean (see pp.50–55) was closely linked to that of Arab regions in North Africa and the Middle East. The classic Arab boat was the dhow, a relatively small ocean-going trading vessel found in the Persian Gulf, northern Indian Ocean, and Red Sea.

The lateen sail

Dhows used an ancient design of sail known as the lateen, which predated the religions of Islam and Christianity. This triangular sail was used with one or two masts, sometimes together with a small headsail based on those of European ships. The lateen sail was hung from a yard – often made of two pieces of wood lashed together – slung from a fairly short mast. The yard was angled about 45 degrees from the horizontal and approximately one-third of the sail area was before the mast.

Compared to medieval European square sails (see p.42), the lateen rig was vastly superior when sailing into the wind.

It enabled ships to steer several degrees closer to the wind. However, handling a lateen sail was labour intensive and so required a larger crew. To operate efficiently when sailing close to the wind, the sail had to be taken from one side of the mast to the other to get a smooth airflow. It was necessary to lift the yard until it was vertical, then haul it behind the mast from one side to the other.

The Arabs continued to use sewn fastenings in the hull construction of dhows long after most of Europe had switched to nails. This was regarded as quaint by European travellers such as Marco Polo, who thought it was "no little peril to sail in these ships", and Vasco da Gama,

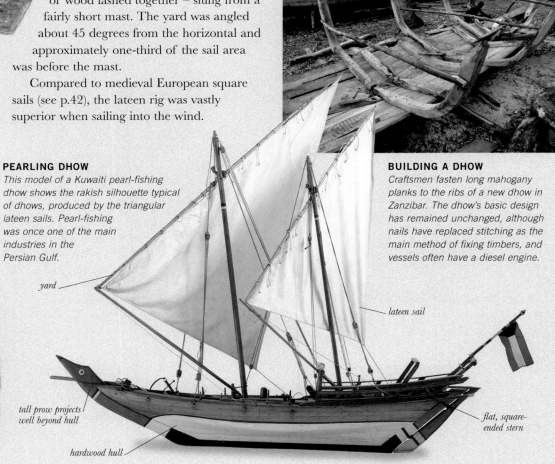

PEARLING DHOW
This model of a Kuwaiti pearl-fishing dhow shows the rakish silhouette typical of dhows, produced by the triangular lateen sails. Pearl-fishing was once one of the main industries in the Persian Gulf.

yard

tall prow projects well beyond hull

hardwood hull

lateen sail

flat, square-ended stern

BUILDING A DHOW
Craftsmen fasten long mahogany planks to the ribs of a new dhow in Zanzibar. The dhow's basic design has remained unchanged, although nails have replaced stitching as the main method of fixing timbers, and vessels often have a diesel engine.

ring

inner ring rotates
to show visible
part of sky

outer ring
sets date
and time

alidade

NAVIGATING THE INDIAN OCEAN
This illustration depicts Arab sailors in the Indian Ocean, as imagined by the Boucicaut Master, an artist active in Paris in 1405–20. The sailors in the foreground are using an astrolabe, which moved with Islam into Europe in the 13th and 14th centuries.

PLANISPHERIC ASTROLABE
Widely used by Arab seafarers, the astrolabe was a device for finding latitude. This Egyptian example was suspended by a ring, and the navigator moved the alidade, or sighting rule, until it lined up with the North Star or the Sun.

who commented that the vessels were "badly built and frail". It has been suggested that the teak often used for construction did not take nails easily. However, a sewn vessel had great strength and flexibility, which was useful in the heavy surf common in the region: the dhow was an excellent example of a vessel designed to fit local needs. During the 15th century, Arab shipbuilders began to adopt the clinker build of overlapping planks common in European ships since the medieval period (see p.34), although the sewn-boat tradition survived in Oman and Yemen well into the 20th century.

The expansion of Islam

Islam, the last of the great world religions to emerge, was founded at Medina and Mecca in Arabia in AD 622. It spread through the Arabian Peninsula to Egypt and along the North African coast. In AD 711, the Moors used their ships to cross the Straits of Gibraltar – the name Gibraltar is a corruption of Jebel al Tariq, the hill of Tariq – and they went on to conquer most of Spain. They took Sardinia in AD 827

and Corsica in AD 850. In the east, Arabs colonized Persia and the Punjab by sea, but their main expansion eastwards was by land, with the conquest of northern India complete by 1290. Gujarati merchants from north-west India probably took Islam across the Indian Ocean, to Malaysia by 1400 and to Sumatra, the Philippines, and many other islands by 1500.

While these regions were converting to Islam, the trading connections of Arab merchants were also expanding. Arab traders travelled much of

the known world, reaching China in AD 727 and sailing into the Atlantic via the Mediterranean. The celebrated Moroccan explorer Ibn Battuta, a Berber from Tangier, sailed along much of the east African coastline in the mid-14th century, and also visited India and southeast Asia.

During the medieval period, the Arabs were advanced maritime pilots and the world leaders in astronomy. They measured latitude by taking Sun sightings with an astrolabe (see left) or a *kamal*. The latter was a wooden square with a string marked with the latitude of places such as Madras and Pondicherry in India or Trincomalee in Ceylon (now Sri Lanka). The navigator lined

VOYAGE TO MECCA
Muslims commonly used ships to complete the hajj, or pilgrimage to Mecca, as shown in this Turkish manuscript dating from 1588.

the top edge of the wooden square with the celestial body and the lower edge with the horizon, then pulled the string up to his eye to give an indication of latitude.

Craft in India

At the edge of the Muslim world, the Indian subcontinent had a much wider range of craft than Arab-controlled areas, due in part to its more varied topography. In the north were the great river systems of the Indus, Ganges, and Brahmaputra, whereas there were many smaller rivers in the centre and south. The long coastline had many towns built along it and numerous estuaries that provided good harbours, so river and coasting transport were particularly well developed. Early craft produced by the indigenous traditions of the subcontinent included log rafts, simple pot boats fashioned from clay, dugouts, and vessels made from animal hide. Sewn-plank boats were probably in use by AD 1000.

Boat-building practices in each region were influenced by those of its trading partners. Arab influence was dominant in the northwest (now Pakistan), where the arid, rocky topography was not unlike that of Arabia; the ships there were all lateen-rigged and had the long, raking stem and stern typical of dhows. The largest of these, the *kotia*, was 21–30m (70–100ft) long and was used to trade as far south as Calicut (now Kozhikode) on the Keralan coast and Zanzibar, off Africa. Further along the Indian coast south of Bombay (now Mumbai), local people also used craft similar to Arab dhows, but they were more influenced by European ships after 1500, adopting larger mizzen sails and a jib sail in the bows. In the far south of India, outrigger canoes like those used in Indonesia were common.

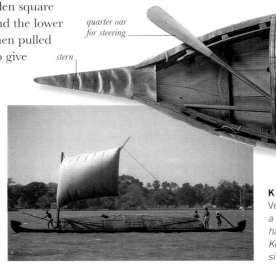

KERALAN CRAFT
Vellam (left) are dugouts with a shallow draught and sail that have plied the backwaters of Kerala in southwestern India since medieval times.

BANGLADESHI CANOE
The rivers of Bangladesh have a long and varied tradition of man-powered craft, including the cargo-carrying canoe pictured above, which may be either paddled or punted with a pole. River transport is of huge importance in this marshy, low-lying region, which is prone to flooding.

Chinese craft

By contrast with other parts of Asia, China had always been isolated from the rest of the world. It was cut off by marshes, mountains, deserts, and rainforests and was largely self-sufficient in its culture and almost all resources. The country's topography played a large part in the development of several unique types of craft, from the diminutive sampan to huge junks (see pp.60–61).

China consisted of a vast low-lying area penetrated by three great river systems: the Yellow River or Huang He in the north; the Yangtze or Chang Jiang in the centre; and the Pearl River or Xi Jiang in the south. These rivers all flow from west to east. In the fifth century BC, work began on a canal to link them, providing China with a strategic north–south connection. The Grand Canal was used to transport rice, manufactured goods, soldiers, and taxes of grain around the Chinese empire. It was rebuilt and extended many times by later emperors, and eventually

GRAND CANAL, CHINA
The Grand Canal (above) extends for 1,750km (1,100 miles) through eastern central China and was built in stages over hundreds of years. In this 18th-century painting on silk (left), Emperor Yang Di of the sixth century AD is opening the latest stage of the canal.

SAMPAN
There are many types of sampan, derived from the Chinese for "three planks". Each is adapted for a different task and to the conditions of its river, canal, or lake. This modern one from Lake Dongting, Hunan Province, is adapted for storing fish.

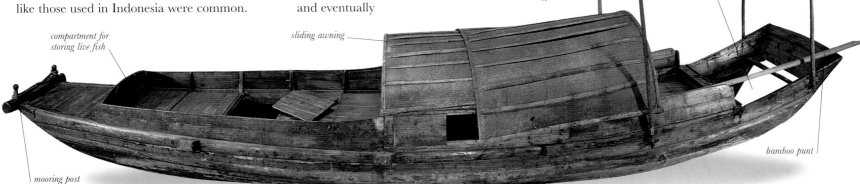

it became the world's largest canal network. In southern China, many towns and cities were built along canals. These busy urban highways were crowded with flat-bottomed sampans, barges, rafts, and houseboats.

Many types of craft had been used in China in prehistoric times, such as log boats in more remote areas and hide boats near the heads of the great rivers. Most of these boats seem to have developed from log rafts, which are first mentioned in 472 BC.

The Chinese developed a variety of rudders for steering, which were usually quite large and designed for use at low speeds in the shallow water typical of most canals and lakes. They also developed the *yuloh*, a unique type of long oar or "sweep" that was placed over the stern and used for both steering and sculling without being taken out of the water. According to legend, it was invented by someone washing clothes by a creek who noticed how fish used their tails for propulsion.

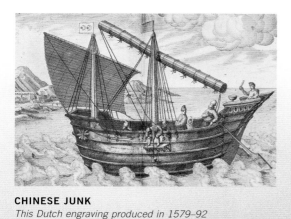

CHINESE JUNK
This Dutch engraving produced in 1579–92 clearly illustrates two features of Chinese junks: the yuloh oar used for steering and the stiffened sails that can be rolled up easily.

JUNK IN HONG KONG
A three-masted junk in full sail heads towards the main business district of Hong Kong, revealing the bamboo sail battens and long, overhanging counter typical of this type of craft. Junks through the ages have been used for virtually every conceivable purpose, including fishing, passenger transport, trade, warfare, and as houseboats and shops.

The Chinese junk

Chinese junks were sailing in the open sea from the fifth or sixth century AD. The first imperial treasure fleets – ocean-going junks despatched to discover new lands and acquire valuable goods – were commissioned in the Yuan Dynasty (1271–1368) and founded trading posts in places such as southern India and Sumatra. The emperors of the Ming Dynasty (1368–1644) extended the fleets. They reached their peak in the early 15th century under Admiral Zheng He (see panel, right), whose unrivalled armada required enormous investment by the emperor and included some of the largest wooden ships ever built. These were said to be 122m (400ft) long and 46m (150ft) wide.

The junk's design originally evolved to suit local conditions. South of the Yangtze, the coast of China is deeply indented with numerous islands and sheltered harbours that provide refuge from summer typhoons. This area produced a craft that rarely had to beach, so it had sharp bows and a deep bottom.

BUILDING A JUNK
A new junk takes shape on Cheung Chau island, Hong Kong. The construction techniques used today would be recognizable to Chinese shipwrights working during the junk's heyday under the Yuan and Ming emperors.

THE VOYAGES OF ZHENG HE

A Chinese Muslim eunuch, Zheng He (1371–1435) was made an admiral by Emperor Zhu Di, the most expansionist leader of the Ming Dynasty. Zheng He was instructed to explore the oceans and search for precious goods. In 1403, he organized the building of an armada of huge nine-masted junks, plus an escort of smaller supply ships, patrol boats, and horse-transports. Zheng He led the treasure fleet on seven expeditions

ZHENG HE
Arguably China's most famous navigator, Zheng He visited 30 nations and travelled 56,000km (35,000 miles) in all.

between 1405 and 1433. The seventh and final voyage, which left in January 1431 comprised 63 ships and nearly 30,000 men. It visited Indochina, Ceylon (now Sri Lanka), India, Persia (now Iran), Zanzibar, the Red Sea, and Java.

Zheng He's impressive fleet, and the silks and spices it carried, caused great excitement as far away as the court of Egypt. Its epic voyages alerted the rest of the world to China's trade potential and acted as a peaceful demonstration of Chinese naval power.

ZHENG HE'S STAR-CHART
The fleet's navigators used star-charts – this one is for the passage between Sumatra and Ceylon – and magnetic compasses.

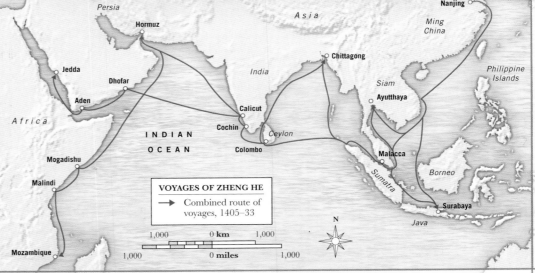

VOYAGES OF ZHENG HE
→ Combined route of voyages, 1405–33

North of the Yangtze, the coast is very different, with flat lowlands, sandbanks, and little shelter. The typical craft there was flat-bottomed with bluff bows. Unlike the vessels of the South China Sea, which traded with other parts of the world, those of northern China had little contact with ships from different cultures and seem to have remained unchanged for many centuries.

In his *Travels*, first published in 1299, Marco Polo describes a large 13th-century junk. It was built of fir, with a single deck divided into 60 cabins, each accommodating one merchant.

The junk had four masts and two more could be set up when required. Marco Polo mentions ships with crews of up to 300, carrying 5,000–6,000 baskets of pepper and moved by large oars, each worked by four men. A large ship might carry 10 small boats slung over the sides for fishing, laying out anchors, or for use as lifeboats.

TREASURE FROM WRECKED JUNK
This pottery statuette of the Buddhist god Kuan-yin was raised from the wreck of a junk that sank off Korea's coast in about 1323. Junks carried huge cargoes of porcelain and silk through the East and South China seas – a trade that peaked between the 12th and 15th centuries.

Design innovations

The characteristic junk rig, which emerged long before Marco Polo's visit to China in the late 13th century, consisted of a sail with horizontal bamboo battens fixed to it at intervals. Not only did these strengthen and stiffen the sail, they enabled part of it to be furled rapidly – like a blind – in strong winds or during an emergency. The battens also served as a ladder for the crew to climb to work on the rig. Sea-going junks usually had sails that narrowed to a peak at the top, whereas river-going junks normally had higher, squared-off sails designed to catch the slightest breeze, which was often blocked by bankside vegetation. The junk's style of rig has proved very successful in east Asia and has been intermittently popular for yachts in the West.

One of the outstanding, albeit less obvious, features of Chinese junks was their internal subdivision by up to 12 bulkheads along the hull. These gave strength to the hull and also contributed to the safety of the ship. According to Marco Polo, their main object was "to guard against accidents which may occasion the vessel to spring a leak … the water, running in at the place where the injury has been sustained, makes its way to a well, which is always kept clear". Occasionally, the crew of fishing junks may even have deliberately flooded several of the watertight hull compartments in order to

JAPANESE SAIL CRAFT
This woodblock print made by Ando Hiroshige in 1833 depicts the departure of a daimyo in a flotilla of boats. Japan developed a network of navigable waterways at a much earlier stage than most European countries.

store live fish. But despite its advantages, the idea of internal subdivision of the hull was not adopted by European shipbuilders until well into the 19th century.

Although the underwater shape of Chinese craft was not dissimilar to those of many other regions, they sometimes had a very angular appearance above water. This was due to the flat-fronted bow (created by the prominent transom, or heavy crosswise timbers) and the often rather square superstructure. It is interesting to speculate that, after the late medieval period, a European shipbuilder or

sailor would have deplored such an angular appearance. In some ways, these Chinese vessels are the natural predecessors of the bulky Chinese and Taiwanese container ships of the late 20th century.

Japanese boats

Japanese culture was even more isolated than that of China until the arrival of Commodore Matthew Perry in Edo Bay in 1853 (see p.198). For several hundred years, powerful shoguns (imperial governors) and *daimyo* (feudal lords) imposed a strict embargo on international trade. In 1542, a Portuguese ship was wrecked off the coast of Kyushu in southern Japan. This chance event (which may have introduced firearms to Japan) did not encourage the Japanese to build similar ocean-going ships of their own. Instead, the country's boats were used mainly on the extensive network of rivers, canals, and lakes, or for island-hopping within the Japanese archipelago. Before the construction of bridges and tunnels in modern times, boats provided the only means of access to the 750 or so inhabited islands in the Inland Sea, a placid body of water separating the islands of Honshu and Shikoku. Japanese vessels bear many similarities to Chinese craft, including boats that resemble sampans or junks. One of the earliest instances of

PLEASURE BOAT
This early photograph taken in the 1890s shows women wearing kimonos being punted along a lake in Japan. Such pleasure cruises, or floating "tea parties", have been popular in Japan since the Edo period in the 17th century, when courtiers and aristocrats began the tradition of boating excursions.

FISHING CRAFT
Japan's inland waterways supported a thriving fishing industry, and various craft were used for this purpose. The vessel in this late 18th- or early 19th-century woodblock print by the artist Masayuki Shinsai, from the series The Eight Views of Omi, *has a typically graceful profile with a high prow, square stern, and long oar.*

boat-building technology being transferred between the two cultures could have been in 220–218 BC, when the Chinese sea captain Hsu Fu left China in search of the fabled "Eastern Isles" for the second time. He probably visited Japan and may have remained there, or possibly continued across the Pacific (some scholars think he even reached North America). There is plenty of other evidence for cultural exchange at this time: Buddhism and Chinese methods of pottery, metalworking, farming, and writing all reached Japan between 300 BC and AD 400.

Many Japanese boats incorporated a system of frameless, edge-joined construction known as *yamato-gata*, which produced a smooth hull. The planks were caulked with a mixture of lime, hemp, and tree oil.

Importance of the sea
A map of the world in about 1500 would demonstrate how important seafaring was to the growth of advanced societies. All of the major literate societies – with the notable exceptions of the Mali and Songhai empires on the River Niger in west Africa – were on or connected to the sea. Soon a movement, beginning in western Europe, would link all these areas together.

SAILING SERENELY
These Japanese boats share several features with Chinese junks, including sail battens and an angular hull with a square counter. Despite trade restrictions during the 16th, 17th, and 18th centuries, local trading vessels such as these contributed to the growth of the Japanese economy.

JUNKS, SAMPANS, AND DHOWS

The Arab world of the Mediterranean, Red Sea, and Persian Gulf produced its own ship, the dhow, characterized by its triangular lateen sail and long rake of the bows and stern. The Chinese and Japanese, on the other hand, developed in very different ways, and the generic term junk belies the great variety of craft in Chinese rivers and seas. They were probably the largest ships in the world in the 15th century – some records say up to 180m (600ft) long.

CHINESE FISHING
This Chinese junk, of around 1840, has an elaborate system of ropes and pulleys for handling fishing nets.

Sampans

The sampan (below) is a small boat, common in China, Thailand, Myanmar, and other parts of the region. It is used for fishing, river transport, harbour services, and as a houseboat. The sampan tanka of Hong Kong is used for port transport.

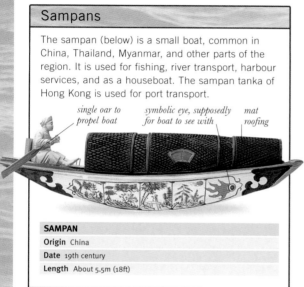

single oar to propel boat

symbolic eye, supposedly for boat to see with

mat roofing

SAMPAN
Origin China
Date 19th century
Length About 5.5m (18ft)

Dhows

The dhow (below) has been common in the Red Sea, Indian Ocean, and Persian Gulf for many centuries. It was used in the east African slave trade in the 19th century. The term dhow is used by Europeans; the Arabs call such a boat a marakab.

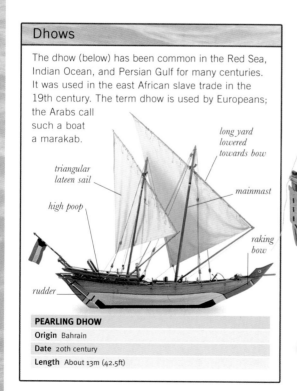

triangular lateen sail

high poop

long yard lowered towards bow

mainmast

raking bow

rudder

PEARLING DHOW
Origin Bahrain
Date 20th century
Length About 13m (42.5ft)

Japanese cargo boats

CARGO BOAT
Origin Japan
Date Early 19th century
Length Not known

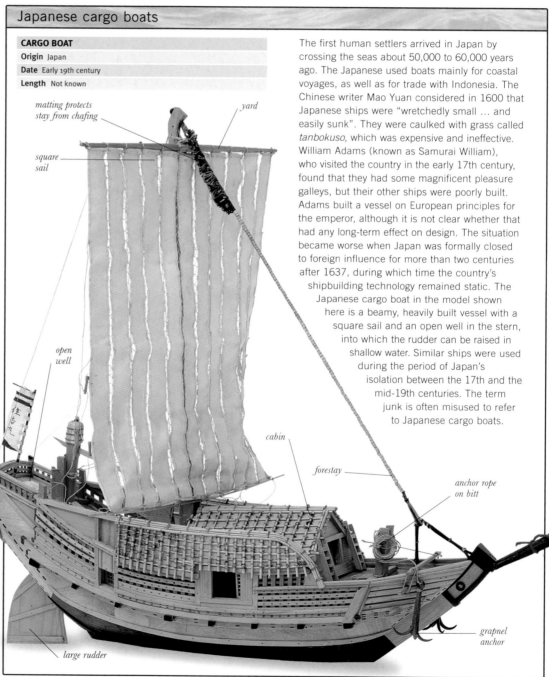

matting protects stay from chafing

yard

square sail

open well

cabin

forestay

anchor rope on bitt

large rudder

grapnel anchor

The first human settlers arrived in Japan by crossing the seas about 50,000 to 60,000 years ago. The Japanese used boats mainly for coastal voyages, as well as for trade with Indonesia. The Chinese writer Mao Yuan considered in 1600 that Japanese ships were "wretchedly small … and easily sunk". They were caulked with grass called *tanbokuso*, which was expensive and ineffective. William Adams (known as Samurai William), who visited the country in the early 17th century, found that they had some magnificent pleasure galleys, but their other ships were poorly built. Adams built a vessel on European principles for the emperor, although it is not clear whether that had any long-term effect on design. The situation became worse when Japan was formally closed to foreign influence for more than two centuries after 1637, during which time the country's shipbuilding technology remained static. The Japanese cargo boat in the model shown here is a beamy, heavily built vessel with a square sail and an open well in the stern, into which the rudder can be raised in shallow water. Similar ships were used during the period of Japan's isolation between the 17th and the mid-19th centuries. The term junk is often misused to refer to Japanese cargo boats.

Chinese pleasure boats

The wealthy Chinese used ships for pleasure as well as business and war. A picture (below) by Captain Drummond of the East India Company, shows a junk with a square cabin amidships and a kind of veranda forward for the passengers. It is also equipped for sailing.

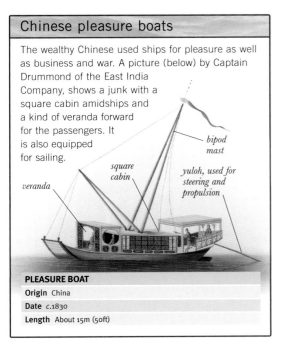

veranda

square cabin

bipod mast

yuloh, used for steering and propulsion

PLEASURE BOAT

Origin China

Date *c.*1830

Length About 15m (50ft)

Chinese war junks

The imperial Chinese used war junks on their coasts and rivers to fight pirates and rebels, as well as external enemies. The Ming Dynasty had a navy with more than 3,000 of them, brightly painted and with flags to show which part of the navy they belonged to. Large junks were propelled by sails and oars or paddles. They proved increasingly ineffective against European invaders in the mid-19th century and finally disappeared around 1900.

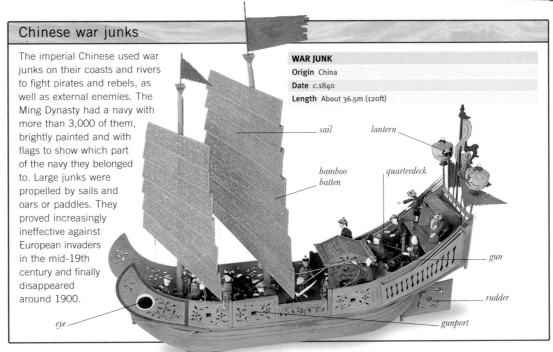

WAR JUNK

Origin China

Date *c.*1840

Length About 36.5m (120ft)

sail

lantern

bamboo batten

quarterdeck

gun

rudder

gunport

eye

Chinese merchant junks

MERCHANT JUNK

Origin China

Date *c.*1938

Length 37–54m (121–177ft)

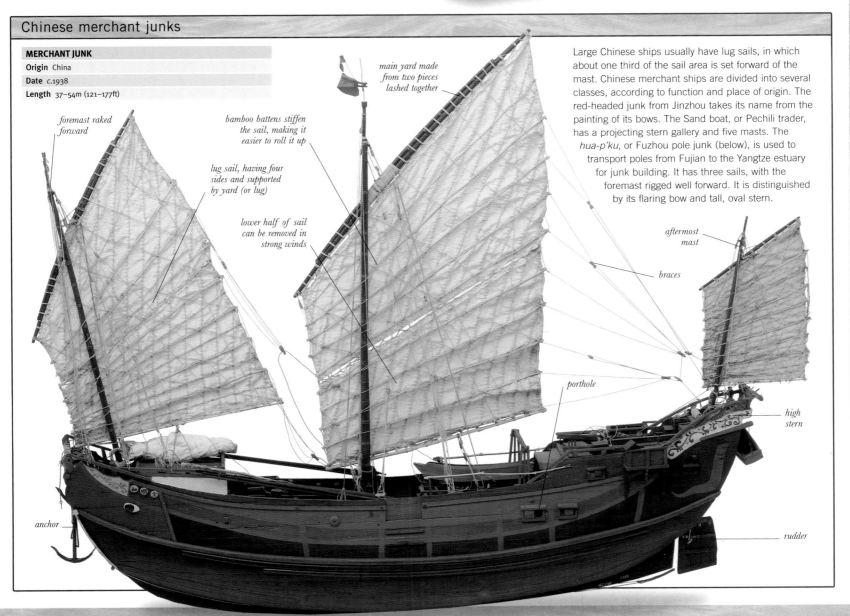

foremast raked forward

main yard made from two pieces lashed together

bamboo battens stiffen the sail, making it easier to roll it up

lug sail, having four sides and supported by yard (or lug)

lower half of sail can be removed in strong winds

aftermost mast

braces

porthole

high stern

anchor

rudder

Large Chinese ships usually have lug sails, in which about one third of the sail area is set forward of the mast. Chinese merchant ships are divided into several classes, according to function and place of origin. The red-headed junk from Jinzhou takes its name from the painting of its bows. The Sand boat, or Pechili trader, has a projecting stern gallery and five masts. The *hua-p'ku*, or Fuzhou pole junk (below), is used to transport poles from Fujian to the Yangtze estuary for junk building. It has three sails, with the foremast rigged well forward. It is distinguished by its flaring bow and tall, oval stern.

3

STRANGE CREATURES
Europeans believed that amazing creatures such as mermaids, griffins, and giants lived in undiscovered lands. Here, the Portuguese navigator Ferdinand Magellan is depicted approaching Tierra del Fuego in 1520.

FERDINAN. MAGALA.

EUROPEAN EXPANSION

DURING THE 15TH CENTURY, European shipbuilders began to blend the best of the European and Arab traditions in the Mediterranean with the descendants of the Viking ships, to produce three- and four-masted ships, ideal sailing vessels for the high seas. They began to develop gun power to allow the ships to fight, but most of their battles were against other European powers, rather than the native peoples they traded with, colonized, or enslaved. The expansion of Europe overseas had a profound effect on the continent itself and on the rest of the world. The Europeans established links with the Far East and set up a world trade in luxury goods, such as spices and tobacco. They took over parts of North and South America, often destroying ancient cultures, and began the forcible migration of millions of African slaves. For the first time, a single continent began to dominate the world. Nearly all of its power, influence, trade, and ideas were borne across the seas in the new multi-masted sailing ships. But Europe itself was far from united, with wars of independence and religion often fought at sea.

OLDEST SURVIVING GLOBE, *c.*1491

> ❝ The Church says that the Earth is flat, but I know that it is round, for I have seen the shadow on the moon, and I have more faith in a shadow than in the Church. ❞
>
> **FERDINAND MAGELLAN**, leader of the first expedition to circumnavigate the globe, **early 1500s**

KEY EVENTS

1492 COLUMBUS CROSSES THE ATLANTIC
Genoese explorer Christopher Columbus leads a Spanish expedition across the Atlantic and discovers the Bahamas, Cuba, and Hispaniola.

1497 NEWFOUNDLAND LANDFALL
John Cabot lands in Newfoundland (it had previously been settled by American Indians and visited by the Vikings and Basques).

1498 SEA ROUTE TO INDIA The Portuguese navigator Vasco da Gama becomes the first European to discover the sea route to India.

1519 FIRST CIRCUMNAVIGATION Ferdinand Magellan sets off on an expedition that will be the first to circumnavigate the globe.

1536 ST. LAWRENCE RIVER EXPLORED
Frenchman Jacques Cartier reaches Montreal on the St. Lawrence River, Canada.

1642 TASMANIA DISCOVERED The Dutch explorer Abel Tasman finds Tasmania and New Zealand while looking for a southern continent.

WONDERS OF THE NEW WORLD
European sailors arriving in tropical Atlantic waters gaze in astonishment as flyingfish rise out of the water and fly past the sails of their ship in this coloured engraving by 16th-century Flemish artist Theodore de Bry.

EARLY EXPLORERS

THE DEVELOPMENT OF THE THREE-MASTED SHIP WOULD ENABLE EUROPEANS TO EXPLORE NEW SEA ROUTES AND DISCOVER NEW LANDS.

Europe was not one of the most developed parts of the world around 1500. Chinese civilization was more technologically advanced, and the Ottoman Empire threatened to engulf Europe from the east and south. The continent was racked with troubles including religious differences, which would lead to the Reformation, beginning in Germany in 1517 and in England in 1534. But the sailing ship would allow Europeans to extend their influence across the world's oceans and make theirs the dominant continent for the next 400 years.

The three-masted ship

From 1450, with the expansion of European trade and horizons, the old types of ship in the north and the Mediterranean became inadequate. A large single mast placed a great deal of strain on a single point on the hull, where it joined the keel, and multiple masts could spread this strain more evenly. A sail that projected too far beyond the sides of the ship would be difficult to control, and one that was too tall would make the ship heel too far. As ships tended to get bigger to make longer voyages and carry larger cargoes, it was necessary to find ways of using more but smaller sails.

The new type of ship that emerged combined the best in Mediterranean and north European design, and it is no coincidence that Spain, which straddles both areas, played a leading part in its

SPANISH PENDANT
This gold and enamel caravel hanging from an emerald cross, made in the 1580s, echoes the caravels that brought gold and precious jewels back from the Americas to Spain.

development. The new ship was largely carvel-built (see panel, p.70), which allowed a great deal of development in the shape and size of the hull, and it was relatively easy to repair without the facilities of a dockyard. The new ship had a rudder, which had originated in northern Europe. It carried more than one mast, as Mediterranean vessels had done since classical times. Most of its sails were square, of a type that had been developed in northern Europe since the Vikings, but it also had the lateen sails of the Mediterranean. It formed one of the greatest revolutions in ship construction.

The three-masted rig made a ship well balanced and more manoeuvrable. When tacking, for example, the foresail could operate in the opposite direction from the others to help bring the bows through the eye of the wind. It allowed a larger number of smaller sails, which were not impossibly large to handle. Square sails could be reduced in area when necessary, and they were best when sailing in a favourable wind. Lateen sails were useful in balancing the rig and sailing closer to the wind. The number and position of the sails could be varied to suit different weather conditions.

PORTUGUESE CARRACKS OFF ROCKY COAST
In this painting in the style of Joachim Patinir from the 1520s, men can be seen working aloft in the rigging of the Portuguese carracks as they sail past a galley on the right.

CARVEL CONSTRUCTION

Around the seventh century AD, Mediterranean shipbuilders began to simplify the system of hull construction. They reduced the size and importance of the pegs that joined one plank to another, placing much greater emphasis on the frame instead. This created a strong hull, but it was labour intensive to build. By AD 1000, they had begun to abandon the pegs entirely. This style of construction, called carvel, was relatively cheap, but it demanded that the frame or ribs of the ship be put in place, at least partly, before the planking was done. The practice of building frame first required more planning but allowed greater flexibility in ship construction, and it led eventually to the use of plans, initially in galleys. There is definite evidence that this was done in Venice in the 15th century, although it may well have begun two centuries earlier. The process was slow to spread, but it was the beginning of the transition of the shipwright from a craftsman into a naval architect, and the use of plans also opened the possibility for much bigger ships.

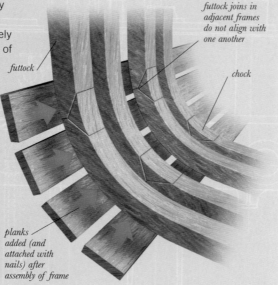

futtock joins in adjacent frames do not align with one another

futtock

chock

planks added (and attached with nails) after assembly of frame

THE CARVEL TECHNIQUE
The frame or rib of a moderate-sized wooden ship is made of separate pieces of timber called futtocks. When attached to the ribs, the side planks are flush, with the edges laid close and caulked to make a smooth, watertight finish.

PRINCE HENRY THE NAVIGATOR
Prince Henry, holding a map, is portrayed with some of the navigators he sponsored at a school at Sagres, Portugal, from 1438 to 1460. From left to right, they are shown holding a quadrant, a model ship, and an astrolabe.

By the second half of the 15th century, the three-masted ship was sufficiently common to appear in paintings of the period. By the early years of the 16th century, it had evolved into several different forms. The generic term ship, or *nao* to the Spanish, came to imply a three- or four-masted vessel with square rig on most of its sails. The carrack was a much larger version, generally a purpose-built warship with very high castles armed with large numbers of small guns. The caravel was a much smaller vessel, closer to Mediterranean principles. In its original version, it had two or three masts, each smaller than the one before it and lateen rigged. Some caravels were designed mainly for use in the Atlantic and were rigged as ships, with square-rigged fore- and mainmasts and a lateen-rigged mizzen.

Early exploration
The Atlantic is the most difficult ocean in the world to cross. It is smaller than the Pacific, but its islands are spread round the edges rather than across its centre. The only route across using short passages is in the north, as used by the Vikings and later the Basques, but the bad weather and cold demanded expert seamanship and a hardy crew. Farther south, the Atlantic was viewed as the edge of the world for many centuries, and it required a great leap of faith to set sail across it without knowing what, if anything, was on the other side. To the south, the coast of Africa was hostile and infertile and offered little except slaves and the possibility of gold.

But, from the 14th century onwards, Genoese, Majorcan, Spanish, and French seaman had ventured forth and found some island groups, such as the Azores, Madeira, and the Canary Islands. Prince Henry the Navigator, third son of King João I of Portugal, was named for his interests in sponsoring exploration rather than any great skill in finding his way around at sea, but his support took Portuguese seamen to the Azores in 1427, up the Senegal and Gambia rivers in west Africa in 1445, and to the Cape Verde Islands in 1446. As the area around the eastern Atlantic islands began to be peopled by the Spanish and Portuguese, it became known as the Atlantic Mediterranean. The islands opened expectations that others might be found, gave some indications of the wind patterns in the area, and eventually formed staging posts for long voyages, such as Christopher Columbus's epic voyage in 1492 (see panel, opposite).

Columbus's later voyages
After his first crossing of the Atlantic in 1492, Columbus made three more voyages, during which he explored the western Caribbean and claimed many islands for Spain, although most were already occupied by the Carib peoples. He also found out more about the wind patterns of the region. On his second voyage, he tried to sail directly back from Guadeloupe to Spain in 1496 and discovered that the winds were contrary that far south. On his third voyage, he went too far south on his westward passage in 1498 and was becalmed in the doldrums. His fortunes also fluctuated when he was on land: he was treated as an almost

PORTULAN CHART
This chart of the Mediterranean, Red Sea (actually shown as red), Black Sea, and part of the North Atlantic was made in Barcelona, Spain, in 1456. Hand-drawn and coloured on vellum, it has rhumb (direction) lines and a compass rose to help sailors plot their course.

COLUMBUS'S FIRST VOYAGE TO THE AMERICAS

The three ships that sailed west from the Canary Islands on 6 September 1492 were tiny by most standards. The flagship, commanded by Christopher Columbus, a Genoese in the service of Spain, was the *Santa Maria* with a crew of 40 men. The *Pinta*, a square-rigged vessel with a caravel hull, was of about 100 tons with a crew of 26, and the *Niña* of less than 100 tons was a true caravel, rigged with lateen sails and had a crew of 24. They were taking on a huge task, to prove Columbus's theory that it was possible to sail westwards to reach the rich trade of China and India, for the Florentine astronomer Paolo Toscanelli had encouraged Columbus in the belief that the world was round and such voyages were possible.

Columbus's travels had already taken him as far north as Ireland, where he learned that the winds were predominantly westerly, and to Madeira and possibly the Canary Islands, where he felt the northeast trade winds, which could carry him across the ocean. Other explorers had tended to set off against the prevailing winds, to make sure that they could get back again, but Columbus had hit on the circular wind pattern of the North Atlantic, which would take him out and get him back. Even so, he knew that he would have to cross several thousand kilometres of ocean, which had never been done before. It might be possible to sail due west, measuring the latitude from the Sun, until an eastern port was reached.

After a month at sea, Columbus turned southwest and on 12 October he sighted land, probably the Bahamas. He explored the islands then went farther to the southwest, where he reached Cuba. The *Santa Maria* was wrecked on the coast of Hispaniola, and Columbus returned home in the *Niña* by a more northerly route via the Azores. He reached Lisbon on 4 March 1493, claiming to have fulfilled his aim and discovered a route to and from India.

FRIENDLY NATIVES
Columbus is given gifts made of gold by natives as he arrives in Hispaniola in December 1492, some of which he presented to the Court at Barcelona on his return to Spain in 1493.

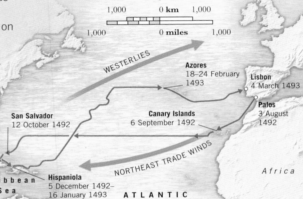

TRAVEL BUSINESS
This letter was written by Christopher Columbus from his home in Seville to his son, Diego, who would also travel to the Americas, discussing his various business affairs.

THE THREE SHIPS
The crews of the Niña, Santa Maria, and Pinta set out across the Atlantic in 1492 in the expectation of reaching China and India.

COLUMBUS'S FIRST VOYAGE

→ Route: 3 August 1492–
4 March 1493

divine hero at the court of Ferdinand and Isabella at Barcelona, but he was also sent home in chains by a royal governor of the new Spanish colony of Hispaniola in 1500.

In some quarters, Columbus was written off as a failure. He had grossly miscalculated the size of the world, believing from astronomical observations that it was 25 per cent smaller than it really was. He had not found the route to the East as he claimed, and maps of the Caribbean predating 1492 indicate other Europeans were there before him. But Columbus's undisputed achievement was to discover viable routes to and from the Americas, routes that would bring the world into a new phase, dominated by interaction between America and Europe.

America is named after the latin version of the Christian name of the Florentine navigator Amerigo Vespucci, who made several transatlantic voyages after 1499. His account of his voyages became influential, and in 1508 he was appointed Chief Pilot of Spain.

Portuguese pioneers

In 1494, the Spanish and Portuguese signed the Treaty of Tordesillas, agreeing that all new discoveries west of a line of longitude 370 leagues (1,770km/1,100 miles) west of the Cape Verde Islands would belong to Spain and all discoveries to the east would belong to Portugal. In fact, this allowed Portugal an as yet undiscovered part of the

DA GAMA'S SHIP
This illustration from the Livro das Armadas, *an early 16th-century manuscript now in the Science Academy, Lisbon, shows Vasco da Gama's ship the São Gabriel leaving for India in 1497.*

VASCO DE GAMA ARRIVES IN INDIA
This fanciful 16th-century tapestry shows the Portuguese explorer Vasco da Gama being received by the king in Calicut, southwest India, on 20 May 1498, some ten months after he and his men left Lisbon.

South American continent, which would later become known as Brazil. In the shorter term, it encouraged the Portuguese in their determination to find a sea route to the East by sailing round the continent of Africa. The Portuguese explorer Bartholemeu Dias had already sailed south in the service of King João II and discovered the Cape of Good Hope in 1488.

In 1497, Vasco da Gama, a Portuguese nobleman who had fought as a soldier before becoming a seaman, was selected by João's successor, Manoel I, to find a sea route to India. He set out from Lisbon in July in the *São Gabriel*, accompanied by three ships and with a total crew of 140–170 men. They sailed as far as Sierra Leone then, instead of travelling down the west coast of Africa and possibly being caught in the doldrums or by the northerly Benguela Current, da Gama turned west until they picked up the southerly Brazil Current. The expedition finally rounded the Cape of Good Hope in December.

In February 1498, da Gama landed at Mozambique to buy fresh food from Arab traders, for after several months at sea the sailors were suffering from scurvy (see p.159). However, here and later at Mombassa, relations between the Arabs and Christians soon became strained and ended in violence. But, they were better received at Malindi, on the coast of Kenya, where da Gama hired a pilot, Ahmad ibn Majid, to guide them across the Indian Ocean. They left the African coast on 24 April and arrived at Calicut, a trading centre on the Malabar coast of India, on 20 May, where, according to da Gama's journal, the King came to look at the ships, "for all the wonder was at seeing so many ropes and so many sails, and because the ships arrived when the Sun was almost set."

Da Gama failed to establish trading links due to local jealousies and the poor quality of the Portuguese goods, and he departed on 29 August. The voyage back across the Indian Ocean was extremely arduous and da Gama had to put down a mutiny. One of the ships, the *São Rafael* was leaking so badly it was abandoned and burned, and only 55 men survived to return to Portugal. But da

Gama had shown what was possible. He made a further voyage to India in 1502–03, and this time he was more successful in establishing trade. In 1517, the Portuguese nobleman Ferdinand Magellan, who had served his king in the Indian Ocean, renounced his nationality and

went to Spain, where he persuaded Emperor Charles V to fund his scheme to reach the Spice Islands (or Moluccas) in the Pacific by sailing west (see panel, above). In one of the greatest voyages of discovery of all time, Magellan proved that this was indeed possible, although he did not survive to return home, and only one of his ships made it back to Spain.

PORTUGUESE AGE OF DISCOVERY
The Monument to the Discoveries in Lisbon was erected in 1960 to mark the 500th anniversary of Henry the Navigator's death. Among the many Portuguese explorers and patrons featured, Prince Henry leads the way, Vasco da Gama is third, and Ferdinand Magellan is fifth.

THE FIRST CIRCUMNAVIGATION OF THE GLOBE

Ferdinand Magellan's fleet of five ships, led by the *Victoria*, left Spain on 20 September 1519, with 241 men on board. They crossed the Atlantic then sailed down the east coast of South America, during which time Magellan had to put down a mutiny. The men spent two winter months camping on shore in Patagonia, then Magellan sought a way through to the Pacific. He finally found a narrow channel, which became known as the Straits of Magellan, and entered the Pacific on 28 November 1520. Magellan headed north along the coast, then turned northwest. He had no idea just how wide the Pacific was and it would be three hard months before he made landfall in Guam, with his men suffering from starvation and scurvy.

MAGELLAN
Ferdinand Magellan learned to navigate when he sailed to India in 1505 with Portugal's Viceroy of the East.

ON THE MAP
The narrow passage through the tip of South America linking the Atlantic with the Pacific now bears Magellan's name.

Having rested and taken on food, they moved on to the Philippines. Magellan explored the islands and bought a cargo of spice, which would more than pay for the cost of the expedition. But he became embroiled in a dispute between the islanders and was killed. Only the *Victoria*, now under the command of Juan Sebastian del Cano with just 30 men, completed the return journey to Spain.

THE ROUTE AROUND THE WORLD
Magellan led his men across the Atlantic and then across the Pacific to the Philippines, where he was killed in a battle between the natives of Cebu and Mactan on 27 April 1521.

Map labels:
- North America
- Europe
- Asia
- PACIFIC OCEAN
- Guadalquivir 20 September 1519
- Seville July 1522
- ATLANTIC OCEAN
- Philippines 13 March–1 May 1521
- Guam 6–9 March 1521
- Moluccas November 1521
- Africa
- INDIAN OCEAN
- PACIFIC OCEAN
- South America
- Pernambuco 6 December 1519
- Rio de Janeiro 13 December 1519
- Australia
- Emerges into the Pacific Ocean 28 November 1520
- Port St. Julian 31 March–August 1520
- Discovery of the Straits of Magellan 21 October 1520
- SOUTHERN OCEAN
- N
- Antarctica

MAGELLAN'S VOYAGE
→ Route: 20 September 1519– 27 April 1521
⇢ Route back to Spain after Magellan's death

JOHN CABOT

The son of a merchant, John Cabot (1455–*c*.1499) was brought up in Venice and sailed to the Levant in Venetian ships. He moved to England with his family in 1484 and became involved with plans for a westward voyage of discovery. In May 1497, he sailed from Bristol with 18 crew in the *Matthew* of about 50 tons. He landed on Cape Breton Island off Canada, but was convinced he was close to the Asian continent. He then explored the island of Newfoundland and returned to England in August 1497. King Henry VII rewarded him with £10 and a pension of £20 a year. He disappeared on a second voyage, which began in 1498.

The English and French in Canada

In March 1496, England's King Henry VII authorized the Venetian navigator John Cabot (see panel, left) to seek out lands "which before this time have been unknown to all Christians". Funded by the merchants of Bristol, he sailed west in May 1497, with the intention of finding a route to Cathay (now China). In June, he landed on Cape Breton Island, Newfoundland, and claimed it for the King. Although he did not find the spices and jewels of Asia, on the return journey Cabot did discover rich stocks of cod off the coast of Newfoundland (see p.250).

French interest in the New World was demonstrated in 1524 when Giovanni da Verrazzano, a Tuscan nobleman in the service of the French monarch François I, sailed north along the unexplored east coast between North Carolina and Maine. He was the first European to explore New York Harbor (the entrance is now called the Verrazzano Narrows), but was convinced that it was the beginning of a passage to the Far East.

In 1534, the French navigator Jacques Cartier left the port of St. Malo, Brittany, with two ships of 60 tons each, carrying 61 men between them, for King François wanted the gold of the New World. Cartier arrived off Newfoundland in May and passed through the Strait of Belle Isle to enter the Gulf of St. Lawrence. He explored the coastline and islands before returning to France. In 1536, he returned with three ships and proceeded up the St. Lawrence River as far as the sites of present-day Quebec and Montreal, where rapids prevented any further progress. Natives from the American Indian village of Hochelaga told him of gold further west, but he was trapped by the ice during the winter and returned to France the

MARINER'S COMPASS
The compass card is mounted on a brass gimbal ring, which helps it to remain level even when the ship is in motion. Most early compass boxes were made of wood, but this one is of precious ivory.

ASCENDING THE ST. LAWRENCE
Having left his ships anchored by the Ile d'Orléans, the French explorer Jacques Cartier rows up the St. Lawrence River towards the American Indian village of Hochelaga (now Montreal, Canada) in 1536.

following year. In 1541, the King appointed the nobleman Jean-François de LaRocque de Roberval to supervise Cartier on his third expedition, with orders to claim the territory for France and search for gold. Cartier sailed early to avoid de Roberval and found what he thought was gold and precious diamonds in the St. Lawrence Valley. De Roberval caught up with him as he returned via Newfoundland and ordered him to Quebec. But Cartier escaped home, where his treasure proved to

MARINER'S MIRROUR
This is the title page of a collection of 16th-century Dutch charts that were translated into English in 1588 and used by British seamen for 100 years.

HENRY HUDSON

The son of a London alderman, Henry Hudson (c.1550–1611) was an experienced seaman by 1607, when he was commissioned by English merchants to look for a northeast passage to the Far East. He made two attempts but did not succeed. In 1609, he went in search of a northwest passage. He reached New York Harbor and went 240km (150 miles) up the river he found there. He did not find a route to the South Seas, but the Hudson River was named after him. In 1610, he tried again. He reached Hudson Bay in the *Discovery*, but she became trapped in ice over the winter, and he and his crew barely survived by eating frogs and moss. In June 1611, the men mutinied and cast Hudson adrift. His exact fate remains a mystery.

be valueless. He was the first European to penetrate deeply into the continent of North America, but French interest in the area would not be renewed for another 50 years.

England's claims to Canada were strengthened by the exploits of Henry Hudson (see panel, left) in the early years of the 17th century. He first came to the fore in 1607 when the Muscovy Company, English merchants trading with north Russia, hired him to look for a northeast passage (a sea route round the north of Europe and Asia to the Pacific). He reached Spitsbergen in his ship *Hopewell* but turned back due to the impenetrable ice. In 1608, he tried again, following the route taken by the Dutch explorer Willem Barents in 1594, but he failed to get beyond the ice of the Barents Sea. Barents, himself, had died in 1597, during his third and final attempt to find the northeast passage.

In 1609, Hudson was hired by the Dutch East India Company of Amsterdam to look for a northwest passage to China (a sea route from

THE DANGERS OF ARCTIC EXPLORATION
Dutchman Willem Barents's second attempt to find a northeast passage to India ended when his ships became trapped in ice north of Russia in 1595. Three of his men had to ward off a polar bear while the others made camp.

the Atlantic to the Pacific via the north of Canada). He did not succeed, but he did enter New York Harbor and explore what is now called the Hudson River. On his return to England, he was placed under house arrest and forbidden to work for the Dutch again. In 1610, he was commissioned by the English East India and Virginia Companies to try again for the northwest passage. He reached Hudson Bay in northeast Canada in the 55-ton *Discovery*, but his crew mutinied the following summer. The *Discovery* returned home in September 1611 with only eight of the original crew of 22 still onboard. But the discovery of Hudson Bay and its potential for a valuable fur trade would lead to the English establishing settlements there.

The Dutch in the East

The Dutch, based at Batavia (now Jakarta) on the island of Java, were the first Europeans to explore the Australian continent. In 1616, Dirk Hartog had landed on an island just off the west coast, and several other navigators sighted the south coast in the 1620s. Abel Janszoon Tasman had already explored the northwest Pacific as far as Formosa (now Taiwan). He was almost 40 years old and an experienced seaman when, in August 1642, he set off into the Indian Ocean to

HUDSON ON THE HUDSON
The English explorer Henry Hudson barters with American Indians in 1609 at the mouth of what became known as the Hudson River. His Dutch ship, the Halve Maan *("half moon"), lies at anchor in the bay.*

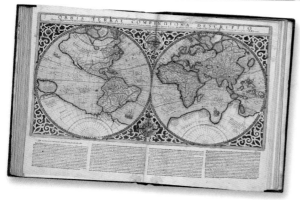

MERCATOR'S PROJECTION
In 1569, the Flemish geographer Gerardus Mercator devised a map projection in which the parallels of latitude and the meridians of longitude are shown as straight lines that cross each other at right angles. The map above is from an atlas published by his son Rumold in 1595.

THE MARINER'S ASTROLABE

For many centuries, Arab astronomers had used the planispheric astrolabe to measure the angle of celestial bodies such as the Sun to the horizon. It consisted of a dial graduated in degrees, with a rotating arm (alidade) fixed to its centre. There was a projection on each end of the arm, bored with a small hole. When these were lined up with the Sun, the light would shine through and the angle could be measured on the scale. The mariner's astrolabe began to appear in the 15th century. It was smaller, usually made of brass or brass and wood, and consisted of a cross inside a graduated circle. The astrolabe could be used to determine latitude using the Pole Star or the Sun.

PARTS OF THE ASTROLABE
The mariner's astrolabe had portions of the disc cut away, to reduce wind resistance, and was heavier at the bottom. This was to help keep it steady when used onboard a ship.

suspension ring
degree scale
pointer gives latitude
rotating alidade
viewing hole
ballast

look for the legendary "great southern continent", on behalf of the Dutch East India Company. He sailed to the west in his ships *Heemskerck* and *Zeehaen* until he reached Mauritius. Then, he headed east below the latitude of 40 degrees S, discovering Amsterdam Island in the southern Indian Ocean. Seven weeks after he set out, he found the southern end of Tasmania, which he called Van Diemen's Landt in honour of the governor of Batavia (it was later renamed after Tasman). But he did not realize Tasmania was an island as he did not find Bass Strait, which separates it from Australia. Heading east again, he landed on Staten Landt (now New Zealand), where some of his men were killed by Maoris. He had a much more friendly reception in Tonga to the north, then he returned to Batavia by way of Melanesia and New Guinea. Tasman had circumnavigated Australia without sighting the mainland. In 1644, he set out again and explored much of the north coast of Australia and the west coast of New Guinea, although he did not realize the latter was an island. It was decided that Australia and New Zealand offered nothing of interest to Europeans, and their native peoples were left mostly undisturbed for the next 140 years.

In many European countries, especially the Netherlands and England, exploration was publicized through the new medium of print, which grew up at almost the same time. The German printer Johann Gutenberg first set up shop in Mainz in Germany in the mid-15th century, to be followed by others in Spain, the Netherlands, and France within the next 30 years.

Explorers such as Tasman published accounts of their voyages, and sea charts and maps of the newly discovered lands were published in atlases. Perhaps the greatest publicist of all was Richard Hakluyt, who brought out *The Principall Navigations, Voyages and Discoveries of the English Nation* in 1587. He gave exaggerated praise to the efforts of Queen Elizabeth I, saying, "…in this most famous and peerless governement of her most excellent Majesty, her subjects through the speciall assistance, and blessing of God, in searching the most opposite corners and

DUTCH UNDER ATTACK
Abel Janszoon Tasman (left) kept a journal of his voyage from the Dutch East Indies to the unknown South Land in 1642. He recorded the attack of his ships by Maori war canoes in New Zealand (below).

quarters of the world, and to speake plainly, in compassing the vast globe of the earth more than once, have excelled all the nations and peoples of the earth".

Hakluyt was typical in that he saw the hand of God behind national success and regarded exploration as an asset to one country, rather than a resource for the whole world. For 150 years after Columbus's voyage in 1492, Europeans vastly increased their knowledge of the globe, especially its coasts, making use of new navigational instruments such as the mariner's astrolabe (see panel, above). There were some gaps, notably in the South Pacific and around the closed societies of China and Japan, but European seamen understood the shape of the world, its wind patterns, and most of the major hazards that were to be encountered in its navigation. Such knowledge allowed the Europeans to spread to the Americas and the Caribbean, to increase trade with the East, and to acquire many islands on the routes to these areas. It allowed them to export some of their surplus populations and gave vast opportunities for trade, cultural contact, and wealth. But contact with the outside world did not always widen European horizons. Religious prejudices were often exported and applied with increased vigour in the New World. And colonial rivalries were to be a primary cause of war between the European powers in almost every decade up to 1815.

TYPVS ORB

SEPT

CIRCVLVS ARCTICVS.

ANIAN regnum.

AMERICA SIVE IN DIA NOVA. Ao 1492. a Christophoro.

Colombo nomine regis Castelle primum detecta.

Noua Francia.

Estotilant.

Groclant.

Tolm.

Chilaga.

QVIVIRA regnu.

Tuchano.

Quiuir̃a.

Cicuic.

Totonte ac.

Canada.

Roquelai.

Norobega.

Terra de Baccalaos.

Dobretan.

Axa.

Tiguex.

Totonte ac.

Ceuola.

Grana Marata.

Marata.

Omet lan.

Calicuas.

Tagil.

Clandia.

La Bermuda.

Santana.

Juan de samp.

Sept cites.

Cozones insula.

C. del engaño.

Las dos hermanos.

Los Bolcanes.

Y de Cedri.

B. de la.

Trimdad.

Cuchillo.

Culiac.

Florida.

Lucaio.

Limana.

TROPICVS CANCRI

Malabrigo.

La farfana.

Mechula.

Hispania.

Cuba.

MAR DEL NORT.

Archipelago di Zamal.

Restinga di ladrones.

Rocca partida.

S. Thomas Anubiada.

R. de cocutula.

Acax catula.

Guada lupe.

y de S. B.

y de c Verde.

Abreojo.

Ins. de los corales.

Cacos.

Grana bra.

Solis.

Los iardi nas Lazaro.

Ins. de los reyes.

CIRCVLVS AEQVINOCTIALIS.

ye de los galopegos.

Quito.

Neyua.

Caribana.

Aúdpari.

y de crespos.

y de hombres blan cos.

Labarbada. Los Bolcanes.

Ins di los Tiburones.

Casma.

Peru.

Tisnada.

Orellana.

Ora.

Fe de.

S. Roque.

Noua Guinea nuper inuenta que an sit insula an pars continentis Australis incertu est.

MAR DEL ZVR.

Insulæ incogni tæ.

Lima.

Cusco.

Amazones.

Brasil.

S. Elena.

P. Segur.

Asenjion.

S. Paulo.

TROPICVS CAPRICORNI.

Coquimbo.

Copaiao.

Giuru matas.

Mepe nes.

B. Real.

C. Frio.

Hanc continentem Australem, nonnulli Magellanicam regionem ab eius inuentore nuncupant.

EL MAR PACIFICO.

y̌ uistas de lexos.

Quinte.

Tara paca.

Chica.

S. Catelina.

Rio de la Plata.

Lucengo. C. de S Maria.

P. de palma Chile.

S. Anna.

Palmares.

C. blanco.

C. de los marmos.

C di 3 puntas.

Archipe lago.

Calis.

CIRCVLVS ANTARCTICVS.

Terra del Fuego.

Estrecho di Magallones.

190 200 210 220 230 240 250 260 270 280 290 300 310 320 330 340 350

80

TERRA AVSTRA

THREE- AND FOUR-MASTED SHIPS

Three-masted ships of the kind developed in Europe in the 15th century were among the great technological advances in world history. The new rig could be balanced more effectively, and sails could be manipulated for greater manoeuvrability. It also allowed more sails to be carried on a given size of ship without the individual sails becoming too large. Three- and four-masted ships were used to explore the world beyond the Mediterranean by sea for the first time – and came to dominate the seas for four centuries.

ARRIVAL OF VASCO
This tapestry records Vasco da Gama arriving at Calicut, India, in 1498.

Early three-masted ships

A round bowl (below) that was made in Malaga, in southern Spain, gives us the first known picture of a modern three-masted ship. Although the proportions are not very accurately drawn, it is clear that the mainsail is by far the largest, suggesting that the other sails were there only for balance. The mainmast is very thick, with a large sail but no sign of a topsail; it also has a platform known as a top above it, for a lookout. The mizzen carries a lateen sail, as was to become common. The foremast is very small and its rigging is unclear, but it seems to carry a small square sail. It has a high forecastle with a projecting beakhead, another soon-to-be-common feature. The raised quarter-deck in the stern is built as an integral part of the ship.

MALAGA BOWL

Origin Spanish-Moroccan	**Date** Early 15th century	
Length Estimated 30m (100ft)	**Tonnage** Not known	
Armament Not known		

Carracks

Spain led the development of the three-masted ship, combining the square sails of Viking tradition with the lateen sail and carvel building of the Mediterranean. The carrack, which evolved from this process, had at least three masts, with a hull that tapered above the waterline and large castles fore and aft. A model of the mid-1400s (below), found near Barcelona, shows a stage in the development. Unusually, it had only two masts and a bowsprit, including a stout mainmast.

MATARO SHIP

Origin Spain	**Date of launch** c.1450
Length About 24m (80ft)	**Tonnage** About 100 tons
Armament None	

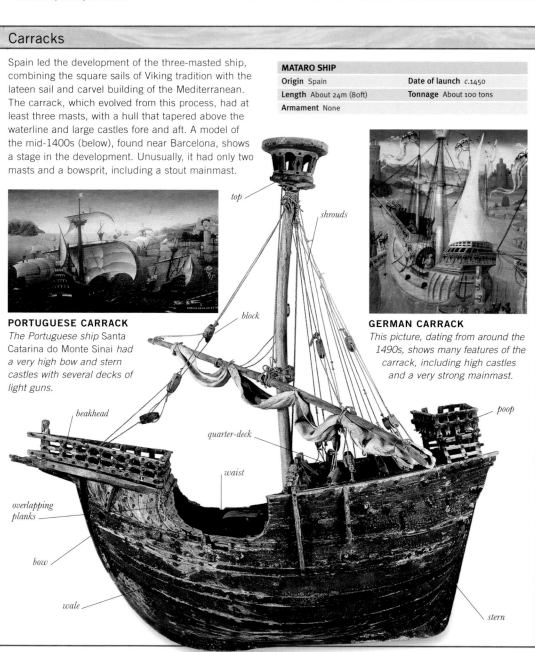

PORTUGUESE CARRACK
The Portuguese ship Santa Catarina do Monte Sinai had a very high bow and stern castles with several decks of light guns.

GERMAN CARRACK
This picture, dating from around the 1490s, shows many features of the carrack, including high castles and a very strong mainmast.

top

shrouds

block

poop

beakhead

quarter-deck

waist

overlapping planks

bow

wale

stern

Naos

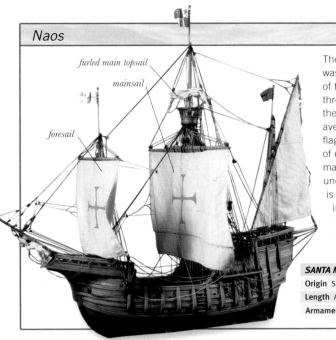

furled main topsail
mainsail
foresail

The *nao* (an old Spanish word meaning "ship") was the classic medium-sized Spanish vessel of the age of exploration, with a fully developed three-masted rig and often a small topsail on the mainmast. The *Santa Maria* (left) was an average ship, built in Galicia and used as the flagship on Christopher Columbus's first voyage of exploration, in 1492. Her sail arrangement – main, main topsail, foresail, square spritsail under the bowsprit, and lateen mizzen – is recorded in Columbus's log. Otherwise, information about the ship is sparse, and models and reconstructions are based on known facts about ships of the time.

SANTA MARIA

Origin Spain	**Date of launch** 1492
Length About 21.3m (70ft)	**Tonnage** About 200 tons
Armament 1 x 9-cm gun (or Lombard), several 4.5-cm guns (falconets)	

Caravels

The *caravela latina* had fore-and-aft lateen sails on all of its masts. Like all fore-and-aft-rigged vessels, it could sail close to the wind. The modified *caravela redonda* (below) had square sails on the foremast or mainmast.

mizzen mast
mainmast
foremast
lateen sail
bowsprit

CARAVEL

Origin Portugal	**Date of launch** c.1490
Length 20.7m (68ft)	**Tonnage** About 140 tons
Armament None	

Warships

The warship was not completely separate from the merchant ship in the 16th century, and almost any kind of seagoing ship could be converted for use in conflict if necessary. But by the early 1500s, kings demanded ever-larger ships for royal prestige, which they had to build for themselves rather than take up from merchants. Meanwhile, the invention of the gunport and the gradual move towards a heavier gun armament meant that fighting qualities had to be planned early in the design of a ship.

Henry VIII of England's *Mary Rose* (below) was one of the first ships to be designed around the gunport and the heavy gun. She also retained a substantial armament of light guns and even longbows. The *Mary Rose* sank off Portsmouth in 1545, while manoeuvring during a battle against the French. Her wreck was recovered in 1982, giving us the clearest picture yet of a Renaissance warship.

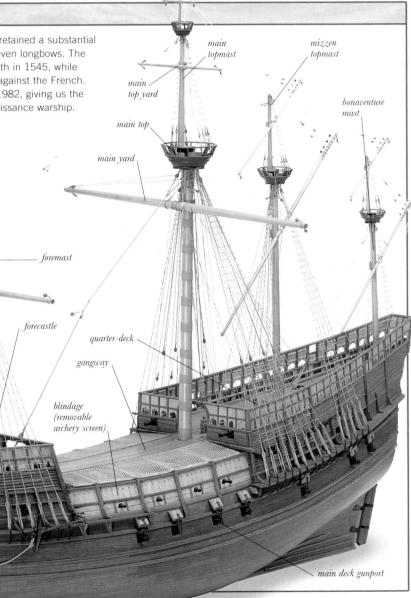

main topmast
mizzen topmast
main top yard
bonaventure mast
main top
main yard
foremast
forecastle
quarter-deck
gangway
forward-firing gun
blindage (removable archery screen)
beakhead
anchor cable
main deck gunport

THE *GREAT HARRY*

Henry VIII's Henri Grace à Dieu, *or Great Harry, was built in 1514 in response to the threat posed by James IV of Scotland. Reputed to weigh 1,500 tons and carry 700 men, 43 heavy guns, and 141 light guns, she was the largest ship of the day.*

MARY ROSE

Origin England	**Date of launch** 1510
Length 32m (105ft) (keel)	**Tonnage** 600 tons
Armament 78 guns	

CONQUISTADOR HELMET

66 Many came also to gape at the strange men, now so famous, and at their attire, arms and horses, and they said 'These men are gods!' 99

FRANCISCO LOPEZ DE GOMARA, on the Spaniards' arrival in Mexico, **1552**

KEY EVENTS

1519 CONQUEST OF MEXICO The Spanish conquistador Hernán Cortés sails from Cuba to Mexico, which he takes for the Spanish.

1531 INCAS SUBDUED The conquistador Francisco Pizarro sails from Panama and invades western South America.

1600 EAST INDIA COMPANY The first East India Company is set up by the English in 1600, with the intention of trading in India and the Far East. The Dutch establish a similar organization two years later.

1607 JAMESTOWN FOUNDED A group of English settlers sail across the Atlantic to establish the first permanent English-speaking colony in the Americas, Jamestown.

1620 LEAVING PLYMOUTH The *Mayflower* leaves Plymouth, England, carrying 102 passengers intending to settle in North America.

SAILING FOR A NEW LIFE
This 17th-century painting by the Dutch artist Adam van Breen depicts the departure of a group of English Puritans from Delft. They sailed from the Dutch port to England, where they joined the Mayflower (see pp.86–87) and voyaged to America for a new life of religious freedom.

COLONIZATION

THROUGHOUT THE 16TH AND 17TH CENTURIES, EUROPEANS ESTABLISHED PERMANENT COLONIES IN NEW LANDS IN THE AMERICAS AND ASIA.

GOLDEN GOD
The Spanish showed little respect for the beliefs of those they conquered. This gold Inca artefact has survived, but countless others were melted down and shipped back to Europe.

Over the course of about 400 years after 1450, Europeans colonized and repopulated North, South, and Central America and the islands of the West Indies (which were collectively known as the New World) and Australia, New Zealand, and southern Africa. For those who embarked on these voyages to distant continents, the future was uncertain. In the days of sail, ocean travel was slow, tedious, uncomfortable, and risky. It offered a host of dangers, including shipwreck, attack by pirates or ships belonging to other nations, and disease. There were also unknown perils to be faced once a journey was completed. Some colonists undertook these voyages voluntarily, expecting to make their fortune or perhaps to win their religious freedom, as was the case with the emigrants to North America in 1620 (see pp.86–87). Others, such as soldiers, convicts, and slaves, sailed to new lands against their will, some in shackles.

Respect for the indigenous peoples varied from place to place. In India, for example, the Europeans were initially traders and had no desire to colonize the subcontinent. In other areas, such as Latin America, the Spanish conquerors, who were known as conquistadors, regarded the natives as heathens who had no rights of any kind. The lure of instant riches was the primary motive for many of those who first sailed to the Americas, no matter what the cost to those they encountered.

The conquistadors

The colonization of the New World began with the island of Hispaniola (now known as the Dominican Republic and Haiti). San Domingo, the first European city to be established in the Americas, was founded on the island in 1496.

HERNAN CORTES

The son of an impoverished noble family, the Spanish conquistador Hernán Cortés (1485–1547) was responsible for the conquest of Mexico. He first crossed the Atlantic in 1506 and helped to administer the island of Hispaniola. In 1511, he served under Diego Velasquez during the invasion of Cuba. In 1519, Cortés sailed to Mexico. He landed on the east coast, where he founded a settlement that became the city of Veracruz. He went on to capture the Aztec capital, Tenochtitlán, imprisoning and executing the king, Montezuma. Cortés returned to Spain in 1540 and settled in Seville, where he died, his achievements largely forgotten.

Christopher Columbus, who had claimed the island for Spain in 1492 (see p.71) wrote: "this land abounds in everything, especially bread and meat. There is no lack of anything except wine and clothing. Of our people here, each has two or three Indians to serve him and dogs to hunt for him and, though perhaps it should not be said, women so handsome as to be a wonder."

But this earthly paradise did

FATAL EPIDEMIC
The conquerors of the Americas carried diseases that proved to be fatal to the native population. This Peruvian Indian is suffering from one such disease, measles.

not last long. The primary reason for the Spanish colonization of the island was wealth. Columbus had found gold when he first visited Hispaniola, and with the arrival of settlers the island's reserves of the precious metal were ruthlessly exploited. So, too, were the native Arawak Indians, whose population declined as a result of diseases that were alien to them and the harsh treatment of their invaders.

The Spanish settlement of the region expanded with the acquisition of Jamaica in 1509 and Cuba in 1511. The first colony on the mainland of Central America was established at Darién, on the Panamanian isthmus in 1510. The Pacific coast of South America was first sighted and claimed for Spain by Vasco Núñez de Balboa in 1513. In 1519, Hernán Cortés (see panel, left) began his conquest of Mexico. He sailed from Cuba with 11 ships, headed by the *Santa Maria de la Concepción*. The vessels carried 110 sailors, 553 soldiers, and 200 Indians. In April 1519, the Spanish ships dropped anchor at San Juan de Ulúa, on the east coast of Mexico, and founded the settlement of Veracruz. Cortés and his men marched on to the capital of the region, the Aztec city of Tenochtitlán. There the conquistador was greeted as if he were a god by the Aztec ruler Montezuma. The magnificent city was built on reclaimed marshland around Lake Texcoco, and it was clear that precious metals were abundant, a factor which motivated Spanish

GOLD EAGLE
This ornate eagle head is a traditional lip decoration, which was fashioned by an Aztec goldsmith. Such precious items were plundered by the Spanish.

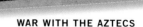

WAR WITH THE AZTECS
This scene from the Codex Duran, an illustrated account of the Spanish conquest of Mexico, which was published in 1580, shows Cortés's soldiers under attack from Aztec warriors.

acquisition of the country. Relations with the indigenous people quickly turned to violence. The Spanish besieged the great city using brigantines mounted with cannon, which they built with the help of Montezuma's opponents, and transported to Lake Texcoco over land and along a specially built canal. Tenochtitlán fell in August 1521. Montezuma was killed, and the Spanish expanded to control the whole of Mexico.

South America was also home to the great Inca civilization, which ruled a large tract of the western part of the continent, including modern Peru, Bolivia, southern Ecuador, and northern Chile. In 1531 another Spaniard, Francisco Pizarro, sailed from Panama with three ships, 185 men, and 27 horses in search of the region's abundant wealth. Exploiting a civil war within the Inca hierarchy, Pizarro's men overcame the inhabitants and murdered their leader, Atahualpa. The Spanish went on to conquer the region in a campaign of notorious brutality. By the end of the 1540s, Spanish settlements stretched down the west coast of South America as far as modern Chile. They also expanded into North America, settling in Florida and California. Just six decades after Columbus had crossed the Atlantic in the *Santa Maria* and claimed the New

DEATH OF AN INCA
The Inca emperor Atahualpa was executed by the Spanish invaders of Peru on 28 June 1533. This illustration of his death is taken from a 1597 manuscript entitled History of the Spanish Conquest.

TERRITORIAL DISPUTE
In 1523 Hernán Cortés fought another Spanish conquistador, Francisco de Garay, for control of the area around the Panuco River. The incident is illustrated in this 1641 engraving.

THE CROSS-STAFF AND THE BACKSTAFF

Navigation using celestial objects is much easier with an accurate method of measuring the angle between objects in the sky such as the Pole Star or the Sun, and the horizon. If the object's movements in the sky are known or predictable, navigators can use its present position to determine their latitude. Since medieval times, Arab mariners had used an instrument called a *kamal* to do this. In the 15th century, European sailors adapted the idea in the form of the cross-staff. The wooden staff was held against the body, and a bar called a cross-piece was moved along the staff until the top end of the bar coincided with the object being measured, and the bottom end aligned with the horizon. A scale marked on the staff then revealed the angle between the two.

Looking directly at the Sun harms the eyes, so English explorer John Davis invented the backstaff, which allowed readings to be taken without facing the Sun.

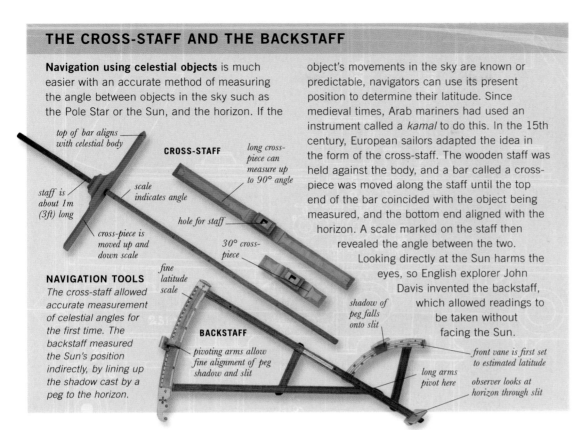

CROSS-STAFF

top of bar aligns with celestial body

long cross-piece can measure up to 90° angle

staff is about 1m (3ft) long

scale indicates angle

hole for staff

cross-piece is moved up and down scale

30° cross-piece

fine latitude scale

shadow of peg falls onto slit

NAVIGATION TOOLS
The cross-staff allowed accurate measurement of celestial angles for the first time. The backstaff measured the Sun's position indirectly, by lining up the shadow cast by a peg to the horizon.

BACKSTAFF

pivoting arms allow fine alignment of peg shadow and slit

front vane is first set to estimated latitude

long arms pivot here

observer looks at horizon through slit

INCA ART
This casket was decorated by Incas shortly after the Spanish arrival in the New World in 1492. The colourful style of painting depicts native people, plants, and animals.

World, Spanish influence had spread over a vast area. They also controlled much of Europe and added the Philippines to their possessions in 1571. In effect, 16th-century Spain was the world's first superpower.

Portuguese expansion

The Portuguese navigator Pedro Alvares Cabral sighted the coast of Brazil in 1500, claiming it for his country under the Treaty of Torsedillas (see p.72). Others, including Amerigo Vespucci (see p.72), who gave his name to the Americas, explored the same coastline, but it was the 1530s before the Portuguese began to settle in the territory.

From the time of Vasco da Gama's voyage to India in 1478 (see p.73), during which he had seen Arab sailors using a device that was adapted in Europe as the cross-staff (see panel, above), Portuguese ships had undertaken an annual voyage from Lisbon to their trading colony of Goa in India. Known as the *Carriera da India*, the trip took about a year. The Portuguese produced elaborate sailing directions for the route and utilized the cyclical weather patterns of the Indian Ocean. The monsoon blew from the northeast in the winter and from the southwest in the summer, so ships scheduled their passages to take advantage of these winds. The standard Portuguese merchant ship of the 16th century was usually known as a carrack, a term that was obsolete elsewhere. According to a decree of 1570, the vessels were between 300 and 450 tons, although larger vessels were possible. The average carrack carried a crew of about 130 men. Some were built in the east, using local supplies of teak. One of the most famous was the *Cinco Chagas*, which was constructed in Goa in 1559–60. She served for 25 years and made many round trips to the east.

GOLD LLAMA
This gold figure, produced by Inca craftsmen, demonstrates the metalworking skills of the native South American cultures.

BOLIVIAN SILVER MINE
This early 17th-century image by the Flemish engraver Théodore de Bry shows the silver mines of Potosí in Bolivia. Huge reserves of the precious metal were discovered in 1545. The Spanish used the mines and employed natives to work in them.

TOBACCO PIPE
In this 19th-century portrait, Walter Raleigh, the English adventurer and explorer, symbolically encircles the globe with his right arm. The leather tobacco pouch and clay pipes are believed to have belonged to Raleigh.

Virginia and New England

The lure of untapped riches also attracted the English to the New World. Humphrey Gilbert was granted the right to travel to Newfoundland and establish a settlement there in 1583. He sailed in his ship, the *Squirrel*, accompanied by the *Golden Hind* and the *Swallow*. Upon arrival, he founded the city of St. John's, the first English colony in North America, although it wasn't settled successfully. On the return voyage to England, the *Squirrel* and her entire crew were lost. In 1584, Gilbert's step-brother, the English sailor and favourite of Queen Elizabeth I, Sir

EXOTIC FRUIT
This 17th-century sketch of a pineapple was drawn by the English mariner John White. It was probably completed on a voyage to the Caribbean with Walter Raleigh in 1585.

INDIAN SETTLEMENT
This "bird's eye view" engraving, showing the Indian settlement of Pomeioc, on the coast of what is now North Carolina, was drawn by John White in 1585.

Walter Raleigh, financed an expedition to survey the east coast of North America, all of which was then named Virginia. The aim was to locate a suitable area for a permanent settlement. The following year, Raleigh's cousin, Sir Richard Grenville, led a flotilla of five ships, *Tyger*, *Roebuck*, *Lion*, *Elizabeth*, and *Dorothy*, to colonize the island of Roanoke, off the coast of what is now South Carolina. The expedition failed, and when a ship returned with supplies for the colony in 1590, no trace of it was found. Its fate remains a mystery.

The English Virginia Company, which was established with the intention of creating a trade monopoly on the east coast of America, chartered three ships, led by the *Susan Constant* (see pp.88–89), to sail to Virginia in 1606. In 1607, the settlers they carried founded Jamestown, on the James River. The colony came close to starvation several times over the next few years, but the leadership of Captain John Smith helped the settlers to organize themselves. Smith was also instrumental in smoothing over the often-fraught relations with the native Indians. Eventually, after several voyages ferrying supplies and new inhabitants from England, Jamestown established itself as the first permanent English-speaking colony in North America.

These initial Virginia colonists were primarily adventurers, hoping for a swift financial return on their voyage. Many did become wealthy, particularly through the establishment of tobacco plantations. However, a later group of colonists, who subsequently became known as the Pilgrim Fathers, had very different aspirations. Their specific intent was to begin a new life, free to practise their Puritan beliefs, which were not tolerated in James I's England. On 16 September 1620, the *Mayflower* left Plymouth, England, packed with 102 passengers. Unlike previous voyages to the New World, the *Mayflower* emigrants included women and children. Sixty-five days after setting sail, the ship reached Provincetown, on the tip of Cape Cod. A colony was

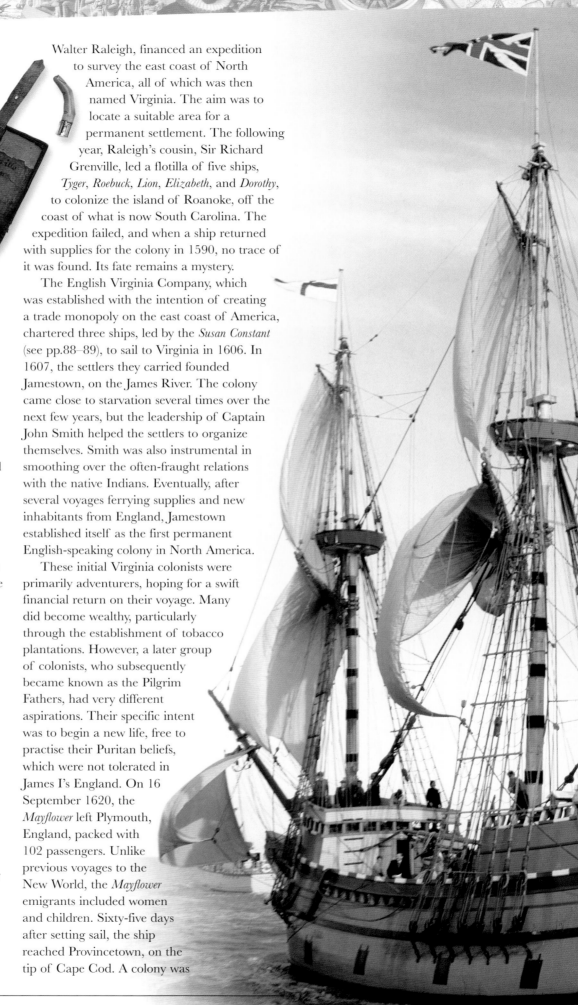

MAYFLOWER II
Before the historic voyage of the Pilgrim Fathers, the Mayflower plied the trade route between England and Bordeaux, France, exchanging cloth and fur for wine and brandy. The replica, Mayflower II (below), was constructed in 1956 and is based at Plymouth, Massachusetts, where the pilgrims first settled.

ARRIVAL IN JAMESTOWN
On 13 May 1607, the English Virginia Company's ships Susan Constant, Godspeed, and Discovery arrived at Jamestown, in Chesapeake Bay. This English painting depicts the landing of the settlers, who are greeted by the friendly native inhabitants.

established on the other side of the bay, named after their English port of departure. William Bradford, who was to become the colony's governor, described the arrival of the pilgrims in his account of the early days of the colony, *On Plymouth Plantation*, which was published in 1650: "Being thus passed the great ocean, and a sea of troubles before in their preparation … they had no friends to welcome them, nor inns to entertain or refresh their weatherbeaten bodies, no houses or much less towns." During the first harsh winter in their new environment, more than half of the pilgrims perished. The eventual survival of the colony was aided by help from the native Wampanoag Indians. Plymouth eventually flourished, and more ships began to carry settlers across the Atlantic. Colonies were established in New Hampshire in 1623; Salem, Massachusetts, which went on to

become one of the primary ports in America in the 18th century, was founded in 1628; and permanent settlements were established in Connecticut in 1633 and Rhode Island in 1636. The descendants of settlers of different parts of the eastern seaboard in the 1640s would eventually fight on opposing sides in the American Civil War: the Puritans of the north; and the plantation owners of the south.

Dutch traders and colonists
Even as they fought for their independence from the Spanish between 1568 and 1648, the Dutch developed a strong overseas trade in Europe and the rest of the world. Like the Hanseatic League before it (see p.45), the Dutch trading community was essentially a confederation of trading cities. The defeat of the Spanish Armada by the English (see p.101) removed the immediate threat to the Dutch, and maritime trade boomed. In 1602,

NEW ENGLAND
This map of 1614 shows the coast of New England. The area was named by Captain John Smith, whose portrait can be seen in the top left corner of the document.

SHIP'S BELL *The ship's bell was essential for summoning the crew and passengers, and in marking the passage of time through watches and parts of watches; its importance is here reflected in its elaborate housing at the forward end of the poop deck.*

ANCHOR *One of the anchors is suspended from the cathead in the bows, to prevent chafing against the wooden hull.*

RIGGING *This view from below shows the mainmast with its circular top. The rope shrouds that help to support the mast form the sides of a triangle. The main yard is just below the top.*

DEADEYE *Shaped like squashed spheres, deadeyes were used in pairs to tighten parts of the standing rigging, such as the shrouds and stays.*

QUARTER-DECK *A view forward shows how narrow the hull is near the stern.*

SWIVEL GUN *Besides her main armament of eight guns, the ship carried light swivel guns on her rails. These were breech loading, with a removable chamber near the rear of the gun.*

PARRELS *These ropes threaded with wooden beads were used to attach yards to masts, allowing the yards to swivel and to be raised and lowered.*

THE LOWER DECK *Most of the passengers lived on this deck, which also housed eight guns. The mainmast and the grating of an open hatch are on the right. There is a step up to the forepeak, for decks were rarely continuous in ships of this time.*

SUSAN CONSTANT

THE *SUSAN CONSTANT* BEGAN HER WORKING LIFE AS AN ORDINARY
THREE-MASTED MERCHANT SHIP. HOWEVER, SHE LATER PLAYED A
SIGNIFICANT PART IN THE EUROPEAN COLONIZATION OF AMERICA.

THE *SUSAN CONSTANT* was launched on the River Thames in 1605. She was chartered a year later for a voyage to North America, but this did not make her unique: Englishmen had tried before to colonize the New World but their attempts had ended in failure. The *Susan Constant*, accompanied by the smaller *Godspeed* and *Discovery*, took on a party of 71 quarrelsome men. Her captain, Christopher Newport, was an experienced explorer but the passengers were woefully ill-equipped. They arrived in Chesapeake Bay in April 1607, after a gruelling 5-month voyage, and Newport left them in the new settlement of Jamestown. Eventually, the colonists, led by Captain John Smith, would just survive, to found Virginia and form the first successful, permanent English-speaking settlement in America. Little is known about the *Susan Constant*. A re-creation in Virginia (shown here) is based on her known tonnage and what is known about standard naval architectural practices of the time.

The centre of activity on the ship was the upper deck, between the mainmast and the steering position. She was steered by means of a whipstaff, just inside the narrow steerage cabin under the quarter-deck, which was also the captain's cabin. At the stern, was the quarter-deck, with the mizzen mast running through its centre. Below the captain's cabin was the gunroom, slightly wider but with the tiller above making it uncomfortable to live in. Below that was a very low breadroom.

SUSAN CONSTANT
The Virginia replica of the Susan Constant is seen here under sail in a strong breeze coming from the port side. Her topsails are furled, and the spritsail under the bowsprit is set, showing one way it might have been used.

Under the main deck in the waist of the ship was the lower deck, with the ship's pumps and most of her eight small guns (known as minions and falcons). Most of the passengers lived there. Forward of that were three decks: the cookroom above; the forepeak for some of the crew below; and storerooms underneath that. There was an open gallery around the outside of the stern and a protruding beakhead in the bows. The ship's decoration was restrained, and in paint rather than carvings.

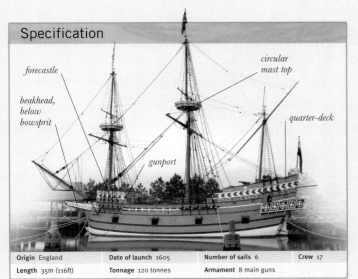

Specification

forecastle

beakhead, below bowsprit

circular mast top

quarter-deck

gunport

Origin England	Date of launch 1605	Number of sails 6	Crew 17
Length 35m (116ft)	Tonnage 120 tonnes	Armament 8 main guns	

STERN CABIN *The captain lived in a narrow, functional cabin in the stern, which housed the whipstaff. He provided the furniture himself.*

COOKROOM *The galley, a brick furnace over which cooking pots could be suspended, was situated high in the bows of the ship.*

BUNKS *Not much is known about living conditions onboard, but the passengers probably slept on straw mattresses in wooden bunks and tried to protect their privacy with canvas partitions. Most lived on the lower deck, among the guns.*

CABINS *The tiny wooden cabins in the aft cabin were probably used by the officers for sleeping. Meals were eaten at the communal table.*

NEW AMSTERDAM
This 1624 engraving by Dutch artist Jooste Hargers is the earliest known image of New Amsterdam (part of modern Manhattan). Among the craft visible are large three-masted Dutch sailing ships and native American canoes.

merchants from Amsterdam formed the Dutch East India Company. Over 1,500 ships bearing the company's seal were constructed in the next 200 years. In 1605, the Dutch took the port of Amboyna in the Spice Islands (now the Maluku Islands) from the Portuguese, establishing a base there. The region proved to be a lucrative source of spices, which were an extremely profitable commodity. By 1609 Dutch ships were trading in Japan, and they remained the only Europeans permitted to deal there until the mid-19th century.

The Dutch had been trading in North America for some time. In 1613 they established the colony of New Netherland, which extended from Delaware in the south to Albany in the north. The first ships carrying settlers arrived in 1626, and the island of Manhattan was purchased from the Algonquin Indians in the same year. The Dutch also took possession of the Cape of Good Hope in 1652, a key staging post on voyages to the East Indies.

TRADING COMPANY
This is the seal of the Dutch East India Company (Verenigde Oostindische Compagnie), a 17th-century economic giant.

Caribbean colonies

With the Spanish firmly established in the Caribbean, their great maritime rivals, the English, sought to expand to the region. English colonization of the Atlantic and Caribbean islands started accidentally in 1609, when the *Sea Venture* was wrecked at Bermuda on a voyage to Virginia. All 150 passengers survived the wreck, building two further ships, in which some continued to Virginia. Others remained at Bermuda, establishing a successful community, which was formally annexed by England in 1612. This stimulated the search for prospective colonies, particularly among the outlying islands of the Caribbean, where Spanish control was weak. English influence expanded to St. Kitts in 1624, followed by Barbados, Nevis, Antigua, and Montserrat over the next decade. The islands had all been discovered by Columbus but remained unoccupied by the Spanish. Barbados was of particular strategic value in the days of sail as it is the easternmost of the Caribbean islands. The French also took the opportunity to colonize the region, settling on the island of Martinique in 1635, followed by Guadeloupe and St-Barthélémy. They also settled in the west of Hispaniola in 1697, forming the extremely profitable outpost of Haiti. These islands were effectively plantations. By the 1640s, sugar cane was the most popular crop in the Caribbean. Both the French and the English garnered huge profits from the trade, and it contributed to the expansion of several European ports, including Nantes.

The start of the African slave trade

Initially, some of the labour for the New World was provided by indentured servants, who had travelled from Europe on a free passage with the agreement that they would work for a specific amount of time in return. Native labour was also used, but the spread of diseases, to which the indigenous inhabitants of the New World had no immunity, dramatically decreased the native population. The huge demand for goods from the Caribbean and the Americas led to an increased requirement for labour, which was provided by the brutal and horrific African slave trade. Spain and Portugal had traded in African slaves before the discovery of America in 1492 and began shipping them to their Atlantic and Caribbean colonies in the 16th century. African slaves were cheap and, if they survived the voyage across the Atlantic, they were hardy. They were utilized in tobacco, cotton, and sugar fields; in the search for precious metals; and as domestic servants. By 1500, about 5,000 slaves were transported to the Americas every year. It is estimated that nearly 300,000 African men, women, and children were exported across the Atlantic between 1450 and 1600. They toiled throughout Spanish America and often outnumbered their owners: in 1590, Chile's population included 9,000 Europeans and 20,000 African slaves.

Already there were protests about the inhumanity of the trade and the conditions on the ships that transported the slaves, which are estimated to have had a mortality rate of up to 80 per cent. Nevertheless, sailors from other nations, such as the Englishman John Hawkins (see panel, above), recognized that the trade was lucrative and attempted to break into it. By the

> 66 Slavery is the beginning of all offences and travails, it is a perpetual death, a living death in which people die even while they are alive. 99
>
> **ALONSO DE SANDOVAL**, Jesuit writer, **1627**

KING OF THE KONGO
This 1686 image shows Don Alfonso Alvares, King of the west African Kongo tribe, greeting Dutch ambassadors. African rulers traded goods, including their own people, with Europeans.

early 17th century, English and French colonies in the Caribbean and along the eastern seaboard of America were just as hungry for slaves to work their plantations as their Spanish counterparts. The grim trade increased still further in the 18th century (see pp.150–51).

The English East India Company

The English East India Company was founded in 1600, with the intent of trading in India, the Far East, and the East Indies. Like its Dutch counterpart, the company constructed its own vessels. The largest of the company's early ships was the *Trades Increase*, a 1,300-ton craft that was built in 1610. Several more ships of about 1,000 tons were built in the next decade, although they sailed badly and by the 1640s they were mostly about 500 tons. The ships were primarily built in England; the main shipbuilder for the Royal Navy in the early 17th century, William Burrell, was an official of the East India Company as well as being their leading contractor.

English interest in the Spice Islands of the East Indies led to sporadic conflict with the Dutch, who were determined to maintain their dominance in the region. In one incident in 1623, 18 English colonists, who had established a settlement in the islands and attempted to gain a foothold in the trade, were tortured and massacred by the Dutch at Amboyna. By 1650, European nations had divided the most desirable areas of the world between themselves. However, the next 150 years witnessed many seaborne wars between Britain, France, Spain, and the Netherlands, in which many of these new colonies changed hands regularly.

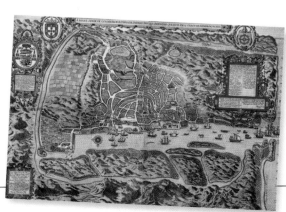

GOA
This map of Goa, on the west coast of India, was engraved in 1595. The Portuguese colony was a key trading post on the route to the East Indies.

SPICE TRADE
This somewhat romanticized view of the spice trade in the Maluku Islands is taken from the French atlas, Cosmographie Universelle, which was created in 1555 for the cartographer and mariner Guilliame le Testu.

CANNONBALLS RECOVERED FROM THE WRECK OF
THE ENGLISH WARSHIP *MARY ROSE*

GUNPOWDER AND SAIL

THE INVENTION OF THE GUN AND THE RISE OF THE GALLEON WOULD LEAD TO FAR-REACHING CHANGES IN NAVAL WARFARE.

> " I send my ships to fight against the English, and not against the winds and the waves. Praise be to God! "
>
> **PHILIP II OF SPAIN**, after the defeat of his Armada, **1588**

Gunpowder is an explosive mixture of sulphur (which gives out intense heat when burned), potassium nitrate (which provides oxygen for combustion), and charcoal (which provides fuel). It was invented by the Chinese in the tenth century AD, but was used mainly for fireworks. In Europe, the first known mention of gunpowder was by the English friar Roger Bacon in 1260. Guns were used in the defence of Florence in 1326 and at the sea battle of Sluys in 1340 (see p.42–43).

In their early days, guns onboard a ship created as many problems as they solved. If the powder was too strong, a gun might explode. It was not easy to find a place to store gunpowder where it would be safe from fire, but would not be ruined by water. The gun itself was difficult to load, and a powerful one was very heavy. If mounted low in the ship, it would reduce the freeboard and make capsizing more likely. If high up, it affected stability. For 150 years after the first known use of guns, they remained secondary to hand-held weapons such as the arrow, spear, sword, and later the musket.

Galleys could be fitted with a limited number of large guns, firing forward over the prow to supplement and to some extent replace the traditional attack by ramming and boarding. They could also carry small swivel guns along the sides above the rowers, designed to kill or wound the crew of an enemy ship.

It was the invention of the gunport around 1500 that allowed the further development of guns on ships. It was easier to cut a hole in the side of a carvel-built ship than a clinker-built one, in which the unity of the planking was a major structural feature. The hole was placed between two of the main frames so that the integrity of the hull was not affected, and it was fitted with a hinged port-lid, which was closed in rough weather or when the ship was heeling to one side. The gunport allowed a ship to carry much heavier guns without mounting them high in the hull and losing stability.

KEY EVENTS

1563 BALTIC WARS BEGIN In the first modern naval war, Sweden and Denmark fight for supremacy in the Baltic region.

1571 BATTLE OF LEPANTO The last naval battle fought between galleys ends in defeat of the Turks by a Christian coalition.

1588 SPANISH ARMADA FAILS Nearly half the ships of the Spanish Armada are lost during an attempt to invade England.

1591 EARLY IRONCLADS Korean Admiral Yi Sunshin invents the *geobukseon*, or turtle ship, an early type of ironclad warship.

1628 SWEDEN'S FLAGSHIP LOST The pride of the Swedish Navy, the 1,300-ton *Vasa*, sinks on her maiden voyage.

1639 DUTCH DEFEAT SPANISH A fleet of Dutch ships defeats the Spanish Navy in the Battle of the Downs on 21 October.

BATTLE OF OLAND
The Battle of Oland, near the island of Gotland on 14 August 1564, was one of seven major naval battles fought between Sweden and Denmark for dominion of the Baltic Sea during the Baltic Wars of 1563–70. In this painting, guns can be seen protruding from the ships' open gunports.

MARY ROSE
Part of an illustrated list of Henry VIII's Navy, this is the only contemporary picture of the Mary Rose after she was rebuilt in 1536 and fitted with 91 guns.

The rise of the English Navy

King Henry VIII of England, who reigned from 1509 to 1547, was one of the first to appreciate the importance of gun power in sailing ships. He increased the size of the small navy he had inherited, building the 600-ton carrack *Mary Rose* of 1510, which handled well and proved to be an impressively stable gun platform against the French during the war of 1512–14. He was influenced by his cousin King James IV of Scotland, who built a large warship, the *Great Michael* of about 1,200 tons in 1511, in spite of the poverty of his kingdom. Henry replied with the *Henri Grace à Dieu* of 1514, of 1,500 tons.

HENRY VIII
In 1534, Henry VIII issued the Act of Supremacy, which declared the king to be the head of the Church of England. He then seized all the property of the monasteries.

In the 1530s, Henry divorced Catherine of Aragon, broke with the Roman Catholic Church, and dissolved the monasteries, releasing a vast amount of wealth into his treasury. He was richer than any English monarch before him, but he had made enemies abroad. War broke out with France again in 1543, and on 19 July 1545 the *Mary Rose* sank

COINAGE
These silver coins were recovered from the wreck of the Mary Rose. In January 1545, the monthly wage of her 200 mariners was raised to six shillings and eight pence (£0.33/$0.6) each. This was a day's pay for an admiral.

while executing a turn during a battle with a French invasion fleet off Portsmouth on the south coast of England.

An illustrated list of Henry VIII's fleet, compiled by the clerk of ordnance Anthony Anthony in 1546 and known as the Anthony Roll, gives a detailed picture of what might be called the first modern navy. It was the king's own navy, not one supplied by subject princes, nobles, or merchant cities, like previous north European navies. It was largely made up of purpose-built warships, not former merchant ships. At first sight, it might seem to be dominated by rowing vessels, like the Mediterranean navies, as 38 out of the 58 craft named could be rowed. But, in fact, 23 of these were very small – the ten "pynnaces" averaged 50 tons and were small sailing ships that could be rowed on occasion. The 13 "roo-barges" averaged 20 tons and were little more than armed boats. The 15 galleasses (see p.100) were much closer to the Mediterranean tradition and were clearly intended for rowing, although more heavily armed than the traditional galley – the *Anne Gallant*, of about 450 tons, had 50 brass and iron guns. But the real core of Henry's fleet was the group of 20 "shippes", from the old *Grace Dieu* to the *Mary James* of 60 tons and 40 men. The ships comprised more than half the tonnage of the navy, twice that of the galleys. They used twice as many men as the galleys, 5,037 against 2,520. More than half of them were of more than 400 tons, making them substantial fighting ships. But they were still a coastal defence force rather than a long-distance or "blue-water" navy. England had no overseas interests at the time, except for Ireland and the French port of Calais, which was subsequently lost by Henry's daughter Mary in 1558.

Naval guns

Although guns were not the only weapons used at sea, their importance increased in the 16th and 17th centuries. Cast guns (see panel, right) came in several types. Short, fat guns, such as mortars and howitzers, were rare onboard ships, except in specialized vessels. Cannons were the most common type of larger guns; the cannon proper fired a ball of 42lb (19kg) in the English Navy, and the more common demi-cannon had one of 32lb (14.5kg). The most common guns of all in the 17th century were culverins – long,

narrow guns with balls of 18lb (8kg) – and demi-culverins of 9lb (4kg). The Dutch introduced intermediate categories of guns, of 12lb (5.5kg) and 24lb (11kg). Smaller guns, mostly for use against personnel, included sakers, minions, and serpentines.

Early carriages, especially for breech-loading guns, were simply fixed beds of wood. Some copied land artillery and were mounted on a

BLOCKS

wooden pulley

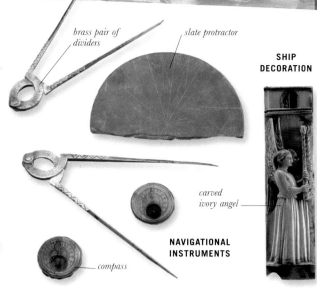

brass pair of dividers — *slate protractor*

SHIP DECORATION

carved ivory angel

NAVIGATIONAL INSTRUMENTS

compass

MARY ROSE ARTEFACTS
The wreck of the Mary Rose was located in the 1970s, and more than 25,000 objects were brought ashore before the hull was raised in 1982. The artefacts include navigational and medical equipment, sailing tackle, and weapons.

pair of large wheels. But later carriages had four small wheels, known as trucks. Heavy ropes were used to restrain the recoil of the gun, and to haul it into place after loading.

GUN TYPES

Early guns were made by craftsmen and often had individual names, such as Mons Meg, which was presented to King James II of Scotland in 1457. Guns could be made in two ways, either by assembling with staves and hoops (hence the term "barrel" of a gun) or by casting in one piece. Wrought guns, made in several pieces, were often breech-loaders, with a detachable chamber that contained the explosive. They were usually made of iron and were quite small, as anything bigger might explode, with dangerous consequences. Larger guns were cast in a copper alloy, commonly known as bronze, and were often heavily

decorated with the emblems of the state or the maker. A cast gun was essentially a tube closed at one end, with a small touch-hole for setting off the powder. It was loaded by ramming gunpowder and shot in from the muzzle. It had a complex breech with a ball or cascable at the end, thicker rings round its length, and a trunnion on each side to form a pivot on its carriage.

Cast-iron guns were much cheaper than bronze ones but were regarded as unreliable until the early years of the 17th century, when the English began to cast them in large numbers. The Swedes, with good supplies of ore, developed iron guns for export and for merchant shipping. Brass guns, however, were retained for prestige on flagships in most navies until near the end of the 18th century.

MUZZLE-LOADING GUN
Henry VIII encouraged the development of a gun-founding industry, and this cast-bronze gun weighing 1,135kg (2,500lb) was made for him in London. It was recovered from the wreck of the Mary Rose.

lion's head decoration — *gun pivots on trunnion* — *barrel cast in single piece*

breech

cascable forms rear end of breech

replica wooden gun carriage

truck (wheel)

KHEIR-ED-DIN (BARBAROSSA)

Born on the Turkish-held Greek island of Lesbos, Kheir-ed-Din (*c*.1483–1546) was descended from European slaves. He went to sea with his elder brother, Aruj, and in about 1504 they began to raid European ships from the North African port of Tunis. From 1510, they were based on the island of Djerba, to the south. In 1518, they took Algiers from Spain and Aruj became Sultan, but later that year he was killed by an invading Spanish force. By 1529, Kheir-ed-Din was in control of the Algerian coast, and in 1533 he was appointed head of the Ottoman Navy by Suleiman I. He harried the Spanish, Venetians, and Greeks by raiding coastal towns, and in 1538 he defeated the Spanish Fleet of Emperor Charles V in a three-day engagement at Préveza in the eastern Ionian Sea.

Barbary corsairs

In the early 16th century, the Ottoman Empire expanded, taking over the North African coast. It was assisted by Kheir-ed-Din (see panel, left), known in Europe as Barbarossa. The epic Christian–Muslim struggle in the Mediterranean culminated in the Battle of Lepanto (see panel, opposite), after which it was less intense. Following the pattern set by Barbarossa, it continued as an informal war on European trade, conducted by the corsairs (or pirates as their enemies called them) based in North African ports such as Algiers, Tunis, and Tripoli. The corsairs developed a fast craft called the *xebec*, which combined rowing and sailing very effectively. It was similar to the Venetian *galeotta*, or small galley, but had a widened hull amidships, which gave it very fine lines. The overhang of the stern was larger than normal, and it had a pointed projection in the bow. In its most common form, it had three masts, with the foremast raked well forward and the mizzen slightly aft. It carried a lateen sail on each mast, plus a triangular jib sail on the bowsprit. The *xebec* was copied by the French and Spanish in the 18th century. Called a chebec, it was sometimes rigged with square sails on the main and mizzen masts.

TORTURING CHRISTIANS
These gruesome prints in a French book show the various ways in which Europeans imprisoned on the Barbary Coast would allegedly be tortured for being Christian.

The corsairs dominated the Mediterranean, and everyone who travelled by sea had to take into account the risk of capture by them. Captives were enslaved, or held to ransom if they were from a wealthy family. Corsairs also operated outside the Mediterranean and reached the northern European coasts and islands, taking advantage of any local naval weakness. In 1631, for example, the village of Baltimore in Ireland was raided and 100 people, almost the entire population, were taken into slavery.

DEATH OR SLAVERY
Spanish crewmen desperately leap into the water as their ship burns, having been attacked by Barbary corsairs. The survivors would have been sold into slavery.

THE BATTLE OF LEPANTO

When two great fleets faced one another off Lepanto at the entrance to the Gulf of Corinth in Greece on 7 October 1571, they seemed evenly matched to the uninformed observer. The Turkish Fleet, inside the Gulf, had about 240 galleys and other vessels drawn up in line abreast in three squadrons, under the overall command of Ali Pasha. The opposing fleet of 200 galleys of the Holy League of Christian states also had three squadrons in its first line and another behind the centre. The Christian Fleet was under the overall command of Don John (see p.100) representing Spain, and the Genoese Admiral Andrea Doria led the right wing. Venice and Malta also sent ships.

However, when the battle began in earnest around midday, the differences between the Turkish and Christian fleets began to emerge. The Christians had more gun power, with the heavy guns mounted to fire forward. Four of their heaviest armed ships, the galleasses, were placed forward of the main fleets. The Turks tried to use their superior knowledge of the shallow waters to outflank the Christians, but their right flank was defeated, and the centre was broken by the galleasses, after which the remaining ships on the Turkish left were forced to withdraw, although half were left behind.

ALI PASHA
The commander of the Turkish fleet, Ali Pasha was beheaded by the Spanish when they boarded his ship.

The casualty figures compare with a 20th-century battle. In all, the Turks lost 200 galleys, with 30,000 men killed or wounded, 3,000 Turks taken prisoner, and 15,000 Christian galley slaves released. The Christians lost 10 galleys, and had 7,500 men killed and 20,000 wounded. Lepanto was the last great galley battle, and marked the end of Turkish expansion towards the western Mediterranean.

BATTLE FORMATION
The Turkish Fleet (on the right) attacked in a crescent, but the Christian allies proved more powerful in the centre and eventually won the day.

Like the Barbary corsairs, the citizens of Dunkirk on the north coast of France also developed small, fast vessels, known as frigates, for raiding in the English Channel, although few details survive. The Barbary and Dunkirk corsairs caused navies to rethink their strategy

MIGUEL DE CERVANTES
Before he became a writer, Cervantes took part in the Battle of Lepanto in 1571, then, in 1575, he was captured by Barbary corsairs and sold as a slave in Algiers. He was ransomed in 1580.

in the early 17th century. However, monarchs preferred large, prestigious warships, whereas merchants wanted small, fast, and numerous vessels to protect their shipping. The English, for example, failed to produce an adequate response until the Civil War of the 1640s, when the Parliamentary side began to copy Dunkirk frigates.

In the Mediterranean, the Knights of St. John were the most determined opponents of the Muslims at sea, whether operating as great fleets or as corsairs. At first, they fought as warrior-monks in the Holy Land in 1118, then based themselves in Rhodes in 1310. They were forced to abandon the island by the Turks in 1523 and took up residence in Malta. They were besieged by a Turkish fleet in 1565 but survived. The knights founded the city of Valletta between two great natural harbours and heavily fortified the area, with the support of the noble families of Catholic Europe. They built up a substantial fleet, mostly of galleys, in the 16th and 17th centuries, and contributed skill and discipline to Christian naval forces.

THE BATTLE OF LEPANTO
This painting by the 16th-century Venetian artist Andrea Micheli depicts the Battle of Lepanto of 1571. This was the last naval action fought by galleys manned by oarsmen.

DON JOHN OF AUSTRIA

Born in Bavaria, the illegitimate son of Emperor Charles V, Don John (1547–78) was brought up in Spain, where his father was also king. His half-brother, Phillip II, became king in 1556. Declining to enter the church, Don John was appointed Captain-General of the Sea, the head of the Spanish Navy, at the age of 21. A daring soldier and a handsome, charismatic leader, he commanded the forces against a Muslim rebellion in Granada. In 1571, he became the Captain-General of the Holy League formed by the Catholic powers against the Turks. He had to use all his skill and charm to keep his fractious allies, including Malta and Venice, united. In October, he defeated the Turks at sea at the Battle of Lepanto. He was ambitious for a kingdom of his own and hoped to marry Mary, Queen of Scots, but he died of typhoid in 1578.

The galley, galleass, and galleon

The oarsman's job on a galley gradually declined from a post of honour to one carried out by the lowest in society. In 1549, those in Venice were divided into three classes. Convicts were completely shaven on the scalp and face. Slaves were prisoners of war, or had been bought in slave markets, and included Turks, Africans, and Moors. They were also shaven, except for a tuft of hair on the head. Volunteers came from the poorest classes in society. They were paid

GALLEY
The 16th-century Venetian bucintoro, *or state galley, shown in this print is being propelled by the* a scaloccio *system of rowing, whereby each oar is pulled by five to seven men.*

wages and wore moustaches to distinguish them from the others, but were chained when rowing. Around the same time, the system of rowing changed to accommodate the lesser skills and enthusiasm of the rowers. Instead of one oar for each man, galleys began to adopt the *a scaloccio* system, in which five to seven men pulled at each oar. One man, the *pianero*, controlled the oar and the others had to keep pace with him.

The larger merchant galleys of Venice during the 15th century were sometimes known as galleasses, and in the middle of the next century a new type emerged bearing the same name. Unlike the low-hulled galley, it had high castles at the bow and stern, so that it had a much heavier gun armament than the galley, and its heavy guns fired in all directions rather than just forward. Galleasses were adopted by most European navies in small numbers. Although quite rare, they were important ships in several battles, including Lepanto, and the Spanish Armada campaign.

The term galleon originated in the second quarter of the 16th century, although it is not always clear what it meant in a particular place or time. The Venetians built a galleon between 1526 and 1530 as a compromise between the long, narrow galley and the cargo-carrying round ship, but their efforts were not successful and, with little interest in the project outside the Mediterranean, they did not develop the idea any further. The Spanish were making galleons by 1540. They were built as warships, and had long, narrow hulls with a relatively heavy armament. They had quite large, although narrow, superstructures

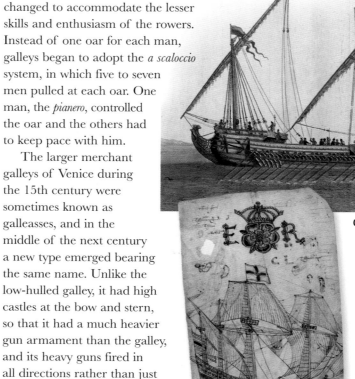

GALLEASS
This French engraving shows a galleass under oar with its sails tightly furled. A hybrid of a galley and galleon, galleasses were developed in the 16th century.

GALLEON
Designed and built in the late 16th century, this full-rigged ship, or galleon, belonged to the English Navy of Queen Elizabeth I.

and were built in substantial numbers from the 1550s onwards. The term was used in Portugal to describe a purpose-built sailing warship that is thought to have evolved from the carrack. The English rarely used the term galleon to describe their own ships, but they took the concept further than anyone else. Under John Hawkins, Treasurer of the Navy from 1577, they began to develop the "race-built" ship with highly characteristic lower stern and bow castles, greatly improving its sailing qualities.

The Baltic wars

In 1563, Sweden and Denmark embarked on the Nordic Seven Years' War, as they fought for control of the maritime trade and invasion routes in the Baltic Sea. Seven major naval battles ensued, including the Battle of Oland in 1564, in which the Danes, supported by ships from the Hanseatic city of Lübeck, defeated the Swedes, who lost their new royal flagship, *Mars*. With neither side gaining supremacy, a truce was finally agreed in 1570 and Denmark retained control of the Sound, a key sea route between the Baltic and the North Sea.

The Dutch, Spanish, and English

In 1566, the Protestant residents of the Netherlands revolted against their Roman Catholic master, King Philip II of Spain. It was a David-and-Goliath struggle on a grand scale

THE SPANISH ARMADA

On 30 May 1588, after many delays, Philip II of Spain's great force, known to its enemies as the Spanish Armada and to the Spaniards as the Invincible Armada, finally sailed from Lisbon. It included around 150 ships carrying about 7,000 sailors, 18,000 soldiers, nearly 1,500 brass guns, and almost 1,000 smaller iron ones. The Spanish had several quarrels with the English, but the most immediate one was that they supported the Protestant Dutch in their rebellion against the

ARMADA ROUTE
Published in 1590 in England, this print shows the track of the Armada through the English Channel, into the North Sea, and then back into the Atlantic to return to Spain.

Spanish crown. The plan was to sail up the English Channel to the Netherlands, where the ships would link up with the main Spanish army fighting the Dutch, and transport it to England. But there was a fatal flaw, even without English intervention: there was no good port in Spanish hands to embark the troops, and a small Dutch force could quite easily prevent it happening. Hindered by heavy weather, the Armada made a slow passage north and did not enter the English Channel until late July. It sailed in an arrowhead formation, keeping close to the English coast, hoping to terrorize the natives and looking for any opportunity to land. On 29 July, the English commanders, Howard of Effingham and Francis Drake, were told of the fleet's approach, and many

COMMEMORATIVE MEDAL
Struck in 1588, this silver medal (both sides shown) commemorates the defeat of the Spanish Armada.

warning beacons were lit along the coast. The English Fleet sailed out and began to attack the Spanish in a series of daytime raids. The English ships were careful not to get too close, knowing that the Spanish had much larger numbers of soldiers for use in a boarding action. Instead, they used gunnery at a relatively long range, moving in closer later in the battle, but after a week of action they had done little real damage. The Spanish ships anchored off Dunkirk, northern France, and were dispersed by English fireships on 7 August.

The Armada retreated by sailing round the north of Scotland and west of Ireland, where many ships were wrecked by storms. In the religious climate of the times, both sides saw that as divine intervention, rather than just luck.

DOOMED CAMPAIGN
This painting by an unknown artist symbolizes the Armada campaign as a whole. In the foreground, a Spanish galleass flying the papal banner is flanked by two English ships.

but also in microcosm. The tiny converted merchant ships and fishing boats of the Dutch were deployed against the great galleons of Spain, raiding naval transports and bases. The Dutch were known contemptuously as the "sea beggars" in their early days, and their reputation was not enhanced when they began to turn to piracy against any shipping they could find. But they seized the harbour city of Briel in April 1572, providing the Dutch rebels under William of Orange with a stronghold. Small ships were a great advantage in Dutch

waters, filled with sandbanks and with numerous islands, marshes, and canals. According to an English traveller, it was: "the great bog of Europe … They are a universal quagmire … full of veins and blood, but no bones in it." Over the next 80 years, the Netherlands were to prove a quagmire for the Spanish in more senses than one, draining their strength and prestige and involving them in other debilitating wars.

The quarrel between England and Spain was partly religious, especially after the accession of Queen Elizabeth I in 1558 confirmed the Protestant succession. Elizabeth herself was conciliatory but her people, inspired by the anti-Spanish activities of Sir John Hawkins, Sir Francis Drake (see panel, right), and many others, hoped for national prestige and plunder

PHILIP II OF SPAIN

King Philip II ruled Spain from 1556 until his death in 1598, during which time the Battle of Lepanto was won by Christian forces, the Dutch began their fight for independence from Spain, and English support for the Dutch led him to send the Armada to invade England.

from the wealthy and rather unwieldy Spanish empire.

In 1587, on the eve of war, Drake launched a pre-emptive strike on the Spanish port of Cadiz, southwest Spain. The English defeat of the Spanish Armada in 1588 (see panel, p.101) removed the immediate threat of invasion of England, but it did not end the war, which dragged on for another 15 years.

ELIZABETH I

The daughter of Henry VIII and his second wife, Anne Boleyn, Elizabeth ascended the throne of England in 1558. She ruled for 44 years until her death in 1603.

RAID ON CADIZ

On 30 June 1596, an Anglo-Dutch Fleet arrived off the coast of Cadiz, southwest Spain. The defending Spanish Fleet was defeated, and troops led by the Earl of Essex plundered the city on 5 July.

Naval tactics of the period were based on the fact that guns were difficult to load, so each gun was fired in succession by turning the ship to bring it to bear. The ship then retreated to reload. A graphic description is given by the English Captain John Smith, founder of Virginia, in his *Sea Grammar* of 1627: "Edge in with him againe, begin with your bow peeces, proceed with your broad side, & let fall off with the wind, to give her also your full chase, your weather broad side, and bring her round that the sterne may also discharge, and your tackes close on board againe!" Broadside guns were not the most important at this time and, according to the English adventurer Sir Walter Raleigh: "a man of war doth pretend to fought most with its prow." All-round firepower was particularly useful when sailing ships confronted galleys. At Cadiz in 1596, an Anglo-Dutch fleet of sailing ships won a battle against Spanish galleys, and when nine Spanish galleys were attacked by the English in the Straits of Dover in 1602 only one escaped. The sailing ship had established its superiority.

FRANCIS DRAKE

Brought up on the River Medway in southeast England, where his father was a Puritan naval chaplain, Sir Francis Drake (c.1540–96) went to sea at the age of 13. In 1564, he sailed with Sir John Hawkins on a slaving voyage, and in 1567 their ships were captured by the Spanish on the coast of Mexico. In 1570–71, Drake took revenge by raiding Spain's possessions in the Caribbean, gaining great popularity in England but being regarded as a pirate by the Spanish. In 1577–80, he became the first English captain to circumnavigate the world. Queen Elizabeth I bowed to popular opinion and knighted Drake on the Golden Hind at Deptford.

THE EIGHTY YEARS' WAR

The Dutch struggle for independence from Spain lasted until 1648, during which time they fought several sea battles with the Spanish, winning some impressive victories and gaining valuable experience of naval warfare.

ALONSO PEREZ DE GUZMAN

Alonso Pérez de Guzmán (1550–1619), also known as the Duke of Medina-Sidonia, inherited his dukedom in 1555 and a vast fortune on the death of his grandfather in 1559. A Spaniard, he gained distinction in the conquest of Portugal in 1580–81, and in 1587 he drove Sir Francis Drake off from his raid on Cadiz. On the death of the Marquis of Santa Cruz in 1588, he was appointed commander-in-chief of the Spanish Armada against England. King Philip II was influenced by his good reputation among the Portuguese, who would form a large part of the Armada, and by his high social and political status. Medina-Sidonia had no wish to take part in the enterprise and had little faith in its success, but he felt obliged to do his duty. With little seafaring experience, he had to rely on the advice of others, but that was common in royal fleets at the time. He managed to get home in his flagship *San Martin* and was not blamed for the defeat of the Armada. He retired to his estates.

SOMERSET HOUSE CONFERENCE
A Spanish–Flemish delegation (seated on the left) negotiated a peace treaty with an English delegation at Somerset House, London, on 19 August 1604, ending England's war with Spain.

England, under its new King James I, made peace with Spain in 1604. However, the Dutch revolt continued, and in 1618 it was linked with a great European struggle, the Thirty Years' War. This produced several small naval battles, but the largest naval encounter of the first half of the century was in the Downs, off the coast of southeast England in 1639, when 100 small Dutch ships confronted 70 much larger Spanish ones. The English, weakened by internal strife that would soon lead to civil war, were unable to defend their territorial waters. The Spanish were thrown into confusion by a

fireship attack by the English and lost many ships. Finally, in 1648, the Spanish were forced to concede Dutch independence. The Dutch had long had the best trading fleet in the world, they had gained a colonial empire in the East (see p.90), they had some of best seamen in the world, and they now had more experience of naval warfare than almost any country. A new naval power had entered the stage.

Naval warfare in the Far East

In the 1580s, the Japanese warlord Toyotomi Hideyoshi began the political unification of Japan. By 1592, he had succeeded and turned his attention to the invasion of neighbouring Korea, capturing the castle at Pusan in the southeast of the country. The Koreans fought back, conducting a campaign of guerrilla warfare against the invaders on land and attacking their supply ships at sea. The Korean Navy had the advantage of a brand new type of warship, the *geobukseon*, or turtle ship. Admiral Yi Sunshin, the commander of the Cholla Left Naval Station at Yosu, had begun their design and construction in 1591 as a means of defence against Japanese pirates. A two-masted galley

KOREAN IRONCLAD
This life-sized replica of a turtle ship resides in the Naval Academy Museum, Korea. When the ship engaged in combat, a cannon could be fired through the mouth of the dragon's head at the bow or embers could be burned to create a smoke screen.

NOCTURNAL
Nocturnals were used by sailors in the northern hemisphere to read the position of the stars like the hour hand of a clock, as they appear to circle anti-clockwise around the Pole Star every 24 hours. This elaborate example was made in 1589 by Amerigo Leone of Rome.

whose deck was covered with iron sheets studded with spikes to deter boarders, the turtle ship was a precursor of the ironclad ships that would take a further two centuries to appear in the West. It was equipped with cannons that could be fired

> ❝ In an instant, our warships spread their sails, turned round in a 'Crane-Wing' formation and darted forward, pouring down cannon balls and fire arrows on the enemy vessels like hail and thunder. Bursting into flame with blinding smoke, 73 enemy vessels were soon burning in a red sea of blood. ❞

YI PUN, on the Korean victory at Hansando, **1592**

through ten gun ports along each side, and one at the stern, and two at the bow. But its most fearsome aspect was the dragon's head at the bow (see left). Archers were carried onboard to shoot burning arrows at the sails and rigging of enemy ships.

In July 1592, Yi Sunshin led a Korean fleet that destroyed 73 Japanese ships in a battle at Hansando, a victory that was recorded by his nephew Yi Pun. He achieved another impressive victory in September 1597, when he led 12 turtle ships against a fleet of over 130 Japanese ships in the Myongnang Straits, sinking 31 of them as the rest retreated. Yi Sunshin was killed by a stray bullet on 19 November 1598 during the final battle of the Hideyoshi invasions, which was won by Korea.

Royal glories

The first half of the 17th century was an age of insecure monarchy in Europe, in which the Spanish faced revolt in the Netherlands, the French king was weakened by a revolt of the nobles known as the Fronde, and the English king was executed in 1649. One royal reaction to this was to demonstrate the glory of monarchy, which included building the largest and most spectacular ship possible as the flagship of the fleet. King James I, who had become the first king of both England and Scotland in 1603, was impoverished for most of his reign, but that did

SAMURAI WILLIAM
In 1598, William Adams arrived in Kyushu, southwest Japan, the first Englishman to visit the country. He built two ships for the feudal lord Tokugawa Ieyasu and taught him navigational skills, for which he was rewarded with the rank and holdings of a samurai.

not stop him building the *Prince Royal*, of 1,200 tons and 55 guns, in 1610. King Gustavus Adolphus of Sweden commissioned the Dutch shipwright Henrik Hybertszoon, who had been in his employ for several years, to build the *Vasa* of 1,300 tons, but she sank before leaving Stockholm Harbour on her maiden voyage in 1628 (see p.106–107). In 1634, James I's son, King Charles I, went considerably further, for he was determined, against expert advice, to build the first 100-gun ship. He authorized his favourite shipwright Phineas Pett to design the *Sovereign of the Seas* of 1,522 tons. She was built at Woolwich on the Thames at a cost of more than £65,000, and was launched in 1637. As a propaganda tool she backfired, for Charles's subjects resented the ship taxes he levied. The French King Louis XIII and his great minister Cardinal Richelieu sought glory by commissioning the *Couronne* of 1635, which was measured at 2,000 tons but carried only 72 guns. She was built in

MAGNIFICENT DECORATION
One means of reflecting the glory of Europe's royals was in the elaborate decoration of their flagships. Sweden's Vasa of 1628 had about 700 carvings. The stern bears the coat of arms of the Kingdom of Sweden, with the personal arms of the Vasa family (a wheat sheaf) superimposed.

France and represented a major shift in French policy, for at that time many French sailing warships were built in the Netherlands.

There were two trends in warship design by 1650: the building of large, heavy ships with as many guns as possible crammed into the broadside; and the development of long, fast frigates (see p.97). Together they produced changes in gunnery. Neither type could turn as well as the ships of an earlier generation, and it was claimed that ships such as the *Sovereign of the Seas*, "being heavy and wieldy withal", would not be able to turn in battle and could use only one broadside: "the same beaten side". Meanwhile there was a silent revolution in gunnery, in which ropes were fitted to make it easier to load the gun inboard in the heat of action, and more men were allocated to the guns. By the 1650s, warships were inclined to stand and fight with their broadsides rather than retreat to reload. They had much greater firepower than their predecessors, both in the number and weight of guns and in the amount of shot that each could fire in a given time. The time was ripe for another revolution in naval tactics, after which the gun would truly be supreme.

GUSTAVUS ADOLPHUS
Known as the Lion of the North, Gustavus Adolphus was a member of the Vasa dynasty that ruled Sweden from 1523 to 1654. Born in 1594, he held the throne from 1611 until 1632.

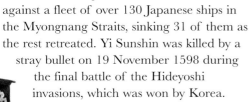

VASA

AS EUROPE'S MONARCHS VIED WITH EACH OTHER
TO PRODUCE THE LARGEST AND MOST ELABORATELY
DECORATED FLAGSHIP, SWEDEN'S *VASA* SAILED INTO
THE ARENA FOR A FEW MINUTES IN 1628.

THE *VASA* WAS BUILT in the Royal Dockyard in Stockholm by Henrik Hybertszoon, a Dutchman who had served the Swedish crown since the beginning of the 17th century. Named after the royal house of Vasa, she was intended by King Gustavus Adolphus to be the pride of the navy and to serve in his wars for control of the Baltic. She was one of the largest ships of the day, but was poorly designed with too much weight high up in the ship. On her maiden voyage on 10 August 1628, she foundered in Stockholm Harbour and sank with the loss of 30–50 lives. Her hull survived in the cold and muddy waters and she was raised in 1961, providing the most complete information available on a 17th-century warship. She is preserved in Stockholm.

From the outside, the *Vasa* presents an appearance of great solidity, even after three centuries in the water. Her hull is dark brown oak, with little trace of the paint that once dominated its upper sides. Decoration is concentrated at the bow and stern. The long beakhead has carved figures on each side, with another carving below, and ends with a lion figurehead, like most warships of the period.

On deck, the ship was steered by a very long whipstaff in a small room just forward of the mizzen mast, with windows that allowed the helmsman to keep an eye on the sails but gave him no view ahead of the ship. Aft of the whipstaff were cabins on three levels. At the highest, well aft on the poop deck above, was a tiny cabin, the function of which is unknown. Below that was a much larger space for officers, and below that was a beautifully decorated cabin for the captain or admiral. Forward of the whipstaff, the upper deck carried light guns towards the bow and stern, the capstan (which was placed well forward), and various attachments for the rigging. Below that was the upper gundeck, with a dozen 24-pounder guns on each side – possibly the ship's downfall as they were too heavy for a vessel of this size, being the same as those on the very similar lower gundeck. Both decks are dark and low, and they provided accommodation for most of the crew. Forward on the lower gundeck are huge riding bitts, vertical posts with a crosspiece to which the cable was attached when the ship was riding at anchor.

The cooking stove is very low in the ship, in the hold just forward of the mainmast. An iron pot was hung above a brick furnace. The orlop deck and the hold were both below the waterline, and the latter would have been filled with barrels.

MOMENTS FROM SINKING
In this imaginative watercolour painted in 1973, the Vasa is depicted with her sails filling for the first time as she sails across Stockholm Harbour, but already she is heeling over and the water is about to reach her gunports.

Specification

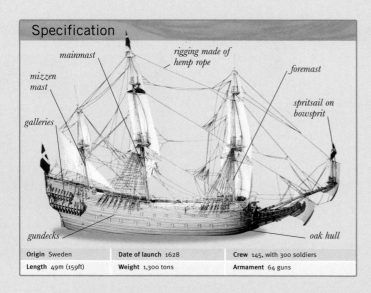

Origin Sweden	**Date of launch** 1628	**Crew** 145, with 300 soldiers	
Length 49m (159ft)	**Weight** 1,300 tons	**Armament** 64 guns	

Labels on diagram: mainmast, mizzen mast, galleries, gundecks, rigging made of hemp rope, foremast, spritsail on bowsprit, oak hull

RIDERS *These strong, internal timbers in the hold helped to support the heavy weight of the guns and gun decks. The marks made by the shipwrights' adzes are clearly visible.*

CAPSTAN *One of three capstans on the Vasa, this one on the upper deck was used for heavy work such as handling the running rigging. As on other ships of the period, the bars of the capstans on the Vasa passed all the way through and had to be set at different heights.*

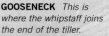

GOOSENECK *This is where the whipstaff joins the end of the tiller.*

CARVINGS *The Vasa carried more than 700 individual pieces of carving, including those on the stern and quarter galleries.*

PAINTWORK *Replica carvings on the roof of the quarter gallery have been painted to show how colourful the ship was when built.*

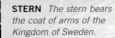

STERN *The stern bears the coat of arms of the Kingdom of Sweden.*

BEAKHEAD *The beakhead helps support the rigging and provides the crew's toilet accommodation.*

GUNPORT LID *Each lid bears a lion's head, which is the right way up when the gunport is open.*

STERN GUNPORTS *Forward and aft firing was considered important in the 1620s. The heavy structure of the lower stern is visible.*

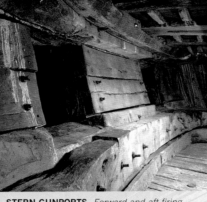

UPPER DECK LOOKING AFT *One of the bitts for attaching the rigging is on the left, and in front are the gratings, which give light to the decks below and access to the hold.*

FLAGSHIP *On the left are two rows of gunports. Above them are the rope shrouds, which support the masts. To the right are the enclosed quarter galleries on two levels, and the elaborate stern is behind them.*

GALLEYS, GALLEONS, AND GREAT SHIPS

The period from 1500 to 1650 saw the culmination and the decline of the rowing galley in the Mediterranean, the birth of the first ocean-going sailing warship, also in the form of the galley, and the first modern sea battles that used the gun as the primary weapon. More masts and sails were added to ships as sailors gained in confidence, and the mass migration to America began, creating a demand for ocean-going ships, freeing new resources, and opening up new markets.

TO THE NEW WORLD
These English ships are arriving in North America in 1584, to found Sir Walter Raleigh's unsuccessful colony at Roanoke.

Galleys

The late medieval galley used the *alla Zenzile* system, with three rowers per bench on each side. In around 1500, the new *a Scalaccio* system was introduced for galleys and galleasses. With five to seven men on each oar, it was more efficient and better adapted to the use of slaves. They could also be sailed when needed, although they were usually confined to short voyages. At the same time, galleys began to adopt forward-firing guns.

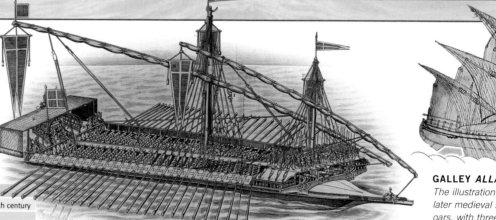

GALLEY *A SCALACCIO*

Origin Mediterranean, probably Italy	**Date of launch** Early 17th century
Length About 46m (150ft)	**Tonnage** Not known
Armament 5 heavy guns in bows	**Crew** 270 rowers, plus soldiers

GALLEY *ALLA ZENZILE*
The illustration above shows the later medieval system of arranging oars, with three men to a bench and an oar each.

Small warships

Although the main navies tended to focus on large prestigious ships during the early 17th century, there was also a need for smaller and faster ships to chase pirates and privateers. The frigate, with a low and narrow hull, was developed by the privateers of Dunkirk, then a Spanish possession. It was adopted by the English and Dutch navies, as pictured here, but they soon built up the sides to carry more guns.

CONSTANT WARWICK

Origin England	**Date of launch** 1645
Length 26m (85ft) (keel)	**Tonnage** 342 tons
Armament 32 guns	**Crew** 140

ENGLISH PINNACE
The early 17th-century English Navy had difficulty defending the coastline against pirates. This plan shows a sailing and rowing vessel for coastal patrols.

Galleasses

Combining the galley with the sailing ship, galleasses led the way to the galleon, which abandoned rowing but adopted the narrow hull. Galleasses were not suitable for rough seas, but some took part in the Spanish Armada campaign (see foreground, below).

SAN LORENZO

Origin Naples (for Spain)	**Date of launch** c.1580
Length Not known	**Tonnage** 600 tons
Armament 50 guns	**Crew** About 640

Galleons

The galleon emerged in Spain and Portugal around the middle of the 16th century, and it soon spread to England, France, and Italy. The word "galleon" is first mentioned in connection with oared vessels, but a Spanish model of about 1540 represents a pure sailing ship. It had a narrower beam than the carrack and was designed for fast sailing. The projecting beakhead in the bow was a common feature. It helped to support the bowsprit, but it became largely decorative on later ships. The English "race-built" galleon had a lower hull for greater speed. The galleon was so successful that it became one of the best-known sailing ships by name, and it began the development that led to the ship of the line and the frigate.

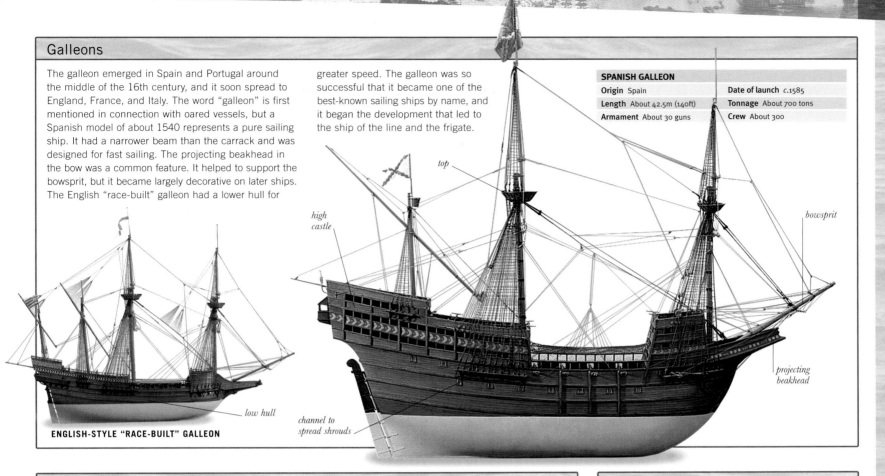

top

high castle

bowsprit

low hull

channel to spread shrouds

projecting beakhead

ENGLISH-STYLE "RACE-BUILT" GALLEON

SPANISH GALLEON	
Origin Spain	**Date of launch** *c.*1585
Length About 42.5m (140ft)	**Tonnage** About 700 tons
Armament About 30 guns	**Crew** About 300

Great ships

PRINCE ROYAL	
Origin England	**Date of launch** 1610
Length 35m (115ft) (keel)	**Tonnage** 1,200 tons
Armament 55 guns	**Crew** 500

King James I, the first monarch to combine the thrones of Scotland and England, revived the idea of large warships as a measure of royal prestige. He built a fleet of "great ships" from 1618 onwards and was followed by his son Charles I. The ships tended to be broader and more heavily armed than the Elizabethan galleons they replaced. They also featured a large amount of decoration. Most of them weighed about 900 tons, but the *Prince Royal* (below) was much larger. The biggest ship of the day, it pointed the way to even larger ships that were to come.

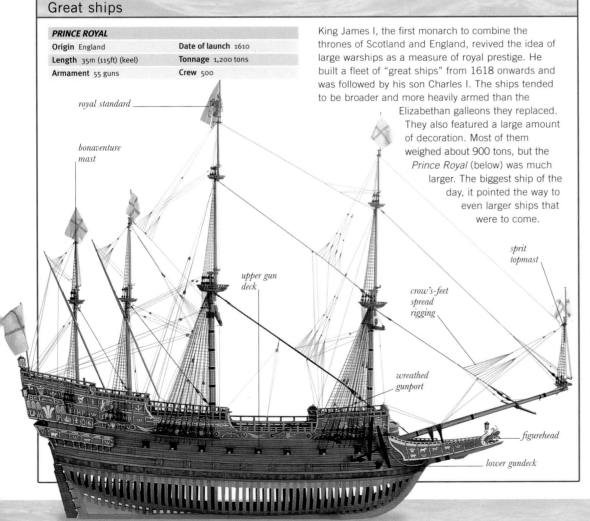

royal standard

bonaventure mast

upper gun deck

sprit topmast

crow's-feet spread rigging

wreathed gunport

figurehead

lower gundeck

Merchant ships

Merchant ships were generally built following the same practices as warships. Compared with merchant ships of the past, they had more masts and sails and, almost invariably, broader and deeper hulls. In the early 17th century, the English took good care to arm their vessels, while the Dutch developed more economical ships. The *Mayflower* (below) was a typical merchant ship of the time before she was taken up by the Puritan migrants, later known as the Pilgrim Fathers, to found a colony in New England.

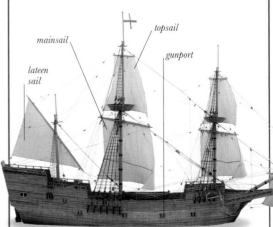

mainsail

topsail

gunport

lateen sail

MAYFLOWER	
Origin England	**Date of launch** Before 1620
Length About 27.5m (90ft)	**Tonnage** About 180 tons
Armament Light guns	**Crew** Not known

4

WARFARE IN THE AGE OF SAIL
J.M.W. Turner's painting depicts one of the greatest naval battles of all time, the Battle of Trafalgar, which was fought in 1805. Ships were more widely used in warfare than ever before during the age of sail.

THE AGE OF SAIL

THE YEARS FROM 1650 TO 1830 witnessed a vast expansion in world trade and led to a huge increase in the construction of merchant ships. Despite the interruptions of warfare, which was almost constant between European powers during this period, maritime trade accelerated the development of industry in Europe, and further increased the continent's wealth and international dominance. It was also an era that saw the birth of a new nation, as the United States declared its independence from Britain in 1776. There was a gradual improvement in sailing ships. Vessels of many different types were constructed, as more was understood about the qualities and functions of different craft. Among the key advances in maritime technology were the steering wheel, copper sheathing (which protected wooden hulls from rotting), and the chronometer. However, seafaring remained a risky profession with many attendant dangers, not least of which were piracy and disease. The 18th century heralded a new wave of exploration, as European mariners, among them Captain James Cook, sailed in search of the mythical *Terra Australis* (southern land), and claimed and surveyed vast tracts of the Pacific.

WARS FOR EMPIRE 112–39

The sailing warship saw a golden age and was used in many European and colonial conflicts. The line of battle • Anglo-Dutch Wars Establishment of navies and shipyards Revolutionary wars in France and America • Battle of Trafalgar • War of 1812

TRADE UNDER SAIL 140–55

Merchant ships carried every kind of cargo, from necessities, such as coal, to valuable luxury goods, such as spices and tobacco. Dutch trade and the *fluyt* • Mediterranean craft • East Indiamen and international trade Slavery and the Triangular Trade • Piracy

EXPLORATION 156–67

The 18th century hopes for new lands in the Pacific created another wave of exploration. First voyages to the Pacific • The expeditions of James Cook • Solving the longitude problem The great French explorers • Effects on indigenous populations • Voyage of the *Beagle*

WARS FOR EMPIRE

THE YEARS BETWEEN 1650 AND 1815 WITNESSED A PERIOD OF INTENSIVE MARITIME WARFARE COMBINED WITH SLOW TECHNOLOGICAL CHANGE.

MEDAL COMMEMORATING THE US WARSHIP *CONSTITUTION*

> "Without a decisive naval force we can do nothing definitive, and with it, everything honourable and glorious."
>
> **PRESIDENT GEORGE WASHINGTON**, to Marquis de Lafayette, **15 November 1781**

KEY EVENTS

1652 FIRST ANGLO-DUTCH WAR The Dutch and English fight over trade rights in the North Sea. The conflict sees the first use of the line of battle in 1653. Two more Anglo-Dutch conflicts follow, the third ending in 1674.

1775 THE CONTINENTAL NAVY FORMED The American Navy is formed to protect the soon-to-be-independent nation against British aggression.

1805 BATTLE OF TRAFALGAR A Royal Navy fleet under the command of Admiral Lord Nelson achieves a decisive victory against the French–Spanish fleet off the coast of Spain.

1812 *CONSTITUTION* DEFEATS *GUERRIERE* The *Constitution* becomes the first American ship to beat a Royal Naval warship in action.

1827 BATTLE OF NAVARINO British and French Mediterranean fleets defeat a Turkish force at Navarino. It is the last great battle between sailing warships.

The causes of warfare shifted in the 17th century. Religion still played a part, but trading rights were at the root of the three Anglo-Dutch Wars, and other causes of conflict included dynastic succession, revolution, territorial struggles, and competition for highly profitable or strategically important colonies. Maritime nations now possessed the degree of organization required to produce navies that could sustain long campaigns over great distances. Warfare, although highly destructive for those involved, was not nearly as terrible on a mass scale as it became in later centuries. Conflicts were rarely fought to a decisive finish, but were settled through negotiation instead.

Although each of the maritime powers of the period retained elements of their own shipbuilding style, and national characteristics continued to be expressed in ship construction, there was increasing convergence of style between different navies' ships. Ideas were exchanged through spying; by emigration of shipwrights from England, Ireland, France, and the Netherlands to Sweden, Spain, and Russia; and by the capture of ships of one navy by another. The English, who were most successful in this last regard, incorporated hundreds of ships into their own fleet.

The newly independent Dutch Republic was Europe's strongest naval power in 1650, having defeated Spain to win its independence. The Dutch were also the world's leading shipbuilders at this time and had a higher proportion of seafarers than any other country. However, their ships were generally small by the

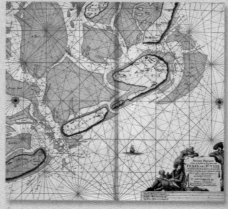

DUTCH NAVAL CHART
This 1682 chart, oriented to the south, shows the main Dutch naval base of Den Helder (top right) at the tip of the West Friesland peninsula.

standards of the era, and there was not a clear distinction between warships and merchant vessels. Power was divided between the five separate admiralties of the different provinces of the Netherlands, rather than centralized.

The other main European maritime power of the era was England. The Republican government, formally headed by Oliver Cromwell as Lord Protector from 1653, had built up its navy during the English Civil War (1642–51), using small, fast ships to combat privateers and gun runners who remained loyal to the Royalist cause. Among the craft used was a fast, low-built type of vessel called a frigate, which was adopted from the mariners of Dunkirk, France. The English transformed the ship into a much more powerful fighting vessel with a forecastle, stronger sides, and often two decks of guns. The Republicans also adopted the concept of the great ship, which was popular among European monarchs. They built several three-deck vessels, although none was large as Charles I's ship the *Sovereign of the Seas* (see p.105).

BATTLE OF THE NILE
Naval warfare between 1650 and 1830 saw ever-larger sailing warships fighting against each other in close proximity. In this painting of the Battle of the Nile (see p.126), the crew of the French flagship L'Orient *are clinging to the remains of their vessel.*

THE FIRST USE OF THE LINE OF BATTLE

In the early 17th century, warships were armed with guns that were able to fire in all directions. However, they took a long time to reload, so once a ship had fired all its guns, it had to withdraw from battle to re-arm. By the 1640s most of the guns were placed on a warship's sides rather than at its bow and stern. The guns themselves had also evolved and could be reloaded without a ship leaving the action of battle.

THE FOUR DAYS' BATTLE

On 11 June 1666, during the Second Anglo-Dutch War, an English line of 56 ships met a superior Dutch line of 80 ships in the North Sea, beginning the Four Days' Battle. The conflict ended in Dutch victory.

In June 1653, at the Battle of the Gabbard in the North Sea, the English Fleet, under its commanders George Monck and Richard Deane, formed a single line of ships, so that all the guns could be deployed without one vessel masking another. According to one contemporary commentator, this new tactic threw the Dutch into "… very great confusion, and the English fought in excellent order".

The line of battle, as it became known, was the standard naval tactic until the Napoleonic Wars (see pp.126–31). It had a profound effect on naval construction, as each warship had to take on the vessel opposite it in the enemy line, however big. This meant that smaller ships no longer had a significant role in battlefleets.

The Anglo-Dutch Wars

As Protestant republics in a Europe that was still predominantly Catholic, the English and Dutch appeared to be natural allies. However, both nations had large merchant fleets and so were fierce trading rivals. In 1651, Oliver Cromwell introduced the Navigation Acts, which stated that only domestic ships could import foreign goods into English ports. If left unchallenged, this would deal a fatal blow to Dutch maritime trade and independence, so they had to resist this English protectionism. As a result, the First Anglo-Dutch War, a purely maritime conflict, began in 1652. Neither side appeared to be stronger than the other until the Battle of the Gabbard, when the English first employed the line of battle (see panel, left), which utilized their larger warships to the best advantage. The 1654 Treaty of Westminster ended the conflict and benefited the English. However, the Dutch had learned a valuable lesson and realized that their ships had to match those of their enemies. The ship of the line, a warship able to maintain its position in battle against the largest opponents, became the main arbiter of naval power. Throughout the period, the minimum size and strength of these ships increased, from 30 guns in the 1650s, to 50 guns in the 1690s, 64 guns by the 1760s, and 74 guns by 1820.

The new English Navy, which had been built by the Republicans, ironically took part in its most lavish pageant when under royal control.

RAID ON THE MEDWAY
In June 1667, the Dutch Fleet sailed up the River Medway, coming within 48km (30 miles) of London, an event documented by the Dutch painter Willem Schellinks. The Dutch cannon above was captured by the English during the war.

MICHIEL DE RUYTER

The greatest Dutch naval commander of the 17th century, Michiel Adrianzoon de Ruyter (1607–76), spent more than six decades at sea and fought in 40 maritime battles. During the three Anglo-Dutch Wars, he won several key victories, including the Four Days' Battle and the daring raid on English naval bases on the River Medway. De Ruyter also demonstrated his skill during the Third Anglo-Dutch War (see p.116), during which he achieved victory against the Anglo-French fleet at the Battle of Texel. He died of wounds he received in a battle with the French off Sicily in 1676.

The occasion was the restoration of King Charles II in 1660, following Cromwell's death. Charles returned to England from Dutch exile aboard the *Naseby*, a three-deck ship named for a Republican victory in the English Civil War. The ship, renamed *Royal Charles*, was fitted with more regal decorations.

War broke out between England and the Netherlands again in 1665, primarily caused by the English Parliament's belief that there were

> **So home, where all our hearts do ake; for the news is true, that the Dutch have broke the chain and burned our ships ... I do fear so much the whole kingdom is undone.**
>
> **SAMUEL PEPYS**, chronicling the Dutch attack on ships in the Medway in his diary, **12 June 1667**

easy pickings to be had from Dutch trade routes and colonies. However, the Dutch were prepared for English aggression, and they fought doggedly and skilfully. Neither side had the upper hand in battle until 1667, when the English Parliament failed to provide enough money to fit out the fleet. In an astounding attack, Dutch ships, commanded by Admiral de Ruyter (see panel, above), broke through a boom laid

across the River Medway and raided the English naval bases at Sheerness and Chatham. The Dutch sank and burned many of the ships anchored there and captured the pride of the fleet, the *Royal Charles*. De Ruyter's intention was to humiliate the English further and attack the south coast naval base at Plymouth in a similar manner, but peace was imminent, and the Treaty of Breda brought an end to the conflict.

FACING THE ENEMY
The Dutch and English fleets face each other on 25 July 1666, off Orfordness on the east coast of England. The English Fleet, in the foreground, consisted of 89 ships, while the Dutch Fleet was made up of 88 ships. The exhausting battle, which lasted more than 24 hours, resulted in an English victory.

BATTLE OF TEXEL
The Battle of Texel was fought on 11 August 1683 between a combined Anglo-French fleet and the Dutch. This painting by the contemporary Dutch seascape artist Ludolf Backhuyzen shows sailors in small boats attacking one another with oars, daggers, and cutlasses, while the main action rages in the background.

In 1670, the English and French forged a secret alliance through the Treaty of Dover. As a result, when France invaded the Dutch Republic in 1672, England was compelled to join the conflict at sea, beginning the Third Anglo-Dutch War. The English and French launched a pre-emptive strike against Dutch shipping. However, the Dutch Fleet had maintained its strength, the French Navy was inexperienced, and the new allies did not complement each other. The Dutch dominated the English Fleet in a series of battles, and the conflict proved unpopular in England because Catholic France under Louis XIV was perceived as an enemy rather than an ally. The two exhausted nations came to terms in 1674, although French forces continued to fight the Dutch until 1679.

During this period there was also conflict in the Mediterranean, where raids by North African corsairs (see p.145) were common. Corsairs were private armed ships licensed by a government to attack its enemy's merchant ships. In the Mediterranean, many corsairs were under licence to the Turks. Strong nations, such as France and Spain, made deals to end these attacks, but smaller nations continued to suffer.

Pepys and Colbert

The French Navy began to revive after Louis XIV assumed absolute power in 1661. The administration of the navy was added to

> 66 It is upon the navy under the good Providence of God that the safety, honour, and welfare of this realm do chiefly depend. 99
>
> "Articles of War" of **KING CHARLES II**

the many portfolios controlled by the great minister Jean-Baptiste Colbert (see panel, opposite). Colbert formed the *Garde de Marine*, training gentlemen's sons at sea until they were commissioned; transferred officers from the army; and recalled others from the Knights of Malta. He also established a register of seamen, who could be called up to serve when required, and instituted a huge shipbuilding programme – by 1672, the French Fleet had 120 ships, most built by Dutch shipwrights. The English master shipwright Anthony Deane was particularly impressed with the *Superbe*, a 76-gun ship built in 1671. The French Fleet continued to expand throughout the 17th century, and by 1675 it consisted of more than 80 ships of over 700 tons, outnumbering the rival English and Dutch navies. The French tended to favour large ships, many with guns spread over three decks.

The burgeoning strength of the French Navy caused serious concern in England. In his capacity as

Secretary to the Admiralty, Samuel Pepys persuaded a reluctant Parliament to invest in 30 new ships in 1677. These warships – of 70, 90, and 100 guns – consolidated the experience that the English Navy had gained over the previous three decades. Charles II, who had renamed the English Navy the Royal Navy, used his own money to enhance the design of the new vessels.

Pepys is perhaps more famous as a diarist, but had worked for the Navy Board in England since 1660. He studied shipbuilding and encouraged a scientific approach to the Navy, although he rarely went to sea himself. One of his key achievements was to regulate the qualifications and appointments of naval officers. He also contributed to the idea that the Navy was a national institution, not a personal possession of the monarch.

Ship decoration

Ship decoration had reached its zenith in the 1630s on ships such as the English *Sovereign of the Seas* and the Swedish *Vasa* (see pp.106–107).

GALLEY *REALE*
Built in Marseilles, France, in 1688, the Reale *was an opulently decorated Mediterranean galley. Its full crew included more than 450 oarsmen.*

However, decoration remained a dominant feature of ship design. Each country had a distinctive national style. The sterns of Dutch vessels were often decorated with friezes, while the French concentrated on elaborate carvings, employing artists such as the master sculptor Pierre Puget to execute designs that became monuments to the lavish reign of the "Sun King", Louis XIV. In England, ship design used local motifs far more, such as wreaths surrounding the upper-deck gun ports, elaborate figureheads, and carved figures on each corner of the stern. From about 1680, decorative styles changed, as ship design had evolved. Stern windows were introduced at quarter-deck level, as were external galleries, which broke up the unity of ship

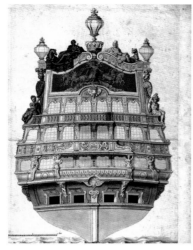

SOLEIL ROYALE
The pride of Louis XIV's resurgent French Navy, the elaborately decorated Soleil Royale *was a magnificent ship. It had three decks and about 100 guns.*

structure by providing a horizontal rather than vertical emphasis. The coats of arms that had dominated the sterns of English warships, for example, were much smaller, to fit into the available space.

With varying success, most nations tried to evolve a vessel that combined the use of sail and oars. Perhaps the best example of such a craft was the North African *xebec* or chebec (see p.96), used by the corsairs. It was also adapted and used by Spain and several other European powers. Mediterranean galleys were still in use by some navies until well into the 18th century, among them the French and Maltese, although they were obsolete in battle. The flagship of the French galley fleet, the *Reale*, was a vessel of great prestige and decoration.

JEAN-BAPTISTE COLBERT

Nicknamed "man of marble" for his public works projects, Jean-Baptiste Colbert (1619–83) became Louis XIV's financial minister in 1661, taking over the running of the Navy in the same decade. He developed a great French Navy from nothing, building the first ships in the Netherlands. By 1677 the French Navy had nearly 200 ships, many of them larger and more efficient than those of England and the Netherlands. On Colbert's death, the French Navy was set to become the world's largest.

COLBERT'S *ATLAS*
This page from Jean-Baptiste Colbert's Atlas *depicts a ship being constructed in Toulon.*

STERN RELIEF DEPICTING WINTER

TRITON (GREEK SEA GOD)

STERN RELIEF DEPICTING SUMMER

GOLDEN DECORATIONS
As head of the French galley fleet, the Reale *was intended to epitomize the splendour of Louis XIV's reign. The gold decorations were inspired by characters and scenes from Greek mythology.*

The English succession

By 1688, James II, who succeeded his brother Charles as king, had lost both popular and parliamentary support after only three years on the throne. His son-in-law, William of Orange, who was Stadtholder (leader) of the Netherlands, armed a fleet and sailed to Torbay, southwest England, where he landed without resistance. He was invited by Parliament to become king, as William III. James was now kept off the throne by the Royal Navy, in which he had taken such a close personal interest.

The French were infuriated by events in England, as they would have preferred the Catholic James to remain as monarch.

SETTING SAIL FOR ENGLAND
The two greatest maritime nations of the 17th century were united in 1688 when William of Orange was invited to invade England and usurp James II. In this painting, William's fleet is shown preparing to leave the Netherlands.

War began 1689, with William leading a coalition against the ever-increasing dominance of Louis XIV. The French Fleet was victorious at the Battle of Beachy Head in the English Channel in 1690, forcing the English to reassess the design of their warships. This resulted in the 80-gun two-deck warship. However, the vessels were too crowded with guns, and after one of them, the *Sussex*, sank in 1694, they were redesigned with three decks, but they proved no more successful.

The English and Dutch rallied to defeat Admiral de Tourville's French Fleet in 1692 at Barfleur and La Hogue in Normandy, destroying many ships, including the *Soleil Royale*. As a result, the French abandoned their attempt to dominate the seas with a great battlefleet. Instead, merchant ports, such as Dunkirk and

COMMEMORATING BATTLE
This Dutch commemorative medal was commissioned to celebrate the combined English and Dutch Fleet's victory over the French at the Battle of La Hogue in 1692.

St-Malo on the north coast of France, were encouraged to fit ships out as commercial men-of-war, or privateers, which were designed to raid English and Dutch trading vessels for profit. This strategy proved highly successful to start with, as it impelled their enemies to build smaller ships to escort merchant convoys. The English briefly favoured the 50-gun ship, in the belief that it could be used either in the line of battle or to escort merchant ships. In fact, it did neither job well. The Dutch also constructed small warships, adding 32 to their fleet between 1691 and 1695.

The birth of the Russian Navy

Despite some obvious disadvantages – he had no professional seamen or officer corps and, unlike other European navies, he had to institute basic training – Tsar Peter the Great (see panel, right) was responsible for establishing an effective Russian navy. After visiting several European nations towards the end of the 17th century, he returned to Russia, taking with him a large group of British and Dutch shipbuilders and sailors. For the next century, the Russian Navy used such foreign talent and experience to consolidate its fleet.

In 1696, Peter mustered 86 ships on the River Don for a naval campaign against Turkey. His capture of Azov allowed the Russian Navy to create an eastern base, but Peter quickly realized that a western port was more urgently required. In 1700, he prosecuted a war against the Swedish, aided by his allies, Denmark and Poland. It was a conflict that was to last two decades. The Tsar's intention was to recover Baltic territories that had been lost to Sweden in the 17th century and open Russia to Europe. On land captured from the Swedes at the mouth of the River Neva, the city of St Petersburg was created, with the naval base of Kronstadt constructed on an island nearby. In 1714, the Russian Navy achieved victory at the Battle of Gangut, gaining control of the Aland Islands and the western coast of Finland. It was Russia's first victory at sea, and it is still commemorated. In 1715, a Swedish attempt to attack Peter's ships off Revel (now Tallinn) was repelled by the Russian galley fleet. Peace negotiations were halted by the death of the Swedish king, Charles XII, in 1718, but terms were eventually agreed in 1721.

Rather than battleships, maritime conflict in the Baltic required oared fighting craft, as these were more effective for fighting in the narrow inlets and shallow estuaries of the region. During the Baltic conflict, the opposing powers used a form of the Mediterranean galley. The Swedish naval architect Fredrik af Chapman (see p.146) developed several classes of rowing gunboat, which were shorter, more robust, and better armed than the old-fashioned galley. These ideas were eventually adopted by powers outside the region, including the French, who saw this type of vessel as a means to invade England during the Napoleonic Wars.

PETER THE GREAT

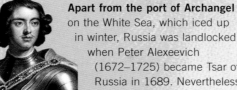

Apart from the port of Archangel on the White Sea, which iced up in winter, Russia was landlocked when Peter Alexeevich (1672–1725) became Tsar of Russia in 1689. Nevertheless, Peter became interested in the sea when he discovered an old boat in a shed, after which he spent much time sailing on lakes and around Archangel. In 1691, Peter brought Dutch shipwrights to Russia to build small frigates and yachts. In 1696, he made it possible for a Russian navy to operate on the Black Sea, when he captured the Turkish stronghold of Azov. The following year he travelled to western Europe, and while there he studied shipbuilding and navigation. He worked in the shipyard of the East India Company in Amsterdam, moving on to England early in 1698, where he worked in the Royal Dockyard at Deptford on the River Thames. Peter returned to Russia with ship models and plans, a number of shipwrights and sailors, and a yacht built at Chatham Dockyard. As Tsar, Peter the Great was determined to drag Russia into the modern age. He was ruthless in his ambitions, suppressing conservative revolts with enormous cruelty. One of Peter's greatest achievements was the Baltic city of St Petersburg, which he founded in 1703 and which gave him the maritime base and opening to western Europe he craved.

PETER THE GREAT IN DEPTFORD

In 1698, Peter the Great arrived in England and worked at the Royal Dockyard at Deptford. This Victorian painting shows the Russian Tsar (left) being visited at the shipyard by the English king, William III (right).

BATTLE OF VIGO BAY

On 12 October 1702, a combined Dutch and English Fleet attacked Spanish and French ships moored at Vigo Bay, northwest Spain. The Dutch-English Fleet annihilated the opposing ships and seized a vast amount of treasure. The Treaty of Utrecht (right) was signed in 1713 and gave the British the colony of Gibraltar.

The War of Spanish Succession

Another great conflict, the War of Spanish Succession, raged across Europe between 1702 and 1714. It was primarily a land war, and the English and Dutch were again allied in an attempt to restrain the French, who were pressing a claim to the Spanish throne, and with it a vast and extremely wealthy empire. Most of the maritime conflict occurred early in the war. In 1704, the English captured the strategic strongholds of Gibraltar and Menorca in the Mediterranean, and there was an indecisive sea battle off Malaga in Spain. The French withdrew their navy and mounted another privateer campaign against English and Dutch merchant ships instead. The Treaty of Utrecht, which ended the war, limited French claims and granted important advantages to Britain, including the *asiento*, the right to trade slaves and other lucrative commodities with Spanish Caribbean colonies.

DEPTFORD, LONDON
One of the Royal Navy's most important dockyards was Deptford in southeast London. This painting shows two views of the launch of the Royal George.

Navies and shipyards

During the 17th century, the major European powers constructed new dockyards to accommodate their great naval fleets and to deal with changing strategic needs. Louis XIV chose a site at Rochefort on the River Charente, to give France a base on the west coast. However, the site was too far upriver to be efficient, so Toulon and Brest were expanded to cope with the needs of the French Navy.

In England, a dockyard opened at Sheerness on the River Medway in 1671, specifically to deal with the Dutch. The English began to construct another dockyard at Plymouth, Devon, in 1690, recognizing that their main adversary was now France. Britain's established yards at Deptford and Woolwich on the Thames began to decline, although there was still much shipbuilding work at Chatham. Portsmouth, on the south coast, expanded and became the main 18th-century British naval base.

Much of Europe was at peace in the 1720s and 1730s. During peacetime, ships were laid up at ports, afloat but with their guns and rigging placed in store. Only a minority, usually the smaller ships, continued to go to sea. Navies were now permanent organizations. In peacetime, most officers were retained on half-pay, while some ordinary seamen were assimilated into the merchant fleet.

SHIPWRIGHT'S ADZE

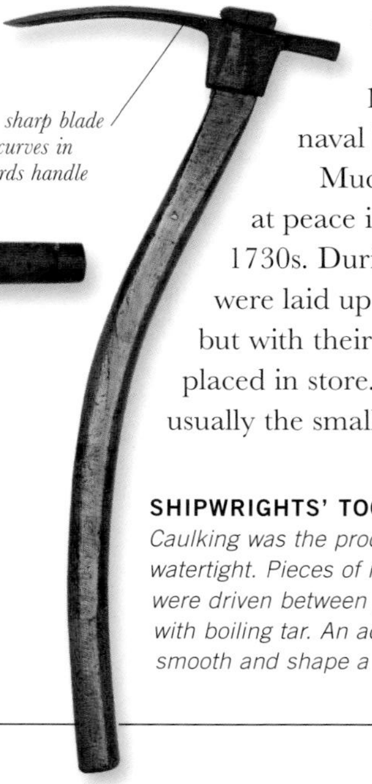

long, sharp blade that curves in towards handle

pitch ladle, used to pour boiling tar into deck seams and make them watertight

caulking mallet, to strike caulking irons

broad-bladed tool, for splitting seams open

jerry iron, for extracting old oakum from seams

caulking iron, used to drive new oakum into seams

CAULKING TOOLS

SHIPWRIGHTS' TOOLS
Caulking was the process of making a ship watertight. Pieces of rope, called oakum, were driven between planks and covered with boiling tar. An adze was used to smooth and shape a ship's woodwork.

THE PRESS GANG

Most navies used compulsion of some kind to recruit men. William Hay recounts being forced into the Royal Navy by a brutal press gang.

I was when crossing Towerhill accosted by a person in seamen's dress who tapped me on the shoulder enquiring in a familiar and technical strain "what ship". I assumed an air of gravity and surprise and told him I presumed he was under some mistake as I was not connected with shipping. The fellow ... gave a whistle and in a moment I was in the hands of six or eight ruffians who I immediately dreaded and soon found to be a press gang.

WILLIAM HAY, **1744**

SHIPBUILDING IN LE HAVRE
Le Havre, Normandy, was a major centre for shipbuilding in the 17th century. The ship in the foreground of this print is being caulked to render it watertight, while those on the right are in various stages of construction.

FORCED RECRUITMENT
This late 18th-century English cartoon shows men being forcibly taken into the Navy by a press gang. These gangs were made up of enlisted sailors and officers.

In these circumstances a fleet could slowly decline, as the French Navy did for a time, or it might be kept up to strength in reserve, which is what the British did with the Royal Navy.

The Royal Navy had been battle-hardened over a long series of wars. It had a competent officer corps and a reserve of merchant seamen who could be recruited by the press gang and popular support. The French had not fitted out

a battlefleet for some years. From its apogee during Louis XIV's reign, the French Navy declined to 48 ships in 1720, compared with Britain's 174. The Spanish had made little impact on naval warfare since the early 17th century, and Dutch naval expansion was constrained by their shallow harbours, which were unsuitable for the ever-larger warships of the age. As a result, the Dutch Fleet declined to 62 ships of all types in 1725.

The French Navy began to revive again in 1730 under Louis XV's naval minister, Jean-Fréderic Phélypeaux, Comte de Maurepas. However, the French realized that they had to give priority to their army, as they would never be able to afford a navy to challenge British maritime dominance. The new French Fleet required fast, well-armed, seaworthy ships rather than the floating fortresses that had been used previously. These ships would pinpoint British weak spots, raiding vulnerable targets such as colonies and troop convoys. The French Fleet could even threaten an invasion of southern

England if defences were not maintained. These tactics instilled constant fear into the British. French ship designers, such as Blaise Ollivier (see panel, above), were extremely creative. They developed vessels that became prominent in all navies for the next century, including the 74-gun ship of the line and a new type of frigate, a fast vessel with one gundeck (see p.123).

Colonial wars

During the mid-18th century, the world's great navies fought several wars, largely in defence of colonies. Empire, particularly in India and the West Indies, proved highly profitable, and sea power was the primary means of defence. The lucrative colonies of the West Indies changed hands many times – for example, Trinidad was originally settled by the Spanish, but the British captured it in 1797.

In India, European trading stations, known as factories, were situated in coastal regions. Naval power was needed to defend them and to escort the merchant ships from which they made their profits. Because the colonies and their industries constituted such a large part of the European economy, particularly in Britain, France, and Spain, the merchants who dealt in the sector had great wealth and political power, so navies became increasingly committed to wars across the globe in their defence.

The Spanish limited trade rights with their Caribbean colonies and claimed the right to search any English ships that entered their waters. Conflict between the two powers flared up in 1739, after an incident in which an English mariner, Captain Jenkins, claimed that a Spanish customs officer in the Caribbean had cut off his ear. He produced the ear before Parliament, and on this flimsy pretext the British declared war, hoping for rich pickings from the Spanish empire.

The War of Jenkins's Ear, as it became known, spiralled into the broader War of Austrian Succession, which began with some British successes. A squadron of six ships, commanded by Edward Vernon, took the Spanish Caribbean port of Puerto Bello, but a subsequent attack on Cartagena in 1741 failed. The Spanish defended themselves with robust vessels, many of which had been built by French émigrés or Roman Catholic refugees from Britain and Ireland. The strength of the Spanish ships was illustrated by an incident in the English Channel in 1740, during which it took three British warships several hours to capture the *Princessa*, a vessel of nominally equal gun power. This forced the British to reassess the design of their warships, but the changes implemented were far from radical. Although France was technically at peace with Britain, it was also allied with Spain.

In February 1744, a Franco-Spanish force sailed out of Toulon, commanded by the 80-year-old French admiral Court de la Bruyère, to meet a British Fleet under Admiral Thomas Mathews. Mathews attacked the combined fleet rather ineptly, and an

PUERTO BELLO CAPTURED
The first naval action of the War of Jenkins's Ear was the British attack on the Spanish colony of Puerto Bello, on the Darien Isthmus. A squadron of warships under Admiral Vernon, whose ship is on the left in this painting, captured the port in November 1739.

indecisive battle followed. Admiral Anson, who had returned from a voyage around the globe (see pp.158–59), formed a squadron to blockade the French port of Brest in 1747, chasing and capturing a fleet of warships and merchant craft off Cape Finisterre. He abandoned the line of battle on the grounds that this was permitted during a pursuit, and his prizes included the French *Invincible*, one of the most efficient of the new 74-gun warships. Admiral Hawke defeated the French in similar circumstances, but the war had reached stalemate, with France, Spain, and their allies victorious on land, and Britain and the Netherlands at sea. The war ended with a compromise peace in 1748.

Many colonial issues remained unsettled and there were intermittent skirmishes between British and French forces in North America and India, which continued with the outbreak of the Seven Years' War in 1756. The naval war took place mainly in the Mediterranean and began well for the French. They attacked and captured Menorca, after the English Admiral John Byng was sent out with a fleet to defend it.

THE STEERING WHEEL

Since the 15th century, a whipstaff had been used to steer large ships. A pivot or "rowle" was set at deck level just above the tiller, through which a staff passed. One end of the staff was connected to the tiller, which in turn was connected to the rudder. The other end was held by the helmsman, who moved it from side to side to steer the ship. This allowed the helmsman to stand a deck higher than the rudder, where he could have a view of the ship's sails. However, it allowed very limited movement of the rudder. One of the greatest maritime innovations of the 17th century was the steering wheel. The first known evidence of a ship's wheel is on a model of an English warship, which dates to about 1705. The wheel allowed the helmsman to stand on the quarter-deck to steer the ship and was more accurate and manoeuvrable than the whipstaff. A second wheel could be fitted to the same barrel to add extra power. In rough conditions, it could take up to four men to operate a wheel.

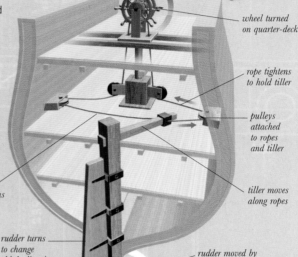

EASTERN WHEEL
The steering wheel was quickly adopted throughout Europe and spread further afield. This example is from a Middle Eastern dhow.

wheel turned on quarter-deck

rope tightens to hold tiller

pulleys attached to ropes and tiller

tiller moves along ropes

rope slackens

rudder turns to change ship's direction

rudder moved by action of tiller

HOW A WHEEL WORKS
A ship's wheel is turned in the direction in which the vessel is to move. It is attached by a system of ropes to the tiller, which in turn is joined to the rudder.

He engaged the enemy in an indecisive battle, in which he adhered rigidly to the line of battle, as ordered. He withdrew to defend Gibraltar, leaving the French to capture Menorca.

The frigate

The standard medium-sized warship at this point was the frigate, which evolved in France in the 1730s, but was widely copied. The first frigates were equipped with three fully rigged masts, 32 guns, and a crew of more than 200. The lower deck was unarmed, which meant that the main gundeck was raised well out of the water. This distribution of weight allowed the ship to heel (tilt away from the wind) efficiently. As with most large ships since the 17th century, steering was achieved with a wheel (see panel, above). The frigate was extremely versatile and swift. It could accompany the main battlefleet in support of larger warships in fleet engagements and carry out strategic reconnaissance, squadron action, blockade duty, coastal operations, and amphibious warfare. Independent of the battlefleet, it could also escort convoys of merchantmen and attack enemy ships.

Influenced by French innovations, the English began to design new 74-gun ships and frigates. By 1760 a revitalized British Fleet had gained unprecedented success in battle and colonial warfare. It was at the forefront of an action to capture Quebec from the French in 1759, and in November that year Admiral Hawke chased a French fleet into Quiberon Bay, off the Atlantic coast of Brittany, and destroyed it.

decorated gold buttons

silk waistcoat embroidered with gold trim

coat lined in white

DRESS UNIFORM
In 1748, officers onboard British warships began to wear ornate uniforms. This dress uniform (for formal occasions) belonged to a lieutenant.

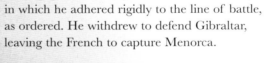

THE *TURTLE*

Designed by the American engineer David Bushnell, the *Turtle* was one of the precursors of the modern submarine. Pedals within the craft operated a propeller on its side, which was used to push it underwater towards an enemy ship. Another propeller on the top of the craft was operated by a handle inside, which allowed the *Turtle* to dive. The submersible carried a limpet mine that contained 70kg (150lb) of explosives. Once the *Turtle* reached its target, the intention was for the pilot to screw the mine into the enemy ship and make a rapid exit.

In 1776, Sergeant Ezra Lee navigated the *Turtle* to a position underneath the British flagship *Eagle*, which was moored in New York harbour. The mission failed because Lee was unable to attach the mine to the *Eagle*'s copper hull.

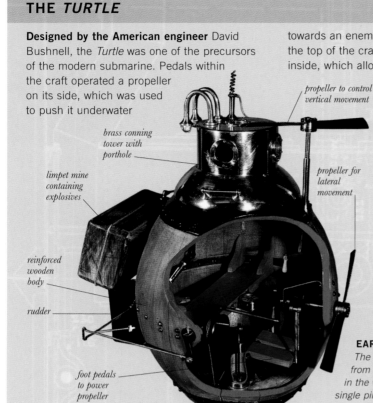

propeller to control vertical movement

brass conning tower with porthole

limpet mine containing explosives

propeller for lateral movement

reinforced wooden body

rudder

foot pedals to power propeller

EARLY SUBMARINE
The oval-shaped Turtle *was constructed from reinforced wood. It floated vertically in the water and contained room for just a single pilot to propel and steer the craft.*

single mast carried square rig

two smaller guns amidships

WRECK OF *PHILADELPHIA*
The Philadelphia *was one of a fleet of gunboats that met British forces on Lake Champlain during the Battle of Valcour Island.*

12-pounder gun on bow

flat-bottomed hull, or "gondola"

CHESAPEAKE BAY
This map shows the French Fleet (left) blocking the entry of the English Fleet to Chesapeake Bay in 1781. The English land forces were compelled to surrender.

carrying tea to Boston and tipped the cargo overboard. This event – the Boston Tea Party – led to British repression of the colonies, causing the American Revolutionary War.

British attempts to dominate the Americans were unsuccessful. At this point, America had no navy in the conventional sense, but instead

The American Revolutionary War

The peace of 1763 ended the Seven Years' War. Britain was in her strongest position ever as a nation, but this dominance was won at great cost, as European allies had been abandoned and none were forthcoming for the next war. France was bent on revenge, having lost its Indian and Canadian colonies to Britain, and George III's determination to tax the American colonies resulted in understandable resentment. In 1768, the sloop *Liberty*, which belonged to the Boston politician John Hancock, was seized by British customs officers. This angered the Americans, who became more determined to free themselves of English rule.

In 1773, acting against levies on goods imported into the American colonies, protesters boarded three British ships

BOSTON TEA PARTY
A turning point in relations between the American colonists and their British oppressors, the Boston Tea Party was the spark that led to eventual independence for America.

JOHN PAUL JONES

The son of a Scottish gardener, John Paul Jones (1747–92) was apprenticed to a shipowner at the age of 13, becoming a master at the age of 21. In 1775, he enrolled as a lieutenant in the Continental Navy, becoming a captain in August 1776.

From France, he led raids on his native coasts in 1778. The following year, in the *Bonnehomme Richard*, he raided the Firth of Forth in Scotland and attacked a large convoy. He fought and won a desperate engagement with the British ship *Serapis*, returning to France and America as a hero.

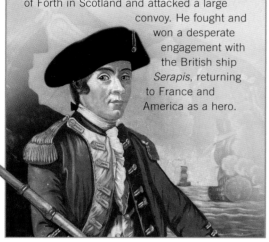

used privateers to disrupt British trade and troop movements. One of the most famous was John Paul Jones, a Scot by birth, who became a revolutionary hero (see panel, above).

In 1775, the Continental Navy was founded. It retained privateers and initially added 13 small warships, including several fast gunboats designed to outmanoeuvre the more cumbersome British invasion craft. Their construction took place at Whitehall, New York State, under the supervision of Benedict Arnold, a wealthy Connecticut businessman. On 10 October 1776, Arnold's flotilla engaged the much larger British Fleet near Valcour Island on Lake Champlain, on the border between Vermont and New York State. Ten American ships were destroyed in the battle, but Arnold succeeded in delaying the British advance. Later in the war, the Continental Navy raided British commerce, prevented the British blockading American ports, and attacked their troop convoys.

The war's emphasis changed dramatically in 1778, when France entered it in support of the Americans, to be followed by Spain, and later the Netherlands. The British Fleet was outnumbered, and for a time the Franco-Spanish Fleet controlled the English Channel and threatened invasion of England.

Naval architecture had reached a plateau in the last few decades of the 18th century, but the British introduced two improvements during the American Revolutionary War: copper sheathing (see panel, below); and the carronade. A new type of gun, the carronade fired a large shot over a relatively short range.

The main fleets moved to American seas after 1780, the only time in the conflict when major naval battles were fought outside European waters. At the Battle of Chesapeake Bay in 1781, a French Fleet, commanded by Admiral de Grasse, prevented British warships from entering the York River to relieve their besieged army. The British, under Admiral Rodney, had partial revenge at the Battle of the Saints in the West Indies in 1782, when de Grasse's French Fleet was heavily defeated. The battle was notable because Rodney abandoned tradition and broke through the enemy line of ships, paving the way for the daring tactics of a later British commander, Admiral Lord Nelson (see p.127). The conflict ended in 1783, and, although the British retained much of their empire, the 13 North American colonies had established themselves as a maritime force and won their independence to become the United States.

Rules of construction

Although there were few theoretical experiments in naval architecture (see panel, p.126) in the 18th century, certain principles of warship construction had emerged. A country with a large empire to defend, such as Britain or Spain, needed slightly smaller and cheaper ships to spread around the seas – although the Spanish also constructed some huge ships. A country

with a small but still effective fleet, such as France or the USA, could concentrate on fewer, well-designed ships. It was accepted that bigger guns, such as the British 32-pounder or the French 36-pounder, were more effective than smaller ones, although very large ones, such as the British 42-pounder, had cannonballs that were heavy to handle. A long ship was better proportioned and sailed more efficiently than a short one, but if a ship was too long it tended to hog (arch) or sag at the ends. As a result, the 74-gun ship, the smallest to carry a full battery of 32-pounders and the longest practicable two-deck ship in rough conditions, was much favoured by the British, while the French moved towards the two-deck ship of 80 guns. With three-deck ships, the British favoured the 100-gun ship until the end of the 18th century, while the French developed the longer 120-gun ship.

At the other end of the scale, there was an increase in smaller ships in most fleets. The fireship had been used since the days of the Spanish Armada (see p.101). It was essentially a small vessel filled with combustible materials that could be launched at an enemy fleet. The bomb vessel was developed in France in the late 17th century, initially for use against North African corsairs. It carried two mortars for shore bombardment and was soon adopted by other nations.

fuse

FRENCH FIRESHIP
Packed with combustible materials, fireships were sent towards enemy lines, where they exploded.

COPPER SHEATHING

The underwater hulls of wooden ships are affected by weeds, which slow them down, and shipworm, a parasite that consumes wood. In the early 17th century, the Dutch naval hero Piet Heijn invented a form of copper covering, but the conventional solution was still to use noxious chemical compositions to deter marine life. In the 1670s, lead plates were tested, but they proved too heavy and caused an adverse reaction with the ships' ironwork. In 1761, the Royal Navy sheathed the hull of the frigate *Alarm* with copper. By 1778, the idea had proved so successful that most navies had adopted the idea, as it allowed ships to operate for much longer periods without maintenance.

thin copper sheets fixed with copper bolts

copper below waterline prevents decay and attack by shipworm

THE RISE OF NAVAL ARCHITECTURE

The design of ships improved steadily as greater scientific understanding was allied to traditional practical skills. Until the 17th century, shipwrights relied on experience to find the best design for a vessel. However, by the end of the century a new science emerged – naval architecture. It was based on both applied geometry and practical experience.

In 1670, the English shipwright Anthony Deane published his *Doctrine on Naval Architecture*, showing that it was possible to calculate the volume of a hull and the height at which it would float in the water. In the next century, advances made by Fredrik af Chapman

(see p.146) made it possible to calculate the stability of a ship before it was built. Models were also constructed and tested by towing them through water. The first school of naval architecture was set up in Paris in 1741, founded by the Inspector General of the French Navy, Duhamel du Monceau. He remained the school's director until his death in 1782.

PLAN OF A FRIGATE
Technical plans called draughts were drawn in detail before vessels were constructed. They usually showed a view of the stern, a view of the side (or sheer) of a ship, and a view of half the ship from below. This draught dates from 1800.

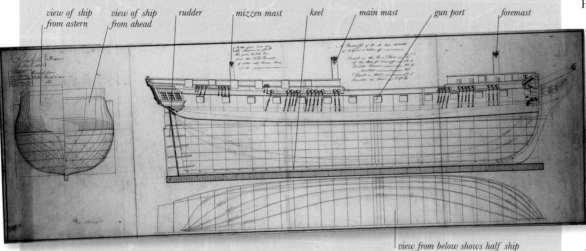

view of ship from astern   view of ship from ahead   rudder   mizzen mast   keel   main mast   gun port   foremast

view from below shows half ship

Local types of fast, seaworthy craft, which had often been initially developed by smugglers and fishermen, were also armed with as many as 14 guns and incorporated into naval fleets. The British used the single-masted cutter, and the French used two-masted luggers, which were also known as *chasse-marées*. The Dutch produced the two-masted, fore-and-aft rigged schooner,

SPANISH SHIPYARD
This painting shows Spanish ships under construction in Seville in about 1740. The port lies on the Guadalquivir River, which flows into the Atlantic Ocean.

which was also developed independently by the Americans (see pp.242–43). All these ships were used for coastal engagements or privateering, due to their speed and efficiency.

Other naval vessels were designed for sturdiness or cargo capacity rather than speed. Troop transports were usually hired from the merchant service, but harbour craft, such as vessels equipped with cranes for maintaining harbour moorings, were often specially designed. Others, such as hulks, which were used for storage, were usually old warships.

The warships of the 18th century had relatively restrained decoration compared with those of the previous century. An order of 1703 attempted to regulate the carvings on British warships. The wreathed gun ports of the last century disappeared, but figureheads were still large. In 1794, the British Admiralty decided to "explode carved works" and abolished the stern gallery, creating the plain type of stern that can still be seen on the British warship *Victory* (see pp. 128–29) today. French ships followed a similar process, although with the advent of

Napoleon austerity and restraint gave way to imperial splendour in the first decade of the 19th century.

Navies and the French Revolution
The French Navy ended the American Revolutionary War with restored prestige. However, it had become somewhat complacent, as established plans by the shipwright Jacques-Noel Sané were agreed as the standard for all future ship construction, thus ending a period of innovation. With the outbreak of the French Revolution in 1789, the French Navy experienced a sharp decline. The main European powers, among them Austria, Prussia, and Britain, declared war on France in 1792–93, fearing that revolutionary ideals might spread. Initially, it seemed that the new republic was doomed to failure at sea. The French Navy had many fine ships, but the majority of its experienced naval officers had fled from the terrors of the revolution, and discipline in the fleet was chaotic. Matters got worse when the supporters of the monarchy handed the great naval port of Toulon to the allies. However, a young artillery major, Napoleon Bonaparte, forced them to withdraw before they could capture or destroy many French vessels. In 1794, the British Fleet under Admiral Howe defeated the French under Villaret de Joyeuse at the Battle of the Glorious First of June in the Atlantic, seizing six ships of the line. But a vital grain convoy from America, which the French Fleet was protecting, escaped from the British warships. By 1798, Napoleon had conquered Italy, forcing the British to withdraw from the Mediterranean region.

By this point, the French Navy had revived in morale, confidence, and skills. The Spanish and Dutch, now allied with France, were defeated by the British in 1797, at Cape St. Vincent, off the coast of Cadiz, and Camperdown, off the Netherlands, respectively. Meanwhile, Bonaparte prepared a fleet of 13 ships of the line and hundreds of merchant ships to transport an

COMBAT AT ABOUKIR BAY
The French warship Le Tonnant *faces the British warship* Majestic *during the Battle of the Nile. Both ships were dismasted and* Le Tonnant *was captured.*

army of 30,000 men to conquer Egypt. Although this would antagonize the Turks, who ruled Egypt, it would augment French control of the Mediterranean and prepare the way for an advance to British India. The French landed in Egypt without difficulty, but Bonaparte soon realized his control of the sea was not absolute in the way that it was on land. Britain's newly promoted Rear-Admiral Nelson (see panel, right) destroyed the French Fleet at anchor in Aboukir Bay, at the mouth of the Nile. The Battle of the Nile, as it became known, had immediate impact. A new coalition, comprising Turkey, Britain, Austria, and Russia, was formed against the French, but it eventually faltered.

Allegiances shifted again when the Danes, Russians, Swedes, and Prussians formed the League of Armed Neutrality in 1801, which isolated the British against the French. A British Fleet was sent to the Baltic, and the Danes were defeated. By this time, as in previous wars, the British were victorious at sea but had no means of prosecuting war against the French on land, and so a compromise peace was agreed.

HORATIO NELSON

The British naval hero Horatio Nelson (1758–1805) first went to sea at the age of 12. By the age of 18, he had received his first commission, and two years later he became the youngest captain in the Royal Navy. He served in the Caribbean and North America during the American Revolutionary War. In 1793, Nelson commanded the 64-gun *Agamemnon*. He was stationed in the Mediterranean, where he lost the sight in his right eye at the siege of Calvi, Corsica. In 1797, his initiative turned the Battle of Cape St. Vincent into a victory, but later in the year he lost his right arm in a raid on Tenerife. In 1798, he took a squadron into the Mediterranean, where, in one of the most uncompromising naval victories of all time, he destroyed the French Fleet at Aboukir Bay.

At the Battle of Copenhagen in 1801, Nelson wiped out the Danish Fleet. He was given command of the Mediterranean Fleet on the resumption of war in 1803. Killed by a musket shot at the Battle of Trafalgar in 1805 (see p.131), Nelson was buried as a national hero.

NELSON'S CEREMONIAL SWORD

TURKISH HAT DECORATION GIVEN TO NELSON

NATIONAL HERO
In this portrait of Nelson, dating from 1800, he is wearing decorations he won for his valour at the Battle of the Nile.

FIGUREHEAD *Fitted in 1803, this was much simpler than the original of 1765.*

GUN *One of the ship's 104 guns protrudes from the hull, although its muzzle is blocked by a tompion and it is not ready to fire.*

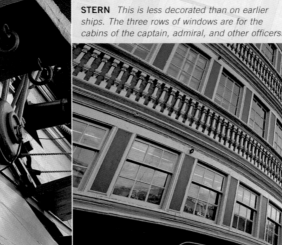

STERN *This is less decorated than on earlier ships. The three rows of windows are for the cabins of the captain, admiral, and other officers.*

ANCHORS *The heaviest of the ship's seven anchors weighs more than 4.5 tonnes. The labour of most of the crew was needed to raise the anchors, by means of the capstans.*

FIRE BUCKETS *This row of leather buckets hangs from the forward edge of the poop.*

RIGGING *One of the most complex areas of the rigging is just under the top on each mast, where the lower yard is held in place by four huge pieces of wood called jeer blocks.*

SHIP'S WHEEL *Aft on the quarter-deck, the wheel is double so that four men can operate it at once.*

CAPTAIN'S CABIN *A three-deck warship such as Victory had large cabins, used for dining and as offices for the admiral and his flag captain.*

GUNDECK *The wide, low gundecks housed the guns, which were the ship's raison d'être. During action, the crew had to use lanterns, as the deck filled with gunsmoke. The gundecks also provided eating and sleeping space for most of the crew.*

GUN LOCK *Pulling the cord of the gun lock created the spark by which a gun's charge was ignited.*

GALLEY *The officers' side of the galley, shown here, has some sophisticated utensils. However, food for the rest of the crew was mostly boiled.*

SICK BAY *Forward on the upper deck, the sick bay had good lighting and ventilation, unlike the operating theatre deep in the ship.*

CARPENTER'S STOREROOM *A ship needed a large amount of spare timber, tar, paint, and other stores, kept in a storeroom well forward in the hold.*

PHOTO PROFILE

VICTORY

THIS BRITISH WARSHIP IS BEST KNOWN AS NELSON'S SHIP AT THE BATTLE OF TRAFALGAR. SHE IS ALSO THE WORLD'S OLDEST SHIP STILL COMMISSIONED IN NAVAL SERVICE.

THE LARGEST BRITISH WARSHIP of her day, HMS *Victory* was ordered by the Admiralty in December 1758, at the height of the Seven Years' War. However, she was not launched until 1765, underwent sea trials in 1769, and was finally commissioned in 1778 as the flagship of Admiral Keppel, to fight a new war against the French. In 1793, during the war with Revolutionary France, *Victory* became flagship of the Mediterranean Fleet. After the victory at Cape St. Vincent in 1797, she was considered old and was sent home to be relegated

AT DOCK
Victory is shown here in the English Channel in 1793. In the same year, she was used by the Royal Navy in the war with Revolutionary France.

to a prison hospital ship. She was revived in 1800, when the Admiralty ordered a "large repair". Re-floated in 1803, she went back to the Mediterranean as Nelson's flagship and led a chase of the French Fleet across the Atlantic and back in 1805. In October that year, Nelson was killed on her decks at Trafalgar (see panel, p.131). Her active career was not over, and she served in the Baltic until 1812. In 1922, *Victory* was put in dry-dock at Portsmouth, where she remains today, restored to her Trafalgar condition.

The area of deck just behind the mainmast is the quarter-deck, where the ship's wheel can be found. Behind and above this is the poop deck. Ahead are the

ship's boats, stowed on booms, and the forecastle with the galley and sick bay under it. Below is the upper deck, which runs from bow to stern and is armed with 30 12-pounder guns. The wardroom, where middle-ranking officers lived, is in the stern of the middle deck, with the Great Cabin and the Captain's Cabin on the two decks above. The rest of the middle deck housed the crew, as did the deck beneath that. Below the waterline, the orlop deck is divided into the bread room, the cockpit, a storage area for the anchor cables, and the storerooms. In battle, this deck held the operating theatre. The lowest part of the ship is the hold, where provisions were stowed.

Specification

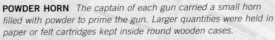

each of the three masts is in three sections

mast sections divided by tops

upper gundeck

middle gundeck

lower gundeck

Origin Britain	Date of launch 1765	Number of sails 37	Crew 850
Length 57m (186ft)	Tonnage 2,142 tonnes	Armament 104 guns	

HOLD *The hold is shown here almost empty, containing a layer of gravel for ballast and a few barrels. However, when full, it could be used to store supplies for a 6-month voyage.*

DINING *The sailors dined on tables between the guns, using wooden bowls or their own plates.*

POWDER HORN *The captain of each gun carried a small horn filled with powder to prime the gun. Larger quantities were held in paper or felt cartridges kept inside round wooden cases.*

BOSUN'S STORE *This housed stores to repair rigging.*

THE BATTLE OF COPENHAGEN
On 2 April 1801, the British Fleet attacked the Danish Fleet off Copenhagen. This painting shows British warships firing broadsides at the moored Danish line visible in the background. In the right foreground are two British vessels, Russell and Bellona, which ran aground in shallow water.

Napoleonic Wars

In 1801, the northern powers of Russia, Prussia, Denmark, and Sweden formed an alliance that represented a challenge to British interests in the Baltic. Britain sent a fleet to the region under Admiral Sir Hyde Parker, with Nelson as second-in-command. In April, the Danish Fleet was destroyed during the Battle of Copenhagen.

However, Britain was more concerned by events in France. Fearing the growing power of Napoleon Bonaparte, who was about to crown himself Emperor of France, the British declared war in 1803. In response, Napoleon built a fleet of barges and threatened to invade England. With hindsight, it is clear that the craft were not seaworthy, but the perceived threat lasted for over two years. In 1805, Napoleon turned to mainland Europe, defeating the Austrians, who had joined the alliance against him, at Ulm and Austerlitz. In October, the combined Franco-Spanish Fleet was defeated at Cape Trafalgar (see panel, opposite).

After Trafalgar, the Royal Navy had to adapt to a new kind of war. In his Berlin Decrees of 1806, Napoleon – now master of most of Europe – declared that ports under his control were closed to British shipping. The British replied by blockading any port that obeyed this edict. In the past, the Royal Navy had blockaded a limited number of large naval ports; now it had to maintain a force that could police dozens of small ports all over Europe. This created a need for more smaller-sized ships, and in the period up to 1812 the Royal Navy expanded to more than a thousand vessels. At the same time, the threat of a French naval revival could not be ignored, for large ships of the line continued to be built in France, the Netherlands, and Italy.

> **"** It [the English Channel] is a mere ditch, and will be crossed as soon as someone has the courage to attempt it. **"**
>
> **NAPOLEON**, 1803

Unlike some previous conflicts, the Napoleonic Wars could not be settled by negotiation, and an alliance of land forces was needed to overthrow the emperor. Navies were peripheral to this process, although they exposed weaknesses in Napoleon's empire. In 1808, the enforcement of the Berlin Decrees triggered a Spanish revolt against French rule. A British army was sent in support of the Spanish guerrillas, supported by British seapower. Further north, Russia refused to accept French dominance, and Napoleon's disastrous invasion in 1812 led to his defeat. Exiled to the island of Elba off Italy in 1814, he escaped to rally his armies. Napoleon was finally defeated at Waterloo on 18 June 1815. He fled from Paris to the coast, but was caught by British ships and sent back into exile.

THE END OF NAPOLEON
This oil painting depicts Napoleon onboard the British warship Bellerophon in July 1815, having surrendered to its captain, Frederick Maitland, off the French coast near La Rochelle. He was later taken to exile on the Atlantic island of St. Helena.

BATTLE OF TRAFALGAR

In late September 1805, Vice-Admiral Lord Nelson joined the British Fleet off Cadiz, Spain, to blockade the large Franco-Spanish Fleet in the port, which was under the command of the Admiral Comte de Villeneuve. Napoleon goaded Villeneuve into putting to sea, although the Admiral was aware that his ships, albeit superior in numbers, lagged behind Nelson's in the seamanship and gunnery skills of their crew.

Nelson had planned to divide his fleet into three divisions, but a shortage of ships caused him to reduce this to one led by himself and another under Cuthbert Collingwood. As they sailed into action against a loosely formed Franco-Spanish line on the morning of 21 October, Nelson considered several strategies: breaking the enemy line in the middle, near the French flagship, *Bucentaure*; cutting off about two-thirds of the line, to be dealt with by Collingwood; or attacking the "head" of the line to prevent an escape to Cadiz. Eventually, he settled for the first option.

REDOUTABLE AT TRAFALGAR

One of the battle's key stages was the arrival of the British "windward" column under Nelson. This painting depicts the French ship Redoutable (centre) trapped between the British ships Victory (left) and Temeraire (right).

BATTLE PLAN

This diagram shows the position of the opposing fleets at noon on 21 October 1805. The British adopted a daring two-column attack on the Franco-Spanish line.

Collingwood raced ahead to attack near the enemy rear, cutting through the line with his flagship, *Royal Sovereign,* at about midday. The first six ships of his division were strung out, suffering heavy casualties before reinforcements could arrive. At 12:20pm, Nelson entered the battle in *Victory*. She raked the *Bucentaure*, causing great damage, but was then engaged by the 74-gun *Redoubtable*.

Nelson had planned the entry to battle carefully, but the fight soon descended into a series of duels between individual ships, sometimes with others in support. It was fought at close range, and many British sailors, including

Nelson, fell to musket fire from the tops of French ships, especially the *Redoutable*, whose captain had trained his men in such combat.

As more ships joined the fighting, the British began to prevail. The French and Spanish ships failed to take any initiatives and began to surrender. The British captured 19 ships of the line and destroyed another, but a storm in the days after the battle meant that all but four of the prizes escaped or were wrecked. The battle was an ambiguous British victory, but confirmed British dominance at sea for nearly a century. Nelson's unorthodox tactics also had a long-lasting effect.

THE DEATH OF NELSON

This painting shows the moment, at about 1:15pm, when Nelson fell onto his flagship's quarter-deck, having been fatally wounded by a shot from a sniper onboard Redoutable.

Map

Portugal
Spain
ATLANTIC OCEAN
Gulf of Cadiz
☐ Site of battle
North Africa

British vessel

Spanish vessel

French vessel

Nelson's "windward" column

wind

Bucentaure

Victory

Redoubtable

squadron under Spanish Admiral Gravina is cut off from main Franco-Spanish Fleet

Royal Sovereign

Temeraire

British advance

French and Spanish survivors return to Cadiz

N

Collingwood's "lee" column

British ships advance to enemy line, then turn to present broadside

main Franco-Spanish line

The new American Navy

The naval power of the United States had remained static since the nation had won its independence. However, from 1785, American merchant vessels, which were no longer protected by British warships, began to suffer significant losses to the Barbary corsairs of North Africa. The United States realized that it needed to develop a naval force to protect its merchant interests in the Mediterranean and the Atlantic. In 1794, US Congress approved the construction of six frigates to be built by

AMERICAN ADMIRALS
This illustration is taken from the 1864 book Naval Heroes of the United States. *Isaac Hull, who commanded the* Constitution *during the War of 1812, is top right.*

CONSTITUTION SAILS FROM HOME
The frigate Constitution *is still in commission today. In July 1997, 200 years after it was first launched, the warship sailed again from Boston Harbor, for the first time in more than a century.*

Joshua Humphreys (see panel, right): *Congress, Constitution, President, United States, Constellation,* and *Chesapeake.* The US Navy was born. Much like the French Navy of the 1730s (see p.121), the Americans were aware that they would not become a major naval power in the immediate future. The main threats the young nation faced on the high seas were attacks on American commerce and port blockades, which prevented maritime trade. With this in mind, the six new frigates were larger, stronger, and faster than any others of the time and had almost as much gun power on one deck as a small ship of the line had on two. They were able to break the blockade of any port using either speed or force and could attack enemy merchant vessels and frigates. From 1798, the new United States Navy fought with France over trade, and, in the early years of the 19th century, conflict continued with the Barbary states.

The War of 1812

The United States found themselves at war with the British from 1812. Like the Anglo-Dutch Wars a century and a half earlier (see pp.114–16), the War of 1812 was primarily maritime in its causes and execution.

JOSHUA HUMPHREYS

Born in Delaware, the American shipbuilder Joshua Humphreys (1751–1838) began his career as an apprentice in Philadelphia. He quickly established himself as a skilled naval architect. When the US Congress decided to establish a naval force, Humphreys was given the job of naval constructor. He agreed with the Secretary of War, Henry Knox, that large frigates should be constructed. The ships that were designed had almost as many guns as a conventional ship of the line and excellent sailing qualities, so that they were able to escape from larger vessels. Humphreys built six highly successful frigates, three of the Constitution class of 44 guns and three of the Constellation class of 36 guns. He was dismissed from office in 1801, but in 1806 he helped to set up naval facilities in Philadelphia.

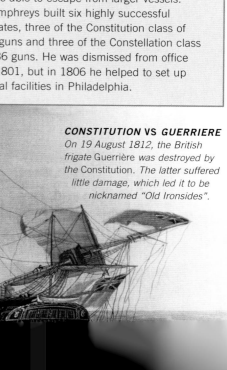

CONSTITUTION VS GUERRIERE
On 19 August 1812, the British frigate Guerrière *was destroyed by the* Constitution. *The latter suffered little damage, which led it to be nicknamed "Old Ironsides".*

The Americans objected to the British habit of searching American merchant ships for deserters from their own navy, and, as a result, President Madison asked Congress to declare war in favour of "free trade and sailors' rights". The British raided the American coast and attacked Washington. At sea, however, the American frigates were triumphant, capturing and destroying a string of inferior ships in highly publicized actions. The battle between the *Constitution* and the frigate *Guerrière* left the British ship shattered by its American opponent. The British rallied somewhat in 1813, when Captain Broke of the *Shannon* challenged the captain of the *Chesapeake*, James Lawrence, off the coast of Boston. Broke defeated the *Chesapeake* in just 15 minutes. In 1815, the war ended. Yet again, the British, who still had the world's most dominant naval force, had to rethink warship design in reaction to the innovations of another navy.

The end of the sailing wars

The Royal Navy faced competition from other nations at the beginning of the 19th century. The French Navy had revived; Russia had a large but inefficient fleet; and the American Navy, although small, was highly effective. The Dutch, Danish, and Spanish navies had been seriously damaged during the Napoleonic Wars

IMPROVEMENTS IN CONSTRUCTION

Early in the 19th century, the British shipwright Robert Seppings developed improvements that allowed larger warships to be constructed. He focused on strengthening the structure of ships. The wooden beams and planks that made up a vessel had traditionally been set at right angles to one another, ignoring the geometric principle that a triangle is more rigid than a rectangle and placing great strain on the hull. Seppings, following the example of some French and American warships, replaced the riders (vertical supports) in the hold with interlocking diagonal braces. He also filled the spaces between the lower ribs of the ship with concrete. Seppings also applied diagonal supports between the gun ports and laid the deck planking diagonally, which lessened the strain on the timbers. Seppings's system of ship construction soon proved its worth on the high seas. Subsequently, the wooden diagonals were replaced by supports made from iron. Seppings also modified the shape of warships. He built up the structure of the ship to create the round bow, which was sturdier than previous designs, and allowed more space for guns to be fitted.

PLAN OF THE WARSHIP *TREMENDOUS*
Robert Seppings constructed the 74-gun warship Tremendous *using his system of diagonal supports in 1811. This plan shows the interior of the ship.*

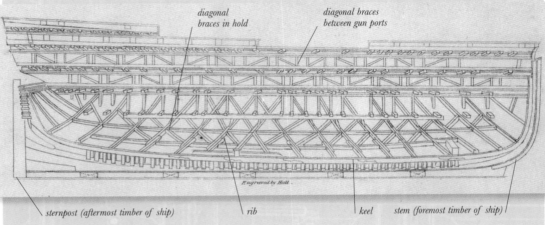

diagonal braces in hold

diagonal braces between gun ports

Engraved by Holl.

sternpost (aftermost timber of ship)   rib   keel   stem (foremost timber of ship)

steering wheel

winch for raising keel

RETRACTABLE KEEL
This 1795 model shows a yacht equipped with Captain Schanck's retractable keel. The model also has a retractable rudder.

retractable keel allows ship to move in shallow water

and were no longer strong maritime powers. Technological progress accelerated after about 1810. The substantial funds poured into navies finally began to converge with the scientific and innovative spirit of the age, and many new inventions were tested. Some were minor improvements, such as new types of pump. Others, such as Captain Schanck's retractable keel (see above), did not catch on. The most important innovation was Robert Seppings's new system of construction (see panel, above).

During the 1820s, the 90-gun two-deck warship replaced the classic 74-gun ship as the standard warship, and three-deck vessels of 120 guns became common. Although nobody was aware of it at the time, the end of the Napoleonic Wars in 1815 ushered in a long period of peace in Europe, with far fewer major conflicts between the great powers.

In 1827, a combined British, French, and Russian Fleet, acting in support of Greek independence, defeated a Turkish force in Navarino Bay, near Pylos, Greece. The battle did much to convince Europeans that they were superior to other cultures, but it also signalled the end of the age of maritime conflict under sail. In less than 20 years, it would be impossible to consider naval action without taking the power of steam into account.

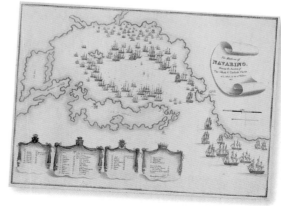

BATTLE OF NAVARINO
This chart shows the position of the fleets at Navarino Bay on 20 October 1827. The allied fleet is about to attack the Turkish Fleet, which is anchored in a semicircle.

THE LAST GREAT BATTLE UNDER SAIL
The Battle of Navarino was the last of the great battles of the age of sail. This 1838 painting of the battle conveys the horror and confusion of maritime conflict.

17TH-CENTURY WARSHIPS

In the late 1600s, huge navies became widespread, and the size of warships increased. Navies were more committed to broadside gun power than before, and attempts to row their ships were all but abandoned. Warships were categorized in several ways, usually by the number of guns they carried or by the number of full decks of guns. Most navies also divided them into "rates". In the English Navy, a 100-gun ship was a first rate, and a third rate usually had about 70 guns.

DECORATED STERN
This painting depicts the Dutch flagship Eendracht, *in about 1670, showing the narrow, highly decorated stern of Dutch ships of the period.*

Galleys

Galleys were no longer as important as they had been in the past, even in their home area, the Mediterranean, as the performance of sailing ships improved even in light winds and the armament of such ships far outclassed that of galleys. However, galleys were maintained until the middle of the 18th century by some naval powers, including France and Spain. The Knights of Malta, warrior monks dedicated to fighting Muslim influence, also had a fleet of galleys. Even the English tried to operate a galley in the Mediterranean for a time in the 1670s. The Russians and the Swedes used a different style of galley during their wars in the Baltic, largely to take part in amphibious operations with armies. The French galleys were manned by convicts as part of the penal system. The flagship *La Reale* (right) was a highly decorated vessel.

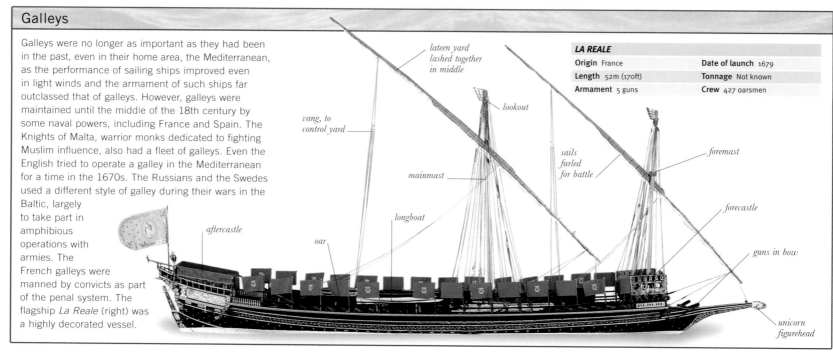

LA REALE	
Origin France	Date of launch 1679
Length 52m (170ft)	Tonnage Not known
Armament 5 guns	Crew 427 oarsmen

lateen yard lashed together in middle

vang, to control yard

lookout

mainmast

sails furled for battle

foremast

longboat

forecastle

aftercastle

oar

guns in bow

unicorn figurehead

Two-decked warships

A two-decked warship carrying between 40 and 80 guns was the standard warship type in western-European navies in the mid- to late 1600s. It had powerful guns, to be effective in a line of battle, but used less timber than the three-decker, so it could be produced in greater numbers. In England, development started with the ships of the *Speaker* class (right) of 1649, with about 50 guns. Larger ships were built over time, culminating in the 80-gun *Boyne* (below) of 1692, but this class was too large to be effective, and later two-deckers had fewer guns. The Dutch also used two-deckers. The 76-gun flagship *Eendracht* blew up at the Battle of Lowestoft in 1666.

quarter galleries

wreathed gunport

SPEAKER-CLASS WARSHIP

BOYNE	
Origin England	Date of launch 1692
Length 47.85m (157ft)	Tonnage 1,160 tons
Armament 80 guns	Crew 490

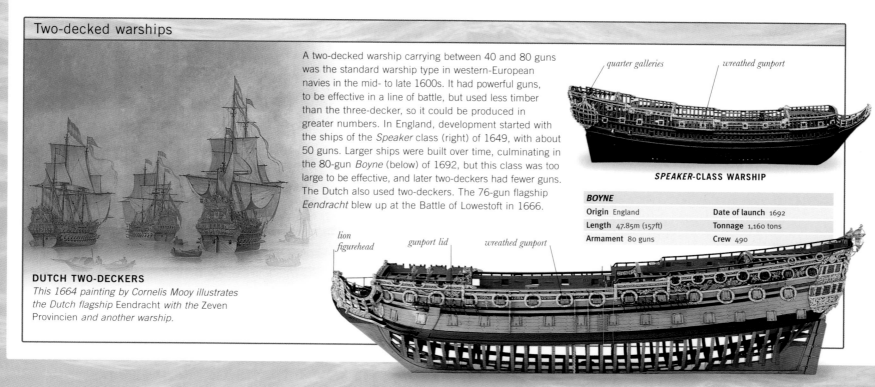

DUTCH TWO-DECKERS
This 1664 painting by Cornelis Mooy illustrates the Dutch flagship Eendracht *with the Zeven Provincien and another warship.*

lion figurehead

gunport lid

wreathed gunport

Three-decked warships

The three-decked warship, descended from the *Sovereign of the Seas* (see p.105) was the most powerful and prestigious vessel of the age, but it was too expensive to build in large numbers. The Dutch built very few because of their shallow waters, but the English and the French had more. These ships might carry as few as 80 guns, but larger ships of 90 to 100 guns were more successful, and the very largest ones were used as fleet flagships. The *St. Michael* of 1669

(below) was one of the smaller English three-deckers, with 90 guns, and her model is the oldest one of an identifiable English ship to survive. The French *Soleil Royal* (right) was built in 1669 and armed with about 100 guns. She was burned in 1692 by English fireships after a battle with the English and Dutch fleets at La Hogue and Barfleur.

SOLEIL ROYAL

ST. MICHAEL

Origin England	**Date of launch** 1669
Length 38m (125ft) (keel)	**Tonnage** 1,101 tons
Armament 90 guns	**Crew** 600

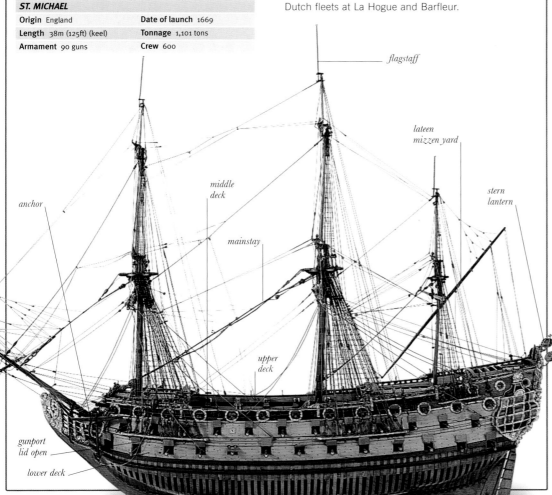

- flagstaff
- lateen mizzen yard
- middle deck
- stern lantern
- anchor
- mainstay
- upper deck
- gunport lid open
- lower deck

Xebec

Although its origins are obscure, by the 17th century the Barbary corsairs of North Africa had evolved a type of sailing and rowing vessel called a *xebec*. Unlike most sailing vessels, its narrow hull allowed it to be rowed well, and its lateen sails were arranged to permit sailing closer to the wind than European ships. A later version was rigged with lateen sails on the foremast, square sails on the main, and a combination on the mizzen. The *xebec* was adapted by the French and Spanish navies and called a chebec.

CHEBEC

Origin Spain	**Date of launch** 1735
Length 31.6m (103ft 9in)	**Tonnage** 247 tons
Armament 30 guns	**Crew** Not known

Bomb vessels

In 1682, the French built a vessel to hit the Barbary corsairs in their bases, using mortars with a high trajectory instead of conventional guns. A strengthened hull could take the weight, and the foremast was omitted. The idea was soon copied by other navies.

- dropped side

BOMB VESSEL

Origin France	**Date of launch** 1682
Length 21.3m (70ft)	**Tonnage** 120 tons
Armament 4 guns, including 2 mortars	

Galley frigates

The original frigate was a small, fast vessel used by the privateers of Dunkirk. Another type, known as the galley frigate, was built in the 1670s to deal with Barbary corsairs and was fitted with oars.

CHARLES GALLEY

Origin England	**Date of launch** 1676
Length 40m (131ft)	**Tonnage** 546 tons
Armament 32 guns	**Crew** 220

Yachts

Although they soon became associated with leisure sailing, yachts were also used as small warships, on diplomatic missions, and to carry messages to and from fleets. The *Mary* (below) was given to Charles II of England by the Dutch in 1661.

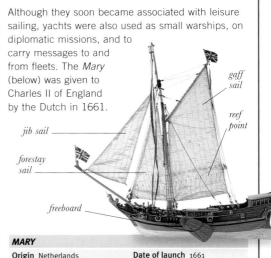

- gaff sail
- reef point
- jib sail
- forestay sail
- freeboard

MARY

Origin Netherlands	**Date of launch** 1661
Length 15.8m (52ft) (keel)	**Tonnage** 100 tons
Armament 7 guns	**Crew** 28

18TH- AND 19TH-CENTURY WARSHIPS

Warship design did not change radically between 1700 and 1800, but it was refined in many ways. Warships of 1800 were about 30 per cent larger than before and usually had lower hulls in proportion to their length, making them better in unfavourable winds. New nations such as the United States produced fine ships; the Russians had many ships but they were poorly built and manned. The traditional naval powers, Britain and France, continued to compete in warship design.

BATTLE OF MALAGA
This painting of the Battle of Malaga (1704) shows English and Spanish warships engaging at close range. Galleys can be seen in the foreground.

Two-deckers

The model below shows a typical British two-decker of around 1730 that would carry 60 guns. Such ships were built according to the Establishment of Dimensions, which made ship design very static. Generally, British ships of the time were crammed with too many guns, and this affected their seaworthiness. In the 1740s, the French began to build bigger two-deckers and hit upon the 74-gun ship, which was the ideal compromise between gun power, strength, economy, and sailing qualities. They intended to use this ship in a new kind of colonial warfare, in which fleets would be sent across oceans. A 74-gun ship could take on a three-decker in battle or chase a frigate with some hope of success. Soon all the major battlefleets were dominated by 74-gun ships, although two-deckers of 64 and 50 guns survived in Britain and the Netherlands.

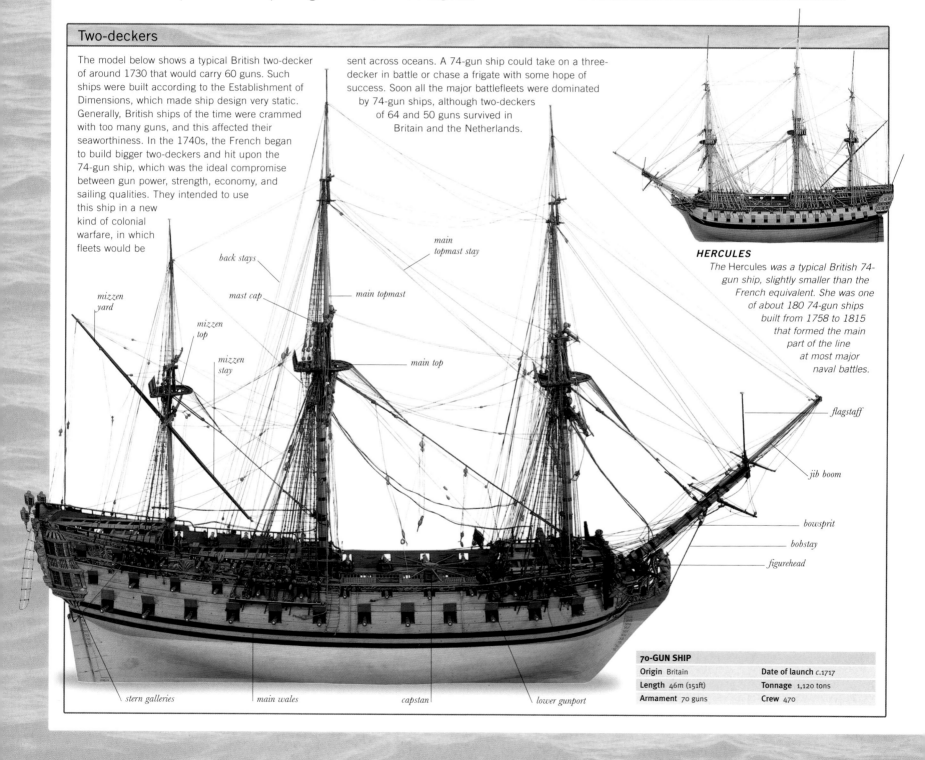

HERCULES
The Hercules was a typical British 74-gun ship, slightly smaller than the French equivalent. She was one of about 180 74-gun ships built from 1758 to 1815 that formed the main part of the line at most major naval battles.

main topmast stay

back stays

mast cap

main topmast

mizzen yard

mizzen top

mizzen stay

main top

flagstaff

jib boom

bowsprit

bobstay

figurehead

stern galleries

main wales

capstan

lower gunport

70-GUN SHIP			
Origin Britain		**Date of launch** c.1717	
Length 46m (151ft)		**Tonnage** 1,120 tons	
Armament 70 guns		**Crew** 470	

Three-deckers

The three-decker remained in favour in most navies as the largest class of warship. Spain's *Santissima Trinidad* (below) was built as a three-decker but later had extra guns added to make her a four-decker.

stay sail

spritsail

gaff mizzen sail

SANTISSIMA TRINIDAD

Origin Cuba	**Date of launch** 1769
Length 57m (186ft 9in)	**Tonnage** 2,153 tons
Armament 136 guns	**Crew** More than 1,000

Frigates

The "true frigate", not to be confused with a vessel of a similar name used in the mid-17th century, evolved in France in the 1740s and was copied by other nations. It had a single deck of guns and good sailing qualities, making it one of the most popular ships. The *Pallas* (left) was a typical British frigate. The *Constitution* (right) was originally built to protect American trade against the Barbary corsairs but found fame in battles with the British in the War of 1812.

PALLAS

dolphin striker supporting bowsprit

CONSTITUTION

Origin United States	**Date of launch** 1797
Length 53.3m (175ft)	**Tonnage** 1,576 tons
Armament 38 guns	**Crew** 460

Bomb vessels

Late 18th-century bomb vessels tended to have the full three-masted ship rig, unlike their two-masted predecessors. Their heavy structure below decks was designed to bear the weight of a mortar and to store ammunition. They were virtually the only ships that required skill in aiming the guns, since they could not be brought up alongside the enemy. In Britain, the guns were usually manned by soldiers rather than sailors.

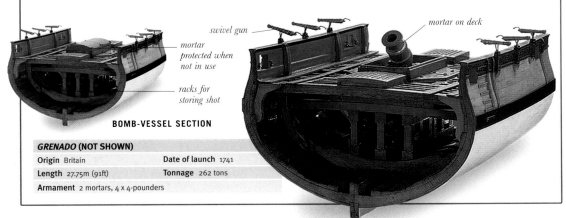

swivel gun

mortar protected when not in use

racks for storing shot

mortar on deck

BOMB-VESSEL SECTION

GRENADO (NOT SHOWN)

Origin Britain	**Date of launch** 1741
Length 27.75m (91ft)	**Tonnage** 262 tons
Armament 2 mortars, 4 x 4-pounders	

Invasion craft

The French built many different types of boats for the projected invasion of Britain in 1803–05. The invasion was never launched, and many of the craft seem rather impractical. Still, the threat kept the British occupied for more than two years.

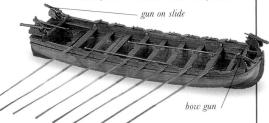

gun on slide

bow gun

CHALOUPE CANNONIERE

Origin France	**Date of launch** *c.*1803
Length 23–24.5m (76–80ft)	**Tonnage** About 100 tons
Armament 4 guns	**Crew** 22 sailors, 130 soldiers

Gunboats

Many types of small craft were built for use in confined waters, such as the Mediterranean and the Baltic. These vessels differed from older galleys in abandoning the traditional projection in the bow and having a much stouter structure. Among the most famous were those designed by Fredrik Af Chapman for the Swedes in their wars against the Russians. Commissioner Hamilton's gunboat (below) was designed to defend the British base at Gibraltar against Spanish attack. A total of 85 were built for various uses.

COMMISSIONER HAMILTON'S GUNBOAT

Origin Britain	**Date of launch** 1805–08
Length 15.4m (50ft 7in)	**Tonnage** 94 tons
Armament 3 x 18-pounder guns	

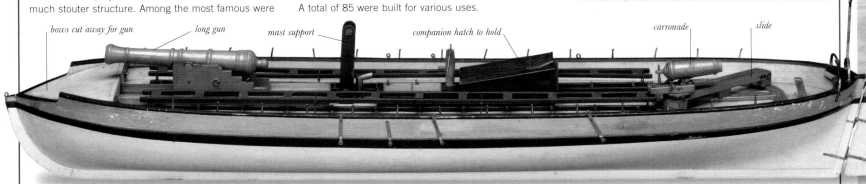

bows cut away for gun   *long gun*   *mast support*   *companion hatch to hold*   *carronade*   *slide*

17TH-CENTURY GOLD COINS

> " Whosoever commands the seas, commands the trade; whosoever commands the trade of the world, commands the riches of the world. "
>
> **SIR WALTER RALEIGH**, *A Discourse on the Invention of Shipping*, **c.1615**

TRADE UNDER SAIL

A WORLD TRADING COMMUNITY HAD TAKEN SHAPE BY 1650. IT WAS DOMINATED BY THE SPANISH, PORTUGUESE, AND DUTCH, BUT OTHER NATIONS BEGAN TO CHALLENGE THEIR POSITION.

After 1648, as their long conflict with the Spanish finally came to an end, the Dutch consolidated their position as the leading commercial power of the age. Imports of grain and timber from the Baltic formed the largest components of Dutch trade, but they also established a vast herring fishing fleet, salting the fish and selling them on in the Baltic and Mediterranean. They assembled cargoes of various kinds of merchandise in the United Provinces (now the Netherlands) for re-export, and their elaborate system of inland waterways allowed goods to be transported from one port to another with ease.

Dutch success depended on several factors that gave them a unique trading advantage. They had a network of merchants around the world, and access to capital that moved into Amsterdam after the decline of the port of Antwerp in the Spanish Netherlands. Above all,

KEY EVENTS

1651 NAVIGATION ACTS The English parliament passes an act that prevents all foreign shipping from using English ports and leads to the Anglo-Dutch Wars.

1667 CANAL DU MIDI Work starts on the Canal du Midi, ordered by Louis XIV, which links the Mediterranean Sea with the Atlantic.

1734 *LLOYD'S LIST* The British insurance company Lloyd's, by now the primary maritime underwriter, starts to publish *Lloyd's List*, a daily newspaper detailing shipping movements.

1768 SHIP SURVEY Swedish shipwright Fredrik af Chapman publishes *Architectura Navalis Mercatoria*, an extensive survey of European shipping.

1794 SLAVERY ABOLISHED France outlaws slavery in its colonies, followed by bans in Denmark in 1803 and in mainland Britain and the USA in 1807.

1825 ERIE CANAL OPENS The waterway linking the Hudson River to the Great Lakes opens, leading to the expansion of New York.

their country was well positioned for trade, being at the mouth of the River Rhine and between the Atlantic and the Baltic. Dutch trading success also relied on mass-produced, economical merchant ships, which, in the words of Sir Walter Raleigh, were built "to hold great bulk of merchandise, and to sail with few men for profit". One of the most successful Dutch merchant ships of the 17th century, a vessel that was to become a symbol of its age, was the *fluyt*.

The Dutch *fluyt*

The *fluyt* was usually quite a small ship of perhaps 300 tons. It had a barrel-shaped appearance, with a prominent bulge in the lower

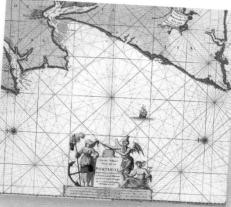

stern and a tumble-home (a sharp narrowing of the hull above the waterline). The compact size and shape of the vessel reduced the duties that had to be paid to harbour authorities for use of their facilities. The *fluyt*'s simple design made it easier for the crew to move around the ship and provided optimum space for freight. The vessel was not designed to carry a specific cargo and was sufficiently adaptable to carry almost anything, although it flourished in the Baltic trade.

The rigging was simple – the upper masts, for example, were easily lowered in rough weather. The *fluyt* carried little, if any, armament, in contrast to English craft, which were fast becoming the main rivals to Dutch merchant shipping. In 1669 the English calculated that Dutch merchant vessels, such as the *fluyt*, cost about 40 per cent of comparable English ships to run. Typically, a Dutch ship had a relatively small crew of one man for every 20 tons, compared with one man for every seven tons on English ships.

MERCHANT SHIPS
In this Dutch painting, various merchant ships are shown assembled in a Mediterranean harbour. The ship with its stern facing out is a Dutch fluyt; other ships include a Mediterranean galley (second left) and a Dutch East Indiaman (far left).

A type of ship called the *oostvarder* was also used by the Dutch to trade in the Baltic. It was slightly larger than *fluyts*, at 300 to 600 tons, and had a shallow draught for entry to river estuaries. For Mediterranean and Far Eastern trades, the Dutch used an armed version of the *fluyt* – the pinnace. A simplified version of the *fluyt* was the *katschip*, known as the cat in English. It had bluff, flat bows and, unusually for the time, no figurehead. The *katschip* had a stumpy rig, and its masts were constructed from a single pole, allowing easy sail handling.

DUTCH RUDDER
A rudder was fitted to the sternpost of a small craft and used to manipulate the direction in which the vessel travelled.

The English response
For the first half of the 17th century, the English continued to favour armed merchant vessels and other kinds of defensible ships, even on coastal and short sea routes. From the middle of the century, English craft did much to undermine Dutch superiority in merchant shipping. In 1651 the Republican parliament passed the

DUTCH LEEBOARD
A leeboard is lowered from the side of a craft and acts like a large oar, providing resistance against the water to lessen sideways drifting of the ship.

Navigation Act, which decreed that merchandise bound for England must be carried on English ships or ships from the country in which the goods originated. It was a punitive piece of legislation that was intended to destroy the Dutch position as carriers to the world and led directly to the three Anglo-Dutch Wars (see pp.114–16).

By the terms of the act, the master and three-quarters of the crew of an English ship had to originate from England. However, Dutch ships captured as prizes by the English were specifically excluded from the Navigation Act, so the English could incorporate thousands of highly efficient Dutch pinnaces and *fluyts* seized during the three Anglo-Dutch Wars into their own merchant service. This also gave English merchants,

shipwrights, and riggers the opportunity to study Dutch construction techniques to improve their own designs. Although England and the Netherlands made peace in 1674, hostilities between the Dutch and the French continued, which allowed the English to penetrate several markets now closed to the Dutch and to expand trade in the Mediterranean. By the end of the 17th century, English shipping was one of the world's fastest-growing industries.

Adaptable ships
All northern European merchant ships of the 17th century carried some fore-and-aft sails (sails that are parallel to the keel), either in the form of triangular staysails that were hung

SPRITSAIL
During the 17th century, the Dutch developed the spritsail, an earlier Greek invention, which can be seen on this coastal craft. A diagonal spar passes across the centre of the sail. Spritsails reduced weight at the top of the rig, but they made it awkward for a craft to move from one tack to the other.

Diversity of craft

In the late 17th century, the
merchant ships of the
French coasts were surveyed
and depicted for the *Rolle
General* of shipping. Among
the vessels shown were a
simple single-masted vessel
with an open hold, tiller
steering, and a single,
square-rigged mast.
Another craft, which was
a type of barque, had a
square, flat stern and two
masts with a single square sail
on each. The *pinnasse*, resembling
the Dutch pinnace, had a flat, square stern
with a row of windows, a figurehead and rail,
and three masts.

Mediterranean craft were subject to a range
of influences, which was evident from the
diversity of craft found in the region. These
ships included vessels that were similar to
northern European ocean-going ships, galleys,
and boats that had evolved from the practices

from the ropes that
supported the masts, or as gaff sails
that were hung from spars, called gaffs,
aft of the lower mizzen mast. Fore-and-aft rig
was mainly used by small trading boats of
100 tons or less. It was more useful than the
square rig used by larger craft, as it allowed
the boat to sail closer to the wind. However,
the benefits of this type of rig were limited,
as the wooden masts and hemp ropes used at
the time created a great deal of drag. The most
common type of rig used was the gaff rig,
which resembled the triangular lateen rig (see
p.57), although it dispensed with the small sail
forward of the mast.

There was little specialization among large
European merchant ships of the 17th century,
and they were adaptable, transforming from
cargo to passenger craft with minimal effort.
Migration to colonies, such as those in the
East Indies, meant that there was a rise in the
number of passengers travelling on merchant
craft. Conditions onboard depended on class.
On the biggest, armed merchant ships, such
as the East Indiamen operated by the Dutch,
French, and English (see p.147), wealthy and
distinguished passengers lived with the officers
in the great cabin. Other passengers, including
troops, servants, and slaves, lived on the decks
among the ordinary seamen. They were
expected to bear such hardship, having no right
to complain about conditions.

Ocean-going merchant ships continued to
reflect the national characteristics of their native
countries, but, like warships, they became more

similar over the years. Most ocean-going
merchant ships of the 17th and 18th centuries
were ship rigged, with three square-rigged
masts. The main exceptions were vessels with
a two-masted rig, which were known as a brig
if the fore-and-aft mizzen sail was attached
directly to the mast, or as a snow if it was fitted
to a spar directly aft of the mast.

DUTCH LOCAL CRAFT

Local craft of all nations in the 17th century
were adapted to regional differences in weather
conditions, such as the wind, and the character
of coastal waters, such as differences in water
depth. They also reflected differences in skills,
materials, and methods of boat building. With
their shallow estuaries and highly developed
inland waterways, the Dutch developed a variety
of highly specialized trading boats that suited
their geographical position. The *schokker*, for
example, was a fishing boat used on the Zuider
Zee. It had a flat bottom and usually had a
rounded stern. The *boeier* had a round bow
and stern and was used on inland waterways
to carry farm produce, although on

Sundays it transported churchgoers. The *botter*
was a fishing boat with a deck that rose sharply
towards the bows, and there were further
regional variations of this type of craft. The *tjalk*
was a flat-bottomed vessel with
rounded ends and was used to
carry freight. Like many other
types of Dutch local craft, it
also doubled as a yacht,
used for pleasure,
rather than
trade.

SMALSCHIP
The smalschip *– which translates
as narrow ship – was one of many
types of Dutch local craft. Its design
allowed it to negotiate constricted
waterways.*

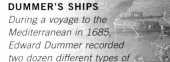

DUMMER'S SHIPS
*During a voyage to the
Mediterranean in 1685,
Edward Dummer recorded
two dozen different types of
ship. Dummer compiled a book
in which he drew meticulous plans
of each vessel, accompanying them
with a pop-up of the craft's structure.*

of Arab seafarers. Among craft identified by an English shipwright called Edward Dummer on a voyage in the Mediterranean was the *Bucentaure*, the ceremonial barge that was used by the *doge* (chief magistrate) of Venice. Dummer also described the well-known Venetian gondola, 10,000 of which are estimated to have been in existence at the time.

One of the most widespread Mediterranean craft was the *tartane*, which was used in Italy, France, and Spain. It featured a prominent projection at the bows and had either a single mast with a lateen sail or two masts, in which case the foremast raked well forward. The *caique* was a common cargo vessel that was used by the Turks, especially in the Bosporus and for island trade. It had a single mast and a square sail. The *gabarra*, which was used by merchants trading from the Spanish ports of Cadiz and Seville, displayed the influence of ancient Roman craft, while the *barca luengo* was an open boat. The *barchetto* was used in Italian ports to transport goods and passengers from ship to shore. The *polacre* had a composite rig with a lateen-rigged foremast and square sails on the

main and mizzen masts – a reversal of the northern European practice in which fore-and-aft rig was placed on the after masts.

Merchant seamen

Merchant ships of all nations were organized similarly. Each ship had a master, who was sometimes known as the captain, although that was strictly a naval title. There were at least two mates (officers), who navigated the ship and supervised the steering. Ships that embarked on long ocean voyages also needed specialists onboard, such as carpenters and coopers. The bulk of the crew consisted of ordinary seamen who entered the profession as ship's boys at an early age. Some were apprentices and were indentured to the master of the ship. Any seaman with the navigation skills necessary for the trade in question could rise to become a

VENETIAN GALLEY
*Bucentaure was the name given to the ceremonial galley of
the doge of Venice. A succession of these were built, the
finest of which was constructed in 1729. The Bucentaure
is shown here at a ceremony celebrating Ascension Day.*

mate. On an ocean-going ship, a mate required a level of literacy and numeracy to make complex calculations. However, for the coasting trades the mate simply had to memorize the features of the coast in question. In the age before telecommunications, the master wielded great power and responsibility. He had to provide rations for his men, suppress mutiny, locate new cargoes away from the home port, and keep the ship afloat and the crew healthy in all manner of adverse situations.

Seamen could make a reasonable amount of money, and they had the chance to see the world, which made them rare creatures in the

NARROW BOAT
*The gondola probably
originated in the 11th
century. The craft is
propelled by an oarsman
positioned at the boat's rear.*

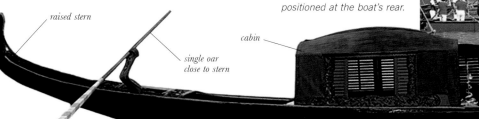

VENETIAN FESTIVAL
*Gondolas still ply the waterways of
Venice. For special occasions, brightly
coloured and decorated craft are used,
rather than the more typical black boats.*

raised stern

cabin

breast hook

*single oar
close to stern*

*asymmetrical wooden
hull is flatter on one
side than other*

CLASHING WITH CORSAIRS
This watercolour by J. Fairbairn depicts sailors boarding a vessel of Barbary corsairs as part of efforts to protect merchant shipping in the Mediterranean. Such violent clashes were frequent in the 16th and 17th centuries.

17th and 18th centuries. But the life of mariners was hard, even if they avoided disasters such as death in battle or from disease or storm, or enslavement by Barbary corsairs. For example, Edward Barlow, an Englishman who first went to sea as an apprentice in 1659 at the age of 17, suffered many setbacks over a period of more than 50 years at sea. He rose to become chief mate of several ships, but he was also pressed into the Royal Navy in 1664 and 1668,

imprisoned by the Dutch in 1674, cheated out of his wages several times, and shipwrecked on the Goodwin Sands in the North Sea in 1675. Not surprisingly, Barlow wrote in his journal of "the hardships of a sailor's life".

Barbary corsairs

From the 1530s until about 1780, merchant ships sailing in the Mediterranean and some parts of northern Europe were plagued by attacks from Barbary corsairs. These were renegade seamen from several nations, but primarily the Berber tribes, who sailed from North African bases such as Algiers, Tunis, and Tripoli. The corsairs cruised the coastal waters of Spain, Portugal, Italy, France, England, and Ireland to intercept ships and seize their cargoes or crew, and they often sacked coastal towns, carrying off people to be sold as slaves in North Africa. Several hundred thousand Europeans were enslaved in this way, but attacks declined after the mid-17th century.

The coal trade

Coal was the primary bulk cargo of the 18th century in British waters. Some parts of the country produced enough coal to satisfy their own needs, but the northeast of England had a surplus that was exported throughout Europe. In ports such as Newcastle, coal was tipped from trucks that ran on wooden rails straight into the hold of a ship, such as a collier brig. In other northern European ports, coal had to be lifted in and out of the ship's hold. Once it had been removed, the coal was often shipped upriver on barges.

The coal trade was of immense importance to the British government for strategic as well as economic reasons. The trade was a major "nursery for seamen", who could then be recruited or pressed into the Royal Navy in time of war. Negotiating the sandbanks of the English east coast required constant attention to seamanship and navigation. Moreover, collier crews were never far from home when they were needed for the navy. This was naturally not the case with the well-travelled crews of bigger merchant ships, such as East Indiamen (see p.147) or their equally large and heavily armed counterparts, which sailed on routes across the Atlantic Ocean, West Indiamen.

COLLIER BRIG
English east coast-colliers were among the most prevalent bulk cargo ships in northern Europe during the 17th and 18th centuries. The vessels had flat bottoms to allow them to moor in shallow waters and unload their cargo of coal onto carts. They could also be beached if necessary.

middle of ship forms squarish cross section

knighthead rises above deck to support bowsprit

stempost is the foremost timber of ship

flat bows

sternpost

individual pieces of timber called futtocks form ribs of ship

cylinders of oak called treenails secure ship's timbers

floor timber

keel

BRIG SKELETON
The wooden frame of a collier brig shows that it had a spacious lower hull, resembling that of its Dutch counterparts such as the fluyt, although its stern was not as high. The collier had an almost square cross section amidships and very broad, flat bows.

CHAPMAN'S SHIPS

The Swedish shipwright Fredrik af Chapman (1721–1808) was one of the foremost maritime architects of the 18th century. In his capacity as the chief naval architect for the Swedish Navy, he designed several new warships, among them innovative rowing craft, and reorganized the country's shipyards.

Chapman also made an important contribution to the concept of maritime architecture as a science. He wrote extensively on the construction, stability, and function of ships. In 1768, he published one of his most

important works: *Architectura Navalis Mercatoria*. The treatise identified and detailed most of the European merchant ships of the age. His classification was based on extensive travel, study, and experience, and his detailed engravings became the benchmark of ship draughtmanship.

EAST INDIAMAN
This East Indiaman was drawn by Chapman and printed in Architectura Navalis Mercatoria. *These were among the largest long-distance merchant ships of the period.*

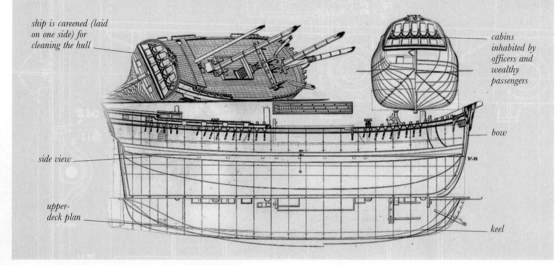

ship is careened (laid on one side) for cleaning the hull

cabins inhabited by officers and wealthy passengers

side view

bow

upper-deck plan

keel

Merchant ships and technology

It was rare for merchant ships to set the technological pace in the 17th and 18th centuries. Innovations such as the steering wheel (see p.123) and copper sheathing (see p.125) were initially tested by navies and subsequently adopted by merchant shipowners, along with navigational instruments such as the sextant and the chronometer, and improvements to the crew's welfare such as the anti-scorbutic diet, which prevented scurvy. Merchant shipowners and seamen were more conservative than navies about new technology and were reluctant to risk their lives, their profits, or their savings on new inventions.

The development of merchant ships was recorded in Fredrik af Chapman's *Architectura Navalis Mercatoria* (see panel, left). The treatise contained engraved plates of many 18th-century European merchant ships. Chapman noted that coastal craft reflected the geographical and industrial characteristics of each nation.

Dutch and English boats still dominated merchant shipping in Europe. The Dutch fly-boat was recognizably descended from the *fluyt* of the 17th century – it still had a bulbous lower bow, although the upper stern was somewhat wider. The Dutch hoy, or *galliot*, had three masts, with both fore-and-aft and square sails on the mainmast and foremast, and a fore-and-aft sail on the small mizzen. Its English counterpart, the ketch or English hoy, was used primarily for ship-to-shore work or local transport on estuaries, for example that of the Thames, and it had two masts and fore-and-aft rig of moderate size. The cutter, on the other hand, had been developed by smugglers in Folkestone, a port on the English Channel; it had a tall mast with both fore-and-aft and square sails. The most unusual rig detailed by Chapman was that of a Dutch *tjalk*. It had a sail resembling the Mediterranean lateen set aft of a single mast, which also carried a staysail and jib forward, as well as square topsails.

In general, merchant shipowners had no great need for speed. The chartered companies, which owned the trading stations in the colonies and contracted merchant ships, were monopolies and so had no fear of competition. In wartime, most merchant ships travelled in convoys that moved at the speed of the slowest ship. It was unusual for a merchant ship to carry perishable goods, and most trades

DUTCH EAST INDIES PORT
Various types of merchant ships, from local coastal craft (left) to large East Indiamen (right), are evident in this 17th-century painting of Surat, India.

LLOYD'S OF LONDON
Situated in the City of London, Lloyd's is of international importance as a maritime insurer. The company began in a coffee house in the 17th century (above), and the huge building it now occupies (above, right) is a major landmark.

were seasonal, so each year a fixed number of round trips were undertaken, with no possibility of slipping an extra voyage into the schedule.

However, fast merchant ships began to evolve in the late 18th century, often on the fringes of the great trades. Perhaps the most well known was the Baltimore Clipper, which operated as a pilot boat, privateer, blockade-runner, or slaver. It had a narrow hull, and its stern extended far deeper in the water than its bows. It remained an important type of merchant vessel in the first decades of the 19th century (see pp.232–33).

Ownership and insurance

Shipping lines did not exist at this point, and the great trading companies chartered individual ships rather than owning them. It was rare for a ship to be owned by one person, unless he was its master. But a family or individual might own shares in one or several ships. In England and the Netherlands, a ship was divided into 16, 32, or 64 shares. A local merchant or shipbuilder might own a number of shares, with the rest held in limited numbers by small investors.

Because the risks of sea travel were so great, marine insurance in one form or another had existed for centuries. It was known among the Ancient Greeks and used by the Hanseatic League. In the 1680s, English merchants began to meet in Lloyd's Coffee House in London, which became a centre for maritime insurance, although the market was not set up on a satisfactory basis until 1719. These events proved to be of global significance and Lloyd's grew rapidly; today, it insures most of the world's ships. Lloyd's also developed other elements of the maritime infrastructure, including *Lloyd's List*, a shipping newspaper, which was started in 1734, and *Lloyd's Register*, a list of merchant ships, which was first published in the 1760s and still continues today.

International trade

The East Indiaman was the largest merchant ship of its time. The vessels were primarily English, Dutch, and French and operated on lengthy trading routes to India and the Far East. East Indiamen were well armed and were of equivalent gun power to a small warship. In the late 18th century, the Royal Navy commandeered five East Indiamen under construction and used them quite successfully as 64-gun ships of the line.

East Indiamen looked as if they had two decks of guns, even if the weapons were not all fitted or operational. This resemblance to warships was encouraged by the authorities in order to protect the ships' precious cargoes on their voyages, which could take over a year. The captains of East India ships had the highest status among merchant captains, and the crews had the privilege of bringing home quantities of goods for private trade.

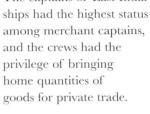

main topcastle

ARMED MERCHANT SHIP
East Indiamen were the largest merchant ships of their time and were often ornately decorated, indicating the wealth of the companies that chartered them.

ornate gold stern carvings

captain's cabin (great cabin)

cabin windows

GUNS *Although they were less well-armed than their naval contemporaries, East Indiamen carried a number of guns on their upper decks (the Amsterdam had 32). This example is stowed out of its firing position to save deck space.*

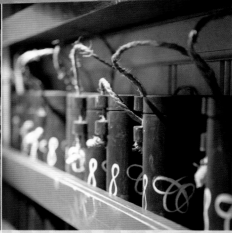

FIREPOWER *This rack holds cases containing gunpowder, which have been precisely weighed. The charges are for an 8-pounder cannon.*

DINING AREA *Officers and the most important passengers dined together in the Great Cabin, which was expensively furnished in comparison with other ships of the period.*

AMSTERDAM

THE *AMSTERDAM* WAS AN EAST INDIAMAN, THE LARGEST TYPE OF MERCHANT SHIP OF THE 17TH AND 18TH CENTURIES. SHIPS SUCH AS THIS CARRIED GOODS BETWEEN EUROPE AND ASIA.

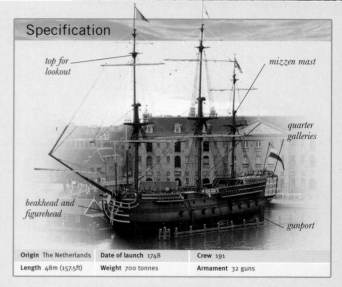

Specification

top for lookout

mizzen mast

quarter galleries

beakhead and figurehead

gunport

| Origin The Netherlands | Date of launch 1748 | Crew 191 |
| Length 48m (157.5ft) | Weight 700 tonnes | Armament 32 guns |

BUILT IN THE SHIPYARD belonging to the Dutch East India Company, in the city after which she was named, the *Amsterdam* was launched in 1748 for the purpose of sailing to distant colonies, such as Batavia (now Java). The ship left the Dutch port of Texel in January 1749, commanded by Captain Willem Klump. However, two weeks after setting sail, he was forced to beach the ship off the coast of southern England. The *Amsterdam* had lost her rudder in a violent storm, and many of those onboard were desperately ill. A large section of the ship's hull survived, buried under about 6m (20ft) of mud and sand, including much of the lower deck and hold. In 1991, a replica of the ship was built using archaeological evidence from the wreck and historical documents and plans. The replica, shown here, is now in Amsterdam's Scheepvaart Museum.

The *Amsterdam* has a layout that is typical of an 18th-century East Indiaman. She has the almost universal three-masted ship rig of the period (which carried three square sails on the fore- and mainmasts, and one square and one fore-and-aft sail on the mizzen). There are two rows of windows in the stern, which illuminate the cabins that the officers and passengers inhabited. Quarter galleries on each side of the hull house the lavatories. The steering wheel is situated on the quarterdeck, just forward of the captain's cabin. There is a gap between the quarterdeck and the forecastle, which is known as the waist. The beakhead at the bow of the ship is short and round, with a relatively long figurehead that follows its shape. The galley is fitted well forward, under the

forecastle. The boat deck, the highest continuous deck in the ship, is well armed, but also has cabins for the ship's passengers. The main capstan, which was used for raising anchors and spars, is aft on this deck. The upper deck was partly used for carrying extra cargo. Most of the crew slept in hammocks on this deck, alongside the 123 soldiers that the *Amsterdam* was transporting to the East Indies. Below the upper deck, the powder stores are situated aft and stores for spare parts forward. The hold, which was used for storage, is the lowest part of the ship.

HOLD *As well as fresh water and provisions, the space below decks was used to store supplies and manufactured goods to be taken out to the East Indies and a cargo of spices to be brought back.*

CAPTAIN'S CABIN *Not much is known about how Captain Klump decorated his cabin. However, he would have had a table to work at, which was lashed to the deck.*

STORE *Far aft on the lower deck is the gun room, where wooden chests full of weapons were stored. The ship's vast tiller passes through this room, connecting with the rudder.*

STERN *The rear end of an East Indiaman, such as the Amsterdam, was decorated ornately. The figures that flank the stern galleries are the ancient Roman gods Mercury (left), who represents trade, and Neptune (right), who symbolizes the sea. The ship flies the flag of the Dutch East India Company.*

SURGEON'S ROOM *East Indiamen often carried a surgeon onboard, equipped with various instruments and potions.*

SEAL *This is the seal of the Dutch East India Company etched into a wooden chest.*

GALLEY *Galley stoves were mostly constructed of brick on 18th-century ships.*

SHIP'S BELL *The iron bell is richly decorated with the vessel's name and the Dutch East India Company's trademark.*

TOP *This platform was used to handle rigging and as a lookout post.*

CREW'S QUARTERS *Most of the sailors and soldiers who sailed onboard the Amsterdam inhabited the upper deck. They slept in canvas hammocks.*

TRADE OF SHAME
Ships involved in the Triangular Trade took goods from Europe to Africa, where they were exchanged for people. This human cargo was transported across the Atlantic to the Caribbean colonies, where the Africans were sold as slaves to plantation owners. Rum and sugar from the colonies were then taken back to Europe.

TRIANGULAR TRADE

→ Route from Europe to Africa and the Caribbean

North America

Britain

Europe

France

GOODS TRADED TO EUROPE

ATLANTIC OCEAN

GOODS TRADED TO AFRICA

MIDDLE PASSAGE

Caribbean Colonies

Africa

Caribbean Sea

west Africa

N

50   0 km   50
50   0 miles   50

The Triangular Trade

One of the most notorious long-distance maritime trades of the 17th and 18th centuries was the Triangular Trade, one element of which was the barbaric traffic of humans. It is estimated that more than 10 million Africans were shipped across the Atlantic Ocean to the Caribbean islands to work on European-owned

SLAVER'S LOG-BOOK
The slave ship Sandown *sailed from London to Sierra Leone, west Africa, in 1793. The ship's captain, Samuel Gamble, wrote of how African slaves were brought to the coast and sold to European slave ships.*

plantations. Ships departed from European ports, such as Liverpool, London, Bristol, and Nantes, with goods to be traded with African rulers and merchants. On reaching west Africa,

and the nations we now know as Nigeria, Ivory Coast, Benin, and Ghana, boats were sent ashore, and the European cargoes were exchanged for men, women, and children.

In 1751, the English slaver John Newton spent five months filling his ship, the *Duke of Argyle*, with slaves. He kept a log-book, which detailed the process: "longboat returned with 11 slaves; viz. 3 men, 1 woman, 2 men boys, 1 boy (4 foot), 1 boy and 3 girls undersized,

SOLD TO SLAVERY

In 1760, at the age of 10, Olaudah Equiano, a native of west Africa, was sold into slavery.

"The first object which saluted my eyes when I arrived on the coast was the sea, and a slave-ship... waiting for its cargo....When I was carried onboard I was immediately handled, and tossed up, to see if I were sound... and I was now persuaded that I had gotten into a world of bad spirits.... Their complexions too differing so much from ours, their long hair, and the language they spoke... united to confirm me in this belief."

OLAUDAH EQUIANO, Autobiography, **1789**

SLAVE SHIP
This model of the slave ship Brookes *shows how its human cargo was stowed. The vessel was intended to carry 450 slaves, although it sometimes carried 600.*

slaves were packed onboard ship with little room to move

NECK COLLAR

IN IRONS
Enslaved Africans were clapped in irons onboard ship. Their ankles were put in fetters that were attached to an iron bar; these prohibited movement and prevented the slaves from rebelling against their captors. Neck collars attached to chains were also used to subdue the imprisoned slaves.

ANKLE FETTERS

> ❝ Aboard ships all possible care is taken to preserve and subsist them [slaves] for the interest of the owners... ❞
>
> **JEAN BARBOT**, slave trader, **17th century**

which makes our number 26." After the slaves had been crammed onto ships, the notorious "middle passage" of the Triangular Trade began. This voyage to colonies across the Atlantic took up to two months. Conditions onboard the slave ships were atrocious. The African captives were chained below deck, with little light or air and no room to manoeuvre. For many, the journey was deadly, with diseases such as smallpox and dysentery rife. Once a ship reached its destination, the slaves were taken ashore and sold for a huge profit, and the ships took on new cargoes, among them sugar or rum, before returning to Europe.

One victim of the slave trade was Olaudah Equiano, who was captured as a child and endured the dreadful middle passage to be sold as a slave in the United States. Equiano later managed to buy his freedom. His autobiography was published in 1789, and was to influence the campaign to abolish the slave trade in Britain (see panel, opposite page).

Tobacco and timber

With the Act of Union in 1707, the Scots were permitted to trade with the English empire and began to dominate the tobacco trade with North America. They had a natural advantage in that ships bound for Scotland passed north of Ireland, avoiding French privateers, and the land passage between the mouths of the rivers Clyde and Forth was the shortest way across Britain, making it easier to re-export goods to Europe. Glasgow established itself on the healthy profits of the tobacco trade, and the Tobacco Lords, as the city's merchants became known, became leaders of this booming economy. Their commercial acumen made them unpopular in the American colonies,

TOBACCO TRADE
These dried tobacco leaves were recovered from the wreck of a merchant ship. The highly lucrative tobacco trade contributed to the rise of Glasgow in the 18th century.

ABOLITION OF THE SLAVE TRADE

Slavery did not trouble the European conscience before the middle of the 18th century, when religious groups began to condemn the practice. In France, philosophers such as Voltaire, Montesquieu, and Rousseau – who were influential in the Enlightenment, a major intellectual movement that pursued rational and humanitarian ideals – vigorously attacked the trade. Meanwhile, the Scottish economist Adam Smith convincingly demonstrated that slavery was an inefficient form of labour, and there were also fears that population increases in the colonies would lead to revolt.

ABOLITIONIST
The politician William Wilberforce (1759–1833) was a leading anti-slavery campaigner in Britain.

In 1792, Denmark banned the import of slaves into its colonies, a law that did not take effect until 1803. The revolutionary government of France abolished slavery in 1794, although the practice was restored in 1802. In January 1807, the American Congress banned the import of slaves, although they made no provision to enforce this measure. In May of the same year, a British bill abolishing the trade became law. In Britain the abolition movement had focused on the traffic of humans from Africa. The abolitionists had been moved by the appalling conditions onboard slave ships and ensured the public became aware of them.

Anti-slavery patrols were a major element of the naval effort of several nations after the Napoleonic Wars ended in 1815. What remained of the slave trade became even more brutal, as slavers retaliated by using faster ships with even more cramped accommodation, sometimes dumping slaves overboard when threatened.

AMISTAD
The schooner Amistad Freedom is a replica of a ship on which a cargo of slaves rebelled after being transported from west Africa in 1839. The incident galvanized support for the abolition of slavery in America.

although they weathered the collapse of the trade during the American Revolutionary War, moving into other trades, such as cotton.

Another trade of great strategic importance was the Scandinavian timber trade, in which timber cut in Scandinavia's extensive forests was bought by British and Dutch merchants to supply markets elsewhere in Europe. Like the coal trade, it involved ships with plenty of cargo space, and a typical ship weighed between 300 and 350 tons. As the primary source of naval stores – including pitch, iron, and tar as well as timber – Scandinavia was an immensely lucrative market, of which the British and Dutch took full advantage.

CRANE AT KARLSKRONA, SWEDEN
The Baltic port of Karlskrona was primarily a naval base, but was also a key port in the Scandinavian timber trade. The huge crane at the port was used to de-mast ships.

Pirates of the Caribbean

By the middle of the 17th century, pirates only occasionally raided the shores of northern Europe, as they were kept in check by the establishment of organized navies. However, piracy remained a problem in many other parts of the world. The European wars of the late 17th and early 18th centuries created gaps in political control of colonies, particularly in the Caribbean, while French and British raiders believed that the wealth of the Spanish Indies was theirs for the taking. Some pirates began as privateers, who were licensed by governments to plunder enemy ships during times of war, often continuing the same trade in peacetime. Anglo-Spanish conflicts continued in the region, maintaining the tradition of Francis Drake (see p.103) in an age when the two nations were not necessarily enemies. Anglo-French hostilities, which continued intermittently throughout the period, created further opportunities for buccaneers. The period was the golden age of piracy, if the term can be applied to such a brutal practice. Nevertheless, the Caribbean pirates of this period are those of popular imagination, though they have little resemblance to their fictional counterparts.

The Welshman Henry Morgan was one of the most successful pirates of the era. Like many of his ilk, he crossed the boundary between respectability and criminality with apparent ease. He began as a privateer in 1662, but crossed the line to piracy with his raid on the Spanish Caribbean ports of Puerto Bello and Cartagena during peacetime. Pirates such as Edward Teach – or "Blackbeard" – operated more traditionally on the open sea, plundering rich merchant ships regardless of nationality and hiding at bases among the Caribbean islands. By 1720, the problem of piracy appeared to be under control, although over the next century it recurred on a small scale during wartime. However, the problem was eradicated from the area by 1830.

PIRATE PISTOL
Pistols were used at close range when pirates attacked and boarded other ships.

FLASHING BLADE
The curved blade of the cutlass was one of the many weapons used by pirates and naval crews during the 17th and 18th centuries.

THE END OF BLACKBEARD
Blackbeard was one of the most feared pirates to sail the Caribbean in the 18th century. In 1718, his ship was captured and he was shot dead by an English naval officer.

FLAGS OF DOOM
Emblazoned on the flags of pirate ships was the skull and crossbones, or Jolly Roger, which appeared in numerous designs on a red or black background.

PIRATE TALES
In the 17th century, a Dutchman called Alexander Exquemelin sailed the Caribbean aboard pirate ships and wrote a graphic account of their bloodthirsty way of life.

Ships were not specifically designed as pirate ships for the Caribbean. Most pirate vessels were former privateers, which could maintain good speeds and were armed, making them ideal for the practice of plunder. Some ships were larger – Blackbeard's *Queen Anne's Revenge* had 40 guns, while Captain Kidd's *Adventure Galley* was 300 tons with 34 guns and 46 oars.

Civil engineering and the rise of canals

As maritime trade grew in the 18th and early 19th centuries, new ports were needed and were sometimes constructed artificially. Glasgow expanded by progressively deepening the River Clyde. In Liverpool, enclosed areas of water called wet docks were built, where ships could unload away from tidal influences. London began to expand its docks in the early 19th century, beginning with the opening of the West India Dock in 1802, followed by London Dock three years later and many more over the next three decades. In Dutch waters, the increasing

WILLIAM KIDD

Born in Greenock, Scotland, William Kidd (c.1654–1701) became a sea captain and then a privateer. In 1695 he was awarded a commission to fight pirates based in Madagascar in his ship the *Adventure Galley*. But he turned pirate himself and captured ships from several nations. He took his richest prize, the French-operated *Quedah Merchant*, in 1698. Kidd is said to have buried a fabulous treasure after his exploits. Under pressure from the East India Company, he was placed on trial for piracy in Boston in 1699. He was hanged in London in 1701.

draught of ships caused difficulties as the ships were not able to navigate the shallow waters. Dutch waterways were also prone to silting up. To combat these problems, devices called camels were used to lift ships over sandbanks, and horse-powered dredgers deepened the water, although these became viable options only once steam power was readily available.

The use of inland waterways and canals was widespread in the Netherlands – the 17th-century ship designer Sir William Petty observed that "In Holland and Zealand, there is scarcely any place of work or business one mile distant

WEST INDIA DOCK
As maritime trade boomed during the 18th century, ports rushed to expand their docking facilities to cope with the increasing number and size of ships. This is an early image of West India Dock on the River Thames in London.

from a navigable water." In France, Louis XIV authorized the construction of the Canal du Midi, which linked the Atlantic with the Mediterranean through southern France. Work began in 1667, and the canal's grand opening took place in May 1681. The use of canals expanded during the 18th and 19th centuries, although the British were slow to appreciate their benefits. However, the British engineers Thomas Telford and John Smeaton demonstrated that a packhorse could carry one-eighth of a ton, a wagon pulled by a single horse could pull five-eighths of a ton on a poor road and two tons on a good one, while a river barge pulled by a horse could carry up to 30 tons. In 1760, the Duke of Bridgewater built a short canal near Manchester, after which hundreds of kilometres were built throughout the country. In Scotland, the Caledonian Canal was constructed along the Great Glen to link the Atlantic with the North Sea, although it proved too narrow for the increasing size of merchant ships by the time it was opened in 1822. In the United States, the Erie Canal, linking the Hudson River to the Great Lakes in the Midwest, opened in 1825 and led to New York becoming the pre-eminent trading centre of the east coast.

Ships and the rise of industry

Historians are divided about whether the industrial changes that originated in Britain in the mid-18th century and continued into the 19th century amounted to a "revolution" or not. However, there is no doubt that the steady development of shipping contributed to these

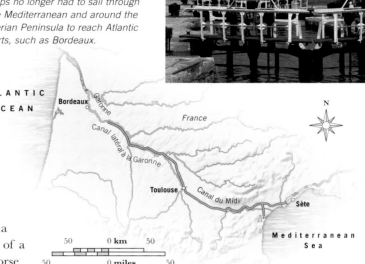

CANAL DU MIDI
The Canal du Midi provided a huge boost to French maritime trade, as ships no longer had to sail through the Mediterranean and around the Iberian Peninsula to reach Atlantic ports, such as Bordeaux.

far-reaching technological, economic, and social changes. Piracy was largely eliminated, insurance was set up on a regular basis, small-scale capital was tapped to finance ships, shipbuilding practices had improved, and large numbers of seamen learned the trade.

Despite numerous wars, merchant shipping continued to expand in the more successful countries, particularly Britain. It allowed the development of a global market, albeit one based primarily on luxury goods and heavily skewed towards the wealthy inhabitants of northern Europe. Shipping drove the development of the cotton trade, which was the focus of industrial development during the 19th century. The merchant ship of 1830 had very little that would have been unrecognizable to a seaman of two centuries before, but it had grown in size, seaworthiness, and efficiency, and existed within a complex and growing infrastructure of merchants, harbours, and canals.

MERCHANT SHIPS

The period from 1650 until the advent of steam, around 1830, saw vast growth in merchant shipping, despite the disruption caused by numerous wars. There was very little specialization of type in merchant shipping, and vessels such as East Indiaman or collier were defined by size or cargo space rather than by any special features of design. Most ships could carry cargo or passengers (or both). Small coastal vessels were more diverse within Europe, reflecting regional variations.

TRADING VESSELS
These Dutch and English armed merchantmen are trading in an Asian port early in the 17th century. This picture was painted by the Dutch artist Hendrik Vroom.

British cargo ships

Compared with a warship, the typical merchant ship of the age had a much squarer hull section, to carry more cargo. British ships of the mid-18th century had absorbed many of the ideas of the Dutch *fluyt*. The ship shown here is a cat or bark, with a broad stern without any kind of figurehead. Like most seagoing merchantmen, it has the full three-masted ship rig, with staysails between the masts and a spritsail hung under the bowsprit.

BARK

Origin Britain	**Date of launch** *c.*1750
Length 30m (98ft)	**Tonnage** About 360 tons
Armament None	

Colliers

Often sailing from ports in the northeast of England, colliers had deep, square hulls for maximum capacity. The *Earl of Pembroke*, whose sails are not shown here, was converted to become Cook's *Endeavour*.

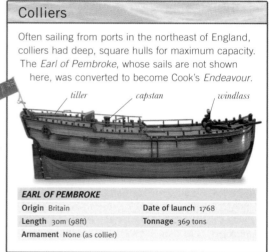

tiller   *capstan*   *windlass*

EARL OF PEMBROKE

Origin Britain	**Date of launch** 1768
Length 30m (98ft)	**Tonnage** 369 tons
Armament None (as collier)	

Fluyts

The Dutch *fluyt*, or *flute*, was the classic merchant ship of the 17th century. It was built to be economical in operation, carrying the largest cargo and smallest crew possible. It had a wide, box-like hull and a high, narrow stern. Its rigging was designed to be operated by very few men, and its narrow upper deck was designed to evade Danish customs dues when passing through the sound into the Baltic, where duties were levied according to the size of the vessel.

mizzen yard

lantern

narrow upper stern

rudder

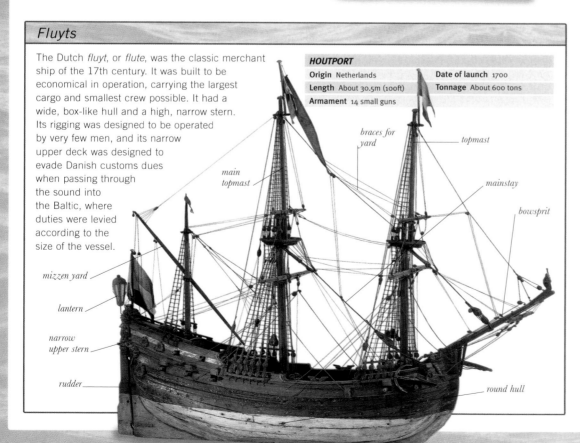

HOUTPORT

Origin Netherlands	**Date of launch** 1700
Length About 30.5m (100ft)	**Tonnage** About 600 tons
Armament 14 small guns	

braces for yard   *topmast*

main topmast

mainstay

bowsprit

round hull

Dutch passage boats

Dutch inland waterways and coastal waters produced a wide variety of craft, some of which influenced ships of other countries – for example, the leeboards used by Thames barges were previously used on Dutch boats. Most Dutch boats had a shallow draft and a very rounded shape, both in cross section and in side view.

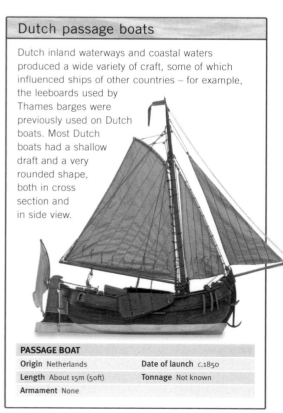

PASSAGE BOAT

Origin Netherlands	**Date of launch** *c.*1850
Length About 15m (50ft)	**Tonnage** Not known
Armament None	

Baltic timber ships

Ships for transporting timber from the Baltic had square underwater hulls, rather like the Dutch *fluyts*, and often had loading ports at the stern. Since the Baltic ports were the main European source of shipbuilding timber, many hundreds of timber ships were built. The details below are for a vessel in Chapman's *Architectura Navalis Mercatoria* similar to the one shown. Typically, timber ships were of about 300 to 350 tons, with simple hulls and an armament of small guns.

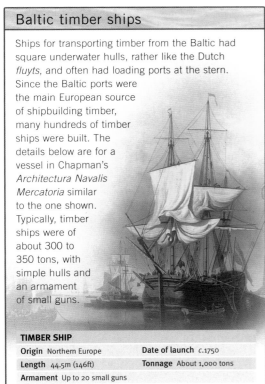

TIMBER SHIP	
Origin Northern Europe	**Date of launch** *c.*1750
Length 44.5m (146ft)	**Tonnage** About 1,000 tons
Armament Up to 20 small guns	

Slavers

Slave ships tended to be faster than other vessels, because, in crude terms, their human "cargo" was perishable. They were fitted with extra-low decks in which the slaves were crammed. The model below, made for French anti-slavery campaigner Abbé Gregoire, shows how slaves were stowed.

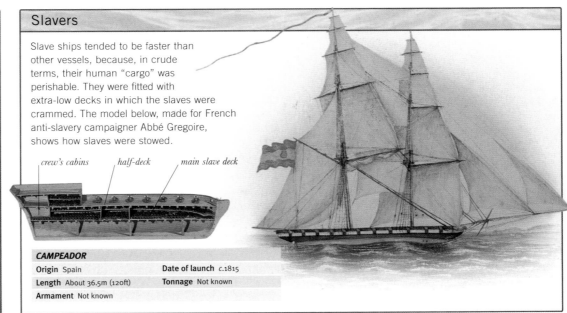

crew's cabins   *half-deck*   *main slave deck*

CAMPEADOR	
Origin Spain	**Date of launch** *c.*1815
Length About 36.5m (120ft)	**Tonnage** Not known
Armament Not known	

East Indiamen

The largest merchant ships of their day, the East Indiamen were equipped for long voyages and able to carry passengers in some comfort, soldiers in less comfort, and goods for trade. Although the Dutch, British, French, and Swedish all had their own styles, the ships had much in common. They were made to look like warships, partly to make the passengers feel safer, partly to fend off local pirates. Ships of the British East India Company were privately owned and operated on charter to the company; they were built in standard sizes that got larger over the years. The *Somerset* (below) made several return voyages from London to India up until 1748. Her lion figurehead is typical of large British ships of the period, mainly warships. Her guns were far smaller than those of a warship of similar size, and her hold was much squarer in cross section, to carry cargo.

square hold   *steering wheel*   *bell*

SOMERSET	
Origin Britain	**Date of launch** *c.*1738
Length 30.5m (100ft)	**Tonnage** 948 tons
Armament 8 x 9-pounder guns, 22 x 6-pounder guns	

British hoys

The hoy was the traditional inshore vessel of southeast England, carrying cargoes out to larger ships at anchor or passengers down the River Thames from London, for example. It was probably influenced by Dutch design, but it had a deeper hull for English waters and had no need for leeboards. The British East India Company employed hoys to service its ships at anchor in the River Thames at Wapping, before the building of the London docks made this less necessary; passenger hoys made trips to emerging English seaside resorts, such as Margate, in Kent. Hoys were locally built and there was much variety among them. The example shown here has a very deep hull and a much more complicated rig than many hoys, which tended to make do with a single-gaff sail aft of the mast and a triangular staysail before it. It has a cabin aft and probably carried passengers.

HOY	
Origin Britain	**Date of launch** *c.*1730
Length 17m (56ft)	**Tonnage** About 100 tons
Armament None	

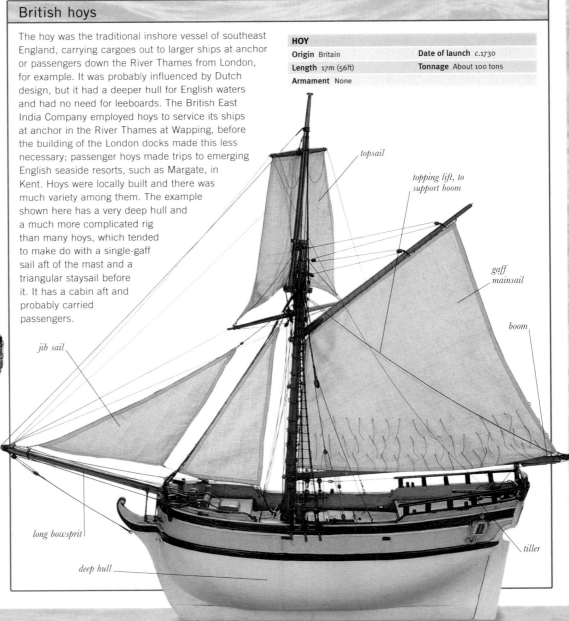

topsail

topping lift, to support boom

gaff mainsail

boom

jib sail

long bowsprit

deep hull

tiller

JOHN HARRISON'S CHRONOMETER H4

❝ Our faithful guide through all the vicissitudes of climates. ❞

CAPTAIN JAMES COOK, describing the chronometer, **1775**

KEY EVENTS

1722 EASTER ISLAND The Dutch explorer Jacob Roggeveen voyages to the South Pacific, where he discovers Easter Island.

1761–62 H4 TESTED John Harrison's H4 chronometer provides accurate longitude readings on a voyage to the West Indies.

1766 FRENCH CIRCUMNAVIGATION Louis Bougainville sets sail on an expedition to the Pacific. He becomes the first French mariner to circumnavigate the globe.

1768 COOK'S FIRST VOYAGE James Cook leaves England on the first of three epic Pacific voyages.

1785 LAPEROUSE TO THE PACIFIC The three-year voyage of the French explorer Jean François Lapérouse begins.

1787 FIRST FLEET Eleven ships set sail from Britain to found a convict colony in Australia.

1831–36 VOYAGE OF THE *BEAGLE* With the naturalist Charles Darwin onboard, the *Beagle* voyages around South America and the Pacific.

EXPLORATION

A NEW AGE OF EUROPEAN EXPLORATION AND COLONIZATION BEGAN AT END OF THE 17TH CENTURY, DOMINATED BY LONG AND ARDUOUS VOYAGES TO THE UNCHARTED PACIFIC OCEAN.

Between 1650 and 1750, the French and British expanded their dominance in North America and the Caribbean. The Scots, who were excluded from trade with English colonies, attempted to found a colony in the Isthmus of Darien (part of modern Panama) in 1698. They chartered Dutch ships and sent out two expeditions, which were financed by thousands of ordinary Scots. The settlement was abandoned in 1700, as a result of disease, hostility from neighbouring Spanish colonies, and the English refusal to trade with them.

By 1730, all the areas of eastern North America accessible by sea were claimed and occupied by European nations. In 1664, the British took the colony of New Amsterdam from the Dutch and renamed it New York, and by the end of the 17th century they controlled a continuous stretch of the eastern seaboard. The French colonized Canada and advanced down the Mississippi River to found Louisiana and New Orleans.

The dominance of Britain and France in Europe in the 18th century was reflected in the explorers of the period. The Spanish concentrated on defending, rather than expanding, their huge empire and mounted only one important voyage of exploration in the 18th century (see p.164). The great

PACIFIC PARADISE
During the 18th century, South Pacific islands were perceived by many Europeans to be utopian societies. This image of Tahiti was painted by William Hodges, who travelled on James Cook's second voyage (see p.162).

Dutch wave of exploration had expended itself. They undertook only one major expedition in the 18th century, led by Jacob Roggeveen, who discovered Samoa, Easter Island, and the Society Islands in 1722. Having profited enormously from lands appropriated in the 15th and 16th centuries, the British and French began to look for other areas that might yield equivalent wealth. They continued to search the cold waters of northern Canada for the Northwest Passage linking the Atlantic and Pacific oceans, a quest that continued into the 19th century (see p.281). However, the main thrust of 18th-century exploration was in a different direction – the South Pacific.

NEW FRONTIERS
One of the primary goals for explorers of the age was the discovery of the mythical southern continent. James Cook's second voyage was undertaken for this purpose. In this painting, his ship, Resolution, is shown battling against the extreme elements, including several huge waterspouts, as it sailed around the coast of New Zealand in May 1773.

AMERICAN COLONIES
This early 18th-century map shows some of the British possessions along the eastern seaboard of America. By 1733, these colonies extended from Canada as far as Georgia in the south.

One of the most successful explorers of the late 17th and early 18th centuries was William Dampier. He was an English buccaneer in the tradition of Sir Francis Drake (see p.103), but he was also a superb navigator. His maritime career was eventful and ranged from raiding Spanish colonies in Central America to discovering and charting islands in the Pacific. In 1697, he published *A New Voyage Round the World*, which was an account of his first circumnavigation of the globe in 1688–91. It became the template for future Pacific voyages and brought Dampier to the attention of the British Admiralty, who allowed him to command an expedition from 1699 to 1701, during which he discovered the islands of New Britain. Dampier's second circumnavigation of the globe, which began in 1703, is chiefly remembered for the fate of one of his crew. The Scottish sailor Alexander Selkirk was abandoned on the island of Juan Fernández, the first stop for ships that had rounded Cape Horn. His experiences became the inspiration for two great works of literature in the 18th century.

The Pacific in literature

In both *Robinson Crusoe* (1719) and *Gulliver's Travels* (1726), the protagonists are shipwrecked on Pacific islands. Daniel Defoe's *Robinson Crusoe* is more obviously based on Selkirk's experiences, while *Gulliver's Travels*, which was written by the Irish writer Jonathan Swift, is actually a complex satire on 18th-century values. Swift's descriptions of the imaginary lands Gulliver visits are explicit. The land of Lilliput is placed "northward of Van Diemen's Land [modern Tasmania] … in the Latitude of 30 degrees 2 minutes south", which, in reality, places the character on the Australian continent. Brobdingnag, the land of the "enormous barbarians", is placed east of the Moluccas (part of modern Indonesia), at the latitude of 3 degrees north, which would place Swift's "great Island or Continent" between New Guinea and Micronesia. Apart from the Pacific location and the theme of shipwreck, the novels contrast starkly. The world Crusoe inhabits is the simplest possible: he is alone for much of the time, eventually building a small community that includes three other men wrecked on the island. However, Gulliver's voyages bring him into contact with highly developed societies. Both novels also fuelled interest in further exploration of the Pacific, and *Robinson Crusoe*, in particular, inspired many young men to go to sea.

Anson's voyage

The first official British venture into the Pacific in the 18th century was an act of aggression, rather than an expedition in the spirit of discovery. However, the voyage resulted in another circumnavigation. On 18 September 1740, six British warships left Portsmouth on the south coast under Commodore George Anson, with the aim of raiding Spanish possessions, such as the Philippines, in the southeast Pacific. Anson's ships were ill-equipped for the voyage and poorly crewed. The army had been asked to provide marines. Reasoning that the soldiers did not have to march, they provided aged pensioners. This proved to be a death sentence for the pensioners, who all perished.

CAPE HORN
This 18th-century French map charts Chile and Argentina. The passage into the Pacific around Cape Horn, at the tip of southern Argentina, was particularly treacherous for sailing vessels, as strong winds and rough seas typify the region.

TAKING A TREASURE SHIP
The purpose of Commodore Anson's Pacific voyage was to plunder Spanish interests. This painting shows the capture of the treasure galleon Nuestra Señora de Covadonga by Anson's smaller ship Centurion in June 1743.

CASTAWAY
This is the title page of a first edition of Robinson Crusoe. The novel drew on Alexander Selkirk's story, although the fictional castaway was stranded for 28 years.

SELKIRK'S ISLAND
After a furious row with William Dampier, Alexander Selkirk requested to be left on the island of Juan Fernández, 700km (440 miles) west of Chile. He was marooned for four years, his only companions being goats and cats.

The squadron had its greatest trial in attempting to round Cape Horn, which took more than a month. The crew's charts were poor and the weather atrocious. The ships were separated, and the crews suffered from exhaustion and disease. At one point, the flagship *Centurion* attempted to turn north, but its position had been miscalculated, and instead of heading into the open ocean it narrowly missed the cliffs of southern Chile. Eventually the three remaining ships met at Juan Fernández – of the others, one had turned back and two had been wrecked.

Anson duly raided Spanish possessions in Chile and Central America and then headed across the Pacific. He reached the Portuguese colony of Macau in November 1742, where he made contact with the Chinese. By this time

Centurion was the only ship left on the voyage. Anson continued to the Philippines, where he captured a Spanish treasure galleon, an event that justified – at least financially – an otherwise disastrous expedition. Three-quarters of the participants, more than 1,300 men, died. The huge death toll led a Scottish naval physician called James Lind to investigate the causes of scurvy, which had been the reason for many of the fatalities (see panel, above).

On Anson's return to Britain in 1744, it took 32 wagons to carry the magnificent Spanish treasure to the Tower of London. An account of the voyage was written by Anson's chaplain, Richard Walters, and it became a perpetual bestseller, stimulating still more interest in Pacific exploration and providing a factual counterpoint to the fiction of Swift and Defoe. However, although it yielded fantastic prizes, the expedition illustrated all too clearly the perils of an extended voyage.

PREVENTING SCURVY

By the 18th century, larger ocean-going ships had a trained medical officer of some kind onboard. Most of these were surgeons, who had a general medical knowledge but were inferior to university-trained physicians. They were often poorly paid and there was a suspicion that only incompetent or inexperienced individuals or alcoholics took the job on.

The biggest single health problem for sailors was scurvy, a hideous disease that began to set in after several months at sea. Its symptoms included weakness, loss of teeth and hair, haemorrhaging, and the reopening of old wounds. As a result of the huge death toll on Commodore Anson's voyage, James Lind undertook an experiment to find a cure. In 1753, he published a treatise in which he described how sailors who were given orange, lemon, or lime juice began to recover from scurvy almost instantly. This was further illustrated during James Cook's first Pacific voyage (see p.161), but it was not until the 1790s that navies recognized the need to supply their sailors with the juice of citrus fruits.

JAMES LIND
Lind was the Scottish doctor who discovered that eating lemons and limes, which contain vitamin C, helped to prevent scurvy. In this image, he attends a toothless victim of the disease.

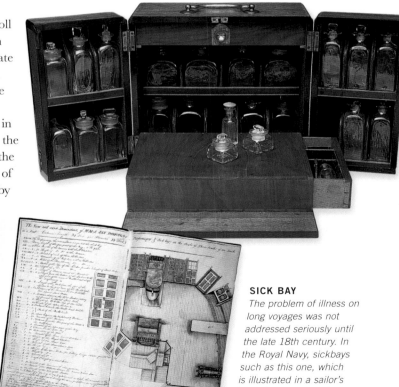

SHIP'S MEDICINE CHEST
The physician or surgeon of a ship undertaking a long voyage had great responsibility, caring for the lives of the entire crew without any outside help. He equipped himself with a medicine chest to deal with minor ailments.

SICK BAY
The problem of illness on long voyages was not addressed seriously until the late 18th century. In the Royal Navy, sickbays such as this one, which is illustrated in a sailor's journal, were compulsory from 1800.

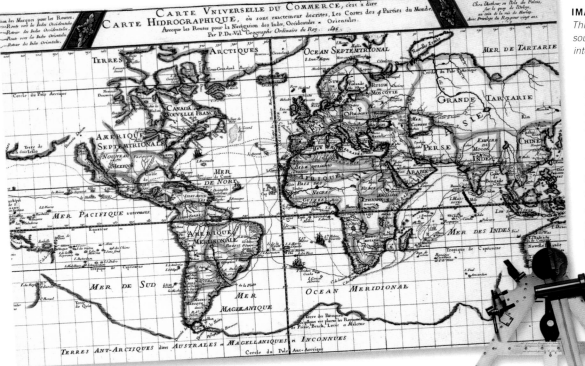

In search of a southern continent

The most prolific period of Pacific discovery began with the end of the Seven Years War in 1763. Britain and France were determined to seize the opportunity to develop new commercial and strategic outposts in the region. Voyages of exploration were still state-sponsored and commanded by naval officers. However, such expeditions were also seen as scientific pursuits for the benefit of all.

Since Ferdinand Magellan first crossed the Pacific in the 16th century (see p.73), interest in the *Terra Australis Incognita* (meaning "unknown southern land") had revived. This mythical continent was first placed on maps by the Alexandrian astronomer Ptolemy in the 2nd century AD, and many believed it existed to counterbalance the huge land masses in the northern hemisphere. Alexander Dalrymple, the hydrographer to the British East India Company, speculated that the continent was 8,000km (5,000 miles) across and sustained a population of 50 million. If colonized, the economy of such a possession "would be sufficient to maintain the power, sovereignty, and dominion of Britain, by employing all its manufactures and ships".

In European eyes, the eastern Pacific was bounded by the long coast of America, much of which had been claimed by the Spanish and was defended obsessively. In the west were the closed societies of China and Japan, with the Dutch East Indies (now Indonesia) and the Spanish Philippines to the south.

The southern Pacific remained largely undiscovered. The vast size of the ocean was a deterrent to travellers, particularly given the problems of scurvy and the difficulty in calculating accurate longitudes. Dutch explorers had found the coast of Australia (see pp.76–77), but, faced with its barren deserts, they took little interest in colonizing their discovery.

One of the first explorers of the new age was the Englishman John Byron. He was a veteran of Anson's voyage, during which he survived a dramatic shipwreck off Chile. Byron crossed the Pacific in 1764 in search of the southern continent, but achieved little on his two-year trip. He was followed in 1766 by his countrymen Philip Carteret and Samuel Wallis, in the *Swallow* and *Dolphin*. These vessels separated after passing through the Straits of Magellan. Carteret went on to sail further south than any previous explorer, discovering parts of the Solomon Islands and Pitcairn Island. Wallis, meanwhile, found many south Pacific islands, including Tahiti in 1767. The first of the great French explorers of the age, Louis Bougainville (see panel, left), was also one of the most successful. James Cook's first voyage (see panel, right) pushed the boundaries of exploration further still.

LOUIS BOUGAINVILLE

The first French explorer to circumnavigate the world was Comte Louis Antoine de Bougainville (1729–1811). After the Seven Years War, in which he served in the army, Bougainville studied plans for French expansion in the Pacific. In 1766, he was given command of two naval ships *Boudeuse* and *L'Etoile*. Bougainville set sail for the Pacific and was welcomed in Tahiti, which he claimed for France. He then sailed west, but was prevented from landing in Australia by the Great Barrier Reef. Bougainville also visited the Solomon Islands, giving his name to the largest of these. In 1771, he published an account of his trip, *Voyage Autour du Monde*.

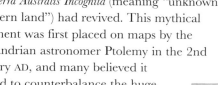

18TH-CENTURY SEXTANT
The sextant was invented in the mid-18th century. It was a vital tool on a long Pacific voyage, as it accurately measured the angle of a celestial body above the horizon, allowing a navigator to calculate a ship's position at sea.

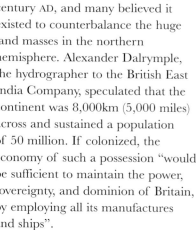

VOYAGE OF DISCOVERY
In June 1768, sailors on Louis Bougainville's epic voyage saw a group of islands to the east of Papua New Guinea. The explorer named the islands the Louisade Archipelago, in honour of the French monarch, Louis XV.

CAPTAIN COOK'S FIRST VOYAGE

On 26 August 1768, Lieutenant James Cook and his crew of 85 left England onboard a refitted collier named *Endeavour*. They entered the Pacific by Cape Horn. Cook's first port of call was Tahiti, where he was to observe the transit of Venus across the Sun in June 1769. However, the primary aim of the voyage was to search for and take possession of the southern continent. Cook arrived at Tahiti in April, where the crew spent three months. *Endeavour* then headed to New Zealand, which had been discovered by Abel Tasman a century before (see p.76–77). Cook

LEAVING WHITBY
Cook chose a collier called the Earl of Pembroke, which was renamed Endeavour, *to pursue his voyage. In this painting, the ship is sailing from her home port of Whitby, England.*

charted New Zealand meticulously, showing that it consisted of two separate islands and was not attached to a greater continent. The expedition moved on to the east coast of Australia. Entranced by the variety and abundance of wildlife collected by the expedition's naturalists, Joseph Banks and Daniel Solander, Cook

named their anchorage Botany Bay. Further along the coast, *Endeavour* struck the Great Barrier Reef and was hauled ashore for repairs. Cook then sailed between Australia and New Guinea and on to the Dutch East Indies. The voyage was a huge success. Despite the loss of 24 men to fever in Batavia, Cook avoided scurvy by insisting the crew eat a balanced diet. After more than two years at sea, Cook returned to England in 1771.

JAMES COOK
Born in Yorkshire, England, in 1728, James Cook worked as a merchant seaman in the coal trade, before joining the Royal Navy in 1755.

COOK'S FIRST VOYAGE

→ Route, 26 August 1768 – 13 July, 1771

Plymouth
August 1768; July 1771
Europe

Batavia
October–December 1770
PACIFIC OCEAN
Tahiti
13 April–13
July 1769

Africa

*South
America*

Cape of Good Hope
14 March 1771

Endeavour River
June–August 1770

New Zealand
8 October 1769

Rio de Janeiro, Brazil
13 November 1768

Botany Bay
May 1770

Cape Horn
25 January 1769

**POSTER CELEBRATING
LANDING IN
BOTANY BAY**

AUSTRALIA

VOYAGE OF *ENDEAVOUR*
Cook sailed more than 48,000km (30,000 miles) on his three-year voyage around the world.

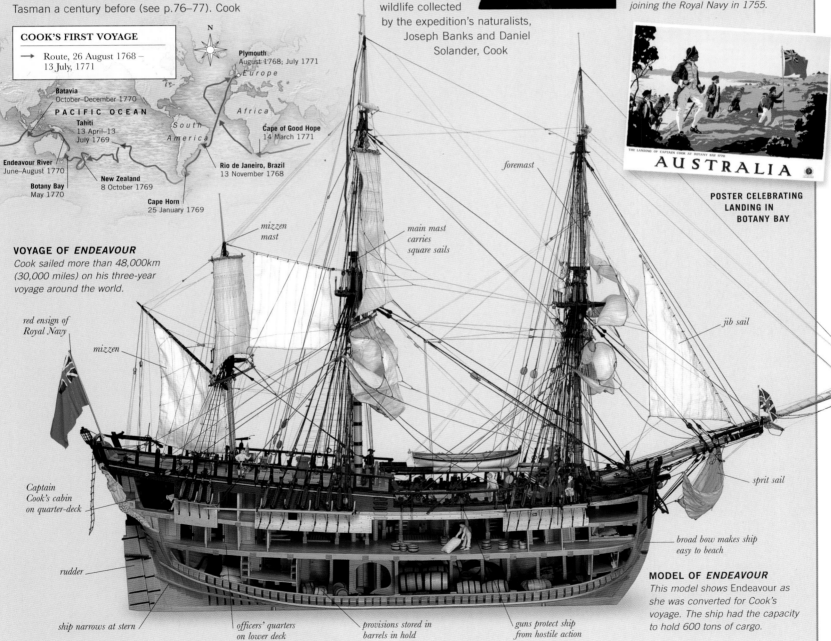

red ensign of Royal Navy

mizzen

mizzen mast

main mast carries square sails

foremast

jib sail

Captain Cook's cabin on quarter-deck

sprit sail

rudder

broad bow makes ship easy to beach

ship narrows at stern

officers' quarters on lower deck

provisions stored in barrels in hold

guns protect ship from hostile action

MODEL OF *ENDEAVOUR*
This model shows Endeavour as she was converted for Cook's voyage. The ship had the capacity to hold 600 tons of cargo.

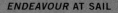

ENDEAVOUR AT SAIL
The Australian replica of Cook's ship, also called Endeavour, sailing between Madeira and the Canary Islands in 1997. The ship is a fully functioning reconstruction of the original exploration vessel.

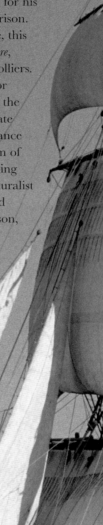

Cook's first Pacific voyage drew on the experience of previous failures and was meticulously planned. His ship, *Endeavour*, is one of the best documented of the explorer's vessels. She had a robust hull with a large cargo capacity and shallow draught – essential for exploration, as it allowed the ship to sail close to shore. Cook's achievement is all the more remarkable when the layout and limited size of the ship are considered. Inside, *Endeavour* was converted to provide deck space for the crew, with officers' cabins aft on the lower deck and quarter-deck. As a large number of scientists and draughtsmen were present on the voyage, all claiming officer status, these quarters were extremely cramped. The great cabin, which was normally reserved for the captain's sole use, had to double as a drawing office. Space was also needed for the natural history specimens collected on the voyage.

After Cook's return to England, *Endeavour* was refitted as a store ship and sold. Her subsequent fate is uncertain, but the wreck of this celebrated ship was discovered lying in shallow water in Newport, Rhode Island, USA, in the late 1990s.

A contemporary of Cook, the French explorer Yves-Joseph de Kerguelen-Trémarec, had mixed success on his voyages to the south seas. In command of two ships, Kerguelen set sail from Ile de France (modern Mauritius) in January 1771. Just over a year later, he sighted a rocky outcrop in the far south of the Indian Ocean. He claimed it as France Australe (southern France), believing he had found the edge of the new continent, but adverse weather conditions prevented him from landing to confirm this. Kerguelen returned to France full of enthusiasm for his discovery and was granted permission to undertake a return trip. On arrival in 1774, he found that his discovery was not the continent that so many had dreamed of.

> **66** A better ship for such service I could never wish for. **99**
> **CAPTAIN COOK**, describing *Endeavour*, **1771**

Instead, it was an isolated archipelago, which Kerguelen named Terre de Desolation, reflecting his disappointment. On arrival in France, he was court-martialled for his lack of success and served four years in prison.

In 1772, Cook left on a second voyage, this time with two ships, *Resolution* and *Adventure*, which, like *Endeavour*, were both former colliers. Once again, his objective was to search for the mysterious southern continent, which the British government was keen to appropriate before either France or Spain. A team of scientists, including the German naturalist Johann Reinhold Forster and his son, Georg, travelled with him. Cook took a copy of John Harrison's chronometer, H4 (see panel, opposite), which proved a successful instrument for calculating longitudes.

In January 1773, *Resolution* became the first ship to cross the Antarctic Circle. This effectively proved that a great, fertile southern land mass was imaginary,

NEW ZEALAND
Throughout his voyages, Cook surveyed and charted the places he saw. This intricately drawn chart of New Zealand was drawn by Cook on his voyage in Endeavour.

and that any continent that did exist must be icy and inhospitable. Cook also charted vast areas of the Pacific before arriving back in England in June 1775. He began the voyage that was to be his last in 1776. The aim of the journey was to search for the Northwest Passage from the Pacific. However, a visit to Hawaii in January 1779 ended in the death of Cook at the hands of the islands' inhabitants.

Enlightenment ideals

Cook's death went some way to dispelling one of the great myths of 18th-century thought, that of the "Noble Savage". Espoused by leading Enlightenment philosophers (see p.151), this was a belief that a tribe or race that remained in its natural state, uncorrupted by "civilization", was more ideal than those living in developed society. At first Tahiti, with its open welcome to European visitors, such as Bougainville and Cook, seemed to provide a model for this notion. However, Europeans soon found that it was as much divided by class and racked by wars as their own societies.

LONGITUDE AND THE CHRONOMETER

By the 18th century, mariners had long known how to calculate their latitude (the position north or south of the equator) by measuring the angle of the Sun from the horizon at noon. However, calculating longitude (the distance east or west) depended on comparing local time with that at a fixed point, for example a ship's home port, or with Greenwich Mean Time (GMT). If the time difference between the two could be calculated accurately, then so could a ship's longitude. Conventional timepieces of the era were unreliable at sea, as the pitch and roll of a ship

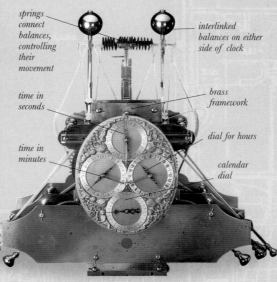

springs connect balances, controlling their movement

interlinked balances on either side of clock

time in seconds

brass framework

dial for hours

time in minutes

calendar dial

JOHN HARRISON
A carpenter and self-taught clockmaker, Yorkshire-born John Harrison dedicated himself to designing an accurate chronometer.

and fluctuations in temperature rendered their mechanisms erratic. Navigational errors resulted in many disastrous shipwrecks.

In 1714, the British set up the Board of Longitude, offering a prize of £20,000 for a device that could measure a ship's position to within 30 nautical miles. The first breakthrough came in the 1730s, with John Harrison's H1, a clock designed with checks and balances to ensure its accuracy over a long period at sea. Harrison went on to design three more of these sea clocks (or chronometers) between 1735 and 1760. Surprised by the accuracy of a pocket watch he designed in 1753, he realized that a smaller device could work more efficiently at sea. The result was H4, which was tested on a voyage to the West Indies in 1761–62, and proved accurate to within one nautical mile.

H1 SEA CLOCK
Weighing 34kg (75lb), H1 was built by John Harrison in 1730–35. The instrument was tested on a 1736 voyage to Lisbon from England and proved to be an accurate marine timepiece. However, Harrison was determined to improve on the design.

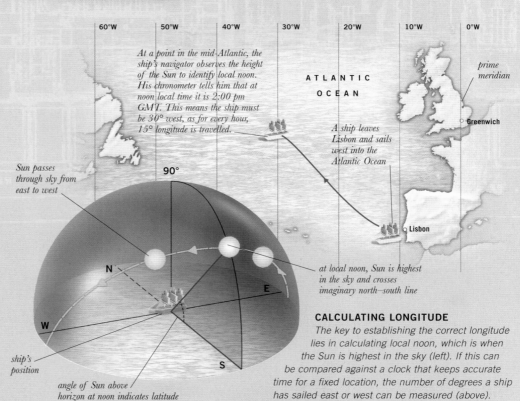

At a point in the mid-Atlantic, the ship's navigator observes the height of the Sun to identify local noon. His chronometer tells him that at noon local time it is 2:00 pm GMT. This means the ship must be 30° west, as for every hour, 15° longitude is travelled.

ATLANTIC OCEAN

prime meridian

A ship leaves Lisbon and sails west into the Atlantic Ocean

Greenwich

Lisbon

90°

Sun passes through sky from east to west

N

E

W

S

ship's position

at local noon, Sun is highest in the sky and crosses imaginary north–south line

angle of Sun above horizon at noon indicates latitude

CALCULATING LONGITUDE
The key to establishing the correct longitude lies in calculating local noon, which is when the Sun is highest in the sky (left). If this can be compared against a clock that keeps accurate time for a fixed location, the number of degrees a ship has sailed east or west can be measured (above).

MUTINY ON THE *BOUNTY*
Captain William Bligh and 18 companions were cast adrift from the Bounty on 29 April 1789. Bligh and his men were given no charts with which to navigate and very few rations.

BLIGH'S BOWL
This bowl was carved by Bligh from a coconut. The rear of the bowl is inscribed with the words "the cup I eat my miserable allowance of".

Mutiny

One of the most notorious Pacific voyages of the 18th century was that of the English ship *Bounty*, which is chiefly remembered for the mutiny that occurred onboard. The ship set sail in 1788, under the command of Captain William Bligh. He was charged with travelling to Tahiti to acquire samples of breadfruit, which it was hoped would be a cheap way to feed the slaves on plantations in the West Indies. Bligh was an expert seaman and navigator and had sailed with Captain Cook on his third voyage. The expedition picked up the breadfruit as planned, but in April 1788 some of Bligh's crew, led by his lieutenant, Fletcher Christian, rose up against him. Along with 18 loyal men, Bligh was put in an open boat, which was just 14m (23ft) long, and cast adrift. There was little possibility of survival. Nevertheless, Bligh and his companions travelled an incredible 6,000km (3,700 miles) in the tiny boat, reaching East Timor 43 days later.

Meanwhile, the mutineers returned to Tahiti in the *Bounty*, where some remained. Led by Christian, nine of the crew, along with several Tahitians, sailed to Pitcairn Island, where they formed a small and quarrelsome community. The mutineers who remained in Tahiti were eventually hunted down, and several were hanged in London.

Theories abound about the reasons for Bligh's failure in the *Bounty* – the lure of Tahiti, personality clashes, and villainy among the crew have all been cited. However, it seems certain that he was not the tyrant he is often perceived to be in popular culture. It was an extraordinary achievement to keep order in a crew for three years or more without any reference to a higher authority. An immensely strong character, such as Cook, accomplished this several times, but not everyone possessed the same skills.

Later voyages

Alejandro Malaspina, a Sicilian in the service of Spain, was one of the most efficient explorers of the age. In 1789, he took command of two ships for a voyage around the Pacific, during which he recorded accurate longitudes

WRECK OF *L'ASTROLABE*
Tragically, Lapérouse's voyage ended in disaster. Debris from L'Astrolabe *was discovered off Vanikaro in the Solomon Islands 40 years later.*

LAPEROUSE AT EASTER ISLAND
On 9 April 1787, Lapérouse's expedition landed at Easter Island, where they measured and sketched the huge statues that dominate the landscape. A bay on the island is named after the French explorer.

for many places for the first time and collected an array of natural history specimens. However, on his return to Spain, his liberal views about the management of colonies and trade fell foul of the authorities. Malaspina was imprisoned, and his achievements had far less impact than they deserved. It was not until 1885 that his journal of his voyage was finally published.

Another successful voyage of exploration in the Pacific was made by the Frenchman Jean François Lapérouse (see panel, above). Despite the work of Cook, Bougainville, and Lapérouse, some parts of America's northwest coast were still unexplored by Europeans at the end of the 18th century. A dispute between Britain and Spain over the ownership of Nootka Sound was settled in Britain's favour. As a result, Captain George Vancouver of the Royal Navy, another of Cook's protegés, was sent to take formal possession of the area and chart it. His two ships, *Discovery* and *Chatham*, sailed eastward into the Pacific, via the Cape of Good Hope. The ships sailed along the south coast of Australia, and on to New Zealand and Tahiti, discovering the Chatham Islands on the way. Vancouver sighted the west coast of America in April 1792 and travelled north from Cape Mendocino, in the Spanish colony of California. The four-year expedition was an enormous success, as the numerous bays and inlets of the Pacific Northwest were charted with great accuracy. The expedition, which covered more than 88,000km (55,000 miles), arrived back in Britain in 1795. Only six of the original 180 men did not return. All of those who perished died in accidents, rather than succumbing to disease.

The convict colony

Since the loss of its American colonies (see p.124), the British government had nowhere to offload people it regarded as undesirable. However, having laid claim to the east coast of Australia, it now intended to dispense with such unsavoury individuals on a grand scale. New South Wales was not the great southern

CONVICT CARGO
Two convicts, their feet and hands chained, take leave of their womenfolk. In the background, a prison guard orders them to board their ship to the penal colony in Australia.

continent that had once been dreamed of, but it could serve a purpose. A large proportion of the British "criminal class", or at least those who escaped hanging, were to be shipped there to build a colony that would serve as Britain's main Pacific base. On 13 May 1787, the 11 ships of the First Fleet, as it was known, set sail from Plymouth, England. The ships, carrying 700 convicts, arrived in Australia eight months later.

Much of Australia was still uncharted. In 1798–89 the British explorers Matthew Flinders and George Bass sailed round Tasmania, proving that it was an island. Flinders was subsequently given the command of the sloop *Investigator* for a full survey of Australia's coast, between 1800 and 1803. A French expedition of 1801–03 under Thomas-Nicolas Baudin surveyed much of the continent's western and southern coastlines. However, despite the achievement of the region's maritime explorers, Australia's development as a viable colony was to come from land exploration.

CONVICT SHIPS

A convict sent to Australia faced a long voyage in harsh conditions with little supplied in the way of nourishment.

[We were] chained two and two together and confined in the hold during the whole course of our long voyage… we were scarcely allowed a sufficient quantity of victuals to keep us alive, and scarcely any water; for my part, I could have eaten three or four of our allowances, and you know well that I was never a great eater…. When any of our comrades that were chained to us died, we kept it a secret as long as we could for the smell of a dead body, in order to get their allowance of provision…

A PRISONER, Australia, **1787**

SYDNEY COVE
Sydney was established as a British penal colony in 1788. This French map shows the area in 1802, by which time it had expanded substantially. After the Napoleonic Wars ended in 1815, up to 3,000 convicts were transported there every year, until the practice ceased in 1840.

BOTANY BAY
The first port of call for Australia's First Fleet was Botany Bay. However, the fleet's commander, Captain Arthur Philip, deemed the bay unsuitable for landing and voyaged further north to settle in what became Sydney.

The effects of exploration

Ships were often the bearers of trade, wealth, and culture, but they also carried disease, oppression, and misery. The various communities "discovered" by the Europeans in the course of the 18th century had lived their lives previously unnoticed by the rest of the world. They were affected by the arrival of European explorers in different ways, and many fared badly. The structures of traditional societies were disrupted by European interest, and native people, such as the Aboriginal people of Australia, were casually dispossessed. Fatal diseases, such as syphilis, influenza, and tuberculosis, spread rapidly, often devastating entire communities.

THE SCOURGE OF SYPHILIS
The huge open pustules carved into this 17th-century French figure represent one of the symptoms of syphilis. Tahiti was particularly affected by venereal disease after the advent of European explorers.

CHARLES DARWIN

After studying medicine at Edinburgh, Charles Darwin (1809–82) moved to Cambridge, where he became interested in natural history. In 1831, he joined Robert Fitzroy's scientific expedition in the *Beagle*. During the five-year voyage, Darwin kept a detailed journal, in which he recorded the flora, fauna, and geology he observed. In the Galapagos Islands, he began to realize that the isolated species of plants and animals he recorded there were the result of "natural selection" and had evolved over thousands of years to suit their habitat. He published his hugely successful account of the voyage in 1839, but omitted his findings on evolution, as he feared the idea was deeply unpopular. Twenty years later, presented with further scientific evidence, he finally published *The Origin of Species*, which outlined the theories he had established on the *Beagle* and changed the perception of the natural world irrevocably.

By 1815, Europeans had explored much of the Pacific region. The interior of Australia was still a mystery, as was the hinterland of some of the larger islands, such as New Guinea, which would remain unexplored for some decades to come. However, most Pacific coastlines and islands were charted reasonably accurately, often using the latest methods of measuring longitude, including the chronometer, which became a standard maritime instrument in the 19th century.

The explorers of the 17th, 18th, and early 19th centuries provided many models of heroism that survive today in both fact and fiction, but, for the authorities who sanctioned their expeditions, the results of the voyages were somewhat disappointing. The importance of the Pacific discoveries did not compare with the discovery of the routes to North and South America. Australia remained marginal in the British economy and strategy long after its annexation. Eventually, dynamic societies emerged in Australia and New Zealand, but it would take more than a century for the Pacific territories to become significant in global affairs.

Two of the last great voyages of discovery during the age of sail were the British voyage of the *Beagle* in 1831–36 and the American Wilkes expedition in 1838–42. The former, led by Admiral Robert Fitzroy, set out to survey the coast of South America and the Pacific. It was equipped with the most up-to-date scientific equipment, and among the scientists onboard was a young naturalist called Charles Darwin (see panel, left). Lieutenant Charles Wilkes was the commander of a naval squadron of six ships and 490 men that left Norfolk, Virginia, USA, in August 1838. His flagship was the three-masted sloop *Vincennes*. The four-year

DARWIN'S INSTRUMENTS
Many artefacts from Darwin's voyage in the Beagle have been preserved, including his notebooks, in which he made meticulous observations, his compass engraved with his name, and his telescope.

voyage – officially known as the United States Exploring Expedition but unfairly dubbed the Everlasting Expedition by sneering critics – surveyed 280 islands in the south and central Pacific and explored Antarctica, confirming that it was a continent.

The nature of exploration had changed by this point. These two great voyages aimed to observe the world in more detail, rather than seek out and exploit new lands and continents. They also heralded an age of new scientific practices.

VOYAGES OF THE PACIFIC
A great era of Pacific discovery began with Jacob Roggeveen's voyage in 1722. Many great explorers followed him, including Lapérouse, Bougainville, and Cook. The Beagle's expedition began an age of scientific discovery. In the painting below, the ship is greeted by the inhabitants of Tierra del Fuego, in the far south of Argentina.

I N D I A N   O C E A N

Kerguelen Islands
Discovered by
Yves-Joseph de Kerguelen, 1772

POCKET GLOBE

Public interest in the expeditions of Pacific explorers was huge. Pocket globes, such as this one, which is decorated with maps of Cook's voyages, were popular in the late 18th and early 19th centuries.

Asia

Bering Sea

Japan

North America

Vancouver Island
Surveyed by George Vancouver, 1788

Hawaii
Captain Cook killed, 1779

PACIFIC VOYAGES

- Louis Bougainville (1767–68)
- Second voyage of James Cook (1772–75)
- Third voyage of James Cook (1776–80)
- Comte de Lapérouse (1785–88)

P A C I F I C   O C E A N

Galapagos Islands
Charles Darwin visits, 1832

New Britain
Discovered by William Dampier, 1700

Society Islands
Discovered by Jacob Roggeveen, 1722

Vanikoro Island
Lapérouse wrecked, 1788

Samoa
Discovered by Jacob Roggeveen, 1722

Tahiti
Discovered by John Wallis, 1767

South America

Marquesas Islands

New Hebrides

Juan Fernandez Islands
Alexander Selkirk marooned, 1705–09

Australia

Coral Sea

Tuamotu Islands

Tonga

New Caledonia

Oparo Islands
Discovered by George Vancouver, 1790

Pitcairn Island
Bounty mutineers land, 1788

Diemen's (Tasmania)

Tasman Sea

Easter Island
Discovered by Jacob Roggeveen, 1722

New Zealand

N

SAIL GIVES WAY TO STEAM
In 1838, J.M.W. Turner painted The Fighting Téméraire, *immortalizing the former Royal Navy flagship as she was towed by a steam tug to Rotherhithe, England, to be broken up. As the 19th century wore on, the major navies began to replace their old wooden sailing ships with steam-powered iron warships.*

THE AGE OF STEAM

THE WORLD WAS TRANSFORMED BY STEAM POWER during the 19th century, on sea as well as land. Shipbuilders began making hulls from iron and steel, and the range and power of ships' guns increased enormously. Communication became faster than ever before, and a global market in food and energy began to develop. This was an age of great engineers, who built bridges, canals, and harbours as well as ships. The great European powers largely avoided wars with one another, but directed their energies to further expansion throughout the world. By the end of the century, only the remotest places did not feel the effects of European or North American technology and culture.

STEAM POWER

THE INVENTION OF THE STEAM ENGINE WOULD CHANGE THE FACE OF SHIPPING FOR EVER.

THE *GREAT WESTERN* STEAMS INTO HEAVY WEATHER WHILE CROSSING THE ATLANTIC IN DECEMBER 1844

> 66 Men might as well project a voyage to the moon as attempt to employ steam navigation against the stormy North Atlantic Ocean. 99
>
> **DIONYSIUS LARDNER**, in a speech to the British Association for the Advancement of Science, **1838**

KEY EVENTS

1782   TWICE THE POWER The Scottish engineer James Watt invents the double-acting steam engine which, combined with his seperate condenser, doubled the power of an engine.

1807   FIRST STEAMBOAT SERVICE Robert Fulton introduces the USA's first commercially successful river steamboat passenger service.

1836   SCREW PROPELLERS PATENTED John Ericsson and Frances Petit Smith both gain patents for their designs for a screw propeller.

1838   ATLANTIC CROSSING The *Sirius* and the *Great Western* both cross the Atlantic Ocean using steam power throughout the entire voyage.

1843   FIRST MODERN SHIP Isambard Kingdom Brunel's *Great Britain* is the first ocean-going screw-propelled iron ship.

1874   TRIPLE EXPANSION TESTED The engineer Dr A.C. Kirk successfully tests his triple-expansion engine in the steamboat *Proponitis*.

1897   QUEEN VICTORIA IS AMAZED Charles Parsons's steam turbine-powered *Turbinia* speeds through the Naval Review at Portsmouth.

The idea of the steam engine has been around since classical times, for Hero of Alexandria invented the aeolipile around AD 100. This consisted of a hollow ball supported by two brackets above the lid of a basin of boiling water. Steam entered the ball through one of the brackets and escaped through two bent pipes, producing a rotary motion. However, it would be several hundred years before the scientific principles Hero had demonstrated would be put to practical use by engineers. At the end of the 17th century, Thomas Savery of Devonshire produced a pumping engine for mines, and another Englishman, Thomas Newcomen, had developed a more efficient version by 1712. The idea of applying steam power to ships was not entirely new either. The French physicist Denis Papin proposed a steamboat in 1690. In 1737, the English engineer Jonathan Hulls produced a plan for a stern-wheel paddle boat using a Newcomen engine, and it is said to have been tried on the River Avon, but it is doubtful that it was successful, in view of the weight and coal consumption of engines of the time.

At the very least, the steam engine needed the improvements made by James Watt before it was practical to be used on water. The atmospheric engines developed by Savery and Newcomen worked by condensing steam in a

JAMES WATT
The Scottish engineer James Watt coined the term horsepower when inventing a new type of steam engine, which was patented in 1769.

cylinder, greatly reducing its volume and creating a partial vacuum that would suck a piston towards it. Watt's main improvement, dating from the 1760s, was the introduction of a separate condenser, into which the steam was pumped, avoiding the wasteful heating and cooling of the cylinder itself. Watt also invented the double-acting engine, in which steam was admitted alternately on both sides of the piston, so that both strokes of the engine were working (see panel, p.172). He, among others, also

EARLY STEAM-POWERED BOAT DESIGN
This model is based on Robert Fulton's steam-powered paddle boat the Clermont of 1807, which plied between Albany and New York on the Hudson River, USA.

connecting rod and crank turn piston movement into rotation

funnel

drive to air pump

boiler creates steam to drive piston

safety valve

paddle shaft

shallow, carvel-built hull

fixed paddles

flywheel stores energy

STOKING THE FIRES
Stokers labour in the fire room of the US battleship
Mississippi in the early 20th century. Teams had to
work around the clock to feed the furnaces – at full
speed, they used up to 16 tons of coal every hour.

developed machinery to translate the up-and-down motion of the engine into a rotary motion, far more suitable for a boat.

This inspired more inventors to try to produce an efficient steamboat. In 1783, the Marquis de Jouffroy d'Abbans operated one for 15 minutes on the River Saône in France. In North America, John Rumsey of Virginia made a trip on the Potomac River in 1786. In the same year, John Fitch of Pennsylvania designed and built a boat with steam-powered paddles that worked in a similar way to those of an American Indian canoe. Fitch began a service on the Delaware River in 1790, but he had no commercial instincts and was bankrupted several times. In Scotland, Patrick Miller and

LINED UP FOR BUSINESS
Paddle steamers line the levee at New Orleans, Louisiana, in 1862. As many as 35,000 steamboats a year docked at the port in its heyday.

William Symington built a two-hulled steamboat propelled by paddle wheels mounted between the hulls, which they successfully trialled on a loch near Dumfries in 1788. Then, in 1802, Symington devised an engine for, and built, the stern-wheeler *Charlotte Dundas* for towing boats on the Forth and Clyde Canal. The

HOW EARLY STEAM ENGINES WORKED

The early steam engine consisted of several elements. Fuel was burned outside the engine to heat water in a boiler to produce steam. The boiler was initially quite simple, a rectangular box held together by internal stays, with a furnace underneath and a large flue, which was big enough for a man to stand in it. The steam entered a cylinder, passing through an eccentric valve, where its high pressure drove a piston. The steam then exited through an exhaust valve, creating a vacuum that drew the cylinder back to its original position. The process was then

repeated. The linear motion of the piston was converted to a rotary motion to drive either a paddle wheel or propeller by means of a beam or lever, and a system of crankshafts and flywheels. The Scottish engineer James Watt introduced a separate condenser for the exhaust steam, to avoid wasting energy by heating and cooling the cylinder. He also invented the double-acting engine in 1782 (see below), in which steam alternately entered the cylinder on the left and then the right, so the piston was pushed both forwards and back.

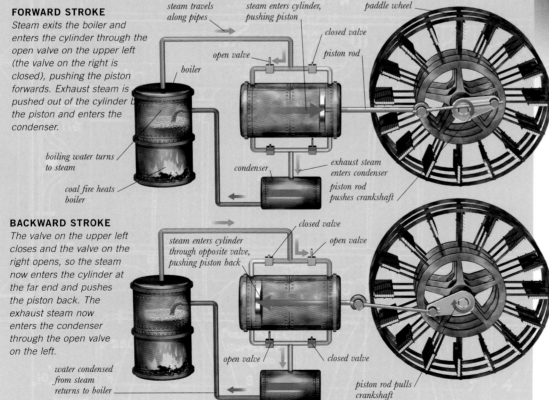

FORWARD STROKE
Steam exits the boiler and enters the cylinder through the open valve on the upper left (the valve on the right is closed), pushing the piston forwards. Exhaust steam is pushed out of the cylinder by the piston and enters the condenser.

steam travels along pipes / steam enters cylinder, pushing piston / paddle wheel / closed valve / open valve / piston rod / boiler / boiling water turns to steam / coal fire heats boiler / condenser / exhaust steam enters condenser / piston rod pushes crankshaft

BACKWARD STROKE
The valve on the upper left closes and the valve on the right opens, so the steam now enters the cylinder at the far end and pushes the piston back. The exhaust steam now enters the condenser through the open valve on the left.

water condensed from steam returns to boiler / steam enters cylinder through opposite valve, pushing piston back / closed valve / open valve / open valve / closed valve / piston rod pulls crankshaft

paddle boat worked, but the canal owners became worried about damage to the banks from her wash and banned her.

The first commercially successful American was Robert Fulton, whose *Clermont* (see p.170) began a passenger service between Albany and New York on the Hudson River in 1807, charging a fare of $7 – $3 cheaper than the stagecoach fare. Meanwhile, in Scotland, Henry Bell was concerned about getting visitors to his hotel in Helensburgh on the Firth of Clyde. Once a millwright, he designed the *Comet*, a 25-ton boat powered by an engine of his own design, and in 1812 it was able to take passengers from Glasgow to Helensburgh at a speed of 6.7 knots. The *Comet* was commercially successful, and Bell extended his services to the Western Highlands and Ireland.

MISSISSIPPI RIVERBOAT
Cotton bales are piled high on the paddle steamer William Carig, *on the Mississippi River near Baton Rouge, Louisiana. The boat is preparing to head downstream to New Orleans, which became the cotton capital of the world in the 19th century.*

RIVER PILOT

Before he became a novelist, Mark Twain (Samuel L. Clemens) worked as a river pilot on the Mississippi. Here, he describes some of the guidance he received from a pilot while training for his licence.

When I stood in her pilot-house I was so far above the water that I seemed perched on a mountain; and her decks stretched so far away, fore and aft, below me… here was a sumptuous glass temple; room enough to have a dance in… 'Do you see that long slanting line on the face of the water? Now, that is a reef. Moreover, it's a bluff reef. There is a solid sand-bar under it that is nearly as straight up and down as the side of a house. There is plenty of water close to it, but mighty little on top of it. Now, look out! Don't you crowd that slick, greasy looking place; there ain't nine feet there; she won't stand it. She begins to smell it; look smart, I tell you! Oh blazes, there you go! Stop the starboard wheel! Quick! Ship up to back! Set her back!' The face of the water, in time, became a wonderful book – a book that was a dead language to the uneducated passenger, but which told its mind to me without reserve… And it was not a book to be read once and thrown aside, for it had a new story to tell every day.

MARK TWAIN, *Life on the Mississippi*, **1883**

The steamboat age had begun, and over the next few years services were set up in other parts of Europe and North America. Following Fulton's success in the New York area, the steamboat spread rapidly to the USA's rivers and coasts, where geographical and economic conditions were highly suitable for its use. The first of the famous Mississippi riverboats was the *Enterprise*, which operated out of New Orleans from 1815; by 1860, there were more steamboats on the Mississippi and its tributaries than in any other part of the world. On the Great Lakes, the first steamboat on Lake Erie was the evocatively named *Walk-in-the-Water* of 1819. The American river steamboat soon developed beyond Fulton's long, open craft to a multi-decked floating hotel, in a sense anticipating the concept of the modern cruise liner by a century.

In Europe, the *Thames* of 1814 made the first seagoing passage, between Glasgow and the River Thames, in 1815. The *Margery* of 1814 operated on the Thames and was the first steamboat to cross the English Channel. By

MARK TWAIN
The American novelist Samuel L. Clemens, seen here relaxing on deck in 1901, took the pseudonym Mark Twain from his days as a river pilot. A crew member in the ship's bow sounding the depth of the river would call out "mark twain" when it was two fathoms deep, and therefore a safe channel. Clemens gained his pilot's certificate on 30 August 1852.

1816, steamers were used in Swedish waters and on the rivers of Prussia (now Germany). Meanwhile, on the Clyde, where one line of steamboat development had originated, more than 50 paddle steamers maintained regular services along and across the river and estuary by 1825, and flourished well into the 20th century. In Australia, the first paddle steamer entered service on the Murray River in 1853, and by the mid-1870s more than 400 steamers were in operation, transporting the growing colony of Victoria's traffic in wool and timber.

In its early stages, steam power could be used in two contexts: in sheltered rivers, estuaries, lakes, and coastal voyages, where it was never far from the shore; and in the open sea as an auxiliary to sail. The second possibility was quite slow to develop. Early steam engines took

STEAMING ACROSS THE ATLANTIC

The 700-ton steamer *Sirius* left the Irish port of Cork on the morning of 4 April 1838, with her officers determined to make the first true steam-powered passage across the Atlantic. They knew that the great Isambard Kingdom Brunel had built his own steamship, the *Great Western* of nearly twice the size, and was not far behind them – in fact, he would leave Bristol on the southwest coast of England four days later.

The *Sirius*'s voyage was not unpleasant for most of the time – her captain waxed lyrical about the rainbows he saw – but the crew had to burn her cabin furniture, spare yards, and even a mast to keep up steam in her boiler. Seasickness struck the passengers of the *Great Western,* and, although her fuel was more than adequate for the journey, her stokers soon became exhausted and had to be bribed with an extra half-dollar.

The *Sirius* arrived off New York on 22 April, but ran aground at Sandy Hook and had to wait for the tide. The *Great Western* had gained on her and arrived in New York on the same day, having taken 14 days compared with the *Sirius*'s 19.

GIVING CHASE
The Great Western steams past Portishead on 8 April 1838, at the beginning of her voyage from Bristol to New York, in which she would beat the Sirius's journey time by five days.

up a large amount of space, especially when they needed paddle wheels on the side of the ship. They consumed large amounts of fuel and required large teams of firemen and engineers to operate them. Multi-skilling was rare in the 19th century, so the engine-room crew would be carried in addition to the seamen.

But in one context the steamship did have a decisive influence on the ocean-going sailing ship. Steam tugs arguably began with the *Charlotte Dundas* or Fulton's steamers, intended to pull other vessels. The name originated with a vessel called the *Tug*, built in Scotland in 1817 for use in the Firth of Forth. By 1825, paddle tugs were common in the major commercial ports. They made it far easier to get sailing ships upriver to ports such as London, and they could be used to manoeuvre ships into place in the new enclosed docks being built in Europe. The use of steam tugs meant that sailing

ships did not have to be kept short to allow them to make short tacks into harbour in unfavourable winds, and helped clear the way for the development of the clipper ship (see p.233) by the middle of the 19th century.
Ships could be towed some way across the open sea until they entered an area with favourable winds.

Extension to the oceans

With emigration from Europe to North America soaring in the 1800s, the transatlantic passenger trade was a profitable one for the shipowner, but a sailing ship had to go out on a very long route, heading south to the Azores to pick up the trade winds, then north along the American coast to the main destinations such as New York and Boston. Unlike other oceans, the North Atlantic has no islands in the middle, so the voyage

would have to be made in a single step, making great demands on the engines of the time. The *Savannah*, built in New York in 1819, had the honour of being the first steamship to cross the Atlantic, but no attempt was made to set up a regular service, for her owners wanted to sell her in Europe. However, during the crossing she used her engines for only about eight hours – the rest of the voyage was made under sail.

The next major advance came with the *Sirius*, built in Leith, Scotland, and the *Great Western*, designed and built in Bristol by British engineer Isambard Kingdom Brunel. Both crossed the Atlantic under steam power alone in 1838 (see panel, left). Shipping magnate Samuel Cunard (see p.202) began his regular service from Liverpool to Halifax and Boston in 1840, and the paddle steamer became an established alternative to the sailing ship on the route.

The screw propeller

Apart from John Fitch's system using paddles in the traditional sense of a kind of oar, early steamships almost invariably used the rotary paddle wheel. Over the years, this became more sophisticated, with gearing that angled each blade in turn to be at right angles to the direction of motion while it was in the water, and perhaps to "feather" itself to create less wind resistance when out of the water. But the paddle wheel was naturally inefficient, in that most of it was out of the water and doing no work at any given moment. It was difficult to use at sea, for in big waves one wheel might be lifted out of the water while the other was deeply

UP ON DECK
The Great Britain *was modified for the Australia run in 1853. She had a cow house and room for 160 sheep, 40 pigs, and 1,200 poultry – although some of the chickens seem to have been free-ranging.*

JOHN ERICSSON

Born in Sweden, John Ericsson (1803–89) served as an engineer in the Swedish Army and became interested in steam power. In 1826, he went to Britain and competed in the 1829 Rainhill trials of locomotives, won by George Stephenson. He then turned his attention to marine matters, and in 1837 he built the *Francis B. Ogden* to test his screw propeller. In 1839, he crossed the Atlantic to promote his propeller and helped design the *Princeton*, the first screw-propelled warship. He is most famous for the *Monitor*, the ironclad turret ship he designed for the US Navy in 1862 during the Civil War.

immersed, making accurate steering impossible. As a ship used up its coal and stores on a long voyage, the paddle wheels would rise further out of the water and become even less efficient.

Inventors began to turn towards the idea of the Archimedes screw, which had been used for raising water and grinding grain for centuries. Both Leonardo da Vinci and the 17th-century English scientist Robert Hooke had recognized that a screw could theoretically be used to

LEAVING BRISTOL TO UNDERGO SEA TRIALS
The Great Britain *carried out her sea trials in the Bristol Channel in 1845. With 18 of her furnaces lit and the engines turning at 16 revolutions per minute, she achieved a speed of 11 knots. Her top speed was 12 knots.*

provide propulsion, and, in 1776, David Bushnell used a type of screw propeller to drive his submarine the *Turtle* (see p.124). Robert Fulton used a similar device in his submarine design of 1800, but it was 1836 before screw propulsion became practical, with the patenting of two separate designs for propellers. Swedish engineer John Ericsson (see panel, left) built several screw-driven ships. His second, the *Robert F. Stockton* of 1838, had two contra-rotating propellers powered by a specially designed two-cylinder engine. British inventor Francis Petit Smith built the *Archimedes* on the Thames in 1839, with a propeller that formed one complete turn of a screw thread (his 1836 patent had two turns).

Brunel took up the screw idea enthusiastically for his second ship, the *Great Britain*. Several designs were considered for her propeller, but the one used had six angular blades. The *Great Britain* was hailed as "the first modern ship". In addition to being both the first ocean-going vessel to be built of iron and to have a screw propeller, she was the largest ship of her day and she also reintroduced the idea of a balanced steering gear in the form of her iron rudder. A central pivot helped balance out the pressure on

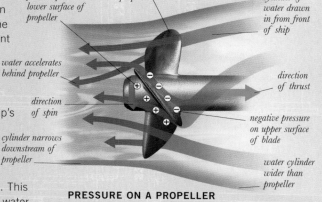

PADDLE VERSUS PROPELLER
On 4 April 1845, the screw-propelled sloop Rattler *and the paddle-driven sloop* Alecto *were coupled up stern to stern. With both ships' engines fully engaged, the* Rattler *(on the left) dragged the* Alecto *astern at a speed of 2.8 knots.*

the surfaces, and made the rudder far easier to turn than a conventional one. The *Great Britain* was launched in 1843, but like many of Brunel's projects she was a technological rather than an economic success. For some years, she inspired few imitators, although in 1850 the Inman Line was founded with the transatlantic voyage of the *City of Glasgow*, another iron screw steamer.

In the meantime, the British Admiralty was inspired by the *Archimedes* and *Great Britain* to take an interest in the screw. In 1845, it staged a tug-of-war between the paddle steamer *Alecto* and its first screw steamer *Rattler* (see above), both of

SCREW PROPULSION

The very earliest propellers, dating from the early 19th century, were widely seen as an inferior means of propulsion to the paddle wheel. However, as more efficient forms were developed, the propeller gradually superseded the paddle wheel, and it remains the most common form of ship propulsion today.

A rotating propeller, driven by the ship's engine, creates a force called thrust that propels the ship forwards. As the blades rotate, a difference in pressure arises between their upper and lower surfaces (see diagram, right). This pressure difference draws a cylinder of water in from the front of the boat and forces it out at the back in a slightly narrower cylinder. The narrowing of the cylinder means that the stream of water exits at an increased velocity, giving the boat forward momentum.

positive pressure on lower surface of propeller

propeller

cylinder of water drawn in from front of ship

water accelerates behind propeller

direction of spin

direction of thrust

cylinder narrows downstream of propeller

negative pressure on upper surface of blade

water cylinder wider than propeller

PRESSURE ON A PROPELLER
As a propeller blade moves downwards, it pushes water down and towards the back of the boat. To fill the space, water rushes in behind the blade. This results in a difference in pressure between the blade's upper and lower surfaces, with a positive pressure on the lower surface and a negative pressure on the upper side.

PROPELLER SHAPES
While William Froude's test propeller (right) had only two blades, later designs (such as the common screw of the 1860s, centre) had four. More streamlined propellers (far right) were designed when it was found that a smooth outline caused less vibration.

FROUDE'S EARLY TEST PROPELLER

COMMON SCREW PROPELLER

THREE-BLADED PROPELLER

ISAMBARD KINGDOM BRUNEL

The son of a French émigré engineer, Isambard Kingdom Brunel (1806–59) led the construction of the first tunnel under the Thames with his father in 1826. His greatest and most lasting achievement was the Great Western Railway, from London to Bristol and on to Cornwall, to which he was appointed engineer in 1833. It was the impending completion of the line to Bristol that inspired his first venture in shipbuilding. Brunel claimed that the company could go much further and link with a steamship service across the Atlantic – the origin of the *Great Western* steamship, which entered service in 1838. The daring and innovative Brunel went on to design the *Great Britain*, the largest ship of her day, made of iron and with a screw propeller. But he overreached himself with the *Great Eastern*, which took up most of his time in the 1850s, and culminated in an eventually fatal illness for Brunel. Despite many commercial failures, he is a symbol of the heroic age of the engineer.

around the same tonnage and horsepower. In fact, the Admiralty had already made up its mind in favour of the screw and the tests were not entirely fair to the *Alecto*, but it provided suitable publicity for the new departure.

Twin-screw, twin-engined ships began to appear from the early 1860s. They had the advantage that the failure of one engine or screw was not fatal, and that, with one engine operating in the opposite direction to the other, manoeuvrability could be greatly increased, which was an added benefit for the longer ships that were being produced.

Development of the propeller continued throughout the century with the aid of practical experience and test tanks, and over this period it took on a far more streamlined shape. Cunard's *Russia* of 1867 was the first screw ship that could compete with the paddle steamers for speed on the transatlantic run, and it was about 1870 before the advantages of the screw propeller were clearly established in all ocean- and seagoing trades – even Brunel reverted and used both a propeller and paddles for his third revolutionary ship.

The *Great Eastern*

In 1851, Brunel began to think of the possibility of a ship that could sail to India round the Cape of Good Hope without refuelling. He had already shown that the water resistance of a ship was proportional to the square of its dimensions, but the space available for fuel was proportional to the cube – in other words, a larger ship could carry fuel for a disproportionately longer voyage. He conceived a huge vessel, 211m (692ft) long and of 18,915 tons – nearly six times as large as any vessel yet built. With support from the Eastern Steam Navigation Company, he began construction on a site at Millwall on the north bank of the Thames, in partnership with the Scottish shipbuilder John Scott Russell. She was fitted with a double bottom and had both paddle and screw propulsion, as well as masts to carry

IRON AND STEEL SHIPS

The first iron steamship was the *Aaron Manby* of 1822, but the great leap came in 1839, when Brunel decided to build his *Great Britain* in iron. In 1846, she ran aground at Dundrum in Ireland, but remained intact where a wooden ship would have broken up. In warship construction, the use of iron was inspired by the desire to keep out enemy shot. Iron ships were at first built in the same way as wooden ones, with iron plates on iron frames. But iron could be bent to shape for frames, and plates could be joined to one another by rivets, making the hull more rigid. Conventional steel of the time was too brittle for shipbuilding, so mild steel was developed. The first seagoing steel ship was the *Rotamahama* of 1879. She also proved her worth by surviving an accident, and by the 1890s steel had totally replaced iron in shipbuilding.

RIVETED IRON PLATES
These two thick iron plates from a 19th-century warship are held together by nine rivets, forming a watertight seal.

sail. Enormous amounts of capital were tied up in the project, and the management structure could not cope with a succession of problems. The partners did not see eye to eye, and costs rose. The ship was so large that she had to be launched sideways, but on the appointed day of 3 November 1857 she stuck fast, although chains were used to haul her towards the Thames. She finally took the water at the end of January 1858. Brunel's death in 1859 coincided with her completion, but there was no market for such a large ship. The *Great Eastern* made several voyages as a cargo-passenger ship but was eventually used for cable-laying (see p.189). She served mainly as a warning about the dangers of expanding too fast, and it would be 40 years before the *Kaiser Wilhelm II* of 1901 exceeded her in tonnage, and nearly 50 before the *Mauretania* of 1907 exceeded her in length.

***GREAT EASTERN* IN SERVICE**
The Steamship Great Eastern in a Choppy Sea *is one of several oils of the ship painted by Henry Clifford, who served as second engineer on the ship.*

Naval architecture as a science

In 1837, the British engineer William Froude became an assistant to Brunel in his work on railway and ship design, but he left the job in 1846 to study hydrodynamics and ship behaviour. Froude carried out experiments on scale models in the River Dart near his home in Devon, and worked out mathematical formulae to apply the results to full-size ships. With the backing of the British Admiralty, he built the first practical test tank at Torquay in 1870. He was the first truly scientific naval architect, and his research made possible the great expansion in the size of ships after his death in 1879.

In the late 19th century, naval architecture was at last developed as a science. Froude's test tank was taken up by the world's navies and commercial shipbuilders, notably Denny of Dumbarton in Scotland (see panel, right), who also developed the possibility of testing the speed of a real ship in a measured mile in the Firth of Clyde. The world's first Chair of Naval Architecture was set up in Glasgow University in 1883, funded by Isabella Elder, widow of the joint inventor of the triple-expansion engine.

Compound and triple expansion

For all his great innovations, James Watt left a legacy of conservatism among mid-19th-century engineers, who held his memory in great respect and accepted his view that there was a practical limit to the efficiency of the steam engine. British marine engineers were also held back by

TESTING TANKS

Naval architects can test how a full-size ship will perform at sea by towing a wax scale model of the hull through a tank of water in carefully controlled conditions, monitoring how it performs, and then applying William Froude's formulae to the results. By varying the speed at which the model is towed through the water and using a wave-generating machine to produce regular or irregular waves, the designers can work out what the actual ship's performance in rolling, pitching, resistance, and engine power would be and improve its lines, if need be, at an early stage. Today's test tanks are computer controlled and use laser measurement systems.

DENNY SHIP MODEL EXPERIMENT TANK
Built in 1882, the Denny Tank is 100m (320ft) in length, 7m (23ft) wide, and 2.7m (8ft 9in) deep. The original model towing carriage was operated by a engineer, who would control its speed and monitor the instruments.

low steam pressure in their boilers. Although high-pressure boilers were used on land, accidents early in the century caused Board of Trade inspectors to be very cautious about ship boilers, and they did not approve of pressures of greater than about 1.4kg/cm² (20lb/in²).

The science of thermodynamics showed that engines with higher pressures were far more efficient. However, the higher pressure could not be used efficiently in a single cylinder. On land, it had long been common to fit two cylinders – a small one to use the high-pressure steam and a larger one to take the lower pressure exhaust steam from the first cylinder. The process had been invented by the English engineer Jonathan Hornblower in 1781 and developed by Scottish engineer William McNaught in 1845 – it was known as "McNaughting" and later

"compounding". David Elder and Charles Randolph, shipbuilders of Glasgow, patented "an arrangement of compound engines adapted for the driving of the screw propeller" in 1853 and began to promote its use. It was taken up in 1864 by the Pacific Steam Navigation Company, operating on the coast of South America, where the extra range of the new engine was a great advantage. By the end of the decade, it was being used by Atlantic liners, and steam pressures of 7.7kg/cm² (110lb/in²) were in use.

The next step was to extend the compounding yet further by using three cylinders to take high-, intermediate-, and low-pressure steam. This system was developed by Dr A.C. Kirk, previously an employee of Elder's company. In 1874, he built the *Proponitis* in Liverpool to test the engine, followed by the *Aberdeen* of 1881, which demonstrated the concept in actual service on the route to Australia. By 1886, 150 sets of triple-expansion engines had been made for the British merchant marine, and by the end of the century it was standard in merchant ships. The triple-expansion engine greatly increased fuel efficiency: the single-cylinder engines of the British ironclad *Warrior* of 1861 needed up to 2.3kg (5lb) of coal to generate one horsepower for an hour; the *Sans Pareil* of

TRIPLE-EXPANSION ENGINE
Often referred to as a cathedral engine because of its vast size – it was as tall as a three-storey building – this particular triple-expansion engine was built around 1890 by David Elder in Glasgow, Scotland, for the liner Orient.

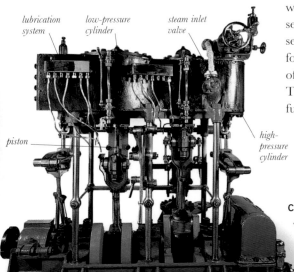

lubrication system

low-pressure cylinder

steam inlet valve

piston

high-pressure cylinder

COMPOUND ENGINE
A compound engine differs from a simple engine in that it has a second cylinder, which catches the steam that escapes from the first cylinder. Both cylinders then drive pistons.

1888, fitted with triple-expansion engines, needed only 1.2kg (2.6lb); and the *Canopus* of 1899 needed just 0.75kg (1.7lb).

The triple-expansion engine was made possible by improved boilers that produced higher boiler pressures, from 10.5 to 17.5kg/cm² (150 to 250lb/in²). The marine boiler was no longer a simple metal box filled with water with a furnace underneath it. The Scotch boiler, the most common type on merchant ships in the late 19th century, was cylindrical to better withstand the great pressure, and its flat ends were braced with iron stays. It also contained tubes to retain the high-pressure gases. Warships of the late 19th century used water-tube boilers, in which small quantities of water were heated in tubes within the boiler. Superheating was used in high-performance ships to raise the temperature of steam above the natural boiling point of water, utilizing waste heat. This helped to reduce the amount of condensation forming inside the engine, and made it run more efficiently. Steam engines were also used to power many auxiliary services, such as electric light, refrigeration, cargo-handling gear, and the gun turrets of warships.

The triple-expansion engine opened a new phase in the steam age. Pioneers such as Brunel had crossed the Atlantic and made long voyages in the face of great difficulties. With the triple-expansion engine, ocean voyages could be completed as a matter of course. By about 1870, three factors – the screw propeller, iron construction, and the triple-expansion engine – were in place to allow the steamship to dominate the world. In 1871, the first sail-less battleship, the British *Devastation*, took to the seas. In 1884, the tonnage of steamships overtook sailing ships for the first time on the British Register. Sail was now mostly confined to coastal trades where the owners could not afford the investment, and to long cargo voyages where speed did not matter. Merchant steamships still

STEAM TURBINE GENERATOR
Parsons's steam turbine of 1889 used high-pressure steam at 200°C (400°F) to drive the generator. The turbine turned 4,800 times every minute, generating 100,000 joules of electrical energy every second – that is, 100 kilowatts.

wires through which electricity leaves generator
governor keeps machine turning at correct speed
steam inlet
powerful magnet turns inside coil
generator
tray catches drips of oil
steam outlet
turbine encasing rows of turbine blades

retained the capacity to carry sail for some years, but even that had largely disappeared by the 1890s. Steam's dominance was almost total.

Parsons and the turbine

The triple-expansion engine encouraged the use of high-pressure steam, and this led to a further development. British scientist Charles Parsons went to great lengths to learn engineering in his youth, and in the 1880s applied his ideas to use the rotary motion of steam engines to drive generators for the expanding electricity industry. This led him to the idea of the turbine engine, which used high-pressure steam to force the rotation of a series of blades on a series of wheels attached to a shaft, whose motion could in turn drive the rotor of an electric generator or a ship's propeller. Parsons built an experimental boat called the *Turbinia*. He took it to Queen Victoria's

Diamond Jubilee Naval Review off Portsmouth in 1897. The little craft raced around at 34 knots and caused a sensation – even the fastest naval destroyers could do only 27 knots.

The turbine engine operated at high speed. It took some time to develop gearing systems, so in the early stages its use was confined to fast ships. It was soon applied to warships, in the destroyers *Cobra* and *Viper* of 1890–1900. The first vessel to use a turbine engine commercially was the *King Edward*, built as a fast passenger ship across the Firth of Clyde in 1901.

In the century that followed, the steam turbine would take to the oceans and complete the steam revolution by providing the main motive power for the most prestigious ships of the age, the fast ocean liners and the dreadnought battleships that vied for supremacy on behalf of their nations.

THE *TURBINIA*
Charles Parsons's Turbinia cuts through the water at more than 30 knots at the turn of the last century. Parsons's revolutionary design was driven by three turbine engines, each connected to its own independent shaft and propeller.

RIVER STEAMBOATS

Steamboats naturally found their first use on rivers and inland waterways, where there were variable winds caused by land features and no room to tack a sailing ship. These vessels could operate against wind and tide, could make as many refuelling stops as necessary, and were in relatively safe and sheltered waters. There was much contact between America and Europe in the development of the steamboat, but there were also many differences in geography, approach, and technology.

European river steamboats

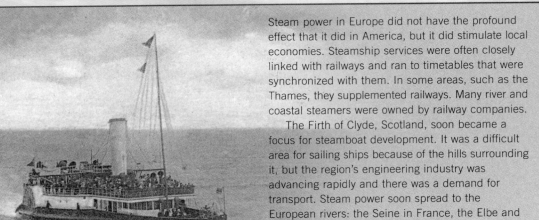

Steam power in Europe did not have the profound effect that it did in America, but it did stimulate local economies. Steamship services were often closely linked with railways and ran to timetables that were synchronized with them. In some areas, such as the Thames, they supplemented railways. Many river and coastal steamers were owned by railway companies.

The Firth of Clyde, Scotland, soon became a focus for steamboat development. It was a difficult area for sailing ships because of the hills surrounding it, but the region's engineering industry was advancing rapidly and there was a demand for transport. Steam power soon spread to the European rivers: the Seine in France, the Elbe and Rhine in Germany, the Danube in Austria–Hungary, and the Neva in Russia, for example. The *Aaron Manby*, the first iron-hulled steamboat, was built for service on the Seine, a river with very strong tides. For the rest of the 19th and much of the 20th century, steamships offered regular services on the Clyde,

APPROACHING CLACTON PIER
This photograph shows the Southend Belle, full of passengers, approaching the pier at Clacton on Sea, Essex.

ROYAL SOVEREIGN
The Royal Sovereign was one of the most popular Thames steamers of the end of the 19th century. She ran from London to Margate in Kent.

ROYAL SOVEREIGN	
Origin Britain	**Date of launch** 1893
Length 91.5m (300ft 2in)	**Tonnage** 891 tons
Propulsion 2 engines, paddles	**Passengers** About 1,000

NEW ORLEANS
William A. Walker painted this scene, entitled Levee, at New Orleans in 1883, depicting the steamboats Natchez and Vicksburg docked in the bustling post-bellum port.

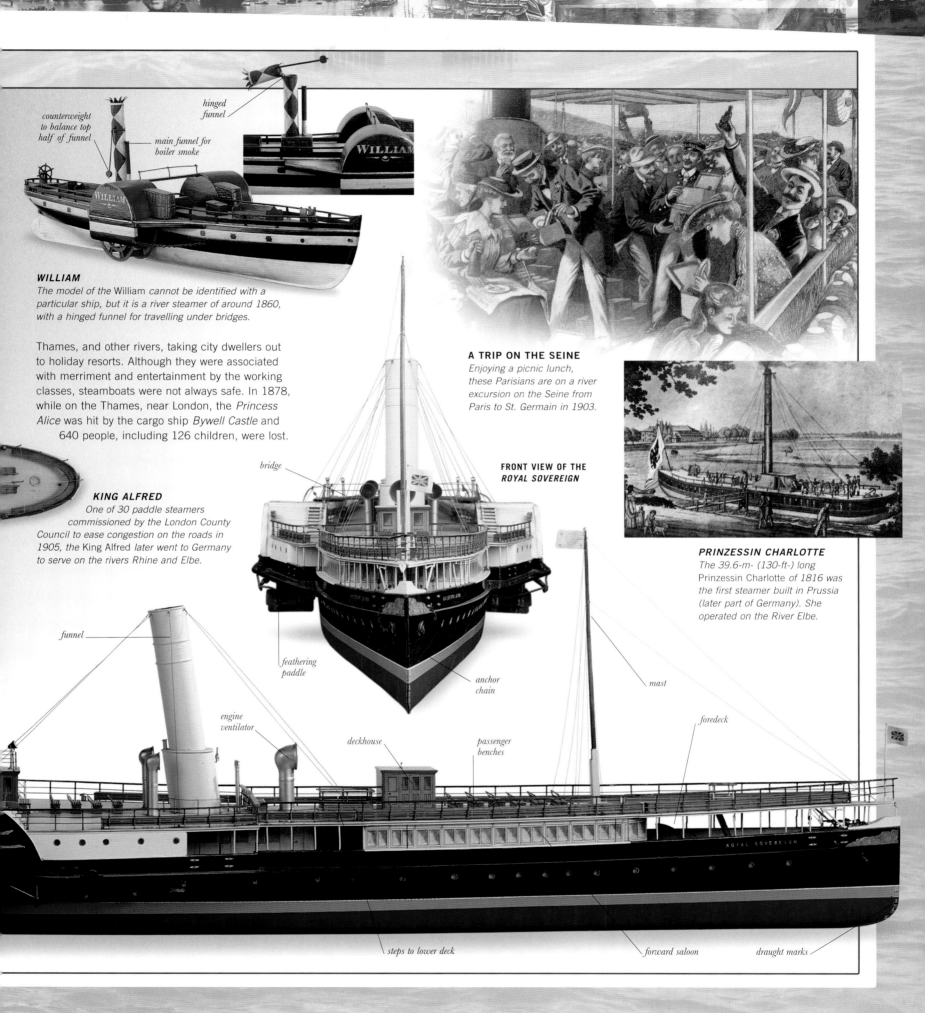

WILLIAM

counterweight to balance top half of funnel

hinged funnel

main funnel for boiler smoke

The model of the William *cannot be identified with a particular ship, but it is a river steamer of around 1860, with a hinged funnel for travelling under bridges.*

Thames, and other rivers, taking city dwellers out to holiday resorts. Although they were associated with merriment and entertainment by the working classes, steamboats were not always safe. In 1878, while on the Thames, near London, the *Princess Alice* was hit by the cargo ship *Bywell Castle* and 640 people, including 126 children, were lost.

KING ALFRED

One of 30 paddle steamers commissioned by the London County Council to ease congestion on the roads in 1905, the King Alfred *later went to Germany to serve on the rivers Rhine and Elbe.*

A TRIP ON THE SEINE

Enjoying a picnic lunch, these Parisians are on a river excursion on the Seine from Paris to St. Germain in 1903.

FRONT VIEW OF THE *ROYAL SOVEREIGN*

bridge

feathering paddle

anchor chain

mast

PRINZESSIN CHARLOTTE

The 39.6-m- (130-ft-) long Prinzessin Charlotte *of 1816 was the first steamer built in Prussia (later part of Germany). She operated on the River Elbe.*

funnel

engine ventilator

deckhouse

passenger benches

foredeck

steps to lower deck

forward saloon

draught marks

Pioneers

Inventors had dreamed of using steam power to propel ships since the early 18th century, but it became practical only after James Watt's improvements made the engine twice as efficient. The next problem was to find a way of transmitting the power to the water. John Fitch used a system of paddles based on the American Indian canoe, but most designers hit upon the rotating paddle wheel in various forms. In Scotland, the *Charlotte Dundas* failed mainly because the owners of the Forth and Clyde Canal objected to her wash on the banks. The *Comet* (right), operating on the River Clyde from 1812, was the first commercially successful passenger steamboat in Europe, taking passengers down the Clyde from Glasgow.

COMET	
Origin Britain	**Date of launch** 1812
Length 40.25m (132ft)	**Tonnage** 205 tons
Propulsion 40-hp engine, paddles	

American steamboats

The steamship played a great part in the development of early 19th-century America by opening up the Great Lakes and rivers, such as the Hudson, Missouri, Mississippi, and Ohio, to settlement and trade. American river boats tended to be less like ships than their European counterparts; they looked more like floating hotels above the waterline. Below the waterline, the hull had little structure, and a truss was often fitted along the length of the ship to give it strength, a practice that the ancient Egyptians had also used. The Americans were less fearful of boiler explosions than the Europeans, and that and the long travelling distances involved allowed the development

of some fast ships. The river steamboat took on an image of glamour and excitement. However, the author Charles Dickens was among critics of the conditions onboard in the early days. Many river services continued well into the 20th century, despite competition from railways. The *Natchez* (below) was one of the fastest ships on the Mississippi. In 1870, she steamed the 1,672km (1,039 miles) from New Orleans to St. Louis at an average speed of 11.2 knots, and in the same year she raced against her great rival the *Robert E. Lee* along the same route. The *Robert E. Lee* won the race.

HENDRICK HUDSON
The Hendrick Hudson *of 1906 was built for the Hudson River. She had the latest compound engine, but her interior was in traditional 19th-century style.*

NATCHEZ	
Origin United States	**Date of launch** 1869
Length 91.75m (301ft)	**Tonnage** 1,547 tons
Propulsion High-pressure engines, paddles	

STEAM AT SEA

From their origins on canals and rivers, steamships soon moved into more open waters, beginning with short passages in northern Europe. At first, they were used mainly on passenger routes, where speed and reliability were advantageous. For Britain, they were an important way of linking with India and the East. In the early stages, this involved travelling through the Mediterranean, before making an overland journey to Suez, and then taking another ship to the destination.

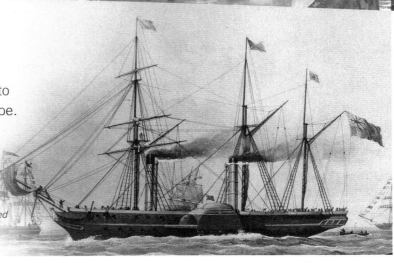

HINDOSTAN
The Hindostan of 1842 inaugurated the service from Suez to Calcutta, causing the Peninsular Steam Company to add Orient to its title.

Paddle steamers

The first paddle-ship services in the open sea included those between the various parts of the British Isles and across the English Channel and the Mediterranean Sea. The *Fernando Primo*, the first steamship to operate in the Mediterranean, was built in 1818. As on the Atlantic, government mail contracts demanded regular services and gave the advantage to steam over sail. Steamships were also used in European colonies in the Far East as early as 1823. The *William Fawcett* (right) was the first ship chartered by the Peninsular Steam Company in 1835, intended for the mail service between England and Portugal.

square-rigged foremast

fore-and-aft-rigged mainmast

tall funnel

sponson

ELIZABETH
Converted from a barge at St. Petersburg in Russia, the Elizabeth was the first to have feathering paddle wheels that changed their angle in and out of the water.

WILLIAM FAWCETT

Origin Britain	**Date of launch** 1828
Length 44.4m (145ft 8in)	**Tonnage** 206 tons
Propulsion 140-hp engines, paddles	

Screw ships

The invention of the screw propeller greatly increased the potential of the steamship at sea, allowing it to operate in much rougher water and far more efficiently. Isambard Kingdom Brunel's 3,270-ton *Great Britain* of 1843 was one of the pioneers of this mode of propulsion, although much smaller screw ships were favoured by most shipowners over the next ten years. Cunard's first iron screw ship, for example, was the *Andes* of 1,440 tons of 1853. Before long, though, rather larger ships were built. Although designed as a paddle steamer, the *Himalaya* (right) was converted to screw propulsion before her completion. She was intended for 200 first-class passengers but was taken up by the Royal Navy as a troopship for use in the Crimean War.

HIMALAYA

Origin Britain	**Date of launch** 1853
Length 103.6m (340ft)	**Tonnage** 3,438 tons
Propulsion 2,500-hp engine, screw propeller	

19TH-CENTURY MORSE TELEGRAPH MACHINE

" More was done yesterday for the consolidation of our Empire than the wisdom of our statesmen, the liberality of our Legislature, or the loyalty of our colonists could ever have effected. Distance between Canada and England is annihilated. "

THE TIMES, on the first telegraphic communication between Europe and North America, **18 August 1858**

KEY EVENTS

1822 FRESNEL LENS INVENTED French physicist Augustin Fresnel invents a multi-prismed lens that dramatically increases the power and visibility of the beam of a lighthouse.

1860 INNOVATIVE LIGHTHOUSE The USA's first offshore masonry lighthouse, at Minots Ledge, Massachusetts, enters service.

1866 COMMUNICATION REVOLUTION The *Great Eastern* completes the laying of the first completely successful transatlantic cable.

1869 SUEZ CANAL OPENS The Suez Canal in Egypt drastically reduces the voyage time between Europe and India and the Far East.

1884 FREIGHT REFRIGERATION The *Elderslie*, the first custom-built refrigerated ship, carries frozen meat from New Zealand to Britain.

1890 LIFEBOAT LAUNCHED The first steam-powered lifeboat, the *Duke of Northumberland*, enters service at Harwich, England.

1895 KIEL CANAL COMPLETED Kaiser Wilhelm II lays the final stone of the Kiel Canal in Germany, linking the Baltic with the North Sea.

MARITIME TRADE

AS THE 19TH CENTURY PROGRESSED, THE WORLD SEEMED TO BECOME SMALLER, THANKS TO ADVANCES IN COMMUNICATIONS AT SEA AND ON THE LAND.

The volume of world trade increased vastly during the 19th century, growing tenfold between 1850 and 1913 alone. New means were needed to build the ships and handle the cargoes and passengers that were generated by the growing trade. Shipping services have always changed to meet people's needs, but now the relationship became closer than ever, as steamships were run to schedule to suit the customers rather than the shipowners, and humanitarians began to take an interest in the great loss of life at sea.

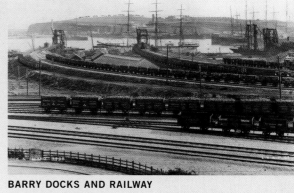

BARRY DOCKS AND RAILWAY
World demand for the premium-quality Welsh coal to power steamships was so high in the 1890s that a coal train from the mines in the Rhondda Valley arrived at Barry Docks, South Wales, every 15 minutes.

Steamships and the railways

Steam had decisive effects on the development of civil engineering, and therefore on ports and other maritime operations. Steam dredgers could dig out channels far faster than the human or horsepowered versions of the 18th century. This allowed the Dutch, for example, to maintain ports such as Rotterdam despite the deposition of silt from rivers, and to cope with ever-larger ships. Mechanical diggers could be used to dig out new, deeper dock basins, and cranes, powered by steam and, later, hydraulics, could lift goods in and out of ships.

Even more decisive was the link between steam and the railways. Britain was the pioneer here, with the first public commercial railway, the Stockton and Darlington, opening in 1825, and by 1850 nearly 10,000km (6,200 miles) were open. France had a similar amount by 1860, while Germany had 11,000km (6,800 miles). The USA completed the great transcontinental railway in 1869, linking the east and west coasts.

Railways could link directly with ships in several ways. The expanding fishing industry depended on getting the catch to market on time, and fishing ports had rail links with the major cities. In Europe, the coal trade provided some of the stimulus for the development of railways, and to some extent trains rivalled ships in bringing coal into the cities. But railways could also bring coal to ports, where it could be exported in great quantities.

LOADING UP WITH SUPPLIES
Dockers carry supplies and cargo onboard the steamship Arawa *in the Royal Albert Docks, London, as she prepares for a voyage to Australia and New Zealand in 1885. To reduce coal consumption on the London–Australia run, she was also rigged for sails, with four masts.*

The development of ports

Ports expanded greatly during the 19th century, largely by developing the facilities of existing ones. Certain ports, such as New York, London, Liverpool, Le Havre, and Marseilles, had to grow fast to cater for the long-distance trades. Others expanded less quickly, but many old ports found a continuing use for local traffic, the coal trade, and fishing. The British, with strong tidal flows and restricted land space, preferred the enclosed wet dock, a large area of useable waterfront constructed behind a relatively small river front, where the level of the water could be controlled. The word "dock" became synonymous with ship loading, and those who worked in the area were known as dockers, comparable with the American longshoremen. The expanding ports, especially London and Liverpool, built miles of new docks down the rivers and towards the sea. Each was a substantial engineering feat. The Royal Albert Dock in London, built in the 1880s, had 23 hectares (56 acres) of dock with a minimum water depth of 8m (26ft) and 7.7 hectares (19 acres) of lock entrance, all of which had to be excavated and lined with stone walls. But dock owners could never stand still in the 19th century, as ever-bigger ships demanded constant improvement.

North European ports had different needs. After much debate, Hamburg, on the River Elbe, rejected enclosed docks in favour of open basins, and in the 1860s it began a programme of construction. This was greatly accelerated by German Unification in 1870, and Hamburg was declared a free port (that is, no duty was payable on goods destined for other countries) in 1888.

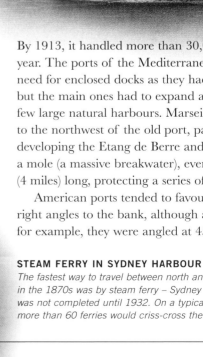

INLAND WATERWAY
In the 19th century, Belgium's network of canals was expanded and improved, linking its inland cities, such as Bruges, above, with the growing North Sea ports of Ostend, Zeebrugge, and Antwerp.

Passenger services were the most obvious way in which rail and sea travel were linked. In some areas the steamships and the railway operated as rivals – on the Mississippi, Missouri, and other rivers in the western USA, river boats were driven out of business as railways were built along the banks. But in many other cases, the steamship operated as an extension of the railway. This was clearest when passenger services, for example across the English Channel or between the Danish islands, were linked to the railway timetable. On a much grander scale, Brunel's first steamship was intended as an extension of his great railway across the Atlantic, as shown by its name, the *Great Western* (see p.174). Perhaps the most extreme example was the train ferry. This was first used across the firths of Forth and Tay in Scotland from 1860, carrying only freight wagons. The first passenger train ferry travelled across the Little Belt between the Danish mainland and islands in 1872, and other services followed, linking the country with Sweden and Germany. The main advantage was that passengers could travel without changing train. Similar services were set up across the Great Lakes in North America, and between the Italian mainland and Sicily.

By 1913, it handled more than 30,000 ships a year. The ports of the Mediterranean had no need for enclosed docks as they had no tides, but the main ones had to expand and there were few large natural harbours. Marseilles expanded to the northwest of the old port, partly by developing the Etang de Berre and constructing a mole (a massive breakwater), eventually 6.4km (4 miles) long, protecting a series of open basins.

American ports tended to favour wharves at right angles to the bank, although at Baltimore, for example, they were angled at 45 degrees to

STEAM FERRY IN SYDNEY HARBOUR
The fastest way to travel between north and south Sydney in the 1870s was by steam ferry – Sydney Harbour Bridge was not completed until 1932. On a typical working day, more than 60 ferries would criss-cross the harbour.

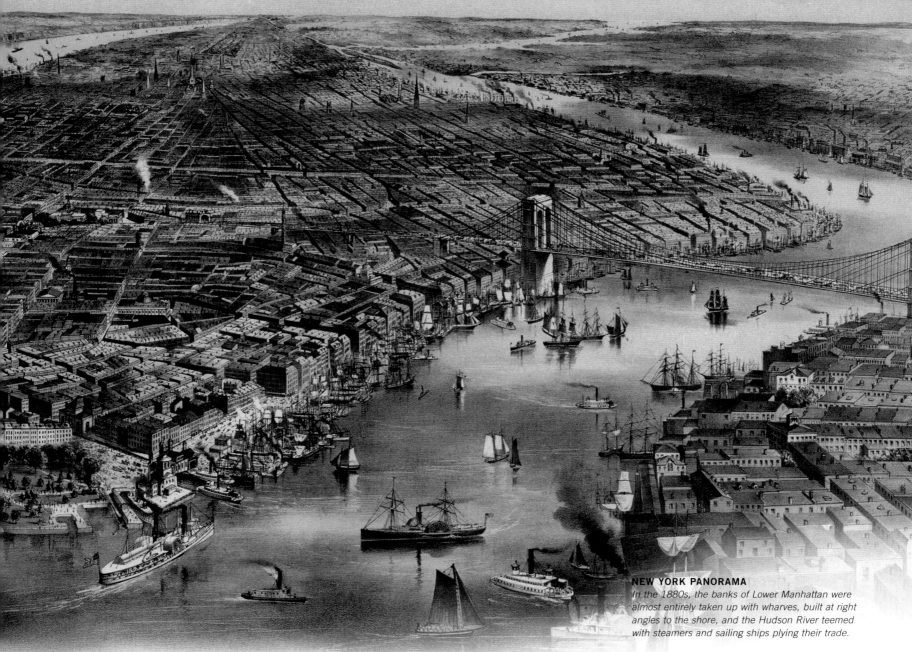

NEW YORK PANORAMA
In the 1880s, the banks of Lower Manhattan were almost entirely taken up with wharves, built at right angles to the shore, and the Hudson River teemed with steamers and sailing ships plying their trade.

allow better access. The original city of Boston was on a round peninsula, lined with small wharves inside a great natural harbour. There was some rationalization of these during the 19th century, but large ships went to newer wharves at east Boston across the harbour. In any case, most of the transatlantic trade went to New York by the end of the century, where the southern end of Manhattan was dominated by the projecting piers that could cater for even the largest passenger liners (see above).

BUILDING THE COLOMBO BREAKWATER
A steam crane deposits 10 tons of concrete on top of the sea berm at Colombo, Ceylon (now Sri Lanka), in 1884 to create a harbour that would attract steamer trade to the island.

Naval ports also had to expand dramatically to cope with steam and iron ships. There were few new naval dockyards in the homelands of the established naval powers, but some of the older ones, such as Deptford on the River Thames, were closed. Others, such as Portsmouth and

Chatham in England, and Toulon and Brest in France, expanded to three or four times their original size to deal with the new ships. The new German Navy built a huge and well-planned yard at Wilhelmshaven on the North Sea, and the Kiel Canal, which linked the North Sea and the Baltic and was completed in 1895, was largely designed for naval use. Another approach was to build breakwaters to enclose large areas of water, as the French did to create a great anchorage at Cherbourg in the English Channel in 1853, followed by a new naval base in 1858.

The large breakwater harbour was also envisaged as a port of refuge near the main shipping routes, where ships could take refuge from storms, and British humanitarians planned

CHARTING THE WORLD

In the 18th century, Scottish surveyor Murdoch Mackenzie pioneered a maritime cartography technique, using the triangulations of land surveyors to establish the base for his work over the sea. This greatly improved the accuracy of marine charts. At that time, most surveys were sponsored by private chart publishers and it was not until 1818 that the British Admiralty's Hydrographic Office began its own surveys under Captain Thomas Hurd. Small vessels, including Fitzroy's *Beagle* (see p.166), were sent to the far corners of the globe to make scientific observations and conduct surveys. Francis Beaufort was appointed Hydrographer of the Navy in 1829, and in 26 years he was responsible for the production of more than 1,446 new charts from around the world.

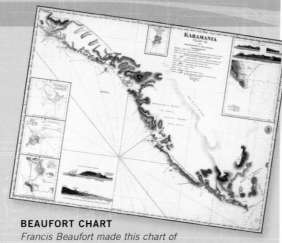

BEAUFORT CHART
Francis Beaufort made this chart of the southern coast of Turkey, from Cape Karaboornoo to Cape Anamour in Karamania, in 1819, when he was a captain in the Royal Navy.

BARGES UNDER CONSTRUCTION
In 1865, these London shipyard workers built barges for P&O's overland service through Egypt. By 1869, the Suez Canal would render the barges unnecessary.

several of these in the course of the 19th century. However, they were not very successful at raising funds, and it was the Royal Navy that financed the large harbours at Dover, Portland, and Alderney because of their strategic value.

The new shipyards

The new ships of iron and steel, powered by steam engines and of ever-greater size, demanded new building facilities. The world's small shipyards continued as they had always done, building wooden coasters, fishing boats, and river craft, but a new breed of large, well-equipped yards began to develop. By the 1890s, Britain became dominant in the shipbuilding market as no nation had been before or would be since. In 1892, more than 80 per cent of world shipbuilding took place in Britain, although this percentage declined over the next 20 years. The American industry was still rooted in wooden sailing ships by 1890, but after the mid-1890s it began to increase its tonnage rapidly. The German shipbuilding industry began to grow at around the same time, producing 465,000 tons per year by 1913.

Within Britain, traditional shipbuilding sites such as the Thames declined, while the northern English rivers (the Tyne, Tees, and Mersey), Belfast in Northern Ireland, and the Clyde in Scotland became world centres for the iron and steel shipbuilding industries. The Clyde boasted some of the most famous yards, such as Fairfield of Glasgow, John Brown of Clydebank, and Denny of Dumbarton. Belfast, dominated by Harland & Wolff's yard, produced many of the largest ships, including the *Titanic* (see p.280).

UNION LINER *SCOT* IN DENNY SHIPYARD
Established in 1847, the firm of William Denny & Bros in Dumbarton, Scotland, became the leading builders of cross-Channel steamers. The Union Line's Scot, seen here approaching completion in 1890, was built for speed and on her maiden voyage reached Cape Town in just 15 days.

HEAVY METAL
Workers in the Clydebank yard of John Brown & Co feed sheets of steel for a ship's hull into a bending machine in 1901. By the end of the 19th century, Scottish shipyards were world leaders in iron-and-steel shipbuilding.

Many different kinds of shipbuilding company were set up over the years, but a characteristic of this period was the involvement of "vertically integrated" steel and armaments firms, such as Krupp in Germany, Armstrong and Vickers in England, and Beardmore in Scotland, which encompassed all the processes from steel production to fitting out. Building iron ships required more capital equipment than building wooden ones, and the cost of that equipment tended to increase as technology improved. Steam and hydraulic riveting machines were in use by the 1890s, and by the end of the century German yards were beginning to adopt what would eventually become the symbol of the industry – the tower crane, used to lift large sections of hull and engine parts.

Germany's shipyards expanded rapidly in the 1890s to cope with the demands of the new navy and the expanded merchant fleet. Krupp's Germania Yard at Kiel employed 1,409 people in 1890 and 2,564 in 1899. The yards created new communities around them, as the owners built houses for the workers (carefully graded for managers, draughtsmen, and skilled and unskilled workers) and often parks and other recreation facilities. In Scotland, the town of Clydebank took its name from the shipyard, and it had a population of 43,000 by 1913.

Charts and surveys

Not only did the rapid growth of trade in the 19th century accelerate the development of ports and the shipbuilding industry, it also led to huge advances in maritime surveying. Accurate marine charts were vital if steamships were to improve their journey times and operate new routes (see panel, left). The Dutch had been the leading maritime cartographers in the 17th century, followed by the French and Scottish in the 18th century. During the 19th century, the governments of major seafaring nations began to sponsor increasingly ambitious surveys.

The electric telegraph

If Brunel's greatest ship was unsuccessful in its intended purpose as a cargo-passenger liner, it soon found a new use that was just as important in the development of shipping in the 19th century: the laying of submarine telegraph cable (see panel, below). Telegraph cables had already been laid between Britain and France in 1851 and across the Mediterranean Sea in 1855, and this was not the first attempt at laying a transatlantic cable. One had been laid by the American *Niagara* and the British *Agamemnon* in 1856, but it stopped working after only 20 days. When the *Great Eastern* left the coast of Ireland in July 1865, she had three holds filled with tightly coiled electric cable and was fitted with special machinery that would lower the cable into the water at a controlled rate.

The *Great Eastern* got two-thirds of the way across the Atlantic when the cable broke and sank. All attempts to recover it failed. In the following year, she tried again and this time reached Newfoundland, where the cable could link up with landlines in the USA and Canada. By 1870, the whole of the world as known to Europeans was linked by cable, which could send messages through Morse code.

The submarine cable was as revolutionary as anything else in the 19th century. For the first time ever, ideas and information could travel instantaneously around the world. Now, information could spread seemingly at the speed of light, rather than the speed of a sailing ship, and shipowners could contact their agents in different countries and arrange cargoes, spawning

STANDING BY FOR ORDERS
This turn-of-the-century engine-room telegraph received orders to speed up, slow down, or stop the engine from the bridge of a steamship, which had a similar telegraph. The orders were transmitted by a wire-and-chain mechanism that linked the two telegraphs.

THE TRANSATLANTIC SUBMARINE CABLE

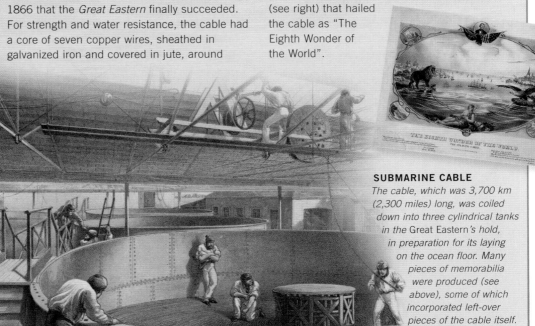

The transatlantic submarine cable was the brainchild of Massachusetts merchant and financier Cyrus W. Field. He first proposed the laying of a telegraph cable along the bottom of the North Atlantic Ocean between Ireland and Newfoundland in 1854, but it was not until July 1866 that the *Great Eastern* finally succeeded. For strength and water resistance, the cable had a core of seven copper wires, sheathed in galvanized iron and covered in jute, around which were wound 10 iron wires, each covered in Manila hemp and gutta-percha. After the first transmission, congratulatory messages were exchanged between the US government and Queen Victoria, and Field was awarded many honours, including a commemorative print (see right) that hailed the cable as "The Eighth Wonder of the World".

SUBMARINE CABLE
The cable, which was 3,700 km (2,300 miles) long, was coiled down into three cylindrical tanks in the Great Eastern's hold, in preparation for its laying on the ocean floor. Many pieces of memorabilia were produced (see above), some of which incorporated left-over pieces of the cable itself.

THE SUEZ CANAL

The idea of a canal through the Isthmus of
Suez, linking the Mediterranean Sea with the
Red Sea and beyond that the Indian Ocean, was
supported by the French under Napoleon in
1800, but was then dropped. The French
diplomat and engineer Ferdinand de Lesseps
took up the idea when vice-consul in Cairo in
the 1820s and 1830s and used his connections
in France and Egypt to advance his plans. In
1859, he formed the Suez Canal Company and
construction began under his supervision.
Because there was only 120cm (4ft) difference
in sea level between the Mediterranean and the

Red Sea, no locks were needed, but the canal,
which is 160km (100 miles) long, still took 10
years to build. The first stage involved the
linking of a chain of five lakes across the
isthmus to form one body of water, Great Bitter
Lake. The second stage of cutting out the canal
made use of the latest steam-powered excavators
and dredgers, but the work was still arduous for
the Egyptian labour force. The canal was
officially opened on 17 November 1869 by the
Khedive (Viceroy) of Egypt, Ismail Pasha, greatly
reducing the travel time between Europe and
south and east Asia.

OPENING CEREMONY
*The official opening of the Suez
Canal was a lavish ceremony
attended by heads of state from
France, Britain, and Russia.*

a new kind of international market and the
tramp steamer (see p.204), which made its living
by picking up cargoes from around the world.

Specialized cargo ships
Oil became important as a fuel in the 1860s as
the Americans exploited their supplies from
fields in Ohio, Pennsylvania, and West Virginia,
480km (300 miles) from the Atlantic across the
Allegheny Mountains. In the following decade, a
Russian field was developed at Baku. Initially, oil

was carried in barrels or canisters as part of a
general cargo, but the Swedish chemist and
inventor Alfred Nobel developed specialized
ships to transport oil across the Caspian Sea to
the Volga, where it joined the railway system.
His third ship, the *Armeniak* of 1883, was a true
oil tanker, with the hull forming the container
for the cargo. Sea transport of American oil
took off in the late 1870s after a pipeline was
opened to take it from the Alleghenies to the
coast. At first, shippers were cautious about the
possibility of explosion and transported the oil
in sailing ships rather than steamships.

It was a German agent of America's
Standard Oil, Heinrich Riedemann, who
ordered the first modern oil tanker from
Armstrong, Mitchell & Co in England in 1886.
The *Gluckhauf* was an adaptation of
the Caspian Sea design to the much
rougher waters of the North

LANDING GOODS IN CALCUTTA
*In the 1860s, Britain imported goods such
as raw cotton, tea, rice, and jute from
Calcutta, northeast India. In turn, Calcutta
imported finished cotton and linen goods
and various industrial products.*

Atlantic, with greater internal subdivision to
prevent the cargo moving too much. She could
carry 2,975 tons of oil, and her triple-expansion
engine was placed at the stern, where it could be
sealed off from the cargo.

Refrigeration was yet another 19th-century
invention that changed the world. Live animals
are the most difficult cargoes of all to transport
by sea, for they need constant feeding and
watering. Before the advent of refrigeration,
the only way to preserve meat was by using salt.
When the first cargoes of refrigerated American
beef sailed in 1874, they were packed in ice and
salt, but this had its limitations. In 1876–77,
the French refrigeration engineer Charles Tellie
equipped the aptly named *Frigorifique* with three
refrigerators and took a cargo of frozen meat
from Buenos Aires to Rouen, although not all
of it arrived in good condition. After 1879, the
technology improved as cold-air refrigeration
replaced methyl ether, and in 1880 the *Strathleven*
exported 34 tons of prime frozen beef and
mutton from Australia to London. After that,
refrigerated cargoes became common, and the
first custom-built refrigerated ship,
the *Elderslie*, was launched in 1884.

LOADING TEA IN COLOMBO
*Chests of Ceylon Pekoe tea are brought to a
wharf in Colombo Harbour, Ceylon (now
Sri Lanka), in the 1880s, in preparation
for loading onboard cargo ships
bound for northern Europe.*

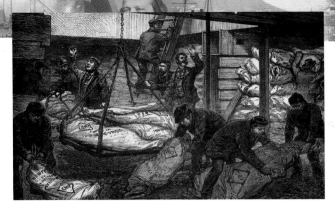

FROZEN FOOD
Dockers unload frozen meat from Australia from the refrigerated hold of the Catania *in Southwest India Dock, Millwall, England, in the 1880s.*

Coaling stations

Worldwide steam shipping required a network of bases where suitable coal could be procured. British shipowners preferred Welsh coal, which burned well in furnaces, but they often had to compromise. By the end of the 19th century, German and American coal was being exported for steamships, and local supplies, from South Africa, for example, were often cheaper to buy.

Shipowners or charterers planned their voyages to take the economics of coal into account. A ship going from northern Europe to Australia, for example, would have enough coal to take it to the Suez Canal (see panel, left). The canal dramatically reduced the length – and hence the cost – of journeys to and from Europe, and Welsh coal was available there, albeit expensive. The ship could then head for Colombo in Ceylon (now Sri Lanka), where British, Indian, and South African coal was available. In Australia, local coal could be bought for the onward or return journey.

COALING STATION
Labourers carry baskets of coal onboard a cargo liner at Port Said, Egypt, at the end of the 19th century. Ships refuelled here before passing through the Suez Canal.

THE PLIMSOLL LINE

In 1876, after a long campaign by the English MP Samuel Plimsoll, Britain passed the Merchant Shipping Act, which subjected merchant shipping to much greater safety regulation. Under the act, it became compulsory for all British merchant ships to have a Plimsoll Line painted on its sides. This indicates six draught levels to which a ship may be loaded with cargo depending on its location and the season, as these variables determine the density of the water.

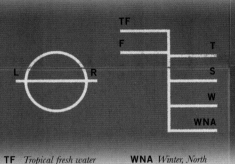

TF	*Tropical fresh water*	**WNA**	*Winter, North Atlantic, for vessels under 100m (330ft)*
F	*Fresh water*		
T	*Tropical sea water*		
S	*Summer, sea water*	**L R**	*Letters indicating registration society (here, Lloyd's Register)*
W	*Winter, sea water*		

Safety at sea

Sea travel has always been recognized as dangerous, but this was taken for granted until the late 18th century, when a combination of the ideas of the Enlightenment philosophers (who emphasized reason and individualism) and the Protestant conscience (according to which protest at poor social conditions was acceptable) led philanthropists to look at ways of saving life, especially from shipwrecks close to shore. The British Humane Society for the Recovery of Persons Apparently Drowned was founded in 1774, followed in 1784 by the Humane Society of the Commonwealth of Massachusetts in Boston, USA. The idea of rescuing survivors from shipwrecks soon followed. The Dutch Frisian Islands had plans for rescue craft by 1769, but it is not clear if they were ever used.

LIFEBOAT DRILL, 1910
If a lifeboat is stationed on a flat beach, it may be far from the sea at low tide. To launch the boat, the crew (here, in the Isles of Scilly) had to haul it to the water on a trailer. Some boats used horses instead.

A CORKING IDEA
In 1789, Henry Greathead designed a boat for the seafarers of South Shields, England, that was "capable of containing 24 persons and calculated to go through heavy broken seas". He was paid two guineas (three dollars) for the design.

The first purpose-built lifeboat, designed by Henry Greathead, operated from South Shields in northeast England from 1789, although his countrymen Lionel Lukin and William Wouldhave also claimed the invention. Greathead's boat was open, with a high bow and stern to ride the waves, and its buoyancy was enhanced by belts of cork around its sides. In the 1830s and 1840s, the Boston inventor Joseph Francis developed numerous innovative lifeboats, including the first iron version, in 1845.

Although there had been locally operated lifeboats in various countries, the first national lifeboat service was founded in Britain in March 1824 as the National

NATIONAL HEROINE
When the Forfarshire ran aground off the northeast coast of England on 7 September 1838, Longstone lighthouse-keeper William Darling and his daughter Grace risked their lives to rescue survivors.

external cork belting

curved keel   *decorated oar*

CORK LIFEJACKET
Invented in 1854 by Captain Ward, an inspector for Britain's RNLI, cork vests gave lifeboat crews buoyancy if they fell overboard. The vests also provided some protection from the weather and spray.

Institution for the Preservation of Life from Shipwreck. The Netherlands followed in November 1824. After a slow start, Britain's lifeboat service developed more rapidly from 1851, and was renamed the Royal National Lifeboat Institution (RNLI). Based on charitable contributions, it provided lifeboats with volunteer crews all round the coast. The US Treasury funded a series of lifesaving stations from 1848, and they carried out many notable rescues, including that of 204 emigrants from the wreck of the *Henry* in 1851.

Lifeboats were propelled by sail and oar until late in the 19th century, when steam engines and motors were fitted to a few. In 1886, the RNLI adopted the self-righting boat designed by George Watson, which would automatically return to the upright position from a capsize

FIRST STEAM LIFEBOAT
The Duke of Northumberland *steams across Harwich Harbour, eastern England, on its inaugural voyage in 1890. The lifeboat was propelled by a revolutionary water-jet system in which water was forced out under great pressure through side vents.*

because it had air trapped in its bow and stern. The first Norwegian lifeboat, the *Colin Archer* of 1893, was designed to cruise offshore for extended periods and assist deep-sea trawlers, rather than be launched to deal with an individual wreck.

However, it is much better to prevent a ship from being wrecked in the first place if possible. One method is to make ships more seaworthy (see panel, p.191). Another solution is the use of lighthouses, which have existed since the famous Pharos at Alexandria was built around 280 BC. Lighthouses could serve two main functions: to guide mariners through a safe channel; and to warn them of dangers, especially isolated ones.

The Eddystone Rocks, 22km (14 miles) off the southwest coast of England, caused many casualties, and three attempts were made to build a lighthouse there before John Smeaton came up with his now classic design in 1759. The lighthouse was made of interlocking granite blocks and had a wide base tapering to a narrow tower. An even more hazardous site was Bell Rock off the east coast of Scotland, which was covered by the tide for most of the time. In 1807, Robert Stevenson, of the famous Scottish family of lighthouse builders, began work on the rock, and the granite tower was completed after great difficulties four years later.

The 19th century saw the building of lighthouses on rocks and coasts all round Europe and North America. Like Bell Rock, Minots Ledge on the US Atlantic seaboard was only exposed at low tide, and between 1832 and 1841 alone it wrecked 40 vessels. In 1847, Captain William Swift of the US Army Topographical Corps began the construction of an octagonal beacon with an iron skeleton frame. It was completed in 1850 but was destroyed by a storm the next year. In 1855, the US Chief Engineer General Joseph Totten began a replacement, a granite tower 31m (102ft) high. The first offshore masonry lighthouse in the USA, it was completed in 1860 and is still in service today (see right).

THE "I LOVE YOU" LIGHTHOUSE
The beacon in the waveswept Minots Ledge Lighthouse, off Cohassset, Massachusetts, USA, flashes in a 1–4–3 identification sequence, earning it the affectionate nickname of the "I Love You" Lighthouse.

LIGHTHOUSE BEACONS

In 1822, the French physicist Augustin Fresnel (1788–1827) published his ideas on glass prismatic lenses and produced a design that concentrated a beam of light in a particular direction. The beam was five times more powerful than the system of silvered reflectors previously used in lighthouses, and if the light was 30m (100ft) above sea level it could be seen up to 32km (20 miles) away. Fresnel lenses, which resembled a giant glass beehive, were soon fitted in all French lighthouses, and the engineer Alan Stevenson installed them in some Scottish lighthouses after meeting with Fresnel, but the US Lighthouse Board did not adopt the design until the 1850s.

Lighthouses originally used wood or coal fires to produce light. In the 18th century, John Smeaton used an arrangement of 24 candles in a chandelier at Eddystone. Oil lamps became common for a time – Bell Rock used spermaceti oil before switching to paraffin in 1877. Electricity was first employed in the South Foreland Light in the Straits of Dover in 1859, at the instigation of Michael Faraday, the great physicist. The first French lighthouse to have an electric beacon was Cap Heve, with a very powerful light for the time of 60,000 candle-power. Each beacon was now given a unique flash sequence, which was marked on charts, so that the lighthouse could be identified at night.

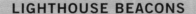

FRESNEL LENS
Grays Harbor Lighthouse in Westport, Washington, USA, had a third order – that is, third most powerful – Fresnel lens installed in 1895. The white beam could be seen 40km (25 miles) away.

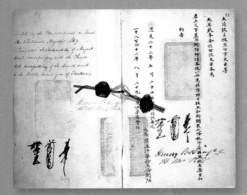

TREATY OF NANKING, 1842

> 66 The Chinese do not know that the foreigners have made their beds on the waves and that their colonies are very near ... they do not realize that armoured ships are like mountains ... 99
>
> **TOIN**, Japanese intellectual, **1800s**

KEY EVENTS

1830 FRANCE TAKES ALGIERS A French naval force captures the port of Algiers, ending Ottoman rule in the region and leading to greater European involvement in North Africa.

1842 HONG KONG CEDED TO BRITAIN The Treaty of Nanking is signed by Britain and China onboard HMS *Cornwallis*. Britain gains Hong Kong and five Chinese ports open up to trade.

1854 JAPAN OPENS PORTS Following Commodore Perry's visits, Japan opens the ports of Shimoda and Hakodate to US trade.

1858 TREATIES OF TIENTSIN SIGNED The Second Opium War ends with China opening 11 ports to Britain, France, Russia, and the USA.

1881 FRANCE CLAIMS VIETNAM France uses gunboats to win sovereignty over Vietnam, thereby extending its control of Indochina.

1882 BRITAIN OCCUPIES EGYPT A revolt in Egypt leads to Britain occupying the country to protect its interests in the Suez Canal.

NEW IMPERIALISM

IN THE 19TH CENTURY, THE EUROPEAN POWERS AND THE USA USED THEIR NAVIES TO EXTEND THEIR EMPIRES AND AREAS OF INFLUENCE.

In August 1816, an Anglo-Dutch fleet, headed by Lord Exmouth in the 100-gun *Queen Charlotte*, arrived off the North African port of Algiers. An emissary demanded the release of Christian slaves, the repayment of ransom money, and the release of the British Consul, who had been detained. Failing to get a reply, the fleet bombarded the port for several hours, and the next day the terms were agreed. More than 1,000 slaves were released. There was nothing new in the technology, but Europe began the new age by asserting itself against what the English novelist Rudyard Kipling would ignominiously later call the "lesser breeds".

The European powers of the 19th century believed firmly in their right and duty to dominate less developed areas of the world for their own use, mostly in competition with one another, but occasionally in co-operation. In the previous century, Europeans – like the Arabs, Indians, Chinese, and Japanese – had used horses, sailing ships, and unrifled muskets. By the second half of the 19th century, Europeans and North Americans used steam power on land and sea, armour-plated ships, rifled guns, explosive shells, and the electric telegraph. Steam power allowed the Americans and Europeans to operate on the great rivers of the world, including the Mississippi, Nile, Irrawaddy, Yangtse, and Congo. The technological and military gap between

RESCUED FROM SLAVERY
This watercolour depicts Africans rescued from the slave ship Albanoz, *under joint Portuguese and Brazilian ownership, by a British anti-slavery patrol in 1845.*

the East and the West was far more obvious than in the past, and it led Europeans to believe in their moral superiority as well.

The decline of slavery

Despite the best efforts of abolitionists (see p.151), the trade in black slaves continued in west Africa. After the end of the Napoleonic Wars, several countries established anti-slavery forces, including Denmark and Holland. Britain sent a task force of 24 sailing ships to patrol the west African coast. Success was patchy, but more than 5,000 people were freed from 23 ships in

COMMODORE PERRY STEAMS INTO JAPAN
In 1853, the sudden arrival in Edo (now Tokyo) Bay of two steam-powered frigates, as part of a flotilla under the command of Commodore Matthew Perry of the US Navy, caused much wonderment among the Japanese.

1829 and sent to Sierra Leone, a colony for liberated slaves. International co-operation, however, was always a problem.

The French government had abolished the slave trade in theory, but did nothing to enforce the ban. The abolitionist movement was much smaller in France than in Britain, and French colonies, starved of slaves by British blockade during the Napoleonic Wars, were hungry for more. The ban was evaded at many levels, and the French slave trade soared in the early 1820s, with 79 ships taking part in 1822. After that, French law was gradually strengthened, and public opinion began to move against it. In the 1830s, the main European governments agreed on a mutual right of search so that it was no longer possible for slave ships to hide under false colours of those countries. But this arrangement did not include the USA. For different reasons, it had already fought to protect its merchant ships from search in 1812–15, and the pro-slavery faction was strong in the Federal Government.

By the 1860s, after slavery had been abolished in much of the world and had led to the Civil War in the USA (see p.216), the attentions of abolitionists turned to east Africa, where Arab slave traders used dhows to service the markets in the north. Zanzibar was the centre of a great trade from the interior of Africa, and from 1841 successive British consuls had used their influence to suppress it. Naval patrols found half-starved slaves crammed into dhows in conditions that were harsh even by the standards of the west African trade.

The anti-slave trade patrols gave European junior naval officers a chance to take part in exciting chases and show a good deal of independence. In the early years, however, they did not use the latest steam technology. Far from established naval bases, there were no facilities for coaling, and sailing ships designed for speed were still faster than steamships. The slave ships' speed caused navies to design faster ships for their own fleets. By the 1850s, faster screw steamships were proving effective against the sailing slavers off west Africa. In the east, the steam and sailing gunboats were the main ships for chasing the dhows.

The Opium Wars

In a campaign which reflects no credit on the British Empire and undermines its idea of a "civilizing mission", the British, and later the French, forced the Chinese government to open its ports to imports of opium. The British East India Company grew opium in India and initially used the crop to pay for its exports of tea from China, although the opium soon showed a handsome profit on its own. The ships used in the 1820s, the opium clippers, were designed for speed and some were ex-slavers. Opium was not illegal in Britain at the time, but the Chinese government consistently attempted to ban it.

The changes in equipment used by European forces over the series of conflicts with China provide a barometer of technological development. In 1834, the British wooden sailing frigates *Andromache* and *Imogene* forced the entrance to the Pearl River past several ancient forts but found themselves trapped, and their commander, Lord Napier, was forced to order a retreat. In 1839, in an attempt to deal with the problem of opium addiction,

OPIUM SMOKERS
From the mid-1700s, the British East India Company cultivated a booming market for imported opium in China, exchanging it for tea, silver, and other goods.

SPOILS OF WAR
This Chinese sword was typical of the treasures looted by the British during the Opium Wars. Porcelain, old bronzes, and statues were also stolen, and an Anglo-French force ransacked the Chinese Emperor's Palace in 1860.

Lin Zexu, the Imperial Commissioner in Canton (now Guangzhou), seized and destroyed 20,000 chests of the drug, triggering the First Opium War. This time the Royal Navy used the latest technology, including steam power and iron ships. At the centre of the fleet was the iron steamship *Nemesis*, built in Britain for the East India Company. Her thin iron plate would not have been effective against European shot, but the Chinese army had not faced a major foreign war for centuries and its weapons were more like fireworks. The *Nemesis* was immune to another of the Chinese defences, fire rafts floated down the river. More conventional wooden sailing ships, led by two 74-gun ships, bombarded the Chinese forts, but even they were towed into position by steamships. The Chinese were forced into many concessions by the Treaty of Nanking in 1842, including giving

Britain sovereignty of Hong Kong island (see panel, right) and opening five ports to trade, but the opium trade was not mentioned.

British policy was often inconsistent in the First Opium War, because of the slowness of communications: it took months for news of changes in policy to reach the theatre of war. This was much less of a problem during the Second Opium War, for the electric telegraph now ran to Alexandria and to Basra in Iraq, and from Bombay to Rangoon in Burma, so a message could be carried in several quick stages to Canton. The dispute began on 8 October 1856, when the crew of the *Arrow*, a Chinese local craft technically under British command, was arrested by Chinese officials on suspicion of piracy. An Anglo-French expedition was mounted in 1857, and under the treaties of Tientsin in 1858 the Chinese were forced to open 11 more ports to trade. The treaties were not fully observed, and in June 1859 the Anglo-French force suffered a reverse when three

THE BRITISH IN HONG KONG

In 1842, as part of the settlement of the First Opium War, the British were granted the island of Hong Kong, near the entrance to the Pearl River and Canton. It had an agricultural population of about 5,000, which grew to 125,000 in 1865 and 300,000 in 1900, partly due to an influx of refugees from the Boxer Rebellion in China. In 1898, the British feared that the increasing range of artillery made them vulnerable, and negotiated the lease of the New Territories for 99 years, to expand the area

TREATIES OF TIENTSIN
Emperor Xianfeng finally agreed to sign the treaties of Tientsin (right) on 26–29 June 1858, thus ending the opening stage of the Second Opium War.

by 920 square km (355 square miles). Britain dominated China's foreign trade in the 19th century, although it had expected to achieve even greater profits. Hong Kong was also a major naval base for Britain throughout its tenure.

HONG KONG HARBOUR
The extensive natural harbour at Hong Kong was perfect for large merchant ships, such as these British vessels pictured at anchor in about 1870.

NEMESIS DESTROYS WAR JUNKS
The steam-powered warship Nemesis (on right) was a devastating weapon against the Chinese in the First Opium War, as shown by this battle in Anson's Bay on 7 January 1841.

gunboats were sunk attempting to force the Pei-Ho River at Taku. Another assault was mounted in August by four French and four British gunboats, while an army attacked Taku from behind. They then advanced to Nanking and Peking (now Beijing), where they raised the Emperor's Summer Palace to the ground and forced China to observe the treaties.

The rise of Japan

As a result of two expeditions in the mid-1850s, the USA secured access to Japanese ports (see panel, p.198). This had a profound effect on the previously closed society of Japan, although there would be more than a decade of civil war, rebellion, coup, and foreign intervention before the full impact would be felt. The future Admiral Togo (see p.273) was present in 1863 (wearing medieval armour and carrying two broadswords and a matchlock musket) when Admiral Kuper of the Royal Navy bombarded Kagoshima in retaliation for the death of a British visitor. The Imperial

THE OPENING OF JAPAN

8 July 1853 was a decisive day in the history of Japan. On that day, a fleet of four "black ships" steamed into Edo (now Tokyo) Bay. They were the American paddle frigates *Susquehanna* and *Mississippi*, towing the sailing ships *Saratoga* and *Plymouth*. The squadron was under the command of Commodore Matthew C. Perry of the US Navy. His mission was to force Japan to accept contact with the modern world. Japan had been a closed society since 1638, but the Americans were exasperated that sailors from their whaling fleets who were shipwrecked in Japanese waters were badly treated, and they also wanted coaling stations en route to China. The Japanese had heard about the power of the West's ships, and how a tiny British force had defeated the Chinese in the First Opium War. Japanese spectators mistook the steamships for burning vessels, and were shocked by the size and number of guns onboard. They mobilized their troops, anticipating war; many fled their homes. Perry made an elaborate show of his naval power but claimed he had come as a peacemaker. He presented his demands, suggesting that rejection would lead to war. The Japanese agreed to think about them by the time Perry returned in the spring.

PERRY'S BLACK SHIP
The discovery that the steam frigates could progress at a speed of 9 knots without any help from the wind was a source of amazement to the Japanese.

Perry came back in February 1854, with three sailing ships towed by three steamers. The Imperial Emissary Hayashi negotiated skilfully on behalf of the Shogun Yoshinobu (the effective head of state, who ruled on behalf of the Emperor). It was agreed to open the ports of Shimoda and Hakodate to the Americans, where they would be able to buy coal and supplies, though the Japanese did not believe that they

COMMODORE PERRY
Matthew Perry (1794–1858) had a distinguished career in the US Navy that lasted nearly 50 years. He served in the War of 1812 (see p.132), and pioneered the Navy's use of steam power.

had agreed to allow trading. Shipwrecked sailors were to be helped, and an American Consul was appointed. Hayashi thought he had done well in avoiding the humiliations that China had endured, but Japanese society and technology would begin to change profoundly.

Japanese Navy was formed in 1869, initially from local craft and obsolete or surplus ships bought from other navies, but in the 1880s it began to order modern battleships and cruisers from the West, especially Britain. Promising young officers were sent to Britain for training, and many of the ideas and practices of the most successful naval power of the age were adapted to Japanese conditions. By the end of the 19th century, the Japanese, unique among nations, had transformed themselves from passive victims of European imperialism to practitioners of their own version of it. In 1894, they used their new fleet of warships to defeat the Chinese at Yalu River (see p.223) and take control of the Yellow Sea.

The British in Egypt

Imperialism saw a resurgence in the 1870s as the new German Empire arrived on the scene, hungry for "a place in the sun", even if all the most desirable colonies had already been taken over. The Turkish Empire, the "sick man of Europe", continued to decay and its decline was accelerated by the Russo-Turkish War (1877–78). In 1878 the European powers met at the Congress of Berlin to negotiate the region's future. As part of the territorial transfers, the British Prime Minister Benjamin Disraeli induced Turkey to give Cyprus to Britain for use as a naval base in the eastern Mediterranean, but the island had no good harbours, and soon a better alternative came along.

Disraeli was succeeded as British Prime Minister by his arch-rival William Gladstone. Although he was an anti-imperialist, Gladstone reluctantly ordered an attack on Alexandria, in Egypt, after anti-European rioting there and an attempt to fortify the city, in order to protect British access to the Suez Canal. The French refused to take part, but Alexandria was bombarded by eight British ironclad warships in a demonstration of raw naval power. The Egyptian army abandoned Alexandria, and the British launched a full-scale invasion to take control of the country. They moved down the Nile towards Khartoum, but had one of their greatest setbacks when General Gordon was defeated and killed by the forces of the Mahdi in 1885. The British returned to the

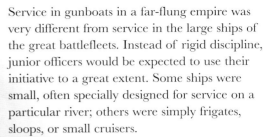

BOMBARDMENT OF ALEXANDRIA

The Condor *was one of eight British ironclad warships that shelled Alexandria on 11 July 1882, in response to a Nationalist uprising in Egypt. The resulting devastation led to the Egyptian army abandoning the port to the British.*

POMP AND CIRCUMSTANCE

This tribute to imperial might is the cover of a music manuscript, a divertimento composed to celebrate Britain's naval and military victories in Egypt in 1882.

area in force under General Kitchener in 1898. Winston Churchill, then a junior army officer, stated the importance of water communication in his book *The River War* (1899): "We were transported by train to Assiout [Asyût]; thence by stern-wheeled steamers to Assouan [Aswan]. We led our horses round the cataract at Philae; re-embarked on other steamers at Shellai; and from there proceeded 400 miles across the desert by the marvellous military railway." Communication was assured by "flat-bottomed gunboats and stern-wheelsteamers, drawing endless tows of sailing boats carrying our supplies".

Troopships and empire

To a large extent, the European empires relied on recruiting native troops to control their colonies. The British had their Sepoys in India, the French had Spahis and Zouaves in North Africa, but they also needed a corps of regular European soldiers and officers to command the native troops. Several shipping lines made their living by moving troops to station in peacetime, including Bibby of Liverpool and the British India Steam Navigation Company, while in war other ships were relieved of their regular passenger or

cargo duties and drafted into service. During the war between Britain and the Boer republics of South Africa (1899–1902), for example, demand for ships was high, and troop-carriers were chartered from companies such as the Union and Castle lines.

Gunboat navies

As well as defending their countries against invasion and protecting the trade routes, the western European, and later the US, navies operated extensively in their countries' empires and spheres of influence. The idea of the gunboat developed during the Crimean War (see p.215) and the Second Opium War.

Service in gunboats in a far-flung empire was very different from service in the large ships of the great battlefleets. Instead of rigid discipline, junior officers would be expected to use their initiative to a great extent. Some ships were small, often specially designed for service on a particular river; others were simply frigates, sloops, or small cruisers.

When France sought to extend its empire in Indochina and declared its sovereignty over Vietnam in 1881, it sent troops down the Red River. In battles with the Vietnamese and the Chinese, who had a proprietorial interest in Vietnam, French gunboats were often involved – in the bombardment of Chilung (Taiwan) and Fuzhou, China, in 1884, for example.

By the end of the 19th century, much of the globe was under the control of the European powers and their descendants, the Americans. Countries such as China and Japan were not formally ruled by the West but had to adopt Western ways or be subjected. The Europeans had achieved this partly because they had largely avoided major quarrels among themselves for nearly a hundred years. The next century would be very different.

WAR IN VIETNAM

French soldiers overcame Vietnamese forces to take control of the city of Tonkin in 1881 (below), leading to a colonial war between France and Vietnam. In this painting (left), the French gunboats La Massue, Le Mousqueton, *and* La Hache *are shown encountering resistance while on patrol on the Red River in 1884.*

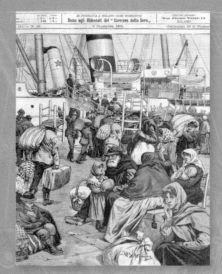

> " Give me your tired,
> your poor,
> Your huddled masses
> yearning to breathe free,
> The wretched refuse of
> your teeming shore,
> Send these, the homeless,
> tempest-tossed, to me:
> I lift my lamp beside
> the golden door. "

EMMA LAZARUS, *The New Colossus*, poem
engraved on the Statue of Liberty, **1883**

KEY EVENTS

1840 CUNARD LINE FOUNDED The British
transatlantic steamship line begins a regular
service, carrying passengers and mail.

1845 IRISH POTATO FAMINE BEGINS The
potato crop in Ireland fails, causing 100,000
Irish to emigrate to the USA in 1846 alone.

1847 HAMBURG–AMERIKA FOUNDED
Germany's Hamburg–Amerika line is started.
By 1900, it had become the world's largest.

1848 AMERICAN PASSENGER ACT The USA
passes an act to regulate conditions endured by
immigrants travelling to the country in steerage.

1892 ELLIS ISLAND OPENS Ellis Island,
New York, takes over from Castle Garden as the
USA's immigrant processing centre.

1897 GERMANY TAKES THE BLUE RIBAND
Kaiser Wilhelm der Grosse breaks the record for
the fastest eastward crossing of the Atlantic.

THE GREAT SHIPPING LINES

THE 19TH CENTURY SAW MIGRATIONS TO THE NEW WORLD ON AN UNPRECEDENTED SCALE, FACILITATED BY THE RISE OF THE STEAM LINER.

Until the 19th century, each merchant ship
was usually owned outright by a number of
small investors, or larger ones who spread
their capital over several ships. The coming
of steam soon caused this to change. The
building and operation of steamships required
more capital, which was raised by joint-stock
companies (where capital provided by
investors, large or small, is pooled in a
common fund). During the mid-1800s, the
law became more favourable to joint-stock
companies in several countries. Another factor
driving the trend towards the new style of

shipping company was that steamships, being
less dependent on the weather, could run to a
schedule. It therefore made good commercial
sense for several ships to operate together, to
maintain a regular service on the route.

The original idea for the shipping line came
from the USA. Perhaps influenced by the "lines"
that ran regular stagecoach routes, the Black
Ball Line offered a fortnightly service between
New York and London in 1816, to be followed
by several other American companies,
exploiting the good sailing
qualities of American ships.

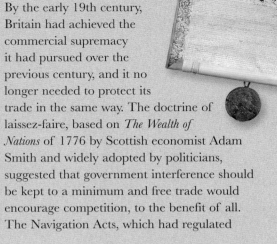

By the early 19th century, Britain had achieved the commercial supremacy it had pursued over the previous century, and it no longer needed to protect its trade in the same way. The doctrine of laissez-faire, based on *The Wealth of Nations* of 1776 by Scottish economist Adam Smith and widely adopted by politicians, suggested that government interference should be kept to a minimum and free trade would encourage competition, to the benefit of all. The Navigation Acts, which had regulated

ROYAL CHARTER
The Peninsular and Oriental Steam Navigation Company was incorporated by the British government in a Royal Charter on 31 December 1840.

British trade since the 1650s, were largely abolished in 1849, and the requirement to have British crews on British merchant ships ended in 1854. At almost the same time, the government felt it necessary to legislate to ensure that there were qualified officers on each ship, and to pass various regulations for safety at sea. The monopoly of the chartered companies

CUNARD'S *UMBRIA* ARRIVES IN NEW YORK
The Umbria carried passengers on the Liverpool–New York route from 1897 to 1905. Emigrants to the USA arriving in New York Harbour knew their new life was about to begin when they saw the Statue of Liberty.

was no longer acceptable, and the East India Company's monopoly was abolished in 1833. Shipping routes were fully opened to competition.

The British government opened the Post Office packet service, the world's largest mail service, to private enterprise (the term "packet" is derived from packets of mail). A mail contract demanded a regular service in good time. It guaranteed a certain amount of revenue on a shipping route, which could be supplemented by carrying passengers and freight, but

penalties for late delivery were severe. In 1839, Samuel Cunard (see panel, below), who had won the transatlantic contract, agreed to pay £500 for every 12 hours his ships were late. In 1837, Arthur Anderson set up steamship service between Falmouth and the ports of Spain and Portugal. His Peninsular and Oriental Steam Navigation Company (P&O) was founded in 1840 and soon extended its services to India, with passengers travelling overland across the Isthmus of Suez, which separated the Mediterranean Sea from the Red Sea and, beyond it, the Indian Ocean.

In a separate development, shipowners began to use special flags, their house flags, to identify their ships. This began at the Lloyds station near Liverpool in 1771, which would hoist a signal to alert an owner that his ship was about to arrive in port, and house flags became common during the Napoleonic Wars. They were virtually universal by the mid-19th century, and, in 1882, Lloyds

PENINSULAR AND ORIENTAL STEAM NAVIGATION COMPANY

HOUSE FLAGS
By the mid-19th century, almost every shipping line had a distinctive house flag.

BLUE FUNNEL LINE

WESTERN CANADA

PACIFIC STEAM NAVIGATION COMPANY

issued the first edition of its *Book of House Flags*. The design and colours of the house flag had even more relevance to steamship lines when they began to apply it to their funnels, and the funnel attained great symbolism by the end of the 19th century. Alfred Holt and Company, based in Liverpool, was commonly known as the Blue Funnel Line and had one of the strongest identities of any cargo shipping company. The distinctive red funnels with black

RECORD-BREAKING PADDLE STEAMER
In 1856, the Cunard Line commissioned its first iron paddle steamer, the Persia, seen here in a plan by David Kirkaldy, chief draughtsman at Robert Napier & Sons, Scotland. The switch to an iron hull increased speed: in its maiden year, the Persia crossed the Atlantic in nine days, a new record.

SAMUEL CUNARD

The son of a family of merchants in Halifax, Nova Scotia, Samuel Cunard (1787–1865) developed his shipping interests and held shares in a transatlantic steamship by 1831. Recognizing the potential of steamships, he went to Britain in 1838 to found a line. He raised capital in Liverpool and Glasgow and had ships built on the Clyde in Scotland by Robert Napier. Although Brunel had pioneered transatlantic services, Cunard won the government mail contract that made the operation viable. His company, the British and North American Steam Packet Line, was later named after its main founder. The first ship, the *Britannia*, made the passage in 14½ days. Despite introducing iron hulls, Cunard was quite conservative in his use of technology. However, his business acumen helped him compete with rivals, such as the American Collins Line.

bands of the Cunard Line became a favourite marketing tool in the company's advertisements.

By the second half of the century, the British steam shipping lines had lost some of their dominance. The largest German line, Hamburg–Amerika, started in the transatlantic trade in 1847, and by the 1880s it was building some of the largest ships in the world. The other great German company, Norddeutscher Lloyd, began in 1856 with operations from Germany to Hull and London. In the 1860s and 1870s, it expanded with services to the USA. The Dutch line Holland America was founded in 1873 under a different name. By its 25th anniversary, it had carried 90,000 cabin and 400,000 steerage passengers to the USA, as well as five million tons of cargo, mostly the traditional Dutch exports of flower bulbs, gin, and herring. The French Messageries Maritime grew out of the state postal service in 1835

CLASS DISTINCTION
As shipping lines competed for the custom of well-heeled travellers, the first-class passenger facilities became ever more luxurious. Shown left is the first-class dining room of the Omrah, built for the Orient Line's Australian service in 1899. By contrast, the facilities available to poorer passengers were more functional, such as the third-class smoking room below.

and took the form of a major shipping line, sponsored by Emperor Napoleon III, in 1853. Its horizons expanded in 1857, when it took on the main services from Bordeaux to Brazil and the River Plate. By 1900 it had 60 ships and was sixth largest in the world.

The first American shipping lines were less successful than their European competitors. In 1848, Edward Knight Collins founded the Collins Line, and two years later it began

PRINZESS IRENE ARRIVES IN NEW YORK
Norddeutscher Lloyd's double screw steamer Prinzess Irene *ran the Italy–USA route. Between 1900 and 1910, more than 2 million Italians emigrated to the USA or Argentina.*

transatlantic services, supported by US government subsidies. His five ships included the *Atlantic* and *Pacific*, larger than any Cunard liners, and faster, more comfortable, and better furnished. But Collins proved to be a better showman than businessman, and his ships were too expensive to run. After the *Arctic* sank in 1854, and then the *Pacific* in 1856, the company was wound up in 1858, leaving the North Atlantic steam trade under British domination for several decades to come.

The impact of the Suez Canal
The opening of the Suez Canal in 1869 (see panel, p.190) had an immediate effect on world shipping. It shortened the distance from London to Bombay by 7,125km (4,425 miles). It made a

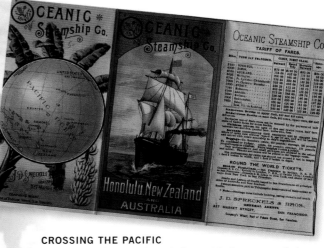

CROSSING THE PACIFIC
Founded in 1881, the Oceanic Steamship Company sailed from San Francisco to Hawaii, New Zealand, and Australia. At the turn of the century, the fare for a first-class cabin on a round trip to Sydney, Australia, was $360.

LOCAL ATTRACTION
Egyptians gather on the banks of the Suez Canal at El Kantara as a cargo liner steams by in 1870, just a year after the canal opened.

steamship voyage to the east much more practicable, for it was largely in the sheltered waters of the Mediterranean and Red seas. The same waters, especially those of the Red Sea, had unreliable winds and were unsuitable for sailing ships. As much as any technological innovation, the Suez Canal ensured the dominance of the steamship on long-distance routes.

CROSSING THE ATLANTIC

Charles Dickens crossed the Atlantic under steam in January 1842 and found it a very uncomfortable experience.

" But what the agitation of a steam vessel is, on a bad winter's night in the wild Atlantic, it is impossible for the most vivid imagination to conceive. To say that she is flung down on her side in the waves, with her masts dipping into them, and that, springing up again, she rolls on the other side, until a heavy sea strikes her with the noise of a hundred great guns, and hurls her back – that she stops, and staggers, and shivers, as though stunned, and then, with a violent throbbing at her heart, darts onward like a monster goaded into madness, to be beaten down, and battered, and crushed, and leaped on by the angry sea – that thunder, lightning, hail and rain, and wind are all in fierce contention for mastery – that every plank has its groan, every nail its shriek, and every drop of water in the great ocean its howling voice – is nothing. To say that all is grand, and all appalling and horrible in the last degree is nothing. "

CHARLES DICKENS, *American Notes,* **1883**

Although Britain was not involved in building the canal, the country's interests in India and Australia meant that it could not afford to ignore its effect on trade routes. Soon two-thirds of the shipping passing through the canal was British. In 1875, as the Egyptian monarchy faced bankruptcy, the British government, led by Prime Minister Benjamin Disraeli, bought seven-sixteenths of the shares. The canal became a major factor in the trade, colonial, and foreign policies of Britain and France over the century after its construction. In 1882, the British occupied Egypt, largely to secure the canal (see p.198), and it remained a protectorate until 1922.

Liners and tramps

By the 1870s, with the advent of the efficient triple-expansion engine, iron and steel ships, the Suez Canal, and the electric telegraph, merchant ships began to evolve into two types – liners and tramps. A liner sailed from port to port on a schedule, carrying passengers, cargo, or a combination of both. For example, from 1881 the French state-owned Messageries Maritime ran a service from Marseilles to Port Said, Mahe in southwest India, the island of Réunion, Mauritius, Adelaide, Melbourne, Sydney, and the Pacific island of Nouméa, servicing its own colonies as well as calling at a few of the more populous British ones. The best-known liners were usually operated by the more prestigious shipping companies, who made some effort to attract wealthy passengers, so the name gradually came to take on a certain amount of glamour and became associated with long- and medium-distance passenger services. It was eventually transferred to any large passenger ship, though the modern cruise ship, with no regular route, is definitely not a liner in the original sense of the term.

If the liner tended to rise in status over the years, its counterpart fell. But the tramp steamer was always inferior in status to the liner, for it was usually smaller, run by a smaller company, and provided less regular employment. The main job of the tramp steamer was to carry a bulk cargo on behalf of a single charterer. Tramps were not passenger ships, although like all ships they were entitled to carry up to 12 passengers without extra certification, so they sometimes carried them on a casual basis.

Each nation had its own coastal trade, and the USA, for example, tended to protect it against foreign competition. Long-distance tramping was largely a British phenomenon, carried out by countless small companies in ports round the country. Unlike liner seamen, the tramp sailor had no way of knowing when he would come home. In an extreme case, the *Queen Louise* of Glasgow, Scotland, spent over four years from 1899 to 1904 away from home waters, visiting India several times, the USA, South America, and Australia. Tramp steamers mostly carried cargoes of coal, but they could also take grain, wood, ore, esparto grass, fertilizer, and rice. Some were chartered by liner companies in busy periods and carried general cargoes on their routes.

Seasickness

Seasickness became a serious problem in the 19th century, for several reasons. A ship proceeding under steam did not have the force of the sails to pin it down and steady it against rolling. Unlike a sailing ship, it might also steam

NO LAUGHING MATTER
As seasickness became more common, satirical magazines, such as the French Le Rire *(left) had fun at the sufferers' expense. But efforts were made to counter it. The print above shows a group of women sharing a seat that was designed in the 1880s to compensate for the pitching and rolling of the ship and thus prevent the onset of seasickness – unfortunately, it didn't work.*

Le Rire

IRISH EMIGRATION

In 1845 and 1846 the Irish potato crop, on which the country was totally dependent, failed due to blight. It resulted in widespread starvation and large-scale emigration across the Atlantic. According to an agent in the west of the country, "Many of the people who go of their own accord are people of some substance, who are able to pay their passage money; but many landed proprietors send out a certain number of persons from their estates, these persons are all poor persons, and the proportions of the two classes are about equal." Other migrants sailed to Liverpool, where they boarded sailing ships. Passengers were crammed into tiny bunks that were compared with dog kennels, fed with inadequate and poor-quality food, and treated brutally if they complained. Conditions on British ships, hastily converted from the timber trade, were worse than those on American ships.

About 20 per cent of the Irish population emigrated during the 1840s, a higher proportion than from any other country or region of Europe. The famine, the British government's failure to help, and the horrors of the voyage across the Atlantic became engraved on the Irish memory, both at home and in the USA.

DESPERATE FOR HELP

Men, women, and children clamour at the gate of a workhouse that is already full to overflowing in 1846. Between 1845 and 1849, around one million Irish people died of starvation or disease.

directly into the wind, creating a very unpleasant motion in rough seas. The range of people who travelled, both for pleasure and as migrants, greatly increased as the century progressed, and voyages were quicker, giving passengers less time to get used to the conditions. As Jerome K. Jerome wrote in *Three Men in a Boat*, "A sea trip does you good when you are going to have a couple of months of it, but, for a week, it is wicked." Seasickness soon became a favourite theme of 19th-century cartoonists (see below, left).

A ship at sea is subject to no fewer than six different movements: pitching, rolling, yawing, surging, swaying, and heaving. Rolling, where the ship repeatedly tips over towards the left and then the right, is often the most dramatic, but it is heaving, the up-and-down motion, that causes passengers the most trouble and is hardest for designers to eliminate. The English Channel ferry *Bessemer* of 1874 was designed to counter seasickness. Her saloon was pivoted so that it could move both sideways and

ENTRY VISA

The visa on the left-hand page of the passport of this Swedish girl, pictured with her mother on the right, grants her unhindered passage throughout the USA for one year.

TRAVELLING STEERAGE

For the poorest emigrants, conditions onboard were spartan, to say the least. These steerage-class passengers on the Red Star Line's Pennland *left the port of Antwerp, Belgium, for a new life in the USA in 1893.*

fore and aft, and her designers intended to fit gyroscopes to control the motion. However, on her first voyage her control gear was not complete, and she collided with a pier in Calais Harbour, France.

Emigration

In the 18th century, many emigrants had been unwilling – soldiers, slaves, indentured servants, or convicts. In the mid-19th century, the largest single group of emigrants were the victims of the Irish Potato Famine (see panel, left), who travelled in despair and ignorance. The majority of emigrants could only afford to travel in steerage, which originally meant the area around the ship's tiller but came to mean a large space below the deck. A sailing ship typically took six weeks to cross the Atlantic, and steerage passengers endured terrible conditions, crowded together in a dim, poorly ventilated, insanitary space, with little food and frequently rancid water. Diseases such as cholera and typhus were a major problem – in 1847, 7,000 people died of typhus during voyages from Europe to the USA, and a further 10,000 died soon after arrival.

In the California Gold Rush of 1848–49 (see p.234) and the Australian one of 1851–52, passengers were adventurers who did not much care what conditions they travelled in as long as they got there in good time. But after that, in the great emigration boom that gathered pace in the second half of

PRICE'S SAFETY CANDLE LANTERN

In the 19th century, many emigrants did not appreciate the danger of fire onboard ships. Price's candlemakers invented a lantern that the crew could lock after lighting the candle.

LEAVING ELLIS ISLAND
*Having passed the US authorities'
health and legal checks, immigrants
would then have to queue for the ferry
that would take them from Ellis Island
to New York.*

CLEAN BILL OF HEALTH
*Third-class and steerage
passengers were required
to undergo a health
inspection before being
given permission to
enter the USA.*

the century, passengers from western Europe
were at least formally willing to go, generally
trying to better themselves rather than escape
from intolerable conditions. This was less true
of Italians fleeing desperate poverty, whose
numbers boomed in the 1880s, or oppressed
minorities, especially Jews from Russia and
eastern Europe. But the conditions in the Irish
famine ships were a low point in the history of
emigration, and after that they generally
improved, partly because of greater government
regulation. In 1848, the US government passed
the American Passenger Act, which stipulated a
minimum space to be allocated to each
passenger travelling steerage to the USA and
required permanently open hatchways. The
replacement of sailing ships by steam also
helped – by 1870, the journey across the
Atlantic had been reduced to two weeks.

Most emigrant passengers were not rich,
and in the 1850s a single steerage-class ticket
across the Atlantic cost British passengers £6,

the equivalent of six months'
wages for a land or factory
worker. Some had saved for
years to pay for the passage;
others were supported by
relatives who had already
emigrated, or by local
landowners who wanted to
reduce pressure on their land.
Occasionally the receiving state
or country, for example
Queensland in Australia, paid the bulk of
the cost. Steamships carried the majority of
transatlantic emigrants by the 1860s, as well as
the largest numbers of those to Australia and
the east after the Suez Canal opened, but the
passengers on liners were carefully segregated
by class, and the comfort of a first-class cabin
was in stark contrast to the conditions in
steerage, albeit at a price – a single first-class
ticket on the White Star Line, for example,
could cost upwards of £10 in the 1890s.

Passengers were also treated differently
according to class on arrival in New York. First-
and second-class travellers did not undergo a
health inspection unless they showed signs of
illness. But third- and steerage-class passengers
had to remain at the immigration processing
station at Battery Park, and from 1892 Ellis
Island, until they had been passed as healthy.

British passengers to India (apart from
soldiers in troopships) were mostly colonial
officials and their families, and P&O
specialized in providing both outward
and home voyages in some comfort.
But the theory that the richest
passengers booked cabins away
from the tropical sun – Port
Out Starboard Home, or
POSH – is apparently a
myth. P&O ships had

THE FIRST FOUR-FUNNELLER
*The Kaiser Wilhelm der Grosse was the first ocean
liner to have four funnels, which were arranged in
two pairs rather than being evenly spaced.*

about twice as many first-class as second-class passengers, reflecting the nature of the trade, and the second class was mainly filled with servants or poorer missionaries. The captain and officers were instructed to give careful consideration to the passengers and become involved with their parlour games and activities. The voyage was a unique experience, which did much to foster the corporate image of P&O.

The growth of the Atlantic liner

In the last decades of the 19th century, the transatlantic liner became a measure of technological progress and national prestige. There was a continuous growth in size from 1888, with the launch of Inman & International Steamship Company's *City of New York* and *City of Paris*, which were the first liners with twin screws and reduced the voyage time

to less than six days. The rising German Empire could not ignore the possibilities of the transatlantic route, especially as up to a million of its citizens were emigrating every decade.

The Germans entered the transatlantic trade on a big scale after 1889, when Kaiser Wilhelm II was shown round the aptly named British White Star liner *Teutonic*. "We must have some of these," he is reported to have said, for German liners up to that time, although numerous, were comparatively small and ill-equipped. Norddeutscher Lloyd of Bremen ordered the *Kaiser Wilhelm der Grosse* from the Vulcan Yard at Stettin. She was designed to be the largest and most powerful ship in the world, and two months after her maiden voyage in September 1897 she became the first German ship to win the Blue Riband for the fastest crossing of the Atlantic, with an average speed

of 22.27 knots. The previous record holder was the British liner *Lucania*, of the Cunard Line. However, the steam turbine engine invented by the British industrialist Charles Parson (see p.179) appeared in the same year, ensuring that a new phase in the transatlantic race would begin early in the next century.

In 1900, the Blue Riband was captured by the *Deutschland*, owned by Hamburg–Amerika, which, with 73 ships, was the largest shipping line in the world. Norddeutscher Lloyd was second largest, and the British India Steam Navigation Company and P&O were third and fourth. However, Britain retained its lead as the world's largest shipping nation, with nearly 14 million tons belonging to Britain and its colonies, compared with 2 million each for the USA and Germany. Britain still controlled over half the world's shipping tonnage.

EARLY ATLANTIC LINERS

Crossing the Atlantic, with its long distances and rough weather, was always one of the greatest challenges to early steamships. The interaction between Europe and America was already an important creative force, but it was accelerated when steamships developed a long enough range to cross the Atlantic. While the paddle ship had its natural disadvantages in rough weather, its replacement by the screw propeller cleared the way for further development. By the end of the 20th century, the liners were the largest ships in the world and the object of intense international competition in speed and comfort.

FROM AMERICA TO FRANCE
The paddle liner Napoleon III *of 1855 was used on the New York-to-Le Havre service by the Compagnie General Transatlantique.*

The pioneers

Moses Rogers, owner of the steamship *Savannah* (below), had no intention of setting up a regular transatlantic service when his ship left New York Harbor on 22 May 1819. She had failed to attract passengers on her intended route on the US east coast between New York, Charleston, and Savannah, and he planned to sell her in Europe. As she approached Ireland, her smoke caused reports of fire. Although her paddle wheels could be unshipped when she was sailing and she used her engines for only 85 hours in a 27-day voyage, her coal was virtually exhausted on arrival. But she was the first steamship to cross the Atlantic in either direction. It was almost 20 years before steam engines were improved enough to allow regular services.

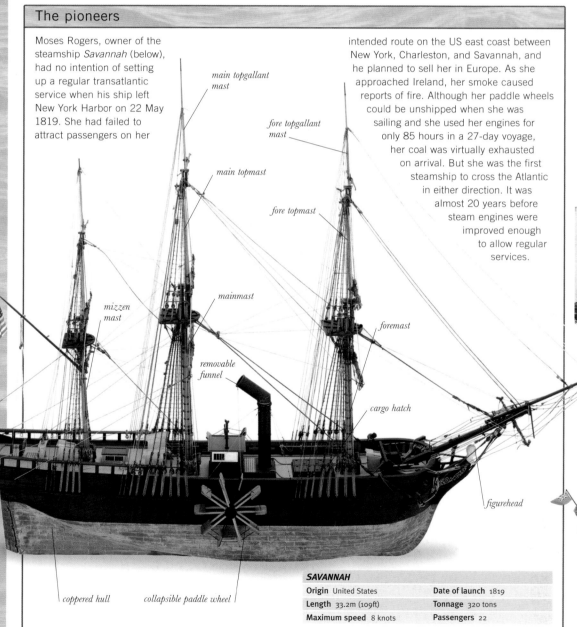

main topgallant mast

fore topgallant mast

main topmast

fore topmast

mizzen mast

mainmast

foremast

removable funnel

cargo hatch

figurehead

coppered hull

collapsible paddle wheel

SAVANNAH		
Origin United States		**Date of launch** 1819
Length 33.2m (109ft)		**Tonnage** 320 tons
Maximum speed 8 knots		**Passengers** 22

The first transatlantic steamers

The idea of regular transatlantic steam travel was visionary but just practicable by the late 1830s. The great civil and railway engineer Isambard Kingdom Brunel initially conceived his first ship, the *Great Western* (below), as an extension of the Great Western Railway, but from London and Bristol to New York. The *Great Western* competed with the smaller ship *Sirius* (below) for the crossing to New York in 1838 and made the faster passage. It demonstrated the possibilities of the route, although it was Cunard, rather than Brunel, who would reap the commercial benefits.

BRUNEL'S *GREAT WESTERN*

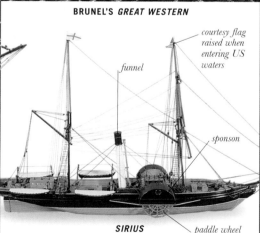

courtesy flag raised when entering US waters

funnel

sponson

SIRIUS

paddle wheel

GREAT WESTERN		
Origin Britain		**Date of launch** 1837
Length 72m (236ft)		**Tonnage** 1,320 tons
Maximum speed 8.5 knots		**Passengers** 148

The first twin-screw steamers

Early passenger steamships had been fitted with a single engine driving a single propeller. Twin engines and propellers had obvious advantages of manoeuvrability and safety, and the Inman Line's *City of Paris* (right) and her sister *City of New York* were the first to be fitted with these on the Atlantic route. They were virtually the prototypes of the great Atlantic liner as it later emerged, setting new standards of speed and comfort. *City of Paris* was the best known of the pair, winning the Blue Riband by making the first crossing of under six days.

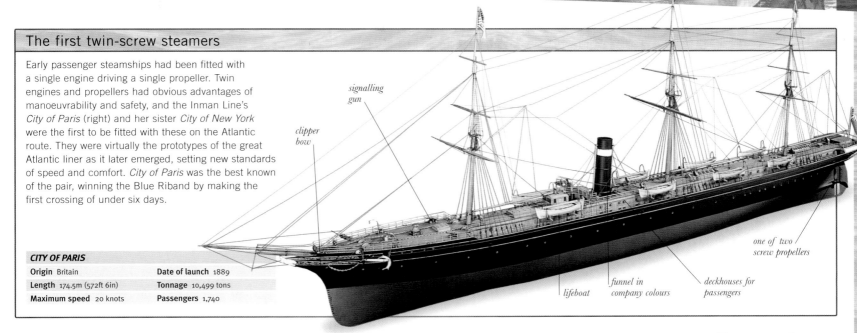

signalling gun

clipper bow

one of two screw propellers

lifeboat

funnel in company colours

deckhouses for passengers

CITY OF PARIS

Origin Britain	**Date of launch** 1889	
Length 174.5m (572ft 6in)	**Tonnage** 10,499 tons	
Maximum speed 20 knots	**Passengers** 1,740	

The first liners

The British government's offer of a mail contract across the Atlantic by steam made regular passenger services viable for the first time, and Samuel Cunard, who was a better businessman than Brunel, was the first to benefit from this. The first of the four vessels to maintain the service, *Britannia* (left), took 12 days and 10 hours on her maiden voyage from Liverpool, England to Halifax, Nova Scotia. The early Cunard ships had none of the luxury associated with the company in later years.

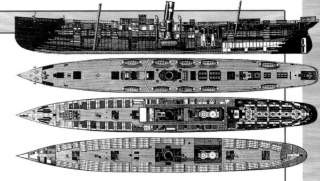

BRITANNIA

Origin Britain	**Date of launch** 1840
Length 64.6m (212ft)	**Tonnage** 1,154 tons
Maximum speed 8.5 knots	**Passengers** 115

PENNSYLVANIA

The 3,000-ton Pennsylvania *was built in 1872 and was the first ship of the American Line. The passenger cabins are in the second-from-bottom diagram.*

Large liners

The North Atlantic run became a focus of national and corporate prestige in the last decades of the 19th century. New nations and companies entered the market, while the older ones invested in new and larger ships in an effort to keep up. Inman's *City of Berlin* (below) was the first liner to be fitted with electric light. Cunard's *Campania* (right) of nearly 13,000 tons took the Blue Riband in 1893.

CAMPANIA

CITY OF BERLIN

Origin Britain	**Date of launch** 1875
Length 148m (486ft)	**Tonnage** 5,491 tons
Maximum speed 15 knots	**Passengers** 1,770

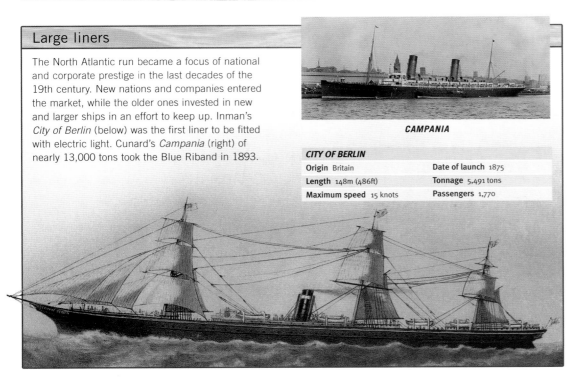

Four-funnel liners

As liners became larger, more engines were used. The number of funnels became symbolic of speed and safety, so shipping companies sometimes fitted false funnels to give an impression of power. *Kaiser Wilhelm der Grosse* (below) represented the new Germany's attempt at transatlantic leadership, and her speed soon enabled her to capture the Blue Riband.

KAISER WILHELM DER GROSSE

Origin Germany	**Date of launch** 1897
Length 191.2m (627ft 3in)	**Tonnage** 14,350 tons
Maximum speed 23 knots	**Passengers** 1,970

CARGO STEAMSHIPS

The cargo steamship of the late 19th century varied in size and status, from the prestigious liners running between the European empires in Africa and Asia, to the tiny coasters that supplied rural communities with necessities. The development of an efficient steam engine allowed world trade to increase tenfold in the 60 years after 1850, and Britain built about 80 per cent of the world's merchant ships.

ROPE JUMPERS
Coal "whippers" unloaded coal from the collier Dunelm *by jumping from a height while holding a rope attached to a load, as seen in this 1877 painting.*

Passenger and cargo liners

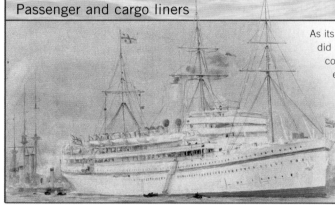

As its name implies, the passenger and cargo liner did not depend on goods as its main living, but it could still carry a substantial amount of cargo, especially when sailing between otherwise isolated points in the European empires in Asia, the Pacific, and Africa. The British India Steam Navigation Company, for example, operated passenger/cargo liners from Europe to various Indian and Far Eastern ports. The French *Messagaries Maritimes* operated from Marseilles to Indo-China, Mauritius, and Tahiti, with various stops along the route. Prices on these routes were controlled by conferences of shipping companies. The P&O ship *Medina* (left) could take 670 passengers – it carried King George V to the Delhi Durbar in 1911 – but it could also carry mail and up to 6,000 tons of cargo on the London-to-Australia service. She was sunk by a U-boat in 1917.

MEDINA	
Origin Britain	**Date of launch** 1911
Length 167.6m (550ft)	
Tonnage 12,350 tons	

Cargo liners

With the new compound engines, the *Agamemnon* (below) and her sisters *Ajax* and *Achilles* could steam using about 20 tons of coal a day. These vessels were the first to compete economically with sailing ships over long distances from Europe to the Far East and were the prototypes of the cargo liner. They could steam 13,680km (8,500 miles) without refuelling and carry 2,800 tons of cargo (three times as much as a typical sailing ship). By 1912, the typical steamer specialized in cargo but could carry up to 12 passengers.

AGAMEMNON	
Origin Britain	**Date of launch** 1865
Length 94.25m (309ft 3in)	
Tonnage 2,212 tons	

NONSUCH
The 1906 Nonsuch *was one of a series of turret ships built in northeast England. The wider deck at a lower level to the rest of the deck was used when mooring alongside in harbour.*

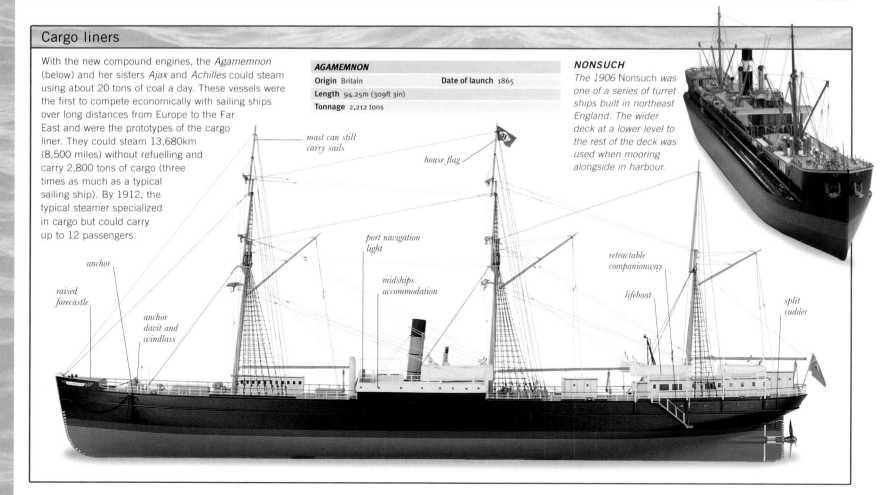

- mast can still carry sails
- house flag
- port navigation light
- midships accommodation
- retractable companionway
- lifeboat
- split rudder
- anchor
- raised forecastle
- anchor davit and windlass

Oil tankers

The first oil tankers originated almost simultaneously in the United States and Russia. Many of the early ones were sail-powered or towed by steamships, for fear that the boiler fires might ignite the oil. The *Looch* (right) was built in Newcastle, England, for the Russian Steam Navigation and Trading Company. By 1912, there were 258 steamers carrying oil around the world.

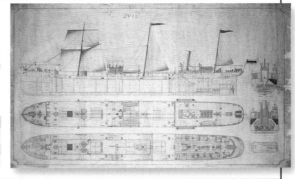

LOOCH

Origin Britain (for Russia)	**Date of launch** 1886
Length 78.9m (255ft 6in)	
Tonnage 1,446 tons	

Coasters

Coasters took many different forms, as they were usually designed for particular areas with their own wind and sea conditions, types of harbour, and cargoes. Clyde puffers (below) were designed to fit into the locks of the Scottish Crinan and Forth and Clyde canals. The name derived from the first generation of ships, which had no condenser and issued a puff of steam with every stroke of the engine.

THE BRITISH *ACTIVE*

Refrigerated ships

In the late 1800s, refrigerated ships made it possible to export cattle from North and South America and frozen lamb from Australia and New Zealand. The *Argyllshire* (below), built near Glasgow, was one of the largest cargo ships built before the First World War and was used in the frozen-meat trade. She was hit by a German torpedo in 1917, but survived until she was scrapped in 1936.

ARGYLLSHIRE

Origin Britain	**Date of launch** 1911
Length 160.4m (526ft 2in)	
Tonnage 10,392 tons	

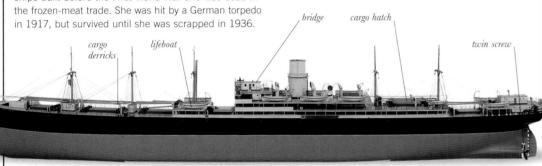

cargo derricks *lifeboat* *bridge* *cargo hatch* *twin screw*

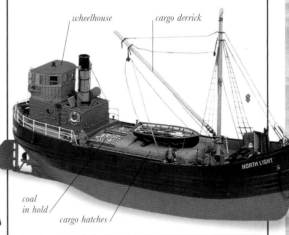

wheelhouse *cargo derrick*

coal in hold *cargo hatches*

NORTHLIGHT

Origin Britain	**Date of launch** *c.*1910
Length 20.3m (66ft 6in)	
Tonnage 100 tons	

Tramps

The tramp steamer was simply a cargo ship without a regular route. Most tramping firms were British, and the most common cargo was coal, although grain, iron ore, and many others could be carried. Tramp steamers might find themselves almost anywhere in the world, as the market demanded, and the international telegraph system was essential to their operation. Three-island tramp steamers had three raised decks; the *Springwell* (below) of 1914 was a typical example. Other ships had

the aftermost and centre islands joined up and were known as welldeckers. If all three joined they were called shelter-decked ships. The engine was usually placed in the centre of the ship because of its weight and that of its fuel.

SIZERGH CASTLE

With a long bridge deck in the centre, the Sizergh Castle had more space for light cargo and was known as a spar-decked ship.

SPRINGWELL

Origin Britain	**Date of launch** 1914
Length 129.75m (425ft 7in)	
Tonnage 5,593 tons	

forecastle (first island) *cargo derrick* *second island* *funnel* *plimsoll line indicates how low vessel is floating* *poop deck (third island)*

NORDENFELDT TWO-POUNDER MACHINE GUN

> 66 You may fire when
> ready, Gridley. 99

COMMODORE GEORGE DEWEY, at the
Battle of Manila Bay during the Spanish-
American War, **1 May 1898**

KEY EVENTS

1854   SIEGE OF SEBASTOPOL The allied
powers of Britain and France besiege the
Russian naval base at Sebastopol in the decisive
action of the Crimean War.

1859   FIRST TRUE IRONCLAD France
launches the *Gloire*, the world's first truly seagoing ironclad warship.

1865   PRESERVATION OF THE UNION The
Confederacy concedes defeat, bringing the
American Civil War (1861–65) to an end.

1866   TORPEDO INVENTED British engineer
Robert Whitehead uses a compressed-air engine
to power the first self-propelled torpedo.

1866   BATTLE OF LISSA An Austrian fleet
uses ramming tactics to defeat the larger Italian
fleet on 20 July 1866, in the eastern Adriatic.

1871   BATTLESHIP WITHOUT SAILS The
Royal Navy launches *Devastation*, the first
battleship powered by steam alone.

1894   BATTLE OF YALU RIVER Japan
defeats China in this decisive naval battle during
the First Sino-Japanese War (1894–95).

1898   *MAINE* SUNK IN HAVANA HARBOUR
The sinking of the US battleship *Maine* was a key
step on the road to the Spanish-American War.

NAVAL WARFARE

ALTHOUGH THE WORLD'S NAVIES WERE SLOW TO REALIZE THE POTENTIAL OF STEAM POWER, ITS ADVENT WOULD TRANSFORM WAR AT SEA.

Steam power was not seen as a great asset to warships at first, for a paddle wheel on the side of a ship would take up about a third of the space usually occupied by guns. However, in 1814 the American Robert Fulton designed the *Demologos*, a steam-powered ship with guns mounted on two pontoon hulls either side of a paddle wheel, for use against the British. It was a French artilleryman, General Henri Paixhans, who first imagined a sea dominated by these smoky little vessels. In 1822, he proposed a fleet of cheap, expendable iron steamships firing explosive shells, but the idea was rejected by the French Navy.

Although Europe as a whole was peaceful in the 1820s, there were a few wars. Thomas Cochrane, already a hero in the Royal Navy (see p.215), went to Greece in 1827 to build a navy for the Greeks to use in their campaign for independence from Turkey. The *Karteria* (see p.224) was built in England and commanded by Captain Frank Hastings. Her engines were unreliable and she was slow under sail, but she carried guns that used red-hot shot warmed in her furnaces.

It was 1835 before the British began to build serious steam warships, in the form of paddle frigates. The prototype was the *Gorgon* of 1,610 tons. She could make a respectable

9 knots, but carried only six guns, albeit heavy ones. When steam enthusiasts claimed that she could defeat a battleship, the Royal Navy's gunnery expert replied that she would not get within range without her machinery and paddles being destroyed. But the paddle frigate had a role as an auxiliary to the fleet, and many more were built, in different sizes.

Screw warships

The advent of the screw propeller changed the picture for the steam warship. A propeller did not interfere with the broadside of a ship and was not vulnerable to enemy fire. In 1846, the British converted four old ships of the line by fitting 450-horsepower engines. They were intended only as blockships for harbour defence, not as seagoing vessels. At the same time, ships under construction were modified into seagoing steam frigates. The French responded with the *Napoleon* of 1850. With a 960-horsepower engine in a hull of 5,120 tons, and an armament of 80 guns, she was the first true steam battleship. Steam was now recognized as essential for warships, but it was still definitely an auxiliary to sail. Most warships had a device whereby the screw could be raised out of the water to prevent drag while sailing (see below), and the funnel could be lowered – hence the British naval order "Up funnel, down screw."

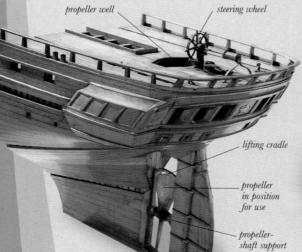

propeller well   *steering wheel*

lifting cradle

propeller in position for use

propeller-shaft support

LIFTING SCREW
To raise a screw propeller, it was first disengaged from the shaft (left-hand picture) and then ratcheted into a well between the lower and upper decks (middle and right-hand pictures).

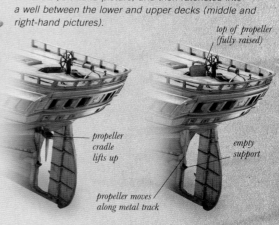

top of propeller (fully raised)

propeller cradle lifts up

empty support

propeller moves along metal track

UNION IRONCLAD WARSHIP
Cannons project from the gun ports of the USS Galena. The ship's thin iron armour proved no match for the guns of the Confederacy's battery at Drewry's Bluff, Virginia, USA, on 15 May 1862.

The Crimean War

In 1853, a dispute between Russia and the Ottoman Empire arose over guardianship of holy places in Palestine. In November, the Russian Black Sea naval squadron, based at Sebastopol, sank the Ottoman fleet at Sinope. In January 1854, the British and French, possessors of the strongest and second-strongest fleets in the world, arrived in the Black Sea to protect Ottoman shipping. France and Britain declared war on Russia in March. Although it was commonly known as the Crimean War, after the peninsula on which the famous land battles, such as Balaclava, were fought, it was the western powers' naval supremacy, partly founded on the use of a large fleet of transports, that allowed them to operate so far from home. Most ships of the line were still wooden and without engines, but they were towed into action by steamboats, as at the bombardment of the Russian naval base at Sebastopol in October 1854. Although such attacks on shore fortifications were surprisingly successful, they revealed the weakness of the wooden ship and increased interest in armour protection. A large fleet of nearly 250 British gunboats was built for inshore operations, all steam-powered. Mines were also used for the first time (see above), in what became the first modern naval war. The war ended in March 1856 with the Treaty of Paris, by which the Black Sea's neutrality was secured.

The birth of the ironclad

With the spread of the iron merchant ship in the 1830s and 1840s, navies took an interest in the new method of construction. Short of building space for wooden ships in the Royal Dockyards, in 1843 the British Admiralty ordered an iron frigate, the *Trident*, followed by the larger *Birkenhead* of 1,918 tons. The French

percussion cap

tethering point

CRIMEAN WAR SUPPLIES
Cannonballs and cannons unloaded from British transport ships at Ordnance Wharf in Balaclava Harbour, Ukraine, await collection by the Army.

INFERNAL MACHINE
Ironclad mines, such as this one recovered by the British (who later added the lettering), were used by the Russians in the Baltic Sea during the Crimean War.

and Americans were quick to follow, but all were premature. These early iron warships were not yet well enough developed to cope with conditions in action because their thin, wrought-iron plates were easily penetrated by shells. During the Crimean War, both the British and the French fitted some of their wooden warships with thicker 10-cm (4-in) iron plate above the waterline, and the French used theirs at the bombardment of Kinburn in October 1855.

THOMAS COCHRANE

The son of an impoverished Scottish aristocrat, Thomas Cochrane (1775–1860) made his name with the Royal Navy sloop *Speedy*, in which he defeated more than 50 ships in the Mediterranean in 1800. As commander of the frigate *Pallas*, he earned a fortune in prize money, but in 1814 he was imprisoned for alleged fraud. This illustration (right) shows him half in naval uniform and half in prison clothes. Cochrane founded the Chilean Navy in 1817, then the Brazilian Navy in 1823, and in 1827, while commanding the Greek Navy, he became one of the first to deploy steam warships.

BRITISH SHIPS AT BALACLAVA, 1855
Balaclava Bay, on Ukraine's Black Sea Coast, was used as a base by the British during the Crimean War. This image by the pioneering English photographer Roger Fenton shows the wooden-hulled warships still in use at that time.

IRONCLAD RIVER GUNBOAT

The USS Essex *began life as a steam-powered ferry, but was converted to an ironclad gunboat in 1861 by the order of her commanding officer William Porter. She was one of the most powerful gunboats on the Mississippi River.*

The success in keeping out long-range enemy shot was exaggerated, but enough to convince Emperor Napoleon III that iron plates on a wooden hull – the ironclad – was the way forward. The French engineer Stanislas Dupuy de Lôme was appointed chief constructor, and he began to build a fully ironclad warship, the *Gloire* (see p.225). Essentially a battleship design reduced to one deck, it was launched in 1859.

The British were quick to respond. They carried out tests of armour plate in 1858 and ordered their first ironclad by the end of the year. The Controller of the Navy, Admiral Baldwin Walker, adopted the design of a large frigate rather than a battleship, but made it half as long again as the *Gloire*. Baldwin's ship, *Warrior*, was launched in

1860 and proved very successful, being 1.5 knots faster than her rival, with a good gun platform because bilge keels added to her stability. Britain's industrial strength thwarted France's attempt to overtake her by means of technology. Ironclads soon became accepted in all fleets. The French already had four under construction by 1860 and ordered 10 more that year. The British had 15 ironclads afloat or under construction by 1861. The new Italian Navy, founded that year after the union of several provinces under the rule of Piedmont,

immediately began the construction of seven ironclads. The USA began only one, the *Stevens Battery*, but it was never completed. Civil war was already developing, and that would demand different kinds of ships.

The American Civil War

Like the Crimean War, the American Civil War (1861–65) is commonly seen as a land war, but the waterborne element was essential to the strategy of both the United States and the Confederates who wanted to secede from the Union.

MONITOR BLUEPRINT

The Monitor *gave its name to a class of ships typified by the central rotating gun turret and a shallow draught.*

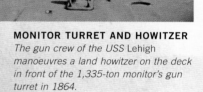

MONITOR TURRET AND HOWITZER

The gun crew of the USS Lehigh *manoeuvres a land howitzer on the deck in front of the 1,335-ton monitor's gun turret in 1864.*

THE FIRST BATTLE BETWEEN IRONCLADS

The USS Monitor *fires a broadside at CSS* Virginia *at Hampton Roads, Virginia, on 9 March 1862. Monitor's turret was hit 24 times during the battle, but she emerged unscathed, only to sink off North Carolina on 31 December. Her wreck, relocated in 1973, is the focus of a conservation programme.*

Exports of cotton and imports of munitions were essential to the non-industrial Confederacy, and Union forces used blockades to try to stop them; the Confederates needed ships that were fast under both sail and steam to get through.

The Union Navy of about 90 ships was in poor condition and unready for war, but the Confederate Navy was almost non-existent. However, the Confederates managed to salvage the lower hull of the frigate *Merrimack*, burned when Union forces abandoned the Norfolk naval base in Virginia. The ship was rebuilt with two layers of sloping iron covering the hull, and guns firing through ports in the side. Renamed *Virginia*, the ship was ready by March 1862, just as the Union Army was attempting to invade the area. On 8 March she steamed out to meet the Union fleet in the James River. She rammed and sank the frigate *Cumberland* and forced the *Congress* to surrender, then burned her, before

RECRUITMENT POSTER
Sailors were needed to man Virginia Coast Guard ships during the Civil War. Their role included bringing supplies and troops to Union garrisons.

night fell. But the *Virginia*'s reign of terror was to last less than a day, for an even stranger-looking craft came into the river. The Union Navy had heard of the rebuilding of the *Merrimack*, and John Ericsson (see p.175) was building the *Monitor* – so called because he regarded her as a warning to both the Confederacy and the other naval powers. Because of the difficulty of turning a ship in the narrow rivers where she was intended to fight, he adopted a rotating turret (see below) with two 11-in (279-mm) Dahlgren guns (see top right). She had a very flat hull and sat low in the water, which made her vulnerable in the open sea.

The *Monitor* and *Virginia* fought an eight-hour engagement at very close range, but neither was able to penetrate the other's armour. Eventually, the *Monitor* used her shallow draught to withdraw over sandbanks, but she had saved the remainder of the Union fleet in the area. On 11 May, the *Virginia* was burned to prevent her falling into Union hands. Both sides continued to build ironclads after the pattern of the original champions.

The Union had to conquer the south mile by mile to win the war, and the best way to do this was to advance down the rivers by steamship.

DAHLGREN GUN DRILL
The crew of the gunboat USS Mendota, a sidewheel paddle steamer, practise firing a Dahlgren gun. Developed in the 1850s by Union ordnance expert John A. Dahlgren, this bottle-shaped gun played a decisive part in the Civil War.

The Mississippi stern-wheeler the *Essex* (see far left) was armoured and fitted with guns and fought its way both up and down the great river on behalf of the Union.

The commerce raider *Alabama* was the most successful Confederate warship. She was built secretly and illegally in Liverpool (Britain was neutral) and was taken over by the Confederates at sea in August 1862. She captured or sank 66 Union merchant ships over the next two years, until she was trapped off Cherbourg, France, by the Union screw-sloop *Kearsarge*. In a rare single-ship action between steam warships, lasting more than 90 minutes, the *Kearsarge*'s superior gunnery sank the *Alabama*. The latter's wreck was discovered in 1982.

AFRICAN-AMERICAN SAILORS
Members of the crew of the USS Vermont, a store ship, pose for a war reporter's camera. The Union Navy employed thousands of freed slaves during the Civil War.

> " Damn the torpedoes. Full speed ahead! "
> **ADMIRAL DAVID GLASGOW FARRAGUT**, onboard USS *Hartford*
> at the Battle of Mobile Bay, Alabama, **5 August 1864**

BOW The bow is decorated in a similar fashion to those of wooden ships.

UPPER DECK The steering wheel is at the rear of the upper deck. Beyond it are two metal binnacles containing the compasses, and beyond them is the wardroom skylight.

SHIP'S BELL With no modern system of communication, the ship's bell was still essential.

GUN TURRET The gun turret, made of iron and lined with wood, carries two 9.2-in (234-mm) guns, which form the main armament of the ship. The guns are behind portals.

ID MARK Each grating on the upper deck has a mark that corresponds to its size.

CABIN The navigation officer's cabin is on the port side of the ship on the lower deck.

SLEEPING QUARTERS The captain's sleeping quarters also includes a bath. The high bed has stowage below.

CAPTAIN'S HEADS A jug of water was used to flush the captain's toilet.

STERN Windows in the stern provide light for the captain's main cabin. The captain's launch hangs from davits at the stern's rear.

LONG ROOM Stretching across the full width of the ship, the long room, or wardroom, reflects 19th-century taste, with a piano, bookcase, and sofas around the sides. It was used for meetings and as a recreation room for the officers.

CAPTAIN'S QUARTERS *The captain's main cabin is on the lower deck, right in the stern. The column on the right houses the steering gear.*

IRON STRUCTURE *The end of a deck beam joins the deck frame and the plates of the hull. The hull is held together by numerous rivets.*

PORTHOLE *Round portholes first came into use in iron and steel ships.*

RUDDER COMPARTMENT *The interior of this compartment, which holds the steering gear, has an iron tiller for emergency use.*

PHOTO PROFILE

BUFFEL

IN 1868, THE DUTCH NAVY ACQUIRED ITS FIRST TURRET-RAM SHIP. ITS DESIGNERS DREW ON THE EXPERIENCE OF OTHER NAVAL POWERS, WHO ALREADY HAD SIMILAR SHIPS.

THE DUTCH NAVY began to modernize itself in the late 1860s, and the *Buffel* (Buffalo) was one of a pair of ships to adopt the latest design features: armoured sides from the *Gloire* and *Warrior*, twin guns in a turret as in the *Monitor*, and a ram bow based on the Italian experience at the Battle of Lissa. The *Buffel* was built by Napier's of Glasgow and her sister *Guinea* was completed in Amsterdam two years later. The *Buffel* was designed as a coast-defence ship and only left Dutch waters for a trip to Antwerp in 1871, but she helped the Dutch Navy train and exercise in the new naval warfare techniques. She was reduced to a barracks ship in 1896 and restored to her original state between 1974 and 1979.

The prominent black hull of the *Buffel* is adorned with gilded decorations at the bows and stern. As a coastal steamship she carries very little rigging – the two light masts were used mainly for signalling. On the upper deck, the wheel is placed near the stern in traditional fashion, although it is some way from the bridge. The after deck is comparatively clear, except for the hatches and companionways down its centre and the area around the funnel, which is surrounded by ventilators to take air to the pair of 1,000-horsepower engines. Forward of that is the light bridge, then the circular turret, with its twin guns normally kept inboard and the portals closed. The deck is also quite clear forward, with the anchors and capstans in the bows.

Below decks, the captain's cabin is at the stern, with his sleeping and bathing room and heads (toilet) to starboard and the officers' galley to port.

UNDER TOW *The partly restored Buffel was towed from Amsterdam to the Maritime Museum in Rotterdam in 1976. Her single funnel and turret are evident here, along with the early form of bridge, a light structure between the sides of the ship.*

Forward of that is the long room, or wardroom, for the officers, with small officers' cabins on both sides of the ship ahead of that. The petty officers lived near the centre of the *Buffel* on either side of the trunking that led the fumes from the engine up to the funnel. The mechanism and armour of the rotating turret also took up a good deal of space below decks, with the crew's mess tables and hammocks on either side and forward of it. Below that deck, just aft of centre, were the engines, with coal stowed near them and provisions stored both forward and aft.

Specification

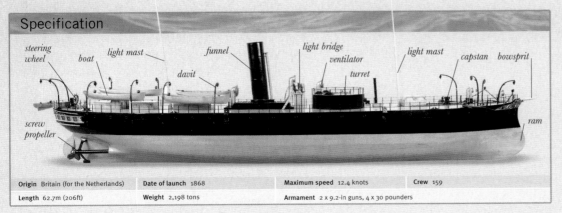

Origin Britain (for the Netherlands)	**Date of launch** 1868	**Maximum speed** 12.4 knots	**Crew** 159
Length 62.7m (206ft)	**Weight** 2,198 tons	**Armament** 2 x 9.2-in guns, 4 x 30 pounders	

The age of the ram

In 1866, Italy, seeking control of the Venetian provinces, fought a war with the Austro-Hungarian Empire, a minor sea power with bases in the Adriatic. The Italians invaded the island of Lissa, covered by a force of 37 fighting vessels, and the Austrians, under Admiral Tegetthoff, attacked with a force of 27. Explosive shells proved ineffective, but the Austrians destroyed the Italian flagship by ramming her with their ironclads (see right).

The Battle of Lissa was the nearest thing to a full-fleet battle in the 19th century after Navarino in 1827 (see p.133) and the first to be fought in the open sea since Trafalgar. Many lessons could have been learned from it, but unfortunately they were the wrong ones – the ram was now seen as a main weapon of naval warfare. Some warships, such as the British *Polyphemus* (see left), were designed around it, and most, except those designed for high speed, were fitted with a ram in some form. The French were fully convinced of the value of the ram and put huge ones on their ships.

However, gun power and range soon increased, and no enemy ship was likely to get close enough to sink by ramming. The ram was in fact more dangerous to one's own side – in 1893, the British battleship *Camperdown* accidentally rammed and sank her flagship, the *Victoria*, with the loss of many lives. Ironically, it was later proved that a projection in the bows contributed to speed (see the *Normandie*, p.308 and pp.306–307), and most merchant ships of today are fitted with bulbous bows.

Ships of the *Warrior* type were a great advance in design, but they had their problems. Their length made them difficult to steer, and the weight of armour tended to reduce the load available for guns. A partial remedy was to armour only the most essential parts of the ship, leaving the bows and stern unprotected, and this became standard on all armoured ships. Another solution was to have fewer guns but to make them larger. This led to the central battery ship, adopted in most navies in the late 1860s after the Royal Navy's *Bellerophon* of 1865.

RAM BOW

The Royal Navy's Polyphemus, *seen here being fitted out at Chatham, England, in 1882, had a distinctive ram bow. The 3-m (10-ft) projection was designed as a secondary means of attack to her broadside torpedoes. Although this ram was successful in trials, it was never tested in action.*

BATTLE OF LISSA
This French print depicts the Battle of Lissa on 20 July 1866, in which the Austrian ironclad Erzherzog Ferdinand Maximilian *rammed and sank the Italian flagship* Re d'Italia. *Many navies later added rams to their ships.*

Several guns were fitted inside a central citadel, arranged on tracks so that they could be moved across the deck as the tactical situation demanded (see Frazer–Woolwich gun in panel, right.)

The problem of the turret

The success of the *Monitor* and her sister ships provoked a reaction among the European navies. Ericsson's vessels were very unseaworthy, and the *Monitor* herself foundered in a storm off Cape Hatteras, North Carolina, at the end of 1862 (for information about saving her wreck, see p.381). An armoured turret was heavy and, unlike the old broadside guns, it had to be mounted high in the ship for the best effect, causing stability problems. In 1867, the Royal Navy's Cowper Phipps Coles designed a masted turret ship, the *Captain* (see p.226). She was caught with all her sails spread by a gale in the Bay of Biscay in September 1870 and capsized. This ended the attempt to combine turrets and sails, and left the field clear for Coles's rival and countryman Edward J. Reed, who had developed the central battery ship. In a bold step, Reed designed the *Devastation* of 1871 with no provision for sails. He had already built several coast defence ships for steam power alone, but the *Devastation* was a fully fledged battleship, armed with four 12-in (305-mm) guns in twin turrets, and a speed of over 13 knots.

Devastation was a success and the general style was copied in other navies, but other problems appeared as the breech loader replaced the muzzle loader, and guns became larger and longer. From the 1880s, guns were carried on barbettes – armoured towers that penetrated deep into the hull and covered the magazines and ammunition supply – for the new explosives of the age made that area even more vulnerable. An armoured shield was built over the gun itself and that became known, loosely, as the turret.

The development of the cruiser

The term frigate, referring to a warship with a single deck of guns, fell into disuse by the mid-1800s because all new battleships, beginning with the *Gloire* and *Warrior*, were built in this way. A new ship emerged to fill the role previously played by frigates. Its main duties included independent cruising, and so it became known as the cruiser. It was generally, although not always, smaller than the battleship and took on the tasks of fleet reconnaissance, commerce protection and raiding, and colonial duties. Speed was important in all these duties,

but generally a heavy armament was not. The cruiser soon developed into three main classes. Large armoured ones worked closely with the fleet or dealt with large enemy raiders. One of the most innovative was the French *Dupuy de Lôme* of 1888, whose armoured protection extended to the sides as well as covering the deck: an 11-cm- (4.5-in-) thick vertical "belt" of steel ran from bow to stern. Such vessels grew in size, and the British *Leviathan* of 1901 was longer than contemporary battleships. The smallest

GUNS VERSUS ARMOUR

Despite advances in gunnery, such as the use of explosive shells, the turret battleships of the 1870s still relied on muzzle-loading guns (see right). It had long been known that a rifled gun, in which the barrel was fitted with grooves to make the shell rotate, gave much greater accuracy and range, and if the gun was of a breech-loading design this made it quite difficult to ram the shell home. The new explosive powders, such as cordite, burned more slowly, which meant that longer barrels were needed to allow full combustion as the shell passed along it, and in the 1880s guns of up to 14.2m (46ft) in length were produced. The gun turrets of the 1890s, mounted on barbettes (see below), were operated by hydraulic power by teams of highly trained men.

At the same time, the effectiveness of armour increased. By the 1880s, ships were

FRAZER–WOOLWICH GUN
This muzzle-loading rifled gun was mounted on a variant of the old-style gun carriage with gearing for running the gun out, and with rails along the deck that allowed it to be moved from one port to another.

built entirely of iron rather than clad in it, and new types of steel were developed to keep out the ever more effective shot. But, on the whole, the gunners won the race – it was rarely possible to build a ship impenetrable by the shot of the age.

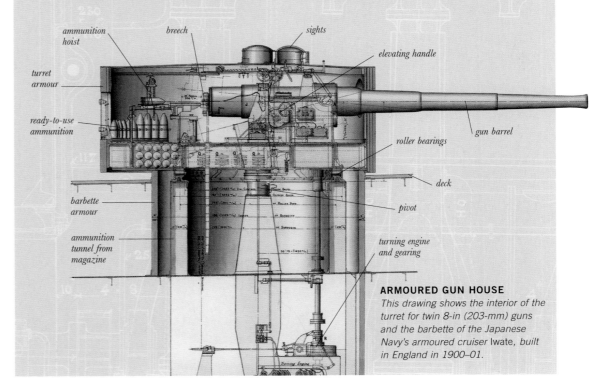

ammunition hoist

breech

sights

elevating handle

turret armour

ready-to-use ammunition

roller bearings

gun barrel

deck

barbette armour

pivot

ammunition tunnel from magazine

turning engine and gearing

ARMOURED GUN HOUSE
This drawing shows the interior of the turret for twin 8-in (203-mm) guns and the barbette of the Japanese Navy's armoured cruiser Iwate, *built in England in 1900–01.*

cruisers were not armoured and were used mainly to protect colonies. In between was another class: the protected cruiser. It had no armour as such, but its coal bunkers were arranged to give protection from shelling.

Defence against the torpedo

The invention of free-running torpedoes in the 1860s (see panel, below) was a development of great significance. These weapons could sink even large ships, and a new type of small, fast boat was created to launch them. France stood to gain more from the torpedo than her rival Britain, which had a stronger fleet, and so the French constructed a large number of swift *torpilleurs*. Britain, conversely, had more to lose.

It was imperative to find defences against the torpedo. For example, the British built huge breakwaters in harbours such as Dover on the southeast coast. Another solution was to fit battleships and cruisers with quick-firing guns for defence against fast craft. The alternative was to make vessels specifically to counter the menace of the torpedo. In 1892, the British produced the first torpedo-boat destroyers, or TBDs, the *Hornet* and the *Havock*. At 27 knots, they were faster than existing torpedo boats and were armed with both guns and torpedoes. They proved very successful and were the basis of the destroyer, one of the classic fighting ships.

The arms race

By the late 1880s, there was a lull in technological progress. Steel armour, rifled guns, the triple-expansion engine, and the rise of the torpedo had all had their effect. The period also marked the beginning of an arms race between the major powers. The British Parliament passed the Naval Defence Act in 1889, adopting the two-power standard, which meant that the Royal Navy should be larger than that of the two next-biggest naval powers combined. In future, British naval strength would depend not on the will of the British taxpayer to finance it but on what the other naval powers did.

Design of the British *Royal Sovereign* class began in 1889, with the first being launched in 1893. Using the barbette system, they had a relatively high freeboard, heavy armour plating, and a main armament of 13.5-in (343-mm) guns, with quick-firing guns for use against torpedo craft. The class formed the basis of battleship design for the next 15 years and became known retrospectively as the pre-dreadnoughts.

WRECKAGE OF THE *MAINE*
On 15 February 1898, the hull of the US battleship Maine was ripped apart by an explosion as she lay at anchor in Havana Harbour, Cuba, leaving 252 people dead or missing.

EARLY TORPEDOES

In the mid-19th century, the term torpedo usually meant a static mine. It was also applied to spar torpedoes, which projected on poles from the bows of attacking craft. In the 1880s, the Brennan torpedo was controlled by wires from the shore and used in harbour defence in Britain. The most effective self-propelled torpedo was invented in 1866 by Robert Whitehead, a British engineer working in Austria. He used a compressed-air engine to drive a propeller and a hydrostatic pressure gauge linked to horizontal rudders to keep the torpedo at the correct depth, with an explosive

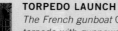

TORPEDO LAUNCH
The French gunboat Condor fires a torpedo with gunpowder from a tube above the waterline.

charge in the nose. The torpedo was a dangerous weapon, for it could sink the greatest of ships. It could be launched by compressed air from a small, fast torpedo boat, built at a fraction of the cost of the ship under attack. In 1896, the Austrian engineer Ludwig Obry added a gyroscope to keep the torpedo on a straight course, giving it a far greater range.

WHITEHEAD TORPEDO
The torpedo carried a 34kg (76lb) explosive charge of guncotton, was 4.8m (16ft) long, and had a range of over 300m (980ft).

plunger, on contact pushes inward and strikes percussion cap   *torpedo casing*   *fin*

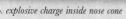
explosive charge inside nose cone   *lifting bracket*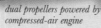
dual propellers powered by compressed-air engine

The new navies

In a war with Denmark in 1863, Prussia (a kingdom in what is now Germany) had been able to muster only three gunboats and had to rely on its Austrian allies for support. In the Franco-Prussian war of 1870–71, the Prussians were unable to prevent a French blockade of their coast, but their armies advanced and defeated the French before it had any effect. The new Germany, united under Prussian leadership in 1870, was far stronger. It became a highly industrialized country, but it was not until Kaiser Wilhelm II came to the throne in 1888 that it began to look to its navy. Admiral Tirpitz planned for a force that would be a significant factor in world affairs.

The Japanese were jolted into modernity after the Perry affair (see p.198) and other western interventions in their country. They began to develop a modern navy, mostly with ships built in Europe, and in 1894 they gained

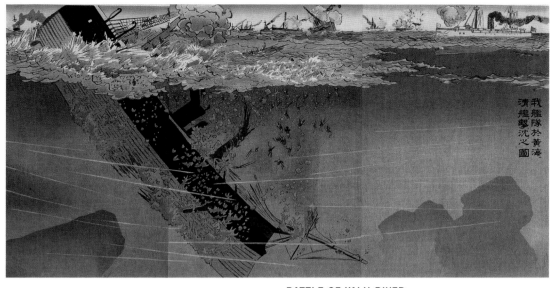

BATTLE OF YALU RIVER
This contemporary print by Japanese artist Kobayashi Kiyochika shows the devastating defeat his country's modernized navy inflicted on the old-fashioned Chinese fleet at the Battle of Yalu River on 17 September 1894.

LANDING IN CUBA
US troops land in Cuba after war was declared against Spain on 24 April 1898. Peace was arranged under the Treaty of Paris on 10 December, under which Cuba was freed from Spanish rule, Puerto Rico and Guam were ceded to the US, and the Philippines were surrendered to the US for $20 million.

in experience when they defeated the Chinese at the Battle of Yalu River, the first naval battle of the Sino-Japanese War (1894–95).

The US Navy had languished since the Civil War ended in 1865, although the country, like Germany, had become a major industrial power. As its expansion west slowed, the USA began to look to its overseas interests, and after 1886 it began to build more battleships and cruisers. The battleship *Maine* was in Havana Harbour in the Spanish colony of Cuba in February 1898 when she blew up. The cause was almost certainly spontaneous combustion of her ammunition, but the USA accused the Spanish of sabotage, and the Spanish-American War began under the slogan "Remember the *Maine*". In May 1898, three months after the explosion, the Americans attacked the Spanish fleet in Manila Bay, sinking all the ships. Two months later, they destroyed a Spanish force of four ships and two torpedo boats off Santiago, Cuba.

End of an era

Steam power, iron and steel construction, long-range guns, and underwater weapons did much to transform the major navies during the 19th century, but some factors remained as they had done for centuries. Despite the threat from underwater, the big ship remained the arbiter of naval power. The ship of the line was eventually replaced by the battleship, but the concept of an expensive, powerful ship remained. Ships were still armed largely with guns, and most of

them were arranged on the broadside, so they still exercised in line of battle as they had done since 1653 – although hardly anyone had any experience of fighting in it. Their guns were capable of long-range fire, though the means of aiming accurately over such distances had not yet been developed. They had gained enormously in firepower, defence, and mobility since the last major war in 1815, but in one respect they were weaker than in the past. The ships needed regular refuelling, so their range was shorter and they depended much more on shore bases. The British remained the main sea power, having seen off several threats by France to overtake them with new technology. But it was the new navies of Germany, Japan, and the USA that were to change the picture in the next century.

LAST OF THE OLD STEAM BATTLESHIPS
In honour of the visit of Queen Victoria to Ireland in April 1900, the Royal Navy conducted a review off Kingstown. The steam battleships that took part were soon to be replaced by a superior class of ship.

EARLY STEAM WARSHIPS

Early steam warships were adaptations of sailing designs with an engine and paddles or propellers added. At first, steam was used only in light winds as an auxiliary to sail, but by the Crimean War it was realized that only steam-powered warships could survive. The American Civil War saw the first use of ironclad warships and turret guns, and it gave rise to many improvisations. Much of the fighting was on the great rivers such as the Mississippi, and this also encouraged some strange designs, including that of the *Monitor* (opposite).

VICTORIOUS IN BATTLE
The screw frigate Kearsarge, *in the service of the Union, sank the Confederate raider* Alabama *off Cherbourg, France, in 1864.*

Pioneers

Although it was not considered suitable for a general naval battle, steam power was soon applied on the fringes of the fleet and in colonial and river warfare. During the 1820s, the British East India Company used the steamer *Diana* in Burma, but the first steamship to see real action was the *Karteria* (right), in the Greek war of independence. Built on the River Thames, she fought very hard against the Turks, claiming the capture or destruction of 24 vessels and firing 18,000 rounds of ammunition. She attracted a good deal of interest in Britain and France.

KARTERIA			
Origin Britain (for Greece)		**Date of launch** 1826	
Length Not known		**Displacement** 400 tons	
Armament 4 x 68-pounder guns			

Paddle frigates

The paddle wheel had several disadvantages in a warship: it obstructed the armament; it was vulnerable to gunfire; and it might make the ship unmanoeuvrable in rough seas. Nevertheless, the world's naval powers built them, largely to supplement more traditional ships. The French built 23 ships of the Sphinx class from 1829 to 1839. The British *Gorgon* (below) was the model for many later ships in the Royal Navy, although they tended to be larger and have more powerful engines.

GORGON			
Origin Britain		**Date of launch** 1837	
Length 54.25m (178ft)		**Displacement** 1,610 tons	
Armament 4 x 42-pounder guns, 2 x 68-pounder guns			

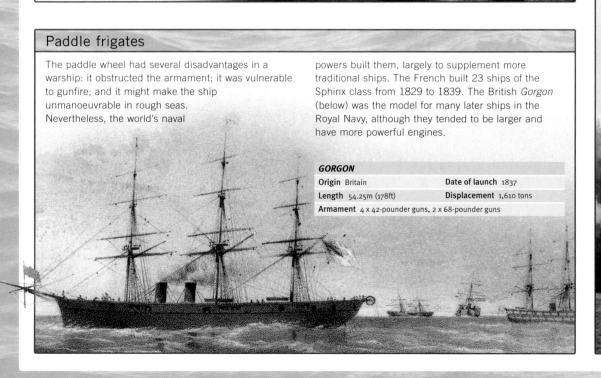

Screw corvettes and sloops

Corvettes and sloops were small ocean-going warships, smaller than frigates, and many of them were fitted with steam engines and screw propellers after the value of the screw propeller was proved in the 1840s. The corvette *Princeton* was the first American screw warship, launched in 1843 with a crew of 166. The *Hartford* served as the flagship of Admiral David Glasgow Farragut in the squadron blockading the western Gulf of Mexico for the Union forces in the American Civil War. Farragut used her during an attack on Mobile, Texas, in 1864, when he gave his famous order, "Damn the torpedoes! Full speed ahead". Another *Princeton* (below) was built later in the century to fulfil some of the role of gunboats in the European navies. She had a crew of 135 to 156.

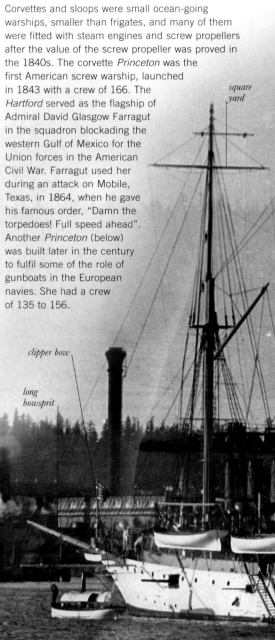

square yard

clipper bow

long bowsprit

Screw ships of the line

In a warship the screw propeller avoided the main disadvantages of the paddle wheel, although at first it was still seen as an auxiliary to sail. The *James Watt* (right) was hindered by unreliable engines.

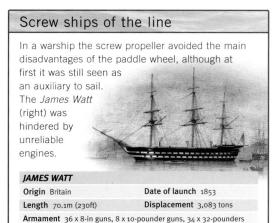

JAMES WATT

Origin Britain	**Date of launch** 1853
Length 70.1m (230ft)	**Displacement** 3,083 tons
Armament 36 x 8-in guns, 8 x 10-pounder guns, 34 x 32-pounders	

PRINCETON

Origin United States	**Date of launch** 1897
Length 62.2m (204ft)	**Tonnage** 1,000 tons
Armament 6 x 4-in guns, 4 x 6-pounder guns, 2 x 1-pounder guns	

funnel

4-in gun barrel

ship's boat hung over side

Commerce raiders

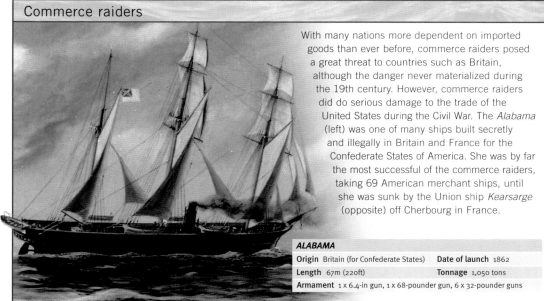

With many nations more dependent on imported goods than ever before, commerce raiders posed a great threat to countries such as Britain, although the danger never materialized during the 19th century. However, commerce raiders did do serious damage to the trade of the United States during the Civil War. The *Alabama* (left) was one of many ships built secretly and illegally in Britain and France for the Confederate States of America. She was by far the most successful of the commerce raiders, taking 69 American merchant ships, until she was sunk by the Union ship *Kearsarge* (opposite) off Cherbourg in France.

ALABAMA

Origin Britain (for Confederate States)	**Date of launch** 1862
Length 67m (220ft)	**Tonnage** 1,050 tons
Armament 1 x 6.4-in gun, 1 x 68-pounder gun, 6 x 32-pounder guns	

Ironclads

Countries on either side of the Atlantic produced very different ships protected by iron armour. The *Gloire* (right) of 1859 and Britain's *Warrior* of 1860 looked relatively conventional from the outside, while the *Monitor* (below) resembled "a cheesebox on a raft", according to naval opinion. Her low hull and turret armament were unsuitable for operations away from the shore, but she was a truly revolutionary warship.

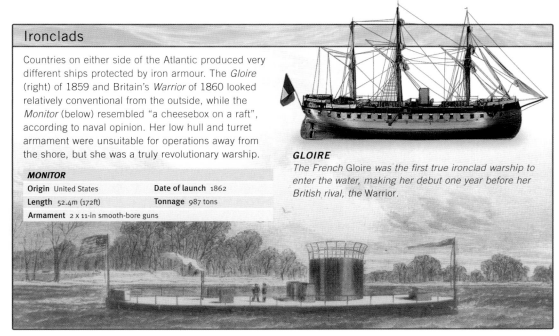

GLOIRE

The French Gloire was the first true ironclad warship to enter the water, making her debut one year before her British rival, the Warrior.

MONITOR

Origin United States	**Date of launch** 1862
Length 52.4m (172ft)	**Tonnage** 987 tons
Armament 2 x 11-in smooth-bore guns	

River gunboats

Steam power opened up the great rivers of the world to naval power. European gunboats operated on the Nile, Yangtze, and Irrawaddy, and the American Civil War was largely fought along river valleys, where industrial power prevailed. The *Cairo* (below) served for the Union on the Mississippi and Ohio rivers. She took part in a battle against Confederate gunboats in June 1862 and was sunk by a mine in December of the same year.

CAIRO

Origin United States	**Date of launch** 1862
Length 53.34m (175ft)	**Tonnage** 512 tons
Armament 3 x 8-in guns, 4 x 42-pounder guns, 6 x 32-pounder guns	

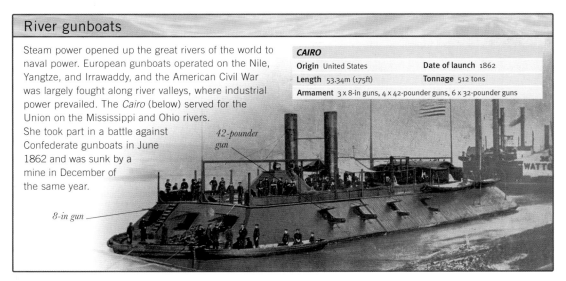

42-pounder gun

8-in gun

IRON AND STEEL WARSHIPS

In the late 19th century, the sail disappeared from major warships, although it was retained on ships in distant imperial stations where coal was in short supply. Larger guns with explosive shells and longer ranges competed with stronger armour plating. New naval powers arose, such as Germany, Japan, and the United States. Initially they followed British and French design, but soon they had ideas of their own. By the beginning of the 1900s, the warship was unrecognizable from what it had been before.

GUN BATTLE
This painting depicts the Battle of Manila, between America and Spain, in 1898, during which the Spanish Fleet was destroyed.

Masted turret ships

The invention of the turret caused a problem for ship designers: it was difficult to combine turrets with sails because both raised the ship's centre of gravity. The British ship designer Cowper Coles tried mounting the guns of *Captain* (below) very low, but this allowed little freeboard and the ship capsized in 1870.

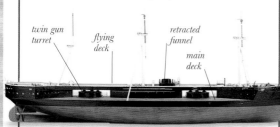

twin gun turret
flying deck
retracted funnel
main deck

CAPTAIN

Origin Britain	**Date of launch** 1869
Length 97.5m (320ft)	**Displacement** 7,767 tons
Crew 500	**Maximum speed** 15.25 knots
Armament 4 x 12-in muzzle loaders, 2 x 7-in muzzle loaders	

Mastless battleships

After the *Captain* disaster, Coles's rival Edward J. Reed designed a seagoing turret ship without sails. He was helped by the fact that engines were now vastly more efficient. The *Devastation* (below) was a success and several other ships followed its basic principles.

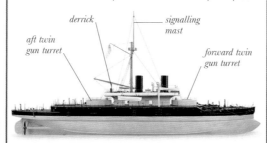

derrick
signalling mast
aft twin gun turret
forward twin gun turret

DEVASTATION

Origin Britain	**Date of launch** 1871
Length 93.5m (307ft)	**Displacement** 9,330 tons
Crew 358	**Maximum speed** 13.8 knots
Armament 4 x 12-in muzzle loaders	

Circular ships

Admiral Popov of the Russian Navy believed that a circular hull would be much more stable and give plenty of room to operate guns, provided they operated in the sheltered waters of the Black Sea. Such ships were unsuccessful and became curiosities.

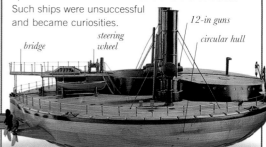

12-in guns
steering wheel
circular hull
bridge

NOVGOROD

Origin Russia	**Date of launch** 1875
Length 36.5m (120ft)	**Displacement** 3,550 tons
Crew 203	**Maximum speed** 8 knots
Armament 2 x 12-in guns, 8 x 3.4-in, 2 x 1-pounders, 1 spar torpedo	

Torpedo boats

After the Whitehead torpedo was invented in 1866, navies began to design small, fast boats from which to launch it. The torpedoes could be dropped over the sides or fired from tubes in the bows. The first British torpedo boat, the *Lightning* (below), was based on steam yachts and designed by John Thornycroft.

The French built large numbers of torpedo boats. Initially they were for local defence, but from the 1880s they began to build seagoing versions.

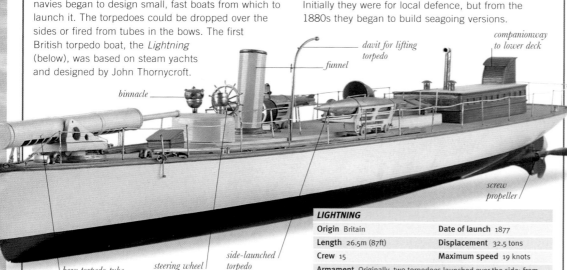

binnacle
funnel
davit for lifting torpedo
companionway to lower deck
bow torpedo tube
steering wheel
side-launched torpedo
screw propeller

LIGHTNING

Origin Britain	**Date of launch** 1877
Length 26.5m (87ft)	**Displacement** 32.5 tons
Crew 15	**Maximum speed** 19 knots
Armament Originally, two torpedoes launched over the side; from 1879, bow-mounted torpedo tube	

Protected cruisers

The protected cruiser was smaller than the armoured cruiser. It often had light armour plating, but its main defence was that its coal bunkers were arranged to absorb enemy shot. *Olympia* (below), whose four main guns were in twin armoured turrets, served as Admiral Dewey's flagship at the Battle of Manila Bay in 1898.

OLYMPIA

Origin United States	**Date of launch** 1892
Length 104.8m (344ft)	**Displacement** 5,865 tons
Crew 447	**Maximum speed** 20 knots
Armament 4 x 18-in guns, 10 x 5-in guns, 14 x 6-pounder guns, 6 x 1-pounder guns, 6 x 18-in torpedo tubes	

Gunboats

Mastless steel ships were universal in Europe by the 1880s, mostly for coastal defence, but the British and other colonial powers continued to use sails in their gunboats, which were used to police colonial waters.

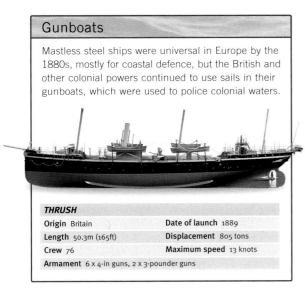

THRUSH

Origin	Britain	Date of launch	1889
Length	50.3m (165ft)	Displacement	805 tons
Crew	76	Maximum speed	13 knots
Armament	6 x 4-in guns, 2 x 3-pounder guns		

Destroyers

In 1892, the British began to build torpedo-boat destroyers that were twice the size of those of their opponents. Other navies soon took up the destroyer, as it became known. The Germans still called theirs torpedo boats, and they were given numbers rather than names. The 12 ships of the S-90 class were strong and seaworthy but slower than some rivals.

S-90

Origin	Germany	Date of launch	1898
Length	63m (206ft 10in)	Displacement	388 tons
Crew	57 to 61	Maximum speed	26.5 knots
Armament	3 x 50-mm guns, 3 x 450-mm torpedo tubes		

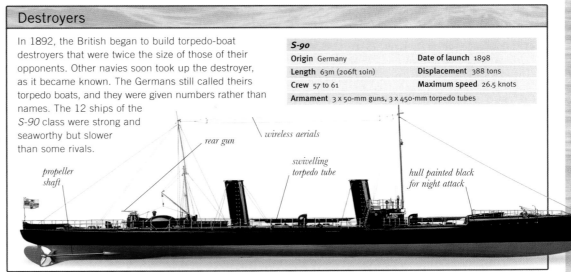

rear gun

wireless aerials

propeller shaft

swivelling torpedo tube

hull painted black for night attack

Armoured cruisers

The armoured cruiser began with the *Gloire* and the *Warrior* and also developed from the old idea of the frigate – a ship that would carry out reconnaissance for the main fleet, escort convoys, and raid enemy shipping. The fully armoured cruiser was designed to take on enemy ships in battle, and some were as big as contemporary battleships. *Leviathan* (right) was one of four *Drake*-class ships, which were among the fastest ships in the world.

LEVIATHAN

Origin	Britain	Date of launch	1901
Length	162.6m (533ft 6 in)	Displacement	14,150 tons
Crew	900	Maximum speed	23 knots
Armament	2 x 9.2-in guns, 16 x 6-in guns, 14 x 12-pounder guns, 3 x 3-pounder guns, 2 x 18-in torpedo tubes		

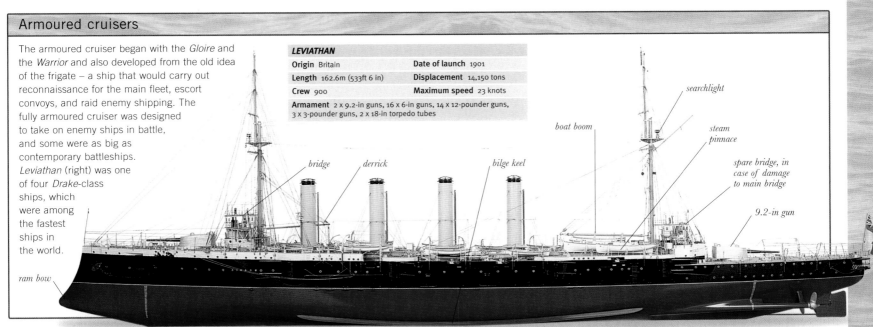

searchlight

boat boom

steam pinnace

spare bridge, in case of damage to main bridge

9.2-in gun

bridge

derrick

bilge keel

ram bow

Battleships

The late 19th century saw a rise in naval competition and the evolution of ships known retrospectively as the pre-dreadnoughts. Britain's *Royal Sovereign*-class ships were equipped with various sizes of gun.

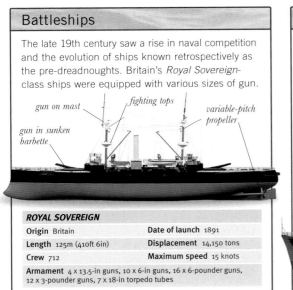

gun on mast

fighting tops

variable-pitch propeller

gun in sunken barbette

ROYAL SOVEREIGN

Origin	Britain	Date of launch	1891
Length	125m (410ft 6in)	Displacement	14,150 tons
Crew	712	Maximum speed	15 knots
Armament	4 x 13.5-in guns, 10 x 6-in guns, 16 x 6-pounder guns, 12 x 3-pounder guns, 7 x 18-in torpedo tubes		

Light cruisers

The light cruiser was unarmoured and generally smaller, cheaper, and faster than other classes. Some were designed to lead destroyer flotillas and some for reconnaissance, and soon they became the most common cruiser type. The *Regensburg* (below) served with the scouting group of the High Seas Fleet in the First World War.

REGENSBURG

Origin	Germany	Date of launch	1914
Length	112.3m (368ft 5in)	Displacement	4,912 tons
Crew	385	Maximum speed	20 knots
Armament	12 x 4.1-in guns, 2 x 19.7-in torpedo tubes, 120 mines		

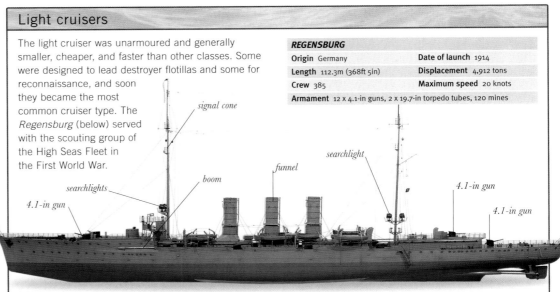

signal cone

searchlight

4.1-in gun

funnel

searchlights

boom

4.1-in gun

4.1-in gun

4.1-in gun

DECK OF THE *PARMA*

Sailing vessels struggled on despite the advent of steam power. This photograph shows the barque Parma in 1933. Despite its gradual decline in trade, sail found a new outlet, as recreational boating increased in popularity during the 19th century.

THE LAST DAYS OF SAIL

THE AGE OF SAIL did not end with the invention of the steam engine. Sailing ships actually became more numerous for many decades after the first steamers ventured onto the oceans. The design of the great clippers was inspired by competition with steam. The latest technology, including iron and steel rigging, was applied in the construction of these vessels, which took the sailing ship to the peak of its performance. The great clipper races, between ships such as the *Cutty Sark* and *Thermopylae*, captured the public imagination and imbued sailing with a romantic image. The late 19th century saw the emergence of huge steel barques, which plied long-distance trades into the 20th century. Sail also survived in the fishing industry. Even in Europe and the USA, where technological progress was fastest, individual fishermen did not often have the necessary capital to invest in new innovations, and many continued to work onboard sailing craft until the 1930s. Meanwhile, sailing for pleasure became increasingly popular, fostered by rising wealth, increased leisure time for the well-off, and rivalry between rich owners. This led to the instigation of organized yacht clubs and races. The sport's appeal widened still further with the advent of smaller vessels, which were built for enthusiastic amateurs of more moderate means.

TRIPLE BLOCK FOR RIGGING

> 66 There is no greater fallacy than to suppose that ships can be navigated on long voyages without masts or sails. 99
>
> **GEORGE NARES**, Royal Navy, **1860**

KEY EVENTS

1812 PRIDE OF BALTIMORE The Baltimore clipper schooner *Chasseur* is launched. One of the most successful craft of her kind, she captures 18 enemy ships in the War of 1812.

1845 *RAINBOW* LAUNCHED The New York-built ship *Rainbow* makes her maiden voyage. She is acknowledged as the first "true" clipper.

1848 GOLD STRUCK Gold is discovered in California and motivates the construction of fast clipper ships. Three years later, gold is found in Australia, prompting another rush, in which many fast sailing ships voyage to the continent.

1851 RECORD BREAKER *Flying Cloud*, an extreme clipper designed by Donald McKay, sails from New York to San Francisco in a record 89 days, 21 hours.

1872 CLIPPER CONTEST The tea clippers *Cutty Sark* and *Thermopylae* race from Shanghai to London. *Thermopylae* wins the race after *Cutty Sark* loses her rudder.

SAIL IN THE AGE OF STEAM

THE 19TH-CENTURY BOOM IN GLOBAL TRADE MEANT THAT, DESPITE THE ARRIVAL OF STEAM POWER, THERE WERE MORE MERCHANT SAILING SHIPS BY THE 1880S THAN EVER BEFORE.

The sailing ship of the 19th century operated on the same principles as its predecessors, although it benefited from new technology. In the 1780s, the English hydrographer Joseph Huddart invented a method of spinning rope that doubled its strength, an obvious advantage when applied to the rigging of a sailing ship. However, during the 1850s the Crimean War cut off supplies of Russian hemp, which was used to make the highest-quality rope. As a result, wire, which was already used in some industries, began to replace traditional rope in the standing rigging of sailing ships. A hemp rope with a circumference of 15cm (6in) has a breaking strain of 12 tons, but a wire rope of the same diameter breaks at 90 tons, a huge improvement to the resilience of a ship's rigging. This advance gave ship designers the option to use either thinner wire rope with the sail configurations that already existed or wire rope of a similar dimension to the traditional rope but supporting a larger sail area. It is possible that such advances in rigging inspired designers to produce the extreme ship designs that appeared in the 1850s (see p.235).

Iron masts were first used on the British warship *Phaeton* in 1827. They eventually became common on merchant ships, particularly in areas, such as Britain, where it was becoming difficult to find trees that were large enough to build masts for the increasing size of ships. A hollow mast constructed of iron or steel offered greater strength, with less topweight.

The 19th century also witnessed the development of iron-hulled sailing ships. However, it was impossible to apply copper sheathing (see p.125) to them because the two metals reacted with each other, weakening the iron. British shipbuilders therefore developed a composite construction, which involved fitting wooden planks on an iron frame. The first ship constructed in this manner was the *Excelsior*, which was built at Liverpool in 1850. The Americans, and some European nations, maintained better timber supplies and remained faithful to the wooden ship for much longer. The construction of wooden ships reached its peak in the United States in 1891, at 144,000 tons.

As the 19th century progressed, competition from steam-powered ships and rising labour costs obliged shipowners to seek out labour-saving devices. One of the most time-consuming manual tasks was reefing, which involved reducing the sail area in heavy winds to ensure greater control of a ship. Self-reefing devices were tried, in which the sail was rolled up using lines that were attached to it, much like a window blind. However, the long-term solution was to divide sails into

FULL SAIL AHEAD
Entitled the Romance of Sail, *this painting by US artist Frank Vining Smith (1879–1967) captures the beauty of the great clipper ship* Cutty Sark. *Such vessels fought back against steam throughout the 19th century, proving their worth on many trade routes.*

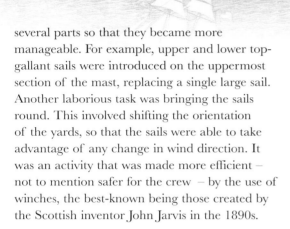

CHESAPEAKE BAY
Schooner-rigged sailing craft were one of the most prevalent sailing vessels along the eastern seaboard of the United States in the 18th and 19th centuries. An abundance of these ships sail around Fort Monroe, in Chesapeake Bay in this mid-19th-century lithograph.

several parts so that they became more manageable. For example, upper and lower topgallant sails were introduced on the uppermost section of the mast, replacing a single large sail. Another laborious task was bringing the sails round. This involved shifting the orientation of the yards, so that the sails were able to take advantage of any change in wind direction. It was an activity that was made more efficient – not to mention safer for the crew – by the use of winches, the best-known being those created by the Scottish inventor John Jarvis in the 1890s.

Baltimore clippers

Despite the onset of steam-powered craft in the 19th century, sailing ships, particularly those that provided fast passages, maintained a hold in certain trades. During the 18th century, most maritime nations developed some form of fast craft, usually for use as privateers or blockade runners in wartime. These vessels often evolved from smuggling or fishing craft and were often fore-and-aft rigged. The British favoured the single-masted cutter, which used a gaff mainsail and triangular jib sails or staysails attached to a bowsprit. Another type of fast vessel was the Bermuda sloop, which originated as a trading vessel around the Caribbean islands. These craft carried a distinctive triangular mainsail, and their influence quickly spread to Europe and America. The French developed the three-masted craft known as the *chasse marée*, which means "chase the tide". It was rigged with four-sided lugsails, which were attached to the mast by means of a diagonal spar. However, it was a vessel that developed along the eastern seaboard of the United States that set the standard for fast sailing craft.

Baltimore clippers were developed in Chesapeake Bay during the late 18th century. Influenced by the Bermuda sloop, these vessels were in fact a type of schooner (see p.242),

rather than "true" clippers, which developed later. Baltimore clippers were usually fore-and-aft rigged with gaffsails on two raked masts, although smaller square sails were sometimes added at the tops. The craft had a great deal of sail area in relation to a relatively small, narrow hull. The stern of a Baltimore clipper was flat and much deeper than its bows. The stem was very sharply angled. At first, they were used as pilot schooners for ships unfamiliar with local waters. However, the Baltimore clippers' finest hour came during the War of 1812 (see p.132), when they proved to be extremely successful privateers. The most renowned of these ships was the *Chasseur*, which earned the nickname Pride of Baltimore, as she captured 18 enemy British ships. When the war ended in 1815, Baltimore

BALTIMORE'S PRIDE
A reconstruction of an early 19th-century Baltimore clipper, Pride of Baltimore II was built in 1988 to replace an earlier replica that was lost at sea. The sleek schooner carries four cannons, which are used to salute ports that she visits, and sails with a crew of 12.

UNRIGGED MODEL OF *SERINGAPATAM*

One of the first Blackwall frigates was the Seringapatam, which was constructed in 1837. This type of ship was in use until the 1870s on routes to India and the Far East.

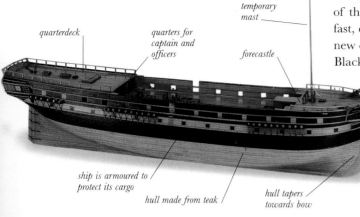

temporary mast

quarterdeck

quarters for captain and officers

forecastle

ship is armoured to protect its cargo

hull made from teak

hull tapers towards bow

The first clipper ships

The term clipper has no precise definition, although it is usually applied to the sharp-bowed, square-rigged ships that evolved in the mid-19th century, culminating in the long, narrow extreme clippers (see p.235). However, there were some significant developments in the 1830s, which influenced later ships. The Baltimore-built *Ann McKim* was launched in 1832 and was certainly a forerunner of the clipper. The vessel's hull resembled that of a Baltimore clipper, but she was much longer and square-rigged. The *Ann McKim* had a successful 20-year career as a merchant ship, sailing on trade routes to South America and China, and developed a reputation as one of the fastest sailing vessels of her time.

On the other side of the Atlantic, British shipowners were also developing fast merchant vessels. In 1833, the British East India Company's monopoly came to an end, which

clippers were largely employed in the slave trade between Africa and the plantations of the Caribbean, as well as to carry opium to China.

meant that there was increased competition on some of the most important trading routes to the East. Britain's primary trading rival was the United States, which was already ahead of the game when it came to developing fast, efficient merchant craft. As a result, a new class of vessel was designed called the Blackwall frigate. The vessels were intended to replace the East Indiamen (see p.147), which they resembled in length and beam. However, the Blackwall frigate had a narrower hull and only a single row of windows at the stern. At the same time, shipbuilders in Aberdeen, Scotland, began to develop a much faster type of coastal craft to compete with steam ships. The result was the schooner *Scottish Maid*, which was built by Alexander Hall for the packet service between Aberdeen and London. The ship's unique bow shape, which became known as the Aberdeen bow, had a sharp cutwater (the angle of the curved timber at its prow, known as the stem). *Scottish Maid* was able to complete the passage between Aberdeen and the mouth of the Thames in as little as 33 hours. Similar vessels were subsequently manufactured for use on both local and international routes.

In 1843, the American shipbuilder John W. Griffiths, who had been impressed by the *Ann McKim*, gave a series of lectures in New York City outlining a different type of hull shape for

the construction of large, fast sailing ships. His theories formed the basis for the construction of the *Rainbow*, launched in 1845 and generally acknowledged as the first "true" clipper. What made *Rainbow*, and her sister ship, *Sea Witch* (see below), so distinctive was the unusually steep rake at the bow. Both ships proved to be highly efficient on trade routes to and from China. The British responded by adopting the Aberdeen bow for their own routes to China. The *Bon Accord* was a square-rigged ship, constructed on the principles of the *Scottish Maid*, although she never made fast passages from the Far East.

ABERDEEN BOW

Thermopylae, *which became one of the most celebrated tea clippers of the 19th century (see p.237), was constructed with a sharp Aberdeen bow. This 20th-century watercolour was painted by Cornelis de Ries.*

SEA WITCH

This "true" clipper was launched in 1847. From her maiden voyage, Sea Witch was a phenomenally successful ship and broke a succession of records. In 1849, she sailed from China to New York in just 74 days. This 19th-century image of the clipper was painted by an anonymous Chinese artist.

The rush for gold

In January 1848, gold was found in California, shortly before the sparsely populated territory was formally annexed by the United States after its war with Mexico. It was almost a year before the news reached the inhabitants of the east coast of America and beyond, but when it did it created the first of the 19th century's great gold rushes, which peaked in 1849.

The overland route across the United States was slow and gruelling, as the railroad had yet to extend across the continent. As a result, many prospectors preferred to travel by sailing ship, despite the fact that the route from New York to San Francisco was 20,000km (13,000 miles) long and involved negotiating the hazardous waters around Cape Horn. It was boom time in California. In 1847–48, San Francisco harbour had welcomed only 13 visiting ships. The following year, almost 800 vessels headed for the Pacific seaboard, nearly all of the them originating from the

SANDRIDGE PIER, MELBOURNE
The Australian city of Melbourne was built on profits from the gold rush. This photograph shows the packed wharves and sailing ships around one of the port's piers, in about 1870.

east coast of America. Initially, the trip to California took six months, but the gold rush had created a demand for ever-faster sailing ships. In July 1849, the *Sea Witch* (see p.233) completed the journey from New York to San Francisco in 97 days. The clipper *Celestial*, constructed in New York in 1850, was the first ship to be built specifically for the gold rush and was followed by many other fast sailing ships.

In February 1851, gold was found in Australia. This time prospectors had no choice but to travel by sea, although the route around

CLIPPER CARDS
With so many fast clipper ships competing to transport prospectors to wealth in Australia and California, vessels were promoted using colourful cards handed out at docks and warehouses.

CITY OF GOLD
San Francisco was transformed by the California gold rush. The British ship Vicar of Bray *arrived at the port in November 1849. Like many other ships that reached San Francisco that year, she was deserted by a crew hungry for gold.*

ROUNDING CAPE HORN

The Polish-born author Joseph Conrad travelled as a crew member on many sailing ships. In the *Nigger of Narcissus*, he described the treacherous passage around Cape Horn:

It was a bad winter off the Cape that year. The relieved helmsmen came off flapping their arms, or ran stamping hard and blowing into swollen, red fingers. The watch on deck dodged the sting of cold sprays, or, crouching in sheltered corners, watched dismally the high and merciless seas boarding the ship time after time in unappeasable fury. Water tumbled in cataracts over the forecastle doors. You had to dash through a waterfall to get into your damp bed. The men turned in wet and turned out stiff to face the redeeming and ruthless exactions of their glorious and obscure fate.

JOSEPH CONRAD, **1897**

CLASSIC CLIPPER
Designed by Donald McKay (see panel, below), Flying Cloud was one of the fastest clippers ever built. On the vessel's first voyage, in 1851, she completed a voyage from New York to San Francisco in 89 days, 21 hours. Three years later, she knocked another 13 hours off the time.

CENTENARY MEDAL
This American medal was cast in 1951 to commemorate the centenary of the record-breaking voyage of Flying Cloud.

the Cape of Good Hope was less hazardous than that around Cape Horn, at the tip of South America. The ships that plied this route were primarily British. As with the journey to California, the prospectors did not care much about conditions onboard; their priority was a fast passage to potential wealth. One of the fastest journeys on the route was that of the iron-hulled clipper *Three Bells*, which made the passage from Glasgow to Adelaide, South Australia, in 99 days in 1851.

Clipper races

For a short period in the 1850s, ships known as extreme clippers were built. These vessels had even sharper bows (which meant that they sacrificed cargo space) and a greater sail area than their predecessors. The ships constructed by the American shipbuilder Donald McKay (see panel, right) probably represent the pinnacle of clipper construction. His *Sovereign of the Seas*,

named after King Charles I's great ship of 1637 (see p.105), was launched in 1852 and was described by a Boston journalist as "the longest, sharpest, most beautiful merchant ship in the world". *Sovereign of the Seas* could sail 640km (400 miles) in a day, but required a huge crew of more than 100 men. McKay's *Great Republic*, launched in 1853, was the largest ship ever built from wood. One of several he constructed to ship emigrants to Australia from Britain (although she never made that voyage), the ship had four masts and a main yard 36m (120ft) long.

Despite such radical advances in clipper construction, hull shape and rigging alone were not enough to produce speed. Much depended on the skill and attitude of the captain, and the

DONALD MCKAY

Born in Nova Scotia, Donald McKay (1810–80) built many of the 19th century's most successful clipper ships. At the age of 16, he was apprenticed to a New York shipbuilder, and in 1840 he moved to Boston, where he constructed some extremely fast vessels. Among these was the *James Baines*, which circumnavigated the world in just 134 days, a record for the time. However, by 1860 McKay realized that the era of the clipper was coming to an end and he began to advocate the use of steamships.

ON THE ROCKS
The three-masted steel cargo ship Guvnor struck the coast of Cornwall during heavy fog in 1912. She was carrying a cargo of nitrates from South America. The cargo was lost but the crew escaped unharmed.

SAILING DOWN UNDER

The sailing ship *Otago* left from the River Clyde for New Zealand on 24 January 1884, with 361 passengers. One passenger described the appalling overcrowding and conditions onboard.

> *My wife, a son turned 11 years, a daughter turned 10 years, and myself were crammed into one of these bunks – the beds being wet through, and utterly unfit for any human being to sleep on. Consequent on damp beds, many of the passengers had to sleep in their clothes for two, three, and, in some cases, even five weeks.*

PASSENGER ON THE *OTAGO*, 1884

ability of his crew. Some captains became famous as "drivers", who strained every nerve and pushed both ship and crew to their limits to achieve a fast passage. During the 1860s, American maritime trade was almost destroyed by the American Civil War, and hardly any new sailing cargo ships were built in the United States. However, the British continued to manufacture wooden clipper ships until the 1870s, particularly to serve in the tea trade. Apart from the prestige

of running a fast ship, there was real economic value in getting the first – and freshest – batch of a year's tea crop to Europe, as it commanded the highest prices. Races between individual tea clippers became legendary, with a prize given for the fastest ship to return to London from China each year. These culminated in the rivalry between the clippers *Thermopylae* and *Cutty Sark*. *Thermopylae*, an Aberdeen-built ship, reached Australia from London in 63 days on her maiden voyage in 1868, a record that was never bettered by another sailing vessel. The *Cutty Sark* was built in the following year, with the intention of challenging the *Thermopylae*. The closest race came in 1872, when the two ships loaded and left Shanghai on the same day. The *Cutty Sark* took the lead, gaining about 640km (400 miles), but disaster struck when she lost her rudder, giving *Thermopylae* the opportunity to win the race. But, in a sense, both ships arrived too late, at least for the tea trade. The Suez Canal (see panel, p.190) had opened in 1869 and gave a great advantage to the faster steam-powered ships on trade routes to the Far East.

Steel and sail

However, there was still life in the sailing cargo ship. Many tea clippers transferred to the Australian wool trade during the 1880s. The same decade saw the development of steel sailing ships. These were usually barque-rigged, which meant that square sails were set on each of the masts, except the aftermost, which was fore-and-aft rigged. Although they did not have the elegant profile of the

TIME FOR TEA
A tea cargo is unloaded from the Loudoun Castle *(left)*, the fastest ship on the China tea route in 1877. The tea was packed in wooden chests for the voyage *(below)*.

clipper ships, steel ships could be constructed on a much larger scale than wooden craft, which allowed them to compete with tramp steamers (see p.204) on cargo size, although not on speed. Such vessels transported cargoes including Australian grain and Chilean nitrate, both of which involved a journey around Cape Horn, through rough seas that a sailing vessel could still cope with better than a steamship.

Scotland's shipyards particularly profited from the construction of steel sailing ships. Among the ships built there were the *France*, the first barque to carry five masts, which was built in 1890 for the French firm of A.D.Bordes. The *Maria Rickmers*, which was built for the Bremerhaven firm Rickmers, followed in 1891, although it was lost at sea in 1892. The Laeisz Line, which was based in the port of Hamburg, built similar ships in Germany, culminating in the massive *Preussen*, completed in 1902.

CHINA CLIPPER
The tea clipper Cutty Sark *was built in Scotland in 1869. She was initially used for the China tea trade but was converted for use in the wool trade. The* Cutty Sark *is the only tea clipper to have survived intact and is preserved at Greenwich, London.*

backstay supports mainmast

mainmast

mizzen mast

wooden upper mast

foremast

steel wire stays

lower mast made of iron

bowsprit made of iron

main shrouds

deck made of teak

sharp bows built for speed

wooden hull constructed over iron frame

FURLING A SAIL
The three-masted Canadian barque Garthsnaid was launched in 1892. This photograph, taken in 1920, shows just how perilous life onboard a large sailing ship was. Four of the crew members have climbed the foremast to furl a sail in heavy seas off Chile.

The *Preussen* weighed more than 5,000 tons and was the largest vessel ever to set sail without the aid of engines. There were more than 100 sailing ships of over 1,000 tons operating from Hamburg by the early 20th century, many of which carried Chilean guano for the chemical industry.

Throughout the 19th century, the rigging of sailing ships evolved (see panel, right). Shipbuilders on the northeast coast of America continued to develop the fore-and-aft schooner rig, applying it to ever-larger ships. The three-masted rig had been standard on schooners plying coastal trades since the 18th century. However, by the 1880s, the four-masted rig became common, followed by five- and six-masted vessels. The climax came with the seven-masted *Thomas W. Lawson*, a schooner built for the coal trade in 1902. Each of her masts was nearly 60m (200ft) high. Although she was 120m (395ft) long and even bigger than the *Preussen*, she needed a crew of only 16 men, as many of the vessel's winches and its steering apparatus were powered by steam. The schooner was one of only three such American vessels to be constructed from steel.

In the last decades of the 19th century, the Americans built large, wooden-hulled, square-rigged ships that followed the tradition of Donald McKay. They were called Down Easters, as they were constructed in Maine, which was east of the major east-coast ports

SAILING RIGS

During the 18th century, most ocean-going vessels were ship-rigged, which meant that they had at least three masts, all carrying square sails. In the 19th century, new sail configurations developed, which combined square and fore-and-aft arrangements. The barque rig was one formation that became increasingly popular: square sails were carried all masts, except the aftermost. The three-masted barquentine carried square sails on the foremost mast, and fore-and-aft sails on the other two. There were benefits of using fore-and-aft sails, as they required less labour, had lighter spars, and created less drag against the wind. Schooners were primarily fore-and-aft rigged, although some carried square topsails.

MODEL OF *WENDUR*
The four-masted ship Wendur *was launched in Scotland in 1884. It was square-rigged on all masts, with jib sails attached to the bowsprit and a spanker hoisted on the aftermost mast.*

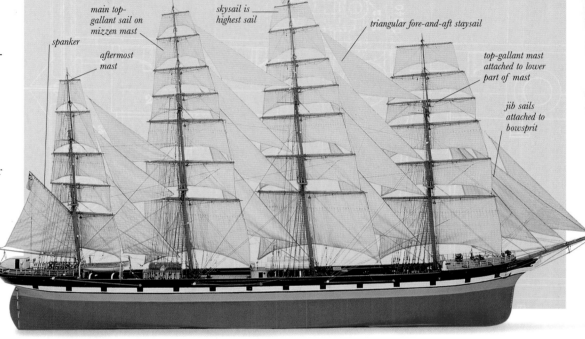

main top-gallant sail on mizzen mast

skysail is highest sail

spanker

aftermost mast

triangular fore-and-aft staysail

top-gallant mast attached to lower part of mast

jib sails attached to bowsprit

of the United States. They mostly operated on grain trade routes between California, the east coast of America, and Europe.

The sailing ship continued to be used on merchant trade routes in the early 20th century, but it was badly affected by the First World War, as it presented an easy target for U-boats. The opening of the Panama Canal (see p.276), which allowed steam ships a manageable passage to the Pacific, also cut the necessity for sailing vessels. However, some ships managed to survive into the 1920s and 1930s. The most successful operator of sailing merchant ships during this period was a Finn, Gustav Erikson. A native of the maritime Aåland Islands, Erikson's shipping company became particularly successful after the First World War, when he was able to purchase many classic sailing ships very cheaply, some of which had already had lengthy careers at sea. Among the ships he ran were the four-masted barque *Lawhill*, the *Pommern*, which had previously been registered to the Laeisz Line, and the huge barque *Moshulu*. By 1939, sailing vessels had all but ceased to exist on transcontinental trade routes. However, the sailing ship survived a little longer in coastal and inshore trades.

HIGH IN THE SKY
The Finnish barque Fahrwohl *was built in Scotland in 1892. Her career as a carrier of nitrates, timber, and grain from South America to Europe lasted more than three decades. This photograph of some of the crew sitting on one of the yards was taken in 1910.*

BUILDING A SCHOONER
The vast size of the four-masted schooner Rachel W.
Stevens *is evident in this picture of the ship being
constructed in Maine, USA. Huge baulks of timber are being
laid along the length of the ship to strengthen the keel.*

Coastal sailing craft

During the First World War, the British
maritime author Alan Moore served as a ship's
surgeon in the North Sea, Mediterranean, and
Red Sea. He used his leisure time to record the
types of local sailing craft he saw, both in their
native waters and on their travels in the wider
world. Among many other examples, he noted
a Turkish single-masted craft called a *tchektima*,
which carried a huge spritsail; a traditional
Mediterranean *polacca* (also known as a *polacre*),
which had three masts, combining lateen and
square sails; ships displaying lateen sails off
Portugal and Gibraltar; and a single-masted
lateen-rigged boat at Jeddah in the Middle East.
However, Moore recognized that sail was only
just surviving among coastal merchant craft and
fishing boats, usually in areas that were least
affected by the war and by the advent of
modern technology. Although traditional hull
shapes might well survive, the addition of a
rudimentary engine reduced the need for sails,
which would render the craft extinct, unless
efforts were made to record and preserve them.
This is illustrated by the fate of the gabbart,
which was the local sailing craft of the
River Clyde, Scotland. These
vessels disappeared in the 19th
century, to be replaced
by the ubiquitous
steam craft known
as Clyde puffers,
and it is difficult to
reconstruct what

they looked like. As Moore wrote in 1925, "The
end will not be sudden. Here and there, in little
lonely havens about the coasts of a few primitive
lands, the white sea wings will linger awhile, but
not for long; the old things
are going from us. These
are the last days."

*mast can be lowered
when passing under
bridges*

*triangular jib
sails attached
to bowsprit*

*diagonal
sprit*

*mizzen sail
attached to
rudder*

*four-sided
fore-and-aft
sail*

THAMES BARGE
*Traditional flat-bottomed
sailing barges operated on
the River Thames well into the
20th century. Their hull shape
allowed them to load and unload
their cargo on beaches.*

bowsprit

SCHOONERS

A schooner has at least two fore-and-aft rigged masts. This type of vessel evolved in Dutch waters in the 17th century, but it later appeared in North America. Schooner rig was ideal for a medium-sized vessel that sailed close to the wind. It enabled sailing ships to compete with steamships, and it became common for trading ships in Europe and America. Later, the schooner was used as a basis for racing yachts, and the name caught the public imagination.

RACING TO GLORY
Pictures such as this, showing the Americas Cup of 1875, gave schooners a popular image of speed, although most were used as working vessels.

Dutch schooners

Although the term schooner was not coined until the 18th century, some Dutch paintings of the 17th century, such as this one, show small, two-masted, fore-and-aft rigged vessels of the schooner type.

EARLY DUTCH SCHOONER

Origin Netherlands	**Date of launch** c.1620
Length Not known	
Tonnage Not known	

Baltimore clippers

European shipbuilders of the 18th century were generally conservative and saw no need for speed, but the Americans were different. The citizens of Baltimore, Maryland, built the first "clippers" for use as pilot boats, smugglers, privateers, and slavers, but they were not the direct predecessors of their namesakes, the clipper ships. The original Pride of Baltimore was the nickname of the *Chasseur*, a privateer that fought the British in the War of 1812. An accurate replica (right) was built in 1988.

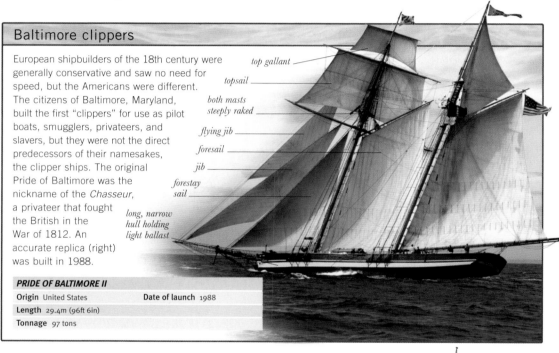

top gallant
topsail
both masts steeply raked
flying jib
foresail
jib
forestay sail
long, narrow hull holding light ballast

PRIDE OF BALTIMORE II

Origin United States	**Date of launch** 1988
Length 29.4m (96ft 6in)	
Tonnage 97 tons	

Slave ships

The fast and nimble schooner, with a low, streamlined hull and large sails, proved ideal for the illicit slave trade after its abolition. Despite its speed, the *Dos Amigos* (below) of Baltimore, Maryland was captured by the Royal Navy off the African coast in 1831.

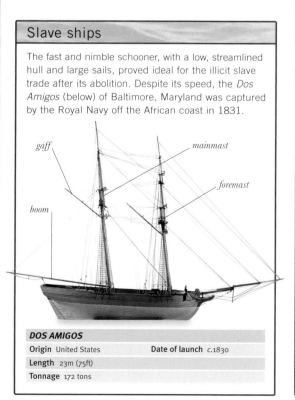

gaff
mainmast
foremast
boom

DOS AMIGOS

Origin United States	**Date of launch** c.1830
Length 23m (75ft)	
Tonnage 172 tons	

Two-masted schooners

The two-masted schooner became the most common in British waters, especially from the 1870s onwards. These boats usually had two topsails on the foremast that could be set when sailing before the wind, and this led to them becoming known as topsail schooners. They had small crews of four or five men, who needed winches to do the heavy work. They operated as far afield as Newfoundland to bring back cod, and they carried coal to many of the smaller ports. The *Victoria* (right) was a typical early two-masted schooner, built in Cornwall, Britain. Later versions had shallower, less rounded hulls.

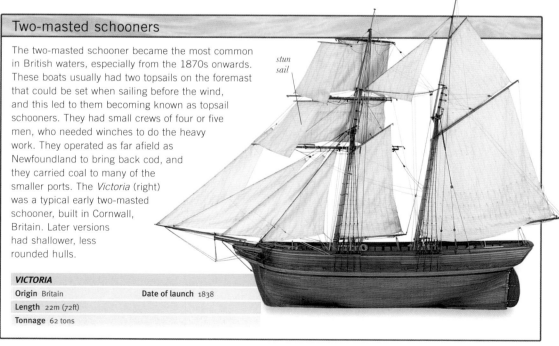

stun sail

VICTORIA

Origin Britain	**Date of launch** 1838
Length 22m (72ft)	
Tonnage 62 tons	

Three-masted schooners

M.A. JAMES

Origin Britain	**Date of launch** 1906
Length 27.25m (89ft 6in)	
Tonnage 97 tons	

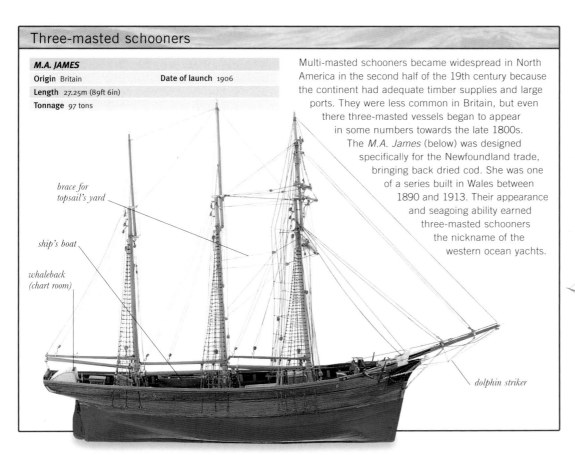

brace for topsail's yard

ship's boat

whaleback (chart room)

dolphin striker

Multi-masted schooners became widespread in North America in the second half of the 19th century because the continent had adequate timber supplies and large ports. They were less common in Britain, but even there three-masted vessels began to appear in some numbers towards the late 1800s. The *M.A. James* (below) was designed specifically for the Newfoundland trade, bringing back dried cod. She was one of a series built in Wales between 1890 and 1913. Their appearance and seagoing ability earned three-masted schooners the nickname of the western ocean yachts.

Four-masted schooners

Unlike the British, the New Englanders had wide harbours and good supplies of timber, and favoured schooners with three or more masts. Insurance restrictions on seagoing wooden steamships caused the shipbuilders of Maine to turn to large coastal schooners. The effect of this was that sailing tonnage exceeded steam in the US coasting trades until 1894. The *Alice M. Colburn* (below) was a typical ship of the type.

ALICE M. COLBURN

Origin United States	**Date of launch** 1896
Length 68.5m (225ft)	
Tonnage 1,603 tons	

Five-masted schooners

After the four-masted schooner, the logical next stage in the development of the American schooner was to add an extra mast. This began with the *Governor Ames* of 1889, built at Waldoborough, Maine, and weighing in at about 1,778 tons. It was ten years before the next came along, and about 60 were built in all. Five-masted schooners were never common in Europe because there was no demand for such large ships and they tended to operate out of the smallest ports. However, in the 1920s the German firm of Vinnen built five of them, each with topsails on two masts. The *Cora F. Cressy* (below) was a casualty of the sea, being abandoned and used as a breakwater at Medomac, Maine, in 1938.

CORA F. CRESSY

Origin United States	**Date of launch** 1902
Length 83.2m (273ft)	
Tonnage 2,499 tons	

Seven-masted schooners

The culmination of the growth of the schooner was the *Thomas W. Lawson* (right), the only seven-masted ship ever built. Six of her masts were identical, and the aftermost one had a larger sail. She was slightly larger than the ship-rigged *Preussen* (see p.245). Steam-powered winches were used to haul up her sails. The *Thomas W. Lawson* wrecked off the Isles of Scilly in 1907.

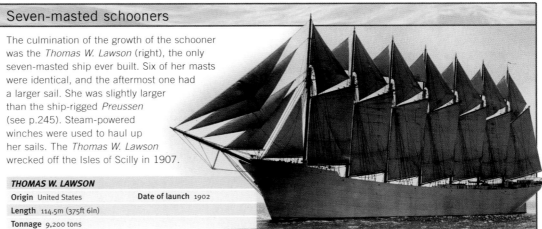

THOMAS W. LAWSON

Origin United States	**Date of launch** 1902
Length 114.5m (375ft 6in)	
Tonnage 9,200 tons	

Bermuda schooners

The seamen of Bermuda evolved a rig in which the gaff that supported the head of the sail disappeared and the sail became triangular. It was simple and required less weight high in the ship. The rig became almost universal for yachts. The Royal Navy also used schooners, such as the three-gunned *Bermuda*. The image shown here depicts an unknown schooner yacht of around 1830.

BERMUDA (NOT SHOWN)

Origin Bermuda (for Britain)	**Date of launch** 1845
Length 24.4m (80ft)	
Tonnage 180 tons	

CLIPPERS AND BARQUES

There is no precise definition of the clipper ship, but it is usually taken to mean a fast-sailing, ocean-going vessel to carry passengers or cargo. Although they kept much of the appearance of older sailing ships, the new ships used new technology such as iron frames and masts, wire rigging, and extra sails. Designed, but not necessarily built, for speed, clippers usually had an underbody that was narrow at the forward end and long and fine at the stern; a large sail area; and a high length-to-beam ratio.

DOCK BUSINESS
Here, sailing ships can be seen loading and unloading at South Street Seaport, New York, in 1900.

Blackwall frigates

Blackwall frigates, built on the Thames near London, were the successors to the East Indiamen. Their finer lines made them faster (frigate originally meant "fast boat") but their appearance was traditional, with stern galleries and painted gunports. The *Owen Glendower* (below) was considered one of the best-looking ships in the trade.

OWEN GLENDOWER	
Origin Britain	**Date of launch** 1839
Length 46.8m (153ft 6in)	
Tonnage 852 tons	

Gold-rush clippers

The gold rushes to California in 1849 and Australia in 1851 created a new demand for fast ships. The *Coeur de Lion* (below), built in Portsmouth, New Hampshire, could sail fast and carry a good cargo. She later traded to Singapore and was sold to European owners.

COEUR DE LION	
Origin United States	**Date of launch** 1854
Length 60.35m (198ft)	
Tonnage 1,098 tons	

China clippers

American ships began to compete in the lucrative China trade from the 1830s, and fast, fine-lined ships were employed. The *Sea Witch* (below) made the passage from Canton to New York in 74 days.

fine-lined hull

SEA WITCH	
Origin United States	**Date of launch** 1846
Length 58.5m (192ft)	
Tonnage 908 tons	

Opium clippers

The opium trade with China (like the tea trade, for example) demanded fast ships. The *Red Rover* (below) was considered the first of the opium clippers. She was rigged as a barque, with two masts fitted with square sails and a mizzen with fore-and-aft sails.

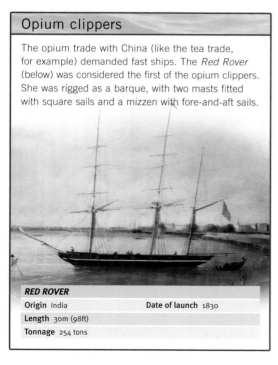

RED ROVER	
Origin India	**Date of launch** 1830
Length 30m (98ft)	
Tonnage 254 tons	

Fast clippers

The great clipper races from China to Europe in the 1860s inspired shipowners to commission some of the fastest sailing ships ever built. The *Thermopylae* (below) was built in Aberdeen, Scotland, and soon proved the fastest clipper on the route. The *Cutty Sark* was built specifically to rival her but lost the most famous race between them, in 1872. The *Thermopylae* seems to have been slightly faster, but the *Cutty Sark* performed better in heavy weather.

THERMOPYLAE	
Origin Britain	**Date of launch** 1868
Length 64.6m (212ft)	
Tonnage 947 tons	

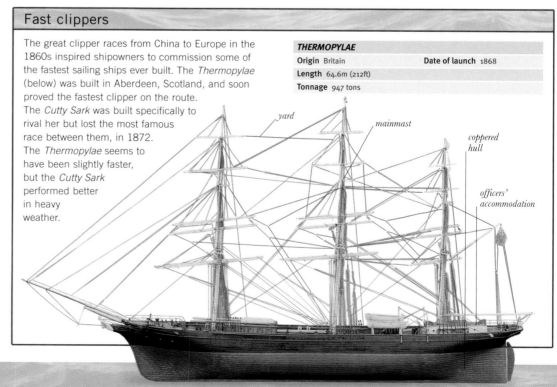

yard

mainmast

coppered hull

officers' accommodation

McKay clippers

The great American ship designer Donald McKay (see p.235) produced many large and fast ships, including the *James Baines* and *Lightning*. But the *Sovereign of the Seas* (right) was his masterpiece, hailed in the press as "the longest, sharpest, the most beautiful merchant ship in the world". On her maiden voyage, she was captained by the builder's brother Lauchlan, who used Matthew Maury's new wind and current charts to sail from New York to San Francisco in 103 days, with a record run of 411 nautical miles in 24 hours and speeds of up to 22 knots. Later, she sailed on charter from Liverpool to Australia, during which she sailed faster than the steamships on the run.

mainmast

deckhouse

shrouds

foremast

anchor

SOVEREIGN OF THE SEAS

Origin United States	**Date of launch** 1852
Length 80.75m (265ft)	
Tonnage 2,421 tons	

Four-masted ships

One way of increasing the sail area of a ship without necessarily using larger sails, which were difficult for a small crew to handle, was to fit more masts. Four-masted vessels might be ship-rigged, with square sails on all masts, or barque-rigged, with fore-and-aft sails on the after-most mast, which was known as the jigger. Barquentines, in contrast, had square sails only on the foremast, with fore-and-aft sails on the others. Four-masted ships became common in the last two decades of the 19th century and were mostly built in British yards. They tended to be built for economy rather than speed and were designed for small crews. The *Wendur* (below), built by Charles Connell in Glasgow, Scotland, had an iron hull like many sailing ships of the period. She was one of the fastest of the four-masted ships.

jigger mast

foremast

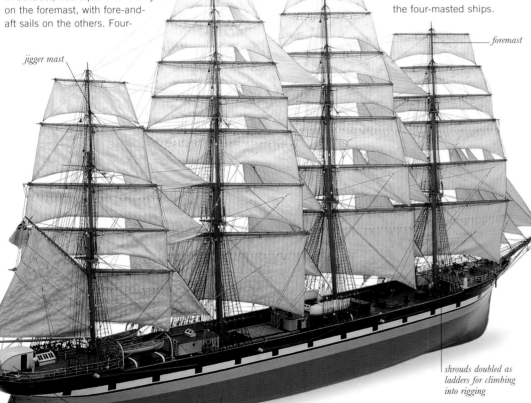

shrouds doubled as ladders for climbing into rigging

steel hull

covered deckhouse

WENDUR

Origin Britain	**Date of launch** 1884
Length 89.2m (292ft 7in)	
Tonnage 2,046 tons	

Down easters

Down easters were wooden sailing ships built in New England for the grain trade with California. One of the biggest square-rigged wooden sailing vessels ever built was the *Roanoke* (below).

ROANOAKE

Origin United States	**Date of launch** 1892
Length 95m (311ft)	
Tonnage 3,539 tons	

Five-masted ships

The *Preussen* (below), built for the nitrate trade with Chile, was the largest sailing ship ever built and the only one to carry square sails on five masts. She was lost in a collision in the English Channel in 1910.

PREUSSEN

Origin Germany	**Date of launch** 1902
Length 124.25m (407ft 8in)	
Tonnage 5,081 tons	

SAILOR'S ENGRAVED SEASHELL

> 66 Towards thee I roll, thou
> all destroying but
> unconquering whale...
> from Hell's heart I
> stab at thee... 99

HERMAN MELVILLE, *Moby Dick*, **1851**

KEY EVENTS

1497 JOHN CABOT AT THE GRAND BANKS
Italian-born English explorer John Cabot reaches
the Grand Banks, off the coast of North
America. The region's abundant supplies of cod
transform cod fishing into an industry.

1596 SPITZBERGEN DISCOVERED
Dutch mariners William Barents and Jacob
Heemskerk discover the Arctic archipelago of
Spitzbergen, opening a new whaling industry.

1713 FIRST FISHING SCHOONER
Andrew Robinson of Gloucester, Massachusetts,
USA, develops the first fishing schooner.

1842 SOUTH-SEAS WHALING PEAKS The
south-seas whaling industry reaches its peak,
with more than 600 whalers operating from
ports on America's eastern seaboard.

1877 FIRST STEAM TRAWLER A converted
English tug called *Messenger* becomes the first
steam trawler. It heralds the expansion of fishing
in the 20th century.

FISHING AND WHALING

THE EUROPEAN DISCOVERY OF FISHING GROUNDS IN THE ATLANTIC, ARCTIC, AND THE SOUTH SEAS HERALDED A PERIOD IN WHICH FISHING AND WHALING BECAME COMMERCIAL INDUSTRIES.

Fishing in one form or another has been practised almost since humans first evolved. Seafood, particularly shellfish, formed a major part of the diet of the prehistoric inhabitants of coastal areas, and some of the earliest ships were developed for the purpose of catching fish. In pre-agricultural societies, river and inshore fishing often proved less dangerous than hunting land-based animals for food. Many of the traditional methods of catching fish – using tools such as spears, hooks, or nets, and basic, small craft – have not changed for millennia, and are still used throughout the world.

FISHING IN GUILIN
In inland China and Japan, traditional methods of fishing still prevail and have been used for many centuries. These fishermen use cormorants to dive for fish that are then pulled from the birds' throats.

Marine mammals, particularly whales, have been prized by many cultures for their products, which include bone, meat, and oil. However, until the commercial whaling industry emerged (see pp.251–55), whales were usually captured only if they swam close to land or they were washed up on shore.

The birth of the fishing industry

The expansion of fishing from coastal shallows to deeper waters probably began with the Vikings, who crossed the Atlantic in about AD 1000 (see p.38). They were followed by the Normans, who spread the method of fishing with baited hooks attached to long lines to England and Ireland. In the Middle Ages, meat was banned during the period of Lent, providing a ready market for fish in Christian countries.

Among the most skilled fishermen of this period were the Basques. By the 15th century, they had extended their range from the Bay of Biscay up the Atlantic to Norway in the west and the Grand Banks, off northeastern America. They voyaged in search of cod, which when salted provided a staple food for Europe's poor. However, it was John Cabot's (see p.74) discovery of the Grand Banks in 1497 that kick-started the Atlantic cod-fishing industry.

During the 14th and 15th centuries, the Hanseatic merchants of Germany (see p.44) controlled much of the fish trade of northern Europe, where the primary catch was herring. They were superseded by the Dutch in about 1500. The creation of fishing fleets also proved advantageous for those who ruled. In the 16th century, the English queen, Elizabeth I, realizing that the industry provided experienced mariners who could be utilized by the state, banned meat on Wednesdays, Fridays, and Saturdays "for the better increase and maintenance of the navy".

PORTUGUESE DORY
The flat-bottomed dory was launched from a larger vessel when it reached cod fishing grounds. Long lines with baited hooks were thrown from the boat to catch fish.

single mast for sail

cork float indicates where line is set

flat bottom

fishing line

oar

SCOTTISH SAILING FLEET
During the age of sail, many coastal communities around the world became entirely dependent on fishing. These Scottish ships, known as fifies, were photographed in 1910, during the period of transition from sail to steam.

North Sea herring

The Dutch North Sea herring fleet, which emerged at the beginning of the 16th century, was the world's first industrial-scale fishery. Their vessel of choice was the *buss*, which was a broad, two- or three-masted ship of between 80 and 100 tons. The *buss* carried a crew of about 15 men and was able to stay at sea for several months, or until the hold was full of fish. The Dutch used drift nets to capture entire shoals of herring. This type of net, which is still used today, is suspended vertically in the sea by floats on its upper edge and metal weights on its lower edge. When hauled in, the herring were gutted and salted to preserve them, before being packed in barrels. By the 17th century, there were up to 2,000 Dutch herring *busses* at work in northern Europe, and 150,000 tons of fish were exported from the Netherlands in 1614 alone. The industry was hugely important to the Dutch in the 17th century, as it employed about a fifth of the population.

Inevitably, other northern European nations took an interest in this lucrative trade, which provided one of the region's basic foods. By the middle of the 19th century, the Scottish herring fishery had risen to a position of prominence. A contemporary observer described how the fishing boats left harbour in the early evening, casting their nets at about dusk. Heavy with herring, the nets were drawn in during the early hours of the morning, a process that could take many hours. The fishing fleets of Norway and Iceland, where herring were known as the "silver of the sea", also developed a successful industry in the 19th century. The Norwegians used long purse-seine nets, which encircle shoals of fish. The ends are then pulled together and the catch hauled in. By 1937, Germany had overtaken other nations to maintain Europe's most successful herring fleet.

DRIFTERS IN THE ENGLISH CHANNEL
This 19th-century painting shows a fleet of herring busses at work in the English Channel. Drift nets have been cast, as can be seen by the floats at the water's surface.

THE HERRING SEASON
Over 1,000 vessels, equipped with drift nets, sailed from the port of Wick in the far northwest of Scotland during the two-month herring season in summer 1880. Thousands of barrels of fish were brought ashore.

SWIFT SCHOONER
Hailing from Lunenburg, Nova Scotia, Bluenose was launched in 1921 and remained a cod fishing schooner for more than two decades. In this 1923 image, she is competing in the International Fishermen's Trophy off the coast of Nova Scotia.

Cod fishing and the Grand Banks

Cod is endemic to the North Atlantic, and one of the most prolific breeding grounds for the species was the Grand Banks, a relatively shallow area of ocean off the coast of Newfoundland (now part of Canada). The Basques, who were skilled fishermen, had discovered these fishing grounds by the early 16th century. They salted and dried the cod to preserve it and built up an extensive export market, trading around Europe. When John Cabot (see panel, p.74) discovered the area,

GRAND BANKS FIGUREHEAD
Brightly painted figureheads adorned many of the fishing boats that sailed to the Grand Banks. This example originated from a French vessel.

CADIZ, SPAIN
As well as being a thriving centre for the fishing industry, the Atlantic port of Cadiz also exported salt – which was used to preserve cod – to many other parts of Europe. This view of the port was painted in 1657.

he described it "swarming with fish; which can be taken not only with the net but in baskets let down with a stone, so that it sinks in the water".

The Grand Banks now opened up to the rest of Europe: the French and Portuguese were the first to exploit the fishing grounds. Over 70 ships had ventured across the Atlantic from La Rochelle by 1550, with more vessels sailing from Brittany. The Spanish went on to dominate the fishery, to be joined in the 17th century by boats from the west of England. After the eastern

seaboard of America was colonized, the citizens of New England and eastern Canada joined the trade.

Sail survived longer in the Grand Banks fishery than in most trades. The two-masted schooner (see p.242–43), a streamlined and extremely fast vessel, was first developed in 1713 by Andrew Robinson of Gloucester, Massachusetts. Schooners soon became the primary fishing vessel on the Grand Banks, and remained so until trawlers (see pp.256–57) replaced them in the 20th century. The ships were also used to transport salt cod to the plantations in the West Indies and to Europe.

Fishing schooners were usually equipped with supplies for a few days. Some ships also carried a number of 6-m (20-ft) flat-bottomed boats called dories (see p.247), which were launched from the main ship with a crew of one or two onboard. Long lines were launched from the dories, which returned to the ship with their catch at the end of each day's fishing. The catch was gutted, dried, salted, and packed in wooden barrels.

Life spent fishing in the perishing-cold conditions and fog banks off Newfoundland was perilous. A staggering 3,800 cod fishermen were lost from the port of Gloucester between 1830 and 1900.

Arctic whaling

For hundreds of years, humans have captured whales and other cetacean species for meat, baleen (the keratin plates in the mouths of certain species), and blubber, which was rendered into oil. The Vikings and the Anglo-Saxons are known to have travelled towards the Arctic in search of whales. But it was the Basques who first discovered in the tenth century how to harpoon whales at sea, a technique that remained unchanged for centuries. In the 16th century, Basque ships of up to 1,000 tons sailed as far as Newfoundland in search of their prey. However, it was the 1596 discovery of the islands of Spitzbergen, by the Dutchmen William Barents and Jacob Heemskerk, that began the Arctic whaling industry. The Dutch and the English began to send regular expeditions to the region. Whaling ships' hulls were strengthened to follow the whales into the Arctic pack ice, where they were plentiful. The voyages concentrated on

capturing the Greenland right whale, which is also known as the bowhead whale, as the species is a slow swimmer and often surfaces close to shore, making it easy prey. Between 1675 and 1721, the Dutch killed nearly 33,000 Arctic whales, an average of about 725 each year.

By the early 18th century, about 250 British whalers, which were subsidized by the government, sailed to the Arctic each year. British ports prospered on the proceeds of

whaling. However, from the middle of the 19th century, the Norwegians began to dominate the trade. The invention of the steam engine also had a significant effect on the whaling industry. In 1859, the *Narwhal*, which operated out of Dundee, was the first of many whalers to be fitted with a steam engine. The additional power of these ships allowed them to pursue and capture many more whales, including faster species that were previously able to escape.

WHALE LOG-BOOK

This log-book is taken from a ship based in Hull on the northeast coast of England. Details of whales observed and killed were noted down. Documents such as this provide a valuable record of whale populations in previous centuries.

flag orders crew to report to ship

mainmast

shrouds give support to masts

foremast rigged with square sails when at sea

bowsprit

BRITISH WHALER

The British typically used three-masted ships with reinforced hulls, such as the one shown in this model, to hunt whales in Arctic seas. This kind of ship was developed from similar Dutch designs.

whaleboat

hull reinforced to protect from pack ice

BLUDGEONED FOR BLUBBER

Whales, seals, and walruses fall victim to the spears of humans in this late 17th-century scene, which is taken from Voyage to Spitzbergen *by Frederick Martens of Hamburg.*

HUNTING A WHALE

The brutal trade of whaling in the frozen waters of the Arctic was hazardous for the humans involved as well as their prey. In freezing conditions, men hunted the whales from small boats using hand-held harpoons.

SHIP'S WHEEL *The wheel is unusual, as it moves in line with the tiller. This was possibly more convenient for long-distance sailing, because it let the helmsman know the position of the tiller at any instant.*

STERN *The stern is decorated with the American eagle and the ship's name and home port. The copper-sheathed hull is green due to contact with air and water.*

HARPOONS *These are the tools of a whaler's trade: harpoons and cutting spades.*

CHARLES W. MORGAN

HAVING ENDURED A REMARKABLE 80-YEAR CAREER IN THE WHALING INDUSTRY, THE *CHARLES W. MORGAN* REMAINS THE ONLY INTACT WOODEN WHALING SHIP IN THE USA.

ENTERING RETIREMENT *The Charles W. Morgan is seen here berthed at Dartmouth, Massachusetts, in 1925. At this point she was maintained by the millionaire Colonel Edward H.R. Green, who was the grandson of one of the ship's owners in the mid-19th century.*

THE CENTRE OF the 19th-century whaling trade in the USA was New Bedford, Massachusetts, where the *Charles W. Morgan* was constructed in 1840–41. She cost $52,000 to build, and came home with a cargo of whalebone and oil worth $56,000 after her first three-year voyage. In the late 19th century, she operated from San Francisco, before returning to her home port in 1904. In all, the whaler made 37 voyages during her eight decades in service, the last of which ended in May 1921. By this time, the whaling trade had long passed its peak. Competition from petroleum, electricity, and steel meant that the profits from the industry were greatly reduced. In 1924, the *Charles W. Morgan* was transformed into a museum at Dartmouth, close to New Bedford. The ship also enjoyed a brief cinema career, featuring in several movies in the 1920s and 1930s. She was taken to Mystic Seaport, Connecticut, in 1941, where she has remained ever since.

The *Charles W. Morgan* was originally ship-rigged, and all three masts were set with square sails. She was re-rigged in about 1880 as a bark, with fore-and-aft sails on the mizzen mast. Aft on the upper deck is the steering wheel, a model known as a "shincracker", which moved across the wheelhouse in motion with the tiller. Forward of the wheel is the compass, which is situated inside a skylight that helps illuminate the cabin below. The deck is flat and equipped with racks to hold implements such as harpoons and lances. Six whaleboats are suspended on davits at the sides of the hull. These small, slim craft were designed for the pursuit of a whale. Also attached to the exterior are platforms, which could be lowered over the side of the ship for the crew to work on. In the centre of the deck is the tryworks, where the whale blubber was rendered. Below deck, the well-furnished master's cabin is aft, as are the quarters inhabited by the mates (officers) and other leading crew-members, such as harpooners (also known as boat steerers). The rest of the crew inhabited the forward end of the ship, separated from the senior crew by the blubber room.

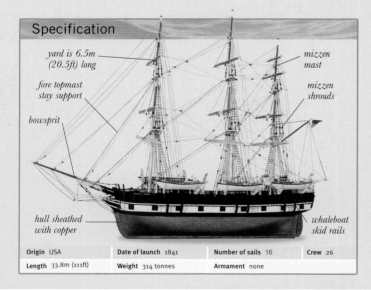

Specification

yard is 6.5m (20.5ft) long

fore topmast stay support

bowsprit

hull sheathed with copper

mizzen mast

mizzen shrouds

whaleboat skid rails

Origin USA	Date of launch 1841	Number of sails 16	Crew 26
Length 33.8m (111ft)	Weight 314 tonnes	Armament none	

RIBS *The tightly packed wooden ribs added strength to the ship's hull.*

MASTER'S STATEROOM *The master lived in relative comfort, with two cabins to himself. He was the only member of the crew who was allowed to possess a gun.*

SLEEPING QUARTERS *Thomas Landers, the ship's master in 1863–67, installed a double bed, as his wife travelled with him on the voyage. The bed was designed to compensate for the roll of the ship.*

MATES' SALOON *Senior members of the crew dined at this table.*

BLUBBER HOOK *The blubber hook was connected to an enormous block and tackle. It was used to lift the portions of blubber and skin cut from a whale's carcass through a hatch in the deck and into the blubber room.*

BLUBBER ROOM *Here, whale blubber was cut up into chunks called horsepieces. The blubber room is situated in the centre of the ship, between the main deck and the hold, effectively dividing it into two.*

TRYWORKS *This is the iron-and-brick boiler to the fore of the ship. It was used to melt the whale blubber into oil, which was then stored in barrels in the hold.*

PLATFORM *These wooden gangways were lowered at the side of the ship for the crew to stand on as they cut the blubber from the carcass of a whale.*

CREW'S QUARTERS *The crew slept on wooden bunks in cramped and spartan conditions. They also used these quarters for eating and for recreation. Their possessions were housed in kitbags and wooden chests.*

DECK LIGHTS *Prisms of glass set into the upper deck provided light beneath. They were equivalent to a 30-watt electric bulb.*

FOREMAST *The rings at the top of the mast were used by lookouts, whose job was to sight the ship's quarry.*

SHIP'S BELL *This was used to mark the time and summon the crew.*

South seas whaling

During the 17th century, the colonists of New England and Canada hunted right whales, which they captured offshore. However, in 1712 a Nantucket fisherman, Captain Christopher Hussey, opened a new chapter in the history of whaling when he encountered and killed a sperm whale. The deep-water creature aroused great interest, as the huge cavity in its head contained abundant oil, called spermaceti, which burned very cleanly and could also be used to manufacture candles. American ships soon began to pursue the whales into the South Atlantic. Sperm-whale oil fetched high prices, and the trade flourished, with Nantucket at its centre. By the time the American Revolutionary War broke out in 1774, there were nearly 400 whalers operating out of ports along the northeast coast of America.

In 1786, the industry expanded further when an English mariner called Samuel Enderby tracked migrating sperm whales into the Pacific Ocean. Soon whalers were hunting as far away as the Galapagos Islands and New Zealand. As a reaction to British attempts to control

the trade, the Americans began to construct larger ships. These vessels could undertake lengthy voyages of up to four years to fill their holds with the precious oil. This development ruined Nantucket – which had already suffered a downturn in fortune as a result of British blockades during the wars that occurred between 1774 and 1815 – because the port's entrance was too shallow to accommodate the new ships.

From this point on, another Massachusetts port, New Bedford, became the principal base for whaling in the south seas. The industry boomed in the first half of the 19th century. By 1842, there were

HARPOONING A WHALE

In his epic novel, *Moby Dick*, Herman Melville vividly describes the moment the eponymous "white whale" is harpooned:

> *The harpoon was hurled .... The oarsmen backed water; the same moment, something went hot and hissing along every one of their wrists. It was the magical line .... It blisteringly passed through and through both of Stubb's hands, from which the hand-cloths, or squares of quilted canvas sometimes worn at these times, had accidentally dropped. It was like holding an enemy's sharp two edged sword by the blade, and that enemy all the time striving to wrest it out of your clutch.*

HERMAN MELVILLE, *Moby Dick*, **1851**

THE FATAL BLOW
As a whaleboat approached its prey, a harpoon was thrown at the whale, which dragged the boat along until it was too exhausted to continue. Standing at the bows of the boat, a crew-member then speared the injured creature to kill it.

MINCING KNIFE
Whalers had a variety of implements onboard to cut up the flesh of their prey. The mincer was about 60cm (2ft) long, and was used to slice lumps of blubber into smaller pieces, called bible leaves, for boiling down.

lance to kill whale

oar

harpooner's rowing position

whale line passes through notched stem

furled mast and sail

harpoon attached to whale line

CHARLES W. MORGAN WHALEBOAT
With a crew of six, small whaleboats were launched from ships such as the Charles W. Morgan (see pp.252–53) and sailed or rowed towards their quarry. Each whaleboat had one harpooner, who sat at the front of the boat.

TWO-FLUE IRON HARPOON

BARBED HARPOON

barbed head lodges into whale's flesh

HARPOONS
Iron harpoons, such as these examples from New Bedford, developed from wooden models. They were attached to a rope before being dispatched. The sharp tips of the weapons embedded themselves into the animals' flesh.

calibrated sight

barbs open when whale is hit

tip loaded with explosives

harpoon pivots on cradle

MECHANIZED EFFICIENCY
The harpoon gun was first developed in Norway in the 19th century. The tip of the harpoon contained a charge that exploded on impact.

HERMAN MELVILLE

The author of the classic novel *Moby Dick*, Herman Melville (1819–91) was born in New York City. In 1841, he joined a whaling expedition on the *Acushnet*. He deserted the ship at the Marquesas Islands in the Pacific and was held captive by a native tribe. After his rescue and return to America, Melville worked as a New York customs officer. His books *Typee* (1846) and *Omoo* (1847) were based on personal experiences. His masterpiece, *Moby Dick*, published in 1851, tells the story of Captain Ahab's obsessive pursuit of the "white whale" that had maimed him. It is the greatest account of whaling ever written.

nearly 600 American ships in commission, compared with fewer than 200 vessels operating from the rest of the world. A typical American whaler had a captain and four mates, each with command of a whaleboat. The harpooners often came from Portugal or the Atlantic islands of Cape Verde. More than 3,000 African-American sailors were employed in the trade, three of whom reached the rank of captain.

The south-seas whaling trade declined from 1846 as the whale population fell. In 1859, petroleum was discovered in Pennsylvania, and soon began to replace whale oil. However, some nations, notably Japan and Norway, continued to pursue whales. In 1868, the harpoon gun was invented, an implement that turned whaling from a contest between an individual and the greatest creature on earth, into organized slaughter.

END OF A WHALE
The crew of this Japanese whaler (photographed in 1902) balance precariously on gangplanks as they dismember a dead whale (a process called cutting in).

INDONESIAN WHALE BOAT
For centuries, the inhabitants of Lamalera on the eastern Indonesian island of Lembata have used small sailing craft, such as this one, to hunt and harpoon sperm whales.

FISHING TECHNIQUES

The Dutch developed the drift net in the 16th century to catch North Sea herring. The nets, measuring up to 60m (200ft) long, were cast from the bows of a boat and hung vertically from floats as the boat drifted on the tide. Shoals of fish swam at the nets and were trapped by their gills. During the 18th and 19th centuries, long-line fishing was a popular method among cod and haddock fishermen, particularly on the Grand Banks. Hundreds of baited hooks were attached to fishing lines anchored on the side of a small craft such as a dory (see p.247).

The first trawl nets, which were used by sailing vessels, were held open by a wooden beam. The net tapered from its opening until it reached a narrow bag, called the cod end, where the fish were trapped. Trawlers required a strong wind to propel the boat and its vast net through the water. The advent of steam-powered fishing craft and the development of otter-board trawling saw the method employed to even greater effect.

DRIFT NET
The crew of a Scottish drifter hauls its catch onboard. Drift nets capture fish that swim in shoals close to the surface, such as herring and mackerel.

TRAWLER NET
Otter-board trawling developed in the 19th century and was initially used by steam trawlers. The huge nets are dragged through the ocean to capture fish that dwell on, or close to, the bottom of the sea, for example, cod and sole. The method is still employed worldwide.

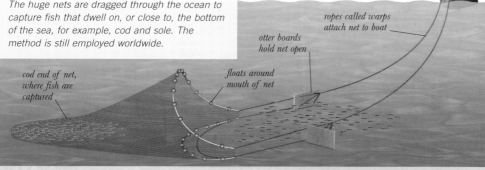

cod end of net, where fish are captured

floats around mouth of net

otter boards hold net open

ropes called warps attach net to boat

ship drags trawl net along

Trawling

Nets have been used to catch fish for centuries. Commercial fishermen have experimented with various kinds of net (see panel, left), but perhaps the most efficient method is trawling, in which a net is dragged through the water by a ship. As far back as the 14th century, English fishermen on the River Thames in London developed a trawl net called the wondrychoun, but it was banned because its mesh was too small and likely to damage fish stocks.

It was not until the early 19th century that trawling began to emerge as a commercial method of fishing. The sailing trawler is believed to have originated at Brixham in southwest England, but its use quickly spread to ports on the North Sea and across the English Channel to Normandy and Brittany. Belgian and German fishing vessels also adopted trawl nets, while the Dutch sometimes used two at once, one suspended from the stern of the boat and the other from the bows. In 1908, trawl nets were first used on the American Atlantic coast, much to the dismay of traditional line fishermen, who saw the method as a threat to the abundant fish stocks in the region. Trawling also spread to the Pacific, where it was adopted by boats in New Zealand in the early 20th century.

Steam fishing

The advent of steam power in the 19th century eventually had an impact on fishing vessels. From the 1860s, fishing boats were towed to their fishing grounds in unfavourable winds by steam paddle tugs. The first steam trawler was a converted tug called *Messenger*, which began to operate out of North Shields in 1877. So profitable was the ship that there were soon 50 similar vessels operating along England's east coast. However, paddle steamers were not very efficient in rough waters, and fishing boats using the screw propeller (see p.174–5) came into use in the 1880s, beginning with the *Zodiac*, which was launched at Grimsby in 1881. Because coal was cheap and abundant, steam trawlers were standard in most fishing fleets in northern Europe and along the Atlantic coast of North America by 1914. Steam power was slightly less advantageous for drifters, as they moved with the tide once they had cast their nets. However, many of these fishing vessels converted to steam power in the early 20th century. The steam fishing boat was a more expensive investment than its predecessor, but it changed the nature of commercial fishing, reaping ever larger catches.

OCEAN BOUNTY
French and English fisherman, onboard the steam trawler Lord Barham *in 1954, unload their catch of approximately 40,000 mackerel in Newlyn, Cornwall.*

A FISHERMAN'S TALE

An English drifterman describes the cramped accommodation onboard his vessel, a converted luxury yacht:

> *Now as regards accommodation, when I was in the* Scadaun *there was only about four or five of us slept aft. All the rest were for'ard in the foc'sle. They had a cookin' stove and a lavatory down there as well. See, ol' Lord Dunraven had built that for his yacht – you know, for towing it about. Mind you, she fished very well. A gentleman by the name of Turkey Goldspink was skipper of her and she had a Low'stoft crew. The cookin' stove down a foc'sle wasn't usual, but most o' the drifters had accommodation for'ard at one time o'day. Yes, they used to sleep four or five down there.*

LOWESTOFT DRIFTERMAN, **1904**

STEAM TRAWLER
Steam trawlers initially resembled their sailing counterparts, complete with masts. The catch was winched up and landed on the deck of the ship.

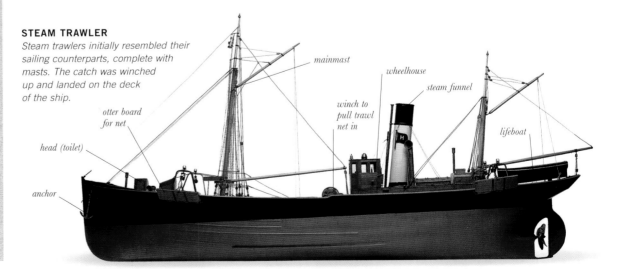

mainmast

wheelhouse

steam funnel

winch to pull trawl net in

lifeboat

otter board for net

head (toilet)

anchor

FISHING BOATS

Although local fishing industries have always been a feature of human societies close to the sea, the expansion into a large-scale regional and world market only began with the Dutch North Sea herring fishery in the 17th century. It continued with the transatlantic trade in cod, although small local fisheries often continued as before. Sail survived longer in fishing boats than in most trades, although steam was beginning to make inroads towards the end of the 19th century due to the competitive nature of the business.

WHITBY BAY
This photograph of Whitby Harbour, northeast England, dates from the 1890s. It shows local fishing craft known as cobles.

Pacific fishing boats

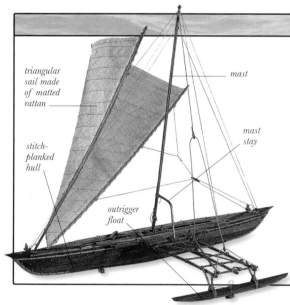

triangular sail made of matted rattan

mast

mast stay

stitch-planked hull

outrigger float

Pacific fisheries of early times were probably based on local craft from various islands and coasts. Over time, Chinese and Japanese fisheries gradually became more extensive: by the late 19th century, Japan had almost 200,000 fishing boats. The most industrialized area, the Pacific Northeast, developed sophisticated modern techniques after its settlement by Europeans, especially after 1850. Fish caught included tuna, swordfish, crab, carp, and halibut. In the meantime, the Pacific islanders maintained their traditional craft well into the 20th century, including this boat from the Gilbert and Ellice Islands, which straddle the equator east of New Guinea.

KIRIBATI OUTRIGGER SAILING CANOE

Origin Gilbert and Ellice Islands	Date of launch c.1960
Length About 5m (16ft 5in)	
Tonnage Not known	

Herring *busses*

The Dutch herring *buss* was first used from the town of Hoorn in 1415. It grew in size over the next century, acquired a round stern with two or three masts, and came to dominate the North Sea fishery.

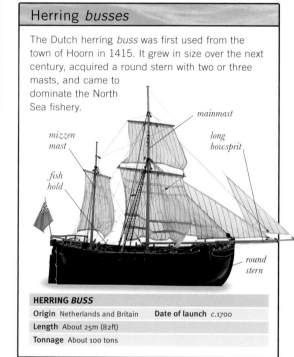

mizzen mast

mainmast

long bowsprit

fish hold

round stern

HERRING *BUSS*

Origin Netherlands and Britain	Date of launch c.1700
Length About 25m (82ft)	
Tonnage About 100 tons	

Zulus

In the extensive Scottish North Sea herring fishery of the mid-19th century, two main fishing vessels evolved: the fifie, with a straight bow and stern; and the scaffie, in which they were steeply raked. In 1879, fisherman "Dad" Campbell of Lossiemouth invented a boat with a straight bow and raked stern, to combine the advantages of the two. It was known as the Zulu, after the Zulu War taking place in southern Africa at the time.

MUIRNEAG

Origin Britain	Date of launch 1903
Length 24.4m (80ft)	
Tonnage About 100 tons	

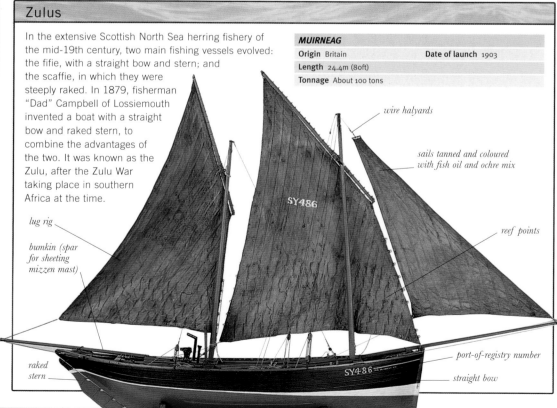

wire halyards

sails tanned and coloured with fish oil and ochre mix

SY486

reef points

lug rig

bumkin (spar for sheeting mizzen mast)

raked stern

port-of-registry number

straight bow

Galway hookers

The Galway hooker was sailed by fishermen using hook-and-line techniques to fish off the west coast of Ireland. It originated towards the end of the 18th century, when an increase in the size of local boats was noted.

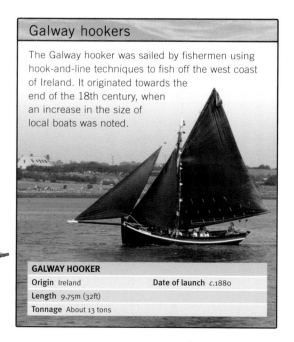

GALWAY HOOKER

Origin Ireland	Date of launch c.1880
Length 9.75m (32ft)	
Tonnage About 13 tons	

Sailing trawlers

The sailing trawler evolved in Brixham in the southwest of England around 1830 and soon spread to the ports of the North Sea. It used the beam trawl, a net that was kept open by a pole across its mouth, because constant winds could not be relied on to keep the sides apart. The *Valerian* (below) was one of the last sailing trawlers to be built at Brixham when there was an attempt to revive the industry after the

VALERIAN

Origin Britain	**Date of launch** 1923
Length 24m (78ft 10in)	
Tonnage 39 tons	

First World War. Although sail did not survive, and was supplanted by steam power and the diesel engine, trawling had established itself as a prominent method of fishing.

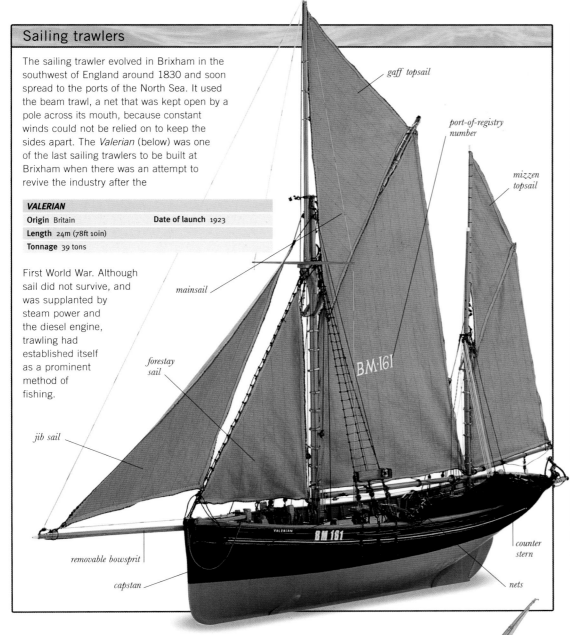

gaff topsail

port-of-registry number

mizzen topsail

mainsail

forestay sail

BM·161

jib sail

removable bowsprit

capstan

counter stern

nets

Breton tunny boats

The fisheries of Brittany in western France include small sardine boats, the *sinagos* of the Gulf of Morbihan, and the *bisquines* of Cancale, with their huge sails of up to 350 square metres (3,767 square feet). The dundees, or tunny boats, had long poles rigged from either side to spread their lines. Their main port was on the Iles de Groix. In the 1930s, many of them were fitted with engines and propellers.

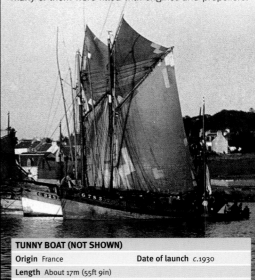

TUNNY BOAT (NOT SHOWN)

Origin France	**Date of launch** c.1930
Length About 17m (55ft 9in)	
Tonnage About 50 tons	

Fishing schooners

The schooners of the northeast coast of America were among the largest and fastest fishing vessels of their day, and competition was intense between different ships and ports. The *Arethusa* (below) had a crew of about 20 and was so fast that she was used as a rum runner during the Prohibition era.

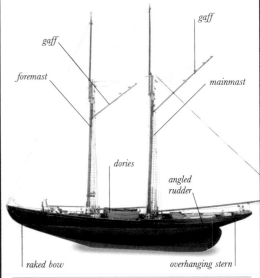

gaff

gaff

foremast

mainmast

dories

angled rudder

raked bow

overhanging stern

ARETHUSA

Origin United States	**Date of launch** 1907
Length 38.8m (127ft 3in)	
Tonnage Not known	

Mediterranean fishing boats

The Mediterranean has relatively few fish compared with the Atlantic, and tuna, or tunny, are commercially the most important of these. Because Mediterranean fishermen have not developed on the same scale as some of their counterparts elsewhere, the traditional craft of Spain, Italy, Greece, and North Africa have tended to survive longer. The *Calypso* (right) is a *lutzu*, a traditional type of Maltese boat used for fishing and for the transport of goods. Like most Mediterranean craft, it is propelled by lateen sails.

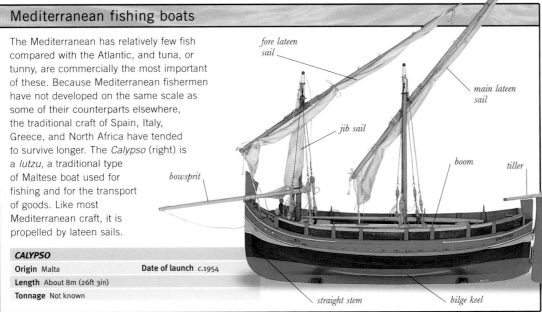

fore lateen sail

main lateen sail

jib sail

boom

tiller

bowsprit

straight stem

bilge keel

CALYPSO

Origin Malta	**Date of launch** c.1954
Length About 8m (26ft 3in)	
Tonnage Not known	

TO SEA FOR PLEASURE

FROM THE BEGINNING OF THE 17TH CENTURY, SAILING BEGAN TO DEVELOP AS A LEISURE ACTIVITY. BY THE 19TH CENTURY, IT HAD ESTABLISHED ITSELF AS A SPORT WORLDWIDE.

THE AMERICA'S CUP

> 66 He who would go to sea for pleasure, would go to hell for a pastime. 99
>
> **18TH-CENTURY FRENCH PROVERB**

KEY EVENTS

1661 FIRST YACHT RACE The first recorded yacht race takes place, between the English King Charles II and his brother James, along the River Thames from Greenwich to Gravesend.

1720 FIRST YACHT CLUB The first organized yacht club, the Water Club of Cork, is formed in southern Ireland. The first English club follows in 1774 in London; and the first European club is established in Sweden in 1830.

1844 NEW YORK YACHT CLUB The first American yacht club is created with just nine founding members in New York.

1851 *AMERICA* WINS The New York-based yacht *America* takes the 100 Guineas Cup at Cowes, on the Isle of Wight. The cup is renamed the America's Cup in her honour.

1898 SOLO CIRCUMNAVIGATION The American sailor Joshua Slocum becomes the first person to sail around the world single-handed in his sloop *Spray*.

Ships and boats have probably been used for leisure since their invention, and there is clear evidence of their recreational use from classical times. A Roman wall painting from the 1st century AD shows a brightly painted craft being rowed by two naked, rather androgynous figures, with another steering. An Egyptian mosaic exists from the same era, which displays a craft with a large cabin and three oarsmen on each side. Centuries later, an English manuscript from the 1400s shows three people playing musical instruments in a small boat, which is decorated with flowers and an awning.

Ceremonial craft also developed to establish the power and majesty of individual rulers or states. The Roman Emperor Caligula is believed to have used two barges, which date from about AD 40 and were excavated in Lake Nemi, south of Rome, in the 1930s. One of the grandest craft was the Venetian galley *Bucentaure* (see p.144),

which first appeared in 1100. On Ascension Day each year, the city's chief magistrate, the *doge*, was rowed in the *Bucentaure* or one of its successors to the entrance of the Venetian lagoon to celebrate the city's association with the sea.

The beginnings of yachting

The Netherlands of the 17th century was probably the first society that was wealthy enough, and close enough to the sea, to develop sailing for pleasure on a large scale, although it remained the preserve of the rich. Dutch ceremonial vessels called *jachts* (from *jachten*, meaning to hunt) first became apparent at the beginning of the 17th century and were soon converted to pleasure craft. An anonymous engraving of 1640 showed a vessel called a *speel-jacht* (pleasure yacht) with the text "Earnings which are often increased by sailing in trade, are consumed again in sailing for pleasure." Dutch

SAILING DUTCH WATERS
Many early Dutch jachts were large sailing vessels that were used as ceremonial craft by government officials. The jacht is the sailing vessel in the centre of this image, which was painted in 1650 by Jan van de Cappelle.

waterways – which are dominated by estuaries, islands, and the Zuider Zee, a large inlet in the northeast of the country – proved extremely suitable for this kind of recreational sailing.

RACING AT SEA
By the early 20th century, yachting was an organized sport with an established calendar of races and regattas. This wooden yacht called Valkyrie was photographed in the 1920s off the coast of New York.

RACING ALONG THE RIVER THAMES
The Cumberland Fleet, formed with the patronage of the Duke of Cumberland, a brother of the English King George III, was one of the first yacht clubs. This late 18th-century image shows the fleet racing along the Thames.

When the English King Charles II left the Netherlands in 1660 to return to England after a period of exile, his Dutch hosts presented him with a *jacht* named *Mary*. Charles adapted the design of the vessel to English waters, which are not as shallow as those of the Netherlands, by deepening the hull and abandoning the leeboards (see p.142). The word *jacht* was quickly anglicized as yacht. Charles and his brother James built a dozen similar craft over the next 25 years, using them for ceremonial, military, and diplomatic purposes. However, like the Dutch, they also adapted them for use as leisure craft. The trend was soon taken up by others in the English aristocracy. Lord Henry Mordaunt built a yacht of more than 500 tons in 1681, which was used by the navy as a small warship two years later. In 1677, an English naval captain

called Jeremy Roch sailed from Devon to London and back in an open sailing boat. Judging by his drawings of the vessel, it measured about 3m (10ft) long, and the configuration of its sails resembled modern yachts. The sport of yachting expanded to France, particularly in royal circles. The English shipwright Anthony Deane constructed two yachts for King Louis XIV in 1674–75.

Sailing for pleasure gained popularity throughout the 18th century, although it was interrupted by military conflict at various points. Fredrik af Chapman's *Architectura Navalis Mercatoria* of 1769 (see p.146) contained plans of 10 "pleasure vessels for sailing", from different parts of Europe, including a 23.5-m- (78-ft-) long frigate (not to be confused with the military vessel of the same name), two schooners, and six yachts, all of which were decorated ornately and fitted with large cabins. Chapman also described other vessels that were used for leisure, including several rowing boats.

Yacht clubs
The first recorded yachting organization was the Water Club of Cork, which eventually became the Royal Cork Yacht Club. It was formed in southern Ireland in 1720. The club used fast vessels that resembled cutters, with a single mast, a gaff rig that utilized quadrilateral sails, and a sharp hull. Club members

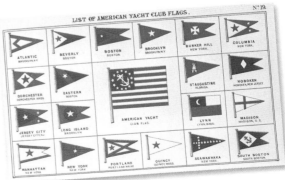

FLYING THE FLAG
Sailing vessels identify their origins by hoisting the flag of their yacht club. This chart shows the ensigns of many of the yachting organizations that existed in the USA in 1881.

dressed in grand uniforms and exercised using naval manoeuvres. The Cumberland Fleet formed in 1775, becoming the Royal Thames Yacht Club in 1823. It was followed by the Royal Yacht Club, which was established soon after the Napoleonic Wars finished in 1815, and based itself in London and Cowes, on the Isle of Wight. King William IV, who was known as the Sailor King, changed the organization's name to the Royal Yacht Squadron in 1833 and it quickly became one of the world's most prestigious yacht clubs. It remains the only yacht club entitled to fly the white ensign of the Royal Navy.

Yacht clubs opened in Scandinavia and continental Europe throughout the 19th century. The Royal Swedish Yacht Club was inaugurated in 1830, and the first French yacht club, the *Société des Régates du Havre*, based in Normandy, followed in 1838. Clubs were set up in different regions of the Netherlands, the nation in which the sport had originated, in 1846, 1847, and 1851, and the first German club was formed in East Prussia in 1855. Italy opened its first club at La Spezia, south of Genoa, in 1879, and Oslo's Royal Norwegian Yacht Club opened in 1883.

The first American yacht was the sloop *Jefferson* of 1801, sailed by George Crowninshield, Jr of Salem. In 1816, he commissioned America's first oceangoing yacht from local shipbuilder Retire Beckett. Named *Cleopatra's Barge*, the brigantine was extravagantly furnished but was also fast and handled well. In March 1817, Crowninshield took her on a six-month cruise of the Mediterranean, but died six weeks after his return. She was sold and became the flagship of Hawaii's King Kamehameha II. Renamed *Ha'aheo o Hawai'i* (Pride of Hawaii), she ran aground on Kauai on 5 April 1824. The wreck was discovered by the Smithsonian in July 1995 and is being conserved. The first American yachting organization, the New York

Yacht Club, was established in 1844. The club was founded with nine initial members, led by John C. Stevens, who met onboard the schooner *Gimcrack*. By 1869, the club had accumulated 42 yachts. Some of these vessels were single-masted sloops (the American equivalent of the European cutter) of 20 or 30 tons, but over a third of the boats were larger, at more than 100 tons, including the publisher J.G. Bennett's 205-ton schooner *Henrietta*. The club shared New York's great harbour with the humbler Atlantic Yacht Club. The Boston Yacht Club was founded in 1866, and the first yacht club on the Pacific coast of the USA opened in San Francisco in 1869. Yacht clubs also emerged in the southern

hemisphere: Australia's Royal Perth Yacht Club opened in 1841, and the 1850s saw yacht clubs open in South Africa and New Zealand.

Yacht design advanced through the mutual exchange of ideas, particularly across the Atlantic. For example, plans of the American sloop *Parole* appeared in the 1882 edition of the British yacht designer Dixon Kemp's *Manual of Yacht and Boat Sailing*, along with those of the sharpie, which had a canoe-like hull, and the sneak boat, which was originally used for duck hunting. All of these craft originated from New York and the city's neighbouring states.

IMPERIAL VESSEL
The steam yacht (see p.266) La Reine Hortense, which belonged to the French Emperor Napoleon III, and was named after his mother, is seen here moored at France's first yacht club, in Le Havre, in 1856.

SHARPIE
A flat-bottomed vessel with a single mast, the sharpie originated among the oyster fishing fleets on the east coast of America. The craft was adapted to leisure use in the 19th century.

Yacht racing

Racing was rare in the early days of yachting. One of the first recorded contests between sailing craft took place between Charles II and his brother James in October 1661. They raced down the River Thames from Greenwich to Gravesend, Kent, and back. The diarist John Evelyn, who was onboard one of the yachts, described how "the King lost it [the race] going, the wind being contrary, but saved stakes in returning." During the 18th century, yacht clubs in England and Ireland raced sporadically, but it was not until the next century that yacht races began to establish themselves as international events.

BUILDING A WINNER

The American marine architects John and Nathaniel Herreshoff were renowned for building fast yachts. This photograph shows the construction of the Rainbow, *which won the 1934 America's Cup.*

Initially, yacht races were grand affairs involving large craft, such as the America's Cup (see panel, opposite). Following the success of the *America*, many new yachts were designed and built for racing. At the forefront of this boom were designers such as the American John Herreshoff and E.H. Bentall, who was based in England.

Races involving small boats or dinghies emerged in the second half of the 19th century, and rapidly gained in popularity, particularly after the end of the First World War. These races usually involved sailing vessels of not more than 4.25m (14ft) in length. Many yacht clubs produced their own class of vessel that suited local conditions, with members encouraged to build and race their own craft.

Yacht races were usually regulated within individual clubs. However, the Yacht Racing Association (YRA) was formed in Britain in 1875 to provide a uniform set of rules. The YRA divided boats into six classes, based on tonnage and ranging from less than 3 tons to more than 80 tons. In 1907, the organization became the International Yacht Racing Union (IYRU), standardizing the sizes and specifications of yachts and establishing racing regulations throughout Europe and much of the world. American yacht clubs raced by their own guidelines until 1925, when they, too, joined the

FULL SAIL

Yachting quickly became popular in Australia, with the first clubs opening there in the mid-19th century. Photographed in Sydney Harbour in 1929, this yacht is racing with the full strength of the wind behind it.

IYRU. Designers soon began to construct yachts based around these rules, interpreting them to the best advantage. This meant that regulations had to be revised constantly to close loopholes or to cope with new technology.

After a period of decline during the First World War, yacht design boomed again in the 1920s. The English marine architect Uffa Fox designed the dinghy *Avenger*, in 1928. It was innovative in that it had a V-shaped hull, which allowed it to cut through the water. Fox's design proved so successful that it soon became standard for racing dinghies. At the other end of the scale, J-class yachts represented the pinnacle of extravagance in sailing yachts. Measuring up to 26m (85ft), these craft required a crew of 24 and were extremely expensive to construct and maintain.

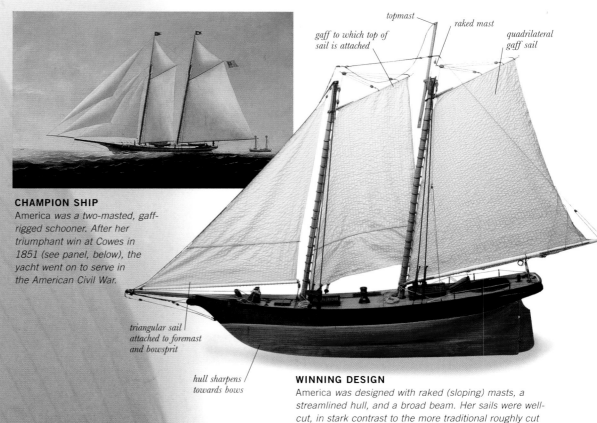

CHAMPION SHIP
America *was a two-masted, gaff-rigged schooner. After her triumphant win at Cowes in 1851 (see panel, below), the yacht went on to serve in the American Civil War.*

topmast
raked mast
gaff to which top of sail is attached
quadrilateral gaff sail
triangular sail attached to foremast and bowsprit
hull sharpens towards bows

WINNING DESIGN
America *was designed with raked (sloping) masts, a streamlined hull, and a broad beam. Her sails were well-cut, in stark contrast to the more traditional roughly cut hand-woven flax used by the ship's British counterparts.*

THE FIRST AMERICA'S CUP

In 1851, the schooner *America*, which was owned by a syndicate headed by John C. Stevens, the founder of the New York Yacht Club, crossed the Atlantic to race against several British ships for the 100 Guinea Cup at Cowes in southern England. Despite the New York crew's lack of local knowledge, *America* won the race eight minutes ahead of her nearest competitor, the much smaller vessel *Aurora*. The crew took the cup, which was renamed in honour of the winning yacht, back to New York, and it soon became the most prestigious prize in yachting. Over the next century, more than 30 yachts, many of them British, unsuccessfully challenged the United States for the prize. It was not until 1983 that the cup was taken from the United States, when it was won by an Australian crew. New Zealand successfully challenged for the trophy in 1995 and 2000, and in 2003 the Swiss yacht *Alinghi* became the first European team to take the prize.

SHAMROCK IV
The English grocery tycoon, Sir Thomas Lipton, financed several yachts named Shamrock *to contest the America's Cup.* Shamrock IV, *photographed here in 1925, lost to the American yacht* Resolute *in the 1920 race.*

VOYAGE AROUND THE WORLD
Joshua Slocum was an exceptional sailor. He became the first person to sail around the world single-handed following an extraordinary three-year voyage in his gaff-rigged sloop Spray (pictured here).

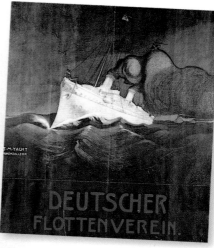

A YACHT FIT FOR A KING
Kaiser Wilhelm's steam yacht Hohenzollern was launched in 1892. It is pictured here on a poster advertising the German Fleet Association, which was based at Dresden.

The quest for single-handed adventure on the high seas continued in the 1920s and 1930s, despite being somewhat overshadowed by the flights of pioneer aviators, including the future record-breaking yachtsman Francis Chichester (see p.369). The French tennis player Alain Gerbault became the first to cross the Atlantic single-handed from east to west in 1924. The American William Albert Robinson sailed around the world in a 9.8-m (32-ft) ketch in 1928, and between 1930 and 1932 the Estonian Ahto Walter sailed an estimated 40,000km (25,000 miles), crossing the Atlantic five times.

Epic voyages

A counterpoint to the social whirl of regattas and races provided by yacht clubs was the pursuit of single-handed sailing. Long and often hazardous voyages were undertaken by solo yachtsmen in small craft, such as yachts or sailing canoes. One of the first of these voyages was undertaken by the Scotsman John MacGregor, who built a canoe called *Rob Roy*. In 1865, he travelled along many of Europe's major rivers, including the Rhine, Danube, and Seine. Later in the same decade, MacGregor toured Norway, Sweden, and Denmark, and in 1868 he took a steamer to Alexandria, Egypt, to canoe through the Suez Canal and down the Red Sea.

Others were inspired to travel even further. The Nova Scotian Captain Joshua Slocum left Boston on 24 April 1895 in his 10.6-m (35-ft) sloop *Spray*. He sailed across the Atlantic to Gibraltar and then travelled south into the Atlantic to sail along the coast of South America and around Cape Horn. By July 1896, Slocum had arrived at Samoa in the Pacific. He then cruised around Australia and headed across the Indian Ocean around the Cape of Good Hope and across the Atlantic for a third time. Despite encountering a tornado along the east coast of the USA, Slocum completed his journey, arriving at Rhode Island in June 1898.

Steam yachts

As with other sailing vessels, leisure craft were changed by the advent of steam. Steam-powered yachts can be traced back to the British industrialist Thomas Assheton-Smith, who built several between 1830 and 1850. However, this type of vessel remained scarce, as the steam engine of the time was noisy, expensive, and unwieldy. The compound engine (see p.178) proved slightly more suitable, although Dixon Kemp argued that 40 per cent of a vessel's space was needed to accommodate such a device.

GERBAULT'S JOURNEY
After reaching New York in 1924, Alain Gerbault, seen here on his yacht Firecrest, continued his epic voyage. He spent over four years at sea and circumnavigated the globe.

> 66 I wanted freedom, open air, adventure, I found it on the sea. 99
>
> **ALAIN GERBAULT,** *Flight of the* Firecrest, **1926**

Steam yachting developed as a pastime for the very rich, who constructed huge vessels. *North Star*, which was built for the American tycoon Cornelius Vanderbilt I in 1855, was one of the first of its kind. She was 83m (270ft) long and cost $500,000, a vast sum for the time. Royalty also took to steam yachting. In Britain, Queen Victoria's steam yacht *Victoria and Albert* was completed in 1855, and other European monarchs, including the German Kaiser Wilhelm and Tsar Nicholas II of Russia, also constructed lavish vessels.

Popular, less extravagant versions of the powered yacht also emerged. As petrol and diesel engines became more prevalent in the early years of the 20th century, smaller vessels, such as cabin cruisers and powerboats, developed. Cruisers were motor-powered leisure craft that were used either on the sea in good weather or along rivers and canals. Many small yachts were fitted with outboard motors after their invention in the late 19th century. However, yachts that were powered purely by sail still remained extremely popular.

Sail training

As steam-powered ships became more ubiquitous, sail training rose in popularity. The aim of the practice was to teach recruits of national or merchant navies "real" seamanship, meaning the skills that were used by sailors on large sailing vessels. Novice mariners were taken

to sea in large sailing ships or put through their paces in harbour in static training ships. In the first half of the 20th century, several nations developed sail training with enthusiasm. The American government built the *Cumberland* in 1904. The Japanese Ministry of Transport built four sailing ships to train recruits for the merchant service, beginning with the *Taisei Maru* in 1904. The Norddeutscher Lloyd Line built several ships, including the *Herzogin Cecilie* and the *Magdalene Vinnen*, as did other lines, such as Rickmers and White Star. The Italian Navy constructed the *Amerigo Vespucci* in 1931, and the French *La Belle Poule* in 1932. The German Navy built several large sailing ships to train cadets, some of which were confiscated by the Allies after the Second World War. Sail training was also viewed by some as a virtue in itself, rather than a precursor to a career at sea. The Australian writer and sailor Alan Villiers renovated an old Danish training ship, the *George Stage*, which he renamed *Joseph Conrad*. He sailed it around the world as a training ship for young men in 1934–36. Many of these sailing ships are still in use today and form the star attractions at tall-ship races.

The skills of amateur yachtsmen were not dismissed, particularly during the 20th century's two world wars. In 1903, the novelist Erskine Childers, whose own yacht *Asgard* became a sail training ship in his native Ireland, published the novel *Riddle of the Sands*. It described a voyage in

which two British yachtsmen discover a German plan to invade England and inspired the formation of the Royal Naval Volunteer Reserve before the First World War. Amateur sailors also found themselves called upon by navies during the Second World War.

GOING ALOFT
Alan Villiers did much to document the sailing ships of the 20th century. He sailed to Australia in 1931–32 onboard the Parma. In this photograph, taken by Villiers, crew-members are climbing the rigging to furl the sails.

RIDING THE TRADES

Alan Villiers served in a variety of sailing ships in the 1920s and 1930s. He vividly described his experiences under sail:

" With the tail of the south-east trade as a light fair wind, we sailed on westwards. We were in a lonely part of the ocean, and sighted no other ships. Day after day the trade wind blew and, upright and lovely, the big four-master slipped quietly along. Her speed was rarely better than seven knots, but it never dropped below five. Flying fish skimmed before the great cut-water, and the conditions were excellent. Week after week the main deck was dry and there was never need to touch a sail. "

ALAN VILLIERS, *The Way of a Ship*, **1954**

RACING AHEAD
Powerboat races first emerged in the early 20th century and proved extremely popular by the 1920s. This powerboat, the Wa Wa, was photographed in 1925 by the New York maritime photographer Edwin Levick.

DEATH OF A U-BOAT
In both world wars, surface ships were attacked by submarines. Here, the crew of the US coastguard cutter *Spencer* use depth charges to thwart an attack on an Allied convoy by the German *U-175*, in April 1943.

THE WORLD WARS

THE FIRST HALF OF THE 20TH CENTURY saw no normal times, only preparation for war, war itself, and the aftermath of war. The basics of ship design changed little during this period, and there was no new type of engine or material for construction. But warship designers had to deal with new factors – the submarine, aircraft, and electronic technologies such as sonar and radar. Sea power played decisive roles in both world wars, especially the second, which was fought across the Mediterranean, the Atlantic, and the Pacific. More people than ever before fought at sea in vastly expanded navies. Maritime blockade threatened starvation to Britain in both world wars and caused the collapse of Germany in the first. Merchant shipping, which suffered terribly in both wars, made slow progress. Competition from air travel was only just beginning, and the ocean liner took on a new and glamorous image in the late 1920s and 1930s in the face of the Great Depression.

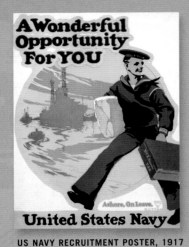

US NAVY RECRUITMENT POSTER, 1917

> 66 A good navy is not
> a provocation to war.
> It is the surest
> guarantee of peace. 99

PRESIDENT THEODORE ROOSEVELT,
Second annual message to Congress,
2 December 1902

KEY EVENTS

1900 UNCLE SAM'S DEVIL OF THE DEEP
The US Navy adopts John Philip Holland's Type
VI submarine design. Britain and Germany
subsequently commission their own submarines.

1905 EAST BEATS WEST Japan defeats
Russia at the Battle of Tsushima and goes on to
win the Russo-Japanese War.

1906 FEAR GOD AND *DREADNOUGHT* The
Royal Navy launches the *Dreadnought*, the most
powerful battleship of its time.

1910 BIPLANE FLIES FROM SHIP American
pilot Eugene Ely successfully launches an
aircraft from the deck of the *Birmingham*.

1911 SOUTH POLE REACHED Norwegian
explorer Roald Amundsen becomes the first
man to stand at the South Pole.

1912 TITANIC DISASTER The White Star
liner *Titanic* hits an iceberg on 14 April and
sinks in 2½ hours with the loss of 1,513 lives.

1914 PANAMA CANAL COMPLETED The
Panama Canal opens, linking the Pacific Ocean
with the Atlantic Ocean via the Caribbean Sea.

THE ROAD TO WAR

INTERNATIONAL RIVALRIES IN THE EARLY 20TH CENTURY WOULD LEAD INEXORABLY TO THE WORST WAR THE WORLD HAD YET SEEN.

The world seemed a much smaller place by the early years of the 20th century, mainly because of the impact of the steamship and the electric telegraph, in alliance with the railway. The effect, however, was not to create a unified world, but one of competing empires. Rivalry between the European powers intensified and found expression in races to build greater navies and larger ocean liners. Although the ensuing conflict, the First World War, had its roots in Europe, it was echoed in the Russo-Japanese War in the Pacific, in liner races across the Atlantic, and even at the North and South Poles.

The Russo-Japanese War

The new age of naval conflict began a long way from Europe. Russia's eastward expansion and the building of the Trans-Siberian Railway brought it into conflict with the rising power of Japan. On the night of 8–9 February 1904, Japanese destroyers launched a pre-emptive strike against Russian forces at Port Arthur (now Lüshun) on the Liaoning Peninsula, northeast China. Two battleships and a cruiser were put out of action. The next morning, the main Japanese fleet, commanded by

UNLOADING SUPPLIES AT PORT ARTHUR
This stereoscopic photo shows soldiers unloading military supplies from cargo ships at Port Arthur, northeast China, during the Russo-Japanese War of 1904–05. When seen through a stereoscopic viewer, the image appears in 3-D.

Admiral Togo (see p.273), fought a short action outside the port, after which the Russians were blockaded. War was formally declared on 10 February. There was much laying of mines over the next few months, and both sides suffered losses. On 10 August 1904, the Russian fleet of 6 battleships, 4 cruisers, and 14 destroyers, led by Admiral Vitgeff, sailed out of Port Arthur to meet Togo, who had 4 battleships, 10 cruisers, and 48 destroyers and torpedo boats. In the Battle of the Yellow Sea that followed, the Russians were damaged by long-range gunnery. After nightfall, the Japanese launched torpedo attacks with little success. The Russians were forced to retreat, either back to

RUSSIAN DEFIANCE
The Russian Porcupine gives Japan's Admiral Togo a bloody hand when he tries to shift it from the Russian naval base of Port Arthur in this Russian propaganda poster from 1904.

ENDS IN DEFEAT
Three Russian military ships sunk by the Japanese Navy lie part-submerged in the Gulf of Bo Hai in the Yellow Sea, at the end of the Russo-Japanese War in 1905.

FUTURE FLAGSHIP
The US Navy battleship Connecticut *steams ahead at high speed during its sea trials in 1906. It became the flagship of the USA's Great White Fleet in 1907, which toured the world in a show of naval strength that was typical of the early years of the 20th century.*

THE BATTLE OF TSUSHIMA

After its voyage halfway round the world to reinforce Port Arthur, Admiral Rozhestvensky's Russian Fleet was met by Admiral Togo's Japanese force at Tsushima Strait, between Japan and Korea, on the afternoon of 27 May 1905. As the mist began to clear, the Russian Fleet was sighted to the southwest of the Japanese Fleet, whereas Togo had expected it to be to the east. Togo ordered his fleet to starboard and across the Russians' path. Then, at 1:35pm, in a surprising and daring manoeuvre, he led the fleet in a great U-turn, bringing his ships on a parallel course with the Russians. The Japanese sailors were better trained and their ships were much faster, and Togo was able to concentrate his fire on each Russian ship in succession and force the fleet away from its original line of advance. At first, both sides inflicted equal damage on each other. Then, at 2:44pm, Rozhestvensky attempted to cut past the Japanese Fleet's rear. Togo turned his ships simultaneously, bringing about a close-range engagement in which the Russian battleships suffered heavy damage. The Russian flagship *Suvarov* was hit and Rozhestvensky was injured. Under the command of Vice Admiral Nebogativ, the Russian Fleet began to fall into disorder. Gun action continued until nightfall, when

WORLD RENOWNED
Italy's Sunday Courier *reports Admiral Togo's landmark victory over the Russians.*

the Japanese torpedo boats began to attack. By the next morning, after another brief engagement, all 45 of the Russian ships, except for four transports, had been sunk, captured, or interned in neutral countries. The Japanese only lost three torpedo boats and had 600 casualties, whereas around 6,000 Russians were killed. It was the most decisive naval action of the age.

THE SINKING OF THE *BORODINO*
Russian sailors struggle to escape from the stricken battleship Borodino, *which was hit by Togo's forces as it tried to escape to the north as night fell on 27 May.*

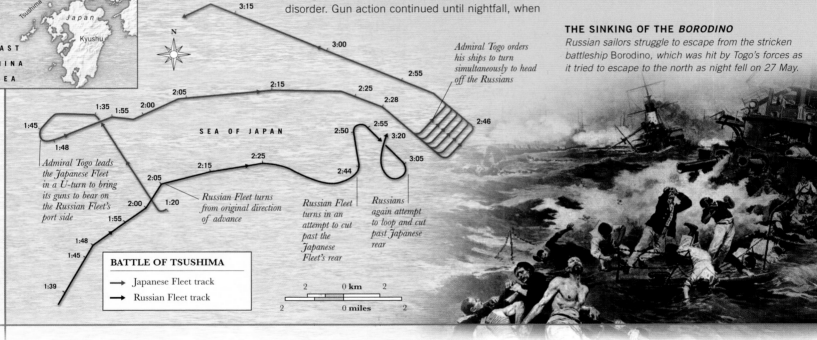

SEA OF JAPAN

Admiral Togo orders his ships to turn simultaneously to head off the Russians

Admiral Togo leads the Japanese Fleet in a U-turn to bring its guns to bear on the Russian Fleet's port side

Russian Fleet turns from original direction of advance

Russian Fleet turns in an attempt to cut past the Japanese Fleet's rear

Russians again attempt to loop and cut past Japanese rear

BATTLE OF TSUSHIMA
→ Japanese Fleet track
→ Russian Fleet track

SEA OF JAPAN — Korea — Tsushima — Tsushima Strait — Honshu — Japan — Kyushu — EAST CHINA SEA — □ Site of battle

Port Arthur, where they were blockaded, or into neutral ports, where they were interned. The Japanese had learned well from the European naval powers, especially the British.

To reinforce the forces in the east, the Russian Second Squadron, headed by five new and two old battleships, left the Baltic in October 1904 for an epic voyage halfway round the world. But it was all in vain as the squadron was destroyed at Tsushima in May 1905 (see panel, above). That

SOVIET CINEMA
Sergei Eisenstein's film Battleship Potemkin, *first shown on 18 January 1926, was commissioned by the Soviet government to celebrate the 20th anniversary of the 1905 uprising.*

September, the Russians conceded Port Arthur to the Japanese in the Treaty of Portsmouth, mediated by President Roosevelt. It was the first time in modern history that an eastern nation had defeated a western one. In Russia, the defeat, and the repression of a mutiny on the battleship *Potemkin* in the Black Sea, sparked an unsuccessful workers' revolution.

Sea power

The works of US Navy officer Alfred Thayer Mahan had been popular since the first publication of *The Influence of Sea Power Upon History* in 1889, and his ideas were well known to naval officers and the better-informed elements of the public. His arguments suggested that commerce raiding was a

ALFRED THAYER MAHAN
US Navy captain and author Alfred T. Mahan argued that all world powers were also naval powers, and that their success was dependent on the strength of their navies. His ideas were hugely influential in the USA, Japan, Germany, and Britain.

diversion from the real naval effort, which should be directed to great fleets of battleships as the main determinant of naval power. This was rather different from the view of Admiral John Fisher, the British First Sea Lord, who envisaged a navy that would defend the homeland by means of submarines and mines, as well as protecting trade with battlecruisers and cruisers. Indeed,

TOGO HEIHACHIRO

Togo Heihachiro (1848–1934) was born into the Satsuma clan, a powerful Japanese family with seafaring interests. He was selected to train for the infant Japanese Navy and spent 1871–73 on the Royal Navy training ship *Worcester* in the Thames estuary. In July 1894, he fired the first shots of the Sino-Japanese War. From 1895, Togo reformed the training of naval officers, and studied tactics. In 1904, as Commander-in-Chief of the Combined Squadrons, he led Japanese forces at the Battle of Tsushima. When Togo died in 1934, he was given a state funeral.

countries to lobby for increased naval expenditure. In Britain, newspapers carried cartoons showing the gunnery progress of the fleet, and crowds demonstrated in the streets demanding more ships be built – "We want eight and we won't wait!" was a popular chant. Even politicians such as Winston Churchill, who had started off opposing increased naval expenditure, were swept up in the movement. As First Lord of the Admiralty from 1911, Churchill presided over the Royal Navy's greatest ever peacetime expansion.

The great arms race

The Germans were wrong-footed by the launch of the *Dreadnought* in 1906. They would have to widen the Kiel Canal to let ships of that size through on their transit between the training area of the Baltic and the operational theatre of the North Sea, and their plans had already committed them to some very different ships. Despite the

the battlecruiser was his favourite ship, conceived when the most likely enemy was seen to be France and the biggest threat was armed raiders that could cut off Britain's food supplies. The battlecruiser was a large cruiser that was as heavily armed as a battleship; it also had the long range of a cruiser, with greater speed but less armour protection. But Fisher also conceived the *Dreadnought* (see panel, p.274), with heavier armour, less speed, and shorter range. This was more consistent with Mahan's idea of sea power, in which great fleets would meet in battle and everything else was subsidiary. The dreadnought concept took hold of the popular imagination and led to the great arms race.

Naval preparations became a matter of great public interest, more than at any other time in history. Navy leagues were founded in several

ARMING GERMANY'S NAVY
The Krupp steelworks in Essen produced Germany's heavy artillery in the build-up to the First World War. These naval guns were destined for the ships of Germany's new fleet.

urgency of the challenge, the German Navy's first ships on the dreadnought pattern, built to a common specification known as the *Nassau* class, were not laid down until the middle of 1907. Their 280-mm (11-in) guns were slightly smaller than the *Dreadnought*'s 12-in (305-mm) guns. No turbines were available, so they had a less efficient triple-expansion engine, but they were well protected with armour up to 300mm (12in) thick, compared with the *Dreadnought*'s 11in (280mm). Unlike the British ships, they were designed for short-range operations in the North Sea, so they could sacrifice fuel stowage and crew accommodation in return for extra fighting qualities. Four ships with 305-mm (12-in) guns were ordered in 1908–09, five more in 1909–11 (the first with turbine engines), and another five in 1911–12. The British responded by increasing the size of the main armament of their battleships, and as a result had to increase their total size as well.

THE ULTIMATE DREADNOUGHT
The arms race resulted in the Royal Navy's Queen Elizabeth *class of dreadnought, laid down in 1912. The 15-in (381-mm) guns could fire 1,920lb (870kg) shells a distance of 25km (16 miles).*

The *Dreadnought* herself, and the nine other ships ordered in the next three years after her launch, had ten 12-in (305-mm) guns on hulls of up to 23,000 tons. The four ships of the *Orion* class, ordered in 1909, were the first of the "Super-dreadnoughts", with 13.5-in (343-mm) guns firing a shell 65 per cent heavier than 12-in (305-mm) guns, on a hull of nearly 26,000 tons. Eight more were ordered in 1910 and 1911.

In 1912, the Admiralty made a further leap, ordering five ships of the *Queen Elizabeth* class, with 15-in (381-mm) guns weighing more than twice as much as a 12-in (305-mm) gun. Despite hulls of 31,500 tons at full load, they had a top speed of 23 knots, only 2 knots less than older battlecruisers. They would remain the most powerful battleships in the world until the 1920s.

BATH TOYS FOR THE BOYS
Even children were caught up in the excitement of the arms race. This pre-war German toy battleship has a brass key in one of its funnels to wind up the motor.

The Germans responded with two ships of the *Bayern* class with 380-mm (15-in) guns, but they were not ready until 1916–17. A separate race developed with the battlecruisers, which were now seen more as a fast squadron of battleships rather than Fisher's original idea of commerce-protection ships. By August 1914, the Royal Navy had 21 dreadnoughts and 9 battlecruisers in service compared with Germany's 15 and 5. The other naval powers, building at a relatively normal rate, had been left behind – the USA had eight dreadnoughts, France and Italy had four each, Austria–Hungary three, and Russia none. The British had maintained their superiority of arms over Germany, but it was not insuperable. A small British squadron might be isolated and destroyed to change the balance of power, or more banal matters such as routine maintenance or accident might narrow the margin.

Roosevelt and the Great White Fleet

Under its ebullient President Theodore Roosevelt, the USA began to take a much greater interest in world affairs. Roosevelt initiated the building of the Panama Canal in 1904 (see panel, p.276), and, in 1906, he was awarded the Nobel Peace Prize for his part in ending the Russo-Japanese War. Another of his ideas, already common among the European powers, was to send ships of the US Fleet to foreign ports, where they would entertain dignitaries and the general public and increase national prestige. Roosevelt's conception was on a grand scale: 16 battleships and their escorts, crewed by 14,000 men, were to sail round the world and call in at capital cities where the Americans had an interest. The fleet sailed from Hampton Roads, Virginia, on 16 December 1907 (see map, opposite).

The fleet called in at Trinidad, where the British reception was frosty, then spent three months cruising around South America, visiting the ports of Rio de Janeiro in Brazil, Punta Arenas in Chile, and Callao in Peru. It then spent two months in San Francisco before crossing the Pacific Ocean, to be greeted by rapturous welcomes in New Zealand and Australia. Next, the fleet's two squadrons sailed north to the Philippines and on to China and Japan. The mission was a diplomatic failure with the Chinese, but improved links with Japan.

THE BIRTH OF THE *DREADNOUGHT*

Western observers drew many different lessons from the Battle of Tsushima. Admiral "Jacky" Fisher, the dynamic British First Sea Lord, saw the possibility of battle at longer range. He appreciated the importance of spotting, or observing the fall of, shot. If guns of different types were all firing at random, it would be difficult to assess the accuracy of the gunnery and direct it closer to the target. Most large warships had a mix of guns, the larger ones mostly being 12in (305mm), with a secondary armament of 6-in (152-mm) or 9.2-in (234-mm) guns in the British case. Fisher decided to abolish the secondary battery and go for an "all-big-gun" armament of ten 12-in (305-mm) guns, with smaller quick-firing guns for use against torpedo craft. He also used a turbine engine to give the ship a speed of 21 knots.

A ROYAL OCCASION
The most powerful battleship in the world, the Royal Navy's Dreadnought *was launched at Portsmouth by King George V on 9 February 1906.*

Fisher fought off criticisms that it would be better for the superior British Navy to continue in the Nelsonian tradition of engaging at close range. With great determination, he had the prototype ship *Dreadnought* built in great secrecy at Portsmouth in under a year. When she took to sea on 3 October 1906, she instantly rendered all other battleships obsolete.

UNDER CONSTRUCTION
The frames of the Dreadnought's *steel hull had just been laid at the Portsmouth Dockyard when this photo was taken on 5 October 1905.*

GREAT WHITE FLEET

→ Route, 16 December 1907–
22 February, 1909

San Francisco
6 May–7 July
1908

Hampton Roads
16 December 1907

Honolulu
16–23 July 1908

Gibraltar
6 February 1909

Port Said
3–7 January 1909

Yokohama
19–23 October 1908

Honolulu
16–23 July 1908

Colombo
14–20 December
1908

Sydney
20–27 August
1908

Auckland
8–15 August 1908

Albany
11–17 September 1908

Melbourne
29 August–3 September 1908

Punta Arenas
1–7 February 1908

Asia

Europe

PACIFIC
OCEAN

*North
America*

Africa

*South
America*

ATLANTIC
OCEAN

INDIAN
OCEAN

PACIFIC
OCEAN

SOUTHERN OCEAN

N

the Germans at the beginning of the century. Moreover, the *Dreadnought* had already been launched, and the American ships were outdated.

International crises

The new German Fleet failed as a deterrent against the British. It was built on the theory that they would not risk a fight with Germany in which they might lose some ships and become vulnerable to another power. In fact, it drove them closer to France. In 1904, Britain and France formed the Entente Cordiale, or "friendly understanding"; then, in 1907, France's ally Russia was brought in to form the Triple Entente. Germany, Austria–Hungary, and Italy were already united in the Triple Alliance of 1882, so Europe was divided into two armed camps.

In 1905, Morocco was one of the last uncolonized areas of the non-European world, and its long Atlantic and Mediterranean coastlines and position opposite the British at Gibraltar made it tempting to Germany. Kaiser Wilhelm II visited the country in March, provoking fears that he intended a takeover. He was forced to withdraw any claims in the face of Anglo-French pressure. In 1911, an even

THE GREAT WHITE FLEET
The flagship Connecticut, *under the command of Rear Admiral Robley D. Evans, leads the Atlantic Fleet battleships on the first leg of its voyage in December 1907. The fleet's two squadrons would travel around 69,000km (43,000 miles) and between them call in at 20 ports during their voyage around the globe.*

more serious crisis began when French troops entered from Algeria to put down a rebellion. In the most famous example of gunboat diplomacy, the Germans sent the *Panther*, originally designed for service on Chinese rivers, to the Moroccan port of Agadir. Again, Britain backed France and the matter was settled by negotiation, in which France ceded rights in the Congo to Germany, and Morocco became a French Protectorate in 1912. Nevertheless, international tension had been heightened.

In 1912 and 1913, there were two major wars in the Balkans, in which rival states fought for possession of the European territories of the collapsing Ottoman Empire (now Turkey). There were some small-scale

ROOSEVELT WELCOMES THE FLEET BACK HOME
President Roosevelt addresses the crew of the Connecticut, *now under the command of Rear Admiral Charles S. Sperry, after reviewing the Great White Fleet as it arrived back at Hampton Roads, Virginia, on 22 February 1909.*

Having stopped off at Ceylon (now Sri Lanka) while crossing the Indian Ocean, the fleet passed through the Suez Canal and arrived at Port Said on 3 January 1909. There it received word of a terrible earthquake that had struck Messina on the island of Sicily on 28 December, killing an estimated 160,000 people. Four ships were immediately despatched to offer aid to the Italians. The fleet reunited at the British colony of Gibraltar to refuel, then crossed the Atlantic to return to Hampton Roads in February 1909, after a voyage of 14 months.

Because the battleships were painted white with gilt scrollwork on the bows, the Atlantic Fleet gained the popular name of the Great White Fleet, echoing Herman Melville's "great white whale". Unfortunately, the ships' colouring made them appear old-fashioned, because European warships were usually painted grey by this time, a practice started by

FRAGILE PEACE
The declaration of war was still a few years off when Tsar Nicholas II of Russia (left) and Kaiser Wilhelm II of Germany held this meeting, but they had already aligned their countries with opposing European factions.

THE PANAMA CANAL

Following his success at Suez in 1869, the French engineer Ferdinand de Lesseps began construction of a sea-level canal across the Isthmus of Panama to link the Pacific Ocean with the Atlantic Ocean via the Caribbean Sea in 1878. But he soon found the hilly topography presented too many difficulties, and his men were decimated by diseases such as malaria and yellow fever. His company collapsed in 1888.

However, such a canal would be of great strategic value to the USA, and in 1903, President Theodore Roosevelt persuaded Congress that they should build a lock-type canal. The railway engineer John Findley Wallace began construction in 1904. He was replaced by John Stevens, who appointed doctors to improve sanitation. The canal was finally completed under Lieutenant Colonel George Goethals, opening to traffic in August 1914. It is 82km (51 miles) long and has six locks, one of which is 26m (85ft) above sea level at the vast, man-made Lago Gatún.

MIRAFLORES LOCK AND GATES

Construction of the Miraflores Locks, the two-step locks on the Pacific side, was ongoing in 1913. The gates of the lower chamber are the tallest in the entire canal.

naval battles, in which the Turks failed to force their way out of the Dardanelles. The Greeks used a seaplane for reconnaissance in February 1913, the first use of an aircraft in this role.

When all-out war finally came in August 1914 after the assassination of the heir to the Austrian throne and a threatened invasion of Serbia by Austria–Hungary, the main causes were not directly nautical. They were based on long-term rivalries and conflicting ambitions between the great land powers of Europe, as well as a system of interlocking alliances that rapidly ranged Germany and Austria–Hungary

against Russia, France, and Britain. But maritime affairs – colonial rivalries and the naval arms race – had worked for 10 years or so to create international suspicions, which destroyed any prospect of peaceful negotiation.

COMING IN TO LAND

Civil aviator Eugene Ely attempts to land his biplane on a wooden platform just 40m (130ft) long and 10m (33ft) wide on the US Navy's Pennsylvania in 1911. The crew had rigged canvas awnings at the sides and in front of the mast to catch the plane in the event of an overrun or a swerve.

Naval air power

The Wright brothers flew their first practical aeroplane in South Carolina on 17 December 1903, but it was not until 1909, after they had won a US government contract and completed a European tour, that their achievements received widespread international recognition. At this time, only visionaries saw naval air power as a means of attacking great warships. Navies first used aircraft for reconnaissance since, despite great advances in almost every other direction, they had no way of seeing beyond the horizon. Early winged aircraft were inhibited by their short range, but the airship seemed a good solution to this. The Germans had their highly efficient rigid airships, the Zeppelins, which had been making regular passenger and mail flights since 1910. But their military applications had mainly been explored by the army, and the Naval Airship Section had only one Zeppelin in service in 1914. The British rigid airship of 1911, the aptly named *Mayfly*, was a failure.

Another possibility was to launch aircraft from ships. This was first tried by American pilot Eugene Ely, who successfully took off in a Curtiss pusher from a platform on the bow of the US cruiser *Birmingham* in Hampton Roads, Virginia, on 14 November 1910. However, landing at sea was still a problem. Floats allowed a plane to land in the water, but affected its performance. Alternatively, the pilot could make for the nearest land.

In his first test, Ely took the latter approach, but on 18 January 1911, he landed his biplane, without brakes, on a purpose-built wooden platform over the after deck of the US Navy cruiser *Pennsylvania*. anchored in San Francisco Bay. A series of ropes secured by sandbags were stretched between boards about 6m (20ft) apart on the deck (see below). Hooks were attached to the plane's landing gear, which caught on the ropes, thus bringing it to a rapid halt. However, this feat was viewed by some US Navy officials as more of a stunt than a convincing demonstration, and it was the British who then took the lead for the next decade. The Royal Navy had a design for a purpose-built aircraft carrier in 1912, although it would take some years of wartime experience for landing techniques to be perfected.

The birth of the submarine

Many pioneers – including the Americans David Bushnell (see the *Turtle*, p.124) and Robert Fulton, the Bavarian officer Wilhelm Bauer, the Frenchman Claude Goubet, and the English clergyman George W. Garrett – had experimented with submarines during the previous two centuries. The idea of a craft that could move invisibly underwater had a good deal of appeal to countries that wanted

MAN AND MACHINE
John Philip Holland emerges from the conning-tower of Holland VI in New York Harbour, USA, in April 1898. This was the prototype of the modern submarine.

INTERIOR OF *U-1*
The German Navy's first U-boat, the U-1 of 1906, has been preserved at the Deutsches Museum, Munich, since 1921. Part of the hull has been removed to reveal the engine and electrical control panel.

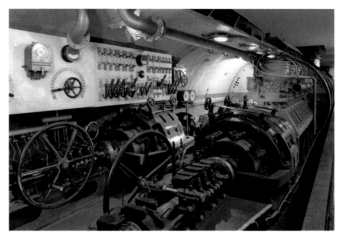

to challenge British naval power, and it was boosted when the development of the torpedo (see p.222) provided a weapon that could be launched underwater. Electric power, unlike steam, could be used under the water, although submarines had to spend a great deal of time on the surface to charge their batteries using steam- and later diesel-powered internal combustion engines.

It was an Irish American, John Phillip Holland, who produced the first practicable submarine at his sixth attempt in 1898. The *Holland VI* was the first to incorporate an advanced streamlined shape with a fixed longitudinal centre of gravity, separate main and auxilliary ballast systems, dual means of propulsion, and to be armed with a torpedo. After two years of trials and a few modifications, the submarine was bought by the US government in April 1900 for $150,000. She entered service in the US Navy, having been renamed *Holland*, in October 1900.

In France, the engineer Maxime Laubeuf produced a type of submarine that was more like a submersible torpedo boat at the turn of the century. Britain was reluctant at first, but followed the USA's lead in 1901 by building submarines under licence from Holland's company. The *Holland 1* was fitted with a single torpedo tube through which a Whitehead torpedo packed with 11kg (25lb) of TNT could be fired with a range of 890ft (275m). In addition to the crew of eight men, three white mice were carried onboard as an early warning system if carbon monoxide leaked from the petrol engine. Holland's designs were also adopted by the Japanese, Russian, and Swedish navies.

The Germans were the last major naval power to realize the potential of the submarine, or *Unterseeboot*, commissioning the *U-1* from the Friedrich Krupp Germaniawerft shipyard in Kiel in 1906. Early submarines had a short range, and their small crews lived and worked in very uncomfortable conditions. *U-1* had a crew of 12 and a range of 50 nautical miles (93km). The British A-class of 1902 had a crew of 11 and could travel 320 miles (515km) at 10 knots on the surface, so even a voyage to the limits of the vessel's range would last only about a day. But larger submarines were soon built, to operate over longer ranges. By 1912, German U-boats had ranges of more than 11,260km (7,000 miles), with crews of 35 men.

HOW A SUBMARINE WORKS

An object will float or sink in water depending on how dense it is. Filling a submarine's ballast tanks with water increases its density. To dive, vents at the top of the outer hull are opened, allowing air to escape from the tanks. The reduced pressure allows water to enter through vents in the bottom. The engine powers the submarine forwards and down, aided by tilting control surfaces called hydroplanes at the front and rear. The vessel sinks until the ballast tanks are full of water and it has achieved neutral buoyancy – the upper vents are then closed. To surface, compressed air is blown into the ballast tanks, forcing water out of the lower vents, and increasing the submarine's buoyancy. The engine propels the submarine upwards, aided by angling of the hydroplanes, until it returns to the surface.

after hydroplanes for depth control

ballast tanks attached to hull

ventilation intake

vent for ballast tanks

conning-tower and mast

casing for crew to walk on

forward hydroplanes

EARLY SUBMARINE
The British D-Class, launched in 1908–11, was one of the first submarines to have diesel-powered engines, giving it a top surface speed of 14 knots. It had two propellers at the rear, wing-like hydroplanes, and saddle tanks for ballast.

compressed air

ballast tanks full of air

outer hull

inner hull

hydroplane rotated for diving

DIVING AND SURFACING
Ballast tanks between the outer and inner hulls are filled with water to submerge the submarine. To bring it back to the surface, the tanks are blown dry with compressed air.

water enters flood ports, filling ballast tanks

direction of dive

vents open, releasing air from tanks

compressed air is released into ballast tanks

hydroplane rotated for surfacing

vents close

water forced out by compressed air

direction of ascent

ballast tanks flooded with water

The great liners

After intense competition between steamship companies in the late 19th century, the next leap forward for the Atlantic liner came with Cunard's *Lusitania* and her sister *Mauretania*, which were the product of rivalries between companies from different countries to build larger, faster, and more luxurious ships (see p.209). German liners boomed after the *Kaiser Wilhelm der Grosse* won the Blue Riband in 1897, and meanwhile the previously British White Star Line was coming increasingly under American ownership. In 1903, Cunard got a loan of £2.6 million from the British government towards the building costs of two new ships, together with an annual mail subsidy of £75,000. In return, the *Mauretania* and *Lusitania* would be manned largely by British naval reservists and be capable of being armed and made available to the Navy in time of war. At nearly 32,000 tons, they were more than 30 per cent bigger than their nearest competitor, the Norddeutscher Line's *Kronprincessen Cecilie* of

NORTH AND SOUTH
While the White Star Line focused its resources entirely on the North Atlantic run, some companies, such as Navigazione Generale Italiana, also offered services to South America.

IMPERIAL EAGLE
Germany's Imperator *entered service in June 1913 as the largest ship in the world. Her eagle figurehead was 3m (10ft) long with a wingspan of 16m (53ft). Sadly, it was damaged in a storm and had to be removed.*

1907, named for the Kaiser's daughter-in-law. They were the first liners to be fitted with the new turbine engines, giving a speed of 25 knots compared with 23 knots for the fastest ships with triple- or quadruple-expansion engines. Their first-class accommodation was promoted as the last word in seagoing luxury. In addition to 563 first-class passengers, the *Mauretania* carried 464 second-class and 1,138 third-class passengers with a crew of 69 seamen and officers, 393 engineers and stokers, and 476 cabin staff. The *Lusitania* won the Blue Riband back from Germany on her second outbound voyage in October 1907, taking 4 days, 19 hours, and 52 minutes to make the crossing. It took the *Mauretania* until 1909 to beat that record, but she went on to hold the Blue Riband for 20 years.

In the early 1900s, ships began to be fitted with wireless telegraphs, the invention of Guglielmo Marconi (see panel, opposite). On 24 January 1909, the wireless proved its worth to shipping when the Italian steamer *Florida* collided with the White Star liner *Republic* in a thick fog about 275km (170 miles) east of New York. The *Republic*'s Marconi wireless operator Jack Binns sent the distress signal CQD ("come quick, danger"), which was received by the White Star liner *Baltic*. The *Republic* sank, but

IN DRY DOCK

The Lusitania's propellers are adjusted during her construction at the John Brown Shipyard in Glasgow, Scotland, in 1906. The Cunard liner had quadruple screw propulsion, powered by four Parsons steam turbine engines.

1,700 lives were saved. Marconi enjoyed further success in July 1910, when the captain of the westward-bound *Montrose* asked his Marconi operator to telegraph Scotland Yard with the message that he suspected that the London cellar murderer Dr Hawley Harvey Crippen was among the saloon passengers onboard. Crippen and his accomplice were arrested by a detective when the *Montrose* docked in Montreal.

Of course, the building of the *Lusitania* and *Mauretania* did not go unnoticed by Cunard's rivals. The White Star Line launched the *Olympic* in 1910 and the ill-fated *Titanic* in 1912 (see panel, p.280), increasing tonnage by 40 per cent, although the new ships were slower and more economical than the Cunard liners. The Germans responded with the Hamburg–Amerika Line's *Imperator*, launched in 1912. At almost 52,000 tons, she was nearly 6,000 tons heavier than the *Titanic* (although her colossal eagle figurehead must have contributed to the load). Her sister ship, the *Vaterland* of 1914, had greater watertight subdivision of the hull in response to the *Titanic* disaster and needed increased beam, giving her a tonnage of 54,300, the largest yet.

Compagnie Générale Transatlantique (a French Line) entered the race in 1912 with its first liner, the *France*. At 23,666 tons, she was small by the latest standards, but as

WIRELESS TELEGRAPHY

In 1894, the Italian scientist Guglielmo Marconi began experimenting with using electromagnetic waves to transmit messages through the air. Using an electric-spark generator invented by German physicist Heinrich Hertz, he concentrated the waves produced into a parallel beam by placing a curved reflector behind the transmitter. The beam was detected by a coherer placed a few feet away, which turned the waves into an electric current that rang an electric bell. By the end of 1902, his wireless telegraph machines were capable of sending radio messages in the form of Morse code 4,800km (3,000 miles) across the Atlantic.

BRIGHT SPARK
Just 22 years old, Guglielmo Marconi sits behind his first wireless receiver in 1896.

stylish as one would expect from her origins. Her first-class rooms were decorated in the manner of Louis XIV and Moorish palaces.

The last of the great pre-war liners made her maiden voyage on 30 May 1914. Cunard's *Aquitania* was neither larger nor faster than her predecessors, but built on their experience. She was beautifully proportioned and fitted, with first-class lounges in the style of the Painted Hall at Greenwich, a French château, and the interiors of Scottish architect Robert Adam. She also had enough lifeboats for her 3,230 passengers and 972 crew.

SHIP'S BELL

Mauretania's forecastle bell now resides at the English National Maritime Museum – the ship's fixtures and fittings were auctioned at Southampton Docks, England, on 14 May 1935. The legendary liner had been sold for scrap after 28 years' service.

ROOM TO LUXURIATE

Acclaimed by many as one of the most beautiful ocean liners ever built, Aquitania's first-class drawing room was decorated in the Adam style, copying some of its features from London's Lansdowne House, designed by Robert Adam in the 1760s.

THE LOSS OF THE *TITANIC*

SETTING OUT TO SEA
The Titanic *steams out of Belfast, Northern Ireland, on the way to undergoing sea trials in early 1912. The massive ship performed well, increasing the confidence of her builders, Harland and Wolff, in her abilities.*

At noon on 10 April 1912, the 46,000-ton White Star liner *Titanic* steamed out of Southampton. She picked up more passengers at Cherbourg in France and Queenstown in Ireland, before heading into the Atlantic with 1,316 passengers and 885 crew. Because of the watertight subdivisions in her hull, the press called her "unsinkable". The maiden voyage was a great social occasion, and passengers included the American financier John Jacob Astor IV, his wife Madeleine, and several other millionaires.

At 11:40 on the night of 14 April, two lookouts at the masthead sighted an iceberg through the darkness. The captain had

> ❝ Not until the last five minutes did the awful realization come that the end was at hand. The lights became dim and went out, but we could see. Slowly, ever so slowly, the surface of the water seemed to come up towards us. ❞
>
> **ROBERT DANIEL**, passenger

previously been warned of the danger, but failed to reduce speed and it was now too late to alter course sufficiently. With a sound like the rolling of thunder, a large part of the *Titanic*'s bottom was ripped out. At first, the crew and passengers were calm, until the magnitude of the problem was appreciated. But, as the ship sank slowly by the bows, it became clear that there was not enough room in the lifeboats for all the passengers. The *Titanic*'s radio operators signalled the old distress code CQD, then switched to the new SOS. The nearby freighter *Californian* failed to respond, and the liner *Carpathia* arrived too late. 1,513 people were lost; around 700 survived.

The *Titanic* disaster was a perfect example of hubris. An arrogant, technologically advanced, class-ridden society headed straight into an avoidable disaster, providing a metaphor for what was to happen in Europe just two years later.

FORTUNATE FEW
Those survivors lucky enough to have been picked up by one of the Titanic*'s few lifeboats then had to row towards the liner* Carpathia, *which had gone to the rescue as soon as she received the distress signal.*

DISTRESS SIGNAL
At 12:45am on 15 April, the final radio message was sent by the Titanic. Wireless operator Jack Phillips used the SOS signal for the first time.

THE FINAL MOMENTS
The Titanic*'s stern rises high as she sinks by the bows. Lifeboat crews had to row hard to get clear of the ship and avoid been dragged down by suction. She finally sank from view at 2:20am on 15 April 1912.*

DISBELIEF
Londoners were brought to a standstill by the news that the unthinkable had happened – the "unsinkable" Titanic had sunk.

Arctic exploration

On 8 July 1879, Lieutenant George DeLong of the US Navy sailed from San Francisco in the *Jeanette* in an attempt to reach the North Pole by way of the Bering Strait. Despite the hull having been strengthened, by 6 September the ship was trapped by pack ice near Wrangel Island in the Chukchi Sea. She drifted with the ice until 12 June 1881, when she was finally crushed and sank near the New Siberian Islands in the Arctic Ocean. The *Jeanette*'s 965-km (600-mile) drift suggested to the Norwegian zoologist and explorer Fridtjof Nansen that a current passed near the North Pole into the sea to the east of Greenland, and that he would be able to use this current to take him as far north as possible before setting out on foot to reach the pole. He needed a ship that would survive the polar pack ice, so he turned to Norwegian naval architect Colin Archer, who designed the *Fram*. Her hull was specially shaped so that, however strong the pressure of the ice, she would be lifted free of it. Although Nansen failed to reach the North Pole in his expedition of 1893–96, he reached latitude 86°13′ N and

ARCTIC EXPLORER
Norwegian explorer Fridtjof Nansen and his crew prepare to set sail in the Fram *from the port of Vardø, northern Norway, on 21 July 1893, in an attempt to reach the North Pole.*

proved the existence of the Greenland Current. Encouraged by his countryman, in June 1903, the Norwegian explorer Roald Amundsen led an expedition on the sloop *Gjoa* to negotiate the Northwest Passage, the long-sought-after sea route through the Canadian Archipelago, linking the Atlantic Ocean with the Pacific, which he finally reached in August 1905. As part of the expedition, Amundsen also established the position (at the time) of the North Magnetic Pole. The first person to reach the geographical North Pole was the American Robert Peary, in 1909. His achievement was hailed as a triumph, but as the Arctic ice has no landmass in the region of the pole, north polar exploration inspired slightly less rivalry than its counterpart at the opposite end of the world.

The race to the South Pole

Antarctic exploration offered no great promise of trade or wealth, unlike expeditions of previous ages. It was fuelled by a hunger for national prestige, and by thirst for knowledge. As Nansen put it, "Man wants to know; and when he does not want to

know, he ceases to be man." The Antarctic offered the most hostile environment on earth. "Great God! This is an awful place," wrote Captain Robert Scott of the Royal Navy, when he finally stood at the South Pole on 17 January 1912. Scott had made the first inland exploration of Antarctica in 1902–04, as part of the *Discovery* expedition, during which he developed techniques for travel by sledge. The

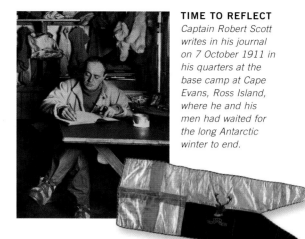

TIME TO REFLECT
Captain Robert Scott writes in his journal on 7 October 1911 in his quarters at the base camp at Cape Evans, Ross Island, where he and his men had waited for the long Antarctic winter to end.

EVER READY
Scott's sledging flag bears his family crest and motto "ready, aye ready". It flew at the South Pole on 17–18 January 1912.

RIVAL EXPEDITIONS
The Norwegian ship Fram *(right), anchored at the edge of the Ross Ice Shelf, encounters the British ship* Terra Nova *early in 1911, before the two expeditions began their race to the South Pole.*

ROALD AMUNDSEN
Captain Amundsen poses in a fur parka in May 1923 for a publicity portrait. He gave many lecture tours before his death in 1928.

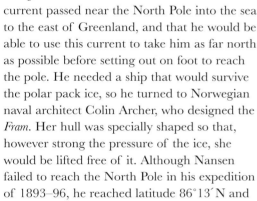

CINECAMERA
Rather than using a professional cameraman like Scott and Shackleton, Amundsen's Antarctic team filmed the expedition themselves on this camera.

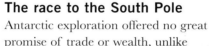

first determined effort to reach the South Pole itself was during the *Nimrod* expedition started in 1907 under the British explorer Ernest Shackleton. He surveyed huge areas and got within 156km (97 miles) of the pole, but was defeated by the topography.

Roald Amundsen had already visited Antarctica several times before he led a Norwegian expedition in 1910–12, sailing on the *Fram*. It was one of the best organized of all time. He carefully chose his 52 sled dogs, and was ready to eat some of them if necessary. He planned for speed rather than research and said in September 1909, "We shall be back from our polar journey on 25 January 1911." He became the first to reach the South Pole on 14 December 1911 and returned to his base at Framheim on the Ross Ice Shelf exactly on schedule, although the return journey proved harder than he had anticipated.

Meanwhile, the rival British *Terra Nova* expedition, led by Captain Scott, set out from the base at Cape Evans on 1 November 1911. His party of four reached the South Pole on 16 January 1912 and were shattered to discover traces of Amundsen's camp from a month earlier. With their food running low, they headed back, but the sledges were hauled by manpower, and illness slowed the men down. All died, to become national heroes in Britain.

On 8 August 1914, Shackleton set out from Plymouth, England, on the wooden barquentine *Endurance* to claim another polar exploration prize for Britain – crossing the Antarctic on foot. On 19 January 1915, the *Endurance* stuck fast in the pack ice of the Weddell Sea, within sight of the continent.

DEATH GRIP
Crushed but still gripped by the pack ice on 27 October 1915, as the sled dogs sit and watch, the Endurance *would eventually sink into the Weddell Sea on 21 November.*

LIFE SAVER
This chronometer was used by Shackleton on the 1,290-km (800-mile) open boat journey on the James Caird *to reach South Georgia Island in 1916.*

She drifted for several months until she was finally crushed and Shackleton ordered the crew to abandon ship. After five months' exposure to the Antarctic winter with little shelter, an escape to Elephant Island on the ship's three boats, and with little food left,

ERNEST SHACKLETON
Ernest Shackleton would live up to his family motto, "fortitudine vincimus" ("by endurance we conquer"), in both 1907 and 1915.

Shackleton took a desperate gamble. On 24 April 1916, he and five crewmen set out in the 7-m (22-ft) *James Caird*, braving 22-m (70-ft) waves to reach South Georgia Island 16 days later. But the only hope of rescue was at the Stromness whaling station on the north of the island. Shackleton and two others trekked for 36 hours over 35km (22 miles) of rugged mountains to raise the alarm. As Raymond Priestley, the civilian geologist and meteorologist on the *Nimrod* and *Terra Nova* expeditions, so aptly put it: "Scott for scientific method, Amundsen for speed and efficiency, but when disaster strikes and all hope is gone, get down on your knees and pray for Shackleton."

> ❝ She was doomed: no ship built by human hands could have withstood the strain. I ordered all hands out on the floe. ❞
>
> **ERNEST HENRY SHACKLETON,** on the *Endurance*, **27 October 1915**

DREADNOUGHTS

The British battleship *Dreadnought* of 1906 was revolutionary in design, combining good long-range armament with the speed of the turbine engine. Tensions were already growing between Britain and Germany, and the new ship redefined the terms of the arms race between them. In the years that followed, the world's naval powers built progressively more powerful warships and started to measure national status in terms of the number and firepower of their large battleships.

BATTLE PRACTICE
The US Navy's super-dreadnought Arkansas fires her 12-in (305-mm) guns prior to the First World War.

Dreadnoughts

The *Dreadnought* herself (below) was rushed in design and construction. She had flaws, the most obvious being that the mainmast was behind the funnel, making life difficult for lookouts. Two of her gun turrets were fitted on the sides, or wings, of the ship, which meant that only one could fire at any given moment. This was a problem that exercised ship designers of all nations over the next few years as they tried to find arrangements that would make the best use of the guns.

The first German ships based on the *Dreadnought* design, the four ships of the *Nassau* class (right), had slightly smaller guns (280mm/11in) than the prototype, but carried 12 of them, with four turrets arranged on the wings. They had triple-expansion engines instead of turbines, but, like most German battleships, had very strong armour, up to 300mm (12in) thick. They were completed in 1910. The French built six ships of the *Danton* class in 1906–11, with a pre-dreadnought armament of 305-mm (12-in) and 240-mm (9.4-in) guns. Their first dreadnoughts, of the *Courbet* class, were launched in 1913–14.

NASSAU CLASS

DREADNOUGHT		
Origin Britain		**Date of launch** 1906
Crew 695–773		**Maximum speed** 21 knots
Displacement 18,110 tons		**Length** 163m (527ft)
Armament 10 x 12-in guns, 24 x 12-pounder guns, 5 x 18-in torpedo tubes		

Battlecruisers

Battlecruisers were originally designed by Admiral Fisher to protect British commerce on the oceans, but they quickly began to take on a role as the fastest and most glamorous ships in the battlefleet. The concept was soon followed in Germany and the USA, but the armour of the British ships proved far too weak in action. The *Queen Mary* was shelled by the German battlecruiser *Derfflinger* at Jutland in 1916 and sank with the loss of nearly all hands.

QUEEN MARY		
Origin Britain		**Date of launch** 1912
Crew 997		**Maximum speed** 27.5 knots
Displacement 26,770 tons		**Length** 217m (703.5ft)
Armament 8 x 13.5-in guns, 16 x 4-in guns, 6 x 3-pounders, 2 x 21-in torpedo tubes		

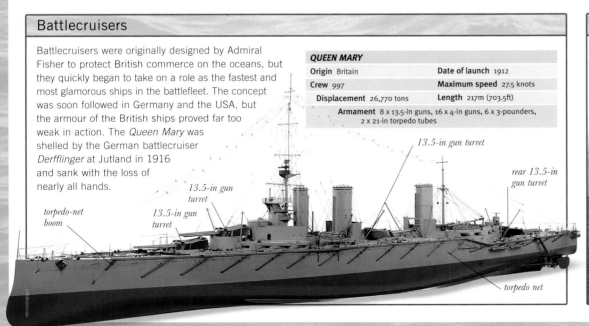

13.5-in gun turret

rear 13.5-in gun turret

13.5-in gun turret

13.5-in gun turret

torpedo-net boom

torpedo net

Queen Elizabeth-class warships

The five ships of the *Queen Elizabeth* class, built between 1912 and 1915, were the culmination of the dreadnought race. They had strong armour, high speed, and the first 15-in (381-mm) guns to be used in such ships. The Germans had only two equivalent ships, of the *Bayern* class, which entered service in 1916–17.

BARHAM		
Origin Britain		**Date of launch** 1914
Crew 925–951		**Maximum speed** 23 knots
Displacement 27,500 tons		**Length** 199m (645.75ft)
Armament 8 x 15-in guns, 14 x 6-in guns, 2 x 3-in guns, 4 x 21-in torpedo tubes		

Super-dreadnoughts

The dreadnought arms race inspired not just the building of more battleships, but also ever-larger ships. With the *Orion* class, which was ordered in 1909, the British went over to the 13.5-in (343-mm) gun, instead of the 12-inch (305-mm). This gave greater range and hitting power, and the vessels were dubbed super-dreadnoughts. The class included the *Conqueror* (below and right) of 1912, and other super-dreadnoughts followed, such as the *Iron Duke*, which served as the British Admiral Jellicoe's flagship at Jutland. The super-dreadnoughts had a new gun-turret arrangement, with one raised higher than the one before or aft of it. This allowed ships to use all their turrets at once for the first time. The Germans followed with the *Kaiser* class, including the *Friedrich der Grosse* (left). Like all German battleships of the period, she was designed for relatively short range and sacrificed living conditions for strength and power. The Americans had anticipated the idea of the *Dreadnought* with the *South Carolina* class, which was begun in 1906. But they were not given the priority of the *Dreadnought*, and the ships were not launched until 1910. The French used 340-mm (13.4-in) guns for their second class of dreadnoughts, the *Bretagne* class, which was completed in 1915–16.

ARKANSAS TURRETS
The American ship Arkansas *was launched in 1912 and in service for 44 years, fighting in both world wars. All six turrets were mounted along the ship's centre line.*

GERMAN *KAISER* CLASS
Launched in 1913, the Friedrich der Grosse *had a 30.5-cm (12-in) gun, a rearranged armament with superimposed turrets aft, and a higher forecastle. Her armour was up to 35.6cm (14in) thick.*

CONQUEROR
The Conqueror *was one of the* Orion *class of super-dreadnoughts and was built on the Clyde in Scotland. She fought at Jutland and was broken up under the Washington Treaty in 1922.*

FRONT VIEW OF THE *CONQUEROR*

spotting top

signal yard

boat boom

boat on davit

spotting top

bilge keel

tripod mast

B turret (13.5-in guns)

4-in guns

gunnery control position

searchlights

cutter

boat boom

A turret (13.5-in guns)

anti-torpedo net

boom for anti-torpedo net

ram bow

anchor

capstan

CONQUEROR

CONQUEROR		
Origin Britain	**Date of launch** 1911	
Length 177m (581ft)	**Displacement** 22,200 tons	
Maximum speed 21 knots	**Crew** 752	
Armament 10 x 13.5-in guns, 16 x 4-in guns, 4 x 3-pounders, 3 x 21-in torpedo tubes		

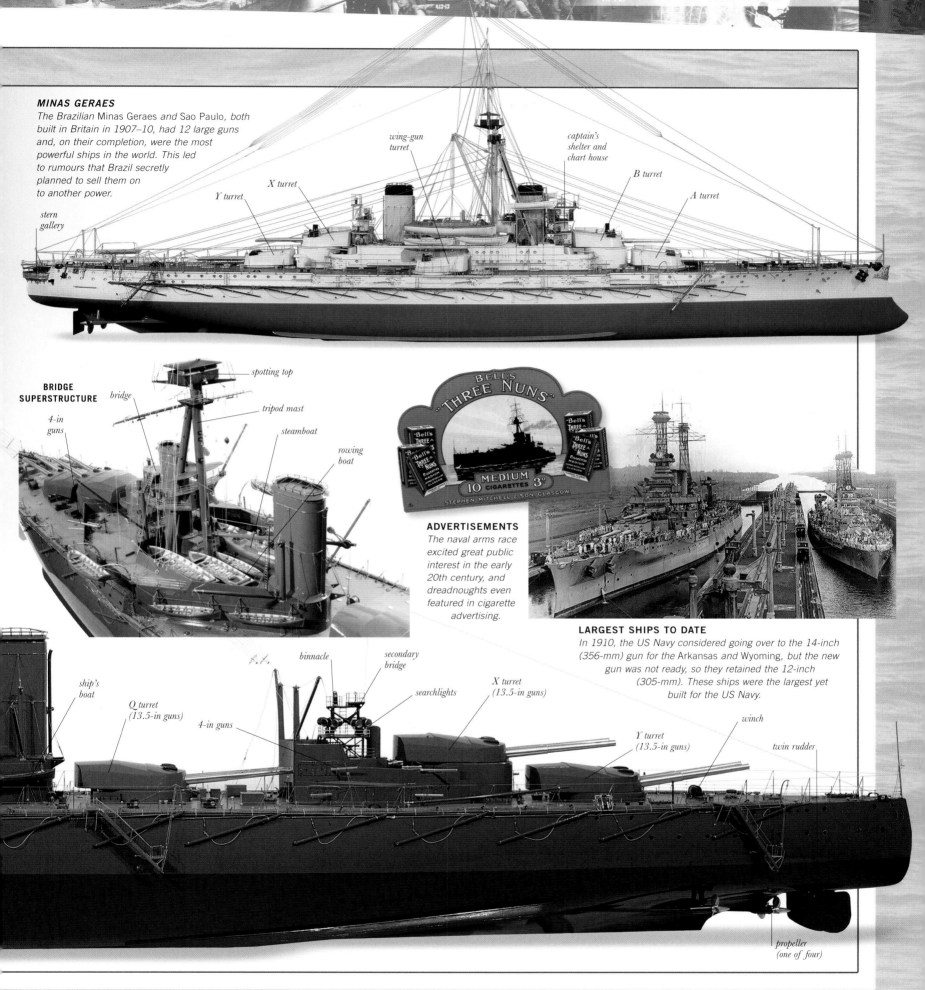

MINAS GERAES

The Brazilian Minas Geraes and Sao Paulo, both built in Britain in 1907–10, had 12 large guns and, on their completion, were the most powerful ships in the world. This led to rumours that Brazil secretly planned to sell them on to another power.

stern gallery

Y turret

X turret

wing-gun turret

captain's shelter and chart house

B turret

A turret

BRIDGE SUPERSTRUCTURE

spotting top

bridge

tripod mast

4-in guns

steamboat

rowing boat

BELL'S "THREE NUNS"

Bell's THREE NUNS

MEDIUM
10 CIGARETTES 3D
STEPHEN MITCHELL & SON GLASGOW

ADVERTISEMENTS

The naval arms race excited great public interest in the early 20th century, and dreadnoughts even featured in cigarette advertising.

LARGEST SHIPS TO DATE

In 1910, the US Navy considered going over to the 14-inch (356-mm) gun for the Arkansas and Wyoming, but the new gun was not ready, so they retained the 12-inch (305-mm). These ships were the largest yet built for the US Navy.

ship's boat

Q turret (13.5-in guns)

4-in guns

binnacle

secondary bridge

searchlights

X turret (13.5-in guns)

Y turret (13.5-in guns)

winch

twin rudder

propeller (one of four)

GERMAN PROPAGANDA STAMP, 1915

> **❝** I am quite homeless. I cannot reach Germany. We possess no other secure harbour. I must plough the seas of the world doing as much mischief as I can, until my ammunition is exhausted, or a foe far superior in power succeeds in catching me. **❞**

VICE-ADMIRAL GRAF VON SPEE, following the British capture of Tsingtao, **1914**

KEY EVENTS

1914   BATTLE OF CORONEL German Vice-Admiral Graf von Spee's China Squadron sinks two British cruisers off Chile on 1 November.

1915   *LUSITANIA* SUNK BY U-BOAT The Cunard liner *Lusitania* is torpedoed by *U-20* on 7 May, resulting in the loss of 1,198 lives.

1915   DARDANELLES DISASTER A flotilla of ships begins the evacuation of troops from the Gallipoli Peninsula, Turkey, after the allies decide to withdraw on 7 December.

1916   DEPTH CHARGES DEPLOYED The Royal Navy introduces depth charges as a weapon against submerged submarines.

1916   BATTLE OF JUTLAND The greatest naval battle of the First World War begins on 31 May. Both Germany and Britain claim victory.

1917   USA ENTERS THE WAR The USA declares war on 6 April, mainly as a result of Germany having resumed its U-boat campaign.

1919   GERMAN FLEET SCUTTLED On 21 June, the German High Seas Fleet sends 74 of its ships to the bottom of Scapa Flow, Scotland.

THE FIRST WORLD WAR

THE FIRST GREAT CONFLICT OF THE 20TH CENTURY, BETWEEN THE WORLD'S GREAT NAVAL POWERS, CHANGED THE NATURE OF WAR AT SEA FOR EVER.

The great naval issue of the First World War was whether the Royal Navy, undefeated for well over a century, could be beaten either on or under the sea. The British Fleet underwent a test mobilization in July 1914, and Winston Churchill, the First Lord of the Admiralty (see panel, p.288), kept the men in service so that the fleet was ready when Britain declared war on 4 August. But another of Churchill's actions had far less successful consequences. Turkey had

bought two battleships from British shipyards and had sent crews to Britain to take delivery of them in July. Unsure of Turkey's intentions and seeing a new asset for the Royal Navy, Churchill had them seized by armed marines on 2 August, a great insult to the Turks. The German battlecruiser *Goeben* and cruiser *Breslau* were already in the Mediterranean. On 3 August, they bombarded two French ports in Algeria then headed for neutral

Turkey, evading a British squadron. The ships reached Constantinople (now Istanbul) and were turned over to the Turks, compensating for the loss of the battleships. It was enough to tip the balance in Turkish politics, and the country eventually entered the war on the German side in October.

Coronel and the Falklands

Apart from its main naval force in the Baltic and North Sea, Germany had small squadrons in the Caribbean, east Africa, and east Asia in early August 1914. The last of these, under Vice-Admiral Graf von Spee, included the modern armoured cruisers *Scharnhorst* and *Gneisenau*.

U-BOATS MEETING
U-35 exchanges news with another U-boat in the Mediterranean in the spring of 1917. Commanded by Lothar von Arnauld de la Perière, the U-35 sank 195 ships, having first allowed the crews to board lifeboats and directed them to the nearest port.

The squadron headed east to rendezvous with the Caribbean force, but instead it met a British force led by two old cruisers, the *Good Hope* and *Monmouth*. The British Admiral Cradock accepted battle knowing the inferiority of his ships; both were sunk in the Battle of Coronel off the coast of Chile on 1 November 1914.

Admiral Fisher, Britain's First Sea Lord, dispatched two battlecruisers, *Invincible* and *Inflexible*, to join three cruisers in chasing the Germans. They found Spee off the Falkland Islands on 8 December. He fought to a finish, but the armoured cruisers were outgunned in turn and sunk. The cruisers *Leipzig* and *Nürnberg* were also sunk, but the *Dresden* escaped, only to be trapped and scuttled near Chile in March 1915.

One of Spee's light cruisers, the *Emden*, had left the squadron at the outbreak of war to raid shipping in the Indian Ocean. She sank or captured 23 merchant ships worth £15 million and caused the diversion of up to 14 British and allied warships in pursuit of her. She was eventually tracked down on 9 November by the more heavily armed Australian cruiser *Sydney*, and was run aground after a short battle. However, the German Navy was already looking at other ways of attacking British trade.

The war in the North Sea

In the North Sea, the British won a minor victory in the first month of the war. Close to the German coast off the island of Heligoland, a skirmish developed between light cruisers and destroyers on both sides. Admiral Beatty's mighty Battlecruiser Fleet arrived and sank three German light cruisers. It was a British victory, but in view of the odds in their favour it was a long way from the "second Trafalgar" that the British press had been encouraged to predict.

gun sight

pivot to change direction and angle of gun

WAITING TO BE RESCUED
Sailors cling to the hull of the capsized German armoured cruiser Blücher *prior to it sinking at Dogger Bank in the North Sea on 24 January 1915. Around 260 survivors were rescued by British ships once the battle ended.*

WINSTON SPENCER CHURCHILL

Winston Churchill (1874–1965) was a British army officer, journalist, and politician before becoming First Lord of the Admiralty in 1911. In a time of great technological change and naval expansion, he encouraged the development of the naval air arm and found money for ever-larger battleships. He showed great energy in mobilizing the fleet when war began in 1914, but fell from office after the failure of the Dardanelles expedition in 1915.

From 1935, he became increasingly suspicious about German rearmament, but his warnings were largely unheeded. He became First Lord again at the outbreak of the war in 1939, and, although largely responsible for the unsuccessful Norwegian Campaign that drove Neville Chamberlain from office in 1940, he succeeded Chamberlain as Prime Minister. He took a personal interest in the naval war, built up the Combined Operations Organization for amphibious warfare, and later wrote a monumental history of the war.

The German Navy had a secure base at Wilhelmshaven, from which it could access the Baltic by way of the widened Kiel Canal. The British had no base of any kind north of the Thames, as one in the Firth of Forth in Scotland was still under construction. It was planned that the great anchorage at Scapa Flow in the Orkney Islands would hold the fleet, but nothing had been done to prepare it. The Royal Navy's vulnerability to attack by submarines was highlighted in September, when three old cruisers, the *Aboukir*, *Cressy*, and *Hogue*, were sunk by the *U-9* off the German coast.

QF 1-POUNDER GUN
Originally installed on ships as a defence against torpedo boats, this British QF 1-pounder was eventually used as an anti-aircraft gun.

Scapa Flow had to be abandoned for some months after a U-boat scare, and the fleet retreated to Ireland and the west of Scotland. Churchill's energies were directed at the anti-submarine defences of the Flow, and the fleet returned early in 1915.

The Germans began to shell English east-coast towns, hoping to lure Royal Navy ships within range of their U-boats. Admiral Jellicoe, commander of the Grand Fleet, was obliged to send his battlecruisers south. On 24 January 1915 at Dogger Bank, a force led by Beatty intercepted a German battlecruiser squadron, which was far inferior in gun power. But the Germans mostly escaped due to signal confusion among the British when the flagship *Lion* was hit, and only the *Blücher* was sunk.

The 1915 U-boat campaign

Since its surface ships could not defeat the British in the North Sea, the German Admiralty decided to try the new weapon, the U-boat.

Until this point, U-boats attacking merchant ships had been required by international law to surface, warn the crew, and give them a chance to escape before sinking the ship, usually by gunfire. On 4 February 1915, Germany declared the waters around Britain a war zone, stating that ships making for British or French ports would be attacked on sight. Soon, casualties among British merchant ships rose to an unacceptable level.

To counter the U-boat threat, at first the British concentrated on destroying them on the surface. They used disguised merchantmen called Q-ships, which would lure the U-boat to the surface before attacking with hidden guns. However, this undermined British claims that U-boat attacks were illegal and gave the Germans an excuse to attack merchant ships without warning. Older destroyers were used to patrol the seas against U-boats, and trawlers and steam yachts were converted into warships. New types of ships were developed, including P-boats, or patrol craft, which were like small destroyers but with a low silhouette to make them look like submarines.

Of all the torpedoes fired in the First World War, the one launched by *U-20* off the south coast of Ireland at 2:09pm on 7 May 1915 caused most damage. It hit the *Lusitania*, causing the great liner to sink in 18 minutes, and killing 1,198 of her passengers and crew. She was carrying a small cargo of ammunition, which gave the U-boat a case for sinking her, but the dead passengers included 128 Americans, and the US public had no hesitation in blaming the Germans. In the face of mounting US pressure, Germany ended the Atlantic U-boat campaign on 18 September, only to redirect the U-boats to the Mediterranean (where American lives would not be at risk) in October. Success for U-boats in

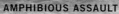

AMPHIBIOUS ASSAULT
British troops with a field gun are tugged towards the beach at Sedd-al-Bahr on Cape Helles at the tip of the Gallipoli Peninsula. The attempted landing there on 25 April 1915 was a disaster, with more than 1,200 allied casualties.

the Adriatic was often spectacular – the leading commander, Lothar von Arnauld de la Perière, sank 195 ships totalling 454,000 tons in just 24 months.

The Dardanelles

After the Battle of the Marne, a land engagement in northern France in September 1914, the German advance was halted, and both sides built enormous lines of trenches. There was stalemate, too, on the Eastern Front, where Germany and Austria-Hungary were opposed by Russian forces. The generals planned massive land offensives that wasted thousands of lives, usually for little reward. At the British Admiralty, Winston Churchill saw another route of attack, against Turkey – the weakest of the enemy powers. If an Anglo-French fleet could enter the Black Sea through the Dardanelles, Turkey could be eliminated

A CALL FROM THE DARDANELLES

Coo–ee–
Won't YOU come ?

ENLIST NOW

ANZAC LANDINGS
Members of the Australian and New Zealand Army Corps land at Anzac Cove on the western side of the Gallipoli Peninsula (above). More than 2,700 New Zealanders – one in four of those who landed – and 8,000 Australians died during the Dardanelles campaign, all of them volunteers.

as an opponent and a route to Russia opened. The British and French would then be able to ship supplies to the huge, but ill-equipped, Russian Army.

Churchill's plan was a clever one, but poorly executed. After bombarding the forts at the mouth of the Dardanelles with heavy guns, an Anglo-French force, including 16 battleships, attempted to sail up the straits on 18 March 1915. It met a mine barrage that damaged the battlecruiser *Inflexible* and sank two other warships. The attempt was abandoned.

It was then decided to land British, New Zealand, and Australian troops at six points on the Gallipoli Peninsula, at the mouth of the Dardanelles on 25 April. At Sedd-al-Bahr, the allies came under heavy fire. Some troops landed using the time-honoured method of rowing ashore in ships' boats. Others, aboard the converted collier *River Clyde*, exited through

THE LAST TO LEAVE
The British battleship Cornwallis *returns fire at the Turkish guns onshore as she prepares to sail out of Suvla Bay. She was the last ship to leave Gallipoli in the evacuation of 19–20 December 1915.*

THE BATTLE OF JUTLAND

On the evening of 30 May 1916, three British naval forces left their North Sea bases. When the Grand Fleet under Admiral Jellicoe, Admiral Beatty's Battlecruiser Fleet, and a squadron from Invergordon met, they would form the most powerful fleet in the world, with 28 dreadnoughts, 9 battlecruisers, 32 cruisers, 77 destroyers, a seaplane carrier, and a minelayer.

Admiral Scheer's German High Seas Fleet intended to show itself off Norway in the hope of luring out and isolating part of the British Fleet. It was numerically inferior in every respect – 22 battleships (including 6 pre-dating the dreadnought era), 5 battlecruisers, 11 cruisers, and 61 torpedo boats. But its ships were expertly built and its crews were well trained.

BRITISH LOSSES
The Queen Mary *(right) explodes at 4:26pm and Admiral Beatty's flagship* Lion *is shelled. The* Lion *had already suffered a direct hit to one of her gun turrets, which killed 98 men.*

WHO WON?
Both sides claimed victory after the Battle of Jutland – known in Germany as the Battle of Skagerrak – and produced souvenirs such as this poster and medal.

Souvenir OF THE VICTORY OF JUTLAND

MAY 31ST 1916.

The two battlecruiser forces met south of Norway and opened fire just before 4:00pm on 31 May. The Germans, believing that they had isolated part of the British Fleet, turned southeast to lure Beatty's ships towards their main force. The Fifth Battle Squadron, supporting the Battlecruiser Fleet, failed to turn with Beatty, so four very powerful ships did not enter the action for a crucial 20 minutes. Shells penetrated the weak armour of the battlecruiser *Indefatigable* and she exploded, killing all but two of her crew. Then another, the *Queen Mary*, blew up. Beatty's superior firepower was at last beginning to prevail when the German battlefleet was sighted heading towards them. Beatty reversed his course, intending to lure the Germans towards the Grand Fleet. Jellicoe's fleet was still cruising in seven columns, and he had to decide which side to deploy them on. Despite poor reconnaissance reports, he made the correct choice by going to port. At about 6:20pm Scheer found the enemy was ahead of him, ready to "cross his T" – to direct the full force of all their guns on his leading ships, which could reply only with their forward guns. Scheer quickly turned away from the trap, and the British lost yet another battlecruiser, the *Invincible*.

Scheer was cut off from his base and turned west to get behind the British, but found them ready to cross his T again. He turned away, ordering his torpedo boats to attack. Jellicoe retreated, allowing the High Seas Fleet to escape. After some night-time action, it eventually made it back to base.

LONE HUNTER
A U-boat surfaces in the open ocean. Germany resumed unrestricted submarine warfare in 1917, and U-boats sunk more than 500,000 tons of British merchant shipping in April alone.

specially cut doors in her side and had to cross a pontoon bridge to reach the shore. The plan proved disastrous as the men were mowed down by machine-gun fire. The troops that did make it ashore failed to progress inland, and were soon cut off on the beaches by the German-trained Turkish Army. After many thousands were lost, the survivors finally withdrew in January 1916. The only large-scale amphibious operation of the war, the Dardanelles campaign was a disaster for the allies. Churchill fell from office, but the greatest side-effect was that Russia remained isolated. Her armies deserted en masse in 1917, leading eventually to the Bolshevik Revolution and Russia's exit from the war.

Jutland and its aftermath

With the U-boat offensive on hold, in spring 1916 the German High Seas Fleet under its new commander Admiral Reinhard Scheer (see panel, right) adopted a more aggressive policy, which led to the Battle of Jutland (see panel, left), the largest naval battle of the war. In the aftermath, the Germans were quick to claim victory, for they had lost only one major ship, the battlecruiser *Lützow*, while their opponents lost three. The British lost more than 6,000 men from a fleet of 60,000; the Germans lost 2,500 from 36,000. The mighty Royal Navy, apparently invincible since Nelson, had been challenged successfully.

> ❝ 'The *Queen Mary* has been blown sky high!' That was splendid; all faces beamed. Might it continue to be so. And continue it did. ❞
>
> **OTTO LOOKS**, Engineer-Commander of the German battlecruiser *Seydlitz* at Jutland, **1916**

The British were much more defensive about the result, for the battle was certainly a disappointment in that the Germans had slipped through their fingers yet again, and exposed several weaknesses as they went. Yet the Germans gave up any serious attempt to dominate the surface of the North Sea and soon reverted to submarine warfare, which eventually led to the American entry into the war.

Jutland was the only full-scale battle of the *Dreadnought* era, mainly because the Germans were cautious about leaving harbour and the British were cautious in battle. It divided the Royal Navy over the next 20 years, as the supporters of Jellicoe and Beatty argued over whose fault the failure was. Jutland was also the last battle in which aircraft played no significant part. Despite the fact that the British seaplane carrier had launched just one flight, which failed to make contact with the enemy, the Royal Navy continued to develop the air weapon. It began to launch fighter and reconnaissance aircraft directly from capital ships and cruisers, and by the end of the war at least 28 ships carried up to three aircraft each. But they were regarded as expendable and the problem of landing on a ship still eluded the Navy. On 2 August 1917, a Sopwith Pup aircraft landed on the foredeck of the battlecruiser *Furious*, while she was under way, but an attempt to repeat this resulted in the death of the pilot.

REINHARD SCHEER

The son of a German pastor and teacher, Reinhard Scheer (1863–1928) entered the German Navy in 1882. He commanded a torpedo-boat flotilla in 1900 and wrote a textbook on torpedo tactics. Scheer was in command of the Second Battle Squadron of the High Seas Fleet at the outbreak of war in 1914; then, in January 1916, he became commander-in-chief when Admiral von Pohl was taken ill. Scheer handled his numerically inferior fleet impeccably at Jutland. He became Chief of Naval Staff in July 1918. On retiring, he wrote two books about the war.

A landing deck was added to the *Furious*, aft of the funnel, but the turbulence created while the ship was under way made landing impossible. Finally, in 1918, the first true flat-top aircraft carrier, the *Argus*, was launched. She performed successfully in trials, but the war ended before she could enter active service.

The 1917–18 U-boat campaign

In January 1917, the German government embarked on a great gamble. It decided to risk war with the USA by reviving the Atlantic U-boat offensive, hoping that Britain would be

DIRECT HIT
A surfaced U-boat torpedoes a merchant ship in early 1917. Around 17,000 British and Commonwealth merchant seamen lost their lives during the First World War.

were sunk in April alone, and Britain, highly dependent on imports, would not last long at that rate.

The British and their allies tried everything they could against the U-boats. Propaganda, in the form of cartoons and posters, was aimed largely at neutral opinion in the USA and Scandinavia. U-boat bases were attacked, notably at Zeebrugge on 23 April 1918, where, despite great heroism by the crew of the Royal Navy cruiser *Vindictive* and her detachment of Royal Marines, an attempt to block the port failed. Mines were laid across the Straits of Dover to prevent U-boats passing, with some success. In 1918, the US Navy began to lay mines across the North Sea between the north of Scotland and Norway, but this task was not completed before the end of the war.

The Royal Naval Air Service (RNAS) mounted airship patrols in areas where U-boats were liable to strike. Although the primitive British non-rigid airships attacked very few U-boats, they were quite successful as a convoy defence. Seaplanes and land-planes

starved out of the war before American troops arrived in Europe. Eight US merchant ships were sunk in February and March, and the USA eventually declared war on 6 April, but it took several months to raise and train a great army and ship it over to Europe. The US Navy was slightly better prepared, immediately sending six destroyers to Queenstown, Ireland, and deploying 12 more to patrol the waters around Britain within a few weeks. In the meantime, the German campaign looked like succeeding: more than 800 ships

PROPAGANDA WEAPON
To promote anti-German feeling and gain public support for the USA to enter the war on the British side, Americans were reminded of outrageous acts such as the sinking of the Lusitania in May 1915.

were also used, and in the second half of 1918 there was a daily average of 189 land-planes, 300 seaplanes and flying boats, and 75 airships available for patrol. Very few ships were sunk in the presence of aircraft, for they forced the U-boat captains to remain submerged for fear of attack. The RNAS was merged into the new Royal Air Force in April 1918.

However, the most important anti-submarine tactic of all was the convoy formation itself, in which a group of merchant ships travelled under the protection of a naval escort. The British Admiralty was reluctant to adopt this, arguing that convoys would cause delays and collisions, and it agreed only under pressure from the Prime Minister, David Lloyd George, in April 1917. From that time, the majority of merchant ships travelled in convoys, and the tactic proved an immediate success. U-boats were forced to take on warships if they wanted to attack, or desist if they did not want to risk being shelled. And escort vessels were now armed with a new anti-submarine weapon, the depth charge (see panel, right). Casualties among escorted merchant ships were very low, while they remained high among stragglers or those allowed to travel without convoy. By the end of 1917, a total of 16,404 ships had sailed in convoys, with the loss of just 147 vessels.

Colonial and river wars
Although the main focus of the naval war was on the Anglo-German conflict in Europe and the high seas, other countries had their own wars to fight. The German and Russian navies skirmished in the Baltic. The Russians also faced the Turks in the Black Sea and on the River

propeller *stabilizer*

fuel tank *gondola*

SEA SCOUT ZERO
This Royal Naval Air Service non-rigid airship was introduced in 1916. It could stay airborne for 17 hours, and its crew of three mostly patrolled for submarines or escorted convoys.

ATLANTIC CONVOY
A convoy zigzags across the Atlantic in 1917, bringing food and supplies to Britain. Merchant ships were escorted by warships to protect them from U-boats.

DAZZLE SHIP IN DRY DOCK
This 1918 woodcut by British artist Edward Wadsworth shows the dazzle camouflage applied to the hulls of many ships from 1917. Geometric patterns distorted the ship's silhouette, making it difficult for U-boats to read its course.

ANTI-SUBMARINE WARFARE

Early submarines were really submersibles and could stay underwater only for relatively short periods. At the surface, they were vulnerable to sighting and attack by aircraft and warships. But, for a ship to be able to find and attack a submerged submarine in its vicinity, new technology was required.

The depth charge was invented by the English engineer Herbert Taylor in 1915 and was in use by the Royal Navy by 1916. The first depth charge was a 140-kg (300-lb) barrel-like canister packed with TNT that was detonated by a hydrostatically controlled pistol set to go off at a certain depth. The pistol operated by the pressure of water against a spring, and the tension of the spring could be calibrated at 1.5-m (5-ft) intervals,

to a maximum depth of 100m (328ft). Once a submarine had been detected and its path and depth estimated, it would be bombarded by charges dropped over the stern of an escort vessel or fired from a launcher on either beam of the ship. A total of 29 U-boats were destroyed in this way, 22 of them in 1918.

DEPTH CHARGE AND LAUNCHER
A crewman onboard a British Q-ship, also known as a "mystery ship" because of its disguise as a merchant vessel, prepares to launch a depth charge.

Danube, and they carried out various amphibious operations. Austro-Hungarian Monitors provided heavy gunfire support in the war against Serbia. They were met by naval forces from Russia, France, and Britain, but nevertheless, by the end of 1915, Serbia had been overrun by Austro-German forces.

Another element of the First World War, reminiscent of the Anglo-French wars of more than a century earlier, was the colonial war. River gunboats supported the British armies on the River Tigris in Iraq, then a Turkish province, but did not prevent a humiliating surrender of 13,000 troops at Kut al-Amara on 29 April 1916. The Japanese, as long-standing British allies, captured German colonies on islands in the Pacific, which they would put to good use as bases in the next major conflict.

The end of the war

In the autumn of 1918, as the USA's armies began to have an effect in Europe, Germany's allies began to collapse one by one, its people approached starvation, and even its great army was on the verge of mutiny. The officers of the High Seas Fleet planned one last operation against the British and Americans, ordering their warships to sea on 3 November. But the crews at Kiel and Wilhelmshaven recognized it as suicide and mutinied in their ports. It was yet another blow to the German state. The Kaiser

fled to the Netherlands, and the German High Command negotiated an armistice with the allies on 11 November.

The British representative at the treaty negotiations, Admiral Lord Wemyss, did not object to harsh terms that France wanted to impose on the German Navy. To the Germans, this was a deliberate humiliation of a navy which had, in its own view, always fought bravely, skilfully and honourably. The best of the High Seas Fleet, 10 battleships, 6 battlecruisers, and 58 smaller vessels, was duly interned at Scapa Flow

while the Treaty of Versailles was negotiated. On 21 June 1919, as the terms of the treaty were about to be announced, the skeleton crews opened up the ships' seacocks and allowed them to sink to the bottom of the Flow. It was the real end of the great naval conflict that began with Admiral Tirpitz's rise to power 30 years earlier.

In the end, the Royal Navy had not been defeated either on or under the sea, but its victory was costlier, slower, more ambiguous, and less satisfying than anyone had expected.

SCUTTLED BATTLECRUISER
On 21 June 1919, 74 ships of the High Seas Fleet were sent to the bottom of Scapa Flow. Scrap merchants subsequently salvaged most of the ships.

EARLY SUBMARINES

For centuries before underwater travel was a practical possibility, sailors and inventors had dreamed of it, for research as well as military purposes – Jules Verne's novel *20,000 Leagues Under the Sea* had fuelled interest in the 19th century, for example. Brave attempts were made to drive submarines by manpower, but it was the invention of the electric motor, combined with the diesel engine to charge it, that made the submarine practicable around the beginning of the 20th century. Submarines were most attractive to navies that were unable to command the surface of the sea with their big ships and soon had a profound effect on naval warfare and strategy in the First World War and after.

ESCAPE ARTIST
In this photograph dating from 1916, the German submarine U-126 shows its gun and gear in the bows for cutting anti-submarine nets.

Experimental craft

There were many attempts at building submersible vessels from the 18th century onwards, including David Bushnell's *Turtle* (see p.124), which attempted to sink a British warship during the American Revolutionary War. The English clergyman George Garret built two boats called *Resurgam*, using steam power even when underwater, but the boiler took up most of the space in the hull and the vessel does not seem to have worked.

RESURGAM	
Origin Britain	Date of launch 1879
Length 13.7m (45ft)	Displacement 30 tons (surfaced)
Crew 2–3	
Armament None	

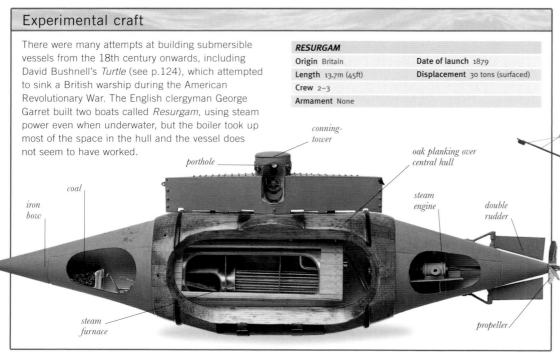

conning-tower

porthole

oak planking over central hull

coal

iron bow

steam engine

double rudder

steam furnace

propeller

Man-powered submarines

Since steam power was very difficult to use underwater, manpower was virtually the only way to power a submarine before the development of the electric motor. The crew of the Confederate submarine *Hunley* (below) operated crank handles to turn a propeller. She holed the *Housatonic* in 1864 but sank soon afterwards with the loss of all hands.

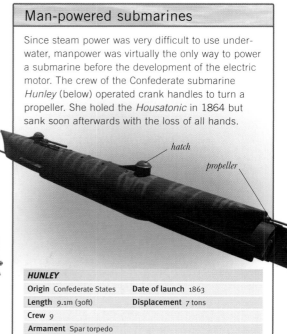

hatch

propeller

HUNLEY	
Origin Confederate States	Date of launch 1863
Length 9.1m (30ft)	Displacement 7 tons
Crew 9	
Armament Spar torpedo	

Prototypes

Several nations – including Greece, Russia, and France – built submarines in the late 19th century. The real breakthrough came with Irish-American John Holland's first successful boats in the 1880s. Holland's ideas were adopted by the US Navy, which took its first boat in 1897. In 1900, the British, alarmed at French developments, began to take an interest, and their first boat, known as *Holland No. 1* (right), was built in the following year. Dedicated to building a battle fleet in the early years of the 20th century, Germany was later than most of the large navies to take an interest in the submarine. The first German submarine, launched in 1906, *U-1*, was used mainly for trials and training.

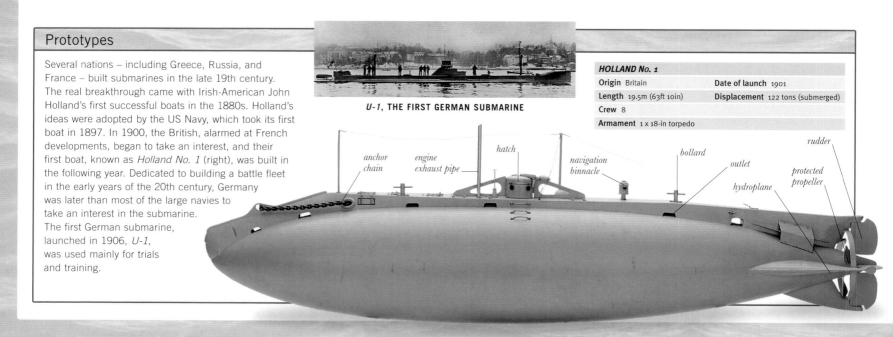

U-1, THE FIRST GERMAN SUBMARINE

HOLLAND No. 1	
Origin Britain	Date of launch 1901
Length 19.5m (63ft 10in)	Displacement 122 tons (submerged)
Crew 8	
Armament 1 x 18-in torpedo	

anchor chain

engine exhaust pipe

hatch

navigation binnacle

bollard

outlet

rudder

protected propeller

hydroplane

Submarines of the First World War

Submarines became a dominant naval weapon of the First World War. The *U-9* sank three old British cruisers in the first days of the war, and the British battlefleet was forced to abandon its anchorage at Scapa Flow for a time. Fleets of battleships had to take care to avoid submarines at sea for fear they might penetrate their base, but submarines were even more effective at attacking merchant ships than warships. During the war, the Germans used U-boats for coastal patrols (*UB* class) and mine-laying (the *UC* class), as well as for longer-range missions (the torpedo-armed *U* classes). The *UC-5* (right), was captured by the British in 1916. Boats grew in size during the war, and the *U-160* class weighed in at 1,002 tons submerged. They operated at increasingly long ranges and had great success in the Mediterranean and the North Sea, as well as moving out into the Atlantic. The British, who had the most to fear from the development of the submarine, developed their own classes – to help carry the war to the enemy or, in the case of the K class, to accompany the main fleet.

U-126
This German submarine belonged to the U-117 class of minelayers. She was launched in 1918, and broken up in 1923.

E CLASS
The British E class, having developed through several stages since the original Holland boat, was very successful.

K CLASS
The British steam-powered K-class submarines were a complete failure. Designed to keep up with the battle fleet, they were involved in many fatal accidents.

white ensign flying over German Imperial ensign after capture

conning-tower

mine

flat deck

pressured hull

UC-5	
Origin Germany	**Date of launch** 1915
Length 33.8m (111ft)	**Displacement** 183 tons (submerged)
Crew 14–16	
Armament 12 mines	

Big-gun submarines

Although the torpedo was the main armament of the submarine, there were several attempts to use aircraft or big guns that could be fired underwater, either to bombard enemy coastlines or to attack their shipping. In the 1920s, two British boats of the *M* classes were adapted to carry guns and even launch aircraft, but they were both lost in accidents. The *X1* of 1923 was even larger, at 110.6m (363ft) long, and she was intended to take on destroyers, but she never worked well and was scrapped. The French *Surcouf* (right) was designed for long-range commerce raiding, with an endurance of 90 days. She was more successful than the equivalent British craft but, despite her impressive armament, she saw little action before being sunk in a collision in 1942.

SURCOUF	
Origin France	**Date of launch** 1929
Length 110m (360ft 10in)	**Displacement** 4,304 tons (submerged)
Crew 118	
Armament 2 x 8-in, 2 x 37-mm guns, 8 x 21-in torpedo tubes, 1 aircraft	

mast — *radio mast* — *conning-tower* — *range finder* — *twin 8-in guns* — *crew on flat deck*

EARLY AIRCRAFT CARRIERS

Within a few years of the Wright brothers' first flight in 1903, naval officers were beginning to look at ways to use aircraft for reconnaissance and even to attack enemy ships and shore installations. Aircraft of the time (apart from airships) had very short ranges, so it was necessary for the fleet to take its aircraft with it. Ways of launching aircraft from the decks were soon discovered, but landing proved far more difficult. Aircraft were cheap in those days, and the pilot could always be picked up from the water. But a ship that could launch and land aircraft would change the face of naval warfare.

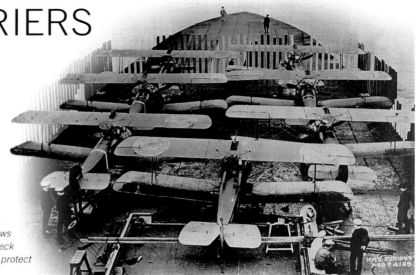

TEMPORARY WINDBREAK
This photograph of 1918 shows screens erected on the foredeck of the British ship Furious *to protect aircraft from the wind.*

Prototype carriers

afterdeck for landing aircraft

gangway between decks

funnel

large central superstructure

dazzle camouflage

crash barrier

forward flying-off deck

FURIOUS	
Origin Britain	**Date of launch** 1916
Length 239.7m (786ft 6in)	**Displacement** 19,513 tons
Maximum speed 29.5 knots	**Crew** 880
Armament 10 x 5.5-in guns, 6 x 3-in guns, 8 aircraft	

Still worried about the problem of landing naval aircraft on ships, the Royal Navy fitted a flat deck to the forward part of the unsuccessful battlecruiser *Furious* (above). A pilot named Commander Dunning managed to land on it by flying round the superstructure at anchor in Scapa Flow in 1916, but the following day he was lost over the side while attempting to repeat the feat. The *Furious* was then given a landing deck aft

of the superstructure, but it proved impossible to use because of irregular air currents. It was decided that only a carrier with a completely flat deck would do.

The British *Argus* was converted from the Italian liner *Conte Rosso* and began her trials in 1918. Since aircraft of the time had very slow landing speeds and were very light, she had arrester wires running fore and aft along the decks rather than across the decks, in an

attempt to prevent the aircraft from being blown overboard. The *Argus* proved far more successful at landing aircraft than anything that had gone before, but she was too late to take part in the First World War. Since torpedo-carrying aircraft were already being developed, she might have been used to launch an attack that anticipated the later assaults on Pearl Harbor and Taranto (see pp.320–21).

ARGUS
With her completely flat deck, the Argus looked very strange to sailors – an opinion further compounded by the "dazzle" camouflage that was intended to confuse the enemy. However, she marked a great step forward in naval aviation.

Conversions and seaplane carriers

ARK ROYAL

Origin Britain		**Date of launch** 1915	
Length 111.5m (366ft)		**Displacement** 7,080 tons	
Maximum speed 11 knots		**Crew** 180	
Armament 4 x 12-pounder guns, 2 machine guns, 2 land-planes, 5 float-planes			

It was not difficult to launch an aircraft of the early 20th century from the forward deck of a ship if the wind was right. This was first done from the American ship *Birmingham* at Hampton Roads, Virginia, in November 1910 and from the armoured cruiser *Pennsylvania* in a year later. The pilot in both cases, Eugene Ely, used a Curtiss biplane. The First World War stimulated interest. In 1914–15, Britain converted several passenger ships to crane seaplanes into the water and lift them out after landing. Three of them raided German airship sheds at Cuxhaven in 1914, but on the whole the type was unsuccessful. The *Ark Royal* (left) had a flying-off deck forward but still lifted her seaplanes out of the water.

PENNSYLVANIA
This picture bears witness to Eugene Ely taking off from the foredeck of the Pennsylvania *in 1911. He also landed on the* Pennsylvania, *the first-ever landing on a carrier.*

True carriers

Following the success of the *Argus*, the British launched the very small *Hermes*, the first carrier built as such from the keel up. The British *Eagle*, converted from a battleship and relaunched in 1924, introduced the island superstructure offset to the starboard side, which was to become characteristic of British and American carriers. Other British carriers of the interwar years included the converted battlecruisers *Glorious*, *Furious* (see opposite), and *Courageous*. They had lower-level flying-off decks in the bows from which small aircraft could be launched. Having lost their early lead in naval aviation during the First World War, the US Navy began to catch up after 1922, when the naval collier *Langley* (right) was converted by adding a flat deck above the existing deck. Known as the "covered wagon" to crew and pilots, she pioneered the techniques that allowed the development of the *Lexington* and *Saratoga* in the late 1920s (both converted from battlecruisers), which were to prove essential in the Pacific War. The Japanese carrier *Hosho* (right) was converted from a naval oil tanker to a design partly prepared by a technical mission from Britain before the Washington Treaty ended the Anglo-Japanese alliance. Initially she had a small island, but that was removed in 1923 after trials, setting the pattern for later Japanese development.

HOSHO
The 1922 Hosho *was the first Japanese aircraft carrier. She could transport 21 aircraft at a maximum speed of 21 knots.*

LANGLEY
The "covered wagon", as the former naval collier Langley *was known, was the US Navy's first experiment with carrier techniques.*

EAGLE

Origin Britain		**Date of launch** 1918 (as battleship)	
Length 203.5m (667ft 6in)		**Displacement** 21,630 tons	
Maximum speed 22.5 knots		**Crew** 950	
Armament 12 x 6-in guns, 4 x 4-in guns, 4 x 3-pounder guns, 6 x 21-in torpedo tubes, 21 aircraft			

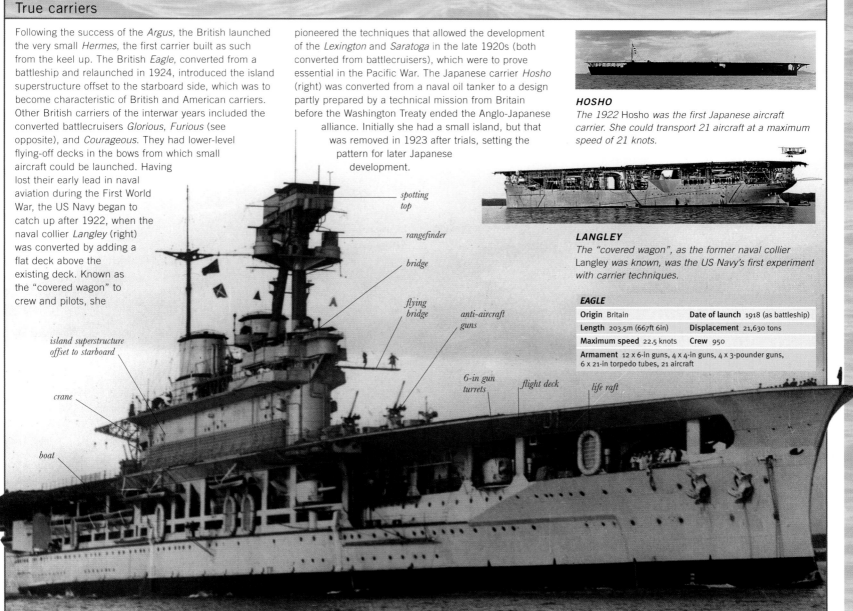

spotting top

rangefinder

bridge

flying bridge

anti-aircraft guns

island superstructure offset to starboard

crane

boat

6-in gun turrets

flight deck

life raft

Cᶦᵉ Gᵉˡᵉ **TRANSATLANTIQUE**
French Line

COUPE LONGITUDINALE
DU PAQUEBOT
NORMANDIE
79.280 Tonneaux

1930s POSTER OF THE *NORMANDIE*

> ❝ The French built a
> beautiful hotel and put a
> ship around it. The British
> built a beautiful ship and
> put a hotel inside it. ❞
>
> **RENE CHAMBRE,** comparing the
> *Normandie* and the *Queen Mary,* **1936**

KEY EVENTS

1921   IMMIGRATION RESTRICTED The USA places quotas on immigration, severely affecting the Atlantic passenger trade. Sailors at Kronstadt mutiny during the Russian Civil War.

1922   WASHINGTON NAVAL TREATY The size of the world's navies is restricted.

1929   WALL STREET CRASH US stock market failure leads to the Great Depression and the closure of many shipyards.

1932   COMPETITION FROM THE AIR The German airship *Graf Zeppelin* begins a scheduled transatlantic service.

1934   NAVAL PACTS TERMINATED Japan announces its intention to withdraw from the Naval Treaties when they expire in 1936.

1935   *NORMANDIE* TRIUMPHS The French liner *Normandie* wins the Blue Riband for the fastest crossing of the Atlantic.

1939   ANGLO-GERMAN AGREEMENT In April, Germany abrogates the 1935 Anglo-German Agreement, escalating naval rearmament.

MAURETANIA LAUNCH
Launched in Birkenhead, England, on 28 July 1938, the Mauretania was the second liner to bear the name and the first to be built from the keel up for the newly formed Cunard White Star Line.

BETWEEN THE WARS

ONCE THE DUST AND SPRAY OF THE FIRST WORLD WAR HAD SETTLED, THE OUTLOOK WAS GLOOMY FOR MOST PEOPLE CONNECTED WITH THE SEA.

None of the great navies took much satisfaction out of the First World War. The 1918 mutiny of the German Fleet led directly to the overthrow of the German Empire and the country's defeat. Mutiny would remain a theme for the next two decades – a revolt of the Soviet Fleet at Kronstadt in 1921 almost toppled the Bolshevik regime; in Britain, a much milder mutiny at Invergordon in 1931 forced a drastic change in economic policy. The British hadn't really defeated the Germans at sea, for the Germans had scuttled their own fleet in Scapa Flow in 1919. The Americans, French, Italians, and Japanese had seen little action in the battleship war. The various navies, which had recruited officers with the expectation of a permanent career, were cut down to much less than their pre-war size. They now had to compete with air forces for limited public funds, although the Americans and Japanese put a good deal of effort into naval aviation.

AMERICA'S FIRST CARRIER
When the Washington Naval Treaty was signed, the US Navy had only one aircraft carrier, the Langley, so it was free to build more.

admirals wanted a large building programme, but the politicians and public believed that the pre-war programme had contributed to the outbreak of the war itself. In 1921, the British agreed to an American request for a conference on naval disarmament.

After much negotiation, a treaty was signed in Washington in February 1922, under which the major navies were allocated battleship tonnages in the ratio of five each for Britain and the USA, three for Japan, and two each for France and Italy. Older battleships would be scrapped to bring the tonnage down. There were similar provisions for light cruisers and heavy cruisers. The treaty included separate allocations for aircraft carriers, which, ironically, encouraged American and Japanese development of naval aviation.

The Washington Treaty

One of the first post-war tasks of the major navies was to decide their role in the new world, traumatized by the war and largely pacifist in its opinions. The Americans were still building ships planned during the war and had a dozen under construction. The Japanese had eight being built or planned. The British feared that they would slip from having by far the world's largest navy before the war to become the third naval power in terms of size, and equipped mainly with older ships that did not incorporate the lessons learned at the Battle of Jutland (see p.290). The British

FIVE-POWER TREATY
The Washington Naval Treaty, ratified by US Congress on 17 August 1923, limited the number of warships held by the USA, Britain, France, Italy, and Japan.

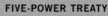

KEEPING TRACK
The US Navy Assistant Chief of Naval Operations, Admiral William Cole (centre), is kept abreast of which of the Atlantic Fleet ships are to be scrapped and which ships are to be maintained under the Washington naval disarmament agreement.

DAVID BEATTY

In 1912, David Beatty (1871–1936) took command of the Royal Navy's glamorous battlecruiser force. He was a daring yet slapdash commander, and the poor gunnery and bad signalling of his fleet led to missed opportunities at both Dogger Bank and Jutland. He took command of the Grand Fleet in 1916 and was deeply disappointed when the war ended without a decisive naval battle. As First Sea Lord and head of the Royal Navy from 1919 to 1928, Beatty was popular and competent, but he failed to regain control of naval aviation or to stop naval arms limitation.

The treaty was a success in its immediate aim and prevented a debilitating and unnecessary arms race between the USA and Britain. The USA did not enjoy its new status to the full, because Congress rarely voted enough money to build or man the ships it was allowed. However, Japan and Italy felt slighted to be rated as second- and third-class naval powers, and this contributed to the rise of warmongers in these countries. Germany was left out altogether, increasing resentment among Germans that their country was being treated unfairly.

The Great Depression and shipping

There was a brief post-war boom in the shipbuilding industries as lost merchant shipping tonnage was replaced, but that was over by 1920. After that, few new ships were needed and the industry stagnated for the rest of the 1920s, only to be hit harder than any other in the Great Depression that began with the Wall Street Crash of 1929. In Britain, still the largest shipbuilding nation by a

JARROW MARCHERS
In October 1936, 200 unemployed men from Jarrow in northeast England marched 480km (300 miles) to London, to deliver a petition to the House of Commons asking that a steelworks be built in their town to bring back jobs.

long way, unemployment in shipbuilding trades was 59.5 per cent in 1932, compared with a national average of 22.9 per cent. The famous "hunger march" from Jarrow in northeast England to London in 1936 was inspired by the permanent closure of Palmer's shipyard in the town. British shipbuilders

NAVAL REDUCTION
Although the damage she received at Jutland had been repaired, under the terms of the Washington Naval Treaty the Royal Navy battlecruiser Lion was scrapped in 1924.

lost their self-confidence, and would never again be the innovative companies that they had been before 1914.

The British merchant fleet also remained the largest in the world, but it was declining, and owners were reluctant to accept new technology such as diesel engines. British tonnage remained stable between 1921 and 1939, whereas Norway doubled its tonnage and Sweden's increased by 50 per cent, mainly due to increases in their liner, refrigeration, and tanker trades. Greek shipping tonnage trebled in the same period. The Germans, having started from a very low base of 700,000 tons after most of their fleet was confiscated at the end of the war, recovered strongly to 4.5 million tons – still a million less than the pre-war figure. The Japanese government heavily subsidized its merchant fleet, introducing a scrap-and-build policy in 1920, in which money raised from scrapping old vessels was put into building new ones – resulting in a doubling of tonnage by 1939.

US merchant shipping had been in decline since the Civil War, despite government attempts to revive it. Ships built hastily in wartime proved to be unsuitable in peacetime. The Merchant Marine Act of 1920 gave US-registered ships preference for carrying many kinds of goods, but failed to stimulate production of any new vessels, and a subsidy of $250 million offered in 1928 produced only 42 new ships, although some were of very good quality. A congressional enquiry showed that the act was poorly drafted, and many shipowners were guilty of malpractice. The Maritime Commission of 1936 authorized loans of up to 75 per cent for new vessels, and some ingenious standard designs were produced, but little had been achieved before the start of the war in Europe in 1939.

The golden age of the liner

In 1921, the USA restricted immigration by the Quota Acts. The great liners no longer carried large numbers of desperately poor immigrants in steerage and were free to take on a new and glamorous image.

DEAD CALM
Despite its fearsome reputation, the Atlantic isn't always stormy. Germany's Europa *cruises serenely in still waters in 1931, belying her great speed.*

THE NEXT GENERATION
The Bremen *and* Europa *were supposed to enter service together in 1929, but the* Europa *was almost gutted by fire in the fitting-out dock and didn't make her maiden voyage until April 1930.*

Britain's Cunard had specialized in cheap emigrant passages and now had to reinvent itself. Existing liners, such as the *Mauretania* of 1907 (see p.278), were reconfigured for the new market, with the old steerage accommodation converted to third class for new-style tourists. Even the first-class market suffered as the numbers of very rich declined in the Great Depression. But in a world traumatized by war, pleasure for its own sake found a ready market, and transatlantic liners offered the enjoyable experience of a voyage filled with dances and games.

Germany was temporarily eliminated from the transatlantic market in 1918, and its best ships, including the great *Vaterland* and *Kaiser Wilhelm II*, were confiscated as war reparations. The most famous new German liner of the 1920s,

THE BLUE RIBAND TROPHY
In July 1935, after nearly 100 years of competition, the Blue Riband prize took on a tangible form. Donated by British politician Harold K. Hale, the trophy is presented to the ship that makes the fastest crossing of the North Atlantic.

GILT TRIP
No expense was spared by the French Line in decorating the Normandie *of 1935 – all the gilt was 24 carat and she exemplified the Art Deco style. These impressive doors separated the smoking room from the grand saloon.*

Norddeutscher Lloyd's *Bremen* of 1929, was built for speed (it could reach 27 knots) and had a new style of decor, which followed the lines of the ship. She took the Blue Riband from the *Mauretania* on her maiden voyage, crossing the Atlantic in 4 days, 17 hours, and 42 minutes, only to lose it to her sister, *Europa*, in April 1930.

The Italia Line's *Rex* was the only Italian ship ever to hold the Blue Riband, steaming from Gibraltar across the Atlantic at 28.92 knots in August 1933, a full knot faster than the new record set by the *Europa* the month before. The *Rex* and her elegant stablemate, the *Conte di Savoia*, did much to popularize first-class travel to the Mediterranean among Americans.

After the Quota Acts, the USA took little interest in the transatlantic trade, which left Britain and France as the main rivals on the

LUXURY LIFESTYLE

In the novel *Gentlemen Prefer Blondes*, Anita Loos' naive heroine Lorelei Lee takes a liner passage from New York to London:

Well Dorothy and I really are on the ship sailing to Europe as everyone could tell by looking at the ocean. I always love the ocean. I mean I always love a ship and I really love the Majestic because you would not know it was a ship, and the steward says the ocean is not so obnoxious this month as it generally is.... Dorothy is up on deck wasting quite a lot of time with a gentleman who is only a tennis champion. So I am going to ring for the steward and have some champagne which is quite good for a person on a boat. The steward is really quite a nice boy and he has had quite a sad life and he likes to tell me about himself.

ANITA LOOS, *Gentlemen Prefer Blondes*, **1926**

ENJOYING THE SUNSHINE
Passengers relax on the sun deck of the Italian Line's Rex. The funnels were painted in the colours of the national flag, red, green, and white.

FASHION PARADE
First-class passengers meet and greet each other by the Rex's grand staircase in this artist's impression by Edina Vittorio from the 1930s.

North Atlantic route. With the market reduced, few new liners were needed in the 1920s, but by the end of that decade the older ships were deteriorating. The French Line's *Ile de France* of 1927 was noted for the catapult used to launch a seaplane during the latter part of the voyage, saving a day with mail deliveries. New ships had oil-fired engines to save labour. Funnels became shorter and less numerous, although they still featured in advertising as company symbols.

The building of France's great liner of the period, the *Normandie*, was supported by government subsidy. Construction was slowed down by the Great Depression, although work never actually stopped. Aimed at the de luxe trade, she was lavishly furnished in the Art Deco style, and her hull design was revolutionary – narrow at both ends, with a bulbous bow below the waterline. On her maiden voyage to New York in May 1935, she captured the Blue Riband, and on her return journey she became the first ship to cross the Atlantic at more than 30 knots.

In Britain, a new Cunard liner of 1930 became a symbol of hope and glamour in the squalor of the depression. It was ordered to be built at John Brown's yard in Clydebank, Scotland, in a town that had massive unemployment. The new ship, No. 534 in the yard's books, was already towering over the slums created in the 19th-century boom when, in December 1931, work was suspended. The government, alarmed at the unemployment situation on Clydeside, forced a merger between the historic rivals Cunard and White Star, offering a subsidy of £9.5 million as an inducement. When work resumed at Clydebank in April

COCKTAIL HOUR
The magnificent cocktail bar of the Queen Mary was situated almost directly under the bridge of the ship, offering passengers a superb view over the bows as they sipped an aperitif or two.

VALUABLE MEMENTO
This lamp from the Queen Mary was presented to a member of her crew by his colleagues in recognition of his service.

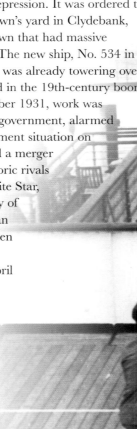

1934, the town was hung with flags, and pipers played as the workers returned to the yard. She was launched by Queen Mary in 1935 and took her name. Traditional in her design but with more powerful engines, the *Queen Mary* took the Blue Riband from the *Normandie* in August 1936. For the next three years, the Blue Riband passed back and forth between the two great liners as each strove to outdo the other, only for the rivalry to cease with the advent of war.

The most luxurious Flying-Boat in the world
IMPERIAL AIRWAYS

EMPIRE DESIGN
Introduced in 1937, Britain's Imperial Airways' Short Empire flying boat had a complex interior layout. Carrying 17 passengers and 5 crew and travelling in stages, it took nine days to fly from England to Sydney, Australia. It also flew to South Africa.

Rivalry with aircraft

Although commercial aviation services began soon after the First World War, they were more of a novelty than a serious rival to railways and shipping. Land aircraft could cross the Atlantic Ocean, as British airmen John Alcock and Arthur Brown did in 1919 and American aviator Charles Lindbergh in 1927, but only if they were specially prepared and carried no payload. The aircraft of the future were thought to be the airship and the flying boat (both of which incorporated nautical terms in their names). Airships were seen as ideal for flight across the oceans. In both Britain and the USA, they had been developed largely by navies during the First World War, for use in sea patrols. But British development stopped in 1930 after the disastrous crash of the R 101 en route to India.

The Germans continued their development of large airships, and the *Graf Zeppelin* of 1928, named for the inventor of the rigid airship, made more than 140 transatlantic trips, starting in 1932, mostly across the Atlantic to Brazil, where there was a wealthy expatriate community. She could carry 20 passengers in the luxurious gondola that hung below the hydrogen-filled gas bag. Her successor, the *Hindenburg*, was even larger and more luxurious, but she was involved in one of the most public disasters of all time when, on 6 May 1937, she burst into flames at Lakehurst, New Jersey. Even though 62 of the 97 people onboard escaped with their lives, this was the end of the airship as a serious rival to the passenger liner.

In the USA and Britain, the flying boat was regarded as the best means of long-distance flight, for it could land on a sheltered stretch of water instead of needing a great runway. The British wanted to improve communication within their empire, particularly by running flights to India and the Far East, with frequent stopovers. The Americans thought of travelling longer distances, across the Pacific and the Atlantic. The culmination of flying-boat development was the huge Boeing 314 of 1938. Pan American Airways called its fleet of Boeing 314s "clippers" in recognition of the nautical associations, and they were also run like a ship. They had a captain as well as first and second officers, radio operators, and flight engineers. The crew stood watches so that they could fly day and night. They operated from an extensive flight deck, and the pilot's compartment was known as the bridge. The flight engineers of the clippers were trained to fit and even make spare parts, for the plane might be many miles from a suitable depot. The passengers travelled in seven separate compartments, in which seats were arranged as in a lounge and could be turned into bunks at night. The stewards could cook meals onboard, as well as distribute them.

Pan American began a regular service from New York to Lisbon and Marseilles in May 1939 with the *Yankee Clipper*. She carried 40 passengers and 12 crew, and a one-way, two-day trip cost $375. Places were limited, and only the rich could afford them, but the service gave a foretaste of what ocean liners might face in the future.

BIRD'S EYE VIEW
The passengers onboard Germany's Hindenburg of 1936–37 were afforded spectacular views of the Manhattan skyline.

IN 2 DAYS TO NORTH AMERICA!
DEUTSCHE ZEPPELIN-REEDEREI

FUN AND GAMES
The chance to play games was all part of the pleasure package offered by the new breed of ocean liners. These energetic bouts of deck tennis took place on the aft deck of the Queen Mary during her maiden voyage in 1936.

SKY LOUNGE
The passenger section of the Graf Zeppelin's gondola was quiet, temperature controlled, and reasonably spacious. The decor was luxurious, as would be expected by the clientele, as only the very rich could afford to fly in her.

Naval aviation

From 1918, British naval aviation was controlled by the Royal Air Force (RAF), which viewed it with scepticism, favouring strategic bombing of enemy cities. After 1924, the Royal Navy was to supply 70 per cent of naval pilots and all the observers, with the RAF supplying aircraft, but aviation was now seen as a dead-end career by most naval officers.

The British aircraft carriers of the First World War were small and slow by later standards. The *Eagle*, completed in 1920, was the first with an "island" superstructure offset to starboard. The *Hermes*, the first carrier built from the keel up, entered service in 1924. Three British battlecruisers, the *Furious*, *Courageous*, and *Glorious*, were converted to carriers in the 1920s and introduced the idea of launching aircraft directly from the hangar below decks. The only modern British carrier built in the interwar years was the *Ark Royal*, ordered in 1935 and commissioned in 1938. She had two complete hangar decks and carried 60 aircraft.

The British failed to develop dive-bombing aircraft. Their carriers had far fewer aircraft than equivalent American or Japanese vessels, and these were generally low-performance. More positively, they adopted the armoured flight deck, made entirely of steel. At the cost of an extra hangar and nearly half the complement of aircraft, the latest British carriers were able to withstand a great deal of punishment.

By 1918, the Americans were paying more attention to British developments in naval aviation. The US Navy's first aircraft carrier, the *Langley*, nicknamed "the covered wagon", was converted from a collier in 1922. The Washington Naval Treaty forced the abandonment of two large battlecruisers, which instead were completed in 1927 as the carriers *Lexington* and *Saratoga*, with enclosed hangars and flight decks of steel with wood planking. These three ships allowed the Americans to gain much experience in fleet exercises, until the next carriers, two of the *Yorktown* class and the smaller *Wasp*, were begun in the mid-1930s.

Despite limitations imposed by budget restrictions, the US Navy had full control of its aircraft. The Bureau of Aeronautics (BuAer) was formed in 1921, and aviation was quickly integrated in the heart of the Navy, becoming a major part of the syllabus of the Naval Academy at Annapolis, Maryland, in 1925. The Japanese had no knowledge of naval aviation until 1921, when a British mission arrived to teach them about

it. Untroubled by either pacifism or isolationism, the Japanese had fewer budgetary constraints than the British or the Americans, but the battleship lobby remained supreme. Admiral Isoroku Yamamoto (see p.322) was one of the first to see that aircraft would dominate future naval battles.

The early stages of Japanese aircraft-carrier development were parallel to those of the USA – a merchant ship, the *Hosho*, was converted in 1922, followed by two battlecruisers banned under the Washington Naval Treaty, the *Akagi* and *Kaga*, completed in 1927 and 1928 respectively. The Japanese carriers had very small superstructures (see left) or none at all. Another carrier, the *Ryujo*, was built in 1933. The Japanese Navy provided the large number

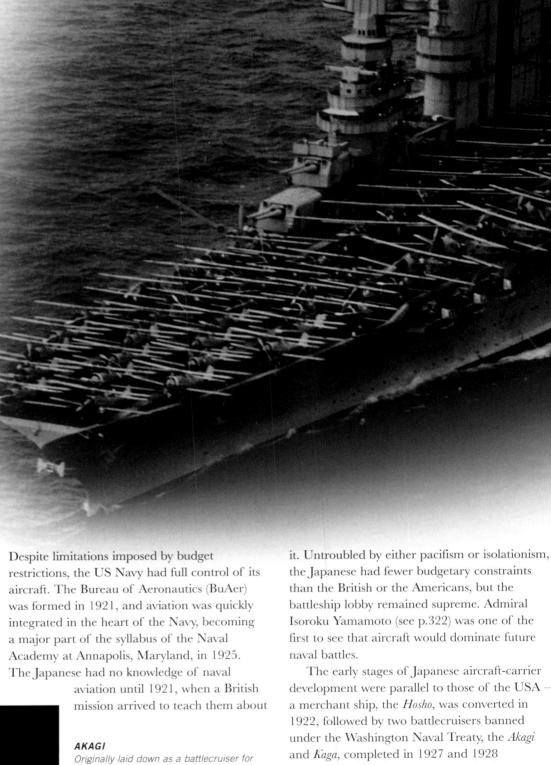

CROWDED FLIGHT DECK
Seen here on exercise in 1935, the US aircraft carrier Saratoga *could carry up to 81 planes. She had a top speed of almost 34 knots.*

AKAGI
Originally laid down as a battlecruiser for the Japanese Navy in 1920, the Akagi *was completed as an aircraft carrier in 1927. She was reconfigured in 1935–38, giving her a full-length flight deck and a small port-side superstructure.*

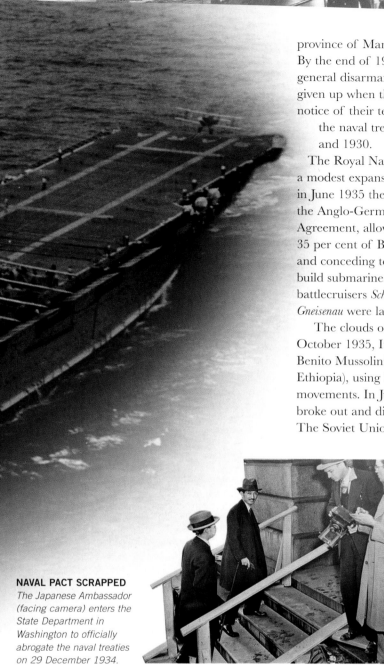

province of Manchuria in 1931. By the end of 1934, any hope of general disarmament had been given up when the Japanese gave notice of their termination of the naval treaties of 1922 and 1930.

The Royal Navy was allowed a modest expansion, although in June 1935 the British signed the Anglo-German Naval Agreement, allowing Germany 35 per cent of British tonnage and conceding to it the right to build submarines. The battlecruisers *Scharnhorst* and *Gneisenau* were laid down the same year.

The clouds of war were gathering. In October 1935, Italy, under the fascist dictator Benito Mussolini, invaded Abyssinia (now Ethiopia), using his fleet to cover troop movements. In July 1936, the Spanish Civil War broke out and divided Europe into three camps. The Soviet Union, and left-wing forces everywhere, supported the Republic but it no longer had any naval power to make this effective. Although the ordinary seamen of the Spanish Navy had secured the ships on behalf of the Republic, it could not run them properly without the officers. On the opposing side, the Nationalist rebels led by General Francisco Franco were supported by Germany and Italy, but only the latter provided any effective sea power. In the middle were nations such as Britain and France, which attempted to enforce "non-intervention" and used their warships, somewhat ineffectively, to patrol the Spanish coast. The Nationalists won the war in March 1939.

Meanwhile, in 1935, Italy began to expand its navy and laid down two battleships and 12 cruisers in the next five years. In Germany in 1938, Hitler approved the naval rearmament programme Plan Z, which would have given a

SPANISH CIVIL WAR
Countries supporting General Franco's Nationalists during the war included Italy, Germany, and Portugal, caricatured in this Republican propaganda poster.

balanced fleet with due proportions of battleships, aircraft carriers, cruisers, destroyers, and submarines by 1948. But submarines and small craft could be built much faster, and in 1939 these dominated the German Navy. In Japan, two huge battleships, the *Yamato* and the *Musashi*, were laid down in great secrecy. First conceived in 1934, they were the first to be built in Japan since the early 1920s. The Japanese carrier force expanded from four to ten in 1938–41.

The USA and Britain got into their stride only on the eve of the Second World War. The Royal Navy had ordered four new carriers in 1936–38 and had won back control of its air arm in 1937. Five battleships of the *King George V* class were ordered in 1937, and modernization of old ships had begun. In the USA, the trickle of orders began with two battleships of the *North Carolina* class in 1937. It became a flood in 1940–41, with six battleships of the powerful *Iowa* class and 10 carriers being started. The accelerating naval programmes were just in time to take part in the greatest naval war in history.

NAVAL PACT SCRAPPED
The Japanese Ambassador (facing camera) enters the State Department in Washington to officially abrogate the naval treaties on 29 December 1934.

of aircrew required by training petty officer pilots rather than expanding the officer corps. It tended to cram a large number of aircraft into a relatively small carrier – a practice that would cause it problems in the future.

Rise of the German and Japanese navies

In 1930, Britain, the USA, and Japan signed the London Naval Treaty, agreeing to tonnage and armament limitations for cruisers, destroyers, and submarines. In January 1933, the Nazis came to power in Germany, determined to wipe out the losses of the First World War and restore the fleet to its due strength. Chancellor Adolf Hitler took Germany out of the League of Nations later that year. Japan had already walked out following its invasion of the Chinese

NAZI BATTLECRUISER
Built as a result of the Anglo-German Naval Agreement of 1935, the 38,100-ton battlecruiser Scharnhorst *flies the naval ensign of Nazi Germany from her stern during the commissioning ceremony on 7 January 1939.*

LUXURY LINERS

American restrictions on immigration greatly reduced the demand for cheap passages across the Atlantic and, therefore, inspired shipping companies to move towards the luxury market in travel for rich tourists and businesspeople. This was encouraged financially by some western European governments. Partly, they wanted large ships that could be converted to cruisers or troopships in wartime. More urgently, though, they saw liners as a valuable way of boosting national prestige, and an intense competition soon developed.

MEETING OF THE GIANTS
This evocative image shows the United States Lines ship America *of 1939 passing her successor, the new* United States *of 1952, in New York Harbor.*

French luxury liners

MAIDEN VOYAGE
The Normandie *arrived to an enthusiastic welcome in New York on her maiden voyage in 1935, having won the Blue Riband.*

INSIDE THE *NORMANDIE*
By 1937, the luxurious first-class lounge studio of the Normandie was fitted with sofas, armchairs, and a writing desk.

The French did not migrate to North America in such large numbers as the British, Irish, Germans, and Italians, but French ships offered a sense of style that was favoured by American passengers in particular. The *Ile de France* of 1927 was the first to use the new Art Deco style, and for Americans tired of Prohibition she claimed the longest bar on any ship.

The *Normandie* was conceived as a follow-up – and the largest, most beautiful ship in the world. She was designed by the émigré Russian Vladimir Yourkevitch, who had built warships for the Tsar. Extra port facilities were prepared for the new ship, including a huge dry dock at St. Nazaire. She was built in secrecy and launched in 1932, to be completed three years later. Externally, she had a concave bow and gently rising forecastle, which gave a streamlined appearance. Like the *Ile de France*, she was designed in the Art Deco style, and the funnel uptakes were split to allow massive internal deck spaces.

William Bertrand, the French Minister of the Marine, wrote of her rivalry with the *Queen Mary*: "Between them there is no place for jealous rivalry, only for fruitful emulation … The contrast between the splendour of these ships and the rigour of the times may be taken as an indication of a determined effort to conquer present economic difficulties and

aft (false) funnel houses domestic animals

officers' cabins

first-class deluxe cabins

café grill

tourist-class smoking room

third-class smoking room

overhanging stern

non-balanced rudder

children's playroom and gymnasium

tourist-class cabins

first-class cabins

boot topping

first-class enclosed promenade

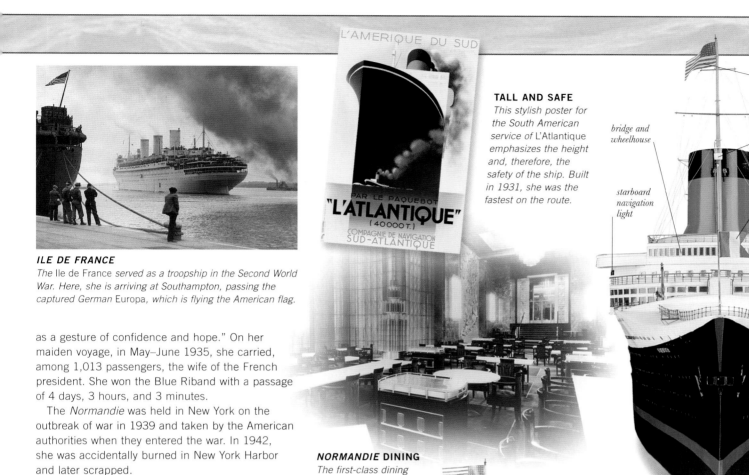

ILE DE FRANCE

The Ile de France *served as a troopship in the Second World War. Here, she is arriving at Southampton, passing the captured German* Europa, *which is flying the American flag.*

TALL AND SAFE

This stylish poster for the South American service of L'Atlantique emphasizes the height and, therefore, the safety of the ship. Built in 1931, she was the fastest on the route.

US flag flown on entering New York Harbor

bridge and wheelhouse

lookout

French ensign

starboard navigation light

port navigation light

as a gesture of confidence and hope." On her maiden voyage, in May–June 1935, she carried, among 1,013 passengers, the wife of the French president. She won the Blue Riband with a passage of 4 days, 3 hours, and 3 minutes.

The *Normandie* was held in New York on the outbreak of war in 1939 and taken by the American authorities when they entered the war. In 1942, she was accidentally burned in New York Harbor and later scrapped.

NORMANDIE IN PROFILE

The great length of the Normandie *is shown well in this side view of a model, which also highlights the dramatic effect of her curved bow and her three raked funnels.*

NORMANDIE DINING

The first-class dining saloon was the largest room on the Normandie, at 93m (305ft) long. This corner is decorated with bas-reliefs by artist Raymond Delamere.

FRONT VIEW OF THE NORMANDIE

midships funnel

forefunnel

lifeboat

sun and sports deck

boat deck

promenade deck

forecastle deck

NORMANDIE		
Origin France		**Date of launch** 1932
Length 313.8m (1,029ft 6in)		**Tonnage** 79,280 tons
Maximum speed 29 knots		**Crew** 1,345
Passengers 828 first class, 670 tourist class, 454 third class		

bilge keel

powerboat

bridge and wheelhouse

winter garden

bow anchor

L'AMERIQUE DU SUD

PAR LE PAQUEBOT
"L'ATLANTIQUE"
(40000 T.)
COMPAGNIE DE NAVIGATION
SUD-ATLANTIQUE

German liners

The Weimar Republic in Germany, banned from large armament programmes after the country's defeat in war, hoped to regain some prestige by re-entering the transatlantic race. Norddeutscher Lloyd built two ships simultaneously: the *Bremen* (below) on the Weser, and the *Europa* in Hamburg. The ships were launched on consecutive days, but the *Europa* was delayed by a fire during fitting out, so the *Bremen* began the express service across the Atlantic alone in 1929, to take the long-standing Blue Riband record from the ageing *Mauretania*.

BREMEN			
Date of launch 1928		Maximum speed 28.5 knots	
Length 286m (938ft)		Tonnage 51,656 tons	
Crew 990			
Passengers 2,400			

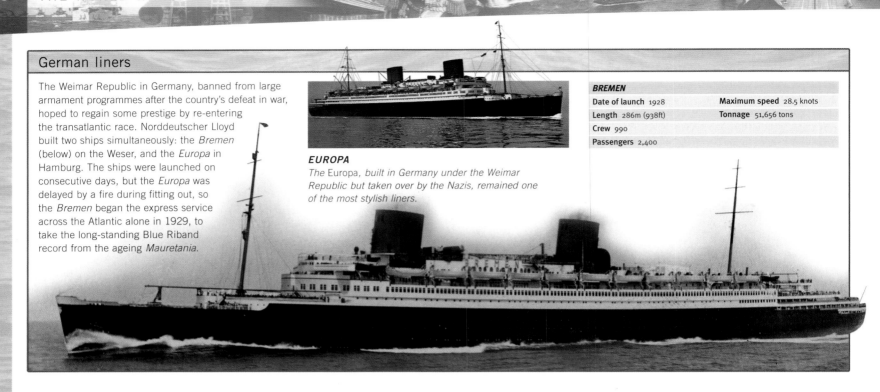

EUROPA
The Europa, built in Germany under the Weimar Republic but taken over by the Nazis, remained one of the most stylish liners.

Italian liners

Mussolini's Italy was as keen as any other nation to win international prestige with its Atlantic liners. Italy offered cultural attractions to American tourists, and there was a strong market in the families of emigrants who had done well in America. The *Rex* (below) and the smaller *Conte di Savoia* (right) were built in Genoa and Trieste respectively, and provided a service between Genoa and New York. The *Rex* was originally to be called *Guglielmo Marconi* after the inventor of radio (see p.279). She became the only Italian winner of the Blue Riband in 1933, with an average speed of nearly 29 knots from Gibraltar, and held it until 1935. She was laid up during the Second World War and, like her sister ship, damaged by allied bombing in Italian waters and scrapped.

REX			
Date of launch 1931		Maximum speed 29 knots	
Length 248m (814ft)		Tonnage 51,062 tons	
Crew 756			
Passengers 2,258			

SLOW AND STABLE
The Conte di Savoia *was slightly slower than the* Rex *but had a system of gyroscopic stabilizers that had some success in reducing rolling and, therefore, seasickness.*

British liners

Built among the slums of Clydeside during the great depression, and launched in the presence of King George V, the *Queen Mary* (below) carried great symbolism for the British people, although her exterior design was criticized for being too old-fashioned. Unlike many of the great European liners, she survived the Second World War to be preserved in Long Beach, California.

QUEEN MARY

Date of launch 1934	Maximum speed 32 knots
Length 310.6m (1,019ft)	Tonnage 80,744 tons
Crew 1,101	
Passengers 2,139	

American liners

The United States Lines were formed in 1921 after the United States Mail Steamship Company failed to meet its contracts with the US Shipping Board. Its most notable ship in its early years was the ex-German *Vaterland*, renamed *Leviathan*, which weighed in at nearly 60,000 tons. The *Leviathan* began a transatlantic service under new owners in 1923. The *America* (below) was launched in 1939 but was diverted from the North Atlantic to Caribbean services because of the Second World War. After Pearl Harbor, she served as a troop transport and began the first transatlantic service in 1946.

STREAMLINING *AMERICA*
The sharp bow of America, seen here while she was under construction, was designed to cut through the water at great speed.

AMERICA

Date of launch 1939	Maximum speed 24 knots
Length 220.4m (723ft)	Tonnage 26,454 tons
Crew 643	
Passengers 543 cabin class, 418 tourist class, 241 third class	

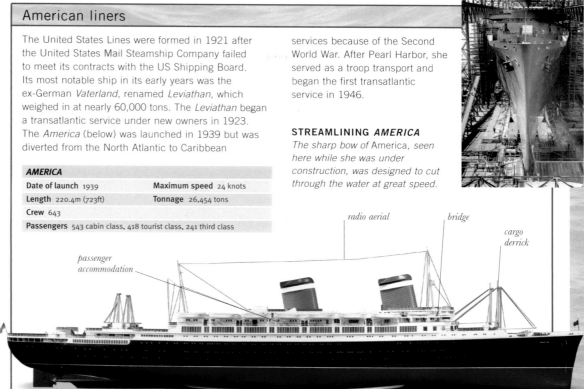

passenger accommodation
radio aerial
bridge
cargo derrick

Canadian liners

The route across the Atlantic to Canada was slightly less glamorous and competitive than the one to New York, although it did produce some fine vessels. The *Empress of France* (right) was run by the Canadian Pacific Line, an offshoot of the Canadian Pacific Railway Company, which also operated shipping services from Canada across the Pacific Ocean. Built as the *Alsatian* for the Allan Line, she was the first liner with a cruiser stern, which curved forwards rather than backwards. After surviving the First World War as an armed merchant cruiser, she was taken over by Canadian Pacific in 1919. The liner was renamed and refitted to modern standards of comfort. She was laid up in 1931.

EMPRESS OF FRANCE

Date of launch 1914	Maximum speed 19 knots
Length 183m (600ft)	Tonnage 18,481 tons
Crew 500	
Passengers 263 first class, 504 second class, 848 third class	

EMPRESS OF BRITAIN
Twice the size of the Canadian Pacific Line's next-biggest ship, the Empress of Britain was launched in 1931. She operated from Southampton to Quebec from May to November, then went on a round-the-world cruise for the remaining four months.

radio aerial
bridge
moveable crow's nest
passenger galleries
cargo derricks
anchor

BEACH MINE

> 66 They came, rank after relentless rank, 10 lanes wide, 20 miles across, 5,000 ships of every description. 99

CORNELIUS RYAN, describing Operation Neptune in *The Longest Day*, **1959**

KEY EVENTS

1939 WAR BREAKS OUT Britain and France declare war after Poland is invaded by Germany.

1940 FALL OF FRANCE Between 26 May and 4 June, over 300,000 English and French soldiers are evacuated from the beaches at Dunkirk as the German army advances.

1941 WOLF PACKS IN THE ATLANTIC In spring 1941, German U-boats start attacking Allied shipping in packs, to great effect.

1941 *BISMARCK* SUNK The German battleship *Bismarck* is sunk by the Royal Navy on 27 May, boosting British morale.

1941 PEARL HARBOR ATTACKED The US naval base at Pearl Harbor, Hawaii, is bombed by Japanese aircraft on 7 December. The USA officially enters the war.

1942 BATTLE OF MIDWAY The US Navy achieves a major victory in the Pacific when it defeats a Japanese carrier force on 4–7 June.

1944 D-DAY LANDINGS Allied forces land on five beaches in Normandy, France, on 6 June, spearheading Operation Neptune.

1945 VICTORY IN EUROPE The Russian Army reaches Berlin, and Hitler commits suicide on 30 April. Germany surrenders on 7 May.

1945 JAPAN ATOM BOMBED The USA drops atomic bombs on Hiroshima and Nagasaki, and the war in the Pacific ends on 15 August.

THE SECOND WORLD WAR

THE SECOND WORLD WAR SAW BATTLES FOUGHT IN SEAS AROUND THE WORLD, MANY OF THEM INVOLVING NEW FORMS OF NAVAL WARFARE.

The Second World War began at sea at 7:30pm on 3 September 1939, less than eight hours after Britain had entered the war and two days after Germany precipitated the conflict by invading Poland. Lieutenant Fritz-Julius Lemp of *U-30* disobeyed Hitler's orders and sank the liner *Athenia* en route from Liverpool to Canada. Nineteen crew and 93 passengers were lost. The Germans covered for the error by claiming that the *Athenia* was an armed merchant cruiser, and so the second U-boat war began. The next great U-boat success was early in the morning of 14 October when *U-47*, under the command of Günther Prien, penetrated the ill-prepared defences of Scapa Flow in Scotland and sank the British battleship *Royal Oak* with great loss of life.

Poland was quickly subdued and there was little land action in Europe. At sea, as in 1914, German surface warships attacked British commerce. The most important was the pocket battleship *Graf Spee*, commanded by Captain Hans Langsdorff, which sank 50,000 tons of shipping in the South Atlantic and Indian Ocean. Langsdorff was found by three British and New Zealand cruisers, the *Ajax*, *Exeter*, and *Achilles*, and he also disobeyed orders in taking them on, believing them to be destroyers. Langsdorff retreated into neutral Montevideo and, thinking he was trapped by an increasing number of British ships, scuttled the *Graf Spee* on 17 December.

ANTI-AIRCRAFT GUNS
A mixed battery of anti-aircraft guns are deployed aboard the US battleship Arkansas *in 1944. Although she had been superseded by aircraft carriers, her guns made her a suitable escort for convoys crossing the North Atlantic.*

The Norwegian campaign
Six months of so-called Phoney War, when little fighting took place, ended on 9 April 1940. Britain's First Lord of the Admiralty Winston Churchill planned to mine neutral Norwegian waters to stop supplies of iron ore reaching Germany, but the Germans forestalled this. Daringly, they launched a seaborne invasion without

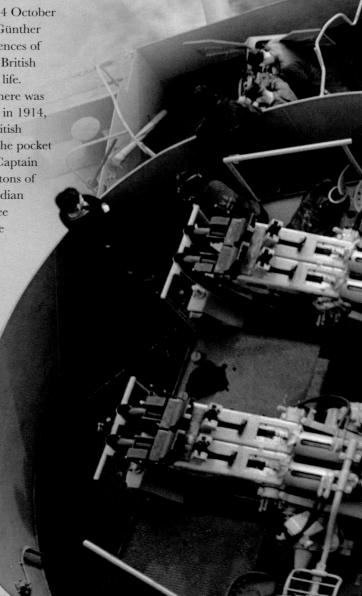

OILY SURVIVORS
Sailors clinging to a life raft from the Royal Navy aircraft carrier Glorious, *sunk leaving Narvik on 8 June 1940, are rescued from the oil-covered waters of the Norwegian Sea by the German cruiser* Hipper.

Glowworm rammed the German cruiser *Hipper* and the battlecruiser *Renown* fought indecisively against the battlecruisers *Scharnhorst* and *Gneisenau*, but the German landings were successful.

On 10 April, a destroyer flotilla under the British Captain Bernard Warburton-Lee attacked Ofot Fjord, in northern Norway, sinking three German destroyers and some merchant ships. On 13 April, the British ships returned with the battleship *Warspite*, and sank the remaining eight German destroyers. British and French troops landed in an attempt to take Narvik, which had great strategic importance as a port for the iron-ore trade, but they were poorly led, with inadequate air support, and had to be withdrawn in June. On the way out, the captain of the British carrier *Glorious* made the mistake of taking on the *Scharnhorst* and *Gneisenau*, and his ship was sunk on 8 June.

Dunkirk and Operation Sea Lion

The next stage of the war began on 10 May 1940 (the day that Churchill became British Prime Minister) when Germany launched a devastating attack on France through neutral Belgium, the Netherlands, and Luxembourg. The Allied armies were soon defeated, and the British, with a substantial number of French troops, were cut off at Dunkirk in northern France.

Despite doubts about risking destroyers in an area where the Luftwaffe was dominant, the Royal Navy, under

command of the sea. Using all the German surface fleet and half the U-boats, the attack was divided into seven groups – two to take Denmark and five to attack various Norwegian ports. Neither country was ready to fight, and the Germans encountered serious resistance only on the passage to Oslo, where the German cruiser *Blücher* was sunk. The British destroyer

BOURRASQUE SINKS
The French destroyer Bourrasque *sinks after hitting a mine on the way back from Dunkirk on 30 May. She had about 1,200 men aboard, many of whom died.*

> ❝ And our great-grandchildren, when they learn how we began this war by snatching glory out of defeat, and then swept on to victory, may also learn how the little holiday steamers made an excursion to hell and came back glorious. ❞
>
> **J.B. PRIESTLEY**, in a BBC Radio Broadcast, **5 June 1940**

TO THE RESCUE
At a mere 4.4m (14ft) long, Tamzine was the smallest vessel to take part in Operation Dynamo, the evacuation of Dunkirk, between 26 May and 4 June 1940. She ferried many soldiers from the Dunkirk beaches to deep-water vessels before being towed back across the Channel to England by a Belgian trawler.

OPERATION DYNAMO
Soldiers wade out to a waiting rescue ship during Operation Dynamo. All their equipment had to be left behind on the beaches of Dunkirk in the rush to evade capture by the rapidly advancing German Army.

Admiral Bertram Ramsay, began to mobilize for an evacuation. A fleet of "little ships" – barges, fishing boats, and motor yachts – used in the operation created a valuable morale-boosting legend, although in fact about two-thirds of the 338,226 men rescued between 26 May and 4 June embarked directly onto warships and ferries, and the little ships' role was largely to transport men from the beaches to the larger ships. Of the 861 vessels used, 243 were lost.

As France surrendered, Churchill and his admirals were determined not to let the French fleet fall into German hands, for it might tip the balance of power against Britain. Admiral Jean-François Darlan's forces were bombarded by the British in the Algerian port of Mers-el-Kebir on 3 July. Three French battleships were sunk and one escaped in an event that created tension between the allies.

The Germans prepared Operation Sea Lion for an invasion of Britain in the autumn of 1940, intending to land their troops on a broad front of England's south coast. But they had lost most of their destroyer force in Norway, and the invasion barges were hastily improvised. With inferior naval forces against a determined and alert enemy, the Germans would first have to gain command of the skies over the Royal Air Force (RAF). This they failed to do in the Battle of Britain, which lasted until October. Instead, the Luftwaffe began to bomb Britain's major cities in the Blitz of September 1940 to May 1941.

The Battle of the Atlantic
Although the U-boat campaign began on the first day of the war, it became more serious after the Germans captured Norway and the fall of France gave them bases with direct access to the Atlantic. In the winter and early spring of 1941, the German captains enjoyed their "happy time", when British and Canadian escorts were weak and the U-boats sank up to 700,000 tons of shipping a month. Taking advantage of the significant growth in U-boat production, Commander Karl Dönitz (see panel, above) had introduced the wolf-pack tactic, in which a number of

SIGNALLING A MERCHANTMAN
A sailor semaphores a merchant ship as it slowly passes a naval control base on the east coast of England on 30 November 1939. Inward-bound convoys had to stop and take pilots onboard to steer them through the minefields.

KARL DONITZ

Karl Dönitz (1891–1980) joined the U-boat service in 1916 and took command of his own boat in 1918. He remained in the Weimar Republic's small navy after the First World War, and was not sorry when Adolf Hitler came to power in 1933 and revived the German Navy and U-boats. As a captain, he commanded the first operational flotilla in 1935 and was in charge of the U-boat arm at the start of the Second World War. He devised the tactics of surface attack at night and U-boat wolf packs, which were to cause the British and their allies so much trouble. In 1943, he took command of the German Navy. When Hitler committed suicide in 1945, Dönitz held the post of Führer for one week.

U-boats would attack a convoy at once. They often attacked at night on the surface, to avoid detection by Asdic (also known as sonar) below the waves. Since invasion was less likely now that the British Army had recovered from defeat in France, and the Blitz was failing to cow the population, Churchill saw that the U-boat was the only realistic way that Britain could be defeated. "We must assume that the Battle of the Atlantic has begun," he declared on 6 March 1941. But the British were beginning to prevail. More escort ships became available, including 50 old destroyers from the USA which

LIFE ON AN ESCORT SHIP

The conscript seamen of the Second World War often had to endure appalling conditions in the stormy North Atlantic, as James Lamb on the Royal Canadian Navy corvette *Candytuft* discovered:

> *By noon on the second day we were mindless automatons, so numbed mentally and physically by the incessant violence of our world as to have become inured. We no longer cared whether we lived or died; it seemed no longer to concern us. But for all of that, life went on within the beaten hulls of our ships; watches changed, men ate a little and slept as best they could in the frightful din of the hurricane. We had been washed bare of everything on the upper deck; the Carley floats gone, the whaler stove in, but still our ship lived.*

JAMES B. LAMB, *The Corvette Navy*, **1977**

COMMERCE RAIDER
The crew of a U-boat line up on the deck, observed by officers in the conning tower, as it arrives at the German naval base at Kiel in the Baltic after a successful mission raiding British merchant ships in the Atlantic.

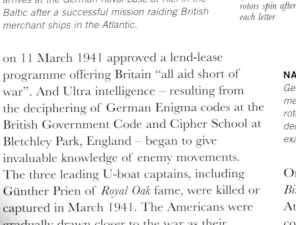

spare light bulbs

viewing windows on lid show encoded letters

rotor cylinder carries four alphabetical rotors

alphabetical lightboard shows final encoded letter

keyboard on which message is typed

plugboard settings are changed daily

light filter plate

position of rotors controls encoding of each letter; rotors spin after each letter

NAVAL ENIGMA MACHINE
Germany's Enigma machines enabled an operator to type a message then scramble it by means of three (or later four) rotors, which displayed different letters of the alphabet. To decode the message, the receiver needed to know the exact settings of the rotors, which changed daily.

on 11 March 1941 approved a lend-lease programme offering Britain "all aid short of war". And Ultra intelligence – resulting from the deciphering of German Enigma codes at the British Government Code and Cipher School at Bletchley Park, England – began to give invaluable knowledge of enemy movements. The three leading U-boat captains, including Günther Prien of *Royal Oak* fame, were killed or captured in March 1941. The Americans were gradually drawn closer to the war as their warships escorted merchantmen in certain areas, while their troops occupied Greenland to protect the naval bases and relieved the British in the occupation of the strategic base in Iceland.

On 18 May 1941, the great German battleship *Bismarck* left port and slipped out into the North Atlantic with the cruiser *Prinz Eugen*. British convoys were diverted, and the German ships were intercepted off Iceland by the battlecruiser *Hood* and the new battleship *Prince of Wales* on 24 May. A salvo from *Bismarck* penetrated the British battlecruiser's weak deck armour, and the

DESTROYER ESCORT
The destroyers escorting Convoy PQ-18 reached the safety of the White Sea on 18 September 1942. With 27 of the original 40 ships surviving the journey, this was the biggest convoy yet to reach Russia.

CONVOY PQ-18 AT FULL STRENGTH
This was the typical formation adopted by Allied Convoy PQ-18 and its escort ships when at full strength on the voyage from Scotland to Russia in September 1942. If the convoy was threatened by enemy aircraft, some of the destroyers would close in to the positions shown by the arrows.

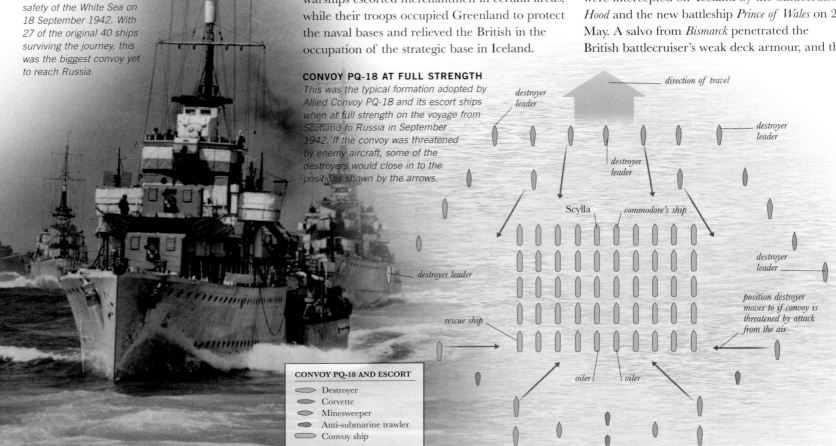

direction of travel

destroyer leader

destroyer leader

destroyer leader

destroyer leader

destroyer leader

Scylla

commodore's ship

destroyer leader

rescue ship

oiler

oiler

position destroyer moves to if convoy is threatened by attack from the air

CONVOY PQ-18 AND ESCORT
- Destroyer
- Corvette
- Minesweeper
- Anti-submarine trawler
- Convoy ship

ship exploded. The German ships escaped detection in the Atlantic for a time, until torpedo bombers from British aircraft carriers damaged *Bismarck*'s steering on 26 May. She was surrounded by ships from the British Home and Mediterranean Fleets and sunk on 27 May.

After the German invasion of Russia in July 1941, supply ships were sent to the northern ports of Murmansk and Archangel, escorted by British warships. This was one of the hardest duties for the Royal Navy, not only because of the severe weather. As well as U-boats, the Arctic convoys were in range of German aircraft and had to face the risk of attack by the remaining German capital ships. An erroneous report that the *Bismarck*'s sister ship, the *Tirpitz*, was at sea caused the Admiralty to order the escort to abandon Convoy PQ-17 in July 1942, and 23 merchant ships were lost as a result. In response, the most heavily defended convoy thus far, Convoy PQ-18, set out for Archangel in September. The Luftwaffe succeeded in sinking 10 ships, but lost 41 planes to the escort's anti-aircraft fire. U-boats sank three more ships, but at the cost of three of their own number.

In December 1943, the *Scharnhorst*, the last effective German capital ship, was found by British forces in Norwegian waters and sunk; the *Tirpitz* had already been disabled by midget-submarine attack in September 1943, thanks to intelligence from the Norwegian Resistance, and was sunk by RAF bombing in 1944.

In the Atlantic, the U-boats had a boost after the USA entered the war in December 1941, in response to the Japanese attack on Pearl Harbor (see panel, p.321). The American eastern seaboard was largely unprotected, and for the Germans there was a second "happy time", with 121 Allied ships sunk in June alone, often within sight of a friendly shore. But by July, the Americans had reorganized their defences, and the U-boats went to the mid-Atlantic instead for the climax of their war. Land-based air patrols were very successful in forcing the U-boats to avoid the surface, but their effective range was limited and there was an "air gap" (or "black pit") in the middle of the ocean. In late 1942 and early 1943, the Germans exploited this to

CATAPULT LAUNCH
As danger threatens, a Hawker Sea Hurricane fighter is readied for launch from the catapult aircraft merchant ship Empire Tide. *This ship was one of the few to survive the attacks on Convoy PQ-17 in July 1942, and she rescued many men whose ships had been sunk.*

the full, using picket lines of boats to find the convoys and direct attacks on them. In March 1943, two British-bound convoys, HX (Halifax) 229 and SC (Slow Convoy) 122 were attacked by dozens of U-boats and lost 21 ships.

EVACUEE CHILDREN
Thousands of British children were evacuated during the war. These girls are embarking for Canada in 1941. The card game shown above featured an evacuee "happy family".

The German defeat in the Atlantic
The Allies introduced new weapons, technology, and techniques in 1942–43, one of the most significant of which was radar (see panel, below). The military value of radar was appreciated as soon as the war started, although in Britain priority was given to developing land-based anti-aircraft equipment until after the Battle of Britain. Early radar sets gave range and bearing on separate scales, but from 1941 the plan position indicator was used, giving a bird's eye view of the area being surveyed, with the position of the aerial in the centre. By 1943, short-wavelength radar sets were able to detect targets as small as the hull of a partially surfaced submarine, and this had a decisive effect on the Battle of the Atlantic.

RADAR

The idea of bouncing a radio signal off a target to detect a ship or aircraft developed in Britain, France, Germany, and the USA in the late 1930s. The rotating antenna of a radar alternately sends out short pulses of radio waves then listens for their echoes. The returning echoes trigger a signal in a cathode-ray-tube display and, as the speed of radio waves is a constant, the time for them to return reveals the distance of the object. In a radar display, the returning signal is displayed by a line sweeping out a circle on the display. The line brightens when it receives strong echoes, and the echoes' position on the line indicates the time taken to receive the pulse, and therefore an object's distance.

RADAR DISPLAY
A navigator onboard a US aircraft carrier plots the positions of vessels in its vicinity, while on an operation in August 1945.

LIFE IN A U-BOAT

Of the many hardships of a submariner's life, being attacked with depth charges, as described by Heinz Schaeffer in his book *U-977 – 66 Days Underwater*, was probably the worst.

> *By the time we have had 16 hours of it we have long given up counting the depth charges. During this time no one's had any sleep, and we've all dark rings under our eyes. Plenty of bulbs have broken, but we don't change them – with the emergency lighting we can only guess the position of the various installations. The darkness makes it all the more frightening ...*
> *Stand by for depth-charge attack! They are falling right alongside now. A roar and a crash in the control room enough to crack our eardrums – fragments of iron fly around – valves smash to bits. In spite of oneself one can't help stretching a hand towards one's escape-gear.*

HEINZ SCHAEFFER, *U-977*, **1950**

Radar could also be used to detect the approach of aircraft, or to give ranges of surface targets, more accurately than optical rangefinders. By 1945, a large ship might have six radar systems, for surface warning, air warning, height-finding, range-finding at long and short ranges, and anti-aircraft fire control.

New Allied anti-submarine weapons included the Hedgehog and the Squid. The depth charge, which was introduced in the First World War (see p.292), had the inherent flaw that it was dropped several minutes after the last Asdic contact, giving the submarine time to take evasive action. British scientists experimented with "ahead-throwing weapons" that would be launched while still in Asdic contact. The Hedgehog was rushed into service in 1941. It fired 24 small bombs

AFT CREW QUARTERS OF *U-505*
The cramped conditions onboard were made even worse by having to store enough food to last 48–59 men for over 100 days at sea. Fruit and vegetables were stored in crates beneath the bunks, and hams hung from the ceiling.

that would land in a circular pattern ahead of the ship, to explode on contact. Only in the second half of 1944, after more training, did the Hedgehog reach its full potential, sinking 13 U-boats, with a 30 per cent success rate. The Hedgehog was also used by the US Navy, with more success due to better training of the operators – it accounted for the six Japanese submarines sunk by the destroyer escort *England* at the end of May 1944.

HEDGEHOG
Mounted on the forecastle of an escort ship, the Hedgehog fired a pattern of 24 x 35-lb (16-kg) bombs, which would explode on contact with a U-boat.

The Hedgehog's rival, the Squid, came into service in 1943. It was a three-barrelled mortar fitted in the bows of the ship, firing depth charges 250m (825ft) ahead in a predetermined pattern. Ships fitted with two Squids apiece were credited with a 40 per cent success rate in 1945.

The merchant ship losses in the Atlantic, and the need to ship armies across the Atlantic and the Pacific, demanded new shipbuilding techniques, mostly pioneered in the USA. Steel ships had been held together by rivets since their inception, but welding offered a smoother and stronger join using less weight of metal. After an initial investment, it was more economical than riveting and allowed much more flexibility in prefabrication. Ships were usually constructed individually even if they shared some common

ELECTRIC MOTOR ROOM OF *U-505*

When submerged, U-505 was propelled by two Siemens electric motors (shown left), using energy stored in batteries. When surfaced, the control panel on the right enabled the motors to be switched to generators, propelled by diesel engines to create electricity for the batteries.

average convoy now had 30 to 50 ships in columns and an escort of about eight warships. In April 1943, the Convoy ONS (Outward North Slow) 5 steamed through a concentration of 11 U-boats and sank five of them with little loss. The tide had turned, and Admiral Dönitz had to urge his commanders on against mounting losses, saying, "If there is anyone who thinks that fighting convoys is no longer possible, he is a weakling and no real U-boat commander." But by the end of May, 27 U-boats had been sunk, and Dönitz temporarily withdrew the wolf packs from the North Atlantic. They returned in July, but by then new merchant ships were coming out of British and American yards at a faster rate than the U-boats could sink them.

On 4 June 1944, the US Navy scored a great success, when an Atlantic task group led by the carrier *Guadalcanal* attacked *U-505* with depth charges. The U-boat was boarded and captured by men from the destroyer *Pillsbury*, then towed to Bermuda where she was kept in great secrecy until the end of the war.

Allied victory in the Battle of the Atlantic was not final, because German technology never stood still. By the end of 1944, the Germans had developed the snorkel, which enabled U-boats to stay underwater for longer periods. This allowed a new inshore campaign in British waters in the last months of the war. The Germans were also actively developing hydrogen peroxide engines, which would have allowed much greater speed underwater and range. On 7 May 1945, the last U-boat of the war was sunk, just as the German armies were about to surrender. In all, 619 U-boats were destroyed by ships, aircraft, and mines in five-and-a-half years of war. They in turn had sunk 2,775 Allied ships, of more than 14 million tons combined.

SALVAGING *U-505*

Sailors from the US escort carrier Guadalcanal, which led the task force that captured the U-505 in the Atlantic on 4 June 1944, salvage the damaged U-boat in preparation for towing her to Bermuda.

features, but the new programmes were based on a standard ship. The famous American Liberty ships, armed merchant ships of 7,200 tons, were built to a simple British design using identical parts made in hundreds of factories across the USA. Between 1941 and 1945, 2,711 Liberty ships were built at shipyards such as Henry Kaiser's (see panel, right), taking just 60 days, on average, from keel-laying to launch.

In March 1943, U-boats sank 82 allied merchant ships totalling 476,349 tons in the North Atlantic. In response, the Allied air forces deployed the long-range Consolidated B-24 Liberator bombers, plugging the air gap. The

LIBERTY SHIPS

Nine Liberty ships at the California Shipbuilding Corporation outfitting yard are readied for delivery to the US Maritime Commission in December 1943.

HENRY J. KAISER

Born in Sprout Brook, New York, USA, Henry Kaiser (1882–1967) became a photographer's apprentice, took over the company by the age of 20, and then moved west to found a construction company in Washington State. He took on government contracts in Vancouver and Cuba and led the combine that built the Hoover Dam in the 1930s. Although he had never built a ship before, he set up shipyards in Seattle and Tacoma in 1939. Using mass-production methods and welding instead of riveting, he built more than 1,400 Liberty ships, as well as small aircraft carriers and other ships. He excelled at labour relations and set up healthcare schemes for his workers.

The war in the Mediterranean

With France occupied and Italy entering the war on the German side in June 1940, the position of the British Mediterranean Fleet became precarious. The British were determined to retain control of the sea so that they would be able to send shipping through the Suez Canal, rather than use the longer route round the Cape of Good Hope. The Italians, who had slender resources and no real

RACING AGAINST TIME
Working in a maze of scaffolding, tools, and wires, shipbuilders at Henry J. Kaiser's Portland yard begin work on the 10,500-ton Liberty ship *Joseph N. Teal* on 25 September 1942. They launched the ship just 10 days later, shattering all previous shipbuilding records.

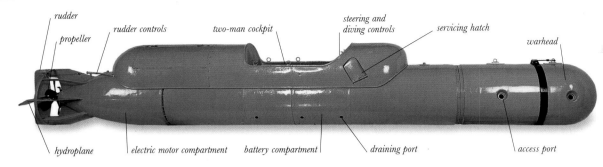

rudder

propeller

rudder controls

two-man cockpit

steering and diving controls

servicing hatch

warhead

hydroplane | electric motor compartment | battery compartment | draining port | access port

wish to fight, soon proved to be easier opponents than the Germans. Malta was defended against air attack, the Italian offensive from Libya into Egypt was held back, the Italian invasion of Greece was unsuccessful, and British forces stationed in Malta disrupted Italian supply lines. The main British Fleet was based at Alexandria, Egypt. On 11 November 1940, their carrier *Illustrious* launched 21 Swordfish torpedo bombers against the Italian Fleet in the harbour of Taranto, southeast Italy, putting three battleships out of action. Fleets could no longer hide safely in port, and the Japanese saw the way forward for their own tactics.

The Luftwaffe and the German Army began to intervene in the Mediterranean at the end of 1940 and soon proved far more formidable than the Italians. The British defeated the Italian Fleet off Cape Matapan, south of Greece, on 28 March 1941, sinking several ships. But in May, ordered to support British forces in Crete against an airborne invasion and then withdraw them, the Royal Navy suffered some of its heaviest losses of the war, including three cruisers and six destroyers sunk, and an aircraft carrier, three battleships, six cruisers, and seven destroyers damaged. They were hard pressed to keep Malta supplied with food and oil, and each convoy to the island was an epic battle against aircraft and ships. In Operation Pedestal in August 1942, a carrier was lost and

THE "HUMAN TORPEDO"
During the Second World War, the Italians produced the Maiale ("pig") submersible to penetrate harbour defences. It was crewed by two frogmen, who would attach the torpedo's warhead to an enemy ship's hull.

two more damaged, and nine out of 14 merchant ships were lost. The damaged tanker *Ohio* eventually limped into harbour on 15 August to give the island its only supply of fuel.

The British aircraft and submarines based in Malta disrupted seaborne supplies to the German Army in North Africa led by Erwin Rommel. In November 1942, the British Eighth Army under Bernard Montgomery was able to advance westwards, having defeated the Afrika Korps at El Alamein on the coast of Egypt. In the meantime, the largest amphibious operation of the war so far was being prepared. A US Navy task force of 102 ships left Hampton Roads, Virginia, in October, landing troops at three points on the Atlantic coast of Morocco two weeks later. British warships and transports sailed

ARABIC ANTI-NAZI POSTER
This Allied propaganda poster depicts Royal Navy ships in the Mediterranean cutting off the Nazis' seaborne supply routes to North Africa.

through the Straits of Gibraltar to land British and American troops in Algeria. The landings were successful despite the loss of some US Coast Guard vessels. The Germans, trapped between the Allied forces, were forced to evacuate North Africa in April 1943, and the war took a new turn in the Allies' favour.

The Japanese advance in the Pacific
In 1941, Japan's ongoing war with China and its determination to take control of all of southeast Asia were leading to conflict with the USA. In a daring attempt to put the US Pacific Fleet out of action, Admiral Isoroku Yamamoto,

SWORDFISH LANDING ON *ILLUSTRIOUS*
Despite its antiquated appearance (it was introduced in 1934), the Swordfish torpedo bomber proved so successful as a strike aircraft that the Royal Navy used it throughout the Second World War, including the action at Taranto in 1940.

THE ATTACK ON PEARL HARBOR

It was a quiet morning on 7 December 1941 as officers and men had breakfast in their ships and barracks in the great US naval base at Pearl Harbor, Hawaii. They did not know that primitive American radar had picked up some strange signals from the northwest, or that a destroyer had sunk a midget submarine just outside the harbour that morning. The peace was shattered at 7:55am when a force of 183 Japanese aircraft began to drop bombs and torpedoes. Ships were

sunk or caught fire, aircraft were destroyed on the ground, and installations were bombed. The Japanese had attacked without declaring war or giving any warning, although there is some evidence that US intelligence suspected that it was going to happen. There was a lull after about half an hour, then a second wave of 176 aircraft arrived. By this time, the Americans had begun to rally, and anti-aircraft guns were manned. The second wave did less damage and suffered more casualties, but the Americans had lost more than 200 aircraft and had 3,681 casualties.

On the face of it, Pearl Harbor was a tactical success for the Japanese – they put five of the eight US battleships in the

harbour out of action. But the aircraft carriers were away on exercise, and these ships would dominate the war to come (see panel, p.325). The attack also infuriated the USA and ensured that it was fully committed to the war.

SALVAGED BINOCULARS
These binoculars were retrieved from the bridge of the US battleship Arizona, *which was the first ship to be sunk during the raid on Pearl Harbor.*

BLAZING BATTLESHIPS
A rescue launch attempts to pick up survivors from the US battleships West Virginia *and* Tennessee *as they sit low in the water, having been crippled in their berths.*

TAKE-OFF
Japanese bombers are readied for take-off onboard one of the six aircraft carriers that took part in the attack on US naval base at Oahu, Hawaii.

DORIE MILLER
Untrained in firearms because of the US Navy's segregation policies, messman Dorie Miller took over a machine gun on the West Virginia *and was officially credited with downing two Japanese planes.*

THE HERO OF PEARL HARBOR

DORIE MILLER

JAPANESE NAVAL SEXTANT

horizon mirror

adjustable eyepiece

Sextants were essential to Japanese naval officers to calculate latitude, so they could navigate their ships around the Pacific Ocean.

scale showing degrees north or south of equator

JAPANESE PROPAGANDA

This Japanese propaganda poster accuses the USA of having ulterior motives for wanting Australians to resist the Japanese advance in southeast Asia.

the naval commander-in-chief (see panel, below), conceived the attack on the US naval base at Pearl Harbor in December (see p.321). The USA declared war on Japan the day after the attack. In the same month, the Japanese took US bases at Guam and Wake in the central Pacific, and their army overran the British in Hong Kong and landed on the Malayan (now Malaysian) Peninsula to attack Singapore. Churchill had sent the capital ships *Repulse* and *Prince of Wales* eastwards in the misguided hope that they would deter the Japanese. Instead, on 10 December, they were attacked and sunk off the coast of Singapore by land-based aircraft. Worse was to come on 15 February 1942, when the British garrison of Singapore surrendered. By that time, Japanese forces had advanced 4,000km (2,500 miles) south of their homeland, taking the Philippines from the Americans, and the islands of the Dutch East Indies (now Indonesia). Their advance had been so rapid that they were unsure what to do next. They were 320km (200 miles) from the north coast of Australia, and their

REFUELLING AT SEA

A crew member clings on for dear life as the US Navy oiler Neosho *refuels the aircraft carrier* Yorktown *in heavy seas, before the Battle of the Coral Sea in May 1942.*

carrier aircraft bombed Darwin on 19 February, in the first of 64 raids on the city. The airfield and harbour were seriously damaged, and 243 people were killed. On 27 February, a force of American, British, Australian, and Dutch cruisers and destroyers under the Dutch Rear-Admiral Karel Doorman met a Japanese naval force in the Battle of the Java Sea. Most of the Allied force was sunk, including the flagship, the cruiser *De Ruyter*. The Battle of the Coral Sea in the South Pacific on 7–8 May was of a different complexion. It was the

ISOROKU YAMAMOTO

Yamamoto (1884–1943), originally known as Isoroku, was born to an impoverished family but graduated high in the class of 1904 in the Japanese Naval Academy. He fought at Tsushima in the following year and adopted the name Yamamoto, from a powerful clan, on the death of his father in 1913. In 1919 he was sent to study in the USA for two years, and he visited Europe in 1923, before becoming naval attaché in Washington in 1926. In 1930 he was appointed to the Japanese Naval Air Corps headquarters as a rear-admiral and later took command of a group of aircraft carriers, which he exercised thoroughly.

Using his experience of western ways and naval air power, Yamamoto planned the December 1941 raid on Pearl Harbor. He was killed in April 1943 when his aircraft was intercepted by US fighter planes.

MULBERRY HARBOURS

After the failure of a raid on Dieppe in 1942, the Allies realized that they would not be able to capture a port intact. They began to design the Mulberry Harbours, which could be prefabricated in Britain and erected quickly elsewhere. The first element was the breakwater, created either by sinking old merchant ships in a line or by floating concrete pontoons. Within this protected space, floating piers led out to deep water, where ships could unload. Two Mulberries were assembled in Normandy soon after D-Day in June 1944, but the one on Omaha Beach was wrecked in a storm, so the one at Arromanches on Gold Beach had to take a great deal of traffic. Floating pontoons became common after the war, for example in yacht marinas.

FLOATING PIER
A US army truck drives along an articulated steel roadway supported on pontoons towards Omaha Beach shortly after D-Day. The Mulberry Harbour here was destroyed by a storm 10 days after it was built.

LANDING IN NAPLES
With her boots slung around her neck, an American army nurse wades ashore at Naples on 4 November 1943, while her shipmates form a human chain to unload their battle gear from the infantry landing craft.

strong in Italy's mountainous terrain. Mussolini was rescued from prison and set up as puppet ruler of a Nazi state in northern Italy. A further Allied landing at Anzio, south of Rome, in January 1944 was not followed up by a swift inward advance, and progress remained slow. The Allied forces finally advanced into northern Italy in January 1945, assisted by partisans of the Italian Resistance, who captured and executed Mussolini in April.

Churchill had doubts about a direct attack on France, after the failure of an Allied raid on Dieppe in August 1942, organized by Chief of Combined Operations Louis Mountbatten (see panel, below), in which over 900 Canadian troops lost their lives. But, at the Quebec

first real aircraft-carrier battle, in which ships of opposing sides never saw one another. The Americans lost the large carrier *Lexington*, the Japanese the smaller *Shoho*, but the Japanese thrust towards Port Moresby on New Guinea was stalled and would never be resumed.

The invasion of Europe

The Western Allies conferred in the Moroccan port of Casablanca in January 1943 and decided to attack the Italian-German Axis through Italy rather than launching an immediate invasion across the English Channel. An invasion of Sicily was planned – and, unlike at the Narvik landings of 1940, this time the troops and landing craft crews were carefully trained. American and British forces landed on the southeastern corner of the island on 10 July 1943. Despite bad weather and some resistance, things went according to plan and several lessons were learned – concerning, for example, the use of naval gunfire support and the need for air co-operation. On 3 September, the Allies crossed the Straits of Messina to Italy and mainland Europe, and six days later they landed in force at Salerno, south of Naples. The dictator Benito Mussolini was overthrown, and the Italians surrendered. In October, Italy changed sides and declared war on Germany. But Italy was not the "soft underbelly" of Europe, as Churchill had suggested. Germany poured troops into the country, and resistance was

INVASION OF SICILY
Tanks roll off an amphibious landing craft onto a beach on the southeast coast of Sicily on 20 July 1943, 10 days after British and American forces landed on the island, opening the way to Italy.

LOUIS MOUNTBATTEN

Louis Mountbatten (1900–79) was a great-grandson of Queen Victoria and the son of a First Sea Lord. He entered the navy as a cadet in 1913 and served in the battlecruiser *Lion* from 1916. In 1939, he took command of the new destroyer *Kelly*, which after a series of daring exploits was sunk off Crete in 1941. Churchill appointed him Chief of Combined Operations, promoting him three grades to vice-admiral. He was responsible for developing the Mulberry Harbours before he left to become Commander-in-Chief, Burma, in 1943. In 1979, he was killed by an Irish Republican terrorist bomb in his fishing boat off Ireland.

THE D-DAY LANDINGS

At dawn on 6 June 1944, American, British, and Canadian troops struggled ashore, often under heavy fire and through beach obstacles and mines, on five main beaches in Normandy, northern France, code-named Omaha, Utah, Gold, Juno, and Sword. This was Operation Neptune, the naval part of Operation Overlord, the largest combined military operation of all time and the main Allied counterattack against German-occupied Europe. Paratroopers had already landed overnight to secure vital positions, and resistance in the area had been weakened by bombing over the previous few months. Admiral Ramsay, who had supervised the evacuation of Dunkirk, was now in charge of the naval operation under the Supreme Allied Commander, US General Dwight D. Eisenhower. More than 112,000 British sailors

took part in the attack in warships, converted merchantmen, landing craft, and barges, alongside nearly 53,000 Americans and 5,000 other allies.

Despite meticulous reconnaissance, training, and planning, some things still went wrong. The greatest problem of all was the weather, and the forecasters agonized about whether a gap in the bad conditions on the morning of 6 June would be enough to let the landings succeed. British and Canadian forces had problems at Juno Beach, where many of the tanks did not arrive as planned and a quarter of the craft were lost or damaged in landing or withdrawal.
In the American sector, things were worse. The Utah Force landed on the wrong beach by mistake, which proved a blessing as it was less heavily defended than the correct one. But on Omaha Beach, the most difficult of the five landing sites because it was surrounded by high cliffs, there was near disaster, caused initially by failures among the

AMPHIBIOUS LANDING
Soldiers disembark from a Higgins boat, a mass-produced landing craft that was specially designed to swiftly transport men and equipment through the surf towards a beach.

landing-craft crews. The first wave should have landed nine companies, evenly spaced along the beach, but the units became scattered on approach. Some men disembarked in water up to their necks and were met with a hail of bullets as they tried to reach the beach. Despite sustaining over 3,000 casualties, the Americans rallied and by nightfall had secured a 3-km (2-mile) beachhead. By the end of D-Day, Operation Neptune had put 132,175 soldiers ashore.

TOP SECRET MAP
Code-named Sword, this was the easternmost of the five D-Day landing beaches. The map detailed the hazards in each landing section.

GOLIATH TANK
This German remote-controlled tank, although never used, was meant to be filled with explosives and used against an Allied landing.

WADING INSHORE
US troops struggle towards the shore of Omaha Beach on D-Day, weighed down by their backpacks and under heavy machine-gun fire.

NORMANDY BEACHHEAD
Trucks carrying troops and supplies stream up Omaha Beach, which was secured by US forces on 6 June 1944. The barrage balloons were to protect the operational area from strafing by low-flying enemy aircraft, but in the end none appeared.

food. Allied landing craft were used again: during the liberation of the Netherlands in February 1945, as the Germans opened the North Sea dykes; and in the crossing of the Rhine into Germany in the same month. Eventually, the Nazis were trapped between the British and Americans to the west and the Russians in the east. Hitler committed suicide on 30 April as the Russian Army took Berlin, having appointed Dönitz Führer. Dönitz spent a week trying, unsuccessfully, to negotiate a peace settlement with the Western Allies, excluding the Russians. Germany surrendered unconditionally on 7 May 1945, ending the war in Europe.

The US counter-attack in the Pacific

Despite the strategic setback of the Battle of the Coral Sea in May 1942 (see pp.322–23), the Japanese still believed that they could defeat the US Pacific Fleet in battle, destroying its

Conference in August 1943, plans for an invasion in 1944 went ahead. Rather than crossing the Straits of Dover, the shortest route to France, the Allies decided to land in Normandy, where there were suitable beaches and the element of surprise might prove useful. The Belgian architect and yachtsman Hugo van Kuyck, who had joined the US Army in 1942, was given the task of charting the Normandy coastline. He developed the Van Kuyck Chart, which takes into account the tidal variation at a given point. These charts, together with aerial photographs showing the exact position of the German troops and the defences they had put into place, enabled detailed maps of the Normandy beaches to be produced, so that the Allied commanders were familiar with the area before the invasion.

The greatest invasion fleet in history – 1,213 warships, 864 merchantmen, and 4,126 landing craft – was assembled at ports all round the British coast from South Wales to Suffolk. The Normandy landings of 6 June 1944, later christened D-Day, were highly successful (see panel, opposite), but the land campaign became bogged down. D-Day was followed by another landing of mainly American forces in the south of France in early August 1944, and Paris was finally liberated on the 26th of that month.

Meanwhile, the Allied navies had to keep the land forces in France and the Low Countries supplied through the artificial harbour at Arromanches (see Mulberry Harbours panel, p.323). A pipeline under the ocean, known as Pluto, was intended to supply the Allies with fuel,

but the ingenious idea did not work well. Ports captured from the enemy, such as Cherbourg (in France) and Antwerp (in Belgium) were usually heavily damaged but were repaired as quickly as possible to bring in fuel, reinforcements, and

US AIRCRAFT-CARRIER TECHNIQUES

On US Navy aircraft carriers, there was not room to stow all the planes in the hangars below, where they were taken in giant elevators with their wings folded, so many had to remain on deck in all weathers. When carrier aircraft were taking off or landing, the ship steamed into the wind to give the maximum airflow. Each plane took off under its own power, dipping momentarily as it left the deck.

After a mission, each plane would be guided onto the deck by the landing officer, who waved short bats to suggest changes in course. The pilot would hope to pick up one of about six arrester wires stretched across the deck with the hook at the rear of his plane. If he did not, he would crash into a net, which might do some damage to the plane. Once a plane had

landed safely, a crash barrier would be lowered to allow the aircraft to be parked forward and clear the deck for the rest to land. US carrier crews, known as Airedales during the Second World War, wore coloured vests according to their function – plane handlers, maintenance teams, first-aid men, refuellers, firefighters, and so on.

FLIGHT DECK
Parked lanes pack the after deck of the US carrier Essex *in the Pacific in May 1943, while several more wait with wings folded to be taken to the hangar below.*

aircraft carriers, and thus control the ocean. Admiral Yamamoto ordered the invasion of the US-held Midway Island in the central Pacific in June 1942. But the Japanese naval commanders made several fatal mistakes in planning the operation. They underestimated US radio intelligence, not knowing that their naval codes had been cracked and that the USA was forewarned. They deployed forces for a simultaneous diversionary attack on the Aleutian Islands, Alaska, which the US Pacific Fleet, under its new commander Admiral Chester Nimitz (see p.328), ignored. And they divided the Midway strike force into four different groups, each under one aircraft carrier, so they could not support one another. However, the Japanese force still numbered 200 ships, and Nimitz had to rely on the air power of his three carriers and the Boeing B-17 bombers stationed at Midway to avoid defeat. Battle was finally joined between the American and Japanese fleets off Midway on 4 June (see panel, opposite).

After their victory at Midway, the Americans began to exploit its new advantage in the Pacific. On 7 August 1942, marines landed on the island of Guadalcanal, near the end of the Solomon Islands chain in the southwest Pacific, to secure the island's vital airstrip. The Japanese naval counter-attack took the form of raids by cruisers and destroyers along the "slot" between the islands. These engagements were the closest to traditional naval battles of all encounters in the Pacific during the war, and the channel north of Guadalcanal became known as Ironbottom Sound because of the number of ships of both sides sunk there. Despite heavy losses, the Americans finally secured the island on 15 November.

The US Navy was highly successful in both submarine and anti-submarine warfare in the Pacific. Its submarines sank well over a thousand Japanese merchant ships, accounting for more than five million tons, for the Japanese Navy followed a crude interpretation of Alfred Thayer Mahan's sea-power theories (see p.272) and believed that commerce raiding

SUICIDE MISSION
Black smoke billows from a kamikaze plane, which hit the US carrier Bunker Hill *near Okinawa, northwest Pacific, on 11 May 1945, causing extensive damage.*

航空機の力が戦ひの勝敗を決する

AIR POWER
"The power of fighter planes determines the victory of war," exhorts this Japanese poster, urging factory workers to produce more planes.

THE BATTLE OF MIDWAY

The crews of the Japanese aircraft carriers *Akagi*, *Kaga*, *Soryu*, and *Hiryu* must have felt satisfied at 10:00am on 4 June 1942, as they refuelled their planes and reloaded them with bombs and torpedoes. Their plan to invade the US-held island of Midway seemed to be going well. Bombing raids on the island early that morning had devastated it. US B-17 heavy bombers had bombed the Japanese strike force already that morning, but failed to score any hits. Attacks by the torpedo planes of the US carriers *Enterprise*, *Hornet*, and *Yorktown* had been beaten off with enormous losses. One US squadron had been wiped out, and many of the planes that had escaped had to ditch in the sea due to lack of fuel. An attack on Midway would

YORKTOWN UNDER ATTACK
Already listing to port as the result of an earlier attack by the Japanese carrier Hiryu's dive bombers, the US carrier Yorktown suffers a direct hit from Hiryu's torpedo bombers at 2:40pm on 4 June 1942. The black puffs are anti-aircraft shells exploding.

soon be launched, to give the Japanese a base from which land aircraft would be in range of the US naval base at Pearl Harbor.

However, just after 10:00 am, dive bombers from the *Enterprise* and *Yorktown* burst through the clouds to find the Japanese carriers in their most vulnerable state, with fuel and ammunition on the deck. American bombs hit the *Kaga*, *Soryu*, and *Akagi*, and they quickly became blazing wrecks. The first two sank that afternoon; the *Akagi* stayed afloat for longer. There was no other 20-minute period in the Second World War in which the balance of power changed so rapidly, not just in the immediate battle but across the largest ocean in the world. But the battle was not yet over. Planes from the *Hiryu* attacked and torpedoed the *Yorktown* (which

was finally sunk by a torpedo from a Japanese submarine on 7 June). The *Hiryu* was attacked and fatally damaged late in the afternoon of 4 June. The Japanese had no air cover left, and Admiral Yamamoto was forced to abandon the invasion. Now, the Japanese Navy was inferior to the US Navy in carrier air power, and Japan would never make up the difference against the might of US industry. From this moment on, the initiative in the Pacific war lay with the USA.

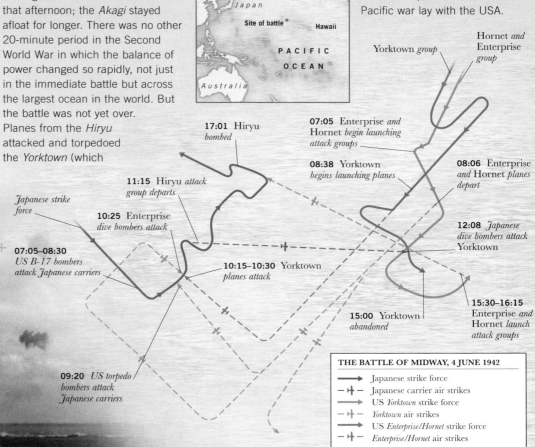

17:01 Hiryu *bombed*

11:15 Hiryu *attack group departs*

10:25 Enterprise *dive bombers attack*

Japanese strike force

07:05–08:30 *US B-17 bombers attack Japanese carriers*

09:20 *US torpedo bombers attack Japanese carriers*

07:05 Enterprise *and* Hornet *begin launching attack groups*

08:38 Yorktown *begins launching planes*

10:15–10:30 Yorktown *planes attack*

08:06 Enterprise *and* Hornet *planes depart*

12:08 *Japanese dive bombers attack* Yorktown

15:00 Yorktown *abandoned*

15:30–16:15 Enterprise *and* Hornet *launch attack groups*

U S A
Japan
Site of battle • *Hawaii*
PACIFIC OCEAN
Australia

Yorktown *group*

Hornet *and* Enterprise *group*

THE BATTLE OF MIDWAY, 4 JUNE 1942	
→	Japanese strike force
–⊬–	Japanese carrier air strikes
→	US *Yorktown* strike force
–⊬–	*Yorktown* air strikes
→	US *Enterprise/Hornet* strike force
–⊬–	*Enterprise/Hornet* air strikes

and protection was an inferior form of warfare. Japan's vital and yet vulnerable supply lines were severed long before the end of the war. The Japanese Navy also failed to deploy its own submarines effectively against American supply lines, which could have been equally vulnerable to attack in the Pacific.

Japan lost Admiral Yamamoto on 18 April 1943, after US radio intelligence decoded details of his inspection tour of Japanese forces in the southwest Pacific. Lockheed Lightning P-38

long-range fighters dispatched from the US air base at Guadalcanal intercepted his aircraft over Bougainville Island and shot it down.

The Americans launched a new offensive in the Pacific, attacking from two directions. The southern

KAMIKAZE PILOTS
These Japanese pilots pose for posterity before setting out to crash their bomb-laden planes onto US Navy warships in 1944.

thrust, led by General Douglas MacArthur, was from island to island in the Solomons group, and then on to New Britain and New Guinea, often bypassing Japanese bases on the way. The Central Pacific Drive, under the command of Nimitz, was via much smaller islands such as Tarawa, Kwajalein, Eniwetok, Saipan, and Guam. Each island was isolated and devastated by naval gunfire before the marines

CHESTER W. NIMITZ

Chester Nimitz (1885–1966), below right, entered the US Naval Academy almost by accident in 1901, when places at the Military Academy at West Point were not available. He served in gunboats, destroyers, and submarines before the First World War and studied diesel engines in Germany. He set up a submarine base at Pearl Harbor in 1920 and commanded the cruiser *Augusta* on the China Station in the 1930s. In 1939, as head of the Bureau of Navigation, he was responsible for personnel and proved a good judge of character. After Pearl Harbor, he became Commander-in-Chief, Pacific, and rallied the fleet to fight the Battle of Midway.

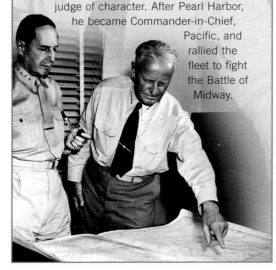

FORMAL SURRENDER
Japan surrendered on 14 August 1945 (above), but the formal surrender document wasn't signed until 2 September. The ceremony was held on the US battleship Missouri, *anchored in Tokyo Bay (right).*

landed. But the Japanese soldiers, who would rather die than face the shame of capture, fought bitterly, and the battle would often end in a suicide charge. The liberated island would then serve as a base for the launch of air strikes against the next island to be invaded. In October 1944, as the two American attack forces converged on the Philippines, the Japanese launched a counter-attack, which led to the Battle of Leyte Gulf of 23–26 October. By most standards, this was one of the greatest battles ever fought, involving two million tons of

shipping and 183,000 men, nearly four times the number at Trafalgar. The Japanese lost three carriers and three battleships, mostly to air attack. The Americans also suffered casualties from the new Japanese weapon, the Kamikaze or suicide pilots, who would deliberately crash planes loaded with explosives into US warships to blow them up, but they now had no serious naval opposition in the Pacific.

The American effort in the Pacific was enormous in its extent. New techniques for refuelling warships at sea were developed to cope with the vast distances. The British arrived back in the ocean in 1944 with their own Pacific Fleet, but they soon found that they were outclassed in both resources and techniques. The island of Iwo Jima, south of Japan, was stormed by US marines on 19 February 1945. The fighting was fierce, and most of the Japanese soldiers continued to the death – just 216 of the island's 21,000-strong defending garrison were taken prisoner. Despite heavy

> 66 The work, my friend, is peace. More than an end of this war – an end to the beginning of all wars. 99
>
> **FRANKLIN D. ROOSEVELT**, undelivered address for Jefferson Day, **13 April 1945**

losses, the marines prevailed, and on 17 March 1945 Nimitz reported, "The Battle of Iwo Jima has been won. Among the Americans who served on Iwo, uncommon valour was a common virtue." The island gave the USA a base from which its bombers could devastate the major Japanese cities. Okinawa, an island southwest of Japan, provided a second base, once the American attack, launched on 1 April, finally succeeded in June. Again, the Japanese fought back hard: on 6 April alone, 700 Kamikazes attacked the US fleet.

On 12 April, the US President Franklin D. Roosevelt died, to be succeeded by Harry S. Truman. Truman was persuaded that the Japanese would only be forced to surrender if the USA used its new weapon, the atomic bomb. He gave the go-ahead on 25 July, and the bomb, delivered by the US cruiser *Indianapolis*, was dropped from the B-29 Superfortress bomber *Enola Gay* onto Hiroshima on 6 August 1945. Another bomb was dropped on Nagasaki by the *Bockscar* three days later. More than 212,000 civilians were killed within five days of the blasts. On 14 August, Emperor Hirohito accepted an Allied demand for Japan's surrender on the condition that he could remain emperor. The formal surrender was signed on 2 September. The Second World War had ended, and the face of warfare had changed for ever.

OKINAWA BARRAGE
Rockets from a US Navy infantry landing craft are fired at the Japanese positions on the island of Okinawa, in the northwest Pacific, just before the invasion by US Tenth Army forces in April 1945.

VETERANS RETURN
American soldiers and sailors onboard the Queen Elizabeth *cheer as she steams into New York Harbor in 1945.*

BATTLESHIPS

In the Second World War, battleships no longer dominated naval warfare as they had in the First World War, due to the increasing threat from aircraft and submarines. The naval-disarmament treaties meant there were far fewer battleships than in the previous war, but the individual ships were mostly much larger and became symbols of national prestige. The small number of ships meant that there were no battle fleets in the old sense, and duels between battleships became rare. Towards the end of the war, guns were used mostly for shore bombardment. All major naval powers suffered heavy losses in their battleships and battlecruisers.

HEAVY GUNS
This photograph shows the US battleship Missouri *firing a salvo of 16-in (406-mm) shells from her forward turret in 1944.*

Bismarck-class battleships

Germany resumed the construction of full-sized battleships with the *Bismarck* (below) and *Tirpitz* in 1936. They were not as big as the German Navy wanted, but they became the most powerful European ships of the Second World War, with high speed, good armour protection, and 380-mm (15-in) guns. The *Bismarck* sank the *Hood* (see right) before she was sunk herself on 27 May 1941. The *Tirpitz* was bombed and sunk in November 1944.

BISMARCK		
Origin Germany	**Date of launch** 1939	
Length 248m (813ft)	**Displacement** 41,700 tons	
Maximum speed 29 knots	**Crew** 2,092	
Armament 8 x 380-mm guns, 12 x 150-mm guns, 16 x 105-mm guns, 16 x 37-mm guns, 12 x 20-mm guns		

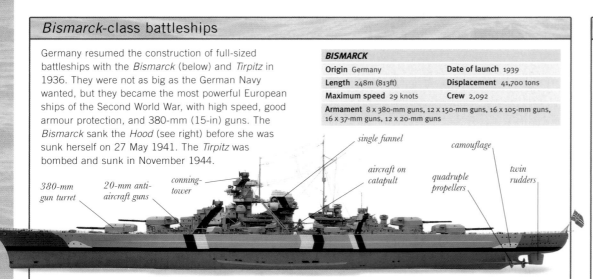

380-mm gun turret

20-mm anti-aircraft guns

conning-tower

single funnel

aircraft on catapult

camouflage

quadruple propellers

twin rudders

Battlecruisers

No true battlecruisers were built during the Second World War, but the German *Scharnhorst* and *Gneisenau* were sometimes considered as such. *Hood* (right) was the pride of the Royal Navy but had weak deck armour. She was sunk by *Bismarck* (see left) in 1941.

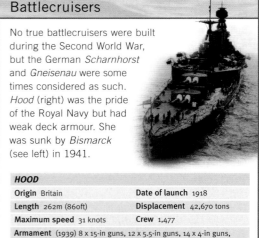

HOOD		
Origin Britain	**Date of launch** 1918	
Length 262m (860ft)	**Displacement** 42,670 tons	
Maximum speed 31 knots	**Crew** 1,477	
Armament (1939) 8 x 15-in guns, 12 x 5.5-in guns, 14 x 4-in guns, 24 x 2-pounder guns		

King George V-class battleships

Believing that naval treaties would soon restrict the size of guns, in 1935 the British went ahead with building five ships carrying 14-in (356-mm) guns. The ships were originally planned to have 12 guns, but this would have caused stability problems, so they were built with 10 guns in an unusual format of two quadruple turrets and one twin turret. The *King George V, Prince of Wales, Duke of York, Anson,* and *Howe* were faster and better armoured than previous British battleships, but they were outclassed in arms.

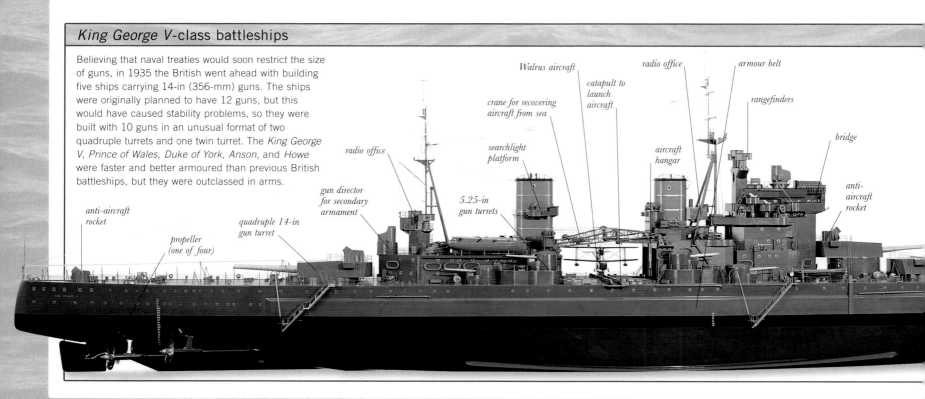

Walrus aircraft

radio office

armour belt

catapult to launch aircraft

rangefinders

crane for recovering aircraft from sea

bridge

radio office

searchlight platform

aircraft hangar

anti-aircraft rocket

gun director for secondary armament

5.25-in gun turrets

anti-aircraft rocket

quadruple 14-in gun turret

propeller (one of four)

Pocket battleships

In 1929, while still restricted by the Treaty of Versailles, the Germans began to build three ships, the *Deutschland* (subsequently renamed *Lützow*), *Admiral Scheer*, and *Admiral Graf Spee* (below), which were planned as a class of eight. They were known as armoured ships and, later, heavy cruisers in Germany, but the British called them pocket battleships, because they were lighter than conventional battleships of the period – to save weight, the designers had used welding and diesel engines. The ships were faster than any battleship, but their armour was weak and they found it difficult to engage more than one target at a time. Although originally intended to face the Soviets in the Baltic, their engines gave them a long range, which made the British suspect that they were meant for use on the high seas, where only three British battlecruisers could hope to catch up with and defeat them.

ADMIRAL GRAF SPEE

Origin Germany	**Date of launch** 1934
Length 186m (610ft)	**Displacement** 11,700 tons
Maximum speed 28 knots	**Crew** 1,150
Armament 6 x 280-mm guns, 8 x 150-mm guns, 6 x 105-mm guns, 8 x 37-mm guns, 6 x 20-mm guns	

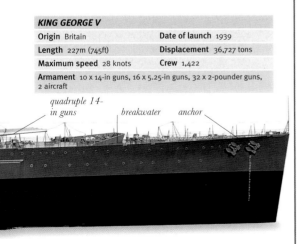

PRINCE OF WALES

KING GEORGE V

Origin Britain	**Date of launch** 1939
Length 227m (745ft)	**Displacement** 36,727 tons
Maximum speed 28 knots	**Crew** 1,422
Armament 10 x 14-in guns, 16 x 5.25-in guns, 32 x 2-pounder guns, 2 aircraft	

quadruple 14-in guns *breakwater* *anchor*

Iowa-class battleships

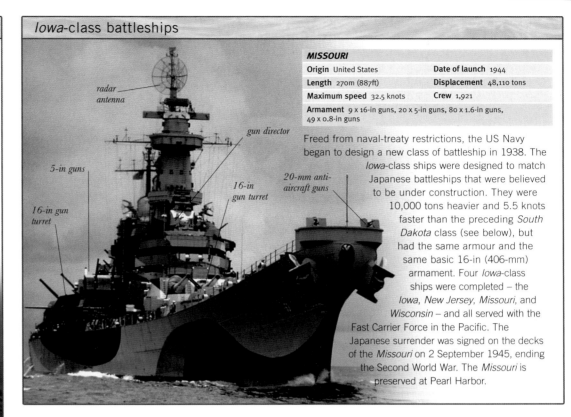

radar antenna

gun director

5-in guns

16-in gun turret

16-in gun turret

20-mm anti-aircraft guns

MISSOURI

Origin United States	**Date of launch** 1944
Length 270m (887ft)	**Displacement** 48,110 tons
Maximum speed 32.5 knots	**Crew** 1,921
Armament 9 x 16-in guns, 20 x 5-in guns, 80 x 1.6-in guns, 49 x 0.8-in guns	

Freed from naval-treaty restrictions, the US Navy began to design a new class of battleship in 1938. The *Iowa*-class ships were designed to match Japanese battleships that were believed to be under construction. They were 10,000 tons heavier and 5.5 knots faster than the preceding *South Dakota* class (see below), but had the same armour and the same basic 16-in (406-mm) armament. Four *Iowa*-class ships were completed – the *Iowa*, *New Jersey*, *Missouri*, and *Wisconsin* – and all served with the Fast Carrier Force in the Pacific. The Japanese surrender was signed on the decks of the *Missouri* on 2 September 1945, ending the Second World War. The *Missouri* is preserved at Pearl Harbor.

South Dakota-class battleships

The four *South Dakota*-class battleships carried 16-in (406mm) guns and had some innovations, such as steeply sloping armour and propellers protected in tunnels, but they were quite slow vessels. They provided fire support and anti-aircraft cover for many operations from November 1942 until the raids on Japan in August 1945.

ALABAMA

Origin United States	**Date of launch** 1942
Length 207m (680ft)	**Displacement** 37,970 tons
Maximum speed 27 knots	**Crew** 1,793
Armament 9 x 16-in guns, 20 x 5-in guns, 12 x 1.1-in guns, 12 x 0.5-in guns, 3 aircraft	

Yamato-class battleships

Construction of the *Yamato* and *Musashi* began in 1937 and 1938 respectively, and they were the largest and most powerful battleships ever built. Their 460-mm (18.1-in) guns had a range of 42km (26 miles), firing a projectile twice as heavy as the British 14-in (356-mm) gun. However, both ships were sunk by American air bombardment before they could show their full potential. The *Yamato* (below) was hit by 9 to 13 torpedoes and six bombs before sinking on 7 April 1945.

YAMATO

Origin Japan	**Date of launch** 1940
Length 256m (840ft)	**Displacement** 62,315 tons
Maximum speed 27 knots	**Crew** 2,500
Armament 9 x 460-mm guns, 12 x 155-mm guns, 12 x 127-mm guns, 24 x 25-mm guns, 4 x 13.2-mm guns	

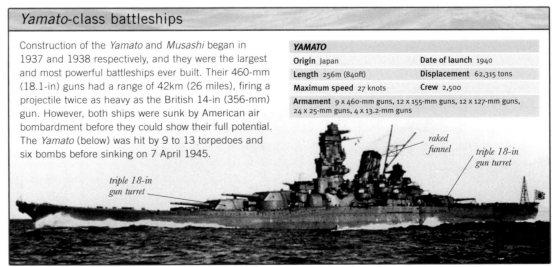

raked funnel

triple 18-in gun turret

triple 18-in gun turret

AIRCRAFT CARRIERS

The aircraft carrier became a dominant weapons system in the Mediterranean and Atlantic wars, and even more so in the Pacific. It could attack fleets in harbour (as at Taranto and Pearl Harbor) or at sea (as at Midway). Small carriers were built for specialized tasks such as anti-submarine warfare with low-performance aircraft, but the largest ships, the fleet aircraft carriers, could operate the fastest fighters to defend the fleet and launch torpedo- and bomb-carrying aircraft against sea and shore targets.

A CROWDED DECK
This photograph, taken in March 1943, shows aircraft with their wings folded on the deck of the American aircraft carrier Essex.

American carriers

The Americans had experience of large carriers at the start of the war, having built the *Yorktown* class. They tended to use these to carry the maximum number of aircraft, compared with the British who used far smaller numbers. The *Essex* class was an enlarged version and was mass-produced. Other US classes of fleet carrier included: the *Independence* class, converted from cruisers to speed production in 1942–43; and the *Midway* class, with armoured decks. All US carriers had heavy anti-aircraft armament to fight off Japanese kamikazes; later *Essex*-class ships were planned with 18 quadruple 40-mm (1.575-in) guns and 35 twin 20-mm (0.787-in) guns – a total of 142 guns.

spotting top

bridge

hangar cover

5-in gun turret

YORKTOWN			
Origin United States		Date of launch 1937	
Length 251.4m (824ft 9in)		Displacement 19,875 tons	
Crew 2,175		Maximum speed 32.5 knots	
Armament 8 x 5-in guns, 16 x 1.1-in guns, 24 x 0.5-in guns, 96 aircraft			

HORNET
Built at Newport News, Virginia, in 1943, the Hornet was one of the first of the Essex class, *the largest group of fleet carriers of the war.*

Japanese carriers

Japanese carriers either had a small superstructure (from which the ship was navigated) or none at all. Unlike America, Japan never had the resources for large-scale production. The largest group was the *Unryu* class, but only three of these were completed before the war ended. The *Hiryu* (below) was unusual as its superstructure was to port. She was sunk at the Battle of Midway in 1942 (see p.327).

HIRYU			
Origin Japan		Date of launch 1937	
Length 227.4m (746ft)		Displacement 17,300 tons	
Crew 1,101		Maximum speed 34.3 knots	
Armament 12 x 5-in guns, 31 x 25-mm anti-aircraft guns, 73 aircraft			

British carriers

During the early 1930s, the British operated several old carriers, built or converted from First World War ships. The *Ark Royal* (below) was their first modern, purpose-built carrier, and she had a very active career before being sunk by a U-boat in 1941. Her successors, the six ships of the *Illustrious, Implacable,* and *Indomitable* classes, had armoured decks. They had one deck less than the *Ark Royal* and carried far fewer aircraft, but the armour proved useful when under attack by bombers and kamikazes. The British also built smaller, unarmoured light fleet carriers to transport fighter aircraft, but most were not completed until after the war.

ARK ROYAL			
Origin Britain		Date of launch 1937	
Length 244m (800ft)		Displacement 22,000 tons	
Crew 1,580		Maximum speed 31 knots	
Armament 16 x 4.5-in guns, 32 x 2-pounder guns, 3 x 3-pounder guns, 60 aircraft			

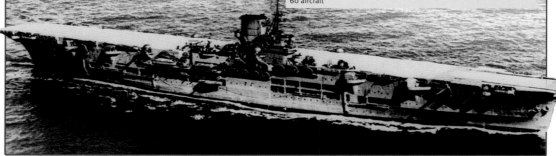

ESCORT VESSELS

The Western allies were unprepared for the U-boat war that intensified in the Atlantic after the fall of France in 1940. They adapted many different types of ship for use as anti-submarine escorts. Air patrols were very useful in attacking U-boats on the surface, so small aircraft carriers were developed. A good escort vessel needed to be faster than the submarines, to carry sonar and later radar to detect them, and to carry weapons.

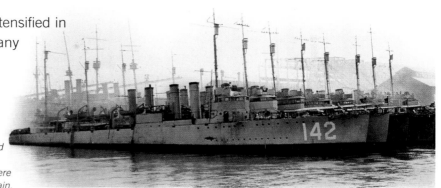

WARTIME GIFTS
These American destroyers were laid up at the Mare Island Navy Yard in California in 1919. Some of them were revitalized in 1940 and given to Britain.

Destroyers

The British adapted old First World War destroyers for escort duties and were given over 50 old US ships, known as the *Town* class, in 1940. Both types were very uncomfortable at sea, but more modern destroyers were needed with the main fleets. The Americans preferred the destroyer escort, based on the conventional destroyer design but with lower speed and less gun and torpedo armament. It proved highly successful in the Pacific.

As soon as the *Flower* class proved inadequate for operation in the Atlantic, the British began to develop a larger type, eventually called the frigate. By the end of the war, the frigate had become the standard anti-submarine vessel. It was relatively cheap but had just enough speed and armament to do the job and was large enough to operate on the oceans.

WOLVERINE		
Origin Britain		**Date of launch** 1919
Length 95m (312ft)		**Displacement** 1,325 tons
Crew 127		**Maximum speed** 34 knots
Armament 4 x 4.7-in guns, 1 x 3-in AA gun, 6 x 21-in torpedo tubes, 70 depth charges, Hedgehog anti-submarine mortar		

bridge

blast shield

whaler

dinghy

torpedo tubes

searchlight

torpedo tubes

4.7-in gun

blast shield

Escort carriers

Escort carriers were designed to carry a small number of low-performance aircraft to protect an individual convoy against submarines. The British merchant aircraft carriers, such as *Empire McAlpine* (below), carried cargo as well as aircraft. They were succeeded by larger escort carriers, dozens of which were built, mostly in the United States, for the American and British navies.

small bridge *swordfish aircraft* *aircraft lift*

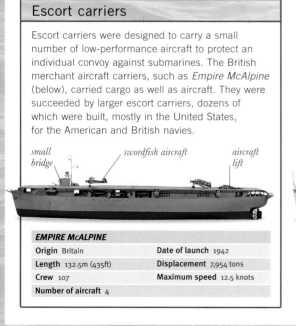

EMPIRE McALPINE	
Origin Britain	**Date of launch** 1942
Length 132.5m (435ft)	**Displacement** 7,954 tons
Crew 107	**Maximum speed** 12.5 knots
Number of aircraft 4	

Sloops

The sloop was the main type of British anti-submarine vessel between the wars, emerging as a result of the experience of the First World War. It had a fairly heavy gun armament and was quite successful but too expensive for mass production. HMS *Amethyst* (below) became famous in 1948, when she escaped advancing Chinese communists on the River Yangtze.

4-in gun in twin turret *lattice mast* *4-in gun in twin turret*

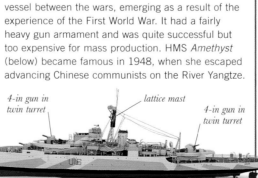

AMETHYST	
Origin Britain	**Date of launch** 1943
Length 91.3m (299ft 6in)	**Displacement** 1,350 tons
Crew 192	**Maximum speed** 19.75 knots
Armament 6 x 4-in guns, depth charges	

Corvettes

Just before the war, the British developed the design of a whaling ship for use as an escort in the North Sea. The resulting *Flower*-class ships soon had to be used in the North Atlantic, for which they were not really suitable. After some adaptations, they filled the gap until larger ships came along. *Sackville* (below) took part in several convoy battles.

SACKVILLE	
Origin Canada	**Date of launch** 1941
Length 62.5m (205ft)	**Displacement** 1,085 tons
Crew 85–109	**Maximum speed** 16.5 knots
Armament 1 x 4-in gun, depth charges	

MERCHANT SHIPS

Most of the merchant ships that supplied Allied civilians and armies in the Second World War were of pre-war construction and drew on a technology that did not differ greatly from that of the early 20th century. They included the traditional types, such as cargo and passenger liners, tramps, tankers, and Atlantic liners. Wartime construction was mostly of economical prefabricated ships, which could be built very quickly to replace tonnage lost to U-boats, aircraft, and mines.

SAFETY FROM MINES
Here, a convoy of British merchant ships in the North Sea can be seen sailing in narrow lines, seeking protection from minefields.

Atlantic liners

In 1939, the normal transatlantic trade was interrupted and British liners began troop-carrying, ferrying more than a million Americans to the war in Europe. The *Queen Elizabeth* (below) could take up to 15,000 soldiers. After the war, she began her career as a luxury liner.

QUEEN ELIZABETH

Origin Britain	**Date of launch** 1938
Length 314.25m (1,031ft)	**Tonnage** 83,763 tons
Maximum speed 29.5 knots	

Liberty ships

"Standard" ships had been built in the First World War using fixed designs and economical methods of production. This idea was taken up with the Liberty ships of the Second World War, which were built in great numbers in the United States and Britain. They had a substantial anti-aircraft armament but no frills of any kind. The first one took 245 days to build, but this was eventually cut to just ten days, and one was even built in four days and 15 hours. The Liberty ship was succeeded by the Victory ship, and standard designs for other types such as oil tankers were also produced.

A.J. CASSAT

Origin United States	**Date of launch** 1944
Length 128.8m (422ft 8in)	**Tonnage** 7,210 tons
Maximum speed 11 knots	

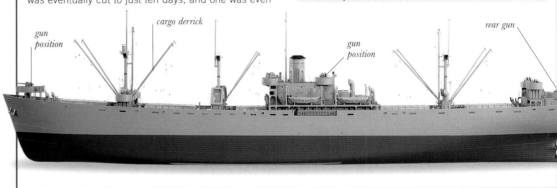

gun position · *cargo derrick* · *gun position* · *rear gun*

Tramp steamers

In wartime, British tramp ships joined oil tankers and cargo liners of many Allied nations in being forced to abandon their regular routes and form convoys, under the control of the Ministry of Shipping and escorted by naval ships. Tramp steamers tended to be put in slower convoys than the faster liners, taking three weeks or more to cross the Atlantic and suffering badly from U-boat attacks. The *Harpalyce* (below) was built in Sunderland, northeast England, for the Gowland Steamship Company. She was torpedoed in August 1940 and sank with the loss of 37 lives.

HARPALYCE

Origin Britain	**Date of launch** 1940
Length 137.4m (450ft 10in)	**Tonnage** 5,169 tons
Maximum speed 10.5 knots	

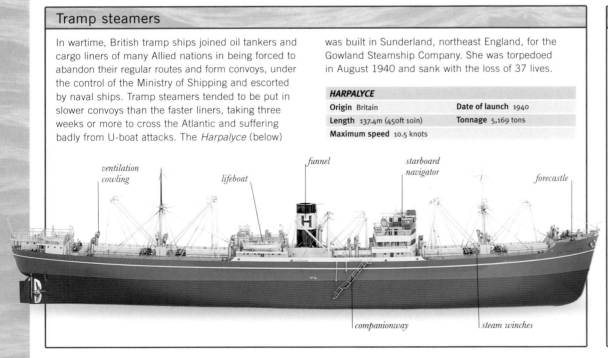

ventilation cowling · *lifeboat* · *funnel* · *starboard navigator* · *forecastle* · *companionway* · *steam winches*

Oil tankers

Because of the vast and unprecedented consumption of fuel by aircraft, ships, and military vehicles, oil tankers were particularly vital in wartime. The British register listed 420 of them in 1939, a total of nearly 3 million tons, while the United States had 389 on the high seas, of 2.8 million tons. The *British Gratitude* (below) was fitted with several guns for defence against surface ships and aircraft, as well as torpedo nets and paravanes for minesweeping.

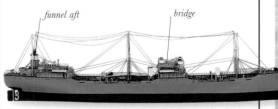

funnel aft · *bridge*

BRITISH GRATITUDE

Origin Britain	**Date of launch** 1942
Length 143.25m (470ft)	**Tonnage** 8,463 tons
Maximum speed 12 knots	

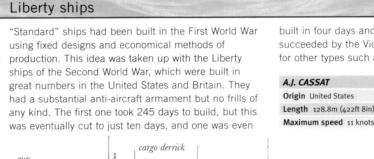

LANDING CRAFT

No nation had much experience of landing an army on a hostile shore in 1939, although the United States Marines had more practice than most. The Japanese built more than 3,000 of their *Diahatsu* landing craft for their advances in the Pacific in 1941–42. As well as the increase in shore defences, the task of landing an army was made more difficult by the need to land heavy equipment, such as tanks, to conduct a campaign ashore.

SICILIAN INVASION
This photograph shows Landing Craft (Tank) being loaded with troops and equipment as US forces prepare to invade Sicily.

Infantry landing craft

The Germans were unprepared when they thought they had the opportunity to invade Britain in 1940. Their landing craft were improvised and were never really tested before the invasion plan was cancelled. Small personnel-landing craft, such as the Landing Craft Assault developed by the British and Americans, could carry about 30 troops for a commando raid or for the early stages of a mass landing. The Landing Craft Infantry (Large) was designed in the United States at the request of the British Admiralty. Most would have to be built in the USA

and then cross the Atlantic under their own power, because of a shortage of shipping space. There was no opening bow door as in other landing craft, and the men landed by climbing down gangways on each side of the bow. This allowed a better hydrodynamic shape and, therefore, a greater speed, but it was more useful for the second wave of a landing than for the first assault, in which the men would have to disembark quickly while under fire. The DUKW, or "Duck", was an amphibious vehicle, equally at home on land or water. It was also used in landings and for ferrying supplies from ships anchored offshore.

LCI			
Origin United States		**Date of launch** 1942–44	
Length 48.3m (158ft 6in)		**Displacement** 209 tons	
Crew 29		**Maximum speed** 15.5 knots	
Load 209 troops or 75 tons of cargo			

Tank landing craft and ships

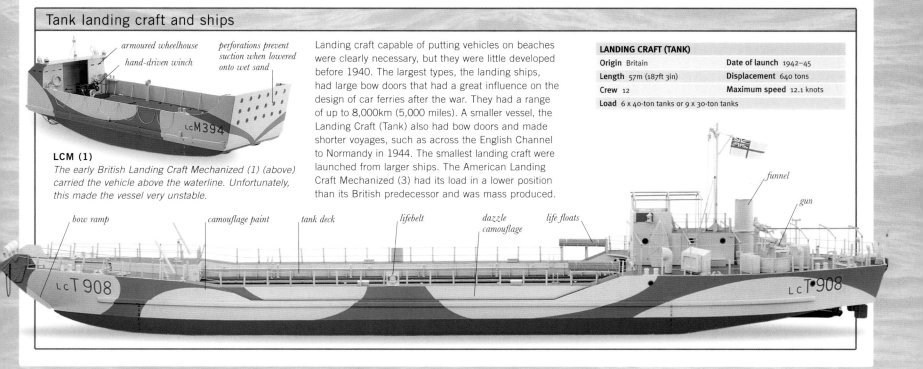

armoured wheelhouse
hand-driven winch
perforations prevent suction when lowered onto wet sand

LCM (1)
The early British Landing Craft Mechanized (1) (above) carried the vehicle above the waterline. Unfortunately, this made the vessel very unstable.

Landing craft capable of putting vehicles on beaches were clearly necessary, but they were little developed before 1940. The largest types, the landing ships, had large bow doors that had a great influence on the design of car ferries after the war. They had a range of up to 8,000km (5,000 miles). A smaller vessel, the Landing Craft (Tank) also had bow doors and made shorter voyages, such as across the English Channel to Normandy in 1944. The smallest landing craft were launched from larger ships. The American Landing Craft Mechanized (3) had its load in a lower position than its British predecessor and was mass produced.

LANDING CRAFT (TANK)			
Origin Britain		**Date of launch** 1942–45	
Length 57m (187ft 3in)		**Displacement** 640 tons	
Crew 12		**Maximum speed** 12.1 knots	
Load 6 x 40-ton tanks or 9 x 30-ton tanks			

bow ramp   *camouflage paint*   *tank deck*   *lifebelt*   *dazzle camouflage*   *life floats*   *funnel*   *gun*

8

UNDER PRESSURE
Ocean-going yacht racing is a competitive and expensive sport. Other watersports have become more accessible in recent decades, as more of us take to the waves.

THE GLOBAL AGE

ALTHOUGH SHIPS ARE NO LONGER the only means of traversing long distances across the world, many people still view them as a romantic way to travel, and in the global economy they are just as vital as they ever were. The volume of world trade is almost 10 times what it was in 1950, and 95 per cent of it is transported by sea. Container ships are being built which will carry the equivalent of 18,000 road vehicles, and an oil tanker can hold a cargo up to half-a-million tonnes. Some modern aircraft carriers accommodate more aircraft than the entire air force of some nations, while a single guided-missile submarine has a destructive power that is twice that of all the weapons used in World War II. Although ships are often taken for granted, epic round-the-world voyages still attract massive media attention, as do the negative aspects of shipping, such as oil spills that threaten the environment.

USS *NAUTILUS* POSTER

66 *Nautilus* underway on
nuclear power. 99

COMMANDER EUGENE P. WILKINSON,
signalling from the *Nautilus* on her maiden
voyage, **17 January 1955**

KEY EVENTS

1950–53 KOREAN WAR The first major
confrontation of the Cold War pitches the USA
and its allies against communist China, and
sees an audacious amphibious landing.

1954 NUCLEAR SUBMARINES The
nuclear-powered USS *Nautilus* enters service,
immediately raising the stakes of the Cold War.

1956 SUEZ CRISIS A British and French
naval assault on Egypt is halted by American
intervention, establishing a new world order.

1962 CUBAN MISSILE CRISIS The United
States blockades communist Cuba and almost
goes to war with the Soviet Union.

1964–75 VIETNAM US Navy ships play a key
role in support of democratic South Vietnam
during its long and bloody war with communist
North Vietnam.

1982 FALKLANDS WAR Britain dispatches
a huge naval task force to reclaim its South
Atlantic colony after an Argentinian invasion.

1991 END OF THE COLD WAR The collapse
of the Soviet Union leaves the USA as the
world's only maritime superpower.

2003 THE INVASION OF IRAQ American
and British naval forces take part in the invasion
in March. In October, on board the US carrier
Abraham Lincoln, George W. Bush declares
"major combat operations in Iraq have ended."

THE NEW WARSHIP

THE ARRIVAL OF THE ATOMIC BOMB AT THE CLOSE OF THE SECOND WORLD WAR MARKED THE END FOR ONE TYPE OF NAVAL WARFARE. BUT SHIPS WOULD STILL HAVE AN IMPORTANT ROLE TO PLAY IN THE NUCLEAR AGE.

The introduction of
powerful nuclear weapons
meant that a conflict
between superpowers
now seemed more likely
to involve a series of swift
nuclear exchanges rather
than a prolonged series
of battles on land and
sea. As a result, there have
been no major battles
between the world's great
navies since 1945. Apart
from occasional ship-to-
ship encounters, most
conflicts have seen navies acting in support
of air and land forces. The period after the
Second World War also saw rapid development
of sophisticated new conventional weapons
for use by and against warships. One of the
most devastating has been the guided missile
(see panel, p.342), which can home in on a
target automatically. Radar and anti-
submarine warfare have also advanced in this
period, and, with such swift technological
change, traditional categories of warship have
disappeared or changed beyond recognition.
For example, after the war, the US Navy
maintained four *Iowa*-class battleships for
use in shore bombardments, but they were
mothballed after an explosion on the *Iowa*
in 1989. Similarly, the British scrapped their
last battleship, *Vanguard*, in 1960. The cruiser
became a large, general-purpose vessel,
while the modern destroyer is an anti-
aircraft ship carrying long-range missiles.
The frigate, revived by the British in the
1940s for anti-submarine work, is the most
prolific surface warship of modern times.
Minesweepers were renamed minehunters
to reflect the varied techniques they used,
and have since transformed into mine
countermeasures vessels.

GUNS OF THE *MISSOURI*
*The 16-in (406-mm) guns of Iowa-class
battleships were the most powerful ever built,
but missile technology made such huge
weapons almost obsolete.*

Electronic information
has become the key to
most modern naval
warfare, and since
about 1960 the control
station has moved from
the bridge to the action
information office or
operations room. Here,
the captain or senior
weapons officer sits
among computers that
provide data and control
the ship's weaponry.

The start of the Cold War

With the end of the Second World War,
the rivalry between the Soviet Union and the
USA, each with its satellite states and allies,
developed into a global confrontation. This
Cold War lasted more than 40 years, during
which the two superpowers never fought directly,
although regimes or guerrilla movements
supported by the opposing sides often did.
One of the first naval incidents of the new era
occurred in 1946, when communist Albania
fired on two Royal Navy cruisers, *Orion* and
Superb, in the Corfu Channel off Greece. In the
same region, a British destroyer was damaged
beyond repair by Albanian mines.

Another early Cold War skirmish was the
Yangtze Incident of 1949. The Royal Navy
sloop *Amethyst* was attacked and trapped on
the Yangtze River by Chinese communists,
during their takeover of the country.
Damaged by gunfire, the *Amethyst* made
a dramatic escape to Hong Kong.

READY FOR ACTION
*F4U Corsairs and an early helicopter sit amid snow onboard
the US attack aircraft carrier* Valley Forge, *off Korea in 1951.
The Korean War helped re-establish the role of aircraft
carriers, and navies in general, in the nuclear age.*

The Korean War

The first open conflict of the Cold War took place in Korea, a country that had been divided since 1945 between a communist north and a capitalist south. On 25 June 1950, North Korean forces, with the approval of China and the Soviet Union, poured over the border into South Korea – by September, their opponents were confined to Korea's southeastern corner. On 15 September, an international fleet of 230 ships under US General MacArthur landed marines at Inchon with United Nations backing. They captured the capital, Seoul, and advanced into the North before China intervened, driving back UN forces to begin a three-year stalemate.

At the time, aircraft carriers were out of favour in the United States, largely because they lacked the support of the US Air Force. The

THE F4U CORSAIR
The Corsair's folding wings made it ideal for use on carriers between the end of the Second World War and the arrival of jets. Ships could carry up to 100 of these fighters.

Americans had just one carrier in the region at the start of the war, but soon built up a substantial task force, including British and Australian vessels. Their aircraft proved vital in fighting for air superiority over the North and bombing in support of ground troops. When the war ended with a restoration of the original border in 1953, the carrier's credibility was fully restored.

Decolonization

The Second World War exposed the insecurity of far-flung colonies. Japanese successes in the Far East, the Pacific, and Burma (Myanmar) destroyed the myth of European invincibility, encouraging

long propeller blades

wings fold for stowing on and below deck

bend in wing allows for short landing gear and long propeller blades (for maximum thrust)

sturdy landing gear

liberation movements. While French Indo-China (now Vietnam) was under Japanese occupation, a communist guerrilla movement had developed under the leadership of Ho Chi Minh. In

LANDING AT INCHON
Operation Chromite, the amphibious landing of almost 70,000 troops in the treacherous waters of Inchon Bay, was a tactical masterstroke by General MacArthur. It was the largest such operation since the Second World War and caught North Korean forces completely off guard.

February 1946, the French Navy landed troops to re-establish authority in the colony, backed by gunfire from its ships. This triggered a bitter eight-year war, in which the French used small gunboats in the river systems of the Mekong Delta and along the coast. Three French aircraft carriers – the *Lafayette*, *Bois Belleau*, and *Arromanches* – were used to bombard enemy positions ashore. After the battle of Dien Bien Phu, France conceded independence in 1954 – but, like Korea, the new Vietnam was split into a communist north and a capitalist south, sowing the seeds of later conflict.

Elsewhere, Britain faced problems of its own. Since 1919, it had ruled Palestine under a League of Nations mandate, with a promise to create a homeland for the Jewish people. After the Second World War, thousands of displaced Jews were determined to settle there, but the British were undecided about how best to establish the new nation. To placate Arab opinion, they patrolled the coast, stopping ships carrying illegal immigrants. By March 1947, they had eight warships on station, with other ships employed to follow suspicious vessels heading for Palestine. There were many confrontations, culminating in the 1947 boarding of the *Exodus 1947*, a ship that had sailed from Europe with 4,500 Jewish refugees aboard. Approaching Palestine, it was escorted by four destroyers and boarded by British troops. In the ensuing fight, three refugees were killed and 27 injured. The incident focused world attention on the problem, and in 1948 the state of Israel was declared.

The end of European colonialism was also evident in the Suez crisis. In 1956, General Gamal Abdel Nasser seized Egypt's Suez Canal, in response to the withdrawal of Western finance

REFUGEES FROM EUROPE
Released from detention in Italy after the intervention of US President Truman, the refugee ship Fede *docks at Haifa with a thousand Jewish migrants on board.*

from the Aswan Dam. Britain, France, and Israel plotted to bring down Nasser and restore the canal to its previous status. Their invasion outraged the world (see panel, below).

Far Eastern colonies were the scene of further flashpoints. In 1963, the Indonesian government claimed parts of newly independent Malaysia. Guerrillas began to infiltrate the Malaysian Peninsula and the island of Borneo, and Britain mobilized a large force, including the aircraft carrier *Victorious*, to aid the Malaysians. Much of the fighting was done by small craft in rivers and coastal waters. At the end of the conflict, in 1966, Britain announced its intention to withdraw from disputes "east of Suez", concentrating on the North Atlantic.

Britain had withdrawn from India in 1947, leaving Muslim Pakistan split in two by India, but tension between the nations led to several wars. As East Pakistan fought for independence in 1971, the Indian carrier *Vikrant* bombed Pakistani positions in the area and enforced a blockade. This was just one of several naval actions leading to the creation of Bangladesh.

ACROSS THE BLACK RIVER
French soldiers come ashore after a dangerous river crossing, in 1952, during the war in Indochina. These commandos went on to destroy a key Viet Minh railway bridge, but in the end their efforts were in vain.

THE SUEZ CRISIS

Following a secret agreement with Britain and France to topple General Nasser and regain control of the Suez Canal, Israel invaded Egypt on 30 October 1956. Within days, a joint French and British task force had assembled off Port Said, ostensibly to enforce a cease-fire and secure the canal. It comprised 34 French warships, including the battleship *Jean Bart* and aircraft carriers *Arromanches* and *Lafayette*, and more than a hundred British ships including the carriers *Ocean* and *Theseus*, both hastily converted to land troops by helicopter, and *Eagle*, *Albion*, and *Bulwark* carrying conventional aircraft.

After a paratroop operation to seize control of nearby Gamil airport, French and British forces landed east and west of the canal early on 6 November, while Royal Marine Commandos assaulted the canal by helicopter. Carrier aircraft stood by, ready to support the ground forces if needed. Egyptian resistance was overcome, but

US President Eisenhower was infuriated by this display of imperialism. He threatened to withhold a much-needed loan to Britain, and this, alongside threats of forcible intervention from the Soviet Union, forced Britain and France into a humiliating withdrawal. It was the end of the old imperialism as a global force and the beginning of US dominance.

BLOCKING THE CANAL
In response to the British, French, and Israeli attack, Egypt sunk some 40 ships along the Suez Canal. They took months to clear.

New weapons

The development of new weapons systems after the Second World War spurred a rush to find equally effective new defences. In any conflict, a ship is a coherent, easily identifiable, and immensely valuable target, but it is a difficult one for a conventional bomber to hit. As a result, the guided missile (see panel, below) has become the biggest threat to ships in modern naval warfare – essentially because it can react to the ship's movements after launch.

Guided missiles first entered use late in the Second World War. The Luftwaffe developed the Henschel Hs 293, a radio-controlled glider bomb, which sank the British cruiser *Spartan* in the Mediterranean in January 1944. In a sense, the Japanese Kamikaze (see pp.326–28) was also a guided missile, albeit one that used a pilot

instead of a computer to reach its target. A modern warship carries a variety of missiles for attack and defence – anti-ship, anti-aircraft, anti-missile, and even anti-submarine. They are almost always propelled by rockets, which need little maintenance, produce high speeds, and can be started in a hurry. The most powerful of all are nuclear-armed ballistic missiles (see opposite) such as Polaris and Trident. These use rockets to launch them on a trajectory that will bring them to land at the target, perhaps even arcing outside the atmosphere en route. They have become the primary strategic deterrent for the world's major powers. Cruise missiles, such as the Tomahawk, have wings to provide lift, and are propelled all the way to the target. They are less expensive, and most use conventional warheads. They can be launched from ships and submarines against static land targets, and were used in both Gulf wars.

To keep up with the increasing threat to naval vessels, radar defences have also advanced. They can now be linked directly to a ship's weapons systems, making anti-aircraft gunnery far more

effective, as it can track incoming missiles. However, attackers can saturate a target with more missiles than its guns can cope with, and for this reason a new generation of flak defences has been created, capable of generating a "wall" of flak around a vessel under attack. The move towards missile-based warfare reached such extremes that some British frigates of the 1970s were built without any main gun armament. However, the Falklands War (see p. 350) showed that guns could still be useful in shore bombardment and for firing across the bows of suspect ships.

SUBMARINE INSIGNIA
All US nuclear submarines have flags and patches that are a source of pride and unity to the crew. This is the badge of the Will Rogers, *the last Polaris-missile carrier to be commissioned. It shows the comedian and actor after whom the boat was named.*

GUIDED MISSILES

The guidance system used in a missile depends on its role. Early anti-aircraft missiles, such as the American Terrier and British Sea Slug, followed a radar beam from ship to target. Their air-launched equivalents, such as the US Sidewinder, home in on heat from a target's engine. The Australian Ikara anti-submarine missiles carried a homing torpedo that was dropped in the water near the target.

Surface missiles, whether ballistic or cruise, are guided by inertial navigation. Using onboard instruments, they keep track of their precise position and guide themselves to the target. Anti-shipping missiles, such as the French Exocet and the US Harpoon, combine inertial guidance with radar. They gain altitude, acquire the target by radar, then dive, level off, and skim the waves to get under the target's defences.

SATELLITE-GUIDED MISSILES
The latest generation of missiles, such as these US Tomahawks, can be precisely guided to their targets using the Global Positioning System, made possible by orbiting satellites.

THE CUBAN MISSILE CRISIS

After Fidel Castro's rebels seized power in the 1959 revolution, Cuba's relations with America deteriorated rapidly – not helped by US backing of an ill-fated invasion in 1961. Eighteen months later, President Kennedy was shown aerial photographs of Soviet missiles on Cuba, within striking distance of the US mainland. In an address on 22 October, he declared a maritime "quarantine" of the island, and sent the Navy to enforce a blockade.

The world held its breath on 24 October 1962, as American warships headed to intercept a group of Soviet cargo ships steaming towards

CLOSE ENCOUNTER
The US warship Barry *steams alongside the Soviet vessel* Ansov *as it leaves Cuban waters at the height of the missile crisis.*

WITHIN RANGE
A CIA map shows the threat to mainland USA posed by Soviet nuclear missiles stationed on Cuba.

Cuba. However, Soviet leader Nikita Khrushchev ordered his ships to turn back at the last minute. The United Nations was then able to mediate an agreement in which the USSR withdrew its missiles, while the United States agreed not to invade Cuba again. In the aftermath, shock and relief contributed to a new mood of co-operation and disarmament.

intercontinental ballistic missile (ICBM), caused a change in strategy. If armies were eliminated and ports devastated in a nuclear exchange, old battle strategies would be irrelevant. The nuclear arms race between the United States and the Soviet Union resulted in several years of extraordinary tension, culminating in the Cuban Missile Crisis (see panel, left), the most dangerous and direct confrontation of the entire Cold War. Throughout this period, navies began to take increasing responsibility for nuclear deterrence. While ground-based missiles might be eliminated in a surprise first strike, and manned bombers might be shot down, a nuclear ICBM fired from a submerged submarine would offer no warning. The first successful test of such a missile, the US Polaris, took place in 1958; 10 Polaris-equipped vessels were in service by 1961 and 23 by 1964. The British adopted the system following the 1962 Nassau Agreement, building their own boats to carry the missiles. France, anxious to retain military independence from America, took the harder path of designing both submarines and missiles for its six-boat Force de Dissuasion. The Soviets naturally responded in kind, building 34 ships of the Yankee class in the ten years after 1963. Their missile-carrier programme culminated in the huge 25,000-ton Typhoon class of 1983 – the largest submarines ever built. Meanwhile the Americans replaced Polaris with Trident, which also required much larger boats, and the British followed with the modern *Vanguard*-class submarines. Replacements for Trident are now being considered by the US and the UK.

Battle of the Atlantic, in which troops and supplies would be carried to Europe in the face of a Soviet submarine threat. The British were also alarmed by the new Soviet *Sverdlov*-class cruisers, which were far bigger than the warships of any other nation. But by the late 1950s, the arrival of hydrogen bombs, many times more powerful than the first generation of atom bombs, together with an almost unstoppable delivery system in the form of the

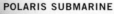

POLARIS SUBMARINE
The US Polaris-missile-carrying submarine Robert E. Lee *was commissioned in Newport News, Virginia, on 16 September 1960.*

THE ULTIMATE DETERRENT
US President John F. Kennedy (centre, out of uniform) inspects a Polaris-missile hatch on the nuclear submarine Thomas Edison *in May 1962. A few months later, he was forced into a game of nuclear brinkmanship with the Soviet Union – one that nearly led to war.*

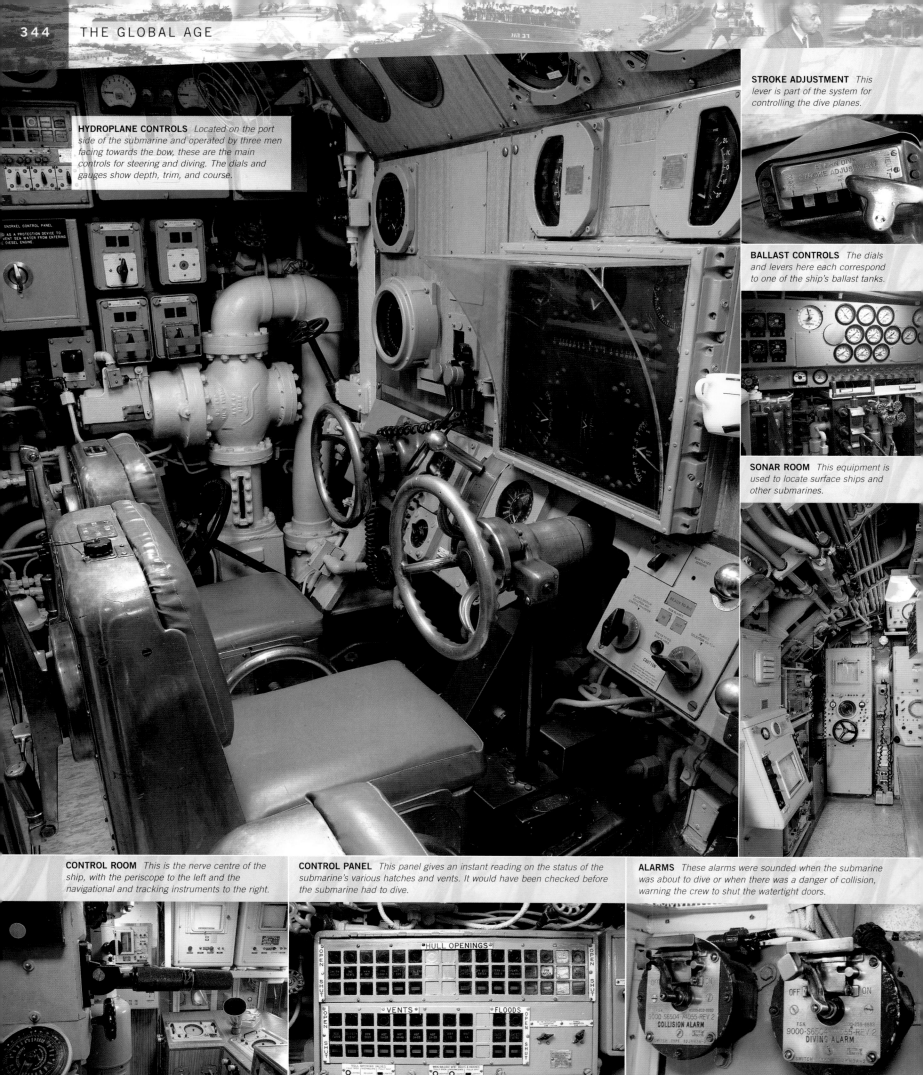

HYDROPLANE CONTROLS *Located on the port side of the submarine and operated by three men facing towards the bow, these are the main controls for steering and diving. The dials and gauges show depth, trim, and course.*

STROKE ADJUSTMENT *This lever is part of the system for controlling the dive planes.*

BALLAST CONTROLS *The dials and levers here each correspond to one of the ship's ballast tanks.*

SONAR ROOM *This equipment is used to locate surface ships and other submarines.*

CONTROL ROOM *This is the nerve centre of the ship, with the periscope to the left and the navigational and tracking instruments to the right.*

CONTROL PANEL *This panel gives an instant reading on the status of the submarine's various hatches and vents. It would have been checked before the submarine had to dive.*

ALARMS *These alarms were sounded when the submarine was about to dive or when there was a danger of collision, warning the crew to shut the watertight doors.*

WARDROOM The dining and recreation area for the captain and officers, this room is nearly four times the size of the wardroom of conventional submarines of the time.

WATERTIGHT Doors such as this were closed in times of action or emergency.

DIALS These dials indicated the amount of water in the submarine's ballast tanks.

COUNTER-MEASURES This gear was used to foil attempts to track the ship.

HATCH The wheel on this hatch was used to lock it in place against the water pressure from outside the submarine.

`PHOTO PROFILE`

NAUTILUS

THE *NAUTILUS* WAS A REVOLUTIONARY SUBMARINE, WHOSE LAUNCH IN THE EARLY PART OF THE COLD WAR SIGNALLED THE ADVENT OF A NEW KIND OF UNDERWATER WARFARE.

THE WORLD'S FIRST nuclear submarine, the *Nautilus* was the main project of US Admiral Hyman G. Rickover (see p. 347). In January 1955, she made a voyage of 2,222km (1,381 miles) in just under 90 hours, setting a record for the longest submerged distance covered in that time. In 1958, after several attempts, she was the first submarine to reach the North Pole. She travelled more than 800,000km (500,000 miles) using three nuclear cores, until she was decommissioned in 1980 and preserved in Connecticut. Unlike her successors, which were designed entirely for underwater use, the *Nautilus* has a flat area on the upper surface of her hull. She is simple in appearance, with no sign of the gun armament visible on earlier generations of submarines.

The bridge, from which the ship was steered when on the surface, is at the top of the conning-tower. Accommodating a nuclear reactor requires a hull with a large cross-section. *Nautilus* has room for two decks, with storage areas and batteries under them. Directly below the conning-tower, on the upper deck, is the periscope room. Forward of that are the captain's and officers' quarters, with the crew's mess and the galley below. The control room, from which the ship was navigated underwater, is directly below the conning-tower on the lower deck. The torpedo room is in the bow. Aft of the conning-tower is the reactor, with the engine behind. Between them, they occupy about a third of the interior. Aft of the engine are the crew's sleeping quarters. Each man had his own bunk, in contrast to earlier submarines, in which men from different watches used the same bed in turn. For the first time in a submarine, there is some attempt at decoration, with panelling to hide some pipes and ducts; but, like all submarines, *Nautilus* is generally functional, with instruments in every space. In many ways, *Nautilus* set the pattern for future nuclear submarines, which came to dominate naval warfare, either as torpedo-carrying attack submarines or as nuclear missile carriers.

Specification

conning-tower also called the sail of the ship

periscope

flattened area on upper part of hull, on which crew could stand

Origin USA	**Date of launch** 1954	**Maximum speed** 23 knots
Length 98.6m (323ft 6in)	**Tonnage** 4,092 tonnes	**Maximum depth** 213.4m (700ft)
Crew 116	**Armament** 6 x 21-in torpedo tubes	

LAUNCH
Draped with flags for her launch in January 1954, Nautilus plunges into the Thames River at Groton, Connecticut, after being christened by Mamie Eisenhower.

TORPEDO Torpedoes were the main armament of the Nautilus. Some were kept in tubes, but this one was a spare, ready to be loaded after another had been fired.

TORPEDO COMPARTMENT On the left are the after doors of two of the torpedo tubes.

GALLEY The ship's galley was fitted in stainless steel for ease of cleaning and maintenance. The Nautilus also had a laundry, ice cream and drinks machines, and a juke box.

CREW'S QUARTERS The three tiers of bunks gave minimal headroom.

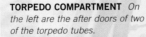

The Vietnam War

Following the French withdrawal and the partition of Indo-China in 1954, the USA became involved in supporting and arming the new state of South Vietnam. In 1962, with support for the communists increasing in South Vietnam, President Kennedy sent in military advisers, and on 31 July 1964 the US destroyer *Maddox*, carrying out electronic surveillance off North Vietnam, was attacked by three patrol boats. A torpedo missed the destroyer, and one of the Vietnamese boats was sunk. The captain of the *Maddox* reported another attack two nights later – although it later transpired that the lookouts and radar operators had largely imagined it. However, the incident was sufficient to obtain congressional and public support for direct American intervention in the war between the two Vietnams.

WATER PATROL
These Vietcong troops were photographed during a patrol in a traditional shallow sampan in Vietnam's maze of coastal river estuaries. Despite weaker technology, the Vietcong's guerrilla tactics bogged down US forces in a long and unwinnable war.

The war is best known for its vicious guerrilla campaign, but the US Navy had an important role. Carriers stationed offshore launched incessant bombing raids against the North – 148,000 sorties had been flown by the end of 1966. The Vietnamese retaliated with missiles, fighters, and anti-aircraft fire, downing more than 400 naval aircraft between 1965 and 1968. The US Navy also used Patrol Boats River (PBRs) on the Mekong Delta and other waterways. Made from plastic, they had highly responsive water-jet propulsion and machine-gun armament. The four-man crew was commanded by a senior petty officer. At the peak of the war in the late 1960s, some 250 of these craft were in service alongside traditional sampans and land forces.

AMPHIBIOUS ASSAULT
A landing craft takes US soldiers of the Second Battalion, Third Marines ashore near Hue, South Vietnam, during 1967's Operation Bear Chain. This was the 34th amphibious assault in barely two years.

The campaign was politically divisive in the USA and took a great toll on all sides. It ended with the North Vietnamese advance on Saigon, the capital of South Vietnam, in April 1975. Amid widespread terror and panic, helicopters of the US Seventh Fleet evacuated 15,000 Americans and Vietnamese to waiting carriers. Soon the world would see equally disturbing scenes as refugees from oppression or poverty took to overcrowded, dangerous boats in the hope of finding a better life elsewhere.

US naval forces were also humiliated at the hand of communist forces elsewhere. In January 1968, the lightly armed intelligence ship *Pueblo* was forced to surrender to North Korean ships. Her crew was later released unharmed, but the North Koreans retain the ship to this day as a trophy.

HANCOCK INSIGNIA
The Hancock was one of many US aircraft carriers to provide valuable air support to the troops on the ground in Vietnam. She was also involved in the final evacuation of Saigon.

PREPARING FOR LAUNCH
A flight deck director signals an F-4 Phantom II fighter into position for a catapult launch from the deck of the US aircraft carrier Midway, *during operations off Vietnam in August 1970.*

Amphibious warfare

After the experiences of Korea and Suez, development of vessels suitable for amphibious warfare was a high priority for Western navies. The first amphibious craft, developed in the Second World War, had included tank and infantry landing craft. These were now supplemented by vessels developed from the aircraft carrier template. The Royal Navy's Landing Platform Docks *Fearless* and *Intrepid* combined a floating dock, which could be used to launch landing craft, with a helicopter pad. America developed the *Iwo Jima* and *Tarawa* classes, resembling small aircraft carriers and capable of landing up to 2,000 men.

SURFACING AT THE POLE
Both the USA and the USSR used their nuclear submarines for propaganda purposes. The Nautilus *dived under the ice to surface at the North Pole in 1958, followed four years later by the Russian* Leninsky Komsomol *(shown here). The* Nautilus *was also the first submarine to circumnavigate the globe underwater.*

Atomic engines

Directly after the Second World War, the British tried the German idea of using hydrogen peroxide fuel to allow submarines to stay underwater for long periods – but it proved highly unreliable and expensive. The true revolution in submarines came with nuclear power (see p.348), which first saw service aboard the US Navy's *Nautilus* in 1954 (see pp.344–45). Nuclear submarines, able to stay submerged for weeks or even months at a time, and carrying a deadly payload of nuclear missiles, were the key to the Cold War stalemate. The first British nuclear submarine, launched in 1960, was named *Dreadnought*, but any echoes of the revolutionary 1906 battleship were undermined by her reliance on an American reactor. By the 1960s, the Soviets had a strong fleet of conventional submarines, but they soon followed the Americans and British into the nuclear age. Nuclear submarines on both sides diversified into gargantuan missile-carriers or boomers, and smaller, faster hunter-killers intended to track and destroy the missile-carriers during a conflict. However, nuclear submarines have not been

entirely free of problems. The Russians, in particular, have suffered repeated accidents, notably the loss of the *Kursk* in 2000. At the end of the Cold War, Russian vessels transferred to the Indian Navy were known ironically as the Chernobyl class.

With nuclear engines making submarines harder to find, anti-submarine technology had to develop too. The Asdic-based active sonar system has been supplemented by a passive version, which is towed up to 0.5km (0.3 miles) behind a vessel and is able to pick up propeller noise from a ship or submarine many kilometres away. Helicopter-launched homing torpedoes can then fix on the target.

Despite the huge amounts invested in them, submarines saw little action during the Cold War – they were peripheral to the amphibious warfare of the period. However, this in itself was a sign of success – their effectiveness as a deterrent may have helped to avert a war between the rival superpowers.

PROPAGANDA COUP
Submarine firsts such as trips to the Pole, commemorated in this Soviet stamp, were driven by the need of the Cold War rivals to show off their technological prowess.

HYMAN G. RICKOVER

Hyman G. Rickover (1900–86) was the architect of the American nuclear submarine programme. A Polish-born immigrant, he attended the US Naval Academy and Columbia University, where he studied engineering. After service on submarines, he headed the electrical section of the Bureau of Ships in Washington during the Second World War. He was appointed to the nuclear programme in 1946, and by 1949 he was at its head. The first nuclear power plant was begun in 1950, and the *Nautilus* was laid down in 1952. Rickover remained head of the nuclear submarine programme until his retirement, with the rank of Admiral, in 1982.

NUCLEAR POWER

The nuclear engine onboard a submarine or battleship may have an exotic fuel source, but it operates on a 19th-century principle. Inside the reactor core, atoms of radioactive uranium are split apart in a process called nuclear fission, generating large amounts of energy. This is used to turn water into steam, and pressure from the steam drives a traditional turbine, linked to the propeller shaft. Diverted steam drives another turbine to produce electricity.

Nuclear power plants are more expensive than diesel engines, but they have many advantages – particularly on submarines. They are not dependent on air for combustion, and

CONTROL ROOM
The reactor onboard the US aircraft carrier George Washington is monitored 24 hours a day for the slightest irregularity.

have an almost unlimited range – an American nuclear aircraft carrier can steam 360,000km (200,000 miles) without refuelling. Nuclear power can also be highly dangerous – the reactor is carefully shielded from the rest of the ship during operation and must be carefully handled during decommissioning.

NUCLEAR POWER
A nuclear engine uses heat exchangers to transfer energy between three systems: a primary system of water pumped through the reactor core; a secondary system that drives the turbines; and a cooling circuit.

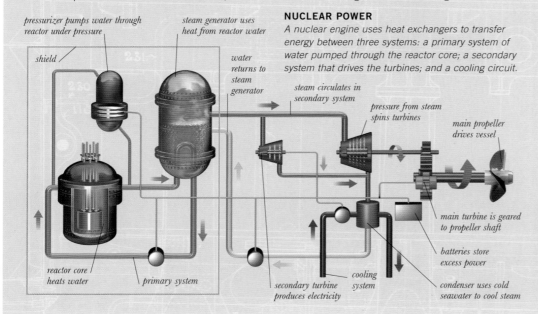

pressurizer pumps water through reactor under pressure

steam generator uses heat from reactor water

shield

water returns to steam generator

steam circulates in secondary system

pressure from steam spins turbines

main propeller drives vessel

main turbine is geared to propeller shaft

batteries store excess power

reactor core heats water

primary system

secondary turbine produces electricity

cooling system

condenser uses cold seawater to cool steam

Aircraft carriers

Many countries took up naval aviation for the first time after the Second World War, using decommissioned British or American aircraft carriers. For example, Brazil acquired the *Minas Gerais* in 1960 after she had first passed through both the British and Australian navies.

However, naval aviation was changing rapidly. The introduction of faster but heavier jet aircraft called for longer and larger aircraft carriers. In 1945, the fastest piston-engined fighter, the Corsair, flew at 757kph (470mph). By 1960, the McDonnell Douglas Phantom had a speed of 2,278kph (1,415mph) and weighed more than five times as much. The aircraft that smaller carriers could launch were rapidly becoming out of date, and ultimately only the

US Navy could build carriers large enough to service the fastest jets. At the slower end of the scale, the development of the helicopter meant that most modern ocean-going warships carried at least some form of aircraft by the 1960s.

The first ever jet landing on an aircraft carrier was made by a prototype Sea Vampire onto the Royal Navy's *Ocean* in 1946, and British invention in the field continued from there. Unable to compete with US carriers for length, Britain revived the catapult for assisting aircraft launches – using steam from the engine to power it – and invented the angled deck, which allowed landing and launching at the same time with less risk of accidents. The Royal Navy rarely had the money to develop such innovations fully, but many were adopted by the Americans. The cancellation of a new carrier in 1966 was expected to signal the end for British naval aviation, but the arrival of the innovative Harrier jump jet (see below) in the 1970s meant that three ships of the *Invincible* class, originally conceived as helicopter carriers, could carry jets.

US carriers continued to grow throughout the 1950s and 60s, reaching a plateau with the arrival of the nuclear-powered *Nimitz* class in 1968. These 90,000-ton ships carry about 90 high-performance aircraft. A dozen carriers are maintained in service, dwarfing any other force in the world. Their ability to operate without reliance on a welcoming host nation has often proved useful. In 1986, when President Reagan ordered the bombing of Libya for alleged terrorism, France refused overflight rights to British-based US bombers, necessitating a long flight with mid-air refuelling; American carriers based in the Mediterranean faced no such problems. They also had a role in the 2001 war in Afghanistan.

LAUNCH RAMPS
A raised launch ramp at the end of an aircraft carrier helps planes such as this Sea Harrier to gain lift during take off. During flight operations, the carrier heads straight into the wind in order to increase the relative air speed.

engine nozzles can pivot to direct thrust down or backwards

external fuel tank

lightweight carbon-fibre airframe

JUMP JET
The Harrier and Sea Harrier are vertical/short take off and landing (VSTOL) aircraft, ideal for operating onboard ship or away from conventional runways. The Royal Navy phased them out in 2011.

Soviet developments

Frustrated by its impotence during the Cuban Missile Crisis and the 1967 Arab-Israeli War, the USSR began to build up its surface fleet during the 1970s, under the guidance of Admiral Sergei Gorshkov (see panel, right). By the end of the decade, it had 35 cruisers, 85 destroyers, and 159 frigates, plus two helicopter carriers and two *Kiev*-class aircraft carriers holding 32 planes each. It also had nearly 70 ballistic missile submarines and more than 300 others. This rapid build-up caused President Ronald Reagan to make plans for a 600-ship US Navy after he took office in 1981, although he never quite achieved that figure, and the Cold War came to an end due to the internal collapse of the communist bloc, rather than any direct

OCEAN GIANTS

The US Navy's Midway *dwarfs an auxiliary and another warship as she refuels in the middle of the Indian Ocean. Completed in 1945, the 295-m (968-ft)* Midway *is still 37m (124ft) shorter than the later Nimitz-class carriers.*

confrontation. Despite the build-up of the Soviet Navy, the Americans have maintained decisive naval superiority throughout most of the world since the end of the Second World War. US Navy ships have been able to operate at long range, partly because of nuclear power on the larger vessels and submarines, but also because of sophisticated techniques for replenishing and refuelling at sea.

RUSSIAN NAVY

The demise of the Soviet Union has left Russia with the legacy of a huge surface fleet. Here, ships are moored at St. Petersburg during a review of the fleet.

SERGEI GEORGIYEVICH GORSHKOV

One of the few Russian naval officers to serve with distinction in the Second World War, Sergei Georgiyevich Gorshkov (1910–88) graduated from the Naval Academy at Frunze in 1931. Commanding naval forces in the Black Sea, he helped liberate the Ukraine, Romania, and Bulgaria, reaching the rank of rear-admiral at the age of 31.

In 1956, Gorshkov was appointed head of the Soviet Navy. Arguing for a more efficient submarine force and a stronger surface fleet, he oversaw an unprecedented naval expansion. In 1976 he published *Sea Power and the State*, outlining his theory of naval power. Gorshkov's influence declined in the 1980s, but he remained in office until his death.

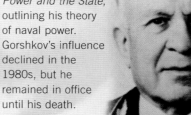

NAVAL WARFARE IN THE FALKLANDS CONFLICT

On 2 May 1982, as the British task force approached the Falkland Islands, the Argentine cruiser *General Belgrano* and its escorts were patrolling near an exclusion zone declared by the British. The task force commander judged they posed a substantial military threat,

LAST VIEW
The periscope camera of the Conqueror *caught this image of the* Belgrano *during the attack.*

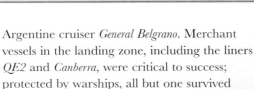

so the nuclear submarine *Conqueror* was ordered to torpedo the cruiser, resulting in the loss of more than 300 lives. A political row later focused on the position and intentions of the *Belgrano* at the time of the sinking, but the Argentine Navy took no further part in the war.

Two days later, the incident was avenged when the destroyer *Sheffield* was sunk by an air-launched Exocet missile. The British lost another destroyer, two frigates, two landing ships, and the container ship *Atlantic Conveyor* in the next few weeks, with several hundred men. The most purely naval war since 1945, the Falklands conflict was also the first to be dominated by guided missiles.

SINKING THE ANTELOPE
On 23 May 1982, the Type 21-frigate Antelope *was struck by two bombs from an Argentine jet while guarding San Carlos Water. Both failed to detonate, but one was later triggered by attempts to defuse it.*

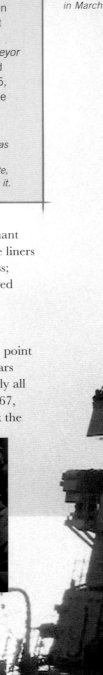

TOMAHAWK LAUNCH
A Tomahawk cruise missile streaks into the sky above the US warship Winston S. Churchill *during operations off Iraq in March 2003.*

Task force to the Falklands

Britain, the world's greatest maritime power for more than 300 years, withdrew progressively from overseas commitments after the Second World War. By 1982, the Royal Navy, although still the largest in Europe, was thinly spread. The military rulers of Argentina mistakenly concluded that Britain would no longer defend its South Atlantic colony in the Falkland Islands, and mounted an invasion, seizing control on 2 April. British reaction was intense – the First Sea Lord, Admiral Sir Henry Leach, advised that the islands could be recovered, and the government dispatched a task force that grew to include 2 aircraft carriers, 23 destroyers and frigates, 8 amphibious warfare vessels, 21 auxiliary craft, and 43 merchant ships. Despite supply lines 11,000km (7,000 miles) long, the Royal Navy defended an exclusion zone from early May. Troops landed at San Carlos Water, to the rear of Argentinian defences, and crossed inhospitable terrain to liberate the capital, Port Stanley, on 14 June. Fierce fighting resulted in many deaths, and several ships were sunk on both sides, including the

Argentine cruiser *General Belgrano*. Merchant vessels in the landing zone, including the liners *QE2* and *Canberra*, were critical to success; protected by warships, all but one survived unscathed (see panel, above).

Middle Eastern conflicts

The Middle East has been a major flash point since 1945, and although most of the wars fought there have been land-based, nearly all have produced some naval action. In 1967, Egyptian boats armed with missiles sank the

MISSILE CONTROL ROOM
The Tomahawk Strike Team onboard the US guided missile cruiser Shiloh *man their positions in the ship's combat information centre.*

Israeli destroyer *Eliat* off Port Said, causing navies to look at the possibilities of small, missile-armed vessels as a means of attack and defence. The British intervened to protect Kuwait from Iraqi attack in 1961, while the Iran–Iraq War of 1980–88 turned oil tankers into targets for both sides. In 1988, the US cruiser *Vincennes* mistakenly shot down an Iranian civil airliner with a guided missile.

In August 1990, the Iraqis under Saddam Hussein invaded Kuwait, and a multinational force assembled to repel them. Carrier-launched aircraft played a large part in the bombardment of shore targets. The threat of mines affected strategy off the coast, but the small Iraqi Navy was destroyed early in the conflict.

During the 2003 war in Iraq, aircraft carriers were even more important, since American and British forces had few land bases in the

region. At one stage, a sandstorm put most airbases out of action, but the US carrier *Abraham Lincoln* was able to steam clear of it in order to maintain the attack. British troops also made amphibious landings.

Fighting terrorism

Since the Cold War ended in 1989, the Western powers have faced no single coherent enemy. Naval forces have, however, intervened in wars connected to the break-up of former communist states, as in Bosnia during the 1990s.

As the prevailing threat to many nations has shifted towards unpredictable acts of terrorism, so the role of navies has changed once again. Britain's former First Sea Lord was blown up on his yacht by the IRA in 1979 (see p.323), while in 1985 the Italian cruise ship *Achille Lauro* was taken over by Palestinian terrorists and a Jewish passenger was murdered. In October 2000, the US destroyer *Cole* was attacked off Yemen by al-Qaeda bombers in a dinghy, and 17 sailors were killed.

For defence against such incidents, the larger navies have specialist teams, of which the US Navy SEALs are probably the best known. Founded in 1961, they served in Vietnam before taking on a mainly anti-terrorist role. The name is an acronym from their role in sea, air, and land warfare.

A great deal of modern naval activity involves operations to intercept illicit cargoes, such as drugs, guns, or people. For example,

AMPHIBIOUS LANDINGS
Royal Marines of 40 Commando come ashore in Kuwait onboard a landing vehicle from the Royal Navy's amphibious helicopter carrier Ocean, *which was commissioned in September 1999.*

Libya's 2004 curtailment of its weapons of mass destruction programme was partly triggered by the British and American seizure of parts en route to Libya. Such concerns bring the world's major navies into ever-closer contact with security services and customs agencies. Piracy off the Somali coast has greatly increased since 2003. Early in 2011, 47 ships and 800 seamen were being held hostage. World navies have found it difficult to agree a common policy on dealing with this menace.

ATTACK ON THE *COLE*
US Marines patrol the waters around the US destroyer Cole in the aftermath of the al-Qaeda bombing in the waters off Aden, Yemen, in October 2000. Damage to the vessel's hull is still clearly visible.

ISLAND SUPERSTRUCTURE *This area contains many of the command-and-control facilities, including radar and other electronic equipment. The ship is steered from the forward-facing bridge, while aircraft on deck are directed from the side-facing windows of the primary flight-control area. The island is painted with the ship's number and is also decorated with awards for bravery and excellence.*

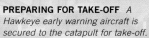

BRIDGE *The bridge provides navigation facilities for the captain or officer of the watch. It is also the station for the helmsman or woman steering the ship.*

PRIMARY FLIGHT CONTROL *All take-offs and landings are coordinated from this position overlooking the flight deck by the air boss in charge of all the ship's aircraft.*

CATAPULT CONTROL *A retractable pod allows the catapult crew to see what is happening on deck while protecting them from moving aircraft and their exhausts.*

CATAPULT *A shuttle (left), which can be attached to a plane's undercarriage, runs along a track in the deck (right). The shuttle is propelled along the track by a steam piston.*

PREPARING FOR TAKE-OFF *A Hawkeye early warning aircraft is secured to the catapult for take-off.*

TAKING OFF *An F/A-18 Hornet strike fighter is catapulted into the air. The deflection shield that has been raised behind it is cooled by sea water.*

DIALS *These gauges show steam pressure in the catapult.*

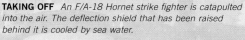

LANDING *An F-14 Tomcat can be seen here landing on the deck. The ship needs a headwind of at least 27 knots for landing and 22 knots for take-off.*

ARRESTING *An aircraft picks up one of four arrester wires with its tailhook to bring it to a sudden halt. If it had missed completely, the pilot would take off again and attempt another landing, a practice called touch and go.*

ARRESTING-GEAR ROOM *Below decks, huge pistons provide the power to stop the aircraft. If a plane lands too far off centre, the arrester wire has to be replaced.*

OPERATIONS ROOM *Staff in this room watch television pictures of the flight deck. They also use radar to control aircraft movements and protect the carrier from attack.*

ENGINE CONTROLS *The two reactors are controlled remotely. The ship can run for a year on a piece of fuel the size of a drink can.*

PUMPING FUEL *This is the No. 3 pump room, where fuel (known as JP5) for the aircraft and other engines is filtered and pumped up to the flight deck.*

FUEL SAMPLES *This JP5 fuel has been bottled for laboratory analysis.*

PHOTO PROFILE

GEORGE WASHINGTON

MODERN-DAY AIRCRAFT CARRIERS ARE THE WORLD'S LARGEST MILITARY VEHICLES. THE *GEORGE WASHINGTON* IS ONE OF SEVERAL CARRIERS IN SERVICE IN THE US NAVY.

ONE OF TEN SHIPS of the *Nimitz* class, the first of which was completed in 1975, the *George Washington* was built at Newport News in Virginia. Like other ships of the class, she has two nuclear reactors that allow her to operate for up to 18 years without refuelling. However, the carrier's 85 aircraft, which include fighter, strike, and transport planes, early warning aircraft, and helicopters, are much hungrier for fuel.

After being commissioned, in July 1992, *George Washington* made six deployments to the Persian Gulf and Mediterranean Sea. She was present at ceremonies to mark the 50th anniversary of D-Day in 1994, and in 1996 she hosted a conference of the warring factions in Bosnia & Herzegovina.

The flight deck of the *George Washington* is 1.8 hectares (4.5 acres) in area and is usually filled with aircraft landing, taking off, and being moved around, serviced, refuelled, and armed with weapons. For the uninitiated, this deck can be a dangerous place. The landing deck is angled to the port side to allow other activities to go on while aircraft are landing. A plane landing on the ship's flight deck is stopped when its tailhook catches an

MOBILE AIRBASE
Aircraft carriers have the strategic benefit of providing a mobile aircraft platform that can operate anywhere in international waters.

arrester wire, causing it to decelerate much more quickly than during an ordinary landing. On transport planes, passengers face backwards to reduce the physical shock. There are four catapults for launching aircraft: two right in the bows, which can be used while other aircraft are landing; and two more at the forward end of the angled deck. To the starboard side is the island superstructure, which overlooks the deck and houses the bridge and primary flight-control area.

Immediately below the flight deck are vast hangars, reached by the four huge aircraft lifts. These provide shelter and maintenance facilities for the aircraft. Below the hangars are facilities for the ship's combined crew and air wing of about 6,000 people. These include hospitals, galleys, and mess areas (15,000 meals are prepared each day for enlisted men and women alone), and a gymnasium.

Specification

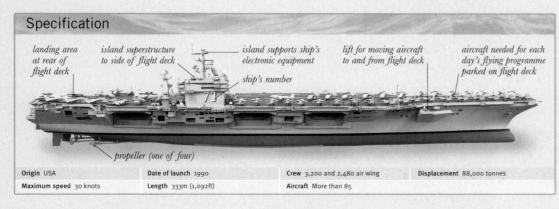

landing area at rear of flight deck

island superstructure to side of flight deck

island supports ship's electronic equipment

ship's number

lift for moving aircraft to and from flight deck

aircraft needed for each day's flying programme parked on flight deck

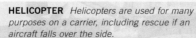

propeller (one of four)

Origin USA	Date of launch 1990	Crew 3,200 and 2,480 air wing	Displacement 88,000 tonnes
Maximum speed 30 knots	Length 333m (1,092ft)	Aircraft More than 85	

WEAPONS *The ship's aircraft can carry various weapons for air, sea, and land operations, including bombs, rockets, guided missiles, and torpedoes.*

HELICOPTER *Helicopters are used for many purposes on a carrier, including rescue if an aircraft falls over the side.*

MAINTENANCE *The engine-maintenance bay can be seen here, with the engine of an F-14 Tomcat in the foreground and an F/A-18 Hornet engine behind.*

PROPELLER SHAFT *This shaft drives one of the ship's four propellers.*

BRIEFING ROOM *Each seat is marked with an individual pilot's call sign.*

THE BAKERY *The bakery provides bread for the crew of 6,000. A row of ovens can be seen behind the two cooks kneading dough.*

OPERATING THEATRE *The ship has to be ready for almost any kind of illness, accident, or battle casualty. In an average year, the medical team sees over 10,000 patients and performs more than 100 surgical operations.*

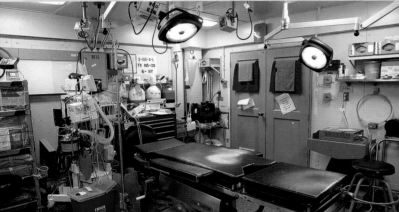

ANCHOR CHAINS *The two anchor chains run through the bows and are also stored there.*

WATER FOUNTAIN *American warships are alcohol-free, but drinking water is provided for the crew on all decks.*

DECK LIFT TO HANGAR *The ship's lifts can each carry two aircraft at a time. They can also be used to take containers of stores and spare parts to and from the hangars. Nimitz-class ships have four lifts in all.*

AIRCRAFT HANGAR *This is packed with aircraft undergoing maintenance by servicing crews, whose vests are colour-coded according to their jobs – for example, a green vest is worn by a maintenance petty officer, while a plane captain wears brown.*

MODERN WARSHIPS

Modern naval warfare is dominated by the aircraft, the submarine, and the guided missile. Nuclear submarines and aircraft carriers are the true capital ships of the age, although the surface warship, in the form of the destroyer and the frigate, still has a place. Most naval operations are directly connected with the shore, so amphibious warfare vessels are far more important than in the past. The proliferation of smaller navies has created a demand for cheap, small- and medium-sized ships, also used by the larger naval powers for inshore operations.

NEW CARRIER
The French aircraft carrier Charles de Gaulle *is shown here in the shipyard at Brest in 1997.*

Minesweepers

In the 1950s, fearing that the Soviets would mine their harbours in wartime, western European navies ordered large numbers of small minesweepers. They were often built in wood or fibreglass to reduce the danger from magnetic mines. One of a class of 118, HMS *Bronington* (below) was commanded by Prince Charles in 1976 and is now preserved in Manchester.

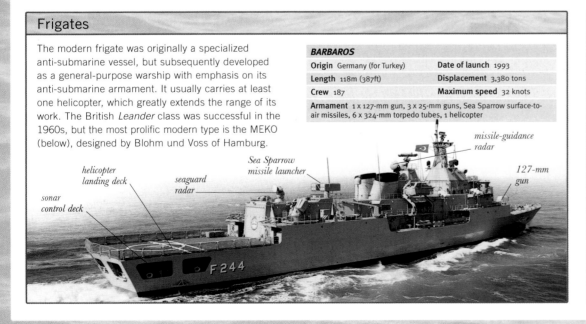

BRONINGTON

Origin Britain	**Date of launch** 1953
Length 46.3m (152ft)	**Displacement** 360 tons
Crew 29	**Maximum speed** 15 knots
Armament 1 x 40-mm gun, 2 x 20-mm guns, minesweeping gear	

Destroyers

As missiles and aircraft made direct combat between surface ships increasingly unlikely, the role of the destroyer in torpedo warfare began to disappear. The ship began, instead, carrying long-range anti-aircraft missiles to protect a fleet or convoy. HMS *Sheffield* (below) was one of the Royal Navy's Type-42 class destroyers. She was hit by an Argentine Exocet missile in the Falklands War and later sunk.

SHEFFIELD

Origin Britain	**Date of launch** 1971
Length 125m (410ft)	**Displacement** 3,850 tons
Crew 312	**Maximum speed** 30 knots
Armament 1 x 4.5-in gun, 2 x 20-mm guns, Sea Dart surface-to-air missiles, 1 helicopter, 6 x 12.75-in torpedo tubes	

ARLEIGH BURKE
The US Navy's Arleigh Burke-*class destroyers, introduced in 1991, are among the world's most sophisticated. They were designed to carry the Aegis integrated combat system.*

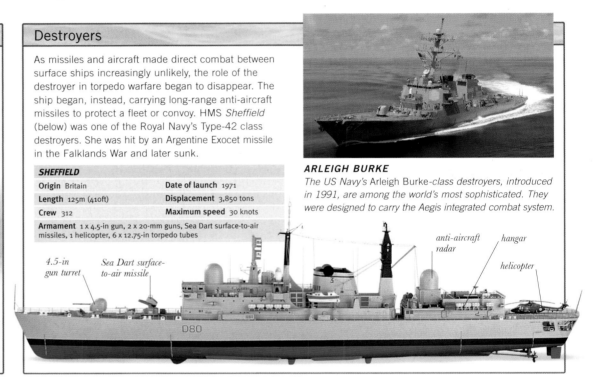

4.5-in gun turret

Sea Dart surface-to-air missile

anti-aircraft radar

hangar

helicopter

D80

Frigates

The modern frigate was originally a specialized anti-submarine vessel, but subsequently developed as a general-purpose warship with emphasis on its anti-submarine armament. It usually carries at least one helicopter, which greatly extends the range of its work. The British *Leander* class was successful in the 1960s, but the most prolific modern type is the MEKO (below), designed by Blohm und Voss of Hamburg.

BARBAROS

Origin Germany (for Turkey)	**Date of launch** 1993
Length 118m (387ft)	**Displacement** 3,380 tons
Crew 187	**Maximum speed** 32 knots
Armament 1 x 127-mm gun, 3 x 25-mm guns, Sea Sparrow surface-to-air missiles, 6 x 324-mm torpedo tubes, 1 helicopter	

sonar control deck

helicopter landing deck

seaguard radar

Sea Sparrow missile launcher

missile-guidance radar

127-mm gun

F244

Cruisers

The Soviet *Sverdlov*-class cruisers caught the attention of the West in the 1950s. The United States built or converted cruisers to carry anti-aircraft missiles in the 1950s or 1960s, but after that the type had no real role and was replaced by the destroyer and frigate.

SVERDLOV

Origin Soviet Union	**Date of launch** 1950
Length 210m (689ft)	**Displacement** 13,600 tons
Crew 1,250	**Maximum speed** 32.5 knots
Armament 12 x 152-mm guns, 12 x 100-mm guns, 30 x 37-mm guns, 10 x 533-mm torpedo tubes	

Aircraft carriers

The aircraft carrier proliferated in the years after the Second World War. Smaller navies, such as the Dutch and Canadian, were able to buy redundant American and British ships to get their first experience of naval aviation. But as aircraft became larger and faster, by the 1970s only the Americans could afford great numbers of full-size aircraft carriers; they built a dozen ships of the huge *Nimitz* class of more than 90,000 tons. The Soviets built the *Kiev* class of helicopter carriers, but their only true aircraft carrier was the *Kuznetsov* of 1985 In the early 1960s, the French came up with the *Clemenceau* and *Foch*, which were replaced by the *Charles de Gaulle* (below), the world's largest, most advanced non-American carrier. In 2011 she took part in the bombing of Libya.

CHARLES DE GAULLE

Origin France	**Date of launch** 1994
Length 261.2m (857ft)	**Displacement** 36,600 tons
Crew 1,256, plus aircrew/marines	**Maximum speed** 27 knots
Armament 4 surface-to-air missiles, 4 x 20-mm guns	**Aircraft** 34 aircraft, 4 helicopters

INVINCIBLE

The British *Invincible*-class aircraft carriers are smaller than their US or French counterparts but were successful with Harrier aircraft during the Falklands War of 1982.

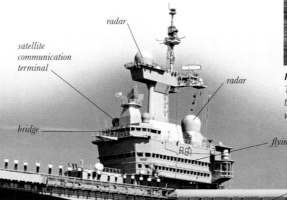

radar

satellite communication terminal

radar

bridge

flying control

foredeck for aircraft take-off

angled deck allows aircraft to overshoot

landing deck

Amphibious warfare vessels

Navies with global interests – especially those of the United States, Britain, and France – have kept up large amphibious warfare forces in order to intervene anywhere in the world. Compared with Second World War vessels, these tend to have longer range, since they are not designed for specific operations. Many carry helicopters, which can be used to land troops. Some have docks in the stern, to load landing craft with heavy vehicles, and others use bow ramps and doors, as did their predecessors. The assault ships of the American *Tarawa* class, including the *Nassau* (below), were built in the 1970s and have taken part in many campaigns, such as Vietnam and Iraq, alongside the smaller *Iwo Jima*-class helicopter carriers.

NASSAU

Origin United States	**Date of launch** 1978
Length 237m (778ft)	**Displacement** 38,761 tons
Crew 892, plus 1,903 troops	**Maximum speed** 24 knots
Armament 2 Sea Sparrow surface-to-air missiles, 3 x 5-in guns, 6 x 20-mm guns, helicopters or Harrier aircraft	

satellite communication terminal

bridge

radar

Harrier jump jets

Boeing CH-46A helicopter

landing deck

dock for landing craft

Nuclear submarines

Since the Americans built the *Nautilus* in the 1950s, nuclear-powered submarines have dominated the world's navies, although diesel-electric versions are still used by smaller navies. Nuclear submarines come in two types: attack submarines (SSNs), for use against enemy ships, and SSBNs, carrying nuclear-armed missiles. The Soviet *Kursk* missile submarine (below) was lost in 2000 in the Barents Sea.

KURSK

Origin Soviet Union	**Date of launch** 1994
Length 153m (502ft)	**Displacement** 16,000 tons
Crew 130	**Maximum speed** 28 knots
Armament 24 nuclear ballistic missiles, 6 torpedo tubes	

FLAG OF PANAMA

> 66 Containerization has been as dramatic and as important as the change from sail to steam. 99
>
> **MICHAEL GREY**, *Lloyd's List*, **1983**

SHIPS IN THE CONSUMER AGE

IMMEDIATELY AFTER THE SECOND WORLD WAR, IT SEEMED THAT THE COMMERCIAL SHIPPING INDUSTRY WOULD RETURN TO ITS PREVIOUS STATE, BUT MASSIVE CHANGE WAS COMING.

At the end of the Second World War, the British merchant fleet was still the largest in the world, although with only 22 per cent of world tonnage in 1948 compared to 26 per cent in 1939. Britain also had the largest ship-building industry in the world, partly because the German and Japanese shipyards lay in ruins. Technology was changing only slowly, and few wartime innovations had any real effect. Radar was fitted to merchant ships,

GERMAN RECOVERY
In the early 1950s, West Germany saw an economic boom. New shipyards such as this one in Hamburg sprung up to build new and larger vessels.

but they still had steam engines and needed large crews.

But behind this facade, the commercial world was already changing. The Soviet Union, China, and their satellite states were excluded from most global trade, but elsewhere the influence of the United States tended to create a world of free trade rather than competing

KEY EVENTS

1956 SUEZ CRISIS Temporary closure of the Suez Canal prompts a rethink in shipping, leading to the use of larger vessels that are capable of making longer voyages.

1958 AIR TRAVEL The Boeing 707 spells the end for passenger liners, forcing their owners to turn their attention to cruising.

1958 CONTAINERIZATION British and US shipping lines both begin integrated shipping services using standardized containers.

1959 ARRIVAL OF THE SUPERTANKER The Japanese vessel *Universe Apollo* is the first oil tanker heavier than 100,000 tons.

1966 TRANSATLANTIC CONTAINERS The American SeaLand line begins containerized shipping between the United States and Europe.

1973 OIL CRISIS Ships are driven to convert to diesel engines due to unstable oil supplies.

2009 *OASIS OF THE SEAS* The world's largest cruise liner, with more than 6,000 passengers, enters service.

2009 HOSTAGES The US navy rescues hostages from the *Maersk Alabama*, which had been seized by Somali pirates.

empires. World commerce boomed – it reached a level of 524 million tons by 1950, doubled by 1960, and doubled again by 1968. The longest boom in history continued until the early 1970s, when the 1973 Oil Crisis, during which a shortage of the fuel led to huge price rises, and a series of recessions took their toll. Since the 1980s growth has been steadier, and about 95 per cent of international trade still travels by sea. The world merchant fleet topped 100 million tons for the first time in 1955, and by 2009 there were more than 853 million tons registered, with 74,951 ships listed in *Lloyd's Register of Shipping*, an annual publication that details merchant vessels.

Changes to merchant shipping began to accelerate in the mid-1950s, as new roads were built to feed the automobile boom and road transport began to take over from rail. As heavy road vehicles are best kept away from city centres, new ports on fresh sites outside the major cities began to be developed, and traditional city-centre docks declined. The temporary closure of the Suez Canal after the 1956 crisis (see p.341) forced ship owners to think about longer alternative routes that could be made economical only with larger ships. Increased affluence and a consumer boom in the United States and western Europe, combined with rising wage costs, made it ever

more attractive for manufacturers to produce goods in cheaper parts of the world and transport them to market by ship. Meanwhile, new shipbuilding industries arose from the devastation of Germany and Japan, soon challenging the established shipyards.

Arrival of the supertanker

Until the 1950s, oil tankers rarely weighed more than 20,000 tons, but from then until the 1970s they grew rapidly. The Japanese constructed most of the record-breakers of the era, including the *Sinclare Petrolore* of 56,000 tons. which was built in 1956; the *Universe Apollo*,

CONTAINER GIANTS
This huge cargo ship belongs to the Danish Maersk Line, which is planning even larger ships that will be able to carry up to 18,000 containers. Ships such as this one are vital to the global economy in the 21st century.

which broke the 100,000-ton barrier in 1959; and the *Idemitsu Maru*, which became the first tanker of more than 200,000 tons in 1966. The 1970s saw two French vessels, the *Batillus* and *Bellamya*, break the half-million-ton limit. The largest tanker in the world today is the *Jahre Viking*. She was built in Japan as the *Seawise Giant* in 1976, but was sunk by a missile attack in the Persian Gulf during the Iran–Iraq war. She was later refloated, rebuilt, and renamed, and now has a weight of some 564,000 tons. At 458m (1,504ft) long, the rebuilt *Jahre Viking* is almost twice the length of the *Titanic* and could engulf the Eiffel Tower laid on its side with room to spare. But despite this exception, the Oil Crisis of 1973 and the sheer difficulty of handling such large vessels meant that later supertankers were less ambitious – most large modern tankers are between 200,000 and 285,000 tons. Such huge ships are enormously expensive to build, but the rising cost of oil means they can pay for themselves in just a handful of transatlantic journeys.

Containers and consumerism

The cargo container is a potent symbol of the modern world, and has transformed merchant shipping. It is uncompromisingly rectangular, and its functional doors and corrugated sides make it irredeemably ugly to many eyes. But this successor to the classical amphora and the medieval barrel (see p.44) is key to transporting goods to the world's farthest corners.

One early attempt at integrated transport was the *Container Venturer* of 1958 (see p.367). Designed to operate between England and Northern Ireland, she carried round-topped wooden containers that were used on British railways. At the same time, the American SeaLand shipping line began a service between New York and Florida using 16-m (40-ft) and 8-m (20-ft) containers, suitable for use on US roads. It took time to set up the necessary infrastructure, and it was 1966 before SeaLand's ship *Fairland* made the first transatlantic container voyage, but after that the advance was rapid. With fast turnaround, a modern ship can carry up to ten times as much cargo per year as a predecessor of similar size. Container ship capacity is measured in TEUs – twenty-foot equivalent units. The Maersk Triple-E Class will hold 18,000 TEUs.

Some goods require special vessels to transport them efficiently. Car transporters take vehicles by the thousand from producers, mainly on the Pacific Rim, to consumers in the West.

TOKYO MARU
At just under 200,000 tons, the Tokyo Maru *(right) was briefly the world's largest tanker in 1966. Most of the tanker's functions are run from a control room (above), allowing such ships to operate with a minimal crew.*

HIGH-SPEED CRAFT

Designing a conventional ship to travel at more than about 36 knots is very difficult. A vessel travelling above this speed generates a very large bow wave, and in effect the ship must push itself uphill as it moves forward. Operators of ferry services are under pressure to increase speed and have experimented with several new ship designs to get around the problem.

A hovercraft rides on a cushion of air that lifts it clear of the water, so high speed is possible. But it travels over the waves rather than through them and can be very uncomfortable in rough weather. The hydrofoil has wings beneath the hull, which lift it up at high speed. It is expensive, and this solution is suitable only for relatively small and lightweight vessels. The catamaran uses the ancient principle of twin hulls, and

HOVERCRAFT
This British hovercraft, the Princess Margaret, *which was photographed in 1968, spent 30 years plying the route across the English Channel.*

has proved successful on ferry services, sometimes halving the time required to complete a journey.

The SWATH (small water-plane area, twin hull) is a catamaran variation, with the main deck lifted above the water and supported by two large flotation cylinders immersed deep in the water, below the effects of the bow wave. It may offer a long term solution to the problems of speed and seasickness.

EARLY HYDROFOIL
The hydrofoil Fairlight, *one of the first to enter commercial service, races across Sydney Harbour, Australia. Modern hydrofoils have grown much larger and faster.*

Gas carriers fall into two types, both dominated by the huge tanks along their hull. Liquid natural gas (LNG) carriers are often filled in Indonesia, Malaysia, and Australia. The gas is cooled until it condenses into a liquid and then exported to countries that lack the fuel. Liquid petroleum gas (LPG) is a by-product of the oil-refining process and is used to make plastics. The major trade routes are from oil exporters such as Saudi Arabia and Kuwait to nations such as Japan.

Bulk carriers transport dry cargo in large quantities. The first such vessel to be purpose-built was the 19,000-ton *Cassiopeia*, built in 1955

in Sweden. As with other types of cargo ship, size has tended to increase, but bulk carriers are sometimes limited by the need to use the Suez and Panama Canals. The largest reach 170,000 tons, and far larger ships are planned. Smaller, more versatile carriers of up to 49,000 tons are often equipped with gear for handling their own cargo, such as ore, wood chip, coal, or grain.

New types of ship have created a demand for new ports, often dedicated to a specific cargo. These are usually sited away from city centres, and turnaround time is brief. For example, in 1905 the P&O liner *Banca* spent 172 days in port, 173 days at sea, and 20 days under repair. In 1991 the container ship *Evergrowth* spent 272 days at sea, 93 in port, and none under repair.

GAS CARRIER
The specialist Norwegian tanker Norman Lady *is designed for transporting liquid natural gas chilled to a temperature of -163°C (-261°F).*

cylindrical gas tanks are optimum shape to hold pressurized gas

thick insulation isolates tanks from rest of ship

raised superstructure for unobstructed views

ARISTOTLE ONASSIS

After emigrating from Greece to Argentina in 1923 with just $250, Aristotle Onassis (1906–1975) set up as a tobacco merchant. He soon became Greek consul and bought his first six ships in 1932, switching to the Panamanian flag to avoid restrictions. After the Second World War, Onassis built his first two oil tankers in Norway, and by the mid-1950s he had the largest tanker fleet in the world, using his contacts among the oil-rich rulers of Saudi Arabia. He also sought the company of the famous – Winston Churchill stayed on his yacht, and in 1968 he married Jackie Kennedy, widow of the US president.

Flags of convenience

After the Second World War, a new breed of shipowner, mainly Greek at first, began to challenge the established Western shipping lines. Greek shipowners had been prominent since the late 19th century, and in the 1950s they bought up redundant Liberty ships to run cut-price services and used Norwegian expertise to enter the tanker market. They prospered during the 1956 Suez Crisis and moved into the bulk carrier market in the 1960s.

From the 1960s, other nations came to prominence in the market. Evergreen shipping of Taiwan, for example, was founded in 1968 and moved strongly into the container market after the Oil Crisis. The Chinese Ocean Shipping Company (COSCO) was founded in 1961 and developed into a $17-billion company. The Soviet Union also developed a strong merchant fleet in the 1970s and 1980s, although

CONTAINER TRANSPORT
This vessel is fully loaded with its containers of freight. Nearly half of the world's merchant ships are registered under flags of convenience.

that has since declined. A few European lines, such as Maersk in Denmark and P&O in Britain, have continued to trade effectively. Meanwhile, US shipping lines, largely unsupported by their government, were among the first to adopt flags of convenience.

Many modern shipping lines have no national loyalties – they are free to register their ships in the countries that offer the best terms. The term flag of convenience originally meant a neutral flag flown by a ship in wartime, allowing it to continue business, but since the 1930s it has indicated a nationality used by ships that belong only nominally to the country in question, for

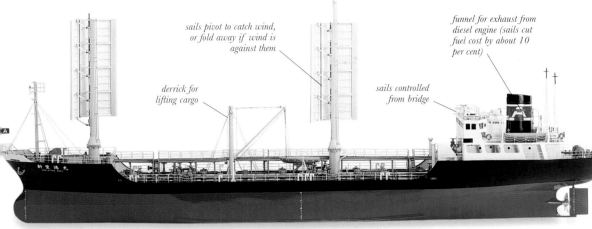

sails pivot to catch wind, or fold away if wind is against them

derrick for lifting cargo

sails controlled from bridge

funnel for exhaust from diesel engine (sails cut fuel cost by about 10 per cent)

RETURN TO SAIL POWER
Some modern ships have made use of old technology. The Shin Aitoku Maru, which was completed in 1980, was the first tanker to be fitted with computer-controlled sails. However, this experimental design was not widely adopted.

reasons of regulation, wage rates, or taxation. Pioneers of the practice included Norwegian shipping magnate Erling Naess, who led the way with supertankers and bulk carriers in the 1950s and 1960s. As early as 1930, he had seen the advantages of registering ships under obscure flags such as that of Panama, to evade the high wages, taxes, and regulations of the more established shipping countries. Naess argued that Western shipowners had to do this in order to survive. Critics claim that flags of convenience create poor employment conditions and low safety standards.

Flags of convenience are difficult to define in law, but it is usually clear which countries provide them. The countries with the highest numbers of ships registered in 1981 were Liberia, Panama, and Honduras. More recently, Belize and Malta have become prominent. Forty-eight per cent of world shipping was registered under flags of convenience by 1998. However, in terms of ownership the league table is very different. Greece was the leading shipowning nation in 1996, followed by Japan, the United States, and Norway. As the global fleet soared in size, the once-mighty British merchant fleet dwindled, until it was only the eighth biggest in the late 1990s.

THE END OF A TANKER
The downside of globalization is shown by rusting hulls of tankers, littering a beach in Chittagong, Bangladesh. Ships are sent to such locations for scrapping and salvage because it is cheap, but the work is dangerous, the waste is hazardous, and the workers are ill-equipped.

Engines and innovations
Despite their increased size, modern merchant ships have very small crews. Electronic navigation and control reduce the workload, and modern engines need little maintenance.

The steam turbine was standard for ocean-going ships after the war. The diesel engine, a type of internal-combustion engine, was first used in 1911 on the Danish ship *Selandia*. It made slow progress among coasters until the 1950s, when supercharging, a method of increasing power, made possible larger engines with greater ranges. Diesel received a major boost during the 1973 Oil Crisis, because it used cheap, low-grade oil in small quantities, and it is now the standard for most merchant ships. Nuclear power was tried with the American *Savannah*, launched in 1962, but it proved too expensive and has yet to be taken further.

The shipping business is highly competitive, and owners are extremely conscious of cost. Advances in technology have allowed them to reduce crews dramatically – the 5,995-ton *Banca* needed a crew of 90 in 1905, but the modern 37,000-ton container ship *Evergrowth* has only 17 crewmen. This means that an enormous ship may typically have just three or four people on duty at once.

Ships have multinational crews and owners, and it is difficult for them to become symbols of national prestige as they did in the first half of the 20th century. Modern shipowners tend to value their privacy. The Greek magnates Aristotle Onassis and Stavros Niarchos were perhaps the last to court publicity – today the airline business tends to attract more flamboyant characters.

In this climate, international regulators find it difficult to keep up with problems and rely on support from the governments in question. The International Maritime Organisation, a United Nations Agency based in London, is the main body for regulating the industry. It finds its workload growing ever larger, with shipping lanes more crowded than ever and less developed countries jumping onto the flag-of-convenience bandwagon in increasing numbers. Vessels operating under these flags account for a disproportionate number of shipping accidents, and the Safety of Life at Sea (SOLAS) convention frequently has to be revised to take account of changing working practices.

CONTAINER TERMINAL
Hong Kong Harbour is a transport hub for the Far East. Here standard containers are unloaded from a ship using huge overhanging cranes. With goods stowed in containers, unloading takes hours, rather than days.

The end of the Atlantic liner

The great liners returned to their peacetime trades soon after 1945, and for a time they boomed. The US government, for example, subsidized the *United States*, whose top speed was a state secret, as she was intended to double as a troop carrier in the event of war.

Transatlantic air services were now available on piston-engined planes, but the journey took about 12 hours. The British Comet jet airliner was too small and its range was too limited to make an impact on the liner business, but in 1958 the picture changed completely. The American Boeing 707 could cross the Atlantic in six or seven hours – a short enough flight for passengers to accept cramped conditions. Within a year, more people were crossing the Atlantic by air than by sea. Regular transatlantic passenger services died out by 1973, although longer-distance trades lasted slightly longer. Fortunately, the end of the old passenger lines coincided with the great post-war leisure boom, and the liners were quickly adapted for cruising. Cruising was invented in the 1830s by Arthur Anderson, founder of P&O, but took time to

PASSENGER MEMENTOES
In the great age of liners, luggage tags and labels frequently had bold, colourful designs. Today, liner ephemera such as this is highly collectable.

become widespread. In the late 1880s, two ships offered cruises in Norwegian waters, and Mediterranean cruises began soon afterwards. This set the pattern for the future – most cruise passengers prefer warm climates, but there is a substantial market for much colder areas, such as Alaska. Cruising flourished in the 1920s and 1930s, although it still had an image of great luxury.

UNDER CONSTRUCTION
The past decade has seen a boom in the building of new cruise ships. Here, the Norwegian Star *nears completion at the Meyer Werft works in Papenburg, Germany. Launched in 2001, she now cruises the waters around Hawaii.*

Today, there is a clear difference between European and American attitudes to cruising. American lines such as Disney tend to see the ship itself as the experience and have ships with elaborate interiors offering all kinds of facilities. Europeans are more interested in visiting ports and sightseeing, perhaps with an educational angle. A strong Soviet cruise fleet was created in the 1980s, as a way to earn foreign currency. The cruise market continues to expand, and although cruising retains its opulent image, it is no longer the preserve of the ultra-rich.

Luxury cruising forms a stark contrast to the world's other sea passengers, who are often among the very poorest people. Refugees from countries such as Vietnam and Albania are

IN THE LAP OF LUXURY
The upper class cabins of the Queen Mary 2, *photographed here before her maiden voyage, mark a return to the days when cruising was a truly opulent experience.*

known as boat people, and often travel in the most desperate and dangerous conditions in the hope of being picked up and transported to a more prosperous nation. Smaller numbers of refugees also hide in containers to reach Western ports, often at great personal risk.

New shipbuilders

Welding and prefabrication, developed to build ships quickly during the Second World War, are the dominant techniques of modern shipbuilding. Plates and parts of frames are cut out automatically from data provided by computer, although bending of plates is still done on machines that have not changed much since the 19th century. Ships are, in effect, constructed from the inside out, around their engines, cabins, and fittings. Sub-assemblies are created under cover using automatic welding, put together to form a vertical slice of ship, and then welded to their neighbours along great seams. This approach requires detailed computer planning for the position of every element and leaves little to the initiative of those on the building berth.

British shipbuilders paid the price of complacency after the Second World War. They were sure that no-one would ever replace their skills and reputation, and at the same time lacked the economic confidence to invest in new machinery. They were already behind the Americans in the technology of prefabrication and welding, and labour relations were appalling. The first challenge came from the rebuilt shipbuilding industries of Germany and Japan, which offered virgin sites, new machinery, dedicated workforces, and, for a time, low wages. They were followed by those of other Far Eastern nations.

In 1996 Japan was the largest shipbuilding nation, but by 2008 had been overtaken by South Korea with more than 50 per cent of world tonnage. In turn, South Korea is likely to be overtaken by China.

The Cunard liner, the *Queen Mary 2*, set sail on her maiden voyage from Southampton, England in January 2004. The immense vessel, which measures 345m (1,132ft) long and weighs 150,000 tons, is symbolic of recent changes to the world of commercial shipping, in which nationalities are blurred and flags have little meaning. Despite being owned by a company with traditional British roots, she was built at a shipyard in St. Nazaire, northern France.

THE LARGEST LINER
The Oasis of the Seas *was completed in Turku, Finland in October 2009. She is the biggest cruise ship in the world and can carry 6,000 passengers. She belongs to the Royal Caribbean Line and has a cruising speed of 22 knots.*

MODERN MERCHANT SHIPS

Merchant ships have become increasingly specialized over the years and are usually built for particular types of cargo, passengers, or routes. They are designed for maximum payload and fuel economy, fast turnaround, and minimum crew. High standards of living in the West and full employment in the Pacific Rim depend on ships that can transport goods economically. The passenger ship has been replaced by the roll-on-roll-off ferry over short distances and by the airliner over longer ones, but the cruise-ship industry continues to grow.

SPECIALIZED TANKER
This tanker is used for transporting chemicals. The crane in the foreground is used for the purpose of unloading the vessel.

Bulk carriers

Bulk carriers are the workhorses of the modern international shipping community, usually chartered by shipbrokers to carry specific cargoes on behalf of individual customers. The successors to the tramp steamers of the past, they are simple, unsophisticated, but highly efficient ships that transport commodities such as coal, grain, and mineral ores such as phosphate and bauxite. Although more than 6,000 of them are in use, they are little known to the general public, perhaps because of a good safety record compared with tankers. They include: ships of up to 80,000 tons, which are known as Panamax ships and are the largest size permitted on the Panama Canal; and Capesize ships, which are even bigger, at up to 150,000 tons. The *Heng Shan Hai* (below) is owned by the Chinese Ocean Shipping Company, or Cosco.

HENG SHAN HAI

Origin China	**Date of launch** 1998
Length 225m (738ft)	
Tonnage 40,215 tons	

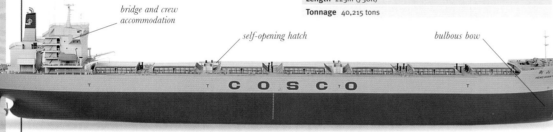

bridge and crew accommodation

self-opening hatch

bulbous bow

Oil tankers

The huge growth of the oil tanker in the 1950s and 1960s was one of the most spectacular features of modern shipping. At 550,000 tons, the *Batillus* and her sister *Bellamya* were the largest tankers ever built, until the oil crisis of 1973 halted development.

ATLANTIC LIBERTY

Origin Japan	**Date of launch** 1995
Length 412.2m (1,352ft 4in)	
Tonnage 164,733 tons	

Gas carriers

Specialized gas carriers emerged in the 1950s on a small scale, but, like most ships, they have grown in size since then. There are two main types. Some carry liquefied natural gas, for example, from Indonesia to Japan, to power industry, generate electricity, and heat homes. In all, 138 ships, of 60,000–80,000 tons each, were employed in this trade in 2004. Liquefied petroleum gas tankers carry by-products of the oil industry from refineries, often to be used in making plastic goods. Unlike other types of ship, their market depends on world petrol consumption rather than any normal supply-and-demand factors within the trade itself. Both types require large and prominent tanks, as well as miles of piping to keep the cargo cool.

AQUARIUS

Origin United States	**Date of launch** 1977
Length 285.3m (936ft)	
Tonnage 95,084 tons	

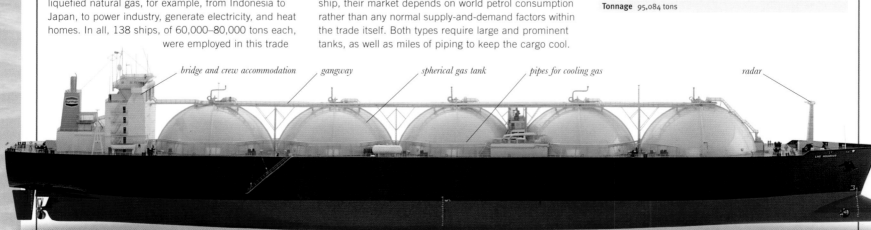

bridge and crew accommodation   *gangway*   *spherical gas tank*   *pipes for cooling gas*   *radar*

Container ships

The container market in 2010 included over 4,800 ships. The most common type is the "handysize", which can take between one and 2,000 6-m (20-ft) units, but there is growth among the largest class: more than 100 ships can carry more than 8,000 containers each. The *Ever Royal* (below), owned by Evergreen Shipping of Taiwan, was built for a round-the-world service.

CONTAINER VENTURER

EVER ROYAL

Origin Japan		**Date of launch** 1993	
Length 294m (964ft 6in)		**Tonnage** 53,359 tons	
Container capacity 4,200 x 6-m (20-ft) containers			

containers stacked on deck — *bridge and crew accommodation*

Heavy-lift ships

Heavy-lift ships were developed mainly by the oil industry for moving equipment. Some use cranes, while others have hulls that can be flooded to submerge them enough to lift the object.

SWAN

Origin Netherlands	**Date of launch** 1981
Length 180.5m (592ft)	
Tonnage 22,788 tons	

Cruise ships

Cruising has flourished since the 1960s. By the end of the 20th century, more than eight million people took part every year. The industry is still expanding despite a short-lived decline in the aftermath of September 11, and in 2003 nearly 400 cruise ships were operating. Ships are almost always purpose-built today. All offer some kind of entertainment, and some make it the main feature. When she was launched, the *Grand Princess* (below), built in Italy, was the pride of the P&O fleet.

GRAND PRINCESS

Origin Italy (for Britain)		**Date of launch** 1999	
Length 290m (951ft)		**Tonnage** 109,000 tons	
Passengers 2,600, plus 1,150 crew		**Maximum speed** 22.5 knots	

QUEEN MARY 2

passenger deck
tennis court
exhaust pipes
passenger deck
bow thrusters
cabins with balconies

P&O

Ro-ro ferries

The roll-on-roll-off (ro-ro) ferry was based on Second World War landing craft and designed to load and unload motor vehicles quickly. The British *Bardic Ferry* (right) of 1957 was the first purpose-built one, but much larger ships were built over the years. There were doubts about their safety after accidents to the *Herald of Free Enterprise* and *Estonia* in the 1980s, because the open car deck can flood very easily, but improvements have been made. Speed is important, and fast craft, such as the *SeaCat* (left) are being developed. Ferries are essential links among the Norwegian fiords, Greek and British islands, and in less developed countries.

BARDIC FERRY

Origin Britain		**Date of launch** 1957	
Length 103.3m (339ft)		**Tonnage** 2,550 tons	
Vehicles 69 commercial vehicles, 13 cars, plus 74 passengers			

SEACAT FERRY

BOHUS

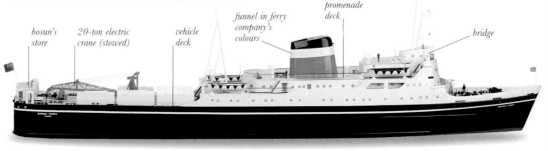

bosun's store
20-ton electric crane (stowed)
vehicle deck
funnel in ferry company's colours
promenade deck
bridge

LIFEJACKET

LEISURE, PLEASURE, AND SPORT

SINCE THE END OF THE SECOND WORLD WAR, THE OWNERSHIP OF MARITIME LEISURE CRAFT HAS EXPLODED, AND MANY NEW WATERSPORTS AND EVENTS HAVE FIRMLY ESTABLISHED THEMSELVES ON THE INTERNATIONAL STAGE.

> 66 There is nothing –
> absolutely nothing – half
> so much worth doing as
> messing about in boats. 99
>
> **KENNETH GRAHAME,**
> *The Wind in the Willows,* **1908**

KEY EVENTS

1958 CUP REVIVAL After a break of two decades, the America's Cup is revived. It is retained by the United States until 1983, when it is won by Australia.

1960 SURFIN' USA The sport of surfing gains popularity in California, USA, having already established a foothold in Australia.

1967 AROUND THE WORLD The English sailor Francis Chichester completes a single-handed voyage around the world in 226 days in *Gypsy Moth IV.*

1973 WHITBREAD TROPHY The first Whitbread Round-the-Word Yacht Race is staged. The Mexican yacht *Sayula II* wins.

1978 RECORD BREAKER Australian Ken Warby breaks the water-speed record, reaching 511.1kph (317.6mph). (The fastest recorded speed for a propellor-driven boat is 330.7kph/ 205.494mph, which was reached by Russ Wicks in 2000.)

2001 VENDÉE GLOBE The Frenchman Michel Desjoyeaux wins the Vendée Globe race in a record 93 days. The British woman Ellen MacArthur is second.

2005 AROUND THE WORLD Ellen MacArthur becomes the fastest person to sail round the world single-handed – a record broken by the Frenchman Francis Joyon in 2008.

Improved living standards in some countries, the opportunity for earlier retirement, new materials for the mass production of boats, electronic technology, and the desire to escape from the confined environment of modern cities, have all contributed to a vast increase in the number of people who use the sea for sport and recreation. Statistically, watersports are enormously popular. For example, in the United States in 1998, 17 million boats were owned and nearly 75 million people (almost a quarter of the population) took part in some form of recreational boating activity. Australia, Britain, France, and New Zealand are just some of the other nations in which yachting and other watersports have boomed. With the increased popularity of such sports, there is great pressure on space in popular yachting areas, such as the south of England. More than 16,000 vessels were based in 14 harbours in the area around the Solent (the stretch of water between the Isle of Wight and mainland England) in 1974, a figure that rose to nearly 28,000 by 1989.

Epic voyages

Besides the many thousands who take part in boating at weekends and during holidays, there are millions more who follow the activities of sailing heroes and heroines, mostly in long-distance voyages or races. They are not voyages of discovery in the historic sense, but they display human endurance at its limits and are particularly popular in

WHITE-WATER RAFTING
The post-war period has seen a diversification of watersports, with adventure activities, such as white-water rafting, gaining popularity. Sports involving boats have also become more accessible, as many leisure craft are now mass produced.

European countries, such as France and Britain. In the spirit of Joshua Slocum in the 19th century (see p.266), mariners have set their sights on single-handed endeavour. One of the most successful such sailors was the former pilot Francis Chichester. In 1966, he began an historic voyage when he sailed his 16-m (53-ft) ketch *Gypsy Moth IV* from Plymouth, England, with the intention of

RACING MONARCH
Watersports are extremely widespread in Scandinavia. By 1989, 40 per cent of Norwegian families had some type of boat. This photograph, which was taken in 2004, shows King Harald of Norway competing in a yacht race off Florida, USA.

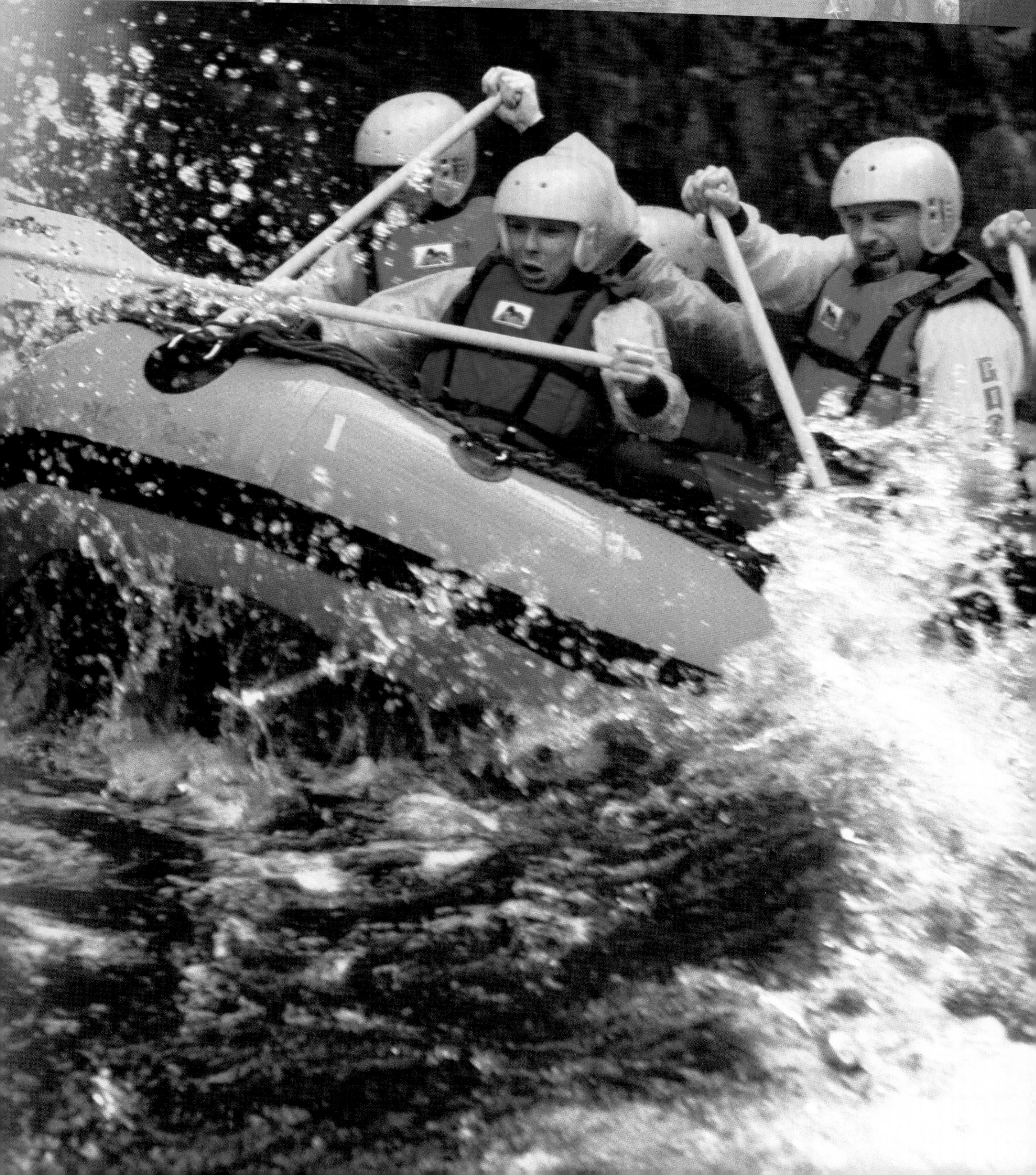

circumnavigating the globe. The voyage wasn't without incident. The yacht's steering mechanism broke 3,700km (2,300 miles) from Australia, and, after a stop-off in Sydney, she capsized. Sailing around Cape Horn, Chichester faced waves that reached 15m (50ft) high. Despite such challenges, on 28 May 1967, after 226 days at sea, half-a-million people welcomed the 65-year-old back to Plymouth at the end of a voyage that broke numerous records. He was the first person to sail around the world single-handed, making just one stop.

Chichester's achievement sparked further record-breaking attempts to sail around the world. In 1968 the British yachtsman Robin Knox-Johnston became the first person to sail the world non-stop, in his ketch *Suhaili*. He travelled more than 48,000km (30,000 miles) in 313 days. In 1971, the Scottish sailor Chay Blyth became the first person to sail solo around the world from west to east, sailing with the prevailing winds against him. The first woman to circumnavigate the globe single-handed was New Zealand-born Naomi James. She finished her voyage in 272 days, arriving back at her port of departure, Dartmouth, England, in June 1978. Her achievement was all the more extraordinary given that James had little sailing experience.

Racing yachts

With the surge in popularity of yachting, many different types of race have emerged, from round-the-world races to small amateur competitions. In 1958, after a break of more than 20 years, the America's Cup (see p.265) was revived. It was dominated by the United States until 1983, when *Australia II* took the

RECORD BREAKER

British yachtswoman Ellen MacArthur gained fame by coming second in the Vendée Globe round-the-world race and is seen here sailing Kingfisher back to the UK.

trophy to the southern hemisphere. The next race was held off Perth, Australia, in 1987. It was the first outside American waters since 1851, and resulted in the cup's return to the United States. New Zealand has also proved successful challengers, winning the trophy in 1995 and 2000. In 2003 the yacht *Alinghi*, representing land-locked Switzerland, took the prestigious prize.

Other internationally renowned yacht races include the biennial Fastnet Race. The 978.5-km (608-mile) contest begins at the Isle of Wight, heads across the Irish Sea, and circles the Fastnet rock off the coast of Cork, before returning to England. The race attracts yachts of all classes and mariners of all abilities, despite its arduous course. The Fastnet Race alternates with the 1,062-km (660-mile) Newport to Bermuda Race. The route starts at Rhode Island and crosses the unpredictable waters of the Gulf Stream, to finish at the northwest Atlantic island of Bermuda. In Australia, the 1,000-km (630-mile) Sydney to Hobart Race was inaugurated in 1945 and has taken place every December since. The Admiral's Cup is a prestigious series of races that has taken place every two years since 1957, in which teams from different nations compete in a series of inshore and offshore races off the English coast. Transatlantic races are also organized. The Observer Single-Handed Transatlantic Yacht Race (OSTAR) was first won by Francis Chichester in 1960. The title was next taken by the French yachtsman Eric Tabarly in 1964 (see panel, below), and his compatriots have won nearly every title since. Another major transatlantic race is the Route de Rhum, which began in 1978 and traverses the ocean from St. Malo, Brittany, to the island of Gaudeloupe in the Caribbean.

Races that involve circumnavigation have also proved to be a thrilling addition to the international yachting calendar. The first Whitbread Round-the-World Yacht Race (now

VIEW FROM ABOVE

This photograph was taken from the top of the 27.4-m (90-ft) mast of the yacht USA during trials for the 1987 America's Cup. Despite USA being a state-of-the-art vessel, the United States was represented by another yacht, Stars and Stripes, which was the eventual winner of the race.

ERIC TABARLY

One of France's greatest yachtsmen, Eric Tabarly (1931–98) began his nautical career as a child, when his father bought a 19th-century yacht called *Pen Duick*. In 1964, he won the Observer Single-Handed Transatlantic Yacht Race in 27 days, 3 hours, and 56 minutes in *Pen Duick II*. Tabarly became a French national hero. Racing *Pen Duick III*, he won several titles in 1967, including the Fastnet and Plymouth to La Rochelle races. He won his last major race, the Transat Jacques Vabre, with fellow Frenchman Yves Parlier in 1997. Tragically, Tabarly fell from his yacht, *Pen Duick V*, and drowned in the Irish Sea in 1998.

known as the Volvo Ocean Race) began in September 1973 and is staged every four years. Crews of up to 12 take on the challenge, which involves navigating some of the toughest sailing routes in the world, among them passages through the Southern Ocean and around Cape Horn. The single-handed Vendée Globe yacht race was first undertaken in 1989. It is a remarkable feat of endurance, which starts in the French port of Sables d'Olonne, Brittany, and follows a course that includes passages in the South Atlantic, Southern Ocean, and around Cape Horn, before returning to France. In 2001 the race was won by the Frenchman Michel Desjoyeaux, who completed the course in a record 93 days. The British sailor Ellen MacArthur arrived in second place, becoming the fastest woman ever to sail around the world.

Dinghies and cruisers

For every vastly expensive boat involved in a high-profile competition, there are hundreds of others that take part in regional regattas and

MULTIHULL YACHTS

Catamarans and trimarans use more than one hull to give stability using principles developed in Polynesia many centuries ago. They can be very fast under sail, like the French trimaran Crepes Whaou *crewed by Franck-Yves Escoffier and Jacques Vabre.*

races, or are used to cruise from port to port. Yacht races are common at most local yacht clubs. Sailing dinghies are primarily used for such competitions, although they are also used in international sailing competitions, for example the Olympics. Dinghies are generally open-decked craft that are constructed with a retractable centreboard or daggerboard. There are many types of dinghy, ranging from basic single-handed learner craft to more responsive high-performance vessels. Some dinghies belong to "one-design" classes, which have been developed for individual clubs to suit their local conditions. Among the most popular training dinghies are the Mirror Class, the Optimist (see left), the American Sunfish, and the French Vaurien, all of which are used internationally. In high-performance classes, larger and faster vessels, such as the Laser 4000 and 5000 and the International 505, are widely used. Another

type of sailing craft that has proved extremely popular, particularly for mariners who yearn for high-speed sailing, is the catamaran. This consists of two narrow hulls that are connected by a fabric area called a trampoline.

The sailing cruiser, which is used for day trips or longer voyages, ranges in length from 5.5m to 114m (18ft to 45ft), and includes accommodation space for the crew. The great majority are single masted with a sloop rig, which has a gaff or Bermuda mainsail set aft of the mast and a headsail to its fore. Cruisers often have a fin-shaped ballast keel, which is weighted with lead or iron. This gives extra stability, and ensures that it is virtually impossible for the vessel to capsize, whatever the weather conditions. Cruiser hulls are constructed of wood, steel, or fibreglass.

diagonal sprit support

four-sided spritsail made from synthetic material

boom, on which sail pivots

mast is light and easy to handle

main body of craft is open

rudder is moved using tiller to steer dinghy

daggerboard slides up and down depending on depth of water

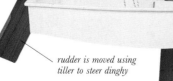

FIT FOR A KID

Optimist dinghies were introduced in the USA in 1947 and today form one of the largest dinghy classes in the world. They are single-handed craft that are very simple to use and suitable for children from the age of eight.

FOUL-WEATHER SUIT
Jackets such as this one are manufactured with light, waterproof materials for use on long sailing voyages and in adverse weather conditions. Many jackets are equipped with satellite-contacting devices that are activated on entering the water.

high-powered light

fluorescent material for high visibility

reflective panel

flare gun for use in emergencies

tag to inflate lifejacket

hook attached to safety line

whistle to attract attention

inflatable life jacket

insulated inner layer

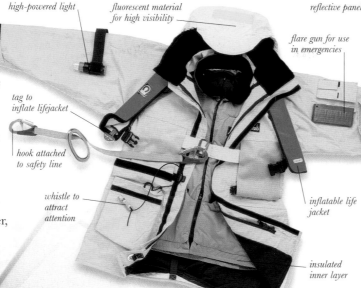

GEARED UP
Protected by all-weather outfits, this sailing crew negotiates the waters around South Island, New Zealand. The correct protective equipment is essential for every sailor and needs to be appropriately selected for the conditions.

The motor cruiser or motor yacht is an increasingly popular type of craft, in fact their numbers have overtaken sail-powered vessels. Without sails to steady them, they can be a rough ride in bad weather, but they are still much used on inland waterways, such as rivers and canals. Hybrid craft, which attempt to perform with equal effectiveness under both sail and engine power, are also available.

Luxury yachts continue to flourish. At the end of 2003, the British company Vosper Thornycroft launched one of the world's largest single-masted vessels, the 76-m (240-ft) *Mirabella V*, which is fitted with everything a wealthy owner could wish for, including a sauna, a gym, and a wine cellar. However, the market is constrained not by a paucity of rich buyers but by the lack of suitable harbours for such vessels and a shortage of trained crew.

Technology and innovation
Since the Second World War, leisure craft have benefited from numerous inventions and innovations. Fibreglass was first used on ships during the war, as it is largely immune to magnetic mines and invisible to radar. From the late 1950s, it was used to mould the hulls of yachts and power boats, which allowed mass production of these craft for the first time and spurred the huge boom in recreational sailing. Most modern sailing craft carry some kind of auxiliary power, either a petrol-driven outboard motor or a diesel engine, as it is virtually impossible to manoeuvre a yacht into a tightly berthed modern marina under sail. Masts are usually made of aluminium, which is strong and light, and sails are manufactured from artificial materials, such as polyester. Standing

rigging is made of wire rope, while sheets and halyards, which are the lines and tackle that control the sails, are made from nylon or polypropylene. New instruments, such as electronic depth sounders and steering systems, aid navigation (see panel, below).

MODERN NAVIGATION
All mariners require equipment to help them navigate their craft. The modern technology boom has seen a surge in devices to help sailors with everything from writing log books to predicting the weather. Most modern yachts sail with a Global Positioning System (GPS) that has a continuous electronic display showing the exact position of the craft. Despite such scientific advances, sailors are often still advised to learn traditional navigation skills, so they know exactly what to do in the event of electronic failure.

GPS SOUNDER SYSTEM
This integrated device contains software that allows mariners to calculate their position at sea, plot a course, and measure the depth of the water.

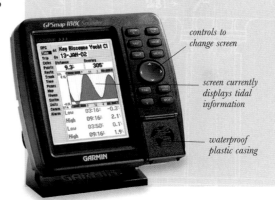

controls to change screen

screen currently displays tidal information

waterproof plastic casing

CHASING THE WIND
Sunbeam dinghies are wooden-hulled racing craft that originated in southern England in the 1920s. This crew is perching on the side of their dinghy to redistribute their weight and prevent the craft from capsizing.

really took off in California in the 1960s. Today, it is an integral element of international popular culture. Windsurfing, which combines elements of both surfing and sailing, emerged in the 1970s and has proved to be a popular modern sport, too.

Canoeing and kayaking are sports that also have their roots in antiquity. Boats in the style of the birch-bark canoe (see pp.16–17) are particularly popular in the United States and Canada and are propelled using a single-bladed paddle. The kayak, which is descended from Inuit craft, differs from the canoe, in that its hull is enclosed and it is propelled using a paddle with blades at either end. Both types of craft are mass produced in fibreglass and are used on rivers that are not navigable by other means. They are also suitable for the open sea.

Sailing schools, training, and marinas

Using a sailing yacht demands a greater variety of skills than any other leisure craft. In addition to having the requisite sailing skills, a skipper needs to be able to navigate, to manoeuvre a vessel into a tight position using engine power, and to supervise the crew during a voyage. Most nations have organizations that regulate the sport and offer structured courses for sailors. In many cases, these qualifications are not compulsory, but it is certainly advisable to undergo some form of training at a recognized sailing school. Britain's Royal Yachting Association offers theoretical and practical training at five levels from Competent Crew, which teaches a learner how to steer, trim the sails, and carry out basic tasks, to Yachtmaster Ocean, which allows an individual to take charge of a yacht in any circumstances. The United States has two major organizations that offer training: the American Sailing Association, which is based in California; and the United States Sailing Association, which is situated in Rhode Island. In France, it is necessary to hold a licence, the *permit à conduire*, to take charge of a boat. One of the most respected French sailing schools is the Centre Nautique, Brittany.

The smallest leisure craft, such as dinghies, surfboards, windsurfers, and rowing boats, require no real harbour facilities. Dinghies can be towed in a trailer behind a car or carried on a roof rack. At most, they need a ramp beside the sea from which they can be launched, but often a beach will suffice. However, larger yachts and motor cruisers need to be kept afloat. Some are kept at swinging moorings, where the boats are anchored to the bottom of the sea. These moorings can be tidal, which means that vessels are left high and dry twice a day and can only be sailed away at high tide. Marinas, which are purpose-built harbours where yachts and other marine craft can be moored, are growing in popularity. Vessels are moored to floating pontoons that rise and fall with the tide. Some marinas, such as that in Calais, France, use the limits of ancient harbours, but others are entirely new constructions. Most contain additional facilities for boats, covering repairs, sales, and charters.

Other watersports

Messing about on the water is not just limited to yachting, and other sports have evolved that have proved immensely popular. Surfing was first practised in the islands of the South Pacific thousands of years ago and was brought to Hawaii during the Polynesian migrations (see pp.20–21). It emerged as a sport in Australia in the early 20th century, but it

BRAVING THE RAPIDS
Kayaking in white water first emerged in the Alpine region of Europe in the 1930s and is today an established international sport. A kayaker sits low in the water and propels the craft using a double-bladed paddle.

RACING THE DRAGON
Victoria Harbour, Hong Kong, is one of many locations that hosts a Dragon Boat Festival every June. The boats are 12m (40ft) long and are decorated to resemble dragons, with the head at the bow and the tail at the stern.

GETTING SOME AIR
A windsurfer takes to the air in spectacular style. Like many modern adventure sports, windsurfing involves a considerable amount of skill.

RIDING THE WAVES
Surfing is an extremely popular and exhilarating sport, and many of its enthusiasts travel all over the world in search of the perfect wave. This photograph was taken in 1995 by the renowned surfing photographer Aaron Chang.

LEISURE AND SPORT CRAFT

Leisure craft are more varied than any other kind, ranging in size from a huge luxury yacht to a 1.8-m (6-ft) dinghy. They draw inspiration from many sources, including the Native American canoe, the Inuit kayak, and the naval fast-attack craft. They are often made from modern materials, but using them may still require traditional skills, such as paddling and sailing. The modern water-leisure industry probably employs and amuses more people worldwide than any past maritime activity.

EARLY LEAD
The yacht Silk Cut *takes an early lead at the start of leg two of the 1997 Whitbread Round-the-World Race in Cape Town, South Africa.*

Dinghies

Many different types of small sailing dinghy have gone on the market. The use of fibreglass for casting lightweight hulls has helped extend their use to more people. Designed by Bruce Kirby and Ian Bruce in 1970, the Laser (right) was selected as an Olympic class in 1996.

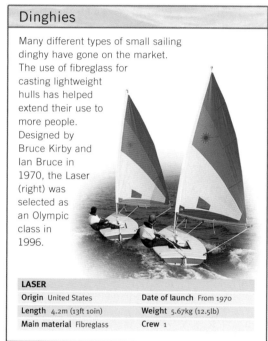

LASER	
Origin United States	**Date of launch** From 1970
Length 4.2m (13ft 10in)	**Weight** 5.67kg (12.5lb)
Main material Fibreglass	**Crew** 1

Sailing cruisers

Thousands of boats are used for weekend and holiday cruising, while larger boats are used for long-distance racing. Tracey Edwards bought the yacht *Maiden* (below) in 1988 and used her to compete in the Whitbread Round-the-World Race with the first female crew.

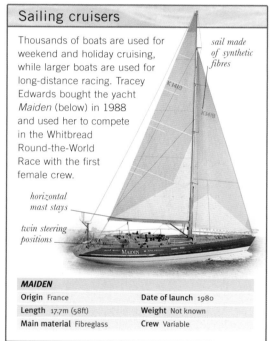

sail made of synthetic fibres

horizontal mast stays

twin steering positions

MAIDEN	
Origin France	**Date of launch** 1980
Length 17.7m (58ft)	**Weight** Not known
Main material Fibreglass	**Crew** Variable

Windsurfers

The windsurfer was born in 1968 when two Californians, Jim Drake and Hoyle Schweitzer, combined their interests in sailing and surfing. The mast was mounted on a universal joint so it had to be supported constantly by the sailor. Schweitzer's board was mass produced in the 1970s. The picture shows a modern fibre-glass windsurfer, but the data is for Drake and Schweitzer's original board.

sail

batten to stiffen sail

boom

transparent panel to aid visibility

mast

mast joint

foothold

board

WINDSURFER (NOT SHOWN)	
Origin United States	**Date of launch** 1968
Length 3m (10ft)	**Weight** Not known
Main material Wood	**Crew** 1

Kayaks

SEA KAYAK (NOT SHOWN)	
Origin International	**Date of launch** c.1990
Length 5.1m (16ft 9in)	**Weight** Not known
Main material Fibreglass	**Crew** 1

The kayak, based on the Inuit design, is the most popular type of canoe in Europe. This photograph shows Steve Fisher riding a waterfall in the Extreme Kayak Final in the Ford Gorge Games in 2002. The slalom kayak (described left) is a type recognized by international canoe clubs.

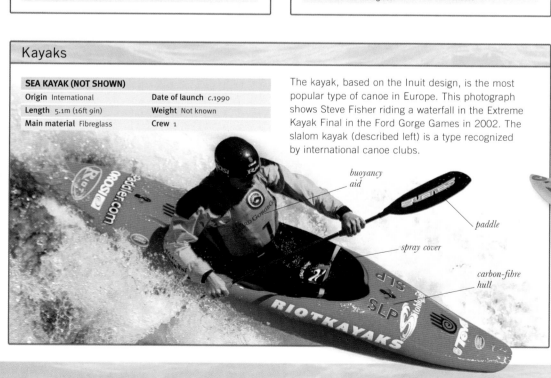

buoyancy aid

paddle

spray cover

carbon-fibre hull

Tall ships

Tall-ship sailing, in traditional vessels similar to those used in the later days of sail, began formally with the organization of races for naval and merchant-sail training ships in the 1950s. The largest sailing vessel ever built in Britain, the five-masted *Kobenhaven*, (right) was originally built as a training ship for the Danish Merchant Service, carrying a crew of 17, plus 60 apprentices.

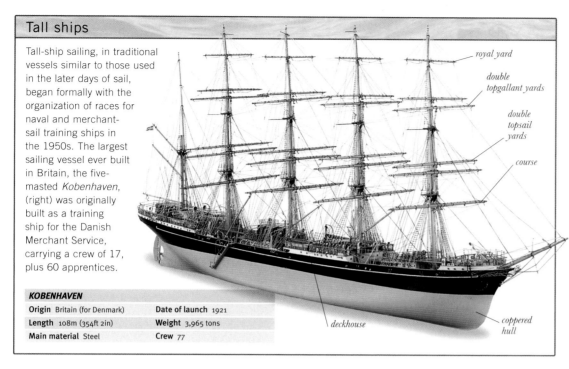

royal yard

double topgallant yards

double topsail yards

course

deckhouse

coppered hull

KOBENHAVEN

Origin Britain (for Denmark)	Date of launch 1921
Length 108m (354ft 2in)	Weight 3,965 tons
Main material Steel	Crew 77

Jet skis

The jet ski, or personal watercraft, was introduced by Kawasaki of Japan in 1973. Although they are not environmentally friendly, jet skis have been produced in considerable numbers.

KAWASAKI 900 STX (NOT SHOWN)

Origin Japan	Date of launch 2002
Length 3.1m (10ft 2in)	Weight 891kg (1,964lb)
Main material Fibreglass	Crew 3

Racing power boats

Power-boat racing is popular in many countries, especially Italy. The CM99 boat, powered by a 2-litre Mercury engine, is used by several teams in the World Championship and can reach 220kph (136.7mph). The picture shows speedboats neck and neck in a race at Swann's Marina in Maryland, USA.

DAC CM99 (NOT SHOWN)

Origin Italy	Date of launch 2003
Length 6m (19ft 8in)	Weight 390kg (860lb)
Main material Carbon fibre	Crew 2

Inflatables

The inflatable boat was based on rubber dinghies used by aircrew during the Second World War. Many have a rigid bottom and are kept inflated almost permanently. As well as for leisure use, they serve as fast raiding craft with navies and as lifeboats.

ATLANTIC 75 RIGID INFLATABLE INSHORE LIFEBOAT

Origin Britain	Date of launch From 1992
Length 7.5m (24ft 7in)	Weight 1,500kg (3,300lb) with 3 crew
Main materials Fibreglass, neoprene rubber	

Motor cruisers

Cabin cruisers became popular in the 1950s, on rivers, canals, and the open sea. With the slogan "the affordable dream", Chris-Craft of Florida began mass producing various types as early as the 1920s.

CHRIS-CRAFT SEDAN

Origin United States	Date of launch c.1956
Length 8.25m (27ft)	Weight Not known
Main material Wood	Crew Variable

Luxury yachts

Luxury powered yachts have been used by the rich and famous – and sometimes by recluses – since the late years of the 19th century, when steam power became practicable for these purposes. Modern boats are usually powered by diesel engines. The industry has boomed during the early years of the 21st century, as the market increased among the wealthy. Most ships are built to the client's specification. The yacht *Eclipse* is owned by the Russian billionaire Roman Abramovitch and is the largest in the world.

ECLIPSE

Origin Germany	Date of launch 2009
Length 170m (560ft)	Weight 13,000 tons
Main material Steel	Crew 70

FRENCH SUBMERSIBLE *NAUTILE*

> *Knowledge of the oceans is more than a matter of curiosity. Our very survival may hinge upon it.*

JOHN F. KENNEDY, letter to the President of the Senate, **29 March 1961**

KEY EVENTS

1943 UNDERWATER BREATHING The French scientists Jacques-Yves Cousteau and Emile Gagnan invent the aqualung.

1954 FACTORY FISHING The first factory ship, *Fairtry*, which is able to trawl for fish, as well as fillet and freeze its catch, is launched in Scotland.

1960 EXPLORING THE DEPTHS The bathyscaphe *Trieste 1* reaches the deepest point on Earth when it descends into the Mariana Trench in the Pacific Ocean.

1961 WARSHIP RAISED The 17th-century Swedish warship the *Vasa*, which sank in 1628, is raised in Stockholm Harbour.

1967 OIL DISASTER The oil tanker *Torrey Canyon* is wrecked in the English Channel. It is the world's first major oil spill.

1986 SAVING THE WHALES The International Whaling Commission agrees to a moratorium on hunting the depleted species.

1992 COD SLUMP The once-abundant stocks of cod disappear from the Grand Banks, off the coast of Newfoundland.

1998 OCEAN AWARE The United Nations declare 1998 the International Year of the Ocean, aiming to promote awareness of the sea and its resources.

2007 EMISSIONS Environmental groups petition the US Environmental Protection Agency about shipping emissions.

SHIPS AND OCEAN RESOURCES

OUR KNOWLEDGE OF THE OCEAN HAS INCREASED THROUGH THE USE OF NEW CRAFT, BUT HAS ALSO LED TO EXPLOITATION OF RESOURCES. HOWEVER, DAMAGE DONE TO THE OCEANS CAN BE REVERSED.

The rapid increase of technology in modern times has led to an expansion in our use of the oceans. They are increasingly used for recreation, to provide us with energy, for scientific research, and trade, and to uncover maritime history. There is no doubt that such increased human activity is damaging this environment, its inhabitants, and its resources in a manner that cannot be sustained. The sea is now the focus of conflict between those who are perceived to exploit its resources and conservationists, who wish to protect its wealth. However, although our knowledge of the oceans has increased since serious study began in the 19th century, only five per cent of the world beneath the surface of the oceans has been explored thoroughly, and there are a possible 50 million undiscovered species inhabiting it.

The origins of marine science

The study of the Earth's seas is called oceanography. One of the individuals credited with creating the science was the American Admiral Matthew F. Maury. He did much research into the effect of weather systems on shipping and, in 1853, proposed a system of recording data that relates to wind and currents. His 1855 publication, *The Physical Geography of the Sea*, was the first great work to be published about the science. At the same time, the British Admiral Robert Fitzroy, who commanded the *Beagle* on its voyage of exploration (see p.166), was instrumental in developing weather forecasts for sailors. However, the

VOYAGE OF THE *CHALLENGER*
This is the frontispiece of At Anchor, an illustrated book about the ground-breaking voyage of the 19th-century ocean-research ship HMS Challenger.

first voyage with a specific oceanographic intent was that of the British ship *HMS Challenger* in 1872–76. During a trip that covered 11,140km (6,900 miles), 362 observation stations were set up around the world. Eleven different measurements were taken at each station, including: the depth of water; a sample of the seabed; a sample of the sea; fauna living at both the surface and at the bottom; water temperature; weather readings; and the strength of the current. It was 1895 before the full results were published, which showed "the currents, temperatures, depths, and constituents of the ocean, the topography of the sea bottom, the geology and biology of its covering and the animal life of the abyssal waters". It provided the first global picture of the oceans and their life and stimulated the development of oceanography, which continued into the 20th century.

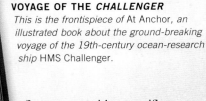

BRENT SPAR PROTEST

Today ships share the oceans with vast structures that harvest oil and gas. In April 1995, the decommissioned Shell oil platform Brent Spar was occupied by activists from the environmental group Greenpeace, who were protesting against the oil company's plan to dump the structure at sea. Shell were eventually vindicated, as their preferred method of disposal was the least damaging.

SPAR 1

JACQUES COUSTEAU

The French oceanographer Jacques-Yves Cousteau (1910–97) transformed underwater exploration. In 1943, in conjunction with Emile Gagnan, he developed the first successful aqualung, which allowed a diver to breathe underwater for up to an hour. In 1950, Cousteau purchased the research ship *Calypso*, from which he explored the world's oceans. His documentaries, such as the film *The Silent World of Jacques Cousteau* (1956) and the television series *The Undersea World of Jacques Cousteau* (1968–74), did much to popularize the idea of underwater exploration and provided valuable records of its remarkable wildlife.

The growth of oceanography

There were practical, economic, and military reasons for the expansion of oceanography as a science from the 1950s. Small research vessels called bathyscaphes and submersibles were developed to explore the ocean's depths, for use by navies, scientific organizations, and industry. These craft reach much greater depths than military submarines, which are not constructed to dive very far, as the immense pressure of the water, which increases the further you descend, limits their design. Vessels of the Russian *Alfa* class reached depths of about 600m (2,000ft), but were withdrawn from service in 1993.

The modern history of the submersible began with the Swiss physicist, August Piccard, who built the bathyscaphe *Trieste* in 1953. The vessel was 18m (59.5ft) long, and consisted of two parts: the main body, which contained ballast and areas filled with petrol to keep the craft buoyant; and a pressurized metal sphere, in which the crew travelled. After several European dives, during which Piccard, accompanied by his son Jacques, took the craft to a depth of 3,690m (12,000ft), the US Navy expressed an interest in *Trieste*, purchasing it in 1958. In 1960, the craft made a

momentous voyage, when it descended 10,912m (35,800ft) into the deepest point in the ocean, the Mariana Trench, off the Pacific Island of Guam. The United States developed the design

of the craft further with *Trieste II*. It was used to investigate the wreck of the American nuclear submarine *Thresher*, which sank east of Boston in 1963. Submersibles now tend to be largely unmanned craft called remotely operated vehicles (ROVs), which are fitted with cameras to record their voyages. *Jason*, the ROV that was used by the American explorer Robert Ballard (see opposite), can descend to 6,000m (20,000ft), and the Japanese *Kaiko* can operate at depths of 10,000m (33,000ft).

DEEP DIVING SUIT

Equipped with a Newtsuit, this French Navy diver is attaching an air line to a submarine in the Mediterranean. The suit keeps the diver's body at normal atmospheric pressure (one atmosphere).

UNSINKABLE SHIP
This photograph shows the prow of the luxury liner Titanic, *which rests at the bottom of the Atlantic Ocean. It was taken during a 1991 expedition to film the ship, which descended to the dark depths of the sea in 1912.*

Exploring wrecks

Many thousands of ships have been lost over the centuries, and their remains provide a vast store of information about seafaring life in the past. Two of the first underwater archaeologists were the English brothers Charles and John Deane, who explored the wreck of the 18th-century British warship the *Royal George* off the south coast of England in 1839–40. They used a diving suit that allowed them to breathe by means of a hose attached to the surface and recovered several artefacts. Over the next century, the wrecks of historical ships were located. They were mostly discovered at inland sites: numerous Viking ships were discovered in Scandinavia in the 19th and early 20th centuries (see pp.32–39); houseboats that are believed to have belonged to the Roman Emperor Caligula were found in Italy in the 1930s; and an Anglo-Saxon ship was unearthed at Sutton Hoo in 1939 (see p.34). The magnetometer, an instrument that recognizes magnetic material such as iron, and techniques such as sonar, which can map the seabed, enable accurate searches for underwater wrecks.

The greatest single landmark in marine archaeology was probably the raising of the *Vasa* from Stockholm Harbour in 1961. It presented a remarkable opportunity to study a 17th-century warship that was almost intact (see pp.106–107). The British warship *Mary Rose*, which sank off Portsmouth in 1545, was raised from the depths in 1982 (see p.81) and has also yielded valuable historical information. In the United States, the Civil War wrecks of the *Monitor* (see pp. 216–17), which was found in 1973, and the *Hunley*, which was found in 1995, have provided vital information about the warships of the period. The

BALLARD AND *BISMARCK*
Robert Ballard explored the Titanic *in 1985 and the German warship* Bismarck, *a model of which he is holding here, in 1989.*

discovery of the *Hunley* is particularly significant, as it was the first submarine to be used successfully in warfare.

Marine archaeology tells us not just about the history of ships, but about the cultures that created them and those who lived onboard. However, the science has its limits, as it tells us only about vessels that sank, and those in deep water can be difficult to reach. Some conditions, for example soft mud, are better for preserving timber, so areas in which the seabed is rocky, such as some parts of the Mediterranean, yield fewer examples of older wrecks. The subject can also create controversy. It is not easy to define who holds the rights to deep ocean wrecks, and there are ethical questions about disturbing ships that contain human bodies, as was the case with the *Titanic*, which was discovered by a Franco-American expedition in 1982.

RED SEA WRECK
A scuba diver explores the wreck of the Zingara, *a German cargo ship that was launched in 1963 and wrecked on a coral reef in the Red Sea in 1984. The vessel lies in a shallow and accessible area of water off the coast of Egypt.*

Equipment that allows individual divers to explore beneath the waves was revolutionized with the aqualung, or self-contained underwater breathing apparatus (scuba). It was developed by the French scientists Jacques Cousteau (see panel, opposite) and Emile Gagnan in 1943. A diving suit called the Newtsuit, which was invented by the Canadian Dr. Phil Nuytten in 1987, can be used to descend to a depth of 250m (820ft). All these advances have benefited such activities as marine archaeology, underwater construction, and recreation.

WRECK OF A GUNSHIP
The wreck of the Monitor *(left) can be clearly seen in this sonar image. It lies 67m (220ft) beneath the ocean. The gold ring (below) is one of many items discovered during the ship's excavation.*

THE *EXXON VALDEZ* DISASTER

Shortly after 9pm, on 23 March 1989, the 300-m (984-ft) oil tanker *Exxon Valdez* departed from its base in Alaska, carrying a cargo of 200 million litres (53 million gallons) of oil. Four minutes after midnight, the ship ran aground in Prince William Sound. Its hull split open, releasing 41.6 million litres (11 million gallons) of oil into the ocean. More than 2,090km (1,300 miles) of pristine coastline, rich in flora and fauna, was affected by the spill, which is widely regarded as one of the most catastrophic ecological disasters ever to have occurred.
Clean-up operations were carried out over four consecutive

THE PRICE OF OIL
Hundreds of thousands of birds were victims of the Exxon Valdez oil spill. Many still suffer the effects of the spill.

summers, at a cost of US$2.1 billion to the ship's owners, Exxon. The disaster led to increased regulation of oil tankers in the United States, including a requirement that tankers were constructed with double hulls to prevent similar events. The *Exxon Valdez* was repaired and continues to operate under the name *Sea River Mediterranean*. Oil deposits remain on some Alaskan beaches affected by the spill.

anchored to the sea floor. Drill ships are also used to explore for oil in deep waters. These contain a central platform, which is equipped with a derrick for drilling. The oil industry has both utilized and inspired innovations from other fields of maritime endeavour. Oil rigs and pipelines are serviced and maintained underwater by ROVs, and floating platforms are controlled by means of "dynamic positioning", which means they can be operated by computer from land. The offshore oil and gas industries have also produced different types of support craft to ferry supplies to rigs and platforms, and vessels that lay pipes to transfer the oil to shore.

Pollution

In ecological terms, carrying goods by sea has less impact on the environment than any other form of transport, but cheap fuel used by ships causes high levels of carbon emissions, which are difficult to control by law. There is also much concern about pollution of the sea from causes other than sea transport or offshore industry, such as waste dumping. However, when tanker disasters, such as the catastrophic

Resources from the sea

In addition to providing food, the exploration of ocean waters also involves a constant search for resources that provide energy. The power of the elements can be harnessed using offshore wind turbines to generate electricity, although some mariners complain that such structures might create new hazards. In deep areas, the seabed is littered with manganese nodules, which can be used in the construction of metal alloys, although there is no economically viable means to extract them. The most valuable of the ocean's resources have proved to be oil and gas. These reserves are becoming increasingly precious as onshore fields are depleted.

Oil reserves beneath the sea were first exploited in the 1920s and 1930s, when drilling extended from the land, taking place on wood platforms and barges close to the Louisiana coast. The first offshore oil platform was floated into the Gulf of Mexico in 1949, with a further 22 fields opening in the region by 1953. Since

then, the technology has extended to other regions, such as the North Sea and the Persian Gulf. There are now offshore oil platforms operating in most of the world's oceans, and vast oil and gas reserves have been discovered in the Pacific Ocean and Caspian Sea.

Before an oil field can be drilled, a geological survey of the potential site is completed. If this proves successful, a mobile exploration rig is towed to the area. In shallow waters of up to 110m (361ft) deep, a jack-up rig is used. This consists of a platform that rests on retractable legs, which are extended to the seabed upon reaching the site. In deeper waters of up to 1,500m (5,000ft), semi-submersible rigs are used. These are floated to the site and partially flooded with sea water, so that the majority of the structure is beneath the surface. They are then

NORTH SEA OIL PLATFORM
At large oil or gas fields, where reserves are extensive, an oil platform is constructed. This is a permanent structure, on which the crew live for months at a time.

incident involving the *Exxon Valdez* (see panel, left), occur, they are damaging, spectacular, and usually highly publicized.

Concern about oil spills began with the wreck of the Liberian-registered tanker *Torrey Canyon* in 1967. The vessel's hull was ripped open when it ran aground off the Scilly Isles in the English Channel, spilling oil on an unprecedented scale. Various attempts were made to minimize the impact of the spill, including several bombing raids that aimed to set fire to the slicks to burn off the oil. However, the spill affected a stretch of coastline 190km (120 miles) long in southern England and 90km (55 miles) long in northern France. It had an appalling effect on the region's wildlife, resulting in the death

of about 200,000 birds. The *Torrey Canyon* disaster highlighted the risk posed by the transport of such vast quantities of oil and led to the development of strategies to deal with large oil spills, although these can also have adverse effects on the environment. Floating booms can be laid around a slick to prevent its spread; huge spongelike devices can be used to soak up the oil; and vessels called skimmers can be deployed, equipped with machinery to suck up or absorb the spill. Excess oil can be burned off, although this has health risks for those who inhabit surrounding areas. Chemicals can be applied to break the oil down, although they could introduce toxins into the food chain. Straw matting, which can be laid on the water's

END OF THE RAINBOW
A diver explores the hull of the Greenpeace ship Rainbow Warrior, *which now forms an artificial reef off the northern coast of New Zealand.*

surface or on land to absorb oil, is more environmentally friendly in some cases, but it is labour intensive to use.

Oil spills, nuclear testing, and the abuse of ocean resources have all been highlighted by environmental organizations. Greenpeace, in particular, has provided many striking images of its seaborne protests. But its demonstrations are not always regarded favourably. In 1985, while moored in Auckland, New Zealand, the pressure group's research vessel, *Rainbow Warrior*, exploded, killing a photographer, Fernando Pereira. The ship had been preparing to protest against French nuclear tests at Mururoa Atoll in the South Pacific. Two French secret agents

RUN AGROUND
In March 1978, the oil tanker Amoco Cadiz *ran aground in appalling weather off the coast of Brittany, France. It is estimated that 260 million litres (69 million gallons) of oil leaked from the vessel, which broke into three parts.*

OIL SLICK
This aerial view shows an oil slick off the coast of southwestern France in April 2003. Five months earlier, the tanker Prestige *broke up 210km (130 miles) off the coast of northwest Spain. The oil that leaked from the vessel affected the coastline from Portugal to western France. The disaster led to calls for single-hulled oil tankers to be banned from sailing in European waters.*

SAVING WHALES
This inflatable boat, which is emblazoned with the Greenpeace logo, is attempting to thwart a Japanese expedition to capture minke whales in the Southern Ocean. Japan hunts whales in the name of "scientific research".

were subsequently found responsible for planting the explosives. The incident sparked international outrage, and New Zealand's Prime Minister at the time, David Lange, described it as "state-backed terrorism".

Modern whaling

Industrial whaling gathered pace after the invention of the mechanized harpoon gun (see p.254). In 1925, the first factory ship was built for the industry, which meant that the catch could be processed onboard, rather than being towed back to land. It is estimated that 1.5 million whales were killed over the next 50 years, with hunters shifting their sights from one species to another as each became less numerous. With strong pressure from conservationists, and the threat of extinction, the

International Whaling Commission (IWC) agreed to a moratorium on whaling in 1986. However, a limited catch is still allowed for scientific purposes. Whale meat commands high prices in Japan, and it is alleged that the catch from their "scientific" whaling is sold at great profit. In 2000, against world opinion, the Japanese extended their catch from minke whales to sperm and Bryde's whales. In 2011, under pressure from the Sea Shepherd organisation, Japan finished the whaling season early. Norwegian ships are also involved in whaling. Conservationists fear that populations of some whale species, which were slowly beginning to recover from the previous mass slaughter, are approaching crisis levels again.

Industrial fishing

Fishermen are the last hunter-gatherers in the modern world. For centuries, they have been imbued with a heroic status, reflecting the arduous, often life-threatening, conditions they confront at sea. In the decades since the Second World War, the fishing industry has changed dramatically, if somewhat paradoxically. In other industries, such as agriculture or manufacturing, technological progress increases production. This is true of the fishing industry, as innovations such as the stern trawler (see below) initially increased catches, although they have also rapidly depleted fish stocks.

One of the key post-war advances in the fishing industry was the factory ship. The first of these vessels, the *Fairtry*, which was four times the size of a conventional trawler, was launched in Scotland in 1954. The ship, and those that followed it, was able to fillet, freeze, and store its catch. The *Fairtry* was also the first fishing vessel to implement stern trawling, which involves pulling the nets in via a ramp at the rear of the ship. This has resulted in nets that are much larger than those used by side trawlers. The Soviet Union, which consciously expanded its

TUNA FISHING
French photographer Jean Gaumy has chronicled the lives of Spanish fishermen. This image shows the crew of a fishing vessel hauling in a thrashing shoal of migrating tuna, as they pass through the Straits of Gibraltar between the Mediterranean and the Atlantic Ocean.

fishing fleet in the 1950s and 1960s, was the first nation to capitalize on this type of vessel, followed by Japan and Spain. By 1970, the Soviets had 400 factory trawlers operating worldwide. One vessel, the 165-m- (540-ft-) long Russian ship *Professor Baranov*, became a familiar sight in the waters of the North Atlantic. The increased production of factory ships, as well as a rise in demand, saw the world's total catch of fish rise from 20 million tonnes a year in the 1950s to 90 million tonnes by 1989.

The right to fish in specific areas is an issue that arouses passions in maritime nations, and had even led to conflict. Between 1958 and 1976, Britain and Iceland fought three "Cod

FACTORY FISHING
This Norwegian fishing vessel, the Sklinabanken *is unloading its catch of herring. The fish have been caught using a purse-seine net, which encircles a school of fish and is then closed, trapping them.*

depth of ocean
liquid crystal display

LOWRANCE

control panel

53.8   30
40
50
60

display reveals presence of fish

X-35M LOG RECORDER
MADE IN U.S.A.

SONAR FISH LOCATION
Modern fishing vessels are equipped with various devices to help optimize their catch. Fishing vessels use sonar systems, such as this one, to locate shoals of fish, and electronic navigation equipment to record sites.

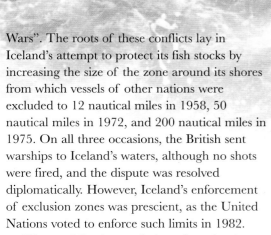

Wars". The roots of these conflicts lay in Iceland's attempt to protect its fish stocks by increasing the size of the zone around its shores from which vessels of other nations were excluded to 12 nautical miles in 1958, 50 nautical miles in 1972, and 200 nautical miles in 1975. On all three occasions, the British sent warships to Iceland's waters, although no shots were fired, and the dispute was resolved diplomatically. However, Iceland's enforcement of exclusion zones was prescient, as the United Nations voted to enforce such limits in 1982.

The need for the regulation of catches is graphically illustrated by the collapse of the Grand Banks cod off Newfoundland (see p.250). Before 1945, the region's average cod catch was about 500,000 tonnes. However, this increased sharply with the introduction of factory ships. In 1968, nearly two million tonnes of cod were caught in the Grand Banks, an all-time high.

From this peak, the catch began to decline, and in 1992 the species, which had once been so abundant in the area, all but disappeared. The Canadian government banned ships from fishing in the area. It was a stark warning about the dangers of overfishing. Other fisheries that once thrived – for example the North Sea and the waters off the east coast of Africa – have displayed evidence that a similar fate awaits them. Regulations and quotas have been put in place in an effort to halt the decline in stocks, but they can be extremely difficult to enforce on

FACTORY FISHING
Since the first factory ships were constructed in the 1950s, this cost-effective method of fishing has spread around the world. This vessel, photographed in Walvis Bay off the coast of Namibia, has the capacity to both catch and process fish so they reach the shore ready for sale.

the open sea, and illegal fishing and poaching does occur. In 2003, the *Viarsa*, a Uruguayan fishing boat carrying an illegal cargo of the Patagonian tooth fish, was chased across the South Atlantic by Australian, British, and South African authorities. The ship and its cargo, which is a protected species, were impounded and taken to Australia.

The demand for fish has never been greater, and the fate of the world's fishing fleets is an emotive subject. Entire communities have established themselves around the fishing industry, and it is, of course, one of the reasons why boats and ships were first constructed.

LIFE ON THE OCEAN WAVES

A solitary fisherman struggles to maintain his balance on the deck of the Spanish side-trawler Rowanlea, *as it battles the waters of the North Sea in January 1998. Fishing remains a hazardous occupation, a reminder that the relationship between humans, ships, and the sea is ongoing and often unpredictable.*

EPILOGUE

HUMAN SOCIETIES MAY APPEAR TO BE LESS CLOSELY CONNECTED WITH THE SEA NOW THAN THEY WERE IN THE PAST. HOWEVER, WE DEPEND ON SHIPS AND THE SEA FAR MORE THAN WE OFTEN REALIZE.

The story of the ship is far from over, even if many people in the West have turned their backs on the sea. A common public perception is that the seas are polluted, or even worse, they are always ready to knock down sea walls and flood us. Reading the popular press, one could easily form the impression that the world's oceans are empty apart from huge oil tankers waiting to run aground and kill thousands of seabirds, missile-carrying submarines with enough destructive power to eliminate civilization several times over, ferries ready to capsize, and amateur yachtsmen in need of rescue by lifeboats and helicopters. Those who use the sea, according to this view, do so only for reasons of self-indulgence. They speak an incomprehensible but easily parodied language, they are detached from ordinary life, and they seem to be increasingly irrelevant.

Although most maritime enterprise takes place out of sight of the land, the ship is as important now as it ever was, perhaps more so. And the sea still has the power to capture the imagination, whether it be the acts of heroism by single-handed yachtsmen or in the leisure pursuits of thousands. The standard of living in the West and the availability of jobs in the East depend on the giant container ships that ply between the two regions.

The car, which often forms the centre of a Westerner's life, depends on vast supplies of seaborne oil, and the central heating and air conditioning that makes him or her indifferent to the weather is fuelled from the same source.

The seas are far from empty. The different interests of merchant shipowners, navies on exercise, fishermen, ecologists, and yachtsmen might compete fiercely in the same waters. If there are fewer merchant ships on the seas, it is only because a single ship can carry as much as 50 ships from half a century ago. If there are fewer professional seamen, it is because these same ships are run with minimal crews. And if the seafaring profession does not carry the same glamour that it once had, it is because it is no longer necessary to go to sea to see the world.

As well as world economies depending on it, the sea is more important than ever for leisure. Taking into account all the small boats in the world, there are probably more seaworthy vessels in existence now than at any time in history. Adding up the leisure users of the sea – including cruise passengers, yacht sailors, ferry passengers, water-skiers, anglers, divers, and tourists – there are probably more people afloat now than ever before. Nautical fiction, by Frederick Marryat and Herman Melville in the 19th century and C.S. Forester and Patrick O'Brian in the 20th, among others, has always been popular and, after a gap of several decades, the film and television industries are reviving an interest. Underwater exploration looks at the last unknown areas of the Earth, and these are very substantial in extent. With the progress of manned space exploration faltering, the sea is an even stronger focus of interest and imagination. The sea floor has shipwrecks that will open new perspectives on the past. The creatures who live in the water are a source of valuable resources and a subject of endless fascination. For 5,000 years, the ship has gradually opened up our minds and supplied us with goods and ideas. It will continue to do so in the future.

THE ENDURING APPEAL OF SAIL
Although sailing ships have long since disappeared from the world's trade routes, they still inspire passionate enthusiasm. This photograph shows the Mexican ship Cuauhtemoc leading a farewell parade of 90 ships taking part in the Cutty Sark Tall Ships race in the Gulf of Gdansk, Poland, in 2003. The sails are backing because the ships are using their engines.

GLOSSARY

In this glossary, terms that are defined within a larger entry are highlighted in **bold** type.

Aberdeen bow A type of pointed bow, developed in the 19th century, originally to avoid taxation, which at the time was based on the depth of a ship's hull. The design led to better seagoing performance and speed, and it was soon widely adopted.

adze A shipwright's tool, similar to an axe but with the blade set at right angles to the line of the handle.

aft The after (or rear) part of a ship or a position towards the stern.

Asdic Underwater sound-ranging apparatus for determining the range and position of a submerged submarine. The name is an acronym for Allied Submarine Detection Investigation Committee. See also *sonar*.

astrolabe A device used for measuring the altitude of the Sun. Some earlier astrolabes were designed to take star sights as well as the Sun sight. It consists of a large graduated ring of brass fitted with a sighting rule pivoted at the centre of the ring.

barque (bark) A merchant sailing vessel rigged with square sails on the fore- and mainmasts and fore-and-aft sails on the mizzen mast.

bathyscaphe See *submersible*.

battlecruiser A class of 20th-century warship with a heavy armament of guns but lighter armour and greater speed than a battleship.

battleship A class of 20th-century warship that carried the greatest number of weapons and was clad with the heaviest armour.

beakhead A projection forward of the bows on a sailing ship. It is beneath the bowsprit and usually highly decorated. The beakhead often holds the heads (or toilets).

beam 1. The measurement across the hull of a ship at its widest part. **2.** A structural timber that forms part of the frame of a ship.

Bermuda sail A sail that is triangular in shape.

bilge keel Two beams or fins fastened lengthwise along the outside of a ship's bilge to reduce heavy rolling. They also support the weight of the hull when it is on a wooden platform for launching and when the ship is in dry dock.

binnacle A wooden or brass case that supports and protects a ship's compass.

bitts Upright wooden posts fixed in the forecastle area of a sailing ship that secure the cable or chain when the ship is at anchor. Smaller bitts are used to attach parts of the running rigging.

Blackwall frigate A term applied to ships built for the Indian trade between 1837 and 1869. Many ships employed in this trade were built at Blackwall on the River Thames, London, England. This and their fine sailing abilities, similar to those of a naval frigate, gave rise to the name. See also *frigate*.

block A pulley enclosed in a wooden shell that is used to alter the direction of a rope in the rigging or to increase pulling power as part of a block and tackle. See also *tackle*.

bow The front section of a ship or boat.

bowsprit A spar extending forward from the bow of a ship, to which the stays of the foremast are fastened.

brig A two-masted sailing vessel that is square-rigged on both the foremast and the mainmast.

brigantine A two-masted sailing vessel that is square-rigged on the foremast and fore-and-aft rigged on the mainmast.

broadside The simultaneous discharge of some or all of the guns fitted on one side of a warship.

canoe A narrow, elongated open boat propelled by paddles.

capital ship One of the most powerful warships in a navy, such as a battleship, battlecruiser, heavy cruiser, aircraft carrier, or nuclear submarine. The term was first used by the English diarist Samuel Pepys in the 17th century.

capstan A rotating, upright cylindrical barrel fitted on larger ships and used for hoisting weights, in particular cables and anchors.

carrack A large sailing vessel in use from the 14th to 17th centuries, usually with elevated structures known as castles at the bow and stern.

carronade A short, fat gun that fires a large ball over a short range.

carvel-built A term to describe a wooden sailing ship built with the hull planks flush rather than overlapping. See also *clinker-built*.

catamaran A boat with two parallel hulls or floats.

caulk To seal a wooden ship by packing the seams of the deck and sides with oakum and pitch or other materials.

centreboard A type of retractable keel used on sailing vessels to prevent drifting downwind. It is also known as a drop keel.

channel A flat, plank-like projection from the side of a sailing ship that is used to spread the shrouds.

chronometer An accurate timepiece, originally used for navigation at sea.

class A group of ships built to the same design.

clinker-built A term to describe a wooden ship or boat built with overlapping planks. See also *carvel-built*.

clipper A fast sailing ship of the mid-19th century with a very sharp bow, a large sail area, and a short beam in relation to its length. Extreme clippers were built with the sharpest bows for the maximum speed. Clippers were mostly used to carry cargo.

cocca A type of late-medieval merchant ship that was used in the Mediterranean Sea.

cockpit 1. An area below the lower gundeck in sailing warships, originally allotted to senior midshipmen and subsequently to the surgeon. In action, it was used as the operating theatre. **2.** The space on a yacht where the steering wheel or tiller is found.

cog (kogge) A clinker-built sailing ship used in northern Europe from the 13th to 15th centuries. It was powered by a single square sail.

commerce raider A warship or merchantman used to capture or sink enemy merchant shipping in order to disrupt maritime trade in time of war.

convoy A group of merchant ships proceeding together in formation under the protection of warships.

corsair 1. A raider (sometimes regarded as a pirate), particularly one operating off the Barbary Coast of North Africa during the 16th and 17th centuries. **2.** A ship operating under government licence off the Barbary Coast to raid enemy trade in wartime.

corvette 1. A fast, lightly armed 20th-century escort vessel, often used for anti-submarine operations. **2.** A small sailing warship used during the 18th and 19th centuries.

counter An arched area of overhang at the stern of a ship beneath the cabin windows. It is usually divided into upper and lower counters.

cruiser A lightly armed fast warship of the late 19th and 20th centuries. A **light cruiser** was not as heavily armed as a regular cruiser.

cutter 1. An 18th-century ship originally used by British smugglers and copied by the Revenue Service and the Royal Navy. **2.** A clinker-built ship's boat, used for communication between ship and shore during the 18th century.

depth charge An anti-submarine weapon originally developed during the First World War. It consists of a canister or barrel filled with explosives and having a hydrostatic detonator activated by pressure to explode at a pre-selected depth. The pressure created by the blast is intended to inflict damage on the target.

destroyer A small, fast warship armed with guns, torpedoes, depth charges, or guided missiles. The original form of this type of ship was the torpedo-boat destroyer of the late 19th century.

dhow A lateen-rigged sailing vessel that originated in the Middle East.

dinghy A small rowing or sailing boat.

displacement The weight of water displaced by a vessel. The size of a warship is usually described by its displacement. See also *tonnage*.

draught 1. The depth of a ship's keel below the waterline. **2.** A drawing that represents the three-dimensional form of a ship's shape.

dreadnought A 20th-century battleship armed with large-calibre guns.

dug-out A simple type of canoe made from a hollowed-out tree trunk.

factory ship A whaling ship or a vessel equipped to process fish at sea.

fathom An old unit of measurement for depth. One fathom is 6ft (1.83m). At one time, depth was measured in fathoms using a rope and also marked in fathoms on nautical charts. Fathoms are now becoming obsolete, and most charts now show depth in metres.

fleet 1. A number of ships sailing together. **2.** The number of merchant ships owned by a shipping company. **3.** The whole of a national navy.

fore–and–aft rig A sail configuration in which the principal sails lie along the same plane from the bow of the ship to the stern lengthwise when in their neutral position. See also *square rig*.

forecastle (fo'c'sle) 1. Originally a structure placed near the bow of a sailing warship on which soldiers stood during battle. On later ships it was a raised part of the ship itself. **2.** An area beneath a raised deck near a ship's bow.

foremast See *mast*.

forepeak The foremost part of a ship's hold.

freeboard The distance measured from the waterline to the main deck of a ship.

frigate 1. A warship with two full decks, with only the upper deck armed with guns, used in the 18th and 19th centuries, mainly for escort duties and reconnaissance. **2.** A 20th-century warship with an anti-submarine or general purpose capability.

futtock A curved piece of timber that forms part of a rib or frame of a ship.

gaff rig A rig on a sailing vessel, in which the upper edge of a fore-and-aft sail is attached to a spar or gaff.

galleas A large, three-masted galley of the 16th and 17th centuries that used both sails and oars for propulsion.

galleon A square-rigged, three-masted sailing ship in use from the 16th to 18th centuries, particularly by the Spanish.

galley 1. An oared fighting ship used mainly in the Mediterranean until the 18th century. **2.** The kitchen of a ship.

global positioning system (GPS) A navigational aid for determining position at sea by comparing radio signals from satellites.

gooseneck 1. A metal joint used for attaching the swinging boom of a sailing vessel to a mast or to the ship's side. **2.** The join between the end of a whipstaff and the tiller.

graving The treatment of the submerged part of a ship's hull to protect it from weeds, shipworm, or decay.

gunport A square hole cut in the side of a sailing warship through which cannons were fired.

gunwale The uppermost piece of timber on the side of a wooden ship or boat, covering the tops of the ribs.

gyroscope The principal component of a **gyrocompass**. A gyroscope is an electrically powered spinning wheel whose axis and plane of rotation remain fixed in space. This creates gyroscopic inertia, which – through further electronic processes – allows the gyrocompass to point to the geographic north as opposed to magnetic north.

heads A naval term for toilets, originating from the time when they were situated at the head of ship in the beakhead. See also *beakhead*.

headsail A general term for a triangular sail carried at the foremost part of a vessel. Specific types of headsail include the Genoa (used on yachts), foresail, and jib.

heaving The up-and-down movement of a ship at sea, a principal cause of seasickness.

heel 1. A term used to describe the motion of a ship or boat as it leans over to one side either due to wind or movement of the sea or when it is turning at speed. Heel is not to be confused with **list**, which refers to a permanent state. **2.** The aftermost part of a ship's keel. See also *keel*.

horsepower (hp) A unit for mechanical power. One horsepower is equivalent to 745.7 watts.

hulk (hulc) 1. A medieval ship of Mediterranean or north European origin with the ends of its planks fitted parallel to the stem- and sternposts. **2.** A ship that has fallen into disuse or been appointed to another task that does not require it to move. Hulks are often used for accommodation (sometimes as prisons) or for storage.

inboard The inside of the structural area of a vessel (and the opposite of outboard). It is sometimes used to describe a marine engine situated inside a boat. The term also indicates a direction of movement towards the centre of a vessel.

ironclad An early name given to a mid-19th-century warship with a hull that was either built from or protected by iron plates.

kayak A type of canoe that was originally built by Inuits. In its traditional form, a kayak has a light wooden frame covered by sealskin. There is a hole in the centre where the occupant (or kayaka) sits, with the edge of the hole laced with sealskin to prevent the influx of water. Modern kayaks are made entirely of plastics with synthetic waterproof coverings.

keel A long, generally straight assembly of timber or metal that forms the lowest part of the hull of a ship along most of its length. It might be made up of several pieces of wood joined together.

knot A unit of measurement for a vessel's speed through water. One knot equals one nautical mile an hour. The term originates from when a line with knots at intervals of 14.4m (47ft 3in) was cast over the side and measured against a 28-second sandglass. The number of knots passed gave the ship's speed. See also *nautical mile*.

landing craft A specially designed, flat-bottomed vessel used to transport troops, vehicles, and equipment between a troopship and the shore. Modern landing craft date from the early 20th century.

lateen sail The standard type of sail in the Mediterranean. It is triangular and attached to a long yard set diagonally fore and aft.

leading edge The edge of a sail that faces the wind.

Liberty ship A prefabricated and mass-produced merchant ship built in the USA between 1941 and 1945 to counter the high losses of merchant ships sunk by U-boats.

line of battle A formation of a fleet before entering into battle. The term originates from a time when sailing warships formed opposing lines to engage one another, thus bringing all their respective broadsides to bear.

liner Originally, a passenger or cargo-carrying merchant ship with a scheduled route. With the decline in passenger sea travel due to competition with aircraft, cruise ships catering purely for the leisure trade have generally adopted the term.

luff 1. The leading edge of a fore-and-aft rigged sail, which is the edge of the sail attached to the mast. **2.** To bring a sailing vessel's bow closer to the wind to decrease power to the headsail.

MAC-ship A type of ship developed during the Second World War to counter enemy air reconnaissance and submarine attack. MAC-ships were merchant vessels, usually grain ships or tankers, fitted with temporary flight decks, from which aircraft could take off or land.

mainmast See *mast*.

man o'war A term applied to a ship specifically built for the purpose of war.

mast A large, tall primary spar placed vertically in a ship or boat. Masts were originally used to attach further yards and spars to carry sails. In modern engine-powered craft, the mast is used for the placement of radar and radio aerials. Until the late 19th century,

ships carried a maximum of three masts: a **foremast** at the front; a **mainmast** (the tallest) in the centre; and the **mizzenmast**, the last, and near the stern. On a two-masted vessel, the mainmast is always the tallest mast.

mast cap A piece of wood at the head of the lower mast to hold the upper mast in place against it.

merchantman A vessel engaged in any form of trade.

minesweeper A vessel designed or fitted out for the clearance of mines, traditionally by trailing a sharp, looped line astern at a selected depth that cut the mooring line of a submerged mine, bringing it to the surface. A more modern method is to use submersibles to detonate mines.

mizzenmast See *mast*.

nautical mile A unit of measurement used in navigation that is equal to a minute of arc (one-sixtieth of a degree) of a great circle on a sphere. One international nautical mile is equivalent to 1,852m (1.151 statute miles). See also *knot*.

oakum Hemp or jute fibre that has been coated with tar.

orlop deck The lowest deck on a sailing warship. Situated below the waterline, the powder magazines were sited there, as well as some of the principal store rooms. The deck also housed the cabins of junior officers and the midshipmen's berth. It was also used as the sickbay during action.

outrigger A secondary hull protruding away from the main hull to provide additional stability. Outriggers were traditionally found on native canoes in the Pacific and Indian oceans.

parrel An arrangement of rollers and flat pieces of wood held together by rope, used to hold a yard against a mast while allowing it to be raised and lowered.

P-boat An anti-submarine patrol boat used during the First World War.

penteconter An ancient Greek galley with 50 oars.

pitch To smear with pitch, a distillation of tar.

Plimsoll line A line painted on the side of a merchant ship that shows six levels to which it may be safely loaded with cargo depending on its current location and varying seasonal conditions that affect water salinity and therefore the boat's stability.

pocket battleship A generic term given to three German cruisers, *Graf Spee*,

Deutschland, and *Admiral Scheer*, which were heavily armoured and armed for their size. Although only 10,000 tons, each carried six 280-mm (11-in) guns in two triple turrets with a secondary armament of eight 150-mm (5.9-in) guns. They had a revolutionary diesel-engine propulsion system that gave them good range and speed.

poop deck The aftermost and highest deck on a ship, fitted above the quarter-deck.

port The left-hand side of a vessel when facing forward towards the bow. It was originally known as larboard, but the term was changed in the mid-19th century to prevent confusion with starboard. See also *starboard*.

pot boat A boat made of clay or similar material for use in inland waterways.

privateer A private vessel fitted out to raid enemy shipping in wartime for the purpose of raising a profit from the sale of captured ships and their cargoes. International laws regulated the circumstances in which warships were allowed to attack merchantmen.

prize money The proceeds from the sale of an enemy ship that were often shared among the officers and crew.

prize rules British legislation governing the distribution of prize money.

Q-ship A merchant ship with hidden armament used to sink U-boats during the First World War.

quarter-deck The highest deck of a ship, apart from the poop, towards the stern. On a sailing ship, it is the part of the upper deck aft of the mainmast.

radar A method, developed just before the outbreak of the Second World War, of detecting objects by sending out radio waves that reflect back on hitting an object, providing information about its bearing and distance. Originally, the signal was presented to the operator through a cathode ray tube but more modern radars have a digital interface. The term radar is derived from radio detection and ranging.

rake 1. A manoeuvre in which a sailing warship positioned itself to enable its guns to fire into the stern or bow of an enemy vessel. The bow and stern were relatively unprotected and thus vulnerable. During action, the decks of a warship would also be cleared, removing obstacles that would prevent a cannonball travelling along the length of the deck and doing great damage. **2.** The angle of the bow or mast of a ship from the vertical.

ram 1. To deliberately collide with another ship. **2.** A long, sharp projection from the bow of a warship

for the sole purpose of ramming an enemy vessel.

reef points Ropes along the length of a sail on either side, which can be tied together to keep part of the sail out of use in strong winds.

remotely operated vehicle (ROV) A small, unmanned submersible that is controlled from another ship or a platform. ROVs are often used in salvage, exploration, and mine-clearing operations. See also *submersible*.

ribs The frames and timbers that extend upwards from the keel to form a ship's rigid framework. See also *keel*.

rig The general arrangement of sails and masts of a particular ship type.

rigging Generally, all the masts, spars, ropes, wires, and chains that form part of the system providing the main motive power of a sailing ship. **Standing rigging** is fixed and is used to support the masts. **Running rigging** supports and controls the yards, sprits, and sails.

rudder The main apparatus for steering a vessel. The rudder is submerged and fixed on or below the stern. When it is moved laterally, the vessel moves to one side or the other. On small ships and boats, the rudder is controlled either by a tiller or wheel. Large modern vessels are usually steered by an electronic device such as a joystick or digital control. See also *tiller*.

schooner A vessel with two or more masts carrying fore-and-aft rig and with the main aftermast taller than the foremast.

screw Another term for propeller. It is so called because a propeller is effectively a rotating screw that transforms engine power into forward thrust through water.

ship of the line A sailing warship built to fight in the line of battle. They were usually all of fourth rate or above, and most were third-rate ships of 74 guns.

shroud Part of the ship's standing rigging, giving support to the mast from behind and either side. See also *stay*.

sloop 1. A sailing vessel with a single mast and fore-and-aft rig. **2.** A general term applied in the 17th and 18th centuries to describe any minor class of warship that was not given a specific classification. By the beginning of the 19th century, the term was applied to two classes, either a **brig sloop** of two masts or a **ship sloop** of three masts. **3.** A term applied during the Second World War to escort ships larger than frigates but smaller than destroyers.

sonar Previously known as Asdic, sonar is an electronic device for the

location of underwater objects, primarily used in anti-submarine warfare and hunting. There are two types of sonar: passive and active. **Passive sonar** is an array of sensors that detects and listens to noise travelling through water. **Active sonar** transmits a sound wave through the water at 1,400m (4,600ft) per second. On hitting an object, the sound wave bounces back, producing an echo that indicates the range and bearing of the target. The term sonar is derived from sound navigation and ranging. See also *Asdic*.

sponson Part of the structure of a ship that supports a box enclosing a paddle wheel.

squadron A division of warships.

square rig A sail plan in which the main driving sails are secured to the yards and lay square to the mast in their neutral position. See also *fore-and-aft rig*.

starboard The right-hand side of a vessel when facing forwards towards the bow. The term probably originated from steerboard, the side of a ship on which a steering oar was placed before the invention of the stern rudder. See also *shroud*.

stay A part of the standing rigging that supports a mast fore and aft and prevents it falling forwards or backwards. See also *shroud*.

steerage A large compartment situated close to the stern and usually just above the propellers. On merchant ships, it was often used to accommodate the crew, and on passenger vessels it housed passengers who could not afford private or shared cabins. Steerage accommodation usually had only basic amenities.

stem (stempost) The primary timber, plate, or other piece of material that forms the bow and joins from the keel. The term is also used to refer to the foremost part of the bow.

submarine See *submersible*.

submersible A small, mobile undersea vehicle often used for underwater science or commercial operations such as exploration or salvage work. It can be either manned or unmanned but has very limited endurance for underwater operations. Larger submersibles capable of diving to great depths are known as **bathyscaphes**. Unlike a submersible, a bathyscaphe has a pressurized cabin that is suspended beneath a tank filled with a buoyant liquid (often petrol). Bathyscaphes have reached depths of 10,912m (35,800ft). A **submarine** differs from a submersible in that it is much larger and able to remain submerged for longer periods of time. It is also

self-sufficient in all aspects, whereas a submersible relies on another ship for deployment and to sustain it during underwater operations.

surging 1. The sudden slackening of a rope or cable to allow it to run out or around a capstan. **2.** A fast movement of a ship through water alternating with a sudden slowing down.

tack A sailing manoeuvre in which a vessel passes its head through the wind so that the wind lies on the opposite side. As a sailing ship cannot sail directly into the wind, it has to sail just off it, making a zigzag course to travel in the general direction it needs to go.

tackle A mechanism in which two blocks are linked by a rope to provide better pulling power for lifting an object. Many varieties are used, depending on the task to be performed. See also *block*.

tiller A horizontal bar fitted to the top of a rudder and used to turn the rudder from side to side. See also *rudder*.

tonnage The gross tonnage of a merchant ship, calculated by dividing by 100 the contents, in cubic feet, of the vessel's closed-in spaces. **Deadweight tonnage** is the measurement of the number of tons of cargo a merchant ship can carry. See also *displacement*.

torpedo A self-propelled underwater projectile launched from a ship, submarine, or aircraft and designed to detonate on impact or in proximity to an enemy vessel.

tramp ship A small cargo ship with no regular route, which delivers and picks up cargo from any destination as required.

transom Transverse timbers bolted to the sternpost of a wooden ship and forming part of the stern.

trawler A fishing vessel that pulls nets behind it, originally along the bottom of the sea.

trireme An ancient Greek or Roman war galley propelled by three tiers of oars on each side.

turtle ship A 16th-century Korean armoured warship fitted with an iron shell to prevent boarding.

U-boat A German submarine. The term derives from the German word unterseeboot.

waist The middle section of the upper deck of a ship between the forecastle and the quarter-deck.

wolf pack In the Second World War, the name given to a group of German submarines that would attack a single vessel or convoy.

INDEX

In this index, page numbers in *italics* refer to the captions of illustrations, while those in **bold** type refer to ship profiles and panel features.

ACKNOWLEDGMENTS

Dorling Kindersley would like to thank the following people for their help in the preparation of this book: the staff of the National Maritime Museum, especially Rachel Giles, Eleanor Dryden, and Fiona Renkin for co-ordinating the project, Enzo di Cosmo, Darren Leigh, Josh Akin, and Ken Hickey for photography at the museum, Simon Stephens and Bernard Bryant for handling and providing information about ship models, Liza Verity and David Taylor for writing the glossary, Jonathan Potts for his comments on Chapter 8, Clive Wilkinson for research, Philippa Mackenzie for co-ordinating photography of the Reserve Collections, and Linda Clarke and the Art and Objects Handling team; Katie Mann, Ellen Nanney, Paul F. Johnston, and Michael R. Harrison at the Smithsonian Institution for all their help; Joanna Chisholm and Polly Boyd for additional editorial work; Alison Gardener for additional design work; Hunny Gahir for editorial and design assistance; Mark Bracey for DTP advice; Kenny Grant for initial design work; and Erin Richards for administrative support.

QUOTATIONS

Every effort has been made to identify and contact copyright holders. The publishers will be glad to rectify, in future editions, any omissions or corrections brought to their notice.

PICTURE CREDITS

Dorling Kindersley would like to thank the following for their help with images: Eleanor Driscoll, Lucy Waitt and David Taylor at the National Maritime Museum Picture Library; Romaine Werblow and Hayley Smith in the DK Picture Library; Giovanni Cafagna at Corbis; Claudia Jew at the Mariner's Museum, Virginia. Also for help in accommodating photoshoots: Fred Hocker and staff at the Vasa Museum, Stockholm; Tracy E. Perkins and staff at the Jamestown–Yorktown Settlement, Virginia; Lt Cdr F. Nowosielski MBE and all at HMS *Victory*, Portsmouth Historic Dockyard; Cees Zevenbergen, Robert Verhoeven, Wouter Heijfield, and staff at the Maritime Museum, Rotterdam; Wanda Bolte and staff at the Scheepvaart-museum, Amsterdam; Sarah Fisher and staff at Mystic Seaport, Connecticut; LCDR Frank Sides, Stephen Finnigan, and staff at the Historic Ship *Nautilus* and Submarine Force Museum, Connecticut. Special thanks to the US Navy, in particular Lt John E. Gay, Lt Garret Kasper, Cdr James W. Graybeal, Lt Cdr Christopher Scholl, USNR, Cpt Martin J. Erdossy and everyone aboard the USS *George Washington*.

Key:
t=top; b=bottom; l=left, r=right; c=centre; A=above; B=below

Abbreviations

AA – The Picture Desk: Art Archive; **BAL** – Bridgeman Art Library, London/New York; **BM:** British Museum, London; **DK:** DK Images; **Hulton** – Hulton Archive/Getty Images; **IWM** – Imperial War Museum, London; **MM** – The Mariners' Museum, Newport News, Virginia; **Mystic** – Mystic Seaport – The Museum of America and the Sea; **NHF** – Naval Historical Foundation, Washington, D.C.; **NMM** – © National Maritime Museum, London

p1 NMM: (F2455). **p2/3 Hulton:** Topical Press Agency/Firmin. **p4/5 Corbis:** Onne van der Wal. **p5 akg-images:** Erich Lessing (5); **Corbis** (7); **NMM:** Greenwich Hospital Collection (BHC0565) (4); Alan Villiers Collection (N61437) (6); **Photo12.com:** ARJ/Bibliothèque Nationale, Paris (3); **AA:** Bibliothèque Nationale, Paris/Harper Collins Publishers (2); National Museum Bucharest/Dagli Orti (1); **Getty Images:** Stone/Kos (8). **p6 DK:** Gary Ombler tl, tc, tr, bl, bc, br. **p7 DK:** Gary Ombler tl, tc, tr, bl, bc, br. **p8/9 AA:** National Museum Bucharest/Dagli Orti. **p9 Corbis:** Stapleton Collection (1); **AA:** Bardo Museum Tunis/Dagli Orti (2). **p10 DK:** NMM/Exeter Maritime Museum/James Stevenson & Tina Chambers tl. **p10/11 Corbis:** Stapleton Collection b. **p11 Corbis:** Archivo Iconigrafico, S.A. crA; **DK:** BM/James Stevenson & Tina Chambers tc. **p12 Alamy Images:** Bryan & Cherry Alexander Photography tc; **Corbis:** Galen Rowell tl; **DK:** NMM/James Stevenson & Tina Chambers bl. **p12/13 BAL:** Giruadon/Lauros b. **p13 DK:** BM/Peter Hayman crA, crB; Pitt Rivers Museum, Oxford tc; **AA:** Dagli Orti br. **p14 Corbis:** Roman Soumar clB; **DK:** NMM/Exeter Maritime Museum/James Stevenson & Tina Chambers bcl; NMM/James Stevenson & Tina Chambers tl; **AA:** Egyptian Museum, Cairo/Dagli Orti br. **p14/15 AA:** Dagli Orti t. **p15 DK:** clB; **AA:** Dagli Orti cr. **p16 Archivi Alinari:** cl; **BAL:** Giraudon/Lauros tr; **© The British Museum:** bl; **DK:** NMM/Exeter Maritime Museum/James Stevenson & Tina Chambers cB; **NMM:** (F2568) bc; (F2570) cr. **p17 Alamy Images:** Craig Lovell tl; **Corbis:** Keren Su cl; **DK:** James Stevenson & Tina Chambers tr; **NMM:** (E9006-150) crB; (F2579) bc; Maker: Kim Allen (F2581) crA. **p18 DK:** BM/James Stevenson & Tina Chambers tl. **p18/19 AA:** Bardo Museum, Tunis/Dagli Orti c. **p19 Corbis:** Bob Abraham crA. **p20 Corbis:** Neil Rabinowitz bl; **DK:** International Sailing Craft Association/Mike Dunning tc; **NMM:** (F3138) tr. **p21 © The British Museum:** br; **Corbis:** Historical Picture Archive tcr. **p22 Corbis:** Gianni Dagli Orti t; **AA:** Musée du Louvre, Paris/Dagli Orti bc. **p23 DK:** BM/Ivor Kerslake cBl; **AA:** National Archaeological Museum, Athens/Dagli Orti br. **p24 Corbis:** Bettmann c; **The Trireme Trust:** Photo: Paul Lipke tr. **p25 BAL:** Instituto da Biblioteca Nacional, Lisbon, Portugal (fl.1299) bc; **The Trireme Trust:** Photo: Paul Lipke t. **p26 Corbis:** Bettmann crA; **DK:** BM/Christi Graham & Nick Nichols br; BM/James Stevenson & Tina Chambers clB; NMM/James Stevenson bcl. **p27 BAL:** Egyptian Museum, Turin, Italy/Alinari tr; **Werner Forman Archive:** bl; **NMM:** (D6014) br; **AA:** Dagli Orti cr; **Science & Society Picture Library:** Science Museum, London cl. **p28 Archivi Alinari:** cBr; **BAL:** BM cl; Museo Archeologico Nazionale, Naples, Italy/Alinari cr; **Corbis:** Archivo Iconografico, S.A. bl; Roger Wood tr; **Science & Society Picture Library:** Science Museum, London c. **p29 Archivi Alinari:** tr, crA, br; **American Academy in Rome:** Museo Nazionale Romano/Ph: Lionel Casson c; **DK:** BM/Christi Graham & Nick Nichols tl; NMM/James Stevenson bl. **p30/31 AA:** Bibliothèque Nationale, Paris/Harper Collins Publishers. **p31 Corbis:** Archivo Iconografico, S.A. (2); Arne Hodalic (3); **Hulton:** (1). **p32 AA:** Historiska Muséet, Oslo/Dagli Orti tl. **p32/33 Hulton:** b. **p33 Corbis:** Bettmann crA; **AA:** Bodleian Library, Oxford/The Bodleian Library (Laud Misc 720 folio 226v) tc. **p34 BAL:** BM br; **DK:** BM tcr. **p35 BAL:** British Library, London, UK (Add 39943 f.2b) crB; **Corbis:** Archivo Iconografico, S.A. bcr; **DK:** Roskilde Viking Ships Museum/Peter Anderson tr, cA. **p36 DK:** Frits Solvang, courtesy of the Universitetets kulturhistoriske museer/Vikingskipshuset l; © University Museum of Cultural Heritage – University of Oslo, Norway cr; Viking Ship Museum, Oslo, Norway/Peter Anderson tr. **p37 Corbis:** Bettmann tl; **DK:** bl; Andy Crawford bcl; **NMM:** (F3030) br; **Vikingeskibsmuseet (Viking Ship Museum, Denmark):** Werner Karrasch tr.

p38 Corbis: Nik Wheeler cl; Werner Forman Archive tc. **p39 Corbis:** Bettmann crA; Ted Spiegel l; Wolfgang Kaehler br; **DK:** Danish National Museum/Peter Anderson crB. **p40 Bibliothèque Nationale De France, Paris:** tl; **BAL:** BM tc; **AA:** Musée de la Tapisserie, Bayeaux/Dagli Orti bl. **p41 AA:** Musée de la Tapisserie, Bayeaux/Dagli Orti tr, b. **p42 DK:** NMM/James Stevenson tcB; **Förderverein Historische Hansekogge Kiel e.V.:** Hans-Georg Billmann bl. **p43 BAL:** British Library, London, UK (Roy 18 E VI f.103v) tl; **DK:**Viking Ship Museum, Oslo, Norway/Peter Anderson bc; **Förderverein Historische Hansekogge Kiel e.V.:** Hans-Georg Billmann crB. **p44 Alamy Images:** Andy Arthur tcl; **Mary Evans Picture Library:** bl. **p44/45 AA:** Hamburg Staatsarchiv/Harper Collins Publishers c. **p45 Corbis:** Steve Raymer crA; **AA:** British Library, London br. **p46 Nationalmuseet (National Museum Of Denmark):** Lennart Larsen br; **NMM:** (F2573) bl; **AA:** Viking Ship Museum, Oslo/Dagli Orti c; **Rex Features:** Rob Walls (RAP) tr. **p47 BAL:** Historika Museet, Stockholm, Sweden bl; **Corbis:** Ted Spiegel clA; **DK:** NMM/James Stevenson c; Viking Ship Museum, Oslo, Norway/Peter Anderson tr; **Vikingeskibsmuseet (Viking Ship Museum, Denmark):** Werner Karrasch br. **p48 BAL:** Corpus Christi College, Oxford, UK (Ms CCC 157 p383) br; **NMM:** (A7445) bl; **AA:** British Library, London tr; Museo Correr, Venice/Dagli Orti cl; **www.undiscoveredscotland.co.uk:** c. **p49 NMM:** (C1883) bl; Greenwich Hospital Collection (F2559) t; **© Kiel City Council:** Image courtesy of NMM (5672) bc; **AA:** Biblioteca Nazionale, Turin/Dagli Orti br. **p50 BAL:** Palazzo Ducale, Urbino, Italy tl; **Corbis:** Underwood & Underwood cA; **Hellenic Maritime Museum:** Makis Skiadaresses br. **p51 Corbis:** Archivo Iconografico, S.A.. **p52 AA:** Bodleian Library, Oxford/The Bodleian Library (Bodley 264 folio 218r) t; Museo Bottacin, Padua/Dagli Orti bl, bcr. **p53 AA:** Biblioteca Nazionale Marciana, Venice/Dagli Orti tc; Museo Correr, Venice/Dagli Orti b. **p54 Corbis:** Archivo Iconografico, S.A. b; **DK:** Warwick Castle/Dave King clA; **AA:** BM tr. **p55 BAL:** British Library, London, UK (Ms Royal 20 All f.1240) clA; **DK:** Pitt Rivers Museum, Oxford/Alan Hills & Geoff Brightling cBr; **NMM:** Georges Prin Collection (D8425) br; **AA:** Topkapi Museum, Istanbul/Dagli Orti cr. **p56 DK:** Pitt Rivers Museum, Oxford/Geoff Brightling tl. **p56/57 Corbis:** Arnie Hodalic c. **p57 Corbis:** Dave G Houser cr; **DK:** NMM/James Stevenson & Tina Chambers bc. **p58 BAL:** Bibliothèque Nationale, Paris, France (Ms Fr 2810 f.188) t; **DK:** Royal Museum of Scotland c; **AA:** Topkapi Museum, Istanbul/Dagli Orti br. **p59 Corbis:** Dean Conger crA; Robert Holmes cAl; **DK:** NMM/Exeter Maritime Museum/James Stevenson & Tina Chambers b; NMM/James Stevenson tc; **AA:** Bibliothèque Nationale, Paris cBr. **p60 BAL:** Private Collection tl; **Corbis:** Michael Setboun b. **p61 42 Degrees South:** Rob Walls tc; **Corbis:** Nik Wheeler cl; **DK:** trB; **National Geographic Image Collection:** H Edward Kim bc. **p62 BAL:** Fitzwilliam Museum, University of Cambridge, UK tc; **Corbis:** Michael Maslan Historic Photographs bl. **p63 Corbis:** Christie's Images t; Underwood & Underwood br. **p64 DK:** Geoff Brightling cl; NMM/James Stevenson & Tina Chambers bl; NMM/Tina Chambers br; **NMM:** (PU8574) tr. **p65 DK:** NMM/James Stevenson & Tina Chambers b; Pitt Rivers Museum, Oxford tr; **NMM:** (PZ1638) tl. **p66/67 Photo12.com:** ARJ/Bibliothèque Nationale, Paris. **p67 AA:** Maritime Museum, Stockholm, Sweden/Dagli Orti (3); New York Public Library/Harper Collins Publishers (1); Terry Engell Gallery/Eileen Tweedy (2). **p68 BAL:** Bibliothèque Nationale, Paris, France/Giraudon/Lauros tl; **p68/69 AA:** New York Public Library/Harper Collins Publishers c. **p69 BAL:** Hermitage, St Petersburg, Russia cA; **NMM:** (BHC0705) br. **p70 NMM:** (3089) bc; **AA:** Marine Museum, Lisbon/Dagli Orti tr. **p71 Corbis:** Stapleton Collection tr; **AA:** General Archive of the Indies, Seville/Dagli Orti cl; Museo de la Torre del Oro, Seville/Dagli Orti b. **p72 AA:** Museo do Caramulo, Portugal/Dagli Orti b; Science Academy, Lisbon/Dagli Orti cAl. **p73 DK:** Peter Wilson bc; **AA:** Arquivo Nacional da Torre do Tombo, Lisbon/Dagli Orti tr; Marine Museum, Lisbon/Dagli Orti tc. **p74 Corbis:** clA; **NMM:** (D9602) cA. **p74/75 Photo12.com:** ARJ/Musée Nationale du Château, Versailles b. **p75 NMM:** (A1730-1) tc. **p76 Corbis:** Bettmann clA, bl; **NMM:** (PX7268) tr. **p77 BAL:** British Library, London, UK (Add 8946 f.52) bc; Private Collection cBl; **NMM:** (8450) crA; (D9258) tl. **p78/79 Corbis:** Archivo Iconografico, S.A. **p80 Maritiem Museum 'Prins Hendrik', Rotterdam, The Netherlands:** Jean Korff br; **NMM:** (BHC0705) c; **Bildarchiv Österreichische Nationalbibliothek, Wien:** (MS 2538 f.109) cr; **Photo12.com:** ARJ tr; **Courtesy of the Trustees of the V&A:** bl. **p81 BAL:** Musée de la Marine, Paris, France/Giraudon/Lauros clB; **DK:** NMM/James Stevenson br; **NMM:** (D3997) tr; **AA:** Private Collection, Italy/Dagli Orti tl. **p82 Corbis:** George HH Huey tl. **p82/83 AA:** Terry Engell Gallery/Eileen Tweedy b. **p83 DK:** BM tcr. **p84 BAL:** tr; **Corbis:** Bettmann clA; **DK:** Michael Zabe tcB; **Institut Amatller D'art Hispànic (Arxiu MAS):** cBl; **NMM:** (PU4865) bl; **AA:** Archaeological Museum, Lima/Dagli Orti cr. **p85 DK:** BM clB; NMM/James Stephenson clA; **Photo12.com:** Oasis/Bibliothèque Nationale, Paris br; **AA:** Museo Casa de Murillo, La Paz, Bolivia/Dagli Orti tr. **p86 BAL:** Private Collection cBl; Wallace Collection, London, UK tcl.; **Corbis:** Stapleton Collection tl; **MM:** bl. **p86/87 Corbis:** Bettmann c. **p87 BAL:** Library of Congress, Washington, D.C., USA br; Private Collection tr. **p88 DK:** Gary Ombler tl, tr, crA, b, cAl, cAr, tcl, tcr, clA. **p89 DK:** Gary Ombler cl, bl, br, bcA, bcB; **Jamestown-Yorktown Foundation, Williamsburg, Virginia:** tr. **p90 Corbis:** Museum of the City of New York tl; **DK:** Kim Sayer clB; **NMM:** (BHC2755) cAr. **p91 BAL:** Min. Defense – Service Historique de l'Armée de Terre, France/Giraudon r; The Stapleton Collection bcl; **AA:** Navy Historical Service, Vincennes, France/Dagli Orti tl. **p92 DK:** Mary Rose Trust/Geoff Brightling tl; **p92/93 AA:** Maritime Museum, Stockholm, Sweden/Dagli Orti. **p94 Corbis:** Adam Woolfitt br; **NMM:** (BHC2763) bcr; **AA:** Magdalene College, Cambridge/Eileen Tweedy t. **p95 Corbis:** Adam Woolfitt tc, tr, tcr; **DK:** Mary Rose Trust/Geoff Brightling br. **p96 BAL:** Christie's Images b; **Corbis:** Christie's Images cl; Hulton-Deutsche Collection tr. **p97 Corbis:** Bettmann c; **Photo12.com:** ARJ/Musée de l'Armée, Madrid bcl; **AA:** Tate Gallery, London/Eileen Tweedy tr. **p98/99 akg-images:** Cameraphoto. **p100 BAL:** Czartoryski Museum, Cracow, Poland cl; **NMM:** (X3) bl; **AA:** Bibliothèque des Arts Décoratifs, Paris/Dagli Orti tr; Bodleian Library, Oxford/The Bodleian Library (Ms Rawl A 102 folio 20r) cA. **p101 BAL:** Private Collection cl; Timothy Millet Collection tr; **NMM:** (BHC0262) b. **p102 BAL:** Private Collection clA; **NMM:** (BHC2951) tc. **p102/103 NMM:** (BHC0270) b. **p103 NMM:** (BHC2662) cr; **AA:** University Library, Cadiz/Dagli Orti tc. **p104 John Hamill:** br; **NMM:** (BHC2787) cl; (D8925) tr. **p105 Corbis:** Bettmann cAl; **DK:** Gary Ombler br; **AA:** Musée du Château de Versailles/Dagli Orti crB. **p106 DK:** Gary Ombler cl, bl, bc, br; **AA:** Cornelis de Vries tr. **p107 DK:** Gary Ombler tl, tr, clA, b, cAl, cAr, tcl, tcr. **p108 British Library, London:** (Cotton MS, Titus A XXVI, f.48v) cr; **Corbis:** Christie's Images bl; **MM:** tr; **NMM:** (BHC0262) br; (F3025) c; (F3026) bc. **p109 DK:** NMM/James Stevenson & Tina Chambers br; **NMM:** Makers: Jim Less & Phillip Wride (D3837-2) tl; Makers: Jim Less & Phillip Wride (D3838-1) tc; Maker: Granville Peter (F2574) bl. **p110/111 NMM:** Greenwich Hospital Collection (BHC0565). **p111 NMM:** (BHC0510) (1); (BHC0811) (2); MOD Art Collection (BHC1906) (3). **p112 NMM:** (B2756) c; (E4707-2) tl. **p113 NMM:** (BHC0510). **p114 NMM:** (BHC0285) cl. **p114/115 NMM:** (A8652 & A8653) b. **p115 NMM:** (BHC0294) tl; (BHC2997) crA; **Louise Thomas:** tc. **p116 NMM:** (BHC0346) tl. **p116/117 Photo12.com:** ARJ/Musée de la Marine, Paris b. **p117 Corbis:** Robert Holmes crA; **© Musée National de la Marine, Paris:** L-S Jaulmes (2001-EE-23(2)) crB; L-S Jaulmes (2001-EE-5(4)) br; L-S Jaulmes (2001-EE-6(3)) cr; **NMM:** (SPB/14) cAr; **Photo12.com:** ARJ/Musée du Louvre, Paris tc. **p118 NMM:** (BHC0325) b; (E2417-2) tc. **p119 Alamy Images:** Popperfoto tc; **BAL:** Archives du Ministere des Affaires Etrangers, Paris, France bc; **Mary Evans Picture Library:** Daniel Maclise cr; **NMM:** (PU5183) cB. **p120 DK:** NMM/Tina Chambers bl, bc, bcl; **NMM:** (BHC3602) cl. **p120/121 AA:** Musée de l'Ancien, Havre/Dagli Orti t. **p121 NMM:** (7301) cl. **p122 NMM:** Greenwich Hospital Collection (BHC0355). **p123 Werner Forman Archive:** tr; **NMM:** (A5399-3) br. **p124 Corbis:** tr; Bettmann bl; **AA:** Science Museum, London/Eileen Tweedy tlB; **National Museum of American History, Smithsonian Institution:** (90-7408) br. **p125 DK:** Musée de Saint-Malo Tina Chambers crB; **NMM:** (C1099) br; (PW3474) clA. **p126 NMM:** (DR2179-37) cl; **AA:** Museo de la Torre del Oro, Seville/Dagli Orti bl. **p127 NMM:** Greenwich Hospital Collection (BHC2889) crA; (D4861-11A) tc; (D8051) cA; (PX8975) b. **p128 DK:** Gary Ombler tr, clA, crA, b, cAl, cAr, tcl, tcr; **Philip Ormerod:** tl. **p129 DK:** Gary Ombler tl, tr, crA, bl, br, bcl, bcr, tcl, tcr; **NMM:** (BHC3696) cBl. **p130 NMM:** (BHC0528) t; (BHC2876) bcr. **p131 NMM:** (BHC0552) cAr; **AA:** Musée de la Marine, Paris/Dagli Orti cB. **p132 Corbis:** Francis G Mayer b; Museum of the City of New York tc; Sygma/Ira Wyman clA. **p133 NMM:** (D7801) clB; (PU6025) crA; (PY8172) br. **p134/135 NMM:** (BHC0622). **p136 © Musée National de la Marine, Paris:** L-S Jaulmes (1980-EE-166(2)) c; **NMM:** (BHC0870) bl; (BHC3307) tr; (D4060-1) crB; Greenwich Hospital Collection (F2449) br. **p137 British Library, London:** (Kings 40 f.93v) tr; **NMM:** (F2561) br; (PU7409) bc; (F2455) cl; (VV538) cr; **AA:** Cornelis de Vries tc. **p138 DK:** NMM/James Stevenson bl; **NMM:** (BHC0340) tr; (D3335-1) crA. **p139 © Musée National de la Marine, Paris:** L-S Jaulmes (2001-DE-122(3)) tl; L-S Jaulmes (2003-DE-237 (3)) cr; **Mystic:** (1966-315-1982) tr; **NMM:** (D4053-1) b; (D7799) tc; Greenwich Hospital Collection (F2489-1 & F2489-2) c & cl. **p140 DK:** BM/Alan Hills & Chas Howson tl. **p140/141 NMM:** (BHC0811) b. **p141 NMM:** (D9255) tc. **p142 DK:** NMM/Exeter Maritime Museum/James Stevenson & Tina Chambers tc, clA; **NMM:** (BHC0853) b. **p143 BAL:** Harold Samuel Collection, Corporation of London, UK br; **NMM:** (BHC0748) tl. **p144 British Library, London:** (Kings 40 f.84) tl; **DK:** John Heseltine bcA; International Sailing Craft Association/Mike Dunning b; **AA:** Musée du Louvre, Paris tr. **p145 DK:** NMM/James Stevenson crB; **NMM:** (BHC2361) bl; **AA:** Eileen Tweedy tl. **p146 Sjöhistoriska Museet (The National Maritime Museum, Sweden):** clA. **p146/147 NMM:** (BHC1933) b. **p147 Corbis:** Hulton-Deutsch Collection tl; **DK:** NMM cr; **Courtesy of Lloyd's of London:** tc. **p148 DK:** Gary Ombler tl, tc, tr, cr, bl, bc, br. **p149 DK:** Gary Ombler cB, bl, br, bcl, bcr, cBl, t. **p150 DK:** Wilberforce House, Hull Museums and Art Galleries/Tina Chambers crB, bc, bcA; **NMM:** (E0064) cAl; (PX9696) tl. **p151 AMISTAD America, Inc.:** Photo: Chad Lyons c; **BAL:** Wilberforce House, Hull City Museums and Art Galleries, UK tc; **DK:** Charlestown Shipwreck & Heritage Centre/Alex Wilson bc; **The Naval City of Karlskrona, Sweden:** br. **p152 BAL:** Private Collection tr; **DK:** NMM/James Stevenson & Tina Chambers cBl; NMM/Tina Chambers cr, cAl; Tina Chambers c, bcA; Musée de Saint-Malo/Tina Chambers tcl. **p153 Alamy Images:** Agence Images tr; **Corbis:** Historical Picture Archive b; **DK:** Tina Chambers clA. **p154 DK:** NMM/Exeter Maritime Museum/James Stevenson & Tina Chambers br; **Maritiem Museum 'Prins Hendrik', Rotterdam, The Netherlands:** Jean Korff bl; **NMM:**

Acquired with the assistance of the NACF (BHC0727) tr; (D3334-1) cr; (F2491) c. **p155 BAL:** Bibliothèque de l'Arsenal, Paris, France/ Archives Charmet tc; Private Collection/ Michael Graham-Stewart tr; **NMM:** (BHC1040) tl; (F2494) br; (F2566) bl. **p156 DK:** NMM tl; **NMM:** MOD Art Collection (BHC2396) crA; **AA:** Private Collection/ Harper Collins Publishers bc. **p157 NMM:** MOD Art Collection (BHC1906). **p158 BAL:** Private Collection/Ken Welsh tc; **Corbis:** Wolfgang Kaehler bl; **Mary Evans Picture Library:** clB. **p158/159 NMM:** (BHC0360) b. **p159 Corbis:** Bettmann tr; **NMM:** (C8423) bcr; (D7562-2) crB. **p160 DK:** NMM/Tina Chambers cA; **NMM:** (F0342) tl; **Photo12.com:** ARJ br; Musée National du Château, Versailles bl. **p161 BAL:** National Library of Australia, Canberra, Australia tcl; **Corbis:** Swim Ink/Percy Trompf cr; **DK:** NMM/James Stevenson, Maker: Robert A Lightley b; **NMM:** (BHC4227) tcrB. **p162 Courtesy of Yves Duflot:** tl. **p162/163 Alamy Images:** Simon Grosset b. **p163 NMM:** (D6783-1) c; (D9254) tl; (PU2851) tr. **p164 Mary Evans Picture Library:** De Vancy bl; **NMM:** (PAH9205) tl; (F1345) tcl; **AA:** Naval Museum, Genoa/Dagli Orti cr. **p165 BAL:** National Library of Australia, Canberra, Australia tc; **Corbis:** Historical Picture Archive cl; **NMM:** (PU2115) b. **p166 Alamy Images:** Vintage Images bl; **DK:** Natural History Museum/Downe House/ Dave King tr; **AA:** br; **The Wellcome Institute Library, London:** tlB. **p167 NMM:** (D3344-1) tr. **p168/169 akg-images:** Erich Lessing. **p169 Corbis:** James Gibson (5); Underwood & Underwood (1); **Hulton:** London Stereoscopic Company (2); **AA:** BM (3); **National Museum of American History, Smithsonian Institution:** (4). **p170 DK:** Science Museum, London b; **Hulton:** Archive Photos/Stock Montage c; **NMM:** (BHC2379) tl. **p171 Corbis:** Underwood & Underwood. **p172 Corbis:** tcr. **p172/173 Corbis:** t. **p173 Corbis:** Bettmann bcl, bcr. **p174 Hulton:** Rischgitz clA; **Courtesy of SS Great Britain:** bl. **p174/175 Courtesy of SS Great Britain:** b. **p175 Corbis:** clA; **DK:** br; NMM/James Stephenson bc; Science Museum, London/John Lepine bcr; **NMM:** (PY0923) tr. **p176 NMM:** (D0283) cl. **p176/177 Hulton** c. **p177 DK:** NMM/James Stevenson cr; **NMM:** (BHC3383) bc. **p178 DK:** NMM bc; **Science & Society Picture Library:** Science Museum, London bl; **Scottish Maritime Museum:** tr. **p179 DK:** tr; **NMM:** (N47745) br. **p180 DK:** NMM/James Stevenson & Tina Chambers c; **Mary Evans Picture Library:** tc; **MM:** cl. **p180/181 NMM:** (F2450) b. **p181 Mary Evans Picture Library:** Le Petit Journal tr; **NMM:** (F2488-1 & F2488-2) tl and tcl; (F2450) c; **Science & Society Picture Library:** Science Museum, London cr. **p182 Corbis:** b; **Mary Evans Picture Library:** cr; **NMM:** (PU6638) tr. **p183 NMM:** (PU6712) tr; (PAH8979) br; **Science & Society Picture Library:** Science Museum, London c, cr. **p184 DK:** NMM/Tina Chambers tl. **p184/185 Hulton:** London Stereoscopic Company c. **p185 Hulton:** crA. **p186 Corbis:** Sean Sexton Collection tl; **NMM:** (A8573-G) bl. **p186/187 Corbis:** Historical Picture Archive t. **p187 NMM:** (P39490) bc. **p188 Corbis:** Hulton-Deutsch Collection bl; **NMM:** (B5097) crB; (F0138) tc. **p189 DK:** NMM/James Stevenson & Tina Chambers cAr; **Library Of Congress, Washington, D.C.:** (3g02388) crB; **NMM:** (G10577) tl; (PX8273) bc. **p190 Hulton:** Otto Herschan cA; **NMM:** (D7209) bl. **p191 British Library, London:** Samuel Bourne (OIOC Photo 11/(37)) b; **Corbis:** Kit Kittle crA; **NMM:** (58-5575) tl; (C3277) c. **p192 DK:** NMM/Tina Chambers tr; **Hulton:** cAr; FJ Mortimer b; **Royal National Lifeboat Institute:** cl. **p193 Corbis:** Onne van der Wal tr; Richard Cummins bcr; **Royal National Lifeboat Institute:** tl. **p194 Public Record Office:** tl. **p194/195 AA:** BM b. **p195 NMM:** (A1818) tr. **p196 NMM:** (d9622-1) tc; (d9811) c. **p196/197 NMM:** (792) b. **p197 Corbis:** Bettmann tr; **NMM:** (P3038) c. **p198 MM:** tr, c. **p199 Corbis:** Hulton-Deutsch Collection clA; **NMM:** (BHC0643) tc; **Photo12.com:** c; ARJ br. **p200 AA:** Domenica del Corriere/Dagli Orti tl. **p200/201 National Museum of American History, Smithsonian Institution** b. **p201 P & O Art Collection:** tc. **p202 Hulton:** bl; **NMM:** (D4033) clA; Pope Collection (RP-10-29) tr(*Blue Funnel*); Pope Collection (RP-12-18) tr(*P&O*); Pope Collection (RP-13-3) tr(*Pacific Steam*); Pope Collection (RP-15-12) tr(*Western Canada*). **p202/203 Corbis:** b. **p203 NMM:** (F2429) crA; (G10514) tc; **National Museum of American History, Smithsonian Institution:** br. **p204 Alamy Images:** Popperfoto tl; **Mary Evans Picture Library:** Le Rire bc; **Hulton:** crB. **p205 Hulton:** c; Archive Photos/Byron Collection/Museum of the City of New York br; **NMM:** (B7392) cr; **Statue of Liberty/Ellis Island, National Monument:** cB. **p206 Corbis:** Bettmann tl; **Statue of Liberty/Ellis Island, National Monument:** clA. **p206/207 Hulton:** b **p208 National Museums Liverpool:** (Model No: 391/Accession No: 37.37) br; **NMM:** (PU6695) crB; (PY9008) tr; **Science & Society Picture Library:** Science Museum, London bl. **p209 DK:** cr; **Hulton:** cB; **National Museums Liverpool:** (Model No: 411; Accession No: 32.91) tr; **NMM:** (P17506) br; (PU6787) bl; (PY0228) cl. **p210 NMM:** (C9298) crB; (PV2097) clA; (PW1185) tr; (F2446) b. **p211 Courtesy of Caldercraft/JoTika Ltd:** crA; **DK:** NMM/ James Stevenson b; **NMM:** (BHC3171) tr; (D7538) crB; (D7540) tc; (F3143) cl. **p212 NMM:** (E0067-2) tl; (F2430-1) bc; (F2430-2) bcr; (F2430-3) br. **p213 Corbis:** James Gibson. **p214 NMM:** (C3953). **p215 Corbis:** Hulton-Deutsch Collection tr; **NMM:** (D9752) cAr; (PW3719) br. **p216 Corbis:** tl; Medford Historical Society Collection cr; **MM:**cAr. **p216/217 MM:** b. **p217 Corbis:** tc, cl; Bettmann tr. **p218 DK:** Gary Ombler tl, tr, cA, cl, cr, b, cAl, cAr, tcl, tcr. **p219 DK:** Gary Ombler tl, tr, bl, tcl, tcr; **Maritiem Museum 'Prins Hendrik', Rotterdam, The Netherlands:** cr. **p220 NMM:** (C5861). **p221 NMM:** (C8659) crA; (F2428) bc; **Photo Scala, Florence:** Museo del Risorgimento, Milano © 1990 tl. **p222 NMM:** (F2427) cB; **The Royal Navy Submarine Museum:** bl. **p222/223 Corbis:** Bettmann c. **p223 Corbis:** cl; Philadelphia Museum of Art tr; **NMM:** (PW1222) br. **p224 Corbis:** Bettmann bl; **NMM:** (A2472) cl; **NHF:** US Naval Academy Museum Collection: Gift of George R Thompson, 1924 (KN-10867) tr. **p224/225 MM:** b. **p225 © Musée National de la Marine, Paris:** P Dantec (1993-DE-45(2)) cr; **NMM:** (BHC3423) tl; **NHF:** (NH 61568) br; Navy Art Collection, Washington, D.C.: Donation of RAdm JW Schmidt (NH 85593-KN) tc; US Navy Art Collection, Washington, D.C. (NH 76324-KN) crB. **p226 Corbis:** tr; **NMM:** (F2451) bl; (F2453) c; (F2452) cl; (F2444) cr; **NHF:** Collection of PayM William R Pattison (NH 93400) br. **p227 NMM:** On Loan from Swires & Son (F2552) tl; (F2556) c; (F2447) bl; (F2448) tr; (F3145) br. **p228 NMM:** Alan Villiers Collection (N61437). **p229 MM:** (1), (3); **NMM:** (N21886) (2). **p230 DK:** tl. **p231 MM**. **p232 MM:** tl; **Courtesy of Pride of Baltimore, Inc.:** Photo by Jerome Bird r. **p233 BAL:** Peabody Essex Museum, Salem, Massachusetts, USA br; **NMM:** Green Blackwall Collection (D9898) tl; **AA:** Cornelis de Vries cr. **p234 Reproduced courtesy of the Australian National Maritime Museum:** clA, clB; **Courtesy of Maritime Heritage Prints – John Stobart Galleries, Boston:** b; **NMM:** (P39487) tc. **p235 Corbis:** Bettmann t; **MM:** br; **NMM:** (E4522-1) cB. **p236 Gibsons of Scilly**. **p237 Corbis:** tcr; **DK:** NMM/James Stevenson crA, bc; **Hulton:** Rischgitz clB. **p238/239 NMM:** (P7148). **p240 DK:** NMM/James Stevenson & Tina Chambers c; **NMM:** (P7145) bl . **p241 DK:** NMM/James Stevenson & Tina Chambers br; **NMM:** (C1057/A) t. **p242 Corbis:** Christie's Images tr; **Mystic:** (162-6-1967-122) bl; **NMM:** Acquired with the assistance of the NACF (BHC0770) cl; (F2563) br; **Courtesy of Pride of Baltimore, Inc.:** Photo by Roger Stevens cr. **p243 Courtesy of Maine Maritime Museum, Bath, Maine:** tr, bl; **MM:** crB; **NMM:** (BHC1161) br; (F2558) tl. **p244 Corbis:** Bettmann tr; **Mystic:** (1962-5-1967-121) cr; **NMM:** Green Blackwall Collection (BHC3532) cl; (BHC3580) bl; (D2867-2) br; **National Museum of American History, Smithsonian Institution:** (84-10064) c. **p245 DK:** NMM/ James Stevenson & Tina Chambers bl; **MM:** br; **Mystic:** (1962-21-1967-135) tr; (1976-21-1967-135) cr. **p246 DK:** Reproduced courtesy of the Australian National Maritime Museum tl; **NMM:** (N21886) r. **p247 Corbis:** Dallas & John Heaton c; **DK:** NMM/James Stevenson & Tina Chambers br. **p248 AA:** Naval Museum, Genoa/Dagli Orti bl. **p249 NMM:** (D4456/10). **p250 DK:** NMM/James Stevenson & Tina Chambers bl; **MM:** t; **AA:** Biblioteca Nacional, Madrid/Dagli Orti cB. **p251 DK:** Town Docks Museum, Hull/ Frank Greenaway tr, tc; **NMM:** (BHC1035) br; **AA:** Musée de la Marine, Paris/Dagli Orti bl. **p252 Corbis:** Schenectady Museum/Hall of Electrical History Foundation crA; **DK:** Gary Ombler tc, tr, bl, br, bcl, bcr, tcl, tcr; **Mystic:** (1941-626) clB; Claire White Peterson (1992-1571) tl. **p253 DK:** Gary Ombler cl, c, cr, bl, br, bclA, bclB, bcr, t. **p254 DK:** Gary Ombler c, bl; New Bedford Whaling Museum/ David Lyons crB; Scott Polar Institute/Frank Greenaway br; **NMM:** (C8557-18) crA. **p255 Corbis:** Bettmann bl; HS Hutchinson cr; **DK:** NMM/James Stevenson & Tina Chambers bc; **NMM:** (PY3425) t. **p256 Hulton:** Fox Photos cB. **p256/257 Hulton:** t. **p257 DK:** br; **Hulton:** Fox Photos crA. **p258 Corbis:** Michael St Maur Sheil br; **NMM:** (F2550) cl; Maker: Alistair Brown (F2562) cr; (F2564) bl; **Private Collection:** Photo by Frank M Sutcliffe tr. **p259 Mystic:** (1989-2021) br; **NMM:** Royal Collection Trust (F2492) bc; Maker: E Prowse (F2578) c; (N30345) tr. **p260 Corbis:** Sygma/Quemere Erwan tl; **p260/261 MM:** b. **p261 Corbis:** National Gallery Collection; By kind permission of the Trustees of the National Gallery, London tr. **p262 BAL:** Private Collection br; Royal Thames Yacht Club, London, UK t. **p263 Corbis:** Historical Picture Archive c; **MM:** b. **p264 MM:** tcl. **p264/265 Hulton:** Fox Photos c. **p265 Corbis:** Bettmann br; **DK:** NMM/James Stevenson & Tina Chambers crA; **Smithsonian American Art Museum, Smithsonian Institution:** *Yacht America* by Charles S. Raliegh (1973.150_1b) tc. **p266 Courtesy of The New Bedford Whaling Museum:** tl; **Corbis:** Bettmann bl; **Photo12.com:** Bertelsmann Lexicon Verlag tr. **p267 MM:** bl; **NMM:** Alan Villiers Collection (N61533) crA. **p268 Corbis**. **p269 Hulton:** Keystone (3); **IWM:** (Q45319) (2); **MM:** (1); **popperfoto.com:** (4). **p270 Corbis:** br; Hulton-Deutsch Collection cB, cAr; Swim Ink tl. **p271 MM**. **p272 Corbis:** crB; Swim Ink bcl; **Hulton:** cr; **AA:** Dominica del Corrier/Dagli Orti tr. **p273 akg-images:** tr; **Corbis:** cAl; **AA:** IWM b. **p274 DK:** IWM/Andy Crawford tc; **Hulton:** c; **NMM:** (P39545) bl. **p275 Corbis:** Bettmann tr, bcr; **NHF:** (NH 1836) cl. **p276 Corbis:** HN Rudd c; **MM:** b. **p277 Deutsches Museum München:** tr; **The Royal Navy Submarine Museum:** clA. **p278 Corbis:** Christie's Images tcl; Swim Ink tcr; **National Museum of American History, Smithsonian Institution:** bl. **p278/279 NMM:** (A2885) c. **p279 Corbis:** Bettmann cr; **DK:** NMM / James Stevenson cB; **NMM:** (G10839) br. **p280 Corbis:** Bettmann clB; Hulton-Deutsch Collection br, t; Ralph White cr; **NMM:** (PY5224) bl. **p281 Corbis:** br, tcr; Bettmann cBl; **© Fram Museum, Oslo:** Image courtesy of NMM (E0826) bl; **Hulton:** tclB; **NMM:** (E0580) crA. **p282 Corbis:** Sean Sexton Collection tclB; Underwood & Underwood br; **NMM:** (D5337) clA. **p283 Hulton:** Three Lions crA; Topical Press Agency c; **NMM:** (F2557) bl; **NHF:** (NH 50155) br; (NH 63636) tr. **p284 Hulton:** Topical Press Agency cl; **NMM:** (F3145) tr; **NHF:** Courtesy of Mr Franklin Moran (NH 64508) tl. **p284/285 NMM:** (F3145) b. **p285 NMM:** (D1649-6) t; (F3145) cl; **NHF:** (NH 57682) cr; **AA:** IWM c. **p286 Corbis:** Austrian Archives tl. **p286/287 IWM:** (Q45319). **p288 DK:** IWM/Andy Crawford cBl; **Hulton:** tcB; Spencer Arnold b. **p289 Australian War Memorial:** *Christmas Tour of Duty concert, Dili* 1999 by Sharpe, Wendy. Oil on canvas, 121.6 x 136.8 cml (ART91179) c; **Corbis:** tr; Bettmann bl; **Hulton:** cr. **p290 Hulton:** c; **NMM:** (E4606-1) tcB; **AA:** IWM/ Eileen Tweedy tcl. **p290/291 Corbis:** F Schensky b. **p291 Corbis:** tr. **p292 Corbis:** David Pollack clB; **DK:** IWM /Andy Crawford crB; **Hulton:** c; **IWM:** (Q19954) bl; (Q20343) tl. **p293 Corbis:** crA; **National Gallery Of Canada, Ottowa:** tl; **AA:** br. **p294 Tim Brown:** cr; **Corbis:** Bettmann tr; **Deutsches Museum München:** cB; **NMM:** (F2504) bc; **The Royal Navy Submarine Museum:** cl. **p295 Hulton:** cr; Topical Press Agency cA, cl; **The Royal Navy Submarine Museum:** tcr, br. **p296 NHF:** (NH 42236) c; (NH 42238) tr; (NH 63225) b. **p297 Hulton:** tl, tr; **National Air and Space Museum, Smithsonian Institution:** (SI-98-15497) b; **NHF:** (80-G-351904) crA; (NH 63545) crB. **p298 Mary Evans Picture Library:** tl. **p298/299 Hulton:** Keystone c. **p299 Corbis:** crB; Bettmann bc; **Hulton:** Topical Press Agency cA. **p300 Hulton:** b; Keystone tr; **NMM:** © Unknown (BHC2537) clA. **p301 Corbis:** Hulton-Deutsch Collection bcl; Swim Ink/Bernd Steiner c; **Hulton:** Fox Photos cr; **MM:** tr. **p302 Corbis:** Historical Picture Archive bcl; Underwood & Underwood tr; **DK:** Judith Miller/DK/Cobwebs cAr; **MM:** clB. **p302/303 Corbis:** Bettmann bc. **p303 Hulton:** Fox Photos br; **National Air and Space Museum, Smithsonian Institution:** (SI 98-20248) tc; (SI-98-20504) cr. **p304 NHF:** (80-G-65192) tr; (NH 73059) bl. **p305 Corbis:** Bettmann c; **NHF:** (NH 97536) br; **Courtesy of The Museum of World War II, Natick, Massachusetts:** tc. **p306 Corbis:** Schenectady Museum/Hall of Electrical History Foundation tc; **Hulton:** London Express c; **MM:** cl; **p306/307 NMM:** (F2454/F2569) b. **p307 Corbis:** KJ Historical tc; **Hulton:** Fox Photos c; Keystone tl; **NMM:** (F2569) cr. **p308 Hulton:** General Photographic Agency tc, cr; Topical Press Agency b; **MM:** cA. **p309 Corbis:** Neil Rabinowitz clA; **Hulton:** Sasha blA; Topical Press Agency br; **MM:** tr, crA. **p310 DK:** IWM/Andy Crawford tl. **p311 popperfoto.com**. **p312 Hulton:** b; **AA:** tl. **p313 akg-images:** cr; **DK:** IWM/Andy Crawford tcl; **Hulton:** Fox Photos br; Keystone cl. **p314 Corbis:** Bettmann tc; **DK:** IWM/Geoff Dann tcr; **IWM:** (A10296) bl. **p315 Corbis:** Bettmann bc; **DK:** IWM/ Andy Crawford c; **Hulton:** Keystone cl; **IWM:** (A9421) tr. **p316 Museum of Science and Industry, Chicago, Il:** tr, cB; **NMM:** (P39674) bl. **p317 Corbis:** cl; Acme Photo br; Hulton-Deutsch Collection cr. **p318/319 Corbis:** Bettmann. **p320 DK:** IWM/Geoff Dann tl; **Hulton:** Fox Photos crA; Keystone b; **Courtesy of The Museum of World War II, Natick, Massachusetts:** cBl. **p321 Corbis:** t; Bettmann cr; **NHF:** (80-G-71198) bcl; **Courtesy of The Museum of World War II, Natick, Massachusetts:** c, clB, bcr. **p322 Corbis:** bl; **DK:** IWM/Andy Crawford tcl; **NHF:** (80-G-13106) tr; **Courtesy of The Museum of World War II, Natick, Massachusetts:** clA. **p322/323 Corbis:** Bettmann b. **p323 Corbis:** Bettmann tr; Hulton-Deutsch Collection br; **Hulton:** Keystone cA. **p324 Corbis:** Bettmann tr; **Hulton:** Archive Photos b; **Courtesy of The Museum of World War II, Natick, Massachusetts:** cl, cAr. **p325 Hulton:** Keystone tl; **NHF:** (80-G-68097) br. **p326 Hulton:** MPI b; **Courtesy of The Museum of World War II, Natick, Massachusetts:** cAr. **p327 Corbis:** clB; **Hulton:** Keystone bcr. **p328 Corbis:** Hulton-Deutsch Collection cl; **DK:** IWM/Andy Crawford tc; **Hulton:** Keystone/Central Press bl; **NHF:** (USA C-1189) tr. **p329 Corbis:** Bettmann/Philip Gendreau. **p330 DK:** NMM/Tina Chambers cl; **Hulton:** Keystone cr; **NMM:** (F3049) b; **NHF:** (80-G-K-4546) tr. **p331 Alamy Images:** Popperfoto clB; **Hulton:** London Express clA; **NHF:** (80-G-704702) br; (80-G-K-443) crB; (80-G-K-4575) tc. **p332 Hulton:** Keystone cr; **NHF:** (80-G-K-698) tr; (NH 73063) bl; (NH 81313) cl; (NH 85716) br. **p333 Corbis:** Hulton-Deutsch Collection br; **NMM:** (F2490) c; (F2560) bl; (F2567) bc; **NHF:** Courtesy of RAdm Ammen Farenholt, USN (MC) (NH 42537) tr. **p334 DK:** NMM/James Stevenson cr; **Hulton:** Central Press tr; Topical Press Agency cl; **NMM:** (F2485) bl; (F2575) br. **p335 Hulton:** Archive Photos/AE French tr; **NMM:** (F2503) clB; (F2572) bc; **NHF:** (NH 97260) c. **p336/337 Getty Images:** Stone/KOS. **p337 Alamy Images:** Buzz Pictures (3); **Corbis:** Macduff Everton (2); **Greenpeace Images International:** SIMS (4); **NHF:** (80-G-428267) (1). **p338 Corbis:** Swim Ink/Erik Nitsche tl; **NHF:** (80-G-K-12603) cA. **p339 NHF:** (80-G-428267). **p340 DK:** Gary Ombler tr; **NHF:** (80-G-420027) b. **p341 Corbis:** Bettmann bl, br; Hulton-Deutsch Collection tr. **p342 Corbis:** Yogi, Inc./ Robert Y Kaufman c; **Courtesy of US Navy:** Photographer's Mate Airman Nicholas C Messina bl. **p342/343 Corbis:** Underwood & Underwood b. **p343 CIA/Center for the Study of Intelligence:** tcr; **Corbis:** Bettmann cA, br. **p344 DK:** Gary Ombler tl, tr, crA, crB, bl, bc, br. **p345 Alamy Images:** Popperfoto clB; **Corbis:** Bettmann/Philip Gendreau crA; **DK:** Gary Ombler tl, tc, tr, bl, br, bcl, bcr, tcl, tcr. **p346 Corbis:** Bettmann/Frank Johnston trB; **Hulton:** Keystone tc; **NHF:** (NH 76187-KN) cBr; Photographed by PH2 Kevin J Freedman (NH 97635) bl. **p347 DK:** c; **Corbis:** Bettmann br, t. **p348 DK:** Gary Ombler tc, bc; **Military Picture Library:** Robert Kravitz bl. **p349 Corbis:** Robert Garwood & Trish Ainslie t; Steve Raymer bc; **The Royal Navy Submarine Museum:** br. **p350 Rex Features:** JTH clA; Sipa Press tc; **Courtesy of US Navy:** Photographer's Mate 2nd Class Bob Houlihan bc. **p350/351 Rex Features:** CNP c. **p351 Corbis:** Sygma br; **Courtesy of US Navy:** Photographer's Mate 1st Class Arlo K Abrahamson tr. **p352 DK:** Gary Ombler tl, tr, crA, cr, clB, cB, crB, bl, bc, br, cBl, cBr. **p353 DK:** Gary Ombler tl, tr, clB, bl, br, bcl, bcr, tcl, tcl; **Courtesy of US Navy:** Photographer's Mate 3rd Class Summer M Anderson crA. **p354 DK:** Gary Ombler tl, clA, clB, cBl, tcl; **Courtesy of US Navy:** Photographer's Mate Airman Jessica Davis bl. **p355 DK:** Gary Ombler. **p356 Courtesy of Blohm & Voss GmbH:** bl; **Corbis:** Sygma/Eric Bouve tr; **James W Goss:** cl; **Hulton:** Topical Press Agency br; **NMM:** Maker: John Haynes (F2567) cr; **Courtesy of US Navy:** crA. **p357 Corbis:** Sygma/Aim Patrice cA; Yogi, Inc./ Robert Y Kaufman br; **Military Picture Library:** tr; **Courtesy of US Navy:** Photographer's Mate 2nd Class Michael Sandberg bl. **p358 Corbis:** Bettmann c; **DK:** James Stevenson & Tina Chambers tl. **p358/359** Maersk Line **p360 Corbis:** Dean Conger clB, bc. **p360/361 Corbis:** Craig Aurness t. **p361 Corbis:** Carl & Anne Purcell c; Dean Conger tc; **DK:** NMM/James Stevenson & Tina Chambers br. **p362 Corbis:** Bettmann/Adam Scull clA; **Magnum:** Ian Berry b; **Getty Images:** Image Bank/Greg Pease tc. **p363 DK:** NMM/James Stevenson & Tina Chambers tl; **Getty Images:** Image Bank/Lee Man Yiu br. **p364 Corbis:** Dave Bardruff b; Stapleton Collection tc. **p365 Rex Features:** Tim Rooke tc, trB; **Press Association:** DPA/RCI br. **p366 NMM:** (F2551) cl; (F2571) b; **Courtesy of Port Aransas ISD:** cr; **Getty Images:** Stone/Don Spiro tr. **p367 Courtesy of Color Line, Norway:** bcl; **NMM:** (D6923-1) tlB; (E0228-1) c; On Loan from P&O (F2486) br; (F2487) tc; **Rex Features:** James D Morgan tr; Tim Rooke crA; **Louise Thomas:** blA. **p368 DK:** tl; **Rex Features:** Tim Rooke crB. **p369 Alamy Images:** Buzz Pictures. **p370/371 Corbis:** Roger Ressmeyer b. **p371 Corbis:** Owen Franken br; Reuters tc. **p372 DK:** bl; **Getty:** AFP tc. **p372/373 Corbis:** Cordaiy Photo Library Ltd/Jonathan Smith b. **p373 Corbis:** Onne van der Wal tr; **DK:** tc; **Courtesy of Garmin (Europe) Ltd:** br. **p374 Corbis:** Earl & Nazima Kowall bl; Kipa/Rault Jean Francis tl; **Rex Features:** DPP cr. **p375 Alamy Images:** Buzz Pictures tl; **Corbis:** Aaron Chang b. **p376 Corbis:** Newsport/ Jonathan Selkowitz bl; **DK:** cl; Philip Gatward br; **Getty Images:** Allsport/John Gichigi tr; **NMM:** (F2553) c. **p377 Alamy Images:** Boating Images Photo Library/Keith Pritchard cl; **Corbis:** Lowell Georgia cr; **Rex Features:** Action Press br; **MM:** c; **NMM:** (F2565) tc; **Rex Features:** DPP tr. **p378 BAL:** Royal Geographical Society, London, UK c; **DK:** Frank Greenaway tl. **p379 Greenpeace Images International:** SIMS. **p380 Corbis:** Bettmann clA; **Science Photo Library:** Alexis Rosenfeld bc. **p380/381 Alamy Images:** Paul Ives t. **p381 Corbis:** Bettmann crA; Sygma/Rien tr; **NOAA:** Monitor Collection bc, br. **p382 Corbis:** Michael St Maur Sheil bcl; **Rex Features:** Sipa Press tc, clA. **p383 Corbis:** Sygma/ Greenpeace tcr; **Magnum:** Bruno Barbey b; **Rex Features:** Sipa Press cr. **p384 DK:** bc; **Magnum:** Jean Gaumy bl; **Rex Features:** John Cunningham tl. **p385 Corbis:** Peter Johnson cB; **Magnum:** Jean Gaumy t. **p386/387 Magnum:** Jean Gaumy. **p388/389 PA Photos:** European Press Agency.

Endpapers: **Magnum:** Jean Gaumy.
Background Water Texture: **Louise Thomas**.